To Students

Writing is a great journey, a voyage through the world of ideas. That's why this writing text is entitled *Odyssey*. The title is meant to represent the journey of writing: the process of transferring thoughts to paper, with its many loops and detours, explorations and discoveries.

Odyssey is designed to help you grow as writers and to develop skills you will need in every area of your school life and beyond. The approach is based on three fundamental premises about learning to write:

The best way to learn is to write. The more you write, the more comfortable and confident you become with the process. Thus, this book gives you countless opportunities to write, whether sketching out ideas or drafting paragraphs, essays, or sentences.

Writing well requires both creativity and critical thinking. Before you can effectively express your ideas about a subject on paper, you must understand the subject, be able to analyze it from several perspectives, recognize its significance, and articulate your ideas about it. Thus, you'll find writing samples throughout the book that embody these qualities. You'll even see how a writer thinks a subject through, moving through all the stages of the writing process to a final draft. And you'll have many opportunities to be creative and think critically yourself.

Good writing is the sum of engaging content and correct form. Writing successfully means expressing solid, interesting ideas in a way that is universally accepted and understood by readers. Thus, you need to learn universally accepted guidelines of grammar and usage to support your ideas, and *Odyssey* guides you in correcting the persistent sentence-level errors that plague all writers.

Described in the next few pages are the special features of this book. Taken together, they will launch you on this journey and guide you on your way.

William Kelly

Deborah Lawton

The Media Connection

Your odyssey through the world of writing is likely to require the use of technology, whether you're surfing a Web site or using a word processing program to compose your assignments. *Odyssey* **offers you a wealth of electronic resources to make your journey smooth sailing.**

Odyssey Multimedia Activity Package with Interactive CD-ROM. This ancillary CD-ROM and workbook offers videos, Web links, exercises, and audio tutorials for each chapter in the text. Look in your textbook for the CD-ROM icons. These alert you to the presence of an additional multimedia activity on the CD-ROM. You can also use the print-based activities in the multimedia activity pack for various other classroom or individual projects, including peer collaboration and research.

Odyssey Companion Website. For additional Web-based exercises, graded quizzes, and interactive activities, visit *Odyssey* on the Web at **http://www.ablongman.com/kelly**

The Longman Writer's Warehouse.
A Complete Grammar and Writing Resource for Developing Writers
Now, developing writers can actually write on the Web—save their work in various stages and see a piece of writing through the complete writing process.

This one-of-a-kind resource offers—

- full coverage of grammar, including diagnostic tests to help students target areas of weakness
- an online writer's journal
- a handbook with thousands of interactive exercises
- extensive research coverage
- a collaborative network
- Web-based activities and links
- multimedia activities including audio, video, and image-based writing assignments

GrammarCoach Software.
This interactive tutorial helps students practice the basics of grammar and punctuation through 600 self-grading exercises in such problems areas as fragments, run-ons, and agreement. IBM diskettes only.

Here's How *Odyssey* Helps You Improve Your Writing

Odyssey is organized into seven parts to help you build your writing skills.

Part 1: **Starting Out (Chapters 1-4).** This section focuses on writing as a means of exploration and discovery, and on the stages of the writing process—generating ideas, composing, and refining.

Part 2: **Using the Patterns of Paragraph Development (Chapters 5-13).** This part focuses on the rhetorical modes, which are the specific techniques that help a writer fulfill the purpose of a paragraph. Examples of these modes are narration, description, example, and process.

Part 3: **Moving On to the Essay (Chapters 14-16).** In this part, you will learn to apply the principles you encountered in Part 1 (writing process) and Part 2 (rhetorical modes) to essay writing.

Part 4: **Developing Sentence Sense (Chapters 17-20).** These four chapters focus on the mechanics of writing correct sentences and avoiding common sentence errors, such as fragments, comma splices, and run-ons.

Part 5: **Understanding Subjects and Verbs (Chapters 21-24).** In these chapters, you will gain practice with subject-verb agreement, and with various verb tenses of both regular and irregular verbs.

Part 6: **Keeping Your Writing Correct (Chapters 25-31).** This part focuses on many important aspects of word usage and mechanics: working with nouns, pronouns, and modifiers; maintaining parallelism; spelling correctly; and using commas, other punctuation, and capitalization.

Part 7: **Connecting Responding to Reading.** Professional writers always say that in order to write better, you need to read more. Thus, in Part 7 you will find 15 readings from both professional writers and student authors. The student writings grew out of assignments like those presented in *Odyssey*. This part also provides guidelines for careful reading and questions that promote critical thinking, discussion, and further writing.

A Conversation with
William Kelly

Q. *What is the biggest stumbling block for new or developing writers?*

A. By far, the biggest stumbling block for new writers—and especially for developing writers—is just plain fear. Nobody wants to fail at a task, to not complete it correctly and well. When it comes to writing, people generally know what they want to say, but many become almost paralyzed at the prospect of transforming those good ideas into an acceptable and understandable form. Some of these people already have had negative experiences with writing, so their past inhibits their ability to perform. And others have had so little experience with writing that they don't know how to begin—never mind to complete the task successfully.

Q. *How can new or developing writers overcome their feelings of inhibition and anxiety as they face the blank page or computer screen?*

A. It may sound simplistic, but one of the best ways for most people to overcome the inhibition and anxiety that a blank page or computer screen creates is to try to lessen their expectations of the finished product a little. I'm not suggesting that anyone plan to do an ineffective writing. But many people focus too much on what the finished product should look like, and this finished product is bound to contrast sharply with the roughness, with all the starts and stops, that mark an early draft. As a result, it's easy to become discouraged and intimidated. A better idea, then, is to assume that the first words you write or type will capture the promise of your ideas. These words won't yet be in the best or most complete form, but they form the foundation you need to fulfill the promise that these ideas hold.

Q. *Do you think that everyone can learn to express their ideas clearly in writing?*

A. Absolutely. If people can think and say their ideas so that others can understand them, then they can write them. What makes writing a bit more complicated is the series of conventions that exist in writing but not in conversation. When you talk, for example, you don't need to worry about spelling or punctuation, complete sentences, or correct paragraphs. Also, if the people listening to you don't understand your point, they can ask you questions and you can supply additional information to fill them in. But the principle is the same whether speaking or writing: to express ideas in such a way that someone else understands the point being made. That means that when people sit down to write, they are generally half way to their goal once they have the ideas. What they simply need is to develop greater mastery of the conventions.

Q. *What is the one most important lesson you'd like students to remember from this book/course?*

A. The most important lesson I'd like students to keep in mind is this: The biggest reason people have difficulty with writing is not lack of ability but lack of practice. Be patient and keep writing. You will get better. You won't be able to avoid it. The truth is that I was not a good student in high school. It wasn't that I lacked ability--in fact, I had been an honor student up until the end of the ninth grade. But after that, I made the ridiculous, conscious decision not to work at my studies anymore. Instead I turned my attention to athletics and socializing. In my senior year, I applied to two local colleges, and fortunately for me, one of them took a chance on me. At that point, I was ready to turn my attention to academics once more, but after my three high school years of self-imposed academic inertia, I struggled greatly. It wasn't until the second semester of my sophomore year in college that I began to reach the level of my true capability again. Throughout my teaching career, I've tried to remember what that struggle was like, how it felt to want to do something but to be unable to reach it immediately. I learned that if I was patient with myself, if I was persistent, if I learned from my mistakes, I could succeed. These lessons form the foundation for my teaching and this book.

Q. *Is there anything else you would like to say to students who are about to begin using this book?*

A. I don't believe that a book has to be tedious to be rigorous. Students who lack knowledge or haven't had practice with writing need a text that talks to them simply, directly, conversationally, with a tone that is encouraging, respectful, and, lighthearted. That's what I want you to find here.

Odyssey

Annotated Instructor's Edition

Odyssey

A Guide to Better Writing
Third Edition
Annotated Instructor's Edition

William J. Kelly
Bristol Community College

Deborah L. Lawton
Bristol Community College

Longman

New York   San Francisco   Boston
London   Toronto   Sydney   Tokyo   Singapore   Madrid
Mexico City   Munich   Paris   Cape Town   Hong Kong   Montreal

VICE PRESIDENT AND EDITOR-IN-CHIEF:	Joseph Terry
SENIOR ACQUISITIONS EDITOR:	Steven Rigolosi
DEVELOPMENT MANAGER:	Janet Lanphier
DEVELOPMENT EDITOR:	Susan Messer
SENIOR MARKETING MANAGER:	Melanie Craig
SENIOR SUPPLEMENTS EDITOR:	Donna Campion
MEDIA SUPPLEMENTS EDITOR:	Nancy Garcia
PRODUCTION MANAGER:	Donna DeBenedictis
PROJECT COORDINATION, TEXT DESIGN, AND ELECTRONIC PAGE MAKEUP:	Elm Street Publishing Services, Inc.
SENIOR COVER DESIGNER/MANAGER:	Nancy Danahy
COVER ILLUSTRATION/PHOTO:	© PlanetArt
PHOTO RESEARCHER:	Moya McAllister/Photosearch, Inc.
SENIOR MANUFACTURING BUYER:	Dennis J. Para
PRINTER AND BINDER:	Webcrafters, Inc.
COVER PRINTER:	Coral Graphic Services, Inc.

For permission to use copyrighted material, grateful acknowledgment is made to the copyright holders on p. 599, which is hereby made part of this copyright page.

Library of Congress Cataloging-in-Publication Data

Kelly, William J.
    Odyssey: a guide to better writing / William J. Kelly, Deborah L. Lawton.—3rd ed. p. cm.
    Includes bibliographical references and index.
    ISBN 0-321-09626-6 (alk. paper)
    1. English language—Rhetoric. 2. English language—Grammar. 3. Report writing. I.
Lawton, Deborah L. II. Title.

PE1408 .K475 2003
808'.042—dc21

Please visit our website at http://www.ablongman.com/kelly

ISBN 0-321-09626-6 (Student Edition)
ISBN 0-321-09627-4 (Annotated Instructor's Edition)

2 3 4 5 6 7 8 9 10—WC—05 04 03

Dedication

To Kevin —
As time goes by . . .

To Michelle —
I can't imagine a better life, thanks to you.

Brief Contents

Detailed Contents

Part Two Using the Patterns of Paragraph Development   93

Part Three Moving On to the Essay   181

Part Four Developing Sentence Sense   263

Part Five Understanding Subjects and Verbs 323

21 Subject–Verb Agreement 324

22 Basic Tenses for Regular Verbs 341

23 Irregular Verbs and Frequently Confused Verbs 353

Part Six Keeping Your Writing Correct   385

27 Adjectives, Adverbs, and Other Modifiers: Using Describing and Modifying Words Effectively   426

28 Parallelism: Presenting Related Items in a Similar Form   446

Part Seven Connecting: Responding to Reading 525

Preface

At some point during the eighth century B.C., scholars believe that the Greek poet Homer first sang his epic poem about the travels of the legendary hero Odysseus. As his audience listened spellbound, Homer presented a story so wondrous, so fantastic, that the name of the poem—*The Odyssey*—eventually came to mean a great journey. Writing is also a great journey, and that's why this text is entitled *Odyssey: A Guide to Better Writing*, Third Edition.

Writing is a voyage of self-expression through the world of ideas. The adventure begins with a few words, drawn from stored reserves of experiences and knowledge, scribbled on paper or typed across a computer screen. It ends as a completed piece of writing that expresses these original ideas in simple, clear, direct, complete, and correct terms. Along the way, the original ideas evolve and grow, the result of unleashed creativity and contact with the world to exchange information and react to the responses of others. Think of *Odyssey* as a guidebook for all the journeys—and all the promise—that writing involves.

The approach in *Odyssey* is based on three fundamental beliefs about writing:

- **The best way to learn to write is by writing.** Confidence leads to competence—the more people write, the more comfortable and confident they become with the process.
- **Writing well requires a combination of sound critical thinking and creativity.** Effectively expressing ideas about a subject on paper involves understanding that subject, analyzing it from different perspectives, recognizing its significance, and articulating key ideas about it.
- **Good writing is the sum of engaging content and correct form.** Writing successfully means expressing ideas in a way that is universally accepted and understood by readers.

To address these fundamental principles, we have included a number of special features in *Odyssey*, all designed to create a greater mastery of writing.

Features of *Odyssey*

Odyssey has been designed with a series of special features to help students learn.

Getting Started... **Q:** Why does it so often seem easier for me to say something than to write it down?

Audio 1.1 **A:** The short answer to this question is that writing often seems harder than speaking because in most cases, it is. Writing holds many challenges that speaking doesn't. For instance, speaking doesn't involve such matters as correct spelling or punctuation. Also, if what you say aloud doesn't make sense, your listener can ask you questions. When you write, you have to anticipate those questions and answer them on the page.

Getting Started... **Q:** The experience was so *vivid*, almost like it was electricity. How can I write about it and capture that sense of full life?

Audio 6.1 **A:** Whenever you want to record in words the vivid sensations you witness or experience, description is the answer. Draw on all your senses—think about what you felt at that time—and you'll be all set.

Chapter-Opening "Getting Started" Q&A

All students have questions about writing and the English language. Many never put these questions into words, however, because they may think they are too simple or too basic to ask. This feature, which begins each chapter, gets at such questions and provides students with answers. Moreover, this brief Q&A exchange will help students get focused on the essence of each chapter: why it matters and what they can get out of it.

Fast Fact If a word is used often enough, it eventually makes it into the dictionary as a legitimate part of the language. And so it happened that the favorite expression of cartoon dimwit Homer Simpson, "Doh!", has recently been added to the Oxford English Dictionary's online edition. It is defined as "expressing frustration at the realization that things have turned out badly or not as planned or that one has just said or done something foolish. Also implying that another person has said or done something foolish."

Fast Fact According to some estimates, the average sentence in American English is about 22 words.

Fast Fact As you write and revise, focus on time and patience. Michelangelo worked three years to create his massive statue, *David,* and four years to paint the ceiling of the Sistine Chapel.

Fast Facts

Learning about language and writing shouldn't be all hard work. Even the hardest-working writers need playful, entertaining moments to keep them going. Thus, several times in each chapter, students will find "fast facts." Although meant to give them a deserved break, they're also tied to the chapter content—sometimes in ways that aren't immediately apparent.

Opportunities for Practice

The only way to learn to write is by doing it. And the only way to learn sentence and grammar-level skills is through plenty of practice. Thus we've supplied a large number of opportunities of meaningful work with writing and with usage. Several types of activities review and provide practice of the skills just introduced in the text.

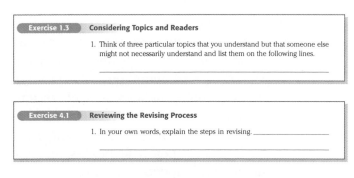

Exercise 1.3 **Considering Topics and Readers**

1. Think of three particular topics that you understand but that someone else might not necessarily understand and list them on the following lines.

Exercise 4.1 **Reviewing the Revising Process**

1. In your own words, explain the steps in revising.

- **Exercises.** These activities check comprehension and offer stimulating practice with the principles just presented. A number of them are *collaborative*, in some cases calling for planning and creating short writings.

Challenge 4.4 **Evaluating Spatial Order in Your Writing**

1. For Exercise 4.11 you described a room in your home. Now turn these details into a paragraph and exchange this paragraph with a partner. Make sure that the description in the paper you receive progresses smoothly and logically. Return the paper to the writer, pointing out any problems that you had in visualizing the scene or the topic.

Challenge 14.6 **Assessing Use of Effective Language in a Rough Draft**

Working with a partner, check the effectiveness of the language in the other paragraphs in the first draft of "Making Their Marks: The Popularity of Tattooing and Body Piercing" (pages 198–199). Circle or highlight any words that are too vague or too general to be effective. Discuss possible replacements.

Discovering Connections 17.1

Using one of the techniques you practiced in Chapter 2, "Generating Ideas through Prewriting," prewrite on one of the following topics:

1. the use of cameras in the courtroom
2. the behavior of tourists

Or, focus on this picture.

Save your work for later use.

Chapter Quick Check: Mastering Subject–Verb Agreement

The following passage contains the various kinds of errors in subject–verb agreement discussed in this chapter. Consider again the ways to correct these errors illustrated in this chapter. Then identify errors in agreement, crossing them out and writing the correct verb form above the incorrect one, as the example shows:

EXAMPLE Several of my friends from my old neighborhood still ~~plays~~ *play* basketball to-

gether two nights a week in the City League.

(1) Speed and convenience seems to be what most customers are look-

ing for when they go grocery shopping. (2) Because everyone, especially

---

Summary Exercise: Mastering Subject–Verb Agreement

The following passage contains the various kinds of errors in subject–verb agreement discussed in this chapter. Consider again the ways to correct these errors illustrated in this chapter. Then identify errors in agreement, crossing them out and writing the correct verb form above the incorrect one.

(1) There is many choices available for the person looking for a laptop

computer. (2) Thanks to price cuts by most major manufacturers, anybody

---

Process Paragraph Checklist

☐ Does the topic sentence clearly state the procedure or technique to be presented?

☐ Does it use the imperative mood (you)?

☐ Is the process divided into simple, logical steps? Do you feel any step should be further subdivided to make it easier for the reader to perform the process? Put a ✓ next to any step that needs to be divided.

☐ Are the steps presented in linear order? Underline any step that is out of linear order, and then draw a line to the spot in the paragraph where it actually belongs.

☐ In your judgment, what is the best part of this paragraph? Explain.

☐ Which detail or example would be even better if it were expanded? Why?

- **Challenges.** These sessions, many of which are also collaborative, emphasize critical thinking, drafting, or revising. They take students to the next level, at which they apply what they've learned by doing their own writing.

- **Discovering Connections.** These opportunities take students even further. Here they are composing their own paragraphs and essays from scratch, always guided by skills introduced in the chapter or earlier in the book. Some include photo prompts, to help students generate ideas.

- **Quick Checks and Summary Exercises.** These present students with all the concepts from a chapter in a single drill. These exercises are found at the end of each chapter in Parts 4, 5, and 6 of the book—where the sentence skills are taught. Quick Checks have 10 items each and are intended to prepare students for the longer Summary Exercises, which instructors may use to assess student mastery of the chapter material.

Checklists

Writers don't automatically know how to evaluate their own work or the work of others. Evaluation is a skill that has to be taught. That's why the book offers checklists—a concrete tool for evaluating students' own work as well as that of another writer. Checklists are included for proofreading, for spelling, for each of the rhetorical modes, and for many other aspects of writing.

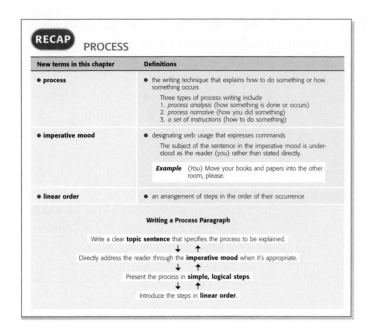

Recaps

These visual summaries appear at the end of each chapter. They review terms presented in the chapter and offer graphic explanations of key concepts.

ESL Notes

These cross-references, appearing at relevant points in the margin, direct ESL students to a specialized appendix, full of grammar and usage tips specifically for them.

ESL Note
See "Writing Paragraphs," especially the section on unity, and "Writing Essays" on pages 585–586.

ESL Note
See "Sentence Basics" on pages 572–574 and "Word Order" on pages 574–575.

As students journey through this book, we hope they will take advantage of all its features and, gradually, discover that they are becoming better writers. Not only will they learn to generate ideas, they will draft effective paragraphs and essays—all flowing from correct, well-crafted sentences. All the tools are here to guide students: explanation, examples, practice, and tools for self-evaluation.

We welcome them to this *Odyssey*. We hope the experience is enjoyable and rewarding.

Collaboration

Because writers need feedback, and because two heads are often better than one, this book encourages collaboration. When students see this icon accompanying an exercise, they are being asked to work with a partner.

Organization of the Text

Odyssey's organization fosters cumulative learning while also allowing for flexible course design. **Part One, Starting Out**, consists of four chapters that employ various enticing activities to focus on the writing process. Chapter 1, "Ensuring Success in Writing," discusses the essential elements of the writing process and the primary purposes of writing. Chapter 2, "Generating Ideas through Prewriting," introduces and provides facsimile examples of five prewriting activities, and Chapter 3, "Composing: Creating a Draft," discusses and illustrates the entire composing stage of writing, from topic sentence to completed draft, emphasizing the difference between writer-centered and reader-centered ideas. Chapter 4, "Refining and Polishing Your Draft," explains and illustrates each step of the revision stage by showing how a first draft becomes an effective final draft. Presented in sequence, these four chapters provide a solid background in and practice with the writing process.

Part Two, Using the Patterns of Paragraph Development, deals with writing paragraphs that feature the traditional rhetorical modes: narration, description, example, process, definition, comparison and contrast, cause and effect, and division and classification. Chapters 5 through 12 explain and illustrate the specific characteristics of the various modes while also emphasizing the **purpose** or aim in a piece of writing. Chapter 13 covers argument, not as a mode but as a purpose, one that writers use a combination of modes to fulfill.

The three chapters making up **Part Three, Moving On to the Essay**, apply the principles of paragraph writing presented in the first two sections to this more complex and detailed form. Chapter 14, "Developing an Essay," focuses on a single essay, shown at every stage from prewriting ideas to polished final draft. Chapter 15, "Examining Types of Essays," discusses ways to use the rhetorical modes to develop entire essays, with argument again presented as a purpose. Chapter 16, "Adjusting Your Process: Timed Writing and Summaries," presents simple, clear, logical steps to perform well on such writing tasks as taking an essay exam, completing a timed writing assessment, and preparing a summary.

The four chapters in **Part Four, Developing Sentence Sense**, focus on writing correct sentences and avoiding the three most serious sentence errors: fragments, comma splices, and run-on sentences. The four chapters in **Part Five, Understanding Subjects and Verbs**, focus on subject–verb agreement as well as different aspects of verb use. The seven chapters comprising **Part Six, Keeping Your Writing Correct**, deal with other aspects of usage and mechanics. Specific topics include working with nouns, pronouns, and modifiers; maintaining correct parallelism and spelling; using commas and other punctuation; and capitalizing words properly.

Part Seven, Connecting: Responding to Reading, is a brief anthology of 15 readings, including 7 pieces by professional writers such as Amy Tan, John Yemma, and Deborah Tannen and 8 writings by students, each accompanied by questions that promote critical thinking, discussion, and writing.

Three practical appendices supplement the lessons in the text. Appendix A, "Writing with a Computer," provides a brief introduction to basic word-processing functions, which can help make the writing process efficient and effective. Appendix B, "Tips for ESL Writers," intended for nonnative speakers of English, covers selected aspects of grammar and usage that ESL students often find confusing. Appendix C, "Exploring the Dictionary," emphasizes good dictionary and vocabulary-building skills through use of a sample dictionary entry as well as stimulating exercises.

New in This Edition

From the moment that we began work on the first edition of *Odyssey*, we have maintained the same goal: to create the most accessible, practical, efficient, and appealing basic writing text possible. Since that initial volume, we have continued to work to improve the text. We used and evaluated the first two editions of the text ourselves. We also asked our students what they thought of the book and how we might adjust it to meet their needs to an even greater degree. In addition, we queried colleagues across the nation for their reactions and suggestions. On the basis of this collective analysis, we have made a number of significant changes in this third edition of *Odyssey: A Guide to Better Writing*. Besides the features already discussed, these changes include:

- new chapter introductions
- increased attention throughout the text to the importance of purpose in writing
- new facsimile examples of prewriting techniques and all stages of the writing process for both paragraph and essay writing, including annotated drafts, peer responses, and instructor's comments
- improved writing assignments throughout the text, most now including a photo as a writing cue
- new discussion and examples of MLA and APA systems of documentation
- six new essays illustrating the modes, two of them five-paragraph essays
- a complete revamp of Chapter 14, "Developing an Essay," tracing a new essay through every stage of the writing process, including peer and instructor comments in facsimile form
- a new chapter on answering essay questions, completing impromptu writing assignments, and writing a summary
- a new chapter devoted exclusively to pronoun use, including pronoun–antecedent agreement
- more than 80 new grammar and usage exercises on high-interest subjects
- seven new reading selections, four of them new student writings

The Media Connection

Your odyssey through the world of writing is likely to require the use of technology, whether you're surfing a Website or using a word-processing program to compose your assignments. *Odyssey* offers you a wealth of electronic resources to make your journey smooth sailing.

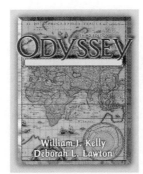

Odyssey Multimedia Activity Package with Interactive CD-ROM

This ancillary CD-ROM and workbook, prepared by Randall McClure of Minnesota State University–Mankato, and Richard Miller of Suffolk University, offers videos, Web links, exercises, and audio tutorials for each chapter in the text. Look in your textbook for the CD-ROM icons. These alert you to the presence of an additional multimedia activity on the

CD-ROM. You can also use the print-based activities in the multimedia activity pack for various other classroom or individual projects, including peer collaboration and research.

Audio 1.1   Video 1.1   Activity 1.1   Weblink 1.1

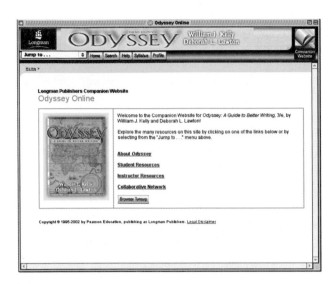

Odyssey Companion Website

For additional Web-based exercises, graded quizzes, and interactive activities, prepared by Randall McClure of Minnesota State University–Mankato, visit *Odyssey Online* at **http://www.ablongman.com/kelly**.

The Longman Writer's Warehouse

This innovative and exciting online supplement is the perfect accompaniment to any developmental writing course. Created by developmental English instructors especially for beginning writers, The Writer's Warehouse covers every part of the writing process. Also included are journaling capabilities, multimedia activities, diagnostic tests, an interactive handbook, and a complete instructor's manual. The Writer's Warehouse requires no space on your school's server; rather, students complete and store their work on the Longman server and are able to access it, revise it, and continue working at any time. For more details about how to shrinkwrap a free subscription to The Writer's Warehouse with *Odyssey,* please consult your Longman sales representative. For a free guided tour of the site, visit **http://longmanwriters warehouse.com**.

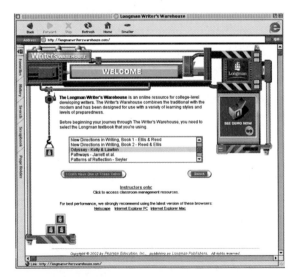

The Writer's ToolKit Plus

This CD-ROM offers a wealth of tutorial, exercise, and reference material for writers. It is compatible with either a PC or Macintosh platform and is flexible enough to be used either occasionally for practice or regularly in class lab sessions. For information on how to bundle this CD-ROM free with *Odyssey,* please contact your Longman sales representative.

GrammarCoach Software

This interactive tutorial helps students practice the basics of grammar and punctuation through 600 self-grading exercises in such problem areas as fragments, run-ons, and agreement. IBM diskettes only.

The Teaching and Learning Package

A complete set of ancillary materials is available with *Odyssey* to ensure that the developmental writing course is a rewarding one for both students and instructors.

Book-Specific Supplements

The ***Annotated Instructor's Edition (AIE)*** includes the answers to all the exercises in the student text, printed directly in the textbook itself for ease of use. 0-321-09627-4

The ***Instructor's Manual and Test Bank***, prepared by Professor Nadine Roberts, Three Rivers Community College, offers teaching tips, sample syllabi, and a wealth of additional material for instructors of developmental English. Reproducible, easily graded quizzes for each chapter in the text are also provided. 0-321-09628-2

In addition to these book-specific supplements, a series of other skills-based supplements is available for both instructors and students. All of these supplements are available either free or at greatly reduced prices.

For Additional Reading and Reference

The Dictionary Deal. Two dictionaries can be shrinkwrapped with *Odyssey* either free or at a nominal fee. The *New American Webster Handy College Dictionary* is a paperback reference text with more than 100,000 entries. *Merriam Webster's Collegiate Dictionary*, Tenth Edition, is a hardback reference with a citation file of more than 14.5 million examples of English words drawn from actual use. For more information on how to shrinkwrap a dictionary with *Odyssey*, please contact your Longman sales representative.

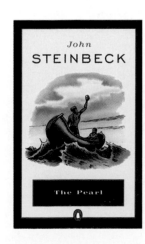

Penguin Quality Paperback Titles. A series of Penguin paperbacks is available at a significant discount when shrinkwrapped with *Odyssey*. Some titles available are Toni Morrison's *Beloved*, Julia Alvarez's *How the Garcia Girls Lost Their Accents*, Mark Twain's *Huckleberry Finn, Narrative of the Life of Frederick Douglass*, Harriet Beecher Stowe's *Uncle Tom's Cabin*, Dr. Martin Luther King, Jr.'s *Why We Can't Wait*, and plays by Shakespeare, Miller, and Albee. For a complete list of titles or more information, please contact your Longman sales consultant.

The Pocket Reader and **The Brief Pocket Reader,** First Edition. These inexpensive volumes contain 80 brief readings and 50 readings, respectively. Each reading is brief (one to three pages each). The readers are theme-based: writers on writing, nature, women and men, customs and habits, politics, rights and obligations, and coming of age. Also included is an alternate rhetorical table of contents. 0-321-07668-0

100 Things to Write About. This 100-page book contains 100 individual assignments for writing on a variety of topics and in a wide range of formats, from expressive to analytical. Ask your Longman sales representative for a sample copy. 0-673-98239-4

Newsweek **Alliance.** Instructors may choose to shrinkwrap a 12-week subscription to *Newsweek* with any Longman text. The price of the subscription is 57 cents per issue (a total of $6.84 for the subscription). Available with the subscription is a free "Interactive Guide to *Newsweek*"—a workbook for students who are using the text. In addition, *Newsweek* provides a wide variety of instructor supplements free to teachers, including maps, Skills Builders, and weekly quizzes. For more information on the *Newsweek* program, please contact your Longman sales representative.

For Instructors

Electronic Test Bank for Writing. This electronic test bank features more than 5,000 questions in all areas of writing, from grammar to paragraphing, through essay writing, research, and documentation. With this easy-to-use CD-ROM, instructors simply choose questions from the electronic test bank, and then print out the completed test for distribution. CD-ROM: 0-321-08117-X; Print version: 0-321-08486-1

The Longman Electronic Newsletter. Twice a month during the spring and fall, instructors who have subscribed receive a free copy of the Longman Developmental English Newsletter in their e-mailbox. Written by experienced classroom instructors, the newsletter offers teaching tips, classroom activities, book reviews, and more. To subscribe, visit the Longman Basic Skills Website at *http://www.ablongman.com/basicskills,* or send an e-mail to *BasicSkills@ablongman.com.*

Competency Profile Test Bank, Second Edition. This series of 60 objective tests covers ten general areas of English competency, including fragments, comma splices and run-ons, pronouns, commas, and capitalization. Each test is available in remedial, standard, and advanced versions. Available as reproducible sheets or in computerized versions. Free to instructors. Paper version: 0-321-02224-6; Computerized IBM: 0-321-02633-0; Computerized Mac: 0-321-02632-2

Diagnostic and Editing Tests and Exercises, Fifth Edition. This collection of diagnostic tests helps instructors assess students' competence in standard written English for purpose of placement or to gauge progress. Available as reproducible sheets or in computerized versions, and free to instructors. Paper: 0-321-11730-1; CD-ROM: 0-321-11731-X

ESL Worksheets, Third Edition. These reproducible worksheets provide ESL students with extra practice in areas they find the most troublesome. A diagnostic test and post-test are provided, along with answer keys and suggested topics for writing. Free to adopters. 0-321-07765-2

The Longman Editing Exercises. These 54 pages of paragraph editing exercises give students extra practice using grammar skills in the context of longer passages. Free when packaged with any Longman title. 0-205-31792-8; Answer key: 0-205-31797

80 Practices. A collection of reproducible, ten-item exercises that provide additional practices for specific grammatical usage problems, such as comma splices, capitalization, and pronouns. Includes an answer key. Free to adopters of *Odyssey.* 0-673-53422-7

CLAST Test Package, Fourth Edition. These two 40-item objective tests evaluate students' readiness for the CLAST exams. Strategies for teaching CLAST preparedness are included. Free with *Odyssey.* Reproducible sheets: 0-321-01950-4; Computerized IBM version: 0-321-01982-2; Computerized Mac version: 0-321-01983-0

TASP Test Package, Third Edition. These 12 practice pre-tests and post-tests assess the same reading and writing skills covered in the TASP examination. Free with any Longman English title. Reproducible sheets: 0-321-01959-8; Computerized IBM version: 0-321-01985-7; Computerized Mac version: 0-321-01984-9

Teaching Online: Internet Research, Conversation, and Composition, Second Edition. Ideal for instructors who have never surfed the Net, this easy-to-follow guide offers basic definitions, numerous examples, and step-by-step information about finding and using Internet sources. Free to adopters. 0-321-01957-1

Teaching Writing to the Non-Native Speaker. This booklet examines issues that arise when non-native speakers enter the developmental classroom. Free to instructors, it includes profiles of international and permanent ESL students, factors influencing second-language acquisition, and tips on managing a multicultural classroom. 0-673-97452-9

The Longman Guide to Classroom Management. Written by Joannis Flatley of St. Philip's College, this first in Longman's new series of monographs for developmental English instructors focuses on issues of classroom etiquette, providing guidance on dealing with unruly, unengaged, disruptive, or uncooperative students. Ask your Longman sales representative for a free copy. 0-321-09246-5

The Longman Instructor's Planner. This all-in-one resource for instructors includes monthly and weekly planning sheets, to-do lists, student contact forms, attendance rosters, a gradebook, an address/phone book, and a mini almanac. Ask your Longman sales representative for a free copy. 0-321-09247-3

For Students

Researching Online, Fifth Edition. A perfect companion for a new age, this indispensable new supplement helps students navigate the Internet. Adapted from *Teaching Online,* the instructor's Internet guide, *Researching Online* speaks directly to students, giving them detailed, step-by-step instructions for performing electronic searches. Available free when shrinkwrapped with this *Odyssey.* 0-321-09277-5

Learning Together: An Introduction to Collaborative Theory. This brief guide to the fundamentals of collaborative learning teaches students how to work effectively in groups, how to revise with peer response, and how to co-author a paper or report. Shrinkwrapped free with *Odyssey.* 0-673-46848-8

A Guide for Peer Response, Second Edition. This guide offers students forms for peer critiques, including general guidelines and specific forms for different stages in the writing process. Also appropriate for freshman-level courses. Free to adopters. 0-321-01948-2

10 Practices of Highly Successful College Students. This popular supplement helps students learn crucial study skills, offering concise tips for a successful career in college. Topics include time management, test-taking, reading critically, stress management, and motivation. 0-205-30769-8

[Florida Adopters] **Thinking Through the Test, by D. J. Henry.** This special workbook, prepared specially for students in Florida, offers ample skill and practice exercises to help student prep for the Florida State Exit Exam. To shrinkwrap this workbook free with your textbook, please contact your Longman sales representative. Available in two versions: with answers and without answers. Also available: Two laminated grids (one for reading, one for writing) that can serve as handy references for students preparing for the Florida State Exit Exam.

The Longman Writer's Journal. This journal for writers, free with *Odyssey,* offers students a place to think, write, and react. For an examination copy, contact your Longman sales consultant. 0-321-08639-2

The Longman Researcher's Journal. This journal for writers and researchers, free with *Odyssey,* helps students plan, schedule, write, and revise their research project. An all-in-one resource for first-time researchers, the journal guides students gently through the research process. 0-321-09530-8

The Longman Writer's Portfolio. This unique supplement provides students with a space to plan, think about, and present their work. The portfolio includes an assessing/organizing area (including a grammar diagnostic test, a spelling quiz, and project planning worksheets), a before- and during-writing area (including peer review sheets, editing checklists, writing self-evaluations, and a personal editing profile), and an after-writing area (including a progress chart, a final table of contents, and a final assessment). Ask your Longman sales representative for more information. 0-321-10765-9

Acknowledgments

As we worked on this third edition of *Odyssey: A Guide to Better Writing*, we benefited from the guidance and support of a number of people, and we offer them thanks. First, we salute John M. Lannon, University of Massachusetts, Dartmouth, and Robert A. Schwegler, University of Rhode Island. They are great teachers, great writers, and great friends.

A number of people at Bristol Community College deserve to be acknowledged for their support. We thank our students for all that they have taught us over the years. We are particularly grateful to the students who allowed us to include their work in this text: Greg Andree, Amanda Beaulieu, Ana Gomes, Larissa Houk, Jane Patenaude, Diane Riva, Josh Trepanier, and Naihsin Weng. Thanks also to Jeremy Wright for sharing his expertise on burning a CD. In addition, we want to express our gratitude to our colleagues at BCC for their continuing interest in our work, including Cynthia Brenner, Rylan Brenner, Sally Cameron, Debra Deroian, Karen Dixon, David Feeney, Tom Grady, Jeanne Grandchamp, Penny Hahn, Jerry LePage, Arthur Lothrop, Diana McGee, Linda Mulready, and Joe Murphy. Thanks also to Jack R. Warner, Associate Chancellor, and Marge Condon, Director, Center for Teaching and Learning, University of Massachusetts, Dartmouth, for their friendship and ongoing support. In particular, we offer thanks to Paul F. Fletcher, Professor Emeritus of English and retired Assistant Dean for Language, Humanities, and the Arts. During our careers, Paul has taught us so much about teaching and about treating both students and colleagues with kindness and respect.

While completing this project, we benefited from suggestions made by a number of top professionals across the country. Their comments helped us shape this third edition of *Odyssey*, and we thank them for their help. They include Marie Connelly, *Cuyahoga Community College;* Frances Secco Davidson, *Mercer County Community College;* Martha Funderburk, *University of Arkansas;* Mary M. Greene, *Tidewater Community College;* Isabel Hansen, *Black Hawk College;* William T. Hope, *Jefferson Community College;* Claudia House, *Nashville State Technical Institute;* Kenneth P. Kerr, *Wor-Wic Community College;* Patsy Krech, *University of Memphis;* Henry G. Papagan, *Lord Fairfax Community College;* Dee Pruitt, *Florence Darlington Technical College;* Merlenc J. Purkiss, *Miami-Dade Community College;* David E. Rogers, *Valencia Community College;* Judi Salsburg, *Monroe Community College;* Justina Thomas, *Delaware Technical and Community College;* Josephine M. Van Wyk, *Millersville University;* and Elizabeth Warner, *Miami-Dade Community College.*

We also salute the fine team at Longman who have devoted their considerable talents to make this edition of *Odyssey* so attractive. Joe Opiela, Vice President and Editor-in-Chief, English, deserves special thanks for his vision and his dedication to this project and its authors. Likewise, we thank Senior Acquisitions Editor Steven Rigolosi for his enthusiasm and determination to make *Odyssey* the best book of its type. We are also very grateful for the hard work of Susan Messer, Development Editor, who has worked so hard to make us look so good. In addition, Donna DeBenedictis, Production Manager, and Sue Nodine, Project Editor for Elm Street Publishing Services, Inc., have done a superb job of transforming the manuscript into its final form. All in all, the third edition of *Odyssey* couldn't have been in better hands at any stage in its development.

And finally, we would like to thank our friends and family for supporting us and our work.

Debbie Lawton would like to thank her Border friends, Mary Beth, Judy, Tom, Barbara, and Michele, for their friendship and support. Above all, she would like to thank her family for their love and encouragement. Her parents, Charles and Virginia Soucy, and her mother-in-law, Elizabeth McCleskey, have always been nearby to lend a helping hand or to give a pat on the back. She has learned much watching her children, Matthew and Amy, grow to adulthood. Her husband, Kevin, continues to be the spirit that guides her in both her work and in life and to him she owes her greatest thanks.

Bill Kelly would first like to offer thanks to his parents, the late Mary R. and Edward F. Kelly. The love and support they offered Bill and his three brothers and the education that they worked so hard to provide established a foundation for future success. His parents-in-law, Flo and Leo Nadeau, also deserve great thanks for always believing in Bill and in his work. He offers special thanks to his son-in-law, Timothy Matos, and his daughters, Nicole Matos and Jacqueline, for their love, inspiration, and hours of mirth. But he reserves the greatest thanks for his wife, Michelle Nadeau Kelly. When she entered his life 30 years ago, she transformed it, and her love and support have made this text—and the rest of his work—possible.

William J. Kelly
Deborah L. Lawton

About the Authors

William J. Kelly earned his Ph.D. in English from the University of Rhode Island. He also received an M.A. in English from Rhode Island College and a B.A. in English from Southeastern Massachusetts University (now the University of Massachusetts, Dartmouth). A classroom teacher since 1975, he began his career teaching junior high school and high school English in the Fall River Public Schools. In 1984, he joined the English Department at Bristol Community College and five years later became the youngest full professor in the history of the college. He has also presented teacher training workshops as well as graduate courses in the teaching of writing. In 1997, the Carnegie Foundation for the Advancement of Teaching and the Council for Advancement and Support of Education named him Massachusetts Professor of the Year, the first time ever a community college professor received this prestigious award. An active freelance writer since 1981, his credits include a three-year stint as a weekly newspaper columnist. He is the author of several other texts, including Longman's *Discovery: An Introduction to Writing* and *Strategy and Structure: Short Readings for Composition*. A runner for more than 30 years, he is also an avid handball player. He lives in Fall River with his wife, Michelle; they are the parents of two daughters, Nicole and Jacqueline.

Deborah L. Lawton has been an advocate of the community college mission for more than 20 years. Her professional life at Bristol Community College has included 5 years as a student affairs professional and 20 years as an instructor of writing, literature, and communication. She is currently Associate Professor of English, and as Assistant Dean, she leads the college's Division of Language, Humanities and the Arts. She holds an M.A. in English from Western Michigan University, a B.A. in English from the University of Massachusetts, Amherst, and an A.A. in Liberal Arts from Greenfield Community College in Greenfield, Massachusetts. She and her husband, Kevin, residents of Swansea, Massachusetts, are the parents of Matt and Amy.

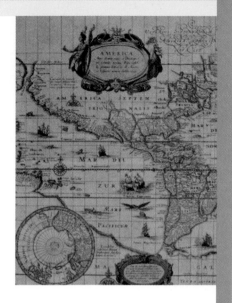

Starting Out

Using the Interactive Companion CD-ROM:

If your text has arrived with the multimedia activity pack to accompany *Odyssey,* you can find additional activities for each textbook chapter on the Interactive Companion CD-ROM. As you work through the book, look for these icons, which direct you to the CD-ROM for more practice and instruction.

Audio
1.1

Video
1.1

Activity
1.1

Weblink
1.1

Ensuring Success in Writing

Q: Why does it so often seem easier for me to say something than to write it down?

A: The short answer to this question is that writing often seems harder than speaking because in most cases, it is. Writing holds many challenges that speaking doesn't. For instance, speaking doesn't involve such matters as correct spelling or punctuation. Also, if what you say aloud doesn't make sense, your listener can ask you questions. When you write, you have to anticipate those questions and answer them on the page.

Overview: Understanding the Importance of Good Writing Skills

Audio
1.2

Writing is an odyssey, a voyage through the world of ideas. Every journey begins with a single step, and you took this first step on your writing odyssey when you opened this book. In your excursion through this world of exploration and discovery, you'll learn how to express your ideas effectively. Each time you write, you'll discover the power of your ideas and the connections between them. As you learn more about yourself and the world of writing, you will also develop greater skills in terms of usage, spelling, and punctuation.

As an introductory discussion topic, ask students to share their academic goals or future career plans. What types of writing will they be required to do?

In addition, your efforts to master writing will gain you some practical rewards. Express your good ideas clearly, directly, and correctly, and you will earn better grades. Do the same on the job, and you will command the respect of your colleagues and supervisors, ensuring your success as a professional. It's that simple.

Weblink
1.1

> **In this chapter you'll discover the basic elements of writing:**
>
> - the three stages of the writing process—prewriting, composing, and revising
>
> - the five interacting components of writing—writer, reader, topic, message, and means
>
> - the purposes of writing—to inform, to entertain, and to persuade

Recognizing the Stages of the Writing Process

Weblink
1.2
A successful piece of writing is much more than the words you see on a piece of paper. In other words, writing isn't just a final product. It is a process consisting of three stages: *prewriting, composing,* and *revising.*

Prewriting is the first stage of the writing process. Think of prewriting as planning. No one would expect a musician, artist, or athlete to perform at top level without some kind of rehearsal, exploration, or warm-up. The same is true of a writer. When you prewrite, you generate ideas on a subject that you can then develop into a piece of writing. Any technique that enables you to examine a subject more closely—for example, thinking, reading, talking to or observing others—can be a good technique. Chapter 2, "Generating Ideas through Prewriting," discusses and illustrates a number of other, more structured prewriting activities.

Fast Fact   The history of the written language extends back at least 5,000 years to the ancient Sumerians.

Weblink
1.3
The next stage of the writing process is **composing**. This stage involves taking the ideas generated during prewriting, expressing them in correct sentences, and then arranging them in paragraph form. Chapter 3, "Composing: Creating a Draft," explains this part of the writing process.

The third stage of the writing process is **revising**. As Chapter 4, "Refining and Polishing Your Draft," illustrates, a final piece of writing actually develops from several earlier versions, called *drafts*. Think of revising as **reseeing**. When you revise, you reexamine and then return to the earlier stages of the writing process, each time creating a more effective draft.

The following figure illustrates the process:

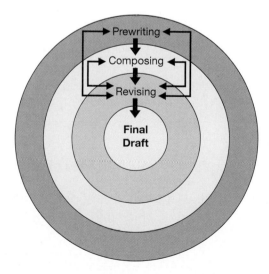

As the illustration shows, when you write, you begin with prewriting and proceed to composing and then to revising. Notice, however, that the arrows in the three outer circles point both ways. That's because the writing process is *recursive*. In other words, as you write, you may move back as well as forward through the process in order to make a piece of writing as effective as possible. For example, if during revision, you notice that your draft needs more detail, you return to prewriting to generate new ideas and then move again to composing to develop those ideas into supporting sentences.

> **Fast Fact** Persistence is one key to success in writing. A number of books that are now considered masterpieces were originally rejected as unpublishable. This group includes *The Chosen* by Chaim Potok, *Lady Chatterley's Lover* by D. H. Lawrence, *Moby Dick* by Herman Melville, and *A Portrait of the Artist as a Young Man* by James Joyce. A total of 27 publishers rejected Dr. Seuss's (Theodore Geisel) first book, *And to Think That I Saw It on Mulberry Street*, and the author considered burning the manuscript.

Exercise 1.1   **Reviewing the Stages of the Writing Process**

Weblink
1.4

1. What is the purpose of prewriting? Answers may vary somewhat.

   The purpose of prewriting is to plan what you are going to write and to generate

   ideas to illustrate or explain your point.

2. What happens in the second stage of the writing process, composing?

   Answers may vary somewhat.

   In the second stage of the writing process, you transform the ideas you have devel-

   oped during prewriting into sentences that you then arrange into paragraphs.

3. What happens when you revise? Answers may vary somewhat.

   When you revise, you take another look at your paper. Often this involves moving

   back through the stages of the writing process, for instance generating new material

   to fill out inadequately detailed sections.

Challenge 1.1   **Exploring Your Attitudes about Writing**

1. How do you feel about writing? On the following lines, briefly explain why you enjoy the act of writing—or why you don't.

   Answers will vary.

2. Now compare your response with a classmate's. On a separate sheet of paper, briefly summarize what the two of you have in common regarding writing.

3. On the following lines, list three things you would like to learn about the writing process. Answers will vary. _____

_____

_____

_____

Understanding the Dynamics of Writing

Audio
1.3

Simply defined, *writing* is an act of communication. It is the act of using words to convey your ideas to someone else. You do the same thing when you speak, but writing is different in two major ways. First, writing is more *deliberate*—more fully thought out—than speech. Second, writing is more *precise*—more carefully crafted word by word for just the right effect.

In the act of writing, five components interact: (1) a writer, (2) a reader, (3) a topic, (4) a message, and (5) the means of expressing that message

Activity
1.1

(written language). The *communication triangle* below shows how the five elements in the writing process interact.

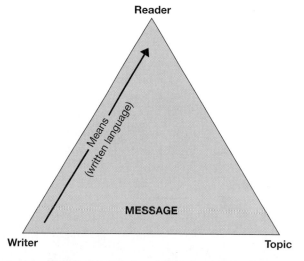

Video
1.1

To understand what writing actually involves, it's important to understand the five components of the communication triangle more fully. When you write, of course, *you* are the **writer**, the person who explores the **topic**, or specific subject, you want to write about. You might do this by drawing on your own experiences, talking to others, or reading and doing research. To convey your understanding of the topic, you use supporting examples, details, and explanations to construct a **message**. The written language you use to express your message is the **means**. And the audience that the paper is directed to, the person or persons whom you want to understand you, is the **reader**.

Imagine that you have written the following paragraph:

One of the most successful and, in some cases, controversial innovations in television programming over the past few years has been Reality Programming. These shows feature so-called ordinary people as they interact in situations and locales arranged by the producers. MTV is sometimes credited with beginning this trend with their show The Real World, in which several young people from diverse backgrounds were brought together to share a house. MTV also has a variation of this formula, Road Rules, which involves a number of young people interacting before the cameras as they travel the country. But reality television hit the mainstream with the introduction of the first Survivor show, which involved people of various backgrounds and ages living on a deserted island. Millions of people watched the participants engage in staged events while they tried to avoid being voted off the island by the other participants. The popularity of the first series led to additional editions of Survivor as well as other shows based on the same theme such as Big Brother, and Boot Camp. Critics have argued that reality shows highlight people's greed and bad behavior. But right now, the success of this kind of programming means that these kinds of shows will be around for a while.

You are the writer. Reality television is your topic. Your message is about the growth of this type of television programming. The specific words you have used to explain the categories of reality shows are your means. The person to whom you are directing this material is your reader.

Exercise 1.2   **Considering the Dynamics of Writing**

1. What are the five interacting components in the communication triangle?

   a writer, a reader, a topic, a message, and the means of expressing the message

2. What are two ways in which writing differs from speech? _____

   Writing is more deliberate than speech; it is more fully thought out. Writing is more

   precise than speech; it is more carefully crafted word by word for the right effect.

3. What does the communication triangle show? Answers will vary somewhat.

   The communications triangle shows how the five components involved in writing

   interact.

Exercise 1.3   **Considering Topics and Readers**

1. Think of three particular topics that you understand but that someone else might not necessarily understand and list them on the following lines.

Answers will vary.

2. Consider everything you understand about the topic *the Internet.* On the lines below, list three details you have thought of that you feel most readers would know, and explain why you think they would know these things.

Answers will vary.

Fast Fact In the first serious study of students who have difficulty writing, researcher Mina Shaughnessy noted that many of these students wrote very short pieces. And why were the papers so short? The students correctly reasoned that the less they wrote, the fewer errors they would make.

Challenge 1.2   **Analyzing Yourself as a Writer**

1. On the lines provided, list three things that make you uncomfortable with writing. Then, put a ✓ next to the one that you consider your biggest obstacle to writing well.

Answers may vary from difficulty with details of spelling, grammar, and punctuation

to general concerns like feeling unable to express thoughts in writing.

2. Working with a partner, make two lists in the spaces provided below. On the left, list what you feel strong writing skills would enable you to do. Then, on the right, list problems caused by weak writing skills.

Answers will vary. Representative answers are given.

Strong writing skills will allow me to . . .	*Weak writing skills mean that I . . .*
enjoy writing	am not making myself understood
get better grades	don't enjoy writing
write more clearly	keep putting off my writing assignments
be happy with what I write	don't get good grades
make my point understood	am not happy with what I write
	spend too much time on each writing assignment

As a journal assignment, ask students to add to the list of goals for improving their writing skills that they began in Challenge 1.2. Students can refer to this list as the course continues and evaluate their progress.

3. Which do you find easier, speaking or writing? Why?

Answers will vary.

Focusing on the Reader

Audio 1.4

As a writer, you need to concentrate primarily on the reader. If your writing doesn't communicate to a reader, then it's not effective. It's that simple.

Sometimes you will know exactly who the reader is. For example, if you are writing a follow-up letter after a job interview, you know that the reader will be the person who interviewed you.

However, for much of the writing you'll do, your reader won't be so clearly identified. In these cases, you must imagine a reader. It may help to think of a specific person, someone you know slightly but not well. The danger in using someone close to you is that you share too much common knowledge. Unless you assume that you are writing to a stranger, you are likely to omit information necessary to communicate with your actual readers.

Sometimes students write as if their instructor were their only reader, and they assume the instructor has knowledge about a variety of subjects. Small group work with opportunities to provide peer feedback can help students consider the needs of an average reader.

For additional discussions of reader-centered writing, turn to Chapter 3.

A second option is to focus on the average reader—someone who is like most of us. Most people know a little about many subjects. However, they don't often know detailed information about them. They don't know the hows or whys. Think of yourself before you learned about your subject. What kinds and amounts of information would you have needed to understand the subject?

For example, imagine that you have just purchased your first DVD player. Before you bought it, you didn't really understand the difference between a DVD version of a movie and a standard VHS videotape. After doing a little research and then buying a DVD player, you now understand a great deal. For example, you know that the digital technology means that the picture and sound are far superior to the picture and sound produced by a videotape. The units are in the same price range as most VCRs, and some DVD players include such features as surround-sound set-up. In addition, you know that the number of DVD titles available for purchase and rental is increasing at a rapid rate.

The average reader is like you were before you ever thought about buying a DVD player. This reader therefore needs to be given the kind of information that helped you understand DVD technology, information that seems ordinary to you now. Keep in mind that the more personal or complex the topic, the more fully you need to explain it.

Exercise 1.4 | **Identifying Your Reader**

Video 1.2

1. Explain why it's not a good idea to imagine a close relative or friend as your reader. _____

   A close friend or relative might have the same information I have, so if I leave out

   important details, neither of us might realize it.

   _____

   _____

2. In your own words, define the average reader. _____

   Answers will vary somewhat.

   The average reader is someone just like you were before you learned about the sub-

   ject you are discussing.

   _____

Exercise 1.5 **Evaluating the Needs of a Specific Reader**

Activity
1.2

1. Look again at the paragraph about *reality television* on page 6. What kind of reader did the writer have in mind? Briefly describe that reader.

The reader is an average reader who is expected to know what reality television is

but isn't expected to have thought very much about how reality television has influ-

enced programming.

2. How are you and the average reader of that paragraph similar? How are you different?

Answers will vary.

3. If the reader of the paragraph on reality television had no access to a television, how would this paragraph need to be changed? Working with a partner, make a list of information you would add. Write your list on a separate sheet of paper.

4. Now, on the same page, make a list of typical writing situations in which you know exactly who your reader is.

Examining the Purpose behind Your Writing

Video
1.3

People write to fulfill three main **purposes** or aims: *to inform, to entertain,* or *to persuade.* A paper explaining the effects of lead poisoning in children, for example, would inform. So would a paper spelling out how to build a stone wall.

A paper about attending a concert or sporting event would clearly entertain. Not all writing that entertains makes you laugh, however. A story about the break-up of a relationship would also entertain because it would arouse your reader's interest and emotions.

An essay suggesting that world powers should work together to reduce harmful emissions from fossil fuels would be persuasive. So would one suggesting that the United States should have a national health care program. As a college writer, you'll frequently be called upon to prepare persuasive writings or *arguments.* Writing that persuades can be particularly difficult to master. For this reason, Chapter 13 is devoted entirely to ways to develop an

Bring a daily newspaper to class, distribute sections to small groups, and ask students to identify informative, entertaining, and persuasive writing in it. Then discuss the following questions: What knowledge do the writers assume their readers have? What details do they include to help average readers understand the hows and whys of their subjects?

effective argument paragraph. In addition, a section of Chapter 15 explains ways to write an effective argument essay.

Often your purposes in writing overlap. An informative paper on lead poisoning might also entertain if it draws the reader in by describing specific cases. It might also be persuasive if it claims that more research money should be devoted to discovering ways to reverse the effects of the poisoning. Although one purpose may be primary, most papers fulfill more than one purpose.

Often students don't think much about the primary purpose of their writing because it is dictated by the assignment. However, it's always important to take a moment to identify that purpose, because purpose determines what you include and also influences the style and tone you adopt.

For example, imagine that your instructor asks you to write a paper that outlines some of the difficulties a first-semester college student might encounter. The primary purpose is to inform. If you instead write a paper in which you assert that college students today have greater opportunities to explore careers than ever before, the paper won't fulfill the primary purpose. Moreover, it won't meet the needs of your reader, who expects different content.

Fast Fact   When it comes to spoken and written communication, the world is becoming smaller every day, as many languages begin to disappear from use. In fact, among the world's 6,800 languages spoken today, linguists believe that 50 to 90 percent could be extinct by the end of this century.

Exercise 1.6   Understanding the Purposes for Writing

Audio 1.5

1. What are the three main purposes for writing?

   to inform, to entertain, and to persuade

2. Why is it important to understand the purpose of a piece of writing?

   It's important to understand the purpose of a piece of writing so that you'll include

   the type of details and language this purpose dictates.

Exercise 1.7   Analyzing the Purpose of a Paragraph

1. Read the following paragraph to determine its *primary* purpose. On the lines below, write that purpose, and explain your answer briefly.

According to recent statistics, more than 50 percent of all marriages in the United States end in divorce. This phenomenon has far-reaching implications, especially for the children of these broken families. In particular, many of these children experience trouble in school. Guidance counselors have reported cases in which elementary school children who were formerly outgoing and affectionate became distant and cold. At the high school level, challenges to authority and physical aggression are two of the most frequent signs of trouble in the house. Overall, divorce usually spells at least a temporary drop in classroom productivity.

The primary purpose of the paragraph is to inform. The writer is explaining the effects of divorce on children.

2. What other purpose does the paragraph fulfill? Explain.

The paragraph also persuades. It presents evidence that divorce can be harmful.

Exercise 1.8   **Listing Details That Are Appropriate to Purpose**

1. Working with a partner, choose *one* of the following three subjects: *a New Year's Eve party, a job interview, a popular vacation destination.* Now, list details you might include in a paper on this topic for each of the following purposes.

   a. Purpose: to inform

   Answers will vary. If students choose a New Year's Eve party, they might describe

   how to prepare for one, how the party evolved, or what ends the party serves.

   b. Purpose: to entertain

   Answers will vary. Students might describe some amusing incidents from New Year's

   Eve parties, or they might describe the most unusual party they ever attended.

c. Purpose: to persuade

Answers will vary. Students could use examples of successful or unsuccessful par-

ties to persuade readers to give or not to give their own New Year's Eve party.

2. Which of the papers for which you've listed examples would you find easiest to write? Why? Which would you find hardest? Why?

Answers will vary.

Challenge 1.3   Considering Approaches to Fulfill a Specific Purpose

1. Working with a partner, make a list of the difficulties that a first-semester college student might face.

Answers will vary. Students may list such problems as choosing courses, covering

expenses, finding time to study, and getting along with roommates.

2. Briefly explain how you might present the difficulties on your list if the purpose of your paper is to entertain.

Answers will vary. Students might give humorous examples of how several first-se-

mester college students dealt creatively with one or more of the problems.

Discovering Connections 1.1

When you see this photo, what do you think of? Do you think of sitting down in your favorite chair, relaxing, reading, talking with someone, or  watching television? Do you focus on a particular coffee shop, diner, or restaurant that you frequent? Does it make you think of a particular person who always seems to have a cup in hand? Or does the symbol make you think of habits in general?

For this assignment, focus on the picture, and discover what you think about it. Using the examples in this chapter to guide you, jot down what you think the average reader would need to know in order to understand your thoughts. Also, write down what your primary purpose would be if you were to write a paper that used these thoughts. Save this work for later use.

Discovering Connections 1.2

For this assignment, think of a first-time experience: a first day on a new job, a first date, the first day at a new school, or the first party you gave. Look again at the sample paragraph on page 6 and the paragraph in Exercise 1.7 on page 12. Then write down examples and details for your own paragraph. What does your reader need in order to understand the experience? Also, indicate the primary purpose for your paper on this topic. Save this work for later use.

 **ENSURING SUCCESS IN WRITING** Activity 1.3

New terms in this chapter	Definitions
● the writing process	● the series of stages in writing, including prewriting, composing, and revising
● prewriting	● when you generate ideas to develop into a piece of writing
● composing	● when you select and then express in sentence and paragraph form some of your prewriting ideas
● revising	● when you create new drafts through reexamining, improving, and polishing your initial version
● draft	● version of a paper
● writer	● the person expressing ideas through the written word
● reader	● the audience to whom a paper is directed
● topic	● the subject of a paper
● message	● the supporting examples, details, and explanations that represent your understanding of the topic
● means	● the written language used to express ideas
● purpose	● the intent or aim of a paper

Steps to Writing Effectively

● Understand the stages of the writing process: **prewriting**, **composing**, and **revising**.

● Understand how the five elements of writing—**writer**, **reader**, **topic**, **message**, and **means**—interact.

● Focus in particular on the **reader**.

● Recognize the **purpose** of any writing assignment.

to *inform*—as in a paper explaining how a movie special effect is created
to *entertain*—as in a paper recalling the first time you drove a car
to *persuade*—as in a paper asserting that recycling should be mandatory throughout the United States

Chapter 2

Generating Ideas through Prewriting

Getting Started... **Q:** I want to write—I really do. I'm just not sure how to start. Why can it seem so hard to begin?

Audio 2.1 **A:** Beginning to write can seem difficult for several good reasons. Some people feel as if they have too much to say on the subject, much more than they could ever organize and express in a piece of writing. Other people find that the vision they hold of the final writing—a completed, effective paper—contrasts so much with the rough ideas from which they will develop the paper that they become overwhelmed and intimidated. Still others feel that they have nothing to say.

Overview: Seeing Prewriting as a Way to Explore Ideas

Audio 2.2 As Chapter 1 discussed, writing is an odyssey through the world of ideas. When you write, you explore the world around you and your relationship to it. As you develop your writing skills, you also develop your creativity and powers of analysis. Through writing, you discover the significance of your ideas and explore the connections among them. This chapter will explore the most creative stage of writing: **prewriting**—the launch of an exciting journey to a new place.

Video 2.1

> **In this chapter you will learn how to use the following prewriting techniques:**
> - freewriting
> - brainstorming
> - clustering
> - branching
> - idea mapping
> - keeping a journal

Understanding Prewriting

Audio 2.3

Actually, you have already begun to explore *prewriting*. In the exercises of Chapter 1, you thought of ideas to communicate what you know about a topic. That activity actually represented an approach to prewriting.

Weblink 2.1

Weblink 2.2

As Chapter 1 explained, prewriting is the first stage in the writing process, which involves two more stages: *composing* and *revising*. When you write, you begin with prewriting and proceed to composing and then to revising. The real work for any piece of writing, however, always begins with prewriting. In order to explain your understanding of a topic, you have to generate ideas that will express that understanding for your reader. Through prewriting, you can discover what you think and know and develop these ideas about your subject.

Activity 2.1

Most writers use a number of informal prewriting activities, such as talking (either with other people or alone into a tape recorder), doodling, and thinking. However, experienced writers also use other, more specific techniques, including *freewriting, brainstorming, clustering, branching, idea mapping,* and *maintaining a journal.*

As you read about each technique, try it out. That way, you'll know which technique—or which combination of techniques—is best for you.

Exercises in this chapter direct students to try prewriting techniques on their own. Alternatively, have students complete these exercises in class, or demonstrate brainstorming, clustering, or branching on the board with everyone contributing ideas.

> *Fast Fact* Writing can get you just about anywhere, including in the *Guinness Book of World Records.* That's exactly what it did for Hakim Syed Irshad of Guirat, Pakistan. He had 602 letters published in national newspapers over almost 40 years. He had 42 letters published in 1963 alone.

Freewriting

Audio 2.4

Video 2.2

Freewriting is a no-holds-barred prewriting technique that involves writing down all your ideas on a subject for a set period of time. Ten minutes is a typical period. To freewrite, simply write everything that comes to your mind, even if it contains errors, drifts from the original subject, or doesn't immediately make sense. Don't stop, even if you get stuck. Instead, rhyme the last word you've written, or write "I can't think" until something different comes to mind. The strength of this method is its ability to help you overcome inhibitions and concerns and to get your ideas starting to flow.

If you do your writing on a computer, you will discover that it is an excellent tool for freewriting. First, set up your program to triple space your document. If you'd like, darken the screen so that you cannot see what you write. This may make you feel less inhibited. Now you can simply type away on your keyboard for ten minutes. When you are finished, print out what you have written. (For more information about using a computer for writing, see Appendix A on page 567.)

A freewriting on a subject such as *a souvenir* might look like this:

> A souvenir-weird word, it sounds French-I'll have to look it up to see. I know it means a special memento. I'm a packrat-save everything, so lots for me to consider. T-shirt from first music festival I was in in middle school-doesn't even fit me anymore, but I keep it shoved in my drawer anyway-reminds me of the good times we all had. How about that little toy truck-my Gramma gave it to me when I was little. Remember a lot from that time period-I wonder why? Mom had taken me to Gramma's apartment-Grampa had died and Gramma was moving and she gave me the truck-it's funny-can barely remember Grampa now, but I can still see Gramma's face when she put the car in my hand. OK, what else-what do I say now? All right, some people would probably think it's stupid, but I have a small paper napkin-came from the restaurant where I went on my first date-kind of goofy thing to keep. And Terry brought me a Can of Sunshine from Florida last year-laugh every time I see the label-wonder if anybody ever opens the cans to see what's inside?

As the highlighted areas indicate, this freewriting holds many promising ideas. Incidentally, no matter what prewriting technique you use, *highlighting, underlining,* or *circling* your best ideas is important. That way you can easily find them later if you want to develop them as topics.

Although these promising ideas are in very rough form, they represent *potential* for constructing a good piece of writing later on. You would then need to develop these ideas by writing additional details about them and drawing connections among them.

Fast Fact In writing and in life, what lies beneath the surface is usually much more than we expect. Mauna Lau and Mauna Kea, volcanoes in Hawaii, are nearly 14,000 feet high. This is less than half the height of Mt. Everest. But when measured from the floor of the Pacific—the base—the Hawaiian volcanoes are some 56,000 feet, meaning that only one-fourth of the mountains are above sea level.

Exercise 2.1 **Understanding Freewriting**

1. In your own words, explain freewriting. __Freewriting is writing that you do on__
   __a particular topic for a given period of time. You don't stop writing even when you get__
   __off the topic or feel that you have nothing more to say.__

2. Which ideas in a freewriting should you highlight, underline, or circle?

Why? <u>You should highlight, underline, or circle those ideas that seem to hold</u>

<u>promise for writing. You can go back to them later and develop them.</u>

_____

Exercise 2.2 **Finding What's Best in a Freewriting Example**

Audio 2.5

1. Take another look at the sample freewriting on *a souvenir* on page 18. What detail especially interests you or makes you curious? Why?

<u>Answers will vary.</u>

_____

_____

_____

2. Which detail or idea about *a souvenir* holds the most potential for development as a topic for writing? Explain why you would want to explore this topic. <u>Answers will vary.</u>

_____

_____

_____

Exercise 2.3 **Trying Freewriting**

1. Now it's your turn. On a separate sheet of paper, freewrite for ten minutes on one of the following topics: *childhood, money, loneliness.*

2. Identify the ideas in your freewriting that show the most promise by circling, highlighting, or underlining them.

3. What specific idea or example in your freewriting has the most potential for development? List it on your paper, and then write three additional details about it.

Challenge 2.1 **Evaluating Freewriting**

1. Exchange your freewriting with a classmate. On the freewriting you receive, put a ✓ next to the ideas that you find the most interesting. Return

the freewriting to the writer, and explain your choices. Put your own work aside for possible later use.

2. What do you like best about freewriting as a prewriting technique? Why?

Answers will vary.

_____

_____

3. Will you use this prewriting strategy again? Explain.

Answers will vary. Some students find freewriting a good way to release creativity;

others find that the pressure to write nonstop inhibits them.

_____

Brainstorming

Audio 2.6

Brainstorming is a more focused prewriting technique than freewriting. To brainstorm effectively, you should deliberately concentrate on a subject and then make a list of every idea that comes into your head about that subject. Brainstorming is an excellent technique when you are working with a partner or a group. Other people's ideas will start sparking your own creative thoughts, and soon you will find that the ideas come more quickly. A set time limit isn't necessary, although some people prefer to work with one. Remember, though, that you list only ideas directly related to the subject. After brainstorming, you may have fewer notes on paper than you do when you freewrite, but the ideas you generate are likely to be more obviously connected.

You can also brainstorm with your computer, if you wish, darkening the screen so that you cannot see what you write. Then type your list, letting your mind lead you easily from one idea to another. When you are finished, print out your list.

After you brainstorm, highlight, underline, or circle ideas that you think have potential as writing topics.

Here is a brainstorming on the subject of *vacation:*

Vacation-Camping

- Cheap compared to staying in a hotel
- borrow or rent a tent and sleeping bags
- food cooked outdoors tastes great
- swimming, fishing, hiking

- many campsites have individual electrical and water hookups
- trailer camping and SUVs-popular choice but really different from tent camping
- even some small RVs cost more than a luxury car or SUV
- everything in these RVs-microwaves, TVs, showers, air-conditioning-more like a hotel
- great to wake up with the sun warming the tent
- aroma of the pine trees is great
- some people are such pigs-leave litter everywhere
- state and national camping areas-good maintenance and security

As you can see, brainstorming generates a listing of related ideas, in some cases more than can be used in one paper. As a result, you have a wide variety of possibilities for further development.

Exercise 2.4   **Reviewing Brainstorming**

Activity
2.2

1. In your own words, explain brainstorming. _____

   Brainstorming means choosing a topic and then listing everything you can think of

   about that topic. Brainstorming is a good technique to use in a group or with another

   person.

   _____

2. Name one way in which brainstorming differs from freewriting.

   The ideas you come up with when you brainstorm are usually more connected than

   ideas that come up in freewriting.

   _____

   _____

Exercise 2.5   **Analyzing a Brainstorming Example**

1. Look again at the sample brainstorming on the subject of *vacation*. What item on the list would you like to learn more about? Why? _____

Answers will vary.

2. Which element or item of this brainstorming would you enjoy reading more about? Why? Answers will vary.

Exercise 2.6   **Trying Brainstorming**

1. Now try brainstorming. On a separate sheet of paper, brainstorm on one of the following topics: *exercise, luck, relaxation*.

2. Go through your brainstorming, and highlight, circle, or underline any ideas that are especially promising.

3. What single idea in your brainstorming seems most promising as a topic? List it, and add three details you could use to develop the idea.

Challenge 2.2   **Evaluating Brainstorming**

1. Exchange your brainstorming with a classmate. On the brainstorming you receive, put a ✓ next to the idea or area that you see as the most promising. Then return it to the writer, and explain your choice. Save your own brainstorming for possible later use.

2. What do you like best about brainstorming as a prewriting technique? What do you like least? Explain.

3. Would you recommend brainstorming as a prewriting technique? Explain.

Answers will vary. Some students may especially enjoy the group aspect of brain-

storming.

Clustering

Clustering is a prewriting technique that visually emphasizes connections among the ideas you develop. Begin by writing a general idea in the middle

Audio 2.7 of the page and circling it. As you think of related ideas or details, write them down and circle each one. Then draw lines to connect the new ideas to the ideas from which they developed. Continue this process until you have thoroughly examined the subject. The result is a series of ideas and examples, with lines showing how they relate to each other. You can then highlight or underline the ideas that hold the most promise.

Look at this clustering on the subject *habits:*

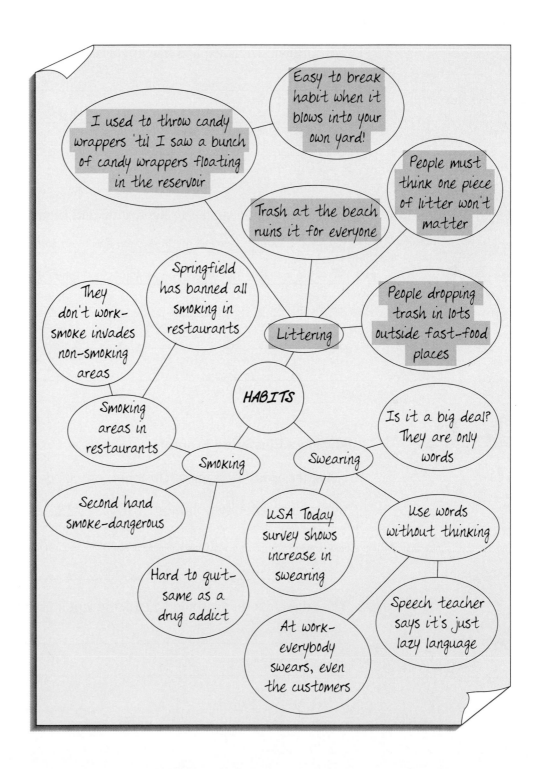

As this example shows, this prewriting technique emphasizes the various connections among related ideas in the material.

Fast Fact Fred Rogers, known to millions as the Mister Rogers in PBS's *Mr. Rogers' Neighborhood*, reported that he is low-tech when it comes to his writing. "I always use a yellow pad and a blue Flair pen." And he prefers silence to do it.

Exercise 2.7   **Reviewing Clustering**

1. In your own words, explain how to develop ideas using clustering.

   Clustering is a way of writing ideas to show the connections among them. When you cluster ideas, you circle them and connect them in groups with lines.

2. How is clustering similar to freewriting and brainstorming? How is it different? Clustering is similar to freewriting and brainstorming in that it helps you come up with ideas for writing. Clustering is different in that it lets you make connections among related ideas.

Exercise 2.8   **Analyzing a Clustering Example**

1. Consider again the sample clustering on *habits* on page 23. Which section or item interests you most? Why? Answers will vary.

2. What three questions would you ask the writer about the idea you chose? Answers will vary.

_____

_____

Exercise 2.9   **Trying Clustering**

1. Now try clustering. On a separate sheet of paper, create a clustering on one of the following subjects: *sports, humor, time.*

2. Circle, underline, or highlight the ideas or examples that interest you most.

3. What single idea holds the most potential for development? Write that promising idea, and add three details about it.

Challenge 2.3   **Evaluating Clustering**

1. Exchange your clustering with a classmate. On the paper you receive, put a ✓ next to the portion that you find most interesting. Return the clustering to the writer, and explain your choice. Save your own paper for possible later use.

2. Does clustering appeal to you as a prewriting technique? Explain.

Answers will vary. Students might find clustering especially helpful because they are

able to make and see connections graphically.

_____

_____

3. What did you like best about clustering? What did you like least?

Branching

Audio 2.8

Branching also visually emphasizes the connections among related ideas. Start by listing your topic on the left side of a piece of paper. Next, write ideas inspired by this topic to the right of it, and connect them to it with lines. As these new ideas lead to related thoughts and ideas, add these to the right again. Working from left to right across the page, let your ideas branch out, with lines showing relationships. Once you complete the branching, highlight, underline, or circle any promising ideas for later development.

Look at this branching on the subject of *competition:*

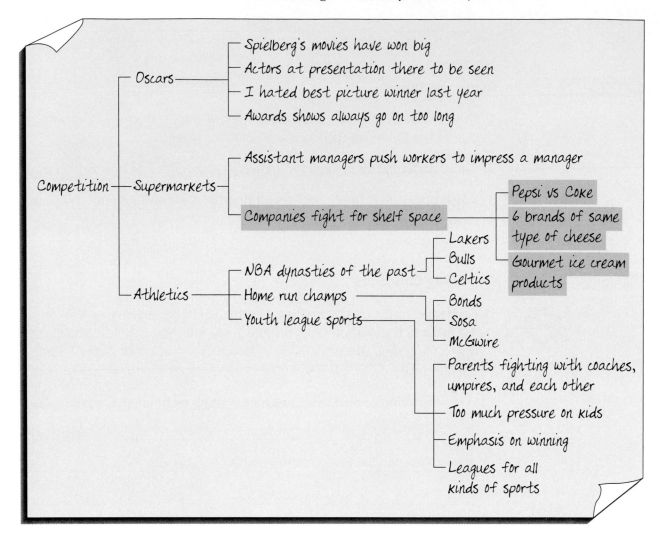

Branching leads you from one aspect of a topic to other, more specific aspects. As an added advantage, each "branch" holds an arrangement of related ideas. This focused organization allows you to concentrate on one area of your topic now and save the other areas for development later on.

Exercise 2.10   **Reviewing Branching**

Activity 2.3

1. In your own words, explain branching. Branching means that you write a topic on the left side of your paper and write your ideas about the topic on the right side. You connect your ideas with lines (branches), and you keep writing new subsets of ideas on the right.

2. How does branching differ from other prewriting techniques?

Branching leads you from general topics to more specific ones at the same time that

it organizes them by their relationships to one another.

Exercise 2.11   **Analyzing a Branching Example**

1. Which section of the sample branching on *competition* on page 26 would you find easiest to develop further? Explain. Answers will vary.

2. Which section would you find hardest to develop further? Explain.

Answers will vary.

Exercise 2.12   **Practice with Branching**

1. Now give branching a try yourself. On a separate sheet of paper, complete a branching on one of the following topics: *pollution, frustration, a holiday celebration.*

2. Highlight, circle, or underline the portions of your branching that might be further developed.

3. What section in your branching holds the most promise for development? List it, and then add three details about this idea or section.

Exercise 2.13   **Evaluating Branching**

1. Exchange your branching with a classmate. On the branching you receive, put a ✓ next to the detail or example that holds the most interest for you. Return the branching to the writer, explaining your choice. Save your own branching for later use.

2. What did you like most about branching? What did you like least?

3. Will you use branching again? Explain. Answers will vary. Some students

may find branching helpful in organizing their thoughts, while others may find it too rigid and confining.

Idea Mapping

Audio
2.9

Idea mapping is a freewheeling prewriting technique that attempts to stimulate multiple aspects of your creativity. When you idea map, you write words *and* create images such as icons, scribbles, sketches, and symbols. According to the theory underlying this technique, the words you include flow from the areas of your brain responsible for logic and analysis. The sketches and doodles you create arise from the areas of your brain responsible for creativity.

To try idea mapping, start anywhere on the page, writing a word or drawing a picture representing the general topic. Then let your mind range freely on the subject, recording your associations in images or words, as seems natural. After you finish, identify the ideas and images that have the most depth and meaning to you; highlight or circle them.

Here is an idea map on the subject *frustration:*

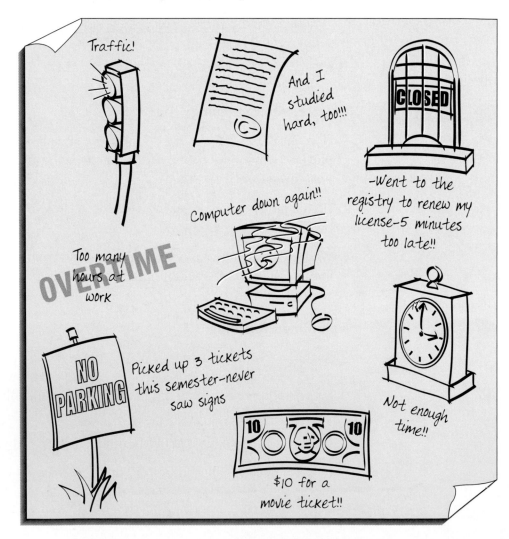

The final step in idea mapping is to translate selected images into words. For example, you might translate the scribbled sketch of the traffic light this way: "All the road construction makes the downtown streets seem more like a parking lot." You might convert the rough drawing of the computer to something like this: "Last night my computer crashed again. This time, I lost almost all my documents." The written version of the image can then serve as an idea to be used in a paper.

Exercise 2.14   **Reviewing Idea Mapping**

1. Explain idea mapping in your own words. _Idea mapping is a freewheeling_ technique that stimulates multiple aspects of your creativity. You write words and draw whatever comes to you, moving randomly back and forth between areas of the brain responsible for these activities.

2. Explain how idea mapping stimulates different aspects of your creativity. You use one aspect of the brain to generate words. You use another aspect to generate sketches or doodles.

Exercise 2.15   **Analyzing an Example Idea Map**

1. In the sample idea map about *frustration* on page 28, what image most interests or intrigues you? Why? Answers will vary.

2. What words most interest or intrigue you? Why? Answers will vary.

Activity
2.4

_____

_____

_____

Exercise 2.16   **Trying Idea Mapping**

1. Look at the scene you see from your vantage point in the classroom, and create an idea map of your thoughts and feelings about the scene. Or, if you prefer, complete an idea map on one of the following subjects: *advertising, time, a first date.*

2. Highlight, circle, or underline the ideas in your map that you feel you can develop further. Remember—translate key images into words.

3. What particular image or idea on your map holds the greatest potential for later development? Write it down, and add three details about it.

Challenge 2.4   **Evaluating an Idea Map**

COLLABORATION

1. Exchange your idea map with a classmate. On the map you receive, put a ✓ next to the idea or image you'd most like to see developed. Return it to the writer with an explanation for your choice. Save your own idea map for later use.

2. What do you like most about idea mapping? What do you like least?

3. Would you recommend idea mapping as a prewriting technique? Explain.

Answers will vary. Artistically inclined students might find idea mapping a particularly

appealing and useful prewriting technique.

_____

Maintaining a Journal

Audio
2.10

Activity
2.5

A journal is an idea book. How you set up your journal is up to you. It can be a notebook that you devote entirely to this purpose or a separate section of a notebook you use for other purposes as well. A computer file is also an ideal place for journal entries. Simply open the file and enter the date at the start of each entry.

As with any other activity, writing becomes easier the more you do it. Writing in your journal every day is one of the best ways to make writing seem as natural as talking and thinking. Use it to respond to discussions and books or articles you read for your classes or for personal enjoyment.

To encourage frequent and regular journal writing, schedule class time for students to read a journal entry of their choosing to a small group of their peers. Ask the listeners to identify a promising topic and raise questions an average reader might have about the topic.

Use it to sort out your feelings about another person or an issue that is important to you. Make no mistake about it: This extra practice will translate into improved writing for you.

Here is a list of topics that you could write about in your journal:

music	confidence	the media	minimum wage
a perfect weekend	dreams	habits	If I were a professor, . . .
high school	deadlines	power	adult responsibilities
the class clown	getting respect	best teachers	best book I've read
security	anticipation	stress	favorite magazine
childhood	success	happiness	best movie of all time
stereotypes	fads	freedom	public transportation
the ideal climate	urban life	worst fears	a special possession
pride	ambition		

Here is a sample journal entry on the subject *television violence:*

Violence on TV—there's a lot of it, that's for sure. Wrestling. It's so obviously fake but do all the people watching know it? Cartoons? The old ones, like the Road Runner, were violent, but the new ones seem to be different. Even the news is violent. It's like the television stations have a camera at every terrible accident or school shooting or riot. Over and over they show that stuff. We talked about this subject in psychology class just yesterday. The big problem is that kids are exposed to this stuff along with adults. My professor says nobody is sure yet. But some experts say kids just become accustomed to the violence. Then when they have problems, they react with violence themselves. I wonder how all the TV and movie violence I've seen has affected me.

Devote at least ten to twenty minutes to each journal writing session. After each one, reread what you've written, and highlight, circle, or underline any ideas that you might want to develop into papers in the future.

Which prewriting technique should you use? The answer, of course, depends on what works for you and makes you feel comfortable. The best way to find out is to explore each technique a few times. Then feel free to adapt or combine any of these techniques to suit your unique style.

Exercise 2.17   **Reviewing a Journal's Purpose**

1. In what ways is writing in a journal similar to keeping a diary? How is it

    different? Explain. <u>Writing in a journal is similar to keeping a diary in that both</u>

kinds of writing are private and personal records, and both are done on a regular

basis. Journal writing is different in that you write about ideas. You respond to read-

ings and discussions, and you explore new ideas.

2. How can writing in a journal help you improve your writing skills?

Writing in a journal means that you are practicing writing—and practicing almost

always leads to improvement.

Exercise 2.18   **Analyzing a Sample Journal Entry**

1. Take another look at the sample journal entry about *television violence* on page 31. What portion of it do you find most interesting? Why?

Answers will vary.

Students can also use their journals to respond to the readings in Part Seven, "Connecting: Responding to Reading" to help them read actively and prepare for class discussions.

2. How is journal writing similar to the other prewriting techniques you've tried? How is it different? Explain.

Answers will vary. Some students may say that journal writing is similar to other

prewriting techniques in that it generates new ideas and helps them see connec-

tions. They may mention as differences that journal writing is long-term, more per-

sonal, and broader in scope.

Exercise 2.19   **Trying Journal Writing**

1. Now try journal writing yourself. On a separate sheet of paper, write a page on one of the following topics: *pets, fame, televised sports.*

2. Reread your journal entry. Circle, underline, or highlight the material you would like to explore in greater detail.

3. What section holds the most promise? Why? On your paper, briefly explain.

Challenge 2.5   **Analyzing Your Writing Rituals**

Audio
2.11

Activity
2.6

COLLABORATION

1. As you worked on your journal entry, what did you notice about your writing habits or rituals? Is the time of day or the place where you write important to you? Do you need noise or silence? What do you use to write—pen, pencil, word processor? Begin your own journal by focusing on one aspect of your writing rituals, and then explore this subject for a page or so.

2. Now exchange your journal entry with a partner to compare answers.

Fast Fact As you work through the writing process, you might find it helpful to consider how a pearl develops. It happens this way: A grain of sand or some other tiny piece of debris irritates an oyster. The oyster reacts by coating the irritant with a lustrous smooth substance. In other words, the oyster turns a tiny thing that initially irritates it into something beautiful.

Discovering Connections 2.1

When you look at this photo, what comes to mind? Does it make you think of a letter you received recently or long ago? Who was it from? What was it about? Why do you remember it? Perhaps it makes you remember a letter you have written—or wished you had. Does it make you think instead of how communication has changed? Now that we have e-mail, does sending a letter seem old-fashioned?

Using the prewriting technique you find most comfortable, explore some of this subject's possibilities. Then highlight, underline, or circle the ideas that seem most promising. Save this material for later use.

Discovering Connections 2.2

For this assignment, think of a pet peeve or annoyance you face regularly. Perhaps it's the person who takes the last cookie and leaves the empty bag in the cupboard. Perhaps it's the driver who keeps a turn signal on for several miles, or the individual who peppers every sentence with expressions such as, "You know what I mean?" Use the prewriting technique that you prefer to explore this topic. Make sure you mark the ideas that have the most potential. Save your work for later use.

 GENERATING IDEAS THROUGH PREWRITING

New terms in this chapter	Definitions
● **prewriting**	● the initial idea-generating stage of the writing process Prewriting techniques include freewriting, brainstorming, clustering, branching, idea mapping, and maintaining a journal.
● **freewriting**	● writing freely about a subject for a set period of time without stopping or worrying about correctness or completeness
● **brainstorming**	● focusing on a subject and listing all related ideas that come to mind
● **clustering**	● writing and circling an idea in the middle of the page, developing and circling related ideas around it, and drawing lines to connect related clusters of ideas
● **branching**	● listing a subject on the left side of the page, writing ideas inspired by that subject to the right, and connecting the branching ideas with lines
● **idea mapping**	● writing words and drawing images about a topic in a random manner across a page and then translating the images into words
● **maintaining a journal**	● writing several times a week in a separate notebook to explore or discover new ideas, respond to points raised in classes, or explore issues important to you

Composing: Creating a Draft

Getting Started... **Q:** I have good ideas about the subject, but right now they only make sense to me. How do I get my ideas in a form that would make sense to a reader?

Audio 3.1

A: Good ideas form the foundation for effective writing. Building on that foundation means taking the time to identify what someone else—your reader—would need to understand your good ideas and then expressing those ideas in correct sentence form.

Weblink 3.1

Overview: Understanding Composing

Audio 3.2

Chapter 2 discussed the first stage in the writing process, showing you various techniques for generating preliminary ideas. This chapter focuses on the next stage: **composing**. If prewriting is the launch of your odyssey, then composing is the main leg of that journey. In this stage of the writing process, you focus on a manageable aspect of a topic and organize your relevant ideas into a coherent message. You compose sentences that support, explain, or illustrate that topic.

> *Fast Fact* **Compose** has several meanings, including separate definitions in relation to such fields as music, art, and printing. If you feel tired after composing for a while, maybe it has to do with the meaning of the word that is associated with writing: "To construct (in words)."

Weblink 3.2

At this stage, your goal is to translate your good ideas into writing that communicates clearly to your reader. The following pages will discuss how to transform your prewriting material into a complete draft that meets your reader's needs. In other words, you will see how to limit your subject and identify the strongest details, examples, and illustrations for support.

> *This chapter focuses on creating the two components that make up a paragraph:*
>
> ● the topic sentence
>
> ● the supporting sentences

Recognizing the Structure of a Paragraph

Audio
3.3

ESL Note
See "Writing
Paragraphs," especially
the section on unity,
and "Writing Essays" on
pages 585–586.

A **paragraph** is a series of sentences that work together to develop one main idea. Paragraphs vary in length, depending on the point you are trying to make. Generally, they are between five and ten sentences long.

What is the role of the paragraph? One way of looking at paragraphs is as the building blocks of essays, the longer pieces of writing you will be expected to write as a college student. (For more on the essay, see Chapters 14 and 15.) As you move from paragraph to paragraph in an essay, you expand your discussion, covering your subject in detail.

It's useful to think of paragraphs in another way: as a miniature version of an essay. Like an essay, a paragraph develops several items of support for its main idea. However, in a paragraph, the scope of your discussion is more limited than it is in an essay.

The following figure shows how a paragraph is arranged:

Have students examine paragraphs in text-books, magazines, and newspapers, or the essays in Part Seven. What do the paragraphs have in common? How are they different? What factors determine the length of the paragraphs? Stress that there is no rule about the number of sentences in a paragraph. Writers always have to identify their readers' needs and determine their purpose for writing.

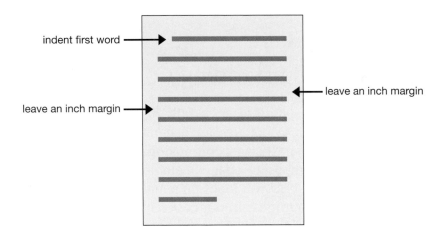

As the figure shows, the first line of a paragraph is *indented* about a half-inch on the paper. This provides a visual cue for the reader that a new idea is being introduced.

Now, look at this sample paragraph. Consider the structure of its content.

> *A sunset two years ago at Horseneck Beach was the most beautiful sight I have ever seen.* During most of the day, the sky was full of clouds, but the temperature was in the 80s, so it was still comfortable. At about 6 P.M., just after I had packed up all my stuff, the sky cleared completely. Instead of heading home, I decided to take a walk to the end of the beach. As I reached the point where the Westport River flows into the bay, I looked out across the bay to see a beautiful rose-colored sun. For the next twenty minutes I watched as the softly glowing sun seemed to sink into the water. I had never seen anything so wonderful, and I probably never will again.

The first sentence of this paragraph answers the reader's unstated question, "What's the point?" It is the **topic sentence**, the sentence stating the main idea. The other sentences are the supporting sentences, sometimes called the *body* of the paragraph. They elaborate on the topic through details and examples. Together, the supporting sentences communicate to the reader why the sunset was so beautiful.

Exercise 3.1   **Reviewing Composing and Paragraphs**

1. In your own words, briefly explain the differences between prewriting and composing. <u>When you prewrite, you come up with ideas that can be developed.</u>

   <u>When you compose, you decide on a main point and organize your ideas into a</u>

   <u>complete message or communication.</u>

   _____

   _____

2. What makes the topic sentence different from the other sentences in a paragraph? _____

   <u>The topic sentence expresses the main idea, or point, of the whole paragraph.</u>

   _____

   _____

Exercise 3.2   **Identifying the Paragraph Break**

1. The following passage runs two paragraphs together. After reading the entire passage, put a / at the point where the second paragraph begins. Then briefly explain why you believe the second paragraph begins at that point.

   > It was so much fun last summer watching the traveling circus set up the big top. First, the twenty members of the circus crew spread out the yellow-and-white-striped canvas, half as long as a football field. They hammered enormous spikes into the ground and tied off one end of the tent. Next, they laid the main tent pole flat, with the center of the tent attached to the top of the 35-foot post. Once this was set, they put several more spikes along each side and tied these sections off. / Then came what everyone was waiting for: the elephants. The canvas seemed almost to come to life as the elephants strained to pull up the pole. The handlers quietly urged the elephants on while the crowd cheered. After five minutes of work, the pole was up, and the crowd applauded while the elephants enjoyed their reward: an extra bale of hay and a shower.

The first section is about the circus crew beginning to set up the big top. A new sec-

tion starts when the elephants are introduced. The whole second section focuses on

the elephants' role in raising the big top.

2. Below are five topic sentences. Choose two of them. On your paper, list three ideas that you would use to support each. Use a prewriting technique if necessary to help generate ideas.

a. Consumers have to be careful to avoid telemarketing scams.

b. An insensitive teacher can have a terrible effect on young children.

c. In most cases, the families of Alzheimer's patients suffer more than the patients themselves.

d. The behavior of adults at youth league games is often offensive.

e. The public is often more honest than the media would have us believe.

Exercise 3.3   **Practice Writing Topic Sentences**

1. Paragraphs a, b, and c lack topic sentences. Read each passage, and then, on the lines after it, write a suitable topic sentence.

a. For example, using the tools of a word-processing program, you can easily produce attractive, error-free documents and letters. With money management software, you can keep track of all your financial transactions and plan for the future. If your computer has a CD-ROM player, you can choose from hundreds of entertaining and challenging games and programs for fun and learning. Even more exciting, by using a modem in combination with your computer, you can purchase a connection to the Internet and join the Cyberworld. There you can shop for everything from software to softballs, communicate with people around the globe, and find fascinating information about any topic you can imagine. Increasingly, the personal computer is becoming a one-stop business and entertainment center in American households.

Answers will vary. Sample answers are given.

Computers enable people to perform a wide range of both routine and

entertaining activities quickly and efficiently.

b. Rent takes a big chunk of my pay. I have to pay $350 a month. In addition, I have to pay for my utilities: heat, lights, electricity, and telephone. That's usually $175 a month. Then, I have to pay for food. Between the groceries I buy and the few meals I eat out, food costs me $300. My school expenses are enormous, too. I receive some aid, but I'm still responsible for $1,000 per semester plus the cost of books. At the end of the month, I have about $10 left.

After I pay my monthly expenses, I don't have much money left.

c. Many of my jobs involve cutting lawns and raking. On some jobs, I also tend gardens. This means regular watering, weeding, and fertilizing of the flower beds, and turning the mulch. I also have to dig up and reseed any problem spots in the lawns. On most days in the spring and summer, I work ten hours straight.

My yard care business keeps me busy with a variety of tasks.

2. Choose a paragraph (five to ten sentences long) from a reading in Part Seven of this book. Identify the topic sentence. Then briefly explain the relationship between the topic sentence and its supporting sentences. Write down the page number of your paragraph so you can find it again easily.

Answers will vary.

Students may find paragraphs without topic sentences. Discuss how topic sentences can help student writers focus and express their ideas in academic writing.

Challenge 3.1   **Analyzing and Developing Supporting Details**

The Challenges in this chapter lead students through the process of drafting a paragraph with an effective topic sentence.

1. Look again at the paragraph on page 36 about the beautiful sunset. Working with a partner, explain on a separate sheet of paper how the rest of the sentences in the paragraph support or explain the topic sentence.

2. Choose one of the following topics. On a separate sheet of paper, list five ideas that could support it. Try your hand at a paragraph, putting your ideas into sentence form. Save the paragraph for possible later use.
   a. the perfect night out
   b. a dangerous activity
   c. dieting

Identifying an Effective Topic

Audio 3.4

Sometimes you know right away what part of a subject you want to focus on. In many cases, however, you will need to work through and evaluate your prewriting material to decide your focus. (See Chapter 2 to review prewriting techniques.)

Video 3.1

For instance, imagine you have been asked to write about *childhood*. The general topic appeals to you. Like many people, you often think about your own childhood, so you certainly have plenty of ideas on the subject. However, *childhood* is far too broad a subject to cover in a paragraph. You aren't sure what aspect of the subject to focus on, so you do the following clustering on the subject:

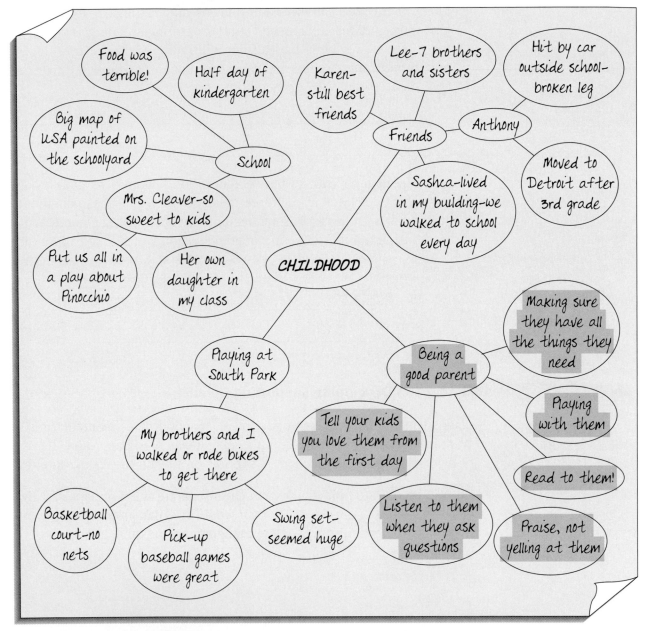

As the highlighted areas of this clustering show, the material on being a good parent is particularly promising. Therefore, an effective topic has emerged: things parents should do to help their children grow into happy adults.

You found an area that interests you and that you have ideas about. Your concern now should be to *limit* your subject, or narrow its scope, enough that you can cover it well in a paragraph. In one paragraph, you could not fully explore all the things parents should do as they raise their children. However, you could explore some key points of child rearing. In other words, narrowing your topic is just as important as coming up with ideas about it.

> **Fast Fact** One of the best ways to discover ideas for writing—reading—is, sadly, becoming less and less commonly practiced. Only 45 percent of Americans read a half-hour or more every day, a number that has dropped from slightly more than 50 percent ten years ago, according to research conducted by NPD Group, a New York–based market research firm.

Exercise 3.4   **Reviewing Topic Focus**

1. What steps should you follow if you don't immediately know the specific

   idea you want to write about? _____

   You should look over your prewriting and decide which idea has the most potential.

   _____

   _____

2. How do you select the prewriting details that you should focus on

   through the rest of the writing process? _____

   When you limit your subject, you focus on a smaller subcategory of it so that you

   can explain or describe it thoroughly in the space you have.

   _____

   _____

Exercise 3.5   **Trying to Focus a Topic**

Students can reserve a section of their journals to record and save additional promising ideas that they may want to develop in later paragraphs or essays.

Select another area from the clustering on childhood on page 40—one that interests you and could be developed. On the following lines, list this topic possibility. If it is too broad, narrow it to a subcategory that can be covered in a paragraph.

Answers will vary. Students might choose the section on being a good parent because it

has substance and research possibilities.

_____

Challenge 3.2   **Developing Your Own Limited Topic**

Choose a prewriting technique and generate ideas for the topic of *greeting cards*. Select the idea in your prewriting that interests you most and that you think is narrow enough to serve as the subject of a paragraph. If necessary, add other details or subcategories of related information. Save this work for later use.

Writing a Clear, Specific Topic Sentence

Audio
3.5

Weblink
3.3

After you identify a suitable subject, the next step is to develop a topic sentence that expresses your specific focus. Writers often place the topic sentence first in a paragraph. That way, readers know immediately what the paragraph will be about and in what direction it is heading. This is a good pattern to follow as you develop your writing skills. Don't be surprised, though, if you occasionally find that the topic sentence fits better elsewhere in the paragraph, perhaps at the end or in the middle.

A typical topic sentence accomplishes two things: (1) It states the topic clearly, and (2) it suggests the direction or tone of the paragraph, often by revealing the writer's attitude toward it. Look again at the topic sentence from the paragraph about the beautiful sunset on page 36:

EXAMPLE

topic | writer's attitude or reaction

A sunset two years ago at Horseneck Beach was the *most beautiful sight I have ever seen.*

The topic is the sunset, and the writer's attitude or reaction expresses how beautiful that sunset was.

As this example shows, an effective topic sentence is more than a simple announcement of your intent. Never write "I am going to write about . . ." or "This paragraph will deal with . . . ." Instead, express in direct terms the particular point you want to make about your subject.

An effective topic sentence is also clear and specific. Consider this version of the topic sentence about the beautiful sunset:

WEAK   A sunset I saw once was special.

This topic sentence is too vague to communicate the main point effectively. The sentence suggests that something was unusual about the sunset, but it doesn't indicate what made it special.

Compare the weak version with the original, effective version:

CLEAR AND SPECIFIC   A sunset two years ago at Horseneck Beach was the most beautiful sight I have ever seen.

This version of the topic sentence is effective because it clearly and specifically identifies when the event occurred and why it was special.

You develop a topic sentence from the prewriting details that you identify as most promising or interesting. Your topic sentence must encapsulate the significance of those ideas and also provide a direction for the rest of the paragraph.

For example, look again at the highlighted material in the clustering on *childhood* (page 40). This information relates to matters of child rearing.

The details all involve things that parents should do to provide children with a greater sense of love and security. Once you determine your attitude and reaction to this topic, you are ready to formulate a topic sentence:

EXAMPLE

topic ⟶ | writer's attitude or reaction

By paying attention to their own behavior, parents can *lay the groundwork for their children's happiness.*

This topic sentence is effective because it is clear and specific and because it answers the reader's implied question, "What's the point?"

Exercise 3.6   **Reviewing the Topic Sentence**

Activity
3.1

1. With most paragraphs, where will you place the topic sentence? Why?

    Most of the time I will place it first in order to give the reader a preview.

2. In your own words, briefly explain the difference between a vague topic sentence and a clear, specific topic sentence. _____

    A clear topic sentence states the topic specifically and gives direction to it. A vague topic sentence is general and directionless. It may not present the topic fully, or it may not give a clear, specific reaction to the topic.

Exercise 3.7   **Analyzing Topic Sentences**

In each of the following topic sentences, circle the topic, and underline the writer's attitude or reaction to it. Study the example first.

EXAMPLE

The (many costs of owning a car) make automobile ownership <u>a luxury some students cannot afford</u>.

Audio
3.6

1. Most people <u>don't spend enough time</u> (planning for their future.)

2. (Poor highway design) is <u>a major reason for auto accidents.</u>

3. (Both major political parties in the United States) seem <u>out of touch with the average person.</u>

4. (Not all top high school athletes) are <u>poor students.</u>

5. (The fierce winter weather) is particularly hard on <u>the poor and elderly.</u>

6. (Better communication) is <u>the key to an improved personal relationship.</u>

7. (Raising the driving age to eighteen) may be <u>one way to reduce the number of car accidents.</u>

8. A (thorough employee training program) translates into <u>a far better environment for workers and customers.</u>

9. (Popular music today) is <u>stale and unimaginative, with each new artist sounding like the others.</u>

10. (A laptop computer's size and portability) makes <u>it a great choice for college students.</u>

Exercise 3.8   **Turning Topics into Topic Sentences**

Below are ten topics. Working with a partner, turn each topic into a topic sentence by adding an attitude or opinion about it on a separate sheet of paper. Write the sentences on a separate sheet of paper, using the example to guide you.

EXAMPLE   melanoma, the most serious type of skin cancer

Melanoma, the most serious type of skin cancer, continues to increase because of our love affair with sunbathing.

Answers will vary.

1. an increase in the number of fatal auto accidents

2. special effects in movies

3. investing in the stock market

4. a better understanding of world geography

5. a reduction in tuition and fees

6. a course in public speaking

7. the amount of money the government allots for education

8. life as a vegetarian

9. interest in astrology

10. the unique landscape of the desert

Exercise 3.9   **Revising Topic Sentences**

The following topic sentences are general and vague. Working with a partner, rewrite them on the lines provided, making sure they clearly focus on a specific topic and express a definite attitude.
Answers will vary. Sample answers are given.

1. I enjoy physical activities.

   Physical activities can improve your mental health.

2. Being laid off is bad.

   Being laid off is particularly hard on men over age fifty.

3. Computers are amazing.

   Computers can put you in touch with people all over the world.

4. Television programming isn't challenging.

   Network television programming offers few programs dealing with important issues

   such as education, government, or the environment.

5. Science is interesting.

   Science interests many people because of the constant potential for discovery in a

   variety of fields.

6. Skateboarding is exciting.

   Over the past few years, skateboarding has become one of the most exciting spec-

   tator sports around.

7. Public transportation is important.

   Public transportation holds great potential to reduce pollution and congested streets

   and highways.

8. Personal counseling can be helpful.

   Personal counseling can help people learn to understand themselves and their be-

   havior.

9. Energy conservation is important.

   Energy conservation is important in order to ensure an adequate supply of power for

   everyone.

10. Working as a construction laborer is hard.

Working as a construction laborer is physically demanding, especially on your back

and legs.

Exercise 3.10 **Evaluating Topic Sentences**

1. Here are several potential topic sentences. Working with a partner, label the effective topic sentences with an *E* and the weak ones with a *W*.

___E___ a. Working in a nursing home has helped me learn the true meaning of dignity.

___W___ b. Housebreaking animals is necessary.

___E___ c. My uncle's best decision ever was to get his general equivalency diploma (GED).

___E___ d. Oil spills are environmental nightmares affecting the world for years.

___W___ e. Many of today's movies are bad.

___W___ f. Golf has increased in popularity.

___E___ g. I trace my decision to major in music education to Ms. Souza, my first music teacher.

___W___ h. The parking situation on campus needs attention.

___W___ i. Winter can be a difficult time.

___E___ j. My friend Alexei knows the secret to having a great party.

2. With the same partner, select one of the topic sentences that you identified as weak.
   a. On a separate sheet of paper, rewrite it. Be sure it focuses clearly on a *specific* topic and expresses a definite reaction.
   b. On the same paper, develop at least three supporting sentences for this topic sentence.

Challenge 3.3 **Developing a Topic Sentence from Your Prewriting**

1. In Challenge 3.2 (pages 41–42), you identified the most promising idea in a prewriting on greeting cards and focused it as a topic. Now, on a separate sheet of paper, write a draft topic sentence based on this limited topic.

2. On your paper, list at least three ideas you could use as support for your topic sentence.

Providing the Best Support for the Topic Sentence

Audio
3.7

After you have developed a clear, specific topic sentence, you need to develop additional sentences that will support, illustrate, or explain it. You can draw much of your raw material from the related prewriting ideas you generated.

Here again is the highlighted clustering on *childhood* from page 40:

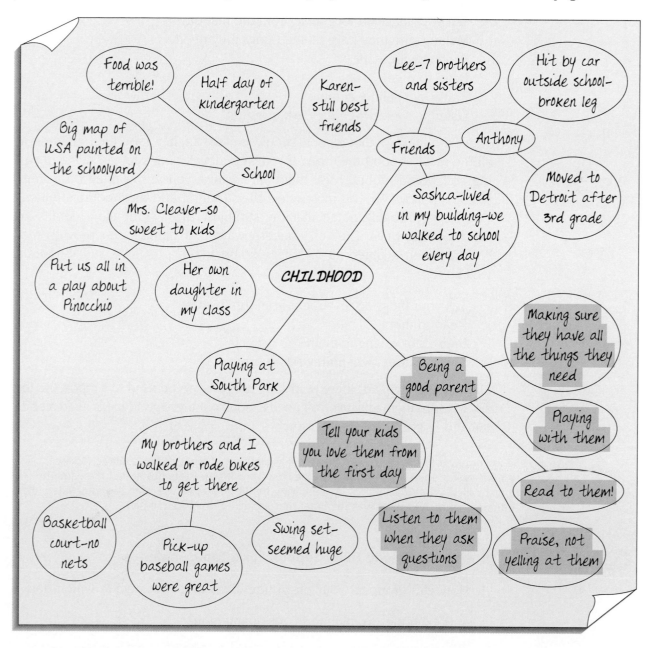

And here again is the proposed topic sentence inspired by the highlighted material:

EXAMPLE

> By paying attention to their own behavior, parents can lay the groundwork for their children's happiness.

With your main idea clearly stated, you need to look back at your prewriting material with a selective eye. You've already identified the most promising section of the clustering. Now your job is to decide which details and examples in that section supply the best support for the topic sentence.

To find out, first list the ideas you have highlighted:

Being a good parent
Tell your kids you love them from the first day
Making sure they have all the things they need
Playing with them
Read to them!
Praise, not yelling at them
Listen to them when they ask questions

These are all ways that parents should behave as they raise their children, so all the ideas support the thesis. If you were developing a longer piece of writing, you would probably use them all. Because you are working on a single paragraph, however, you must select the strongest and most complete items.

You've probably noted that the strongest, most compelling details are the following ones. They all concern ways that parents can provide their children with a blueprint for success and a sense of love and emotional well-being:

Tell your kids you love them from the first day
Read to them!
Praise, not yelling at them
Listen to them when they ask questions

Of course, as they are, these points are not ready to be used to support the thesis. To make them effective, you need to spell out these good ideas in greater detail and in correct sentence form.

Fast Fact To compose the famous word game "Scrabble," out-of-work architect Alfred Mosher Butts relied upon the front page of the *New York Times*. Butts developed the game he first called Criss-Cross Words by identifying the frequency of use of the various letters of the alphabet. And what was the letter that appeared most frequently? **E.**

Exercise 3.11 **Reviewing How to Build Support for a Topic Sentence**

1. How can grouping your prewriting ideas help you decide which details

   and examples to include in your paragraph? _____

   When all the material is grouped, you can determine which group is strongest and has the most specific and detailed examples.

_____

2. Not all the ideas you develop during prewriting can be used in any one

   paragraph. What purpose can the other ideas serve? _____

   You can write an essay and develop the other ideas in separate paragraphs, or you

   can develop them for later papers.

   _____

   _____

Exercise 3.12   **Analyzing the Relationship between Topic Sentence and Body**

1. Choose a paragraph of five to ten sentences from a reading in Part Seven, and identify its topic sentence.

2. On the lines that follow, explain the connection between this topic sentence and its supporting sentences. (Record the page number of the paragraph so you can locate it again easily.)

   Answers will vary.

   _____

   _____

   _____

Exercise 3.13   **Developing Effective Topic Sentences**

For more practice grouping details into categories, have students arrange the details in the prewriting samples in Chapter 2.

1. Here is a list of details from an idea map on credit card purchases:

birthday presents	new coat
shoes	books
CDs	stereo equipment
graduation gifts	pants

   Working with a partner, arrange the details in related categories on a separate sheet of paper. Add more specific details as you wish.

2. After you and your partner identify the grouping with the most potential for development, pinpoint the topic they cover, and write a clear, specific topic sentence.

Challenge 3.4   **Evaluating a Topic Sentence and Grouping Details**

1. Exchange the topic sentence you drafted on greeting cards (page 46) with a partner. Check the topic sentence you receive to make sure it is

clear and specific. Return the topic sentence and any suggestions for changes to the writer. Then make any necessary changes to your own topic sentence.

2. Group the ideas from the prewriting you completed for Discovering Connections 2.1 or 2.2 at the end of Chapter 2 (page 33). Save this work for later use.

Deciding on the Most Effective Arrangement

Video 3.2

Once you select the details and examples that will best support your topic sentence, you must arrange them in a logical, effective order. Ask yourself this question, "How can I present this information so that I hold my reader's attention?"

In the case of the clustering material on child rearing, you believe the following arrangement will accomplish this aim:

2 Listen to them when they ask questions
1 Read to them!
3 Praise, not yelling at them
4 Tell your kids you love them from the first day

Reading to children is important because it sets them up for success in school and beyond. Listening to children is even more important, however, because it tells them that they are important to their parents. But making sure that children hear praise and regular reminders that they are loved is most important of all. As you see it, this order of presentation, working up to your most important point, best lays the groundwork for a convincing paragraph.

Taking the time to sort out your ideas and establish a tentative order is an important step in creating an effective piece of writing. Your final decisions about how to order the details should always depend on what arrangement best draws and holds the reader's attention. In many cases, building from strong to stronger example would help to hold the reader's attention.

Remind students that the order in which they present their information is not a rule but a choice for them to make that depends on their purpose for writing. Also, this is a preliminary choice; for additional information about organizing, see "Organizing Sentences Effectively" on pages 67–75 in Chapter 4.

ESL Note
See "Writing Paragraphs" on page 585.

Exercise 3.14   **Reviewing the Importance of Order in a Paragraph**

1. Once you have grouped the ideas and examples in your prewriting, what should you do next? Why? _____

Once you've grouped the ideas and examples in your prewriting, you should divide them into categories. You can then figure out how to present them in the best order.

2. How will arranging your supporting details in a logical order make your paragraph more effective? _____

You can keep your ideas together in a logical way. You can also build your paragraph

so that it has the strongest possible ending.

_____

Exercise 3.15   **Identifying Strong Supporting Details**

1. Take another look at the examples of good child-rearing practices on page 48. Which one would you find easiest to develop? Why?

Answers will vary depending on which area students find most troublesome.

_____

_____

2. Of the examples listed, which do you think is the strongest? Why?

Answers will vary.

_____

_____

_____

Exercise 3.16   **Arranging Supporting Details in Your Writing**

1. Choose one grouping of details you created on credit card purchases in Exercise 3.13 (page 49). On a separate sheet of paper, arrange this list in an order you could use to support the following topic sentence: *Credit cards make it easy to spend more than you really want to.*

2. Exchange your list with a partner.
   a. On the list you receive, evaluate the order of the details and make any suggestions you think would help the writer develop a better paragraph. Return the list to the writer.
   b. After considering your reader's comments, make any changes you feel are necessary. Put this list aside for later use.

Challenge 3.5   **Ordering and Developing Your Supporting Ideas**

1. On a separate sheet of paper, arrange the prewriting information you grouped in exercise 2 in Challenge 3.4 (page 50) into ordered subcategories. Save this work for later use.

2. Develop one detail from one of the subcategories into a supporting sentence. Write it on your paper.

Making Your Material Reader Centered

Audio
3.8

In order for your reader to understand your ideas, you must present them as **reader-centered writing**. In other words, you must express those ideas fully, in complete sentences, so that the average reader will understand them.

Prewriting ideas are generally not expressed completely or in correct sentence form. They are expressed as **writer-centered writing**, that is, in a raw, unpolished form that makes sense to you but not necessarily to another person.

To understand the difference between writer-centered and reader-centered material, think of your notes for one of your classes. In a psychology class, for example, you might have written the following notation:

WRITER-CENTERED   *Personality types/Jung-way you behave?*

These words have a specific meaning to you because you were in class when your instructor presented the material, and you participated in the class discussion that followed. However, a reader who was not in that class might have trouble interpreting your notes.

Now, look at this reader-centered version of the same material:

READER-CENTERED

Discuss with students the importance of providing concrete details in their writing. As an example, write a writer-centered shopping list on the blackboard, and ask students to rewrite it as a reader-centered list. Also, turn to Part Seven, and have small groups choose an essay and identify reader-centered details that give them a clear understanding of the writer's meaning.

Carl Jung's theories about personality types raise some questions about the way we behave.

As you can see, this version expresses the ideas more thoroughly in complete sentence form. With the ideas spelled out this way, even a reader unfamiliar with psychology can understand what the note actually means.

In addition to expressing your good ideas in correct sentence form, one other step to make your writing more reader centered is to *amplify*. When you amplify, you provide additional specific examples and details to support your ideas. As a way to cue yourself to amplify, you might even consider including the expressions *for example* or *for instance*. When you write one of these expressions, you make a commitment to your reader to provide additional specific details about the information.

Consider the reader-centered example about personality types, but this time with the additional supporting information:

EXAMPLE

Carl Jung's theories about personality types raise some questions about the way we behave. **For example, some people prefer to work independently, while others prefer the company of co-workers. These preferences are connected to a person's personality type, which is identified by an instrument called the Myers-Briggs Type Indicator.**

As you can see, the idea becomes even more reader centered once the information introduced by *For example*, shown in boldface, is added. Even when you don't use *for example* or *for instance*, make sure to supply information to support or explain the point you are making.

Exercise 3.17 **Reviewing Writer-Centered and Reader-Centered Writing**

1. In your own words, briefly explain the difference between writer-centered and reader-centered information. _____

   Writer-centered information is raw and unpolished. It's clear only to the person who

   wrote it. Reader-centered information is complete, polished, and in sentence form.

   It's clear to anyone who reads it.

2. How do you change writer-centered material into reader-centered information? You change writer-centered material into reader-centered information by

   expressing it clearly and thoroughly in complete sentences.

3. How can including the expressions *For example* or *For instance* help you make information even more reader centered? _____

   When you use the expressions *for example* or *for instance,* you make a commitment

   to your reader to provide additional specific details.

Exercise 3.18 **Creating Reader-Centered Sentences**

1. Make a copy of a page of notes you took for another class. Exchange this copy with a partner. On a separate sheet of paper, try to change the writer-centered notes you receive to reader-centered sentences.

2. Return the notes and your reader-centered version to the writer. Review the papers returned to you and circle any detail that your reader failed to understand. Explain the point you meant to communicate.

Challenge 3.6 **Evaluating and Developing Reader-Centered Sentences**

1. Return to the material you developed in Challenge 3.4 (pages 49–50) and Challenge 3.5 (pages 51–52). On a separate sheet of paper, transform all your writer-centered details into reader-centered sentences.

2. Exchange your reader-centered sentences with a partner. On the page you receive, put a + next to each sentence that is reader centered and a ✓ next to any sentence that is still writer centered. Return the page to the writer, and suggest a way to improve the sentences marked with a ✓. Save your own work for later use.

Using a Reader Evaluation Checklist

Activity 3.2

The secret to success in writing is to meet the needs of your reader. In most cases, you can assume that your reader knows a little bit about many subjects but not necessarily a great deal about most subjects. Using a **reader evaluation checklist** is one way to make sure that your supporting information meets the needs of your reader.

To use the reader evaluation checklist below, simply insert the name of your topic in the blanks, and then write your answers to the questions.

Reader Evaluation Checklist

☐ What does the average reader need to know about _____?

☐ What does the average reader already know about _____?

☐ What information would help the average person better understand _____?

☐ What did I find the hardest to understand about _____ at first?

☐ What helped me to figure out _____?

☐ What's the best example or explanation I can give the average person about _____?

As you answer these questions, you will also focus on the examples or explanations that your reader will need to see your point.

Exercise 3.19 | **Understanding Your Reader's Needs**

Activity 3.3

1. In your own words, explain how much specialized knowledge you can expect your reader to possess about most topics. _____

   You can expect your reader to have only a little specialized knowledge about most topics.

2. Briefly explain how using the reader evaluation checklist can help you meet the needs of your reader. _____

As you answer the questions on the list, you'll be providing the information that your

reader needs.

Exercise 3.20　　**Analyzing Your Readers' Needs**

1. On the lines below, list three subjects that you know a great deal about and then three subjects that you wish you knew more about.

I know a great deal about . . .　　　*I wish I knew more about . . .*

a. _____Answers will vary._____　　a. _____

b. _____　　b. _____

c. _____　　c. _____

2. Choose one item from each column in number 1, and then answer the following questions.

a. What details would help you communicate to a reader what you know

about the subject you understand well? _____

Answers will vary.

_____

_____

b. What details would help you understand more about the subject you

want to explore? _____

Answers will vary.

_____

_____

Exercise 3.21　　**Evaluating How Well a Paragraph Meets Readers' Needs**

1. Using the reader evaluation checklist on page 54, read and assess the following paragraph. Use the questions below the paragraph as guidelines.

　　Coffee bars are gaining popularity in cities and towns throughout the country. The trend began a while ago. The shops serve several varieties of coffee and food, and they offer a pleasant atmosphere. Some coffee bars have begun to include various activities to make patrons feel comfortable as they enjoy their favorite brand of coffee.

   a. Did the writer do a good job of providing information the average reader might not know?

   b. What did the writer assume the average reader *did* know?

   c. Are there areas on which the writer still needs to focus?

2. On a separate sheet of paper, write to the writer of the paragraph, suggesting ways to improve this paragraph.

Challenge 3.7 **Rewriting a Paragraph to Meet Readers' Needs**

1. Exchange the note you wrote to the writer in Exercise 3.21 with a partner. Using the comments to guide you, rewrite the paragraph on a separate sheet of paper.

2. Exchange your rewritten paragraph with a partner. Use the reader evaluation checklist on page 54 to assess the paragraph you receive. Make a note next to any point that still needs work, and return the paragraph to the writer.

Developing a Complete Draft

ESL Note
See "Writing Essays" on pages 585–586.

Video
3.3

Using a computer can also help students quickly arrange and organize details in various ways as they begin to compose.

The final step in the composing stage of writing is developing a **complete draft**. This draft combines your topic sentence with selected reader-centered examples and details in the order you have chosen.

   As you develop this initial version, remember that it doesn't have to be perfect. (The next chapter will show you how to revise, or refine and polish, your writing.) At this point, focus your energies on stating your ideas completely and clearly.

   You should make your draft look clean and readable, too. If you have access to a computer, learn how to use it to do your writing. You'll find the flexibility of writing with a computer especially helpful in making changes as you revise. Whether you use a computer or a typewriter, make sure to double-space to leave room to make corrections and additions. If you write by hand, write on every other line. Either way, you'll have room to make corrections and additions as you revise your work.

   Here's a completed draft of a paragraph on the importance of some aspects of child rearing, which developed from the original clustering on childhood. They key ideas from the section on being a parent are underlined:

By paying attention to their own behavior, parents can lay the groundwork for their children's happiness. <u>Reading to children</u> every day is important. Parents also need to spend <u>time interacting with their</u>

children <u>and responding to their questions</u> patiently. They count on their parents to help them make sense of the world around them. Most of all, parents should regularly <u>tell their children that they love them</u> and <u>praise them when they do something well</u>. Nothing is more important to children's future success than the support and interest of their parents.

As you can see, the original writer-centered prewriting material from page 40 has all been changed into reader-centered supporting sentences. Notice also some additional supporting sentences that help clarify and explain the key points. The arrangement follows the order indicated on page 50, with a significant example of good parenting behavior leading to increasingly significant examples. In addition, the final sentence reiterates the main point so it serves as a conclusion.

Of course, this writing can still be improved, but before you can revise, you need a completed draft as a starting point. That's exactly what this paragraph represents.

Exercise 3.22   **Reviewing the First-Draft Stage**

1. What do you do in the final step of the composing stage of writing?

   In the final step of the composing stage, you write a complete draft. You do that by

   combining your topic sentence with reader-centered examples and details that sup-

   port it.

2. What advantage is there in double-spacing your work? _____

   You can make corrections and additions above the lines.

Exercise 3.23   **Analyzing a First Draft**

1. Which aspect of the composing stage have you found easiest? Which is most difficult for you? Explain. Answers will vary.

2. On the following lines, explain what you like most about the first draft paragraph on child rearing. What do you think should be changed?

Answers will vary.

Students can share and discuss their responses to Exercise 3.23 as an introduction to the practice of providing peer feedback.

3. On the following lines, list any examples in this first draft that need improvement. Explain why reading to children is important. Explain how parents should interact with their children and respond to questions. Explain ways parents should show their love.

Challenge 3.8   **Creating a First Draft**

1. Through several Challenges in this chapter, you have been developing your prewriting from Discovering Connections 2.1 or 2.2 in Chapter 2 (page 33). Now write a clear, specific topic sentence for the subject you have developed from this prewriting. Let the model paragraph on child rearing on pages 56–57 serve as a guide.

2. Identify your best details from the reader-centered sentences you developed in Challenge 3.6 (pages 53–54), and turn them into your supporting sentences for a first draft. Save your draft for later use.

Fast Fact If you feel frustrated at the time it takes to complete a first draft, keep this point in mind: It took 70 years to produce the first version of the *Oxford English Dictionary*.

Discovering Connections 3.1

When you look at this photo, what ideas does it inspire? Does it make you think of something you need to throw away? Something you threw away that you now wish you had saved? What was it? Why do you feel this way? How about the expression, "One person's trash is another person's treasure"? Do people sometimes overlook the value in something they discard? Does the picture instead make you think of society's wasteful habits or the mountains of trash that cities and towns accumulate every day?

For this assignment, focus on the photo, prewrite, choose and focus a topic, and compose a draft paragraph (at least five to ten sentences long). Follow the process outlined in this chapter, making sure that your writing is reader centered.

Discovering Connections 3.2

For this assignment, focus on an influential individual you know. Who is it? How did you meet this person? In what ways has this individual influenced you in the past? How does this individual influence you now? Is the influence positive or negative? After you prewrite, compose a paragraph (at least five to ten sentences long), following the steps outlined in this chapter. Concentrate on making your paragraph reader centered.

 RECAP   COMPOSING: CREATING A DRAFT   Activity 3.4

New terms in this chapter	Definitions
● **composing**	● the stage of writing during which you focus on a topic and provide supporting ideas drawn from your prewriting material
● **paragraph**	● a series of sentences that work together to develop one main idea
● **topic sentence**	● the sentence stating the main idea, or topic, of a paragraph and setting the tone or direction for the writing The topic sentence expresses the topic, limits it to a manageable size, and usually reveals the writer's attitude or reaction to the topic. **Example** ⌐ topic ⌐ The new biography of former President Carter is ⌐ attitude or reaction ⌐ fascinating reading.
● **reader-centered writing**	● ideas expressed thoroughly and in complete sentence form so that they make sense to the reader
● **writer-centered writing**	● raw, unpolished ideas that provide enough clues to make sense to the writer but not necessarily to the reader
● **reader evaluation checklist**	● series of questions designed to help writers ensure that their supporting information meets their readers' needs
● **amplifying**	● the act of supplying additional specific examples and details
● **complete draft**	● the first complete version of a piece of writing, including a clear, specific topic sentence plus supporting sentences

The Process of Composing a Draft

Focus a topic.
↓ ↑
Create a **topic sentence**.
↓ ↑
Organize **prewriting ideas** and **examples**.
↓ ↑
Develop **supporting sentences**.
↓ ↑
Restate **topic sentence**.

Chapter 4

Refining and Polishing Your Draft

Getting Started... **Q:** I've worked really hard and developed the best paper I could. Why go back and work on it again?

Audio
4.1

A: Yes, your initial draft was as good as you could make it—at that time. But haven't you ever had a discussion and then, after the discussion is long over, remembered something else you wish you had said? That's how it is with writing, too. After a little time away from your draft and with a little help from a reader, you will probably see several areas in your writing that could still use work.

Overview: Understanding the Revising Stage

Audio
4.2

You can always be sure of one truth about writing: You won't write a masterpiece on the first try. Your best writing takes thought, time, and patience. A good first draft is only the beginning. Once you have completed a solid draft, you must *revise*, or refine and polish, your draft. This chapter explains how to revise your writing and turn something good into something even better.

Revising actually involves three interrelated steps: reassessing, redrafting, and editing. **Reassessing** means checking for *unity, coherence,* and *effective language.* It also involves seeking feedback from an objective reader. **Redrafting** means rewriting to eliminate any problem spots and add needed material. You may need to reassess and redraft more than once in order to achieve the results you want. **Editing** means proofreading your final draft to eliminate any remaining errors. It represents the last leg of your writing odyssey.

Ask students if they have revised their writing in the past and what steps they have usually taken. How is revising different from proofreading? Refer to the illustration on page 3 in Chapter 1; review how revising is a central part of the writing process, which may lead to further prewriting and composing.

This chapter outlines the way to refine and polish your first draft until it represents your best. You will learn that revising involves

- reassessing

- redrafting

- editing

Reassessing: Reseeing Your Work

Video 4.1 By the time you complete a draft, you will probably feel that you've taken your paragraph as far as you can. Let a little time pass, though, and you will undoubtedly find areas that still need work. Putting your initial draft away for a day or two will create a distance and enable you to *resee* your paragraph. When you look at it again with a fresh eye, you'll be better able to reassess it for unity, coherence, and effective language.

> **Fast Fact** Former Beatle Paul McCartney reports that he woke up one morning with the tune for "Yesterday," a song that has gone on to be one of the most-recorded pieces of all time, complete, in his head. It usually doesn't work that way. As McCartney puts it, "Well, you're dead lucky if something like that passes through you."

Maintaining Unity

Audio 4.3 Writing is **unified** when all the examples and details relate directly to the main idea. To make sure your writing is unified, eliminate any material that is not relevant to your topic.

Look at this paragraph about the stressful experience of getting a driver's license:

Underscores and circles are answers for Exercise 4.4 on page 66.

Getting my driver's license was the most stressful (experience) I have ever faced. On that morning, I had my final road (lesson,) I had no problems. In fact, my instructor told me that it was the best of my six (training sessions.) But as soon as the inspector from the Registry of Motor Vehicles stepped into the car, I could feel my heart racing. Stress contributes to the number of people who suffer heart attacks each year in the United States. Bad diet is one of the major contributing (factors) to the number of heart attacks. Heredity is another major (cause.) By the time the (inspector) sat down and put on (her) seat belt, I could feel my shirt becoming damp. When she told me to start up the car, for a moment I couldn't even think what to do. After a couple of seconds, I remembered to turn the key. For the next ten minutes, I felt like I was watching someone else pull out into traffic, turn left and right, complete a three-point turn, and parallel park. After I parked the car back at the (Registry) parking lot, the (inspector) turned to me and said that I had passed. <u>At that point</u>, I was happier and more tired than I had ever been.

Which sentences are not directly connected to the writer's topic, a stressful experience?

You probably identified the fifth, sixth, and seventh sentences. They deal with heart attacks, which are related to stress, but they are irrelevant to the specific experience of getting a driver's license. Once you eliminate these sentences, the paragraph is unified.

Exercise 4.1   **Reviewing the Revising Process**

1. In your own words, explain the steps in revising. _____

   In the revising stage, you look at your writing again. You rewrite any parts that still

   need work. Finally, you proofread to correct any remaining errors.

   _____

2. When you reassess a draft to see if it is unified, what are you looking for?

   When you reassess a draft for unity, you check the sentences to make sure they all

   relate directly to the topic.

   _____

Exercise 4.2   **Eliminating Unrelated Sentences**

Activity
4.1

1. Check the following paragraph for unity. Circle any sentences that do not belong with the others.

   Last summer, I had a great experience working as a soccer coach for the day camp at a local Boys and Girls Club. I was in charge of the indoor soccer games for the youngest group of campers, ages five to seven. (In many countries, soccer is called football.) During the first week of camp, I assigned the fifty kids to different teams and had practice games. They didn't really understand how to play the game, so I spent the first two weeks teaching them basic things like passing and playing defense. (Soccer is the world's most popular sport.) So far, professional soccer has not been especially successful in the United States.)For the rest of the summer, I was able to watch the children as they improved and learned to love soccer. At the end of the summer, all the players gave me a plaque naming me "Most Valuable Coach." I never would have guessed that a simple summer job could have been so rewarding.

2. Use the following lines to explain why the sentences you've circled do not belong. <u>That soccer is also called football is not related to the topic. Soccer's</u>

<u>popularity is not relevant here. The fate of professional soccer in the United States</u>

<u>has nothing to do with the point of the paragraph.</u>

Challenge 4.1   **Assessing Unity in Writing**

Video

4.2

COLLABORATION

Challenges in this chapter will guide students through the steps in the revising process as they provide feedback to a peer and refine and polish their own paragraphs.

1. You completed a draft paragraph for Challenge 3.8 in Chapter 3 (page 58). Exchange that draft paragraph with a partner. Check the paper you receive for unity. Indicate for the writer any sentence that you think does not belong, and return the paragraph to the writer.

2. Check your reader's comments, and make whatever changes you feel are necessary to establish unity in your paragraph. Save your work for later use.

Providing Coherence

For a paragraph to communicate your ideas clearly to a reader, it must be **coherent**. Coherence means a paragraph holds together. All of the paragraph's sentences should be arranged in a logical order and connected so that ideas flow smoothly.

Two elements give a piece of writing coherence: (1) transition and (2) organization of sentences or order of ideas.

Audio

4.4

To help students understand the connections transition provides, have them select an essay in Part Seven and identify the synonyms and transitional expressions the writer used.

Transition   Connecting your supporting sentences smoothly is a matter of supplying *transition*. Writers use three techniques to relate sentences to one another.

1. Repeat key words and phrases or rename them with pronouns.
2. Substitute **synonyms**, words that have similar meanings, for key words.
3. Insert transitional expressions to connect ideas.

The repetitions and substitutions provide a thread of continuity that keeps the main idea uppermost in the reader's mind. Look at the italicized words in the following sentences.

> **EXAMPLE**
>
> *The manager* came out to the front of the *movie theater* to talk to the *crowd* waiting to get into the *building*. She quietly told *the angry people* that a smoke alarm had gone off. *Her* staff was checking to make sure the *facility* was safe.

In the second sentence, *She* takes the place of *The manager*, *the angry people* renames *the crowd*, and the synonym *building* substitutes for *the movie theater*. In the third sentence, *her* refers to *She* and another synonym, *facility*, replaces *building*.

Weblink 4.1

Perhaps the most useful technique for showing the relationships among sentences is adding **transitional expressions** to connect ideas. Here is a listing of common transitional expressions:

Common Transitional Expressions to Illustrate or to Show Cause and Effect

accordingly	consequently	indeed	particularly
after all	for example	in fact	specifically
as a result	for instance	of course	therefore
because	for one thing	overall	thus

> **EXAMPLE**
>
> Injuries resulting from in-line skating have risen dramatically over the past few years. *As a result,* sales of helmets and other safety equipment have also risen.

Common Transitional Expressions to Add, Restate, or Emphasize

again	finally	in conclusion	on the whole
also	first (second, last, etc.)	in other words	too
and	further	moreover	to sum up
besides	in addition	next	

> **EXAMPLE**
>
> For more than two weeks, people in the central part of the state faced intense temperatures and high humidity. *Finally,* a cold front brought relief in the form of three days of much-needed rain.

Common Transitional Expressions to Show Time or Place

above	beyond	lately	soon	until
after	currently	now	then	when
as soon as	earlier	once	there	whenever
before	here	presently	to the left (or right)	where
below	immediately	since	under	

> **EXAMPLE**
>
> The dog raced toward the open gate. *When* the owner shouted, the dog came to a dead stop.

Common Transitional Expressions to Compare or to Contrast

although	despite	in the same way	similarly
and	even though	likewise	still
as	however	nevertheless	though
both (neither)	in contrast	on the other hand	whereas
but	in spite of	regardless	yet

EXAMPLE   The small stores in town can't compete with the prices of the giant home repair center that just opened. *However,* they can provide more personalized service.

As you can see, the italicized words in each of these example sentences signal the connection between ideas.

Consider the boldfaced and italicized words in the following paragraph:

> Good time management is the key to success in college. Setting up **an hour-by-hour breakdown** is the first step. *As* you make your **time plan**, don't forget to include time for meals and for nonschool activities such as exercise. *Once* you establish your **schedule**, you *then* need to follow it closely. *For example, if* you set aside Mondays from 12 to 2 for study time in the library, make sure to follow through on your **commitment**. *If* you follow your **schedule** carefully, you will find the quality of your work improving.

As you can see, transition holds this paragraph together. For example, **time plan** renames **hour-by-hour breakdown**. In the remaining sentences, two other synonyms, **schedule** and **commitment**, also replace **time plan**. In addition, a number of transitional expressions, including *as, once, then, for example,* and *if,* emphasize the connections between the points.

Exercise 4.3   **Reviewing Coherence**

1. What do you check for when you reassess your writing for coherence?

   When you reassess your writing for coherence, you check that your sentences are

   arranged effectively and connected clearly.

2. What techniques can you use to connect your sentences smoothly?

   You can repeat key words or phrases; you can use synonyms; and you can use tran-

   sitional expressions to connect ideas.

Exercise 4.4   **Identifying Transitions**

See pages 62–63 for an illustrated version of this paragraph.

COLLABORATION

1. Return to the paragraph on a stressful experience (pages 62–63). Working with a partner, underline its transitional expressions, and circle any synonyms or renaming words.

2. Choose one of the transitional expressions you underlined, and, on the following lines, briefly explain how it connects ideas in the paragraph.

Answers will vary.

_____

_____

_____

Exercise 4.5   **Using Transitions in Your Writing**

1. Write a paragraph of at least five sentences about your favorite way to relax. Include several transitional expressions from one of the lists on page 65.

2. Choose one of the sentences you have just written. On the lines below, briefly explain how its transition provides connection within the sentence or between sentences.

Answers will vary.

_____

_____

_____

Challenge 4.2   **Evaluating Use of Transitions**

1. Exchange the draft paragraph you completed in Challenge 3.8 of Chapter 3 (page 58) with a partner. Check the paper you receive for adequate use of transitions. Put a ✓ at any point where you feel a transition is needed, and return the paragraph to the writer.

2. Check your reader's comments, and make whatever changes you feel are necessary to connect your paragraph's sentences smoothly.

 Audio 4.5   **Organizing Sentences Effectively**   The second element of coherence is organization. As the previous chapter shows, the order in which you present your ideas can affect how well your reader is able to see your point. Therefore, when you reassess, you should make sure your ideas are effectively arranged. Three common organizational plans for writing are *chronological order, spatial order*, and *emphatic order*.

Fast Fact Be careful not to let your work in developing an effective paper overwhelm you, as it did for novelist John Steinbeck. Disappointed in the tone of an early version of his Nobel prize-winning novel *The Grapes of Wrath,* Steinbeck destroyed the entire draft.

 Audio 4.6   *Using Chronological Order*   Whenever you recall a series of events as they occurred in sequence, you use **chronological order**, or time order.

Look at this paragraph about dealing with jury duty:

Choose a narrative essay listed in the Rhetorical Index. Have students read it, identify the transitional words, and explain the chronological sequence.

> Being called for jury duty proved to be a waste of time for me. When I arrived at the courthouse at 8:30 A.M., I joined about twenty other people in the main courtroom. The court clerk then addressed us, explaining our duties as jurors. After the clerk was done, we watched a brief video about proper conduct in the courtroom. The clerk then told us to wait in that room until we were summoned. Sitting with nothing to do wasn't easy for me. Two days before, my boss had given me a huge new project with a tight deadline. I had been working like mad from that point on. Now I had to watch the minutes tick by. After about forty minutes, another court officer came into the room, told us that we were dismissed, and thanked us for our time. At that point, I picked up my jacket and headed to the door, thinking about my lost morning.

In this paragraph, chronological order and transitional words help the reader keep the events straight. *When* the writer arrived, she went into a courtroom and *then* the court clerk addressed them. *Once* the talk was over, they changed rooms, and *then* they were told to wait. *After* some time passed, the prospective jurors were told that they could leave, and *at that point* the writer thought about the time she had wasted.

Incidentally, in some cases, you break chronological order by deliberately presenting some episode out of order. You use this device, called a *flashback*, to emphasize or explain some point. In this paragraph, sentences seven, eight, and nine, which explain time pressures this prospective juror encountered *before* that morning, constitute an effective flashback. When you include a flashback, make sure to supply sufficient transition, as this passage does, so that your reader will notice that you have switched the order of events.

Exercise 4.6   Reviewing the Importance of Order in Paragraphs

Video
4.3

1. In your own words, briefly explain how a clear, logical ordering of ideas can improve your writing.

   Effective organization helps readers follow your train of thought and understand your point.

2. On the following lines, briefly explain chronological order.

   Chronological order is the arrangement you use when you write about events in the order in which they occurred.

_____

_____

| Exercise 4.7 | **Considering the Uses of Chronological Order** |

1. List three types of subjects that would be best organized in chronological order—for example, a first night at a new job. _____

   Answers will vary. Students might choose subjects like their first meeting with

   someone who became significant in their lives, their first day in the military or in a

   foreign country, or their recollection of a particular sports event.

2. Choose one of the subjects you listed in number 1 and, on the following lines, list at least three steps in that sequence of events.

   Answers will vary. _____

   _____

   _____

| Exercise 4.8 | **Analyzing Chronological Order and Transitional Cues** |

Students can write a list of steps in a process they know well and then scramble them and have another student arrange the steps. Turn to Chapter 8 for more information about using linear order.

COLLABORATION

1. Working with a partner, arrange the following steps in the formation of a thunderstorm in chronological order. Number them *1, 2, 3,* and so forth.

   __6__ Precipitation starts, causing updrafts and downdrafts within the cloud.

   __1__ A cold air mass enters an area of warm air, pushing up the warm air.

   __3__ The condensation causes a cloud to begin forming and heat to be released into the atmosphere.

   __4__ The heat pushes the air higher yet, releasing more heat, condensing more water vapor so that the cloud grows.

   __7__ The violent up-and-down motion within the thunderhead forms storm cells.

   __5__ As the cloud grows, windspeed increases, forming an anvil-shaped cumulus cloud called a thunderhead.

   __8__ The thunderstorm is now mature; thunder, lightning, even hail, accompany heavy rains.

_____2____ The rising warm air reaches dew point and water condenses from the surrounding air.

2. On a separate sheet of paper, explain how you and your partner figured out the order. List any transitional expressions that helped you determine your final order.   Answers will vary somewhat.

Challenge 4.3   **Evaluating the Use of Chronological Order**

1. For Exercise 4.8 (pages 69–70), you developed a three-step sequence for one of three subjects provided. Turn this material into a draft paragraph, and then exchange your paragraph with a partner. Check the sequence of the paper you receive, noting any irregularities, and return the paper.

2. After considering your reader's comments, make whatever changes you think are necessary. Save your work for later use.

Audio
4.7

Using Spatial Order   When you need to explain where one object, place, or person exists in relation to other objects, places, or people, you rely on spatial order. This method of arrangement is used whenever a writer needs to help a reader visualize a particular scene. Through spatial order, items, locales, and individuals can be viewed in an organized, natural way: top to bottom, left to right, near to far.

Look at this paragraph about a newly decorated apartment:

> The biggest transformation I have ever seen in a space was my Aunt Monique's last apartment. When I first saw the place, it was in terrible shape. The wallpaper throughout was torn and stained, with piles of trash in each room. When I returned a month later, the change was unbelievable. The living room was now painted off-white, with a stenciled pattern along the edge of the ceiling. Next to the living room was the kitchen, now decorated with pastel-colored striped wallpaper. Above the new sink and counter, a flowering plant hung. Under the counter were new cabinet doors. Through the door at the far corner of the kitchen was her bedroom. On the floor in front of her bed was a small blue area rug, with matching blue curtains decorating the window next to her bed. It was hard to believe that this apartment was the same place I had seen just a month earlier.

In this paragraph, spatial order is used to help the reader visualize the apartment. After the renovation, the living room walls were newly painted, with stenciling *along the edge* of the ceiling. The kitchen, *next to* the living room, was also newly wallpapered, with a plant hanging *above* the sink and counter and new cabinet doors *under* the counter. The bedroom, which was *through the door* at *the far corner* of the kitchen, was also newly decorated and painted. The curtains on the window *next to* her bed matched the small area rug *on the floor in front* of the bed. As these italicized words illustrate, spatial cues make the scene easier to visualize.

| Exercise 4.9 | **Reviewing Spatial Order** |

Activity
4.2

Briefly explain spatial order. _____

Spatial order is the arrangement you use when you explain where objects are located in

relation to one another.

_____

_____

| Exercise 4.10 | **Analyzing Spatial Order in a Paragraph** |

1. Read the following paragraph. Then, on the lines below it, explain the order in which the parts of the suit have been described.

   The man's Armani suit gave graphic evidence of how difficult his ordeal in the woods had been. The jacket's left shoulder bore a long raveling pull, as though a thorny branch had wrestled with it. The right sleeve was torn almost completely off, and both cuffs were frayed and dirty. A large, purple stain had spread across the midsection of the vest. The pants legs of the suit, from the knees down, were so riddled with tears and holes that they looked shredded. The whole outfit could have been framed and enshrined in the hall of unlikely heroic survivals.

   In this case, spatial order moves from the top down: it begins with the jacket shoulder, moves to the sleeves, and then focuses on the vest; finally, it focuses on the

   pants.

   _____

2. Working with a partner, select transitional expressions that specify location to insert in the paragraph above. Insert them in the space between lines where they fit best. Compare your work with that of another team, and discuss which versions work best.

   Answers will vary.

Exercise 4.11 | **Using and Evaluating Spatial Order Cues**

Ask two student volunteers to complete Exercise 4.11 for the class, using the blackboard to sketch the room. Have the class record transitional words that the volunteers use.

1. Use spatial order to give a partner a tour of a room in your home. As you speak, have your partner sketch the room on a sheet of paper.

2. Switch roles, do the exercise again, and compare sketches. Then answer the following questions on your paper:

   a. How accurate are the sketches?

   b. What transitional expressions related to spatial order helped you and your listener visualize the scenes? Why?

      Answers will vary.

Challenge 4.4 | **Evaluating Spatial Order in Your Writing**

1. For Exercise 4.11 you described a room in your home. Now turn these details into a paragraph and exchange this paragraph with a partner. Make sure that the description in the paper you receive progresses smoothly and logically. Return the paper to the writer, pointing out any problems that you had in visualizing the scene or the topic.

2. Consider the suggestions your reader has made, and then make the changes you feel are called for. Save your work for later use.

Audio 4.8

Ordering for Emphasis   As discussed in the child-rearing example earlier, another way to organize your ideas is **emphatic order** or order of significance. In many cases, especially if you are trying to persuade readers, emphatic order means saving your strongest example for last. In other words, you build from less important to most important ideas. In this way, the examples or details build to a high point and sustain the reader's interest, much the way a story or play does.

Look at this paragraph about mandating the use of seat belts:

> Everyone who drives or rides in a car should be required by law to wear a seat belt. One important reason is that seat belts prevent injuries in minor crashes because they keep the driver and passengers from bouncing around on impact. Even more important, not wearing a seat belt in a car equipped with air bags can lead to serious injuries. Recent studies have shown that unless a person is wearing a seat belt, the sudden expansion of an air bag can slam that person up against the roof of the car. Most important of all, children without seat belts are particularly vulnerable because they are generally too small to brace themselves for any crash. Seat belts keep children from being thrown against the windshield or out of the car in the most serious crashes. Clearly, because seat belts reduce injuries and save lives, wearing seat belts should be mandated by law.

The paragraph begins with a strong reason to mandate the wearing of seat belts: that they keep driver and passengers from bouncing around during minor crashes. This reason is followed by a stronger one: that air bags can be especially dangerous for those not wearing seat belts. This point is followed by an even stronger reason: that they help keep children safe. As you can see, emphatic order sustains the reader's interest as it accentuates the topic sentence.

Exercise 4.12 **Reviewing the Use of Emphatic Order**

1. In your own words, briefly explain emphatic order. _____

   Emphatic order places examples in the order of their importance. You can start with

   the least important example and build to the most important one, or vice versa.

   _____

2. Why is emphatic order effective in persuasive writing? _____

   In persuasion, order of importance helps you build a case by giving increasingly

   convincing (strong) reasons.

   _____

Exercise 4.13 **Identifying Transitions That Emphasize Importance**

1. Read the following paragraph. Working with a partner, underline transitional expressions and phrases that help you see the relative importance of each point in the argument.

   American public schools should adjust the current school calendar and hold classes year round. A calendar calling for ten-week sessions of education followed by two-week vacation periods makes more sense. For one thing, this schedule allows for a concentrated period followed by a rest period. As a result, students and teachers avoid the fatigue they face under the traditional calendar. In addition, the ten-week sessions would help with matters of discipline and order in the schools. For instance, more frequent breaks from school would minimize tensions among students. <u>More important, though,</u> adjusting the schedule would eliminate the long break in the summer. When farming had a larger presence in the United States, the long summer break was necessary so that children could work. <u>In today's world, however,</u> the long summer break creates child care problems for working parents. <u>Also,</u> the long period away from the classroom means students have a greater opportunity to forget what they have learned. Nobody would ever disagree that education is vital to success. <u>Therefore,</u> we should follow a calendar that will give students the best chance to learn.

2. On the following lines, briefly explain how the transitional expressions help emphasize the importance of the supporting material. _____

The transitional expressions one important reason, even more important, *and* most

important of all *emphasize the order of importance for each main point in the sup-*

porting material. The transitional expression because *adds emphasis by explaining.*

Exercise 4.14   Writing and Organizing Reasons in Emphatic Order

As an alternative, complete Exercise 4.14 with the entire class, brainstorming and arranging a list of reasons on the blackboard or computer.

1. Working with a partner, choose one of the following statements and develop a list of at least three reasons for or against it. Write down your reasons on a separate sheet of paper.
   a. Family members should have the right to terminate life support for patients who have been declared brain dead.
   b. People convicted of drunk driving should lose their licenses for five years.
   c. Only high school students with a C average or better should be allowed to participate in extracurricular activities.

2. Now arrange your reasons in emphatic order.

Challenge 4.5   Evaluating Use of Emphatic Order

1. Choose another of the statements provided in Exercise 4.14 and develop a list of at least three reasons supporting or refuting it. Then write a paragraph in which you incorporate them. Exchange your paragraph with a

writing partner. In the paragraph you receive, make sure the order of the sentences stresses the point of the topic sentence. If you think the order should be adjusted, let the writer know.

2. Consider your reader's suggestions, and adjust your own paper accordingly. Save your work for later use.

Choosing Effective Language

When you reassess, you must also reevaluate the language you've used. Your choice of words plays a direct role in how effectively your ideas come across for your reader. Therefore, it's important to make sure that you use **effective language**, in other words, language that is both specific and concise.

Audio
4.9

Keeping Your Writing Specific   To help your reader picture things as you picture them, you must keep your language *specific*, that is, detailed and to the point. When you write *sports car,* for example, the image of a particular car probably comes to mind. However, *sports car* is a general expression; it can conjure up any of dozens of images in the reader's mind. What details does your reader need to see the car as you see it?

To communicate clearly, make such general terms *specific*. For example, replace the general expression *sports car* with a more specific description, such as *shiny new, forest-green Mazda Miata*. This specific language gives your reader an exact picture of what you mean.

Look at this paragraph from writer and poet Maya Angelou's autobiographical narrative, *The Heart of a Woman*. She describes the first time she read her work at the Harlem Writers Guild.

For further discussion of concrete language, see Chapter 6, or turn to descriptive essays listed in the Rhetorical Index.

> I read the character and set description despite the sudden perversity of my body. The blood pounded in my ears but not enough to drown the skinny sound of my voice. My hands shook so that I had to lay the pages in my lap, but that was not a good solution due to the tricks my knees were playing. They lifted involuntarily, pulling my heels off the floor and then trembled like disturbed Jello. Before I launched into the play's action, I looked around at the writers expecting but hoping not to see their amusement at my predicament. Their faces were studiously blank. Within a year, I was to learn that each had a horror story about a first reading at the Harlem Writers Guild.

Which specific details help you picture this scene?

You probably identified particular details, such as *blood pounded in my ears* and *skinny sound of my voice,* which bring the scene to life. Other specific details include the involuntary movement of her knees *pulling my heels off the floor* and the *studiously blank* faces of her listeners.

Audio
4.10

Keeping Your Writing Concise   When you revise, you also need to make sure your writing is *concise*—brief but clear. One way to keep your writing concise is to eliminate deadwood. Deadwood means words and expressions that have no value and add no real meaning. For example, nonspecific words like *a lot, definitely, extremely, quite, really, somewhat,* and *very* combined with weak, vague terms such as *good* or *bad* may make your paper longer, but they do not help you communicate.

Fast Fact If a word is used often enough, it eventually makes it into the dictionary as a legitimate part of the language. And so it happened that the favorite expression of cartoon dimwit Homer Simpson, "Doh!", has recently been added to the Oxford English Dictionary's on-line edition. It is defined as "expressing frustration at the realization that things have turned out badly or not as planned or that one has just said or done something foolish. Also implying that another person has said or done something foolish."

At the same time, concentrate on choosing the best word or two to express your meaning. The English dictionary is filled with words of precise meaning and almost endless variety. Don't specify "a closed-roof car with two or four doors seating four to seven people" when *sedan* will do. Moreover, don't use two or more words when one will do to say the same thing. The following lists suggest ways to turn inflated phrases into concise expressions:

Convert these wordy expressions . . .	*into these concise words*
due to the fact that	because
a large number of	many
in the near future	soon
prior to	before
completely eliminate	eliminate
come to the realization that	realize
with the exception of	except for
in order that	so
at the present time	now
take action	act
the month of January	January
give a summary of	summarize
mutual cooperation	cooperation
make an assumption	assume

What parts of the following paragraph need to be made more concise?

Working as a flagger for a construction company last summer was harder than I really expected it to be. When I first heard about the job, I figured that earning $7 to direct traffic around construction sites would be very easy. I soon found out how wrong I was. On that first morning in the month of June, I reported to the site at 8:15. Due to the fact that I needed to be highly visible to oncoming traffic, the boss handed me a hard hat, a safety vest, and a large orange flag. My station was next to the excavation in the road, and for the next four hours I had to stand in the extremely blazing sun directing traffic with my flag. Minutes seemed like hours as I stood there, listening to honking horns, sweating, and breathing in dust. By lunchtime, I felt that I had been on the job for a week instead of four hours. That's when I came to realize that I was in for a long summer.

As you can see, several sentences need to be made more concise. In the first sentence, *really* can be eliminated, as can *first* and *very* in the second sentence and *extremely* in the sixth. In *the month of June* in the fourth sentence can be shortened to *June,* and *Due to the fact* in the fifth sentence can be changed to *because.* Finally, *came to realize* in the last sentence can be shortened to *realized.*

Here's the same paragraph, this time with the changes:

Activity
4.3

> Working as a flagger for a construction company last summer was harder than I expected it to be. When I heard about the job, I figured that earning $7 to direct traffic around construction sites would be easy. I soon found out how wrong I was. On that first morning in June, I reported to the site at 8:15. Because I needed to be highly visible to oncoming traffic, the boss handed me a hard hat, a safety vest, and a large orange flag. My station was next to the excavation in the road, and for the next four hours I had to stand in the blazing sun directing traffic with my flag. Minutes seemed like hours as I stood there, listening to honking horns, sweating, and breathing in dust. By lunchtime, I felt that I had been on the job for a week instead of four hours. That's when I realized that I was in for a long summer.

This version expresses the same idea, but thanks to the changes, it is more direct and concise.

Exercise 4.15   **Reviewing Specific and Concise Language**

Weblink
4.2

1. On the lines below, briefly explain how to make writing specific. _____

   Specific writing provides clearly worded, exact details rather than vague generaliza-

   tions. It creates a precise image in the reader's mind.

   _____

2. What are two strategies you can use to make your writing more concise?

   1. Eliminate unnecessary and repetitious words.

   2. Don't use two or more words when you can use only one with an exact meaning.

   _____

   _____

Exercise 4.16   **Identifying Overly General Language**

Read the following paragraph. Working with a partner, underline the details that are too general. Then, on the lines below the passage, make up details, and write more specific versions of these sentences.

(1) My favorite job was at Mac and Al's Diner. (2) I worked every weekend for almost three years when I was in high school. (3) On Friday nights, I started at 5 P.M. and worked until 1 A.M. (4) On Saturdays and Sundays, I worked from 6 A.M. to 3 P.M. (5) <u>I never knew what to expect when I went to work.</u> (6) Sometimes I'd be the dishwasher. (7) <u>Other times the boss would have me do other things.</u> (8) <u>I loved the people I worked with.</u> (9) <u>They were great.</u> (10) Many of the customers were there so often, they seemed like family. (11) One couple met at the diner and came in every Saturday night for a big steak dinner. (12) When they finally got married, they invited the entire staff at the diner. (13) Mac and Al closed the place down that day so we could attend the wedding.

Weblink
 4.3

Answers will vary.

_____

_____

_____

_____

_____

_____

Exercise 4.17   **Developing Specific, Concise Language**

For additional practice, write five general expressions on the blackboard, such as *a good dessert, a spoiled child,* or *a scary movie,* and have the class make them more specific and concrete.

1. Transform the following general words into concrete, specific images:

Answers will vary. Sample answers are given.

a. a vacation spot

South Beach in Miami, Florida, USA

b. a CD

Under the Pink by Tori Amos

    c. a sports team

       the St. Louis Cardinals

2. On the lines provided, make the following sentences more concise.

    a. A large number of tourists head to New England during the month of October.

       Many tourists head to New England during October.

    b. The weather forecast calls for really warm temperatures in the near future.

       The forecast calls for warm temperatures soon.

    c. Michelle eventually came to the realization that cutting class definitely had the potential to create problems for her.

       Michelle eventually realized that cutting class could create problems for her.

Challenge 4.6   Evaluating the Effectiveness of Language in Writing

1. Exchange the draft paragraph you worked on for Challenge 4.5 (pages 74–75) with a partner. Check the paragraph you receive to make sure the language is specific and concise. Put a ✓ next to any area you think needs revision, and return the paragraph to the writer.

2. After considering your reader's suggestions, make any changes you feel are necessary. Save your work for later use.

Getting Feedback from an Objective Reader

Audio
4.11

An especially helpful step in reassessing is to seek feedback from an objective reader. Anybody who will read your work and then respond intelligently and honestly to it—a classmate, a family member, a friend—is a potential reader.

To make the task easier for your reader, provide the following reader assessment checklist. This series of questions will guide your reader through an evaluation of your writing. More important, the answers will help you to see how effectively you communicate.

Reader Assessment Checklist

  ☐ Do you understand the point I am making? (topic sentence)

  ☐ Do I stick to that point all the way through? (unity)

  ☐ Are all my ideas and examples clearly connected and easy to follow? (coherence)

  ☐ Are the words I've used specific and concise? (effective language)

  ☐ What changes do you think I should make?

Here is an example of what a peer response to these questions might look like, in this case about the draft paragraph on good parenting presented earlier:

I like your paper—it really made me think. I think the topic sentence is good, and the other sentences are unified and coherent. I think the language you use is one of the best features because it is simple and anybody could understand your point. The only thing I wish is that you gave some specific examples to explain what you mean. <u>Why</u> is it important that parents read to kids? How can parents help their kids make sense of the world? When I read, these are the kinds of questions your writing made me wonder about. If you add this kind of material, your paper would be even better.

As you can see, comments like these can be very helpful in zeroing in on problem spots remaining in a draft.

Exercise 4.18 | **Understanding the Function of Feedback**

Video
4.4

1. Who is a suitable candidate to provide feedback on your paper?

   Anyone who will read objectively and respond intelligently and honestly to your

   paper is a suitable candidate to provide feedback: a classmate, a relative, or a

   friend.

2. How can the feedback you receive from an objective reader help you improve your paragraph? It can help you make your main point clearer, stick to

   the point better, connect your ideas more clearly, and use more specific and concise

   language. Someone may also suggest changes you never thought of.

Exercise 4.19 | **Evaluating the Feedback Process**

1. What do you find most difficult about providing feedback to another writer?

   Answers will vary. Some students may find it most difficult to come up with specific

   suggestions for improving someone else's writing.

2. Which question on the reader assessment checklist do you think is most important? Why? <u>Answers will vary. Many students will choose the first question:</u>

<u>"Do you understand the point I am making?" They may reason that if their message</u>

<u>isn't clear, most of the other questions don't matter.</u>

Exercise 4.20   **Practice in Evaluating and Revising**

1. For Challenge 3.1 (page 39), you developed a draft paragraph on one of three topics. Exchange your paragraph with a partner. Using the reader assessment checklist and sample response above, evaluate the paper you receive.

2. Consider your partner's response. Put a ✓ next to the proposed change that you consider most important to make and then revise your paragraph.

Challenge 4.7   **Evaluating a Partner's Draft**

1. Make a copy of the draft you worked on for Discovering Connections 3.1 or 3.2 at the end of Chapter 3 (pages 58–59). For this assignment, work with a reader who has not previously seen your paper. Complete the following steps with the draft you receive:
   a. Put a **+** next to the topic sentence if it provides a clear direction. Put an **x** next to it if the main point isn't clear.
   b. Now, check the paragraph for unity and coherence. Underline any section or sentence that disrupts the unity of the paragraph, and put a ✓ at any point where an additional transition would help. Note any problems with the order of the sentences.
   c. Check the paragraph for effective language. Circle any vague words and deadwood. Write suggested substitutes above the words. Return the draft to the writer.

Weblink
4.4

2. After evaluating your reader's comments, make any adjustments you feel are needed in your own paragraph. Save your work for later use.

Redrafting

After you have identified what still needs work in your writing, the next step is redrafting, or writing a new version or draft of your paper. As you work through later drafts, you will correct any flaws you've discovered. In addition, you will fill any gaps in content. As page 52 in Chapter 3 indicates, to do this you **amplify**—provide additional, specific details.

Here is a first draft paragraph dealing with medical explorations:

> Research has led to dramatic changes in medical treatment. Technological innovations have helped to turn ideas from science fiction into fact. In addition, researchers continue to develop new devices and treatments designed to prolong life.

As writers reassess, they may need to generate additional examples. Ask students how writers do this. Reinforce that revision may take writers back to the prewriting stage.

A reassessment of this paragraph shows that it is unified, coherent, and organized, but it is far too general and lacks supporting details. To fill these gaps, you need to amplify. In other words, you need to answer the kinds of questions a reader might have. For instance, what *specific* changes in medical treatment have occurred? What *particular* innovations have made the impossible real? What *exactly* are medical researchers working on now?

Now consider this amplified version of the same paragraph:

> Research has led to dramatic changes in medical treatment. *For example, serious surgical procedures such as heart and brain surgery are now commonplace.* Technological innovations have helped to turn ideas from science fiction into fact. *Today, burn victims enjoy faster healing because of the development of artificial skin. Replacement knees, hips, and knuckles mean that people suffering from degenerative joint conditions can now regain greater mobility.* In addition, researchers continue to develop new devices and treatments designed to prolong life. *Prototypes of a completely self-contained artificial heart, powered by a rechargeable battery the size of a book, already exist. Within the next few years, researchers hope to make available a number of other bodily parts, including artificial kidneys and retinas.*

As you can see, the new information, shown in italics, clearly improves the paragraph. This new material specifies the progress that medical researchers have achieved as well as the changes that are on the horizon.

Redrafting is different with every paper you write. With some papers, you'll need to make minor adjustments in several areas. With other papers, you may have to concentrate to a greater degree on one particular point. No matter what you need to add, delete, or correct, however, remember that your goal for redrafting is always the same: to improve your writing.

Fast Fact According to some estimates, the average sentence in American English is about 22 words.

Exercise 4.21 **Reviewing Redrafting**

1. Briefly explain what redrafting involves. _____

   Redrafting involves writing a new version of a paper.

2. In your own words, explain amplifying. _____

Amplifying means supplying additional examples and details to support or illustrate

sections of a writing that are too general to be wholly effective.

| Exercise 4.22 | **Evaluating a Paragraph Draft** |

1. Read the following paragraph, and then evaluate it using the reader assessment checklist on page 79. Write your evaluation on a separate sheet of paper.

> Television programming today is uninspired and boring. For example, none of the comedies are original. The plots are simply recycled versions of earlier comedy shows. Even fairly good shows like *Friends* or *Frasier* stoop to cheap gags like mistaken identities or being locked out of an apartment. The dramas are even worse. *ER* is simply an updating of other shows. The late night talk shows all feature similar routines and the same celebrities selling the same movies, books, or television shows.

2. On the same sheet of paper, redraft the paragraph, making changes you think will improve it.

| Challenge 4.8 | **Analyzing Feedback and Redrafting** |

1. Compare your suggestions for changes in the paragraph from Exercise 4.22 with those of a partner. After comparing answers, adjust your own list to include good points your partner noted.

2. On a separate sheet of paper, redraft this paragraph again, incorporating the suggestions you added to your list.

Acknowledging Your Sources

If in your writing you support your own ideas with information from some other source, you need to acknowledge that source. Otherwise you would be guilty of *plagiarism*, the act of taking or stealing someone else's work and passing it off as your own.

Whenever you come across material in another source that would help you make your point, you can include it with your own words in one of three ways. You can present it word for word as it appears with quotation marks around it. This is called **direct quotation**. A second way to express the information is to present it in a greatly reduced form, called **summary**. Third, you can include your own interpretation or explanation with the material, again in your own words, which is called **paraphrase**.

Regardless of the way you present information from another source, you must acknowledge that source in two spots in your paper. To do so, you follow one of the standard methods of documentation. The Modern Language Association (MLA) system and the American Psychological Association (APA) method are the two most common methods.

The first place to acknowledge your source is immediately after the information you have included. At that point, insert a set of parentheses containing the author's last name. If you are following MLA, you also include the page number, as these examples show:

MLA parenthetical documentation

From a book	The people who make their living at sea understand its tremendous power. For instance, they understand the grave consequences of storm-driven waves. "On a steel boat the windows implode, the hatches fail, and the boat starts to downflood" (Junger 173).
From a newspaper, magazine, or periodical	She had set out to tell the story as accurately as possible. The best of intentions aren't enough with some stories, however, as she found out when she saw the article in print. "But later in the day, when I saw the magazine, the article seemed different to me from the version I had approved with my editor" (Szalavitz 76).

The second place that you must acknowledge your source is at the end of your paper, in a section called "Works Cited," as these examples show. Note that the second (and each subsequent) line of each entry is indented.

Works Cited

For a book	Junger, Sebastian. *The Perfect Storm: A True Story of Men against the Sea.* New York: HarperCollins, 1997.
For a newspaper, magazine, or other periodical	Szalavitz, Maia. "12 Steps Back." *Brill's Content* Jan. 2001: 72–78.

If you use the APA method, you record the information in the text of your paper in a slightly different way, the author's last name plus the *year of publication, preceded by a comma,* rather than a page number, as these examples show:

APA parenthetical documentation

From a book The people who make their living at sea understand its tremendous power. For instance, they understand the grave consequences of storm-driven waves. "On a steel boat the windows implode, the hatches fail, and the boat starts to downflood" (Junger, 1997).

From a newspaper, magazine, or periodical She had set out to tell the story as accurately as possible. The best of intentions aren't enough for with some stories, however, as she found out when she saw the article in print. "But later in the day, when I saw the magazine, the article seemed different to me from the version I had approved with my editor" (Szalavitz, 2001).

And your notations at the end of the paper, presented under the title "References," would also look slightly different from the MLA style. Initials rather than first names are used, and the name is followed by the date of publication, in parentheses, plus a period. Also, you capitalize only the first word of the title of the work as well as any subtitle and proper nouns, as these examples show. Again, make sure to indent the second line (and any other subsequent lines) of each entry.

References

For a book Junger, S. (1977). *The perfect storm: A true story of men against the sea.* New York: HarperCollins.

For a newspaper, magazine, or other periodical Szalavitz, M. (2001, January). 12 steps back. *Brill's Content,* 72–78.

Of course, you have many other types of documents from which you might draw information to support your own ideas, including the Internet. The reference section of your college library contains complete explanations and thorough illustrations of how to acknowledge the source for these kinds of documents following the MLA, APA, and other systems of documentation. If you have questions or need additional guidance, stop by the reference desk for help.

Exercise 4.23   **Reviewing Documentation of Sources**

1. What are the three ways that you can include information from another

   source to support your own ideas? The three methods of recording informa-

   tion from another source are direct quotation, summary, and paraphrase.

2. What are two well-known systems for acknowledging sources?

   Two well-known systems of acknowledging sources are the Modern Language

   Association (MLA) system and the American Psychological Association (APA)

   system.

3. Where can you find more information about other systems of documentation as well as complete guidelines for MLA and APA documentation?

   Information about other systems of documentation as well as complete guidelines

   for MLA and APA documentation can be obtained from the library's reference desk.

Editing

Weblink
4.5

Once you have eliminated the weaknesses in your draft, you are ready for the final step in revising: *editing*. When you edit, you polish that draft to correct errors in your use of English. This means you need to *proofread*, to identify and eliminate any errors in grammar, spelling, and punctuation.

Developing a Personal Proofreading System

The secret to effective proofreading is timing. Plan your time so that you proofread your paper when you are rested. That way, fatigue and familiarity with content won't cause you to see what you *meant to write* rather than what you *have actually written*. When you are tired, for example, you may see *receive* even though you've actually misspelled it as *recieve*.

Also, concentrate on the types of errors that most often appear in papers. Focus on the following proofreading checklist, and you'll eliminate most of the mistakes that trouble writers and distract readers.

Have students review the table of contents and note chapters that focus on types of errors they make frequently. As they begin to develop a personal proofreading checklist, they will have referenced chapters or sections to use when editing.

Proofreading Checklist

☐ Have I eliminated all sentence fragments (*frag*)? (Chapter 18)

☐ Have I eliminated all comma splices (*cs*)? (Chapter 20)

☐ Have I eliminated all run-on sentences (*rs*)? (Chapter 20)

☐ Is the spelling (*sp*) correct throughout? (Chapter 29)

☐   Is the verb tense (*t*) correct throughout? (Chapters 22, 23, 24)

☐   Do all subjects agree with their verbs (*subj/verb agr*)? (Chapters 17, 21, 25)

☐   Do all pronouns agree with their antecedents (pro/ant agr)? (Chapter 26)

Weblink
4.6

Of course, this checklist doesn't cover all the errors writers make. You may have trouble with some other aspect of writing such as double negatives or apostrophe use. Don't worry if you don't yet understand why some of these errors occur. Other chapters in this book will explain how to watch for and eliminate them. The Sentence Skill Locator on the inside back cover shows you where to look for help.

Another secret to effective proofreading is to tailor your checklist to suit your own needs. Concentrate on the items listed above that you find most difficult. Add others that especially trouble your writing. Then you'll have your own personal proofreading checklist that focuses on your particular areas of concern.

Teaming up with a proofreading partner is another way to eliminate errors in your paper. Once you have proofread your paper, exchange it with another reader. This proofreading partner will not be as invested or involved with the writing as you are and so may be better able to find any remaining errors. You can perform the same duties for your partner. The result will be better papers for both of you.

Using Computer Tools to Your Advantage

Weblink
4.7

Video
4.5

Video
4.6

If you are using a computer to do your writing, you probably have an additional proofreading tool: the spell check command. This function checks your spelling against the computer's dictionary and points out words that appear to be misspelled. Sometimes the computer offers a list of words that you might have intended rather than the misspelled word. To eliminate the error, simply select the correctly spelled version. If the computer doesn't offer a possibility, look the word up to find the correct spelling, and then make the changes yourself.

Don't trust the computer to find all your spelling errors, however. Imagine that you have written this sentence: "Suddenly the room became deathly *quite*." The computer doesn't read and reason as you do, so it won't be able to tell that you meant to write *quiet*, not *quite*. Therefore, take full advantage of the spell checker on your computer, but do a final check yourself to make sure, for example, that you don't use *dose* when you really mean *does*.

Exercise 4.24   **Reviewing Editing**

Weblink
4.8

1. In your own words, explain what editing involves. _____

Editing involves polishing your draft: proofreading it and correcting all grammar,

spelling, and punctuation errors.

2. What advantage do you gain by allowing some time to pass before you proofread? You can spot errors that you might miss if you've just finished writing and are either too tired or too close to the draft to be able to see it clearly and objectively.

Exercise 4.25 | **Creating Your Proofreading Checklist**

Weblink 4.9

1. Of the areas of concern noted in the proofreading checklist on pages 86–87, which one has given you the most trouble in the past? Why do you think you have difficulty with this area?

Answers will vary.

2. Which area of concern highlighted in the proofreading checklist troubles you least? Why do you think you find this area easy?

Answers will vary.

Exercise 4.26 | **Editing a Paragraph**

1. Proofread the following paragraph. Correct the errors you find. In the margin beside each error, write the abbreviation from the proofreading checklist on pages 86–87 to identify the type of error (*frag, sp,* and so forth).

This paragraph appears with answers on page 91.

The hardest thing I ever has to endure was my parents' divorce. I was ten when it happened, I had always thought I had the perfect family, but I was wrong. A few days before Christmas, my mother sat down in front of my brother and me and told us that my father was moving out to live with another woman. Every kid wants to have someone they can look up to, and for me that used to be my father. But when I saw how sad my mother looks, I hated my father I wished he were dead. He kept calling the house to talk with me, but I wouldn't talk to him. Two years later, after the divorce was final. I met him by accident downtown. When he seen me, he started to cry and said he was sorry. I couldn't forgive him then and I can't forgive him now. He ruined my prefect family.

2. Working with a partner, compare your editing. Make a note of any errors you missed. Then check your answers against the corrected version on page 91.

Challenge 4.9   **Editing a Partner's Paragraph**

1. After you proofread the draft you worked on for Challenge 4.7 (page 81), exchange your draft with a partner. On the paragraph you receive, put a ✓ before any error you see, write the name of the error next to it, and then return the draft to the writer.

2. After evaluating your reader's corrections, make all necessary corrections.

Fast Fact As you write and revise, focus on time and patience. Michelangelo worked three years to create his massive statue, *David*, and four years to paint the ceiling of the Sistine Chapel.

Examining a Revised Draft

So what happens when you follow the revising guidelines presented in this chapter? Here again is the first draft version of the paragraph on being a good parent that appeared at the end of Chapter 3 (pages 56–57).

> By paying attention to their own behavior, parents can lay the groundwork for their children's happiness. Reading to children every day is important. Parents also need to spend time interacting with their children and responding to their questions patiently. Children count on their parents to help them make sense of the world around them. Most of all, parents should regularly tell their children that they love them and praise them when they do something well. Nothing is more important to children's future success than the support and interest of their parents.

Now consider this revised version of the same paragraph:

> By paying attention to their own behavior, parents can lay the ground-work for their children's happiness. Reading to children every day is important. **It teaches them the basics of the language, from ABCs to sentences and paragraphs. It also makes them familiar with what books can do for them. As a result, when they enter school they'll have a head start that they'll never lose.** Parents also need to spend time interacting with their children and responding to their questions patiently. Children count on their parents to help them make sense of the world around them. **For example, if they ask why the sun shines or why cats and dogs fight, parents should do their best to give an honest answer in terms the children can understand.** Most of all, parents should regularly tell their children that they love them and praise them when they do something well. **The consistent reinforcement when they pick up their toys or share with others helps provide a sense of love and security.** Nothing is more important to children's future success than the support and interest of their parents.

Thanks to the additional supporting material developed during revising, shown here in boldface, this version is far more specific and thorough. This final draft version is clear proof of the power of revision, as the following instructor's comments indicate:

Congratulations—you have done a fine job revising your paper. You have made a number of improvements since I saw the first draft a week ago. I especially like the specific examples you've added. Now in addition to just saying what parents should do to help their children, you explain why through those new examples and therefore show exactly what you mean. When we move on to writing essays, you should consider expanding this paper. All in all it's an excellent first paper.

Discovering Connections 4.1

When you see this photo, what comes to mind? Do you think of a recent success in your life? What was it? Did you have to overcome some obstacle to achieve it? Or does the picture make you think of the opposite, of a time that you hoped for success but didn't achieve it? What happened?

For this assignment, choose some aspect of this topic, prewrite on it, and develop a draft paragraph (at least five to ten sentences long). Then, following the process outlined in this chapter, revise the draft.

Discovering Connections 4.2

> For this assignment, think of a traumatic incident you experienced or witnessed. What happened? Who was involved? When and where did it occur? What caused it? How did you react? How has it affected you since? Prewrite to gather ideas, and then compose a draft paragraph (at least five to ten sentences long) on the subject. Then revise the draft, following the process outlined in this chapter.

Corrected Version of Exercise 4.26, Number 1

had

t & subj/verb agr   The hardest thing I ever ~~has~~ to endure was my parents' divorce. I was

cs   ten when it happened, I had always thought I had the perfect family, but I

was wrong. A few days before Christmas, my mother sat down in front of

my brother and me and told us that my father was moving out to live

he or she

pro/ant agr   with another woman. Every (kid) wants to have someone (they) can look up

to, and for me that used to be my father. But when I saw how sad my

looked

t/rs   mother ~~looks~~, I hated my father. I wished he were dead. He kept calling

the house to talk with me, but I wouldn't talk to him. Two years later, after

saw

frag/t   the divorce was final, I met him by accident downtown. When he ~~seen~~

cs   me, he started to cry and said he was sorry. I couldn't forgive him then

perfect

sp   and I can't forgive him now. He ruined my ~~prefect~~ family.

REFINING AND POLISHING YOUR DRAFT

Activity 4.4

New terms in this chapter	Definitions
● **revising**	● the stage of writing during which you refine and polish a draft Revising means (1) reassessing, (2) redrafting, and (3) editing.
● **reassessing**	● looking closely at a draft to find and correct errors and weaknesses
● **redrafting**	● creating a new version of a piece of writing by correcting problems and incorporating new material
● **editing**	● polishing and proofreading a piece of writing to eliminate errors in grammar, spelling, and punctuation

New terms in this chapter	Definitions
● **unity**	● quality achieved in writing when all sentences relate to the main idea
● **coherence**	● quality achieved in writing when sentences hold together well Coherence comes from logical order and connections that show how ideas interrelate.
● **synonyms**	● words with similar meanings
● **transitional expressions**	● words that connect ideas and show relationships between them
● **chronological order**	● organization in sequence on the basis of time
● **spatial order**	● organization based on location of parts in relation to a whole
● **emphatic order**	● organization based on order of significance, or importance
● **effective language**	● language that communicates well because it is specific (detailed) and concise (brief but clear)
● **plagiarism**	● appropriating someone else's work
● **direct quotation**	● presenting information word for word within quotation marks as it appears in an original source
● **summary**	● presenting information from a source in a greatly reduced form
● **paraphrase**	● presenting information from a source in different words with an interpretation or explanation
● **MLA system of documentation**	● the Modern Language Association's method of acknowledging sources
● **APA system of documentation**	● the American Psychological Association's method of acknowledging sources

The Process of Revising

1 Reassess ⟶

Check for ⟵
● unity
● coherence
● effective language

Seek feedback from objective reader

2 Redraft ⟶

Add new material ⟵

Improve existing material

Delete irrelevant material

3 Edit

Proofread for errors in
● spelling
● grammar
● punctuation

Using the Patterns of Paragraph Development

Chapter 5

Narration

Getting Started... **Q:** I want to tell about something that happened to me. What's the best way for me to tell it so it will make sense to somebody else?

Audio
5.1

A: When you want to tell about something that happened to you—or something that you saw happen to someone else—narration should be the mode you choose. Tell the story as fully as you recall it and in the order in which it occurred, and you'll be all set.

Overview: Understanding the Modes, Purposes, and Importance of Telling Your Story

Audio
5.2

Weblink
5.1

Weblink
5.2

If you've looked ahead in this book or through the table of contents, you've seen names such as *description, example, process, definition, comparison, and contrast, cause and effect,* and *division and classification.* These are the **modes**, writing techniques or patterns that you can use to express your point on a subject. Each enables you to approach and cover a topic in a different way.

As Chapter 1 (page 10) shows, you write to fulfill one of three purposes: to *inform,* to *entertain,* or to *persuade.* The modes are the devices you use to fulfill those purposes. **Narration**, the focus of this chapter, is one of the modes. It's the mode that people use to tell stories, from "Once upon a time . . ." fairy tales to personal experiences to autobiographies and memoirs.

This chapter and the seven that follow examine the modes one by one. As you read this material, you will learn and practice the characteristics of each mode. When you do, keep this point in mind: Most writing relies on a combination of modes to communicate ideas to readers. One mode will dominate and one or more of the others will support it. The longer a piece of writing is, the more likely this will be the case.

Imagine, for example, a writing about the problem of beach erosion that affects states such as North Carolina, New York, and Florida. In such a writing, cause and effect, which focuses on the reasons underlying events, would dominate. However, process might also appear to explain how the ocean gradually claims more and more of the shore. In addition, description might be used to illustrate the changes and comparison and contrast to detail different solutions to the problem.

The focus of Chapter 13 is *argument*. Argument is different in that it doesn't refer to a single mode but to a purpose: to persuade. Simply put, argument is writing that persuades. As Chapter 13 shows, you use whatever combination of modes is necessary to fulfill that purpose.

The focus of this chapter, however, is narration. You use narration whenever you relate a series of events or incidents. For instance, a story about a date gone wrong would focus on narration. So would a paper about a prank or the discovery of a family secret.

> **This chapter will explore the basic requirements for writing an effective narrative paragraph:**
>
> ● providing a topic sentence that establishes a context
>
> ● explaining the events in the story in chronological order
>
> ● recognizing the most effective point of view

Mastering this mode will also enable you to create longer documents that focus on narration.

Discovering Connections 5.1

Discovering Connections 5.2 at the end of the chapter will allow students to apply what they learn in this chapter by composing and revising a narrative paragraph.

Choose one of the following topics, and selecting one of the strategies that you practiced in Chapter 2, prewrite on that topic. Let your mind revisit the events in the episode.

1. an occasion when you lost your temper
2. a time when you felt proud of a family member or friend
3. an episode that required you to try something you had never done before

Save your work for later use.

Writing a Clear Topic Sentence That Establishes a Context

Audio
5.3

ESL Note
See "Sentence Basics" on pages 572–574 and "Word Order" on pages 574–575.

In order to help readers understand the point of a narrative paragraph, the writer must establish a clear direction, or point, for the story he or she is about to tell. The part of the paragraph that provides this needed direction is the topic sentence. The topic sentence establishes a context for the sequence of events that follows. In other words, it sets the scene and orients the reader. As Chapter 3 showed, a typical topic sentence pinpoints both the *topic* and your *attitude* or *reaction* to it. In the narrative paragraph, the topic is the incident, or story. Your reaction is the "spin," or slant, you put on the events you relate.

Look at the topic sentence in this narrative paragraph from *Bird by Bird* in which author Anne Lamott discusses her father:

> I'm sure my father was the person on whom his friends relied to tell their stories, in school and college. I know for sure he was later, in the town where he was raising his children. He could take major events or small episodes from daily life and shade or exaggerate things in such a way as to capture their shape and substance, capture what life felt like in the society in which he and his friends lived and worked and bred. People looked up to him to put into words what was going on.

The topic sentence is *I'm sure my father was the person on whom his friends relied to tell their stories, in school and college.* As you can see, it prepares the reader for the focus of the rest of the paragraph. The opening sentence states that her father was the one whom acquaintances counted on to present their experiences, and the other sentences explain why.

Activity
5.1

Exercise 5.1 Understanding Purposes and Modes and Defining Narration

1. Briefly explain the relationship between purposes and modes in writing.

   In any piece of writing, writers select the mode or modes that will best allow them to

   fulfill their purpose or purposes.

   _____

   _____

Exercise 5.2 Analyzing a Topic Sentence for a Narrative Paragraph

1. Reread the example paragraph by Anne Lamott above. On the lines below, briefly explain how the topic sentence sets the direction and context for the material provided in its supporting sentences.

   The topic sentence tells us in general terms the role her father played. The supporting

   sentences explain the exact nature of that role in terms of the things expected of him.

   _____

2. Choose one of the supporting sentences and briefly explain how it specifies the point made in the topic sentence. _____

   Answers will vary depending on the sentence selected.

   _____

Challenge 5.1   **Preparing to Write a Narrative Paragraph**

Weblink
5.3

Prewrite on the subject of a first date. Then plan a sequence for the most promising details. Finally, write a topic sentence that establishes an appropriate direction and context. Save your work for later use.

Relying on Chronological Order

Audio
5.4

Narration is the mode that focuses on a series of events. For this reason, how effectively you present the sequence will influence how your reader understands it. With narration, **chronological order** is often the ideal choice. As Chapter 4 (pages 67–68) explains, this method of arrangement involves presenting the series of incidents in the order in which they happened. Note the use of chronological order in the following narrative paragraph from "A Sweet Devouring," in which author Eudora Welty discusses how she obtained books to feed her childhood appetite for reading:

Activity
5.2

> All that summer I used to put on a second petticoat (our librarian wouldn't let you past the front door if she could see through you) ride my bicycle up the hill and "through the Capital" (shortcut) to the library with my two read books in the basket (two was the limit you could take out at one time when you were a child and also as long as you lived), and tiptoe in ("Silence") and exchange them for two more in two minutes. Selection was no object. I coasted the two new books home, jumped out of my petticoat, read (I suppose I ate and bathed and answered questions put to me), then in all hope put my petticoat back on and rode those two books back to the library to get my next two.

As you can see, Welty tells her experience in the order of occurrence, making it easier for a reader to understand the story. First, she would put on her petticoat and ride her bicycle, with the two books she had already read in the basket, to the library. Then she would return the books, select two new ones, and pedal home. Once she was home, she would remove her petticoat and read the books. Finally, she would put her petticoat back on and start all over again.

When you write a narrative, you will find certain transitional expressions helpful to show the sequence of events. Some of them are listed below.

Transitional Expressions for Narratives

after	during	later	soon
before	first (second, etc.)	meanwhile	then

Sometimes writers employ a **flashback**, an incident deliberately presented out of sequence, often to give the reader some important background information. Imagine, for example, you were writing about how you finally overcame terrible stage fright in your public speaking course. You had originally developed the stage fright in the first grade when you forgot your lines in the spring play. Including this flashback in your paper would make it easier for your reader to understand how difficult overcoming your anxiety was.

Choosing the Most Effective Point of View

Have students refer to the Rhetorical Index and choose an essay that includes the narrative mode. Ask them to identify and discuss the author's choice of point of view. Why do they think the author chose this point of view? Is it effective? Why?

Any time you tell a story, you select a **point of view**, the perspective from which you relate the experience. Often when you use narration, you will write from a *first person point of view,* that is, from your viewpoint as you participated in or experienced the event. With first person point of view, you use *I, me,* and other words that refer to yourself. Other times, you will write from a *third person point of view,* that is, as an observer rather than as a participant. Because you focus on others with third person narration, you use *he, she, her, they,* and so on.

Consider this narrative paragraph from "They All Just Went Away," an essay by writer Joyce Carol Oates, which features first person point of view:

> I must have been a lonely child. Until the age of twelve or thirteen, my most intense, happiest hours were spent tramping desolate fields, woods, and creek banks near my family's farmhouse in Millersport, New York. No one knew where I went. My father, working most of the day at Harrison's, a division of General Motors in Lockport, and at other times preoccupied, would not have asked; if my mother asked, I might have answered in a way that would deflect curiosity. I was an articulate, verbal child. Yet I could not have explained what drew me to the abandoned houses, barns, silos, corncribs. A hike of miles through fields of spiky grass, across outcroppings of shale as steeply angled as stairs, was a lark if the reward was an empty house.

It's clear from the use of words like *I, my,* and *me* that this passage concerns an incident in which Oates was a participant.

Now, consider this paragraph from Peter Griffin's biography of Ernest Hemingway, *Less Than a Treason.* It describes Hemingway's first encounter with flying.

> Ernest first saw the plane from the window of the taxi he and Hadley took to the field. It was a silver biplane with a tiny cabin with portholes, and a seat for the pilot in the rear. Ernest bought the tickets at a counter in the plane shed, and had them checked by an attendant who stood just ten feet away, by the door to the field. Then, with cotton stuffed into their ears, Ernest and Hadley climbed aboard the plane and sat one behind the other. The pilot, a short, little man with his cap on backwards, shouted contact, and the mechanic gave the propeller a spin.

In this case, the paragraph is related from the third person point of view. In other words, the writer is not a participant but a witness.

Fast Fact Narrative writing has more staying power than you at first might think. The *Guinness World Records 2001* reports that the best-selling diary of all time is *The Diary of Anne Frank,* which has been translated into 55 languages and has sold more than 25 million copies.

Exercise 5.3   **Understanding Chronological Order and Point of View**

**Activity
5.3**

1. How does chronological order help a reader understand a story?

   Chronological order makes a story clearer because readers can understand the

   events as they took place in time.

2. Briefly explain the difference between first person and third person point of view. _____

   First person point of view uses the word *I* and tells the story from the writer's per-

   spective. Third person point of view uses the words *he* and *she* and tells the story

   from an observer's perspective.

Exercise 5.4   **Listing Events in a Narrative Paragraph**

1. Take another look at the paragraph by Joyce Carol Oates on page 98 and then answer this question: How would this passage be affected if it were changed from first person to third person point of view?

   Answers will vary somewhat, although most students will agree that the piece would

   be less effective, that the charm of the piece comes from her voice as the participant.

2. Turn again to Peter Griffin's paragraph about Ernest Hemingway on page 98. Working with a partner, list and number the sequence of events.

(1) Ernest and Hadley saw the plane from the taxi window. (2) Ernest purchased tickets. (3) An attendant check them. (4) Ernest and Hadley stuffed cotton in their ears and climbed in the plane. (5) The pilot said, "Contact," and the mechanic spun the propeller.

Exercise 5.5   **Revising a Narrative Paragraph to Use Flashback**

Ernest Hemingway was excited about the prospect of flying before he actually took the flight described in the paragraph on page 98. Try to imagine an event that would have aroused his interest in flying. Then, on a separate sheet of paper, rewrite the paragraph, including a flashback that describes this earlier, imaginary event.

Exercise 5.6   **Considering Purpose in Narration Paragraphs**

This chapter features several sample narrative paragraphs. The names of the authors of these paragraphs, with the appropriate page numbers, are listed below. Working with a partner, take another look at the paragraphs and then on the lines next to the names list the primary purpose and any secondary purposes for each paragraph.

1. Anne Lamott, page 96

Most students will agree that Lamott's primary purpose is to entertain and her secondary purpose is to inform.

2. Eudora Welty, page 97

Students will probably be divided in their opinions. Some will assert that the primary purpose is to inform and the secondary purpose is to entertain, while others will maintain that the opposite is true. A few students will see persuasion as a secondary purpose, as Welty does suggest that the system should have been easier for children.

3. Joyce Carol Oates, page 98

   Most students will agree that Oates's primary purpose is to entertain and her sec-

   ondary purpose is to inform.

4. Peter Griffin, page 98

   Most students will agree that Griffin's primary purpose is to inform and his secondary

   purpose is to entertain, although a few students may argue for the opposite view.

Challenge 5.2   **Writing a Narrative Paragraph**

Using the notes you completed for Challenge 5.1 (page 97), draft a narrative paragraph of at least 100 words that deals with a first date.

Discovering Connections 5.2

1. In Discovering Connections 5.1 on page 95, you chose a topic for a narrative paragraph and completed your prewriting. Now using the points in this chapter as a guide, develop a paragraph of at least 100 words that tells your reader the series of events involved in the experience.

2. Exchange your paragraph with a partner. If you completed the paragraph for Challenge 5.2 above and you feel this is better, use it for this exercise instead. Evaluate the paragraph you receive, using the narrative paragraph checklist below. Write your answers on a separate sheet of paper, and then return the paragraph and your assessment to the writer.

3. Using your reader's comments to guide you, revise your own paragraph.

Narrative Paragraph Checklist

☐ Does the topic sentence establish a context?

☐ Is the material arranged in chronological order?

☐ Is the point of view used to present the paragraph appropriate?

☐ In your judgment, the best part of this paragraph is _____. Explain.

☐ Which detail or example would be even better if it were expanded? Why?

NARRATION

New terms in this chapter	Definitions
● **narration**	● the writing technique used to relate a series of events or incidents
● **flashback**	● a past event deliberately presented out of sequence to provide background information
● **point of view**	● the perspective a writer uses to tell a story

● the perspective a writer uses to tell a story

Using *first person point of view* makes the writer a participant (I, me, my, mine).

> ***Example*** Suddenly, I heard a car stop outside my window.

Using *third person point of view* makes the writer an observer (she, he, they, him, her, his, them, their, it, its).

> ***Example*** The old woman stood up and reached for her cane.

Writing a Narrative Paragraph

Focus on a subject that includes a **sequence of events**.

↓ ↑

Develop a **topic sentence** that establishes a **context** for the reader.

↓ ↑

Present the events through **chronological order**.

↓ ↑

Choose the most effective **point of view—first person** or **third person**.

Chapter 6

Description

Getting Started... **Q:** The experience was so *vivid*, almost like it was electricity. How can I write about it and capture that sense of full life?

Audio 6.1 **A:** Whenever you want to record in words the vivid sensations you witness or experience, description is the answer. Draw on all your senses—think about what you felt at that time—and you'll be all set.

Overview: Creating a Picture In Words

Audio 6.2

Weblink 6.1

When you write, think of your words as a camera lens through which your reader views the situations or experiences you are presenting. The mode that is perhaps the best to bring into focus the scene in your camera lens of language is **description**.

You use description whenever you try to capture a particular setting, individual, experience, or object in words. A paragraph detailing the feeling of speeding along on a motorcycle would call for description. So would a writing about the frenzy of last-minute holiday shoppers and one dealing with a schoolyard full of children on the first day of school.

> *This chapter will explore the basic requirements for writing an effective descriptive paragraph:*
>
> ● providing a topic sentence that previews your description
>
> ● drawing upon sensory details
>
> ● relying on both objective and subjective description
>
> ● considering spatial order

With these basics mastered, you will be prepared to write longer essays that use description.

Discovering Connections 6.1

Discovering Connections 6.2 at the end of the chapter will allow students to apply what they learn in this chapter by composing and revising a descriptive paragraph.

Select one of the following topics. Then, following one of the strategies that you practiced in Chapter 2, prewrite on that topic. Consider sensory details and location of parts of the scene (or person).

1. an accident scene
2. a nightclub, stadium, workplace, or other facility after closing
3. the best-looking person you've ever met

Save your work for later use.

Previewing the Focus of Description through the Topic Sentence

Audio
6.3

Your reader depends on you to clarify the focus of your writing early on. Your descriptive paragraph will create a vivid impression of an object, person, or place in the reader's mind. To begin it, you need a topic sentence that previews what will be described and suggests your point of view. That way your reader can make sense of the specific details and examples that follow.

Consider the italicized topic sentence in this paragraph from "Total Eclipse," an essay by writer Annie Dillard:

Weblink
6.2

> *The second before the sun went out we saw a wall of dark shadow come speeding at us.* We no sooner saw it than it was upon us, like thunder. It roared up the valley. It slammed our hill and knocked us out. It was the monstrous swift shadow cone of the moon. I have since read that this wave of shadow moves at 1,800 miles an hour. Language gives no sense of this sort of speed—1,800 miles an hour. It was 195 miles wide. No end was in sight—you saw only the edge. It rolled at you across the land at 1,800 miles an hour, hauling darkness like plague behind it. Seeing it, and knowing it was coming straight for you, was like feeling a slug of anesthetic shoot up your arm. If you think very fast, you may have time to think, "Soon it will hit my brain." You can feel the deadness race up your arm; you can feel the appalling, inhuman speed of your own blood. We saw the wall of shadow coming, and screamed before it hit.

The italicized topic sentence tells the reader that the paragraph will describe an experience of great darkness. It also prepares the reader for further discussion of that great darkness (a solar eclipse) that will so swiftly fall upon her and the other observers. The body of the paragraph then provides details and examples that make the scene come alive for the reader.

Using Sensory Details

Audio
6.4

See "Choosing Effective Language" on pages 75–78 in Chapter 4 for a related discussion about using specific and concise language.

Vivid experiences create vivid memories. Think for a moment of the aroma the last time you walked into a bakery or of the sensation the last time the sound of the phone woke you from a sound sleep. **Sensory details**—what you perceive by seeing, hearing, tasting, smelling, and touching—enable you to communicate these experiences to your reader. To write sensory details, choose concrete language that draws in the five senses.

Look at this paragraph from writer Richard Rodriguez's "Aria: A Memoir of a Bilingual Childhood," which features sensory details:

> There were many times like the night at a brightly lit gasoline station (a blaring white memory) when I stood uneasily hearing my father talk to a teenage attendant. I do not recall what they were saying, but I cannot forget the sound my father made as he spoke. At one point his words slid together to form one long word—sounds as confused as the threads of blue and green oil in the puddle next to my shoes. His voice rushed through what he had left to say. Towards the end, he reached falsetto notes, appealing to his listener's understanding. I looked away at the lights of passing automobiles. I tried not to hear any more. But I heard only too well the attendant's reply, his calm, easy tones. Shortly afterward, walking toward home with my father, I shivered when my father put his hand on my shoulder. The very first chance that I got, I evaded his grasp and ran on ahead into the dark, skipping with feigned boyish exuberance.

As you can see, the passage contains a number of sensory details. When Rodriguez notes the brightness of the lights, the sound of his father's voice, and the shiver he felt, he fills the paragraph with a sense of vivid life.

Fast Fact Tests have shown that, of the five senses, smell creates the most complete, lasting memories. Females have the advantage in this regard, since on the whole, females have better olfactory systems than males.

Exercise 6.1   Defining Description

Weblink
6.3

1. Briefly define description. _____

   <u>Description means painting a picture in words so that readers can clearly "see" the</u>

   <u>scene, person, or object you're writing about.</u>

   _____

   _____

2. What are sensory details? How do they help you write effective description?

Sensory details are what you perceive through sight, sound, taste, smell, and touch.

They help you communicate your experiences to your reader.

Exercise 6.2 **Identifying the Role of the Topic Sentence**

1. In Rodriguez's paragraph, how does the topic sentence prepare you for the details that follow? _____

The topic sentence states that he recalls "many times" when hearing his father

speaking English made him uneasy. The reader expects examples to follow.

2. In your view, which sentence in Rodriguez's paragraph provides the best support? Explain. _____

Answers will vary, although many students may choose either sentence three or five,

which deals with the sound of the father's voice, or sentence nine, which deals with

his reaction when his father touched his shoulder. These all give a very concrete pic-

ture of the boy's experience.

Exercise 6.3 **Identifying Sensory Details**

Activity 6.1

Review Annie Dillard's paragraph about a total solar eclipse on page 104. Working with a partner, make a list on a separate sheet of paper of the various sensory details in the paragraph. Beside each detail, write the sense or senses to which it appeals.

Challenge 6.1 **Prewriting for a Descriptive Paragraph**

Weblink 6.4

Prewrite on the subject of a special day or a memorable event in your life. Try to focus on sensory details you remember vividly. Save your work for later use.

Relying on Objective and Subjective Description

Audio
6.5

Activity
6.2

Descriptive writing can be divided into two basic types. **Objective description** concerns actual details and sensations. **Subjective description** focuses on the impressions those details and sensations create. Rarely is a paper completely objective (as a lab report is) or completely subjective (as an essay dealing with a nightmare or intense spiritual experience would be). Most descriptive writing contains a combination of both types.

Consider the details in this paragraph from *The Diving Bell and the Butterfly*, in which author Jean-Dominique Bauby describes the last time he saw his father:

Have students refer to the Rhetorical Index and choose an essay that includes the descriptive mode. Ask them to identify objective and subjective description. Does the author use both types of description? Is this effective?

> Hunched in the red-upholstered armchair where he sifts through the day's newspapers, my dad bravely endures the rasp of the razor attacking his loose skin. I wrap a big towel around his shriveled neck, daub thick lather over his face, and do my best not to irritate his skin, dotted here and there with small dilated capillaries. From age and fatigue, his eyes have sunk deep into their sockets, and his nose looks too prominent for his emaciated features. But, still flaunting the plume of hair—now snow white—that has always crowned his tall frame, he has lost none of his splendor.

Activity
6.3

Bauby uses both objective and subjective description to record this final portrait of his father. The color of the upholstery, the thickness of the shaving lather, and the mottled skin and sunken eyes are all examples of objective description. His father's *brave* reaction to the razor attacking his skin, the image of his white hair as a *flaunting* plume, and his overall *splendor* are examples of subjective description. Unlike the objective details, these subjective ones express characteristics or qualities that are not concrete but rather open to interpretation. Together, these two types of description create a vivid sense of what Bauby's father was like.

Using Spatial Order

Refer to "Using Spatial Order" on pages 70–71 in Chapter 4 for more information about organizing descriptive details.

As Chapter 4 indicates, writers often rely upon **spatial order** to organize descriptive writing. Spatial order locates the described elements logically in relationship to each other. It directs the reader's attention, for example, from left to right, from near to far, or from top to bottom. Spatial order helps your reader to visualize the details of the scene as they actually exist.

Consider the order of details in this descriptive paragraph about a unique restaurant:

> The most unusual restaurant in town is a place called PastaWorks, Inc. It is set up to resemble the inside of a broken-down factory. Near

the main entrance, there are several gigantic machines, each running from floor to ceiling, made of enormous spinning gears. The dining area is spread out behind the machines. This part of the restaurant is wide open, like the inside of a warehouse. Overhead, huge fans and pipes billowing steam hang from the ceiling. The strangest part of the room is the back wall. About twenty feet up is the front half of a real delivery truck. The wall is painted so that it looks as if the truck had crashed right through the wall. On the floor underneath the truck lies a jumble of bricks and truck parts.

Here, spatial order helps the reader bring this unusual place into focus. The description proceeds in an orderly way from the front entrance to the back wall: The gigantic machines are near the entrance, the dining area is behind the machines, the fans and steam pipes are hanging from the ceiling, and the nose of the delivery truck is about twenty feet up on the back wall, above a pile of bricks and truck parts.

Where spatial order is used to organize a descriptive paragraph, transitional expressions that show location help your reader. A few of these transitions are shown below.

Transitional Expressions Showing Location

above, below	in front of, behind	toward, away
close, far	next to, near, between	up, down

Exercise 6.4   Understanding Types of Description and Spatial Order

1. Briefly explain the difference between objective and subjective description.

   Objective description refers to the details and sensations in the world outside you.

   Subjective description refers to the impressions that those external details and sen-

   sations create within you.

   _____

   _____

2. How can spatial order make it easier for your reader to understand your

   description? _____

   Spatial order helps a reader visualize a scene according to the physical relation-

   ships among the objects.

   _____

   _____

| **Exercise 6.5** | **Recognizing the Role of Objective and Subjective Description and Transition in Descriptive Writing** |

1. Reread the paragraph on the unusual restaurant on pages 107–108. Working with a partner, make a list on a separate sheet of paper of all objective and all subjective details.

2. On the lines below, briefly explain the relationship transition plays in the spatial order used in the paragraph on the unusual restaurant.

Answers may vary somewhat, but most students will notice that expressions such as

Near the main entrance, Overhead, About twenty feet up, and On the floor under-

neath maintain spatial order because they provide a visual guide through the restau-

rant, the way a person who had just entered would see it.

| **Exercise 6.6** | **Working with Descriptive Details** |

1. Look again at the paragraph about the restaurant on pages 107–108. Which details—objective or subjective—did the most to catch your attention? Why?   Answers will vary. Some students will respond more to the vivid objective

details while others may identify with the writer's reactions.

2. Working with a partner, make a list of three details, at least one subjective and one objective, to add to the paragraph about the unusual restaurant.

Answers will vary. Representative answers are given.

Subjective: The place feels too much like a factory to be comfortable. There is not

enough soundproofing on the floor, walls, and ceiling.

Objective: The tables are made of weathered oak. The large front window overlooks

a small pond.

| **Exercise 6.7** | **Considering Purpose in Description Paragraphs** |

This chapter features several sample description paragraphs. The specific focus or names of the authors of these paragraphs, with the appropriate page numbers, are listed on the next page. Working with a partner, take another look at the paragraphs and then on the lines next to the names list the primary purpose and any secondary purposes for each paragraph.

1. Annie Dillard, page 104 <u>Most students will agree that Dillard's primary purpose</u>

   <u>is to entertain and her secondary purpose is to inform.</u>

2. Richard Rodriguez, page 105 <u>Most students will agree that Rodriguez's primary</u>

   <u>purpose is to entertain and his secondary purpose, although limited, is to inform.</u>

3. Jean-Dominique Bauby, page 107 <u>Most students will agree that Bauby's primary</u>

   <u>purpose is to entertain and his secondary purpose, although limited, is to inform.</u>

4. An unusual restaurant, pages 107–108 <u>Students may be divided in their view of</u>

   <u>this paragraph, with many arguing that the primary purpose is to inform and the sec-</u>

   <u>ondary purpose is to entertain and others asserting the opposite.</u>

Challenge 6.2   **Writing a Descriptive Paragraph**

Using the prewriting material you completed for Challenge 6.1 on page 106, complete a paragraph of at least 100 words that deals with a special day or memorable event. First, outline a plan for your paragraph, deciding on the best order for your details.

Discovering Connections 6.2

1. In Discovering Connections 6.1 on page 104, you chose a topic for a descriptive paragraph and completed your prewriting. Now develop a paragraph of at least 100 words that describes what you saw, thought, or experienced so that your reader can visualize it. As you write, focus on the points raised in this chapter.

2. Exchange your paragraph with a partner. If you completed the paragraph for Challenge 6.2 above and you feel at paragraph is better, use it for this exercise instead. Evaluate the paragraph you receive using the descriptive paragraph checklist on page 111. Write your answers on a separate sheet of paper, and then return the paragraph and your assessment to the writer.

3. Using your reader's comments to guide you, revise your own paragraph.

Descriptive Paragraph Checklist

☐ Does the topic sentence preview the description?

☐ Does the paragraph use sensory details? List them.

☐ Does it make effective use of both objective and subjective description? Write an *S* above every use of subjective description and an *O* above every use of objective description.

☐ Is it effectively arranged in spatial order or some other order? Explain.

☐ In your judgment, what is the best part of this paragraph? Explain.

☐ Which detail or example would be even better if it were expanded? Why?

 RECAP

DESCRIPTION

 Activity
6.4

New terms in this chapter	Definitions
● **description**	● the writing technique used to paint a picture in words of a scene, individual, object, or experience
● **sensory details**	● information perceived through sight, sound, taste, smell, and touch
● **objective description**	● writing that focuses on actual details and sensations ***Example*** The restaurant featured wood paneled walls and candlelit tables.
● **subjective description**	● writing that focuses on the impressions that details and sensations create within the writer ***Example*** The atmosphere in the restaurant was warm and cozy.

Writing a Descriptive Paragraph

Develop a **topic sentence** that previews the object to be described in the paragraph.

↓ ↑

Include **sensory details** to bring the scene into focus.

↓ ↑

Use a combination of **objective** and **subjective description**.

↓ ↑

Present the details through **spatial order** when appropriate.

Chapter 7

Example

Getting Started... **Q:** I want to make sure that the person who reads my paper understands my point the way I do. What's the best way to make sure this happens?

Audio 7.1 **A:** Whenever you want someone to understand something the way you do, one of the best techniques is to give an illustration or two of the point you are making. In other words, your answer in these situations is example.

Overview: Illustrating Your Point

Audio 7.2 You've probably said it hundreds of times yourself as you explained something: "For example, ..." We use examples to ensure that our points or statements are fully understood. In writing, **example** refers to the use of specific instances to illustrate, clarify, or back up a point.

As a writing technique, example is valuable. Well-chosen examples help make a point powerfully. A paragraph outlining types of fads could be developed through example. A paragraph about college challenges might also use example.

Weblink
7.1

> ***This chapter will explore the basic requirements for writing an effective example paragraph:***
>
> ● providing a topic sentence that clearly states the point you will illustrate
>
> ● choosing examples that are specific
>
> ● selecting examples that are relevant

Once you have mastered the basics of an example paragraph, you will also begin to understand how to write longer essays that use example.

Discovering Connections 7.1

Discovering Connections 7.2 at the end of the chapter will allow students to apply what they learn in this chapter by composing and revising an example paragraph.

Select one of the following topics. Then, employing one of the strategies that you practiced in Chapter 2, prewrite on that topic. Concentrate on useful, effective illustrations or examples.

1. entertaining advertisements
2. ways to spend a Saturday night in the summer
3. difficulties in hunting for a job

Save your work for later use.

Providing a Topic Sentence That States the Point You Will Illustrate

Audio
7.3

In an example paragraph, the topic sentence identifies the general idea that the examples will then clarify and illustrate. It should clearly state the point to be illustrated.

Look at this paragraph from "The Marginal World," an essay by environmentalist and writer Rachel Carson, in which she discusses an area at the edge of the sea:

Activity
7.1

> The flats took on a mysterious quality as dusk approached and the last evening light was reflected from the scattered pools and creeks. Then birds became only dark shadows, with no color discernible. Sanderlings scurried across the beach like little ghosts, and here and there the darker forms of the willets stood out. Often I could come very close to them before they would start up in alarm—the sanderlings running, the willets flying up, crying. Black skimmers flew along the ocean's edge silhouetted against the dull, metallic gleam, or they went flitting above the sand like large, dimly seen moths. Sometimes they "skimmed" the winding creeks of tidal water, where little spreading surface ripples marked the presence of small fish.

As you can see, the topic sentence indicates the focus of the paragraph: the change in the tidal flats as dusk approaches. The sentences that follow then provide specific examples of the various creatures that create the "mysterious quality" she speaks of. When you write, keep in mind that, like Carson, you may need to supply more than a single sentence to make each of your supporting examples clear for your reader.

Incidentally, with example you will often use the transitional expressions *for example* and *for instance*. Although Carson does not use either one in this particular paragraph, they are good cues for you to use. They remind you of the commitment you have to your reader: to provide a convincing illustration of your point.

In addition to these two transitional expressions, you might want to consider the following words when you create a writing that features example. Like *for example* and *for instance,* these other transitional expressions will help you emphasize the significance of the illustrations and details you include.

Transitional Expressions for Example Writing

| after all | in addition | moreover | particularly |
| indeed | in other words | of course | specifically |

Exercise 7.1 **Defining Example**

1. In your own words, explain how example as a mode can help you express your ideas in writing. _____

   Example helps you express ideas in writing because through this mode you can

   offer specific illustrations of your point.

   _____

2. Why are *for example* and *for instance* good transitional expressions to use in an example paragraph? _____

   Each time you use one of those expressions, you are promising to provide a specific

   illustration of your point—something you want to do in example writing.

   _____

Exercise 7.2 **Analyzing the Topic Sentence and Details in an Example Paragraph**

Working with a partner, list the examples used to support the topic sentence in the paragraph about the tidal flats on page 113. Write each example below. Next to each example, explain how it supports the topic sentence.

Activity
7.2

The birds became shadows—their appearance is now different.

Sanderlings scurried and then ran—they behaved differently.

Willets remained still and then flew—they behaved differently.

Black skimmers were silhouetted against the sky—conditions made the scene

look different.

Challenge 7.1   **Preparing to Write an Example Paragraph**

Prewrite on the subject of bad habits. Focus your topic, mark your best examples, and write a clear topic sentence. Save your work for later use.

Providing Specific Examples

Audio
7.4

To stress the importance of using specific details, ask students to brainstorm specific information to help readers understand one or more of these problems in today's schools.

Specific means detailed and particular. Writing **specific examples** means providing enough information so that your reader understands their meaning and significance. Generally, the more specific the information you supply is, the more convincing your examples are.

Imagine you are writing a paragraph about problems in today's schools, such as poor reading skills, lack of discipline in the classroom, students' personal difficulties, and unmotivated teachers. Supplying statistics or specific background about each of these examples would help your reader understand the problems. Simply stating that all of these things are problems would be less helpful and convincing.

Consider the following paragraph about hand gestures from a psychology text by Carol Tavris and Carole Wade:

Activity
7.3

> Even the simplest gesture is subject to misunderstanding and offense. The sign of the University of Texas football team, the Longhorns, is to extend the index finger and the pinkie. In Italy and other parts of Europe this gesture means a man's wife has been unfaithful to him—a serious insult! Anita Rowe, a consultant who advises businesses on cross-cultural customs, tells of a newly hired Asian engineer in a California company. As the man left his office to lead the first meeting of his project team, his secretary crossed her fingers to wish him luck. Instead of reassuring him, her gesture thoroughly confused him: In his home country, crossing one's fingers is a sexual proposition.

Here, Tavris and Wade provide two examples of misunderstood hand gestures to support their point: extending the index and pinkie fingers and crossing fingers. The authors ensure that these examples are specific by using two sentences to explain the first and three sentences to explain the second.

Fast Fact Here are examples of some English words for groups of things—**collective words**—that you don't hear too often: a *bale* of turtles, a *rout* of wolves, a *gam* of whales, a *leap* of leopards, a *crash* of rhino, a *cete* of badgers, and a *dray* of squirrels.

Ensuring That Your Examples Are Relevant

Relevant means appropriate and connected. **Relevant examples** are directly associated with the topic. For a paper on frustrating household chores, examples such as dusting, vacuuming, and washing windows would

Have students refer to the Rhetorical Index and choose an essay that includes the example mode. Ask them to identify and discuss the examples. Are they effective? Why or why not?

ESL Note
See "Writing Paragraphs" on page 585.

be relevant. These tasks are all frustrating because they must be repeated so frequently. However, an example about sweeping up at work would not be relevant. Although this task may indeed be frustrating, it is an on-the-job duty, not a household chore.

Take a look at the following paragraph from "Gray Area: Thinking with a Damaged Brain," an essay by Floyd Skloot, in which he discusses ways that his thinking has been affected because of a brain virus:

> I am so easily overloaded. I cannot read the menu or converse in a crowded, noisy restaurant. I get exhausted at Portland Trailblazers games, with all the visual and aural imagery, all the manufactured commotion, so I stopped going nine years ago. My hands are scarred from burns and cuts that occurred when I tried to cook and converse at the same time. I cannot drive in traffic, especially in our standard-transmission pickup truck. I cannot talk about, say, the fiction of Thomas Hardy while I drive; I need to be given directions in small doses rather than all at once and need those directions to be given precisely at the time I must make the required turn. This is, as Restak explains, because driving and talking about Hardy, or driving and processing information about where to turn, are handled by different parts of the brain, and my brain's parts have trouble working together.

As you can see, Skloot's topic sentence indicates that the focus of the paragraph is how parts of his day-to-day living now overwhelm him. The examples that follow are all relevant because they detail a number of ordinary things that now "overload" him.

Exercise 7.3   **Considering Specific and Relevant Examples**

1. How does making examples specific help to make an example paragraph more effective?

   Specific examples help readers understand the meaning of a general statement.

   They also help convince readers of the validity, or truth, of the general statement.

2. What makes examples relevant?

   Examples are relevant when they are directly connected to your topic.

Exercise 7.4   Explaining Relevance in an Example Paragraph

Look again at the sample paragraph about hand gestures on page 115. Working with a partner, explain why the detailed examples are relevant.

Answers will vary somewhat. Students will likely point out that both extended examples are misunderstood hand gestures and as such are relevant to the topic.

Exercise 7.5   Developing Specific Examples

Reread the examples of problems in today's schools given on page 115. Working with a partner, develop a list of additional examples of problems in U.S. public schools today. Choose one example, and list several ways you could provide specific support for it.

Exercise 7.6   Considering Purpose in Example Paragraphs

This chapter features several sample example paragraphs. The names of the authors of these paragraphs, with the appropriate page numbers, are listed below. Working with a partner, take another look at the paragraphs and then on the lines next to the names list the primary purpose and any secondary purposes for each paragraph.

1. Rachel Carson, page 113 ___Most students will agree that Carson's primary purpose is to inform and her secondary purpose is to entertain.___

2. Carol Tavris and Carole Wade, page 115 ___Most students will agree that entertaining barely edges out informing as the primary purpose in Tavris and Wade's paragraph.___

3. Floyd Skloot, page 116 ___A few students may note that Skloot's piece persuades because it suggests that people don't consider the far-reaching effects a brain injury can have.___

Challenge 7.2   **Writing an Example Paragraph**

Review the prewriting material and topic sentence on bad habits you developed for Challenge 7.1 on page 115. Make sure your examples are specific and relevant. Draft an example paragraph of at least 100 words that develops this topic.

Discovering Connections 7.2

1. In Discovering Connections 7.1 on page 113, you chose a topic for an example paragraph and completed your prewriting. Now develop a paragraph of at least 100 words that provides three or more brief examples of the subject. Consider the points raised in this chapter as you develop your paragraph.

2. Exchange your paragraph with a partner. If you completed the paragraph for Challenge 7.2 above, and you feel that paragraph is better, use it for this exercise instead. Evaluate the paragraph you receive using the example paragraph checklist below. Write your answers on a separate sheet of paper, and then return the paragraph and your assessment to the writer.

3. Using your reader's comments to guide you, revise your paragraph.

Example Paragraph Checklist

☐ Does the topic sentence clearly state the point to be illustrated?

☐ Does the paragraph provide specific examples? Underline any example that you feel needs to be made more specific.

☐ Are all the examples relevant? Put an * next to any example that you feel is not directly connected to the main idea of the paragraph.

☐ In your judgment, what is the best part of this paragraph? Explain.

☐ Which detail or example would be even better if it were expanded? Why?

RECAP   **EXAMPLE**

Activity
7.4

New terms in this chapter	Definitions
● example	● the writing technique that uses specific instances to illustrate, clarify, or back up the point being made
● specific examples	● illustrative material that is detailed and particular
	Example In the center of the room was *the old, dusty, mahogany roll-top desk.*

New terms in this chapter	Definitions
● **relevant examples**	● illustrative information that is appropriate and directly connected

> ***Example***   The *household chores* I find most annoying are *dusting, vacuuming,* and *washing windows.*

Writing an Example Paragraph

Identify the **subject** that you wish to **illustrate**.

↓   ↑

Provide a **topic sentence** that indicates the **specific idea** to be **illustrated**.

↓   ↑

Keep all examples **specific**.

↓   ↑

Make all examples **relevant**.

Chapter 8

Process

Getting Started... **Q:** I understand how this gizmo works, how to use it. But to explain it so somebody else understands how—now that, I'm not sure of. How do I write it for someone else?

Audio 8.1 **A:** Whenever you have to explain a process or procedure for somebody else, process is your answer. That you understand the process or procedure means you are in great shape. Now think back to what it was like *before* you understood the subject. Write out the steps with that perspective in mind, and you'll be all set.

Overview: Explaining How It Happens or How to Do It

Audio 8.2 Whenever you explain how something occurs or how to do something, you are using **process**. There are basically three types of process writing. One type, called *process analysis*, explains such matters as how tornadoes form or how certain foods contribute to cholesterol problems. A second type, called *process narrative*, explains how you as the writer did something, such as organizing a weekend park cleanup or establishing a fitness routine. The most common type, however, often called *how-to writing*, presents instructions for filling out a financial aid form or assembling a gas grill.

Weblink 8.1

Weblink 8.2

This chapter will explore the basic requirements for writing an effective process paragraph:

- including a topic sentence that clearly states the procedure or technique

- using the imperative mood (you) when it's appropriate

- dividing the process into simple, logical steps

- relying on linear order

Once you have mastered these basics, you will begin to understand how to write longer papers involving process.

Discovering Connections 8.1

Activity
2.3

Discovering Connections 8.2 at the end of the chapter will allow students to apply what they learn in this chapter by composing and revising a process paragraph.

Select one of the following topics. Then, using one of the strategies that you practiced in Chapter 2, prewrite on that topic. Concentrate on steps in the process involved.

1. how to make a bed
2. how to stop on rollerblades
3. how to gift wrap a package

Save your work for later use.

Including a Topic Sentence That Clearly States The Process

Audio
8.3

An effective topic sentence for a process paragraph must focus on something that can be adequately explained in a brief space. It must clearly state the specific process—procedure, technique, or routine—to be explained and set a direction that the other sentences in the paragraph will cover.

Take a look at the relationship between the topic sentence and the supporting sentences in the following paragraph from a book on solving children's sleep problems written by Richard Ferber, M.D.:

> Bedtime means separation, which is difficult for children, especially very young ones. Simply sending a toddler or young child off to bed alone is not fair and may be scary for him. And it means you will miss what can be one of the best times of the day. So set aside ten to thirty minutes to do something special with your child before bed. Avoid teasing, scary stories, or anything that will excite your child at this time. Save the wrestling and tussling for other times of the day. You might both enjoy a discussion, quiet play, or story reading. But let your child know that your special time together will not extend beyond the time you and he have agreed upon, then don't go beyond those limits. It is a good idea to tell your child when the time is almost up or when you have only two or three more pages to read, and don't give in for an extra story. Your child will learn the rules only if you enforce them. If both you and he know just what is going to happen, there won't be the arguments and tension that arise when there is uncertainty.

Ferber's topic sentence indicates that the paragraph concerns bedtime for children, specifically how difficult it can be. The rest of the paragraph lays out a procedure that will make a difficult time far easier for both parents and children.

Using the Imperative Mood: You

Activity 8.2   With instructions, it makes sense to address the reader directly, using the **imperative mood**, often called the **command**. When you use the imperative mood, the subject is not stated but *understood* to be the person reading the piece. When you write, "Close the kitchen window," you are actually saying, "*You* close the kitchen window."

Note the use of the imperative mood in this paragraph on how to insert a contact lens:

> Inserting a contact lens is a simple process. First, take the lens out of the fluid it is stored in and rinse it off. Next, place the cleaned lens on the tip of your right index finger. Check the edge of the lens to make sure the lens hasn't turned inside out. It should look like the top of an opened umbrella. Using your left index finger, pull down gently on your lower right eyelid to expose more of the white of the eye. Then carefully place the lens over the iris, or colored part, of your eye. Blink once to make sure the lens is securely in place. If you can see clearly through that eye, repeat these steps for your other eye.

As you can see, the steps of the process are written in the imperative mood. The subject is actually *you*, the person who is performing the steps, but the word *you* is never stated.

Exercise 8.1   Defining Process

1. In your own words, briefly explain process. _____

   Process is writing that explains how to do something or how something happens.

   _____

   _____

   _____

2. Why should you use the imperative mood when writing a set of directions?

   You are telling the reader what to do, so the subject of your sentences is really *you*.

   ("You, the reader, do this.")

   _____

   _____

Exercise 8.2   **Relating the Parts of a Process Paragraph**

1. Briefly explain the connection between the topic sentence and the supporting sentences in the paragraph on how to insert a contact lens on page 122. What does each accomplish?

   The topic sentence (the first sentence) asserts that inserting a contact lens is

   easy. The supporting sentences "prove" this by showing the steps in easy-to-follow

   fashion.

2. In your view, which of the sentences in the paragraph about dealing with bedtime on page 121 does the best job supporting the topic sentence? Why?

   Answers will vary depending upon sentence selected.

Challenge 8.1   **Preparing to Write a Process Paragraph**

Prewrite on how to prepare a favorite meal, iron a pair of pants, or apply makeup. As you list information, think of your reader. Ask questions such as *What are the steps? Have I left out anything a novice would need to know?* Save your work for later use.

Dividing the Process into Simple, Logical Steps

Activity 8.3

Activity 8.4

The key to successful process writing is to separate the process into small, manageable steps and then to spell out these steps in detail. For example, although blood circulates through the human body in a highly complex process, you can describe it fairly accurately in four basic steps: (1) The heart pumps oxygenated blood to body tissues through the arteries and capillaries. (2) The veins carry the blood back to the heart. (3) The heart pumps the blood to the lungs to be oxygenated again. (4) The blood returns to the heart to be circulated through the body again. Breaking the process down into discrete steps, each with its own function, makes the complex process easier for the reader to understand.

Consider how the steps are presented in this paragraph from Simon Winchester's book, *The Professor and the Madman: A Tale of Murder, Insanity, and the Making of the Oxford English Dictionary:*

> The volunteers' duties were simple enough, if onerous. They would write to the society offering their services in reading certain books; they would be asked to read and make wordlists of all that they read, and would then be asked to look super-specifically, for certain words that currently interested the dictionary team. Each volunteer would take a slip of paper, write at its top left-hand side the target word, and below, also on the left, the date of the details that followed: These were, in order, the title of the book or paper, its volume and page number, and then, below that, the full sentence that illustrated the use of the target word. It was a technique that has been undertaken by lexicographers to the present day.

This paragraph breaks down a process—the one that participants in the dictionary project followed—into distinct, easily completed steps. Because each step is explained in specific detail, a reader can understand the process that eventually produced the massive multivolume text that is among the most well-known and most often used reference works of all time.

Fast Fact Before any new word is added to the *Webster's New World Dictionary,* it is first put on "word watch" and its use is then monitored by a thirteen-member editorial team. The word must be widely used for at least three years before it will actually be considered for adoption. Words currently under examination include *irritainment,* entertainment of some kind that is both annoying and compelling, and *starter marriage,* a brief first marriage that ends in divorce, without kids, property, or regrets.

Relying on Linear Order

Activity 8.5

Have students refer to the Rhetorical Index and choose an essay that uses the process mode. Ask them to identify the main steps in the process and list them in sequence. What specific details in the essay help readers understand the process that is explained?

Effective process writing often depends on **linear order**, or the arrangement of steps in the order they occur. Writing about the process of taking a photograph with a 35-millimeter camera would call for linear order: (1) adjust the focus; (2) change the setting to allow the proper amount of light through the lens; (3) push the shutter button to take the picture. Unless the steps are performed in this order, the photograph would probably not turn out well.

Take a look at the order of the steps in this paragraph from a textbook on study skills by James F. Shepherd, which concerns identifying a person's level of concentration:

> When you begin to study, make a note of the time. Then, when you first become aware that your attention is not focused on studying, record the time again. Compare the two times and make a note of how many minutes you studied before you lost your concentration. Next,

spend a few minutes doing something other than studying; you might stand up and stretch or look out the window. When you begin to study again, make another note of how long you concentrate.

As you can see, linear order plays an important role in this paragraph. To analyze your level of concentration successfully, you must follow the various steps in the order presented. If you do any of the steps out of order, you won't be able to establish your own degree of concentration.

Process writing places events in time order sequence. Therefore, transitional expressions that signal that order help your reader. See the list below for transitions useful in a process paragraph.

Transitional Expressions for Process Writing

Beginning	*Continuing*				*Ending*
begin by	as soon as	second step, etc.	until		finally
initially	next	then	while		last

Keep in mind that if you are explaining an unusual or specialized process, you may need to define special terms. In any how-to process paragraph, you will need to specify the materials or tools needed to carry out the process. In most cases, this information should come right after the topic sentence so that the reader will be fully prepared to complete the process.

Exercise 8.3   **Understanding Organization in a Process Paragraph**

1. Why is it important to divide a process into small, manageable steps?

   A process can be very complicated. Breaking it into small, manageable steps makes

   it possible for a reader to understand it.

2. Briefly explain linear order. _____

   Linear order is the arrangement of steps in the order that they occur.

Exercise 8.4   **Explaining Order in a Process Paragraph**

1. Reread the paragraph on creating entries for the *Oxford English Dictionary* on page 124, and then briefly explain how linear order helps the reader understand the process.

Linear order breaks down a complicated process into small steps and shows the re-

lationship between them. Each step had to be completed before volunteers could go

on to the next step.

_____

_____

2. Consider the transitions in the paragraph on monitoring your concentration. Choose one of the transitional words or examples and explain how the transition helps to maintain linear order.

Answers will vary.

_____

_____

_____

_____

_____

Exercise 8.5   **Enumerating Steps in a Process**

1. Take another look at the sample paragraph on pages 124–125 about level of concentration. Working with a partner, list the steps that make up the process on a separate piece of paper.

2. With your partner, list on your sheet the steps involved in tying a shoelace or hanging a picture.

Exercise 8.6   **Considering Purpose in Process Paragraphs**

This chapter features several sample process paragraphs. The specific focus or names of the authors of these paragraphs, with the appropriate page numbers, are listed below. Working with a partner, take another look at the paragraphs and then on the lines next to the names list the primary purpose and any secondary purposes for each paragraph.

1. Richard Ferber, page 121   Most students will agree that Ferber's primary purpose

   is to inform and his secondary purpose is to persuade.

2. Inserting a contact lens, page 122   Students will agree that the purpose in this

   paragraph is to inform.

3. Simon Winchester, page 124 <u>Most students will agree that Winchester's</u>

<u>primary purpose is to inform and her secondary purpose is to entertain.</u>

4. James F. Shepherd, pages 124–125 <u>Most students will agree that Shepherd's</u>

<u>purpose is to inform.</u>

Challenge 8.2   Writing a Process Paragraph

Using the ideas you developed in Challenge 8.1 on page 123, complete a paragraph of at least 100 words on how to prepare a favorite meal, iron a pair of pants, or apply makeup.

Discovering Connections 8.2

1. In Discovering Connections 8.1 on page 121, you chose a topic for a process paragraph and completed your prewriting. Now develop a paragraph of at least 100 words that explains how to perform the action. Use the points presented in this chapter as a guide.
2. Exchange your paragraph with a partner. If you completed the paragraph for Challenge 8.2 above and you feel that paragraph is better, use it for this exercise instead. Evaluate the paragraph you receive using the process paragraph checklist below. Write your answers on a separate sheet of paper, and then return the paragraph and your assessment to the writer.
3. Using your reader's comments to guide you, revise your own paragraph.

Process Paragraph Checklist

☐ Does the topic sentence clearly state the procedure or technique to be presented?

☐ Does it use the imperative mood (you)?

☐ Is the process divided into simple, logical steps? Do you feel any step should be further subdivided to make it easier for the reader to perform the process? Put a ✓ next to any step that needs to be divided.

☐ Are the steps presented in linear order? Underline any step that is out of linear order, and then draw a line to the spot in the paragraph where it actually belongs.

☐ In your judgment, what is the best part of this paragraph? Explain.

☐ Which detail or example would be even better if it were expanded? Why?

 PROCESS

New terms in this chapter	Definitions
● **process**	● the writing technique that explains how to do something or how something occurs Three types of process writing include 1. *process analysis* (how something is done or occurs) 2. *process narrative* (how you did something) 3. *a set of instructions* (how to do something)
● **imperative mood**	● designating verb usage that expresses commands The subject of the sentence in the imperative mood is understood as the reader (you) rather than stated directly. ***Example*** (*You*) Move your books and papers into the other room, please.
● **linear order**	● an arrangement of steps in the order of their occurrence

Writing a Process Paragraph

Write a clear **topic sentence** that specifies the process to be explained.

Directly address the reader through the **imperative mood** when it's appropriate.

Present the process in **simple, logical steps**.

Introduce the steps in **linear order**.

Chapter 9

Definition

Getting Started… **Q:** Even though my idea is a little complex and abstract, I do understand it. How do I write about it so somebody else will also understand it?

Audio 9.1

A: When you understand what something means and you want to communicate that meaning to someone else, definition is the mode to use. With definition, you identify the essence of the topic and you concentrate on expressing this essence in terms that someone who lacks your specific background can understand.

Overview: Making Meaning Crystal Clear

Audio 9.2

No matter what your topic is, your job is to communicate your ideas about that topic clearly and precisely. One writing mode that will help you achieve this goal is **definition**. Through definition, you can specify the meanings of actions, ideas, places, and things.

For example, a paragraph featuring definition could spell out the qualities of a good boss. This mode would also be a natural choice to explain what makes a house a home.

Weblink 9.1

> ***This chapter will explore the basic requirements for writing an effective definition paragraph:***
>
> ● providing a topic sentence that highlights the term to be defined
>
> ● understanding the elements of an effective definition
>
> ● recognizing all the possible meanings of the term defined

Once you have mastered these basics, you will also be prepared to write longer papers involving definition.

Discovering Connections 9.1

Activity
9.1

Discovering Connections 9.2 at the end of the chapter will allow students to apply what they learn in this chapter by composing and revising a definition paragraph.

Select one of the following topics. Then, relying on one of the strategies that you practiced in Chapter 2, prewrite on that topic. Focus on defining the qualities of the term.

1. charisma
2. success
3. a slob

Save your work for later use.

Providing a Topic Sentence That Highlights the Term to Be Defined

Audio
9.3

An effective definition paragraph begins with a topic sentence that highlights the term to be defined. In fact, the topic sentence of a definition paragraph is often a brief definition itself. For example, if you were defining your view of what an *optimist* is, you might begin this way:

EXAMPLE

An optimist is a person who sees good even in the worst situations and believes that, somehow, things will always work out for the best.

As you can see, the topic sentence provides a brief definition of the term, setting the direction for the sentences that will follow.

Look at this paragraph from Robert Jourdain's book, *Music, the Brain, and Ecstasy: How Music Captures Our Imagination,* in which he offers a definition of the musical scale:

Activity
9.2

Like the scale found at the bottom of a road map, a musical scale provides units of measure, but for pitch space rather than geographical space. The basic unit is called a *half-step* (or a *semitone*). Every key along a piano keyboard represents a half-step. From C to C-sharp is a half-step, and so is from E to F. In the scale system we're accustomed to in the West, there are twelve half-steps (and twelve piano keys) in any octave, say, from middle C to the C above.

The topic sentence clearly states the term to be defined, the musical scale. It also refers to another familiar scale—the scale at the bottom of a map— as a way to make this aspect of music easier to understand. The supporting sentences in the paragraph then develop the definition further, explaining the half-step's function within this musical scale.

Understanding the Pattern of an Effective Definition

Audio 9.4 A dictionary definition follows a simple pattern. It first identifies the general class to which the term belongs. Then it gives the special, or distinguishing, characteristics that set the word apart.

EXAMPLE

A zip drive is a [class: *computer device*] that [distinguished characteristics: *enables a user to store large amounts of information on special disks*].

Paragraphs that define should also follow this **pattern of an effective definition**. However, most definition paragraphs call for greater elaboration. Especially with abstract subjects such as fear, you will need to express personal interpretation or experience. For such words, in addition to class and distinguishing characteristics, you should also provide specific, concrete examples and details for support.

Note the elements of definition in the following paragraph from "The Search for Marvin Gardens," by writer John McPhee. In this article, he discusses the classic board game *Monopoly* and the actual by-ways of Atlantic City, New Jersey, whose names make up the blocks on the game board:

> Marvin Gardens is the one color-block Monopoly property that is not in Atlantic City. It is a suburb within a suburb, secluded. It is a planned compound of seventy-two handsome houses set on curvilinear private streets under yews and cedars, poplars and willows. The compound was built around 1920, in Margate, New Jersey, and consists of solid buildings of stucco, brick, and wood, with slate roofs, tile roofs, multi-mullioned porches, Giraldic towers, and Spanish grilles. Marvin Gardens, the ultimate outwash of Monopoly, is a citadel and sanctuary of the middle class.

Discuss with students what other modes writers can use to help them express how they understand or interpret something. Example, narration, and description, for example, are used to support a definition paragraph.

The elements of an effective definition are at work here. The opening sentence indicates that, unlike the other locales on the *Monopoly* game board, Marvin Gardens isn't actually in Atlantic City, New Jersey. The next two sentences specify the distinguishing characteristics of this area. Marvin Gardens is a small planned compound of seventy-two houses on tree-lined private streets in a suburb near Atlantic City. The other sentences then provide additional specific details, including the name of the city that is home to Marvin Gardens. Together this information leads to a complete picture of this small neighborhood made famous by a simple board game.

Exercise 9.1   **Defining Definition**

1. Briefly explain definition. How is a dictionary definition different from a definition paragraph? _____

   Definition is writing that explains the meaning of a term. A dictionary definition

   explains class and distinguishing characteristics. A definition paragraph elaborates

   with examples and details that explore the totality of meaning.

   _____

2. What role does the topic sentence play in a definition paragraph? _____

   The topic sentence in a definition paragraph presents the term to be defined. It is

   often stated as a definition itself.

   _____

   _____

Exercise 9.2   **Identifying the Elements of Definition**

1. In each sentence of definition below, underline the word that is being defined. Then circle the class to which the word belongs, and double underline the distinguishing characteristics that set it apart. Study the example first.

   EXAMPLE   A diplomat is a (government representative) who conducts relationships involving trade, treaties, and other official business with the government of another nation.

   _____ a. A judge is (an elected (or sometimes appointed) public official) who has the authority to hear and decide cases in a court of law.

   _____ b. A gecko is (a tropical lizard) with soft skin, a short, stout body, a large head, and suction pads on its feet.

   _____ c. A monopoly involves (ownership or possession) that gives exclusive control of a service or commodity in a market, making it possible to fix prices and strangle free competition.

_____ d. The <u>nuclear family</u> is a social unit that <u>consists of parents and</u>

<u>the children they raise.</u>

_____ e. A <u>democracy</u> is a form of government in which the <u>people</u>

<u>hold ruling power through elected officials.</u>

2. Working with a partner, develop a sentence definition for the following five terms on a separate sheet of paper. Follow the pattern of the sentence definitions in the first part of this exercise. Use a dictionary if necessary, but make sure to express the definition in your own words.

a. jet ski
b. DVD
c. dialysis
d. eminent domain
e. search engine

Exercise 9.3   **Developing Supporting Details for a Definition Paragraph**

1. On page 130, the following topic sentence is given: _An optimist is a person who sees good even in the worst situations and believes that, somehow, things will always work out for the best._ Working with a partner, list details that could develop this definition more fully. Write the list on a separate sheet of paper.

2. Turn the details that you and your partner generated into sentences to support the topic sentence.

Challenge 9.1   **Preparing to Write a Definition Paragraph**

Prewrite on the subject of maturity. Focus on your best defining details. Then draft a topic sentence. Save your work for later use.

Recognizing the Full Effect of the Term Defined

Preparing an effective definition paragraph may also mean taking into account all the possible meanings for the term you are defining. To do this, you need to consider both the **denotation**, or literal meaning of the word, and its **connotations**—all the associations that also come with the word.

For example, the denotation of _clever_ is its literal meaning, quick-witted and intelligent. When we say a child is clever, that is a compliment. When we say a politician or a criminal is clever, we may imply something negative, such as the person's ability to manipulate or take advantage of others. It is important to keep these kinds of connotations in mind when you are writing a definition paragraph.

Consider the following paragraph from Esther Dyson's article, "Cyberspace: If You Don't Love It, Leave It," in which she offers another way to define *cyberspace:*

> In the same way, you could think of cyberspace as a giant and unbounded world of virtual real estate. Some property is privately owned and rented out; other property is common land; some places are suitable for children, and others are best avoided by all but the kinkiest citizens. Unfortunately, it's those places that are now capturing the popular imagination: places that offer bomb-making instructions, pornography, advice on how to procure stolen credit cards. They make cyberspace sound like a nasty place.

In this paragraph, Dyson takes the term *cyberspace,* an electronic arena that has no real permanent form or structure, and makes it more concrete for the reader by comparing it to a more familiar concept, *real estate.* Her definition works well in part because of what people understand real estate to mean. As she indicates, in terms of denotation, people do think of real estate in terms of land and buildings, property that is owned, rented, or shared. But in terms of connotation, people also think of real estate as something valuable, that can be a source of pride when it is well-maintained and a source of annoyance and fear when it isn't. Through this use of denotation and connotation, Dyson emphasizes that the virtual real estate has the same attributes and qualities as its actual equivalent. As a result, the term that she is using real estate to explain, *cyberspace,* is a bit easier to understand.

One way to ensure that the point you are making is clear for your reader is to supply transition. With definition writing, you may find the following transitional expressions useful:

Transitional Expressions for Definition Writing

accordingly	in addition	in other words	on the whole	therefore
indeed	in fact	in the same way	specifically	thus

Fast Fact Who would have thought that simple definitions could cause any trouble, but that's what happened recently in a New London, Connecticut, court. A Superior Court judge ordered a new trial for a man convicted of felony murder, first-degree robbery, first-degree arson, second-degree arson, and tampering with evidence. The judge made this decision after the jurors admitted that they had consulted a dictionary for definitions of *robbery* and *burglary,* which, according to the judge, amounted to introducing "extraneous material."

Exercise 9.4   **Distinguishing between a Word's Denotation and Its Connotations**

Activity
9.3

1. Explain the difference between a word's denotation and its connotations.

   Denotation is the objective meaning of a word. Connotations are the emotional associations—negative or positive—that the word communicates.

2. Working with a partner, provide a connotation for each of the italicized words on a separate sheet of paper.
   a. an *intense* discussion
   b. *eccentric* behavior
   c. a *cheap* product

Exercise 9.5   **Using Connotations of Words to Create an Attitude**

For each pair of synonyms, write a + beside the word with a positive connotation and a − beside the word with a negative connotation. Then write a sentence using each word so that its meaning and your attitude toward it are clear. Study the example first.

EXAMPLE   __−__ miserly   __+__ thrifty

The miserly old man was so stingy that he deserved his lonely life. My thrifty grandfather at last saved enough to buy me that fishing rod I wanted.

1. __−__ stubborn   __+__ persistent

   Sentences will vary throughout.

2. __+__ quaint   __−__ outlandish

3. __+__ ideals   __−__ illusions

4. __+__ dog   __−__ cur

Exercise 9.6 — **Considering Purpose in Definition Paragraphs**

This chapter features several sample definition paragraphs. The names of the authors of these paragraphs, with the appropriate page numbers, are listed below. Working with a partner, take another look at the paragraphs and then on the lines next to the names list the primary purpose and any secondary purposes for each paragraph.

1. Robert Jourdain, page 130 Most students will agree that Jourdain's primary purpose is to inform and his secondary purpose is to entertain.

2. John McPhee, page 131 Most students will agree that McPhee's primary purpose is to inform and the secondary purpose is to entertain.

3. Esther Dyson, page 134 Most students will agree that Dyson's primary purpose is to entertain and her secondary purposes are to inform and to persuade (to convince the reader to reconsider how cyberspace is perceived).

Challenge 9.2 — **Writing a Paragraph of Definition**

For Challenge 9.1 on page 133, you completed a prewriting on the subject of maturity. Drawing on this material, write a paragraph of at least 100 words defining maturity. Consider the pattern of definition and the connotations of words as you write.

Discovering Connections 9.2

1. In Discovering Connections 9.1 on page 130, you chose a topic for a definition paragraph and completed your prewriting. Now develop a paragraph of at least 100 words that defines that subject. Use the points laid out in this chapter as a guide.
2. Exchange your paragraph with a partner. If you completed the paragraph for Challenge 9.2 above and you feel that paragraph is better, use it for this exercise instead. Evaluate the paragraph you receive using the definition paragraph checklist below. Write your answers on a separate sheet of paper, and then return the paragraph and your assessment to the writer.
3. Using your reader's comments to guide you, revise your own paragraph.

Definition Paragraph Checklist

☐ Does the topic sentence highlight the term to be defined?

☐ Does it include the elements of an effective definition? What are they?

☐ Does it take into consideration both the denotation and connotations of the term?

☐ Underline any examples or details that are too general or too abstract to be effective. Suggest a concrete example that might be used instead.

☐ In your judgment, what is the best part of this paragraph? Explain.

☐ Which detail or example would be even better if it were expanded? Why?

RECAP   DEFINITION

Activity
9.4

New terms in this chapter	Definitions
● **definition**	● the writing technique used to specify the meanings of both concrete and abstract objects, ideas, events, or persons
● **pattern of an effective definition**	● two-step method of defining by first identifying the general class to which the term belongs and then listing its distinguishing characteristics  **Example** A *convertible* is a *car* with a *retractable top*.
● **denotation**	● the direct, specific meaning of a word, as listed in the dictionary
● **connotations**	● the additional, subjective meanings a word suggests, deriving from the associations or emotional overtones it has

Writing a Definition Paragraph

Choose a topic whose meaning needs **clarification** or **delineation**.

↓ ↑

Provide a **topic sentence** that indicates the term to be defined.

↓ ↑

Focus on the **elements of an effective definition**.

↓ ↑

Consider the **denotation** and **connotations** of the term you are defining.

Chapter 10

Comparison and Contrast

Getting Started... **Q:** I want to talk about two topics that have many things in common. I want to make sure that my readers can see all these common points. What's the best way for me to write about these subjects?

Audio 10.1 **A:** When you want to show how two subjects are similar—or for that matter how two subjects are different—comparison and contrast is your answer. This mode helps you point out similarities or differences in a form that makes them clear for someone who is less familiar with the subject than you are.

Overview: Expressing Similarities and Differences

Audio 10.2 Because we often make decisions after considering alternatives, mastering the writing technique that examines alternatives, **comparison and contrast**, is important. To compare is to examine *similarities;* to contrast is to examine *differences.* When you use comparison and contrast, you organize your explanation of one thing relative to another, on the basis of common points.

Comparison and contrast would dominate in a piece of writing discussing similarities and differences between two computer game systems. This mode would also be useful to explore the similarities and differences between two eras in history or two characters in a play. You may find, in fact, that you rely on comparison and contrast a great deal in academic writing, especially with essay examinations.

Weblink 10.1

> ***This chapter will explore the basic requirements for writing an effective comparison and contrast paragraph:***
>
> ● providing a topic sentence that specifies the subjects and indicates the focus
>
> ● establishing a basis for comparison
>
> ● arranging ideas effectively

Once you have mastered these basics, you will be prepared to write longer papers featuring comparison and contrast.

Discovering Connections 10.1

Weblink
10.2

Discovering Connections 10.2 at the end of the chapter will allow students to apply what they learn in this chapter by composing and revising a comparison and contrast paragraph.

Select one of the following topic pairs. Then, using one of the strategies that you practiced in Chapter 2, prewrite on that topic pair. Focus on similarities and differences between the two people, places, or items.

1. two competing brands of the same product
2. two vacation spots
3. two instructors

Save your work for later use.

Providing a Topic Sentence That Specifies Both Subjects and Indicates the Focus

Audio
10.3

The topic sentence of a comparison and contrast paragraph specifies the two subjects to be examined. It also indicates whether the focus is on similarities or differences.

Consider this paragraph from a textbook on macroeconomics by Stephen L. Slavin:

> The big difference between the old Soviet economy and our own is what consumer goods and services are produced. In our economy, the market forces of supply and demand dictate what gets produced and how much of it gets produced. But a government planning agency in the Soviet Union dictated what and how much was made. In effect, central planning attempted to direct a production and distribution process that works automatically in a market economy.

Notice that the topic sentence names the subjects under discussion (the old Soviet economy and our own) and also indicates that the paragraph will contrast the two systems.

Students have learned that an effective topic sentence states or implies the writer's opinion or attitude about the subject (Chapter 3). What is the author's opinion in this example about the old Soviet economy and that of the United States? A topic sentence in a comparison or contrast paragraph will often show the writer's evaluation of the subjects.

Establishing Your Bases for Comparison

Whenever you use comparison and contrast, you need to establish your **bases for comparison**. In other words, once you have chosen your subjects and your focus, you must specify the characteristics or elements you are going to examine.

For example, in a paragraph examining two brands of personal computers, you might examine *purchase price, warranties, types and availability of software,* and *ease of use.* Once you have established these bases of comparison, the next step is to discuss each brand in relation to these features.

To be sure you include comparable information for both brands on every point, you may find it helpful to construct a planning chart first.

	Computer 1	**Computer 2**
Price		
Warranty		
Software		
Ease of use		

Look at this paragraph by N. L. Gage and David C. Berliner, which contrasts experienced physicists with newcomers to the field:

Ask students to identify the topic sentence in this paragraph and explain why it is effective. Also, ask this question: What do you think of a question as a topic sentence? Why?

How do expert physicists differ from novices? One difference is that experts take more time than novices in studying a problem. But once they start to work, they solve problems faster than novices do. The experts also seem more often than novices to construct an abstract representation of the problems in their minds. That is, in their working memory they hold mental representations of the blocks, pulleys, inclined planes, levers, or whatever they need to solve a problem. Expert physicists also tend to classify new problems more frequently. They may decide a problem is a type-X problem, to be solved by using the laws of inclined planes. Or they may see the problem as belonging to the type that deals with forces, pulleys, and blocks, which are always solvable by using some variation of Newton's second law, $F = MA$ (Force = Mass $\times$ Acceleration).

As you can see, the bases for comparison are clear. Expert physicists differ from novices in terms of how much time they spend solving problems and how they study, visualize, and classify problems.

Fast Fact Consider this contrast: Even though this black and white, odoriferous rodent is immediately recognizable to anyone who sees it, not everyone in the United States calls it by the same name. In the North, people refer to it as a *skunk*. People in the South, however, knowing its appetite for *poultry*, refer to it as a *polecat.*

Exercise 10.1 Defining Comparison and Contrast

Activity 10.1

1. In your own words, explain comparison and contrast. _____

   Comparison means exploring the similarities between two things. Contrast means

   exploring the differences.

   _____

   _____

2. What does *bases for comparison* mean? _____

Bases for comparison are those grounds on which you compare and contrast. They

are the features or aspects that you look at in both things.

Exercise 10.2   **Analyzing a Topic Sentence and Bases of Comparison**

1. Take another look at the paragraph on the previous page about expert and novice physicists and then answer the following questions:

   a. How does the topic sentence prepare the reader for the rest of the paragraph?

   The topic sentence prepares the reader for the rest of the paragraph because it

   identifies the topic—expert and novice physicists—and it indicates that the focus

   will be on the differences between the two.

   b. How do the supporting sentences follow through on the promise of the topic sentence?

   The supporting sentences follow through on the promise of the topic sentence be-

   cause they specify the various differences between expert and novice physicists.

2. Working with a partner, list on a separate sheet of paper the bases for comparison in the paragraph on page 139 about our economy versus the old Soviet economy.

Challenge 10.1   **Preparing to Write a Paragraph of Comparison or Contrast**

Prewrite on the similarities or differences between two types of music or two political figures, actors, or professional athletes. Decide on several sound bases for comparison. Construct a planning chart like the one on page 140.

Arranging Your Ideas Effectively

When you write a paragraph in which the comparison and contrast mode dominates, you can choose between two organizational plans. The first alternative, the **block format**, examines all the elements of subject A and then all the same elements in the same order for subject B. Imagine, for example, you were writing a paragraph about two bosses for whom you've worked. If you used the block format, you would first examine one boss in terms of knowledge of the job, patience with workers, and basic fairness. Then you would examine the same criteria in the same order for the second boss.

The other method of arrangement is the **alternating method**. When you follow this format, you switch back and forth between subjects as you examine each point. With the paragraph about your two bosses, you would first discuss how well boss 1 understood the job and then how well boss 2 understood it. Next you would explain how patient boss 1 was and then how patient boss 2 was, and so on.

Note the organizational plan of this paragraph from "Dazzled in Disneyland," an article by Aubrey Menen:

> There are two kinds of legends: with one sort we can get inside them; with the other we are always spectators. I suppose there can be no American male who has not, at some time in his life, found himself alone in the countryside and explored Tom Sawyer island, or fought Indians, or crept on his belly up to a paleface fort. But nobody, I think, at any age plays Water Rat and Toad, or goes into Mole's house, or plays Prince Charming or Cinderella (unless driven to it by sentimental elders). These stories are too complete to have room for the outsider. We would know what to say to Pinocchio if we met him, or the Three Ugly Sisters. But we do not imagine ourselves being these people. A lesser man than Disney would not realize this. But here Tom Sawyer's island is big enough for children to play on; and Pinocchio's village is so small there is not even room in its streets to put one's foot. Once again Disney shows himself a master of the use of proportion.

As you can see, this paragraph is arranged in the alternating format. First Menen discusses the type of fantasies that one participates in, such as the story of Tom Sawyer. Then, for contrast, he brings in imaginings associated with children's stories like *The Wind in the Willows* and Cinderella in which one is a spectator. Then he discusses the size of Tom Sawyer's Island in Disneyland and contrasts it with the size of Pinocchio's village.

Now here is an example of a paragraph from an astronomy textbook by Jay M. Pasachoff arranged in the block fashion:

> Venus and the Earth are sister planets: their sizes, masses, and densities are about the same. But they are as different from each other as the wicked sisters were from Cinderella. The Earth is lush; it has oceans and rainstorms of water, an atmosphere containing oxygen, and creatures swimming in the sea, flying in the air, and walking on the ground. On the other hand, Venus is a hot, foreboding planet with temperatures con-

stantly over 750 K (900°F), a planet on which life seems unlikely to develop. Why is Venus like that? How did these harsh conditions come about? Can it happen to us here on Earth?

Have students refer to the Rhetorical Index and choose an essay that uses the comparison and contrast mode. Ask them to identify the bases for comparison and identify block or alternating format.

This paragraph is arranged in the block fashion. First, the writer discusses various characteristics of Earth, and then he notes the contrasting characteristics of Venus. For information on using these formats in an essay, see "Using Comparison and Contrast to Develop an Essay" on pages 227–228 in Chapter 15.

Transitional expressions are a great help to readers as they follow your organizational plan. A paragraph of comparison will, of course, use different sorts of transitions than a paragraph of contrast. The list below shows some of the transitional expressions you will find useful for each of these techniques.

Transitional Expressions for Comparison and Contrast Writing

Contrast		Comparison	
although	however	also	just as
but	on the other hand	both, neither	like
in contrast	unlike	in the same way	similarly

Exercise 10.3   **Distinguishing between Block and Alternating Format**

1. Briefly explain the difference between the block format and the alternating format for comparison and contrast writing.

   In the block format, you describe all the aspects of the first subject and then (in the

   same order) all the aspects of the second subject. In the alternating format, you

   switch back and forth, describing both subjects in terms of one aspect, both subjects

   in terms of the next aspect, and so on.

2. Working with a partner, consider again the paragraphs on the previous page illustrating the two formats. Then, after discussing the pieces, explain on a separate sheet of paper how, in your view, the effectiveness of these paragraphs might have been affected if the writers had chosen to use a different format.

Exercise 10.4   **Practicing Formatting Bases of Comparison**

1. For the subjects listed below, five types of differences are listed. Number the points of difference in column two so that they match up with the appropriate points of difference in column one.

Fish		*Whales*
1. vertical tail fins	_4_	20 feet to 100 feet long
2. gills take oxygen from water	_5_	thick layer of blubber below skin
3. young develop from eggs released into water	_1_	horizontal tail fins
4. up to 10 feet long	_2_	lung breathers, must surface often
5. body covering of protective scales	_3_	give birth to live young, feed them milk

2. Now on a separate piece of paper, describe how you would develop a paragraph contrasting whales and fish. Would you use alternating or block format? Explain your choice.

Exercise 10.5 **Revising and Evaluating Format**

1. Review the sample paragraph on expert physicists and novices (page 140). Working with a partner, identify the type of format the writer uses.

   The paragraph on expert physicists versus novices is written in an alternating

   format.

2. With your partner, try reformatting the paragraph to use the other format. Now read your version out loud. Which format is more effective? Use the lines below to explain.

   Answers will vary. Many students will think the current format is effective; others may

   feel a block format would be less confusing and would read more smoothly.

Exercise 10.6 **Considering Purpose in Comparison and Contrast Paragraphs**

This chapter features several sample comparison and contrast paragraphs. The names of the authors of these paragraphs, with the appropriate page numbers, are listed below. Working with a partner, take another look at the paragraphs and then on the lines next to the names list the primary purpose and any secondary purposes for each paragraph.

1. Stephen L. Slavin, page 139 _____

   Most students will agree that Slavin's purpose is to inform.

2. N. L. Gage and David C. Berliner, page 140 <u>Most students will agree Gage and</u>

<u>Berliner's primary purpose is to persuade and the secondary purpose is to inform.</u>

3. Aubrey Menen, page 142 <u>Most students will agree that Menen's primary pur-</u>

<u>pose is to persuade and the secondary purposes are to entertain and inform.</u>

4. Jay M. Pasachoff, pages 142–143 <u>Most students will agree that Pasachoff's pri-</u>

<u>mary purpose is to inform and his secondary purpose is to entertain.</u>

Challenge 10.2   **Writing a Paragraph of Comparison or Contrast**

Using the prewriting material you generated for Challenge 10.1 (page 141), complete a paragraph of at least 100 words that compares or contrasts two types of music or two political figures, actors, or professional athletes.

Discovering Connections 10.2

1. In Discovering Connections 10.1 on page 139, you chose a topic for a comparison or contrast paragraph and completed your prewriting. Now develop a paragraph of at least 100 words that examines the similarities or differences between the subjects you chose. As you organize your plan and write your paragraph, remember the points raised throughout this chapter.

2. Exchange your paragraph with a partner. If you completed the paragraph for Challenge 10.2 and you feel that paragraph is better, use it for this exercise instead. Evaluate the paragraph you receive using the comparison and contrast paragraph checklist below. Write your answers on a separate sheet of paper, and then return the paragraph and your assessment to the writer.

3. Using your reader's comments to guide you, revise your own paragraph.

Comparison and Contrast Paragraph Checklist

☐ Does the topic sentence specify the subjects and indicate the focus?

☐ Does the paragraph establish bases for comparison? Make sure that each characteristic or element is discussed in equal detail for each subject. Put an ∗ at any point where an element or characteristic is missing, and write *amplify* above any point that should be discussed in greater detail.

☐ Are the ideas arranged effectively? Would the paragraph be more effective if the ideas were arranged differently or a different format were used? Explain.

☐ In your judgment, what is the best part of this paragraph? Explain.

☐ Which detail or example would be even better if it were expanded? Why?

 **RECAP** ## COMPARISON AND CONTRAST

New terms in this chapter	Definitions
● **comparison and contrast**	● the writing technique that examines similarities and differences between subjects *Comparison* may be used to develop similarities between subjects; *contrast,* to develop differences.
● **bases for comparison**	● the aspects, characteristics, or elements to be examined for both subjects in a paragraph of comparison and contrast
● **block format**	● a method of arranging elements for comparison and contrast in which all ideas about one subject are presented first, followed by all ideas about the second subject
● **alternating format**	● a method of arranging elements for comparison and contrast in which each of the elements or characteristics is discussed for both subjects on a point-by-point basis

Writing a Comparison and Contrast Paragraph

Choose subjects with evident **similarities** or **differences**.

↓ ↑

Provide a topic sentence that specifies the **focus—comparison** or **contrast**.

↓ ↑

Determine the **bases for comparison**.

↓ ↑

Consider either the **block format** or the **alternating format** to arrange your ideas.

**The Block
Format**

Introduction

Subject A
Point 1
Point 2
Point 3

Subject B
Point 1
Point 2
Point 3

Conclusion

**The Alternating
Format**

Introduction

Point 1
Subject A
Subject B

Point 2
Subject A
Subject B

Point 3
Subject A
Subject B

Conclusion

Chapter 11

Cause and Effect

Getting Started... **Q:** I have to explain what made this event happen and what happened as a result of this event. But how do I write about it so that all the reasons or consequences make sense to someone else?

 A: Whenever you want to explain the reasons for some event, situation, or experience or what results from it, the mode that answers your needs is cause and effect. This mode enables you to express the often complex relationships between an event, situation, or experience and what led up to it or resulted from it.

Overview: Explaining Reasons and Consequences

 Nothing happens without a reason or without some kind of consequence. When you explain why things happen and what occurs when they do, the mode you use is **cause and effect**. *Cause* is the *reason* something occurred; *effect* is the *result* of what occurred. Effects always have causes and causes always lead to effects, so in writing, you rarely find one without the other. Often, however, the bulk of the writing focuses on either cause or effect.

A paragraph explaining why NASCAR racing has become so popular would call for a cause and effect approach. So would a writing dealing with the results of a severe drought and one explaining the recent increase in certain antibiotic-resistant bacterial infections.

 This chapter will explore the basic requirements for writing an effective cause and effect paragraph:

- providing a topic sentence that focuses on either cause or effect

- distinguishing between direct and related causes and effects

- avoiding oversimplification of causes and effects

Once you have mastered these basics, you'll be prepared to use cause and effect to write longer papers.

Discovering Connections 11.1

Discovering Connections 11.2 at the end of the chapter will allow students to apply what they learn in this chapter by composing and revising a cause and effect paragraph.

Select one of the following topics. Then, following one of the strategies that you practiced in Chapter 2, complete a prewriting on that topic.

1. cheating in the classroom
2. peer pressure
3. popularity of cell phones and pagers

Save your work for later use.

Providing a Topic Sentence That Focuses on Cause or Effect

 Audio 11.3

With cause and effect writing, an important function of the topic sentence is to make clear if the focus will be on cause or on effect. Consider the following paragraph by writer Alice Walker from her essay, "Looking for Zora":

> There are times—and finding Zora Hurston's grave was one of them—when normal responses of grief, horror, and so on do not make sense because they bear no real relation to the depth of the emotion one feels. It was impossible for me to cry when I saw the field full of weeds where Zora is. Partly this is because I have come to know Zora through her books and she was not a teary sort of person herself; but partly, too, it is because there is a point at which even grief feels absurd. And at this point, laughter gushes up to retrieve sanity.

The topic sentence specifies that the paragraph will focus on cause. It states that Walker's reaction to seeing the unmarked and untended grave of African-American writer Zora Neale Hurston did not match her profound sadness. The supporting sentences then specify why she reacted as she did.

Remember—transitional phrases will help you to clarify which of your supporting statements express causes and which express effects.

Transitional Expressions for Cause and Effect Writing

Cause		*Effect*	
because	since	as a result	if
cause	so that	consequently	therefore
reason	unless	effect	thus

Distinguishing between Direct and Related Causes and Effects

Some causes and effects are more directly connected than others. For example, the primary cause of an automobile accident might be bad weather.

Activity
11.1

For additional discussion of faulty cause and effect relationships, see the section on *logical fallacies* on pages 173–174 in Chapter 13.

However, excessive speed and lack of experience on the part of the driver may be contributing factors. You must distinguish between **direct causes** and **effects** and **related** ones so that you don't overstate a particular cause and effect relationship.

You must also make sure not to confuse cause and effect with **coincidence**, which refers to events, ideas, or experiences that occur at the same time but purely by accident. For example, just because the power went off in your next door neighbor's apartment while you were using your hair dryer, you cannot assume that one event caused the other.

Here is an example of a well-constructed cause and effect paragraph from a chemistry textbook by Cynthia Hahn:

> When a hot object is placed in contact with a cold object, energy is transferred from the hot object to the cold object by means of heat flow. The *temperature* of the hot object *decreases* because its *internal energy decreases*. The *temperature* of the cold object *increases* because its *internal energy increases*. The amount of energy lost by the hot object is equal to the amount of energy gained by the cold object. You know that heat flows spontaneously from hot object to cold, but not from cold to hot.

The opening sentence explains how energy is transferred from a hot object to a cold one. The direct cause of this heat transference, which the other sentences in the paragraph explain further, is a change in the internal energy of the objects. A decrease in internal energy of the hot object leads to an equal increase in the internal energy of the cold object.

Fast Fact Failure to pay attention to details can occasionally cause embarrassing effects, particularly when it concerns language. Recently, graduates of a prestigious New York City high school specializing in science and mathematics received diplomas noting the school's prominence in "science and *mathemetics*." After the error was discovered, corrected versions of the diplomas were made available. Presumably they were prepared by the New York City high school specializing in language arts.

Exercise 11.1   **Defining Cause and Effect**

1. Briefly explain cause and effect writing. _____

   In cause and effect writing, you explain why something happened (the cause) and

   what result it had (the effect).

   _____

2. What specific function does the topic sentence fulfill with cause and effect writing? With cause and effect writing, the topic sentence often identifies

   whether the focus of the writing will be on cause or effect.

   _____

3. What is the difference between a coincidence and a true cause and effect relationship? Briefly explain below; then provide an example of each.

A coincidence means that two things happen, often close together in time, but are

not related. A cause and effect relationship means that one thing happens as a re-

sult of another. If you drop the telephone and suddenly the sky darkens, that's a co-

incidence. If you drop the telephone and then you can't get a dial tone, that's a

cause and effect relationship.

Exercise 11.2 **Listing Causes and Effects**

1. For each cause listed below, write as many effects, or consequences, as you can. Write your consequences in sentence form on a separate sheet of paper. Study the example first. Answers will vary.

EXAMPLE Statement: The drinking age is lowered to eighteen.

Effect 1: The number of fatal car accidents involving teenagers doubles.
Effect 2: The rate of teen alcoholism increases.
Effect 3: Rates of truancy and unemployment among teens increase.

a. Statement: World population doubles in size.
b. Statement: You accept a job in another state.

2. For each statement listed below, provide as many causes as you can. State these reasons in sentence form on your paper. Study the example first. Answers will vary.

EXAMPLE Statement: By 1900, bison nearly became extinct.

Cause 1: In the late nineteenth century, hunters killed hundreds of thousands of bison for thrills or just for their tongues.

Cause 2: In the late nineteenth century, settlers took over much of the bison's grassland habitat.

Cause 3: In the late nineteenth century, smaller bison populations could not reproduce quickly enough to replace herd members killed by hunters.

a. Statement: The water supply in many communities is polluted and unsafe to drink.
b. Statement: Average life expectancy of U.S. citizens has increased.

Exercise 11.3　　**Planning for a Cause and Effect Paragraph**

Working with a partner, exchange your work from Exercise 11.2. Review one another's causes and effects. Place a ✓ beside the statement for which your partner has provided the strongest support. When you get your own work back, look at the list of supporting causes or effects that your partner has checked. Decide on an appropriate order of presentation for these causes and effects. Save your work for later use.

Challenge 11.1　　**Prewriting for a Cause and Effect Paragraph**

Prewrite on the rise to popularity of a type of clothing, music, or dance. Explore either the reasons for the fad or the effects it had.

Avoiding Oversimplification of Causes and Effects

Activity 11.2

When you write about causes and effects, be sure to avoid **oversimplification** of either one. Rarely does an event or situation have a single cause or a single effect.

Think of a serious problem such as juvenile delinquency. If you were to state that children whose parents are lenient will end up as juvenile delinquents, you would be *oversimplifying* a situation that is quite complex. Certainly a lack of discipline in childhood can contribute to bad behavior later in life. But to claim that one situation automatically leads to the other would not be accurate. Other outcomes are possible. (We all know people who were raised in undisciplined environments but who became solid citizens. We all also know individuals who had strict upbringings but still ended up in trouble.)

This paragraph, from Steven Pinker's *Words and Rules*, discusses why identifying the exact pronunciation of a word in English at a particular time in history is difficult:

> We can never say for sure what the pronunciation of a given word at a given time actually was. Just as there are regional accents today (London, Boston, Texas, and so on), there were regional varieties of English centuries ago; indeed, many more of them, because people did not move around as much as we do, did not send their children to melting-pot schools, and had no dictionaries to consult. Also, the written record is haphazard. Most words and pronunciations were in use long before the first literate person chanced to write them down, and many others went to the grave along with their speakers.

As you can see, tracing the exact pronunciation of an English word throughout the history of the language is not a simple matter. To illustrate the difficulty, Pinker provides several reasons for the complexity.

Exercise 11.4 — Understanding Complexity in Cause and Effect

Have students refer to the Rhetorical Index and choose an essay that includes the cause and effect mode. Does the essay focus on causes or effects or both? Ask students to list and identify direct and related causes and effects. Does the author avoid oversim- plifying cause and effect relationships? Explain. COLLABORATION

1. How can you avoid oversimplifying when developing a cause and effect writing?

   You avoid oversimplifying when developing a cause and effect writing by carefully

   examining the issue and considering all the possible reasons leading to it or results

   springing from it.

2. Working with a partner, take another look at Pinker's paragraph about the pronunciation of English words on page 151 and consider the accent that people in your region exhibit. For instance, do people tend to say "gonna" rather than "going to" or "Ah" rather than "I"? Then, on a separate sheet of paper, suggest one reason you think people in your area talk this way and one reaction or judgment you think outsiders might have upon hearing this accent.

Exercise 11.5 — Developing Adequate Causes

 COLLABORATION

1. On page 151, one possible cause of juvenile delinquency is discussed. Working with a partner, make a list on a separate sheet of paper of other possible causes of juvenile delinquency.

2. On the same sheet of paper, write a topic sentence and turn the causes of delinquency that you and your partner have identified into supporting sentences.

Exercise 11.6 — Writing a Topic Sentence and Supporting Sentences

COLLABORATION

Working with a partner, review the strongest list of causes or effects that you identified in Exercise 11.3 on page 151. Have you oversimplified any of your causes or effects? Add further support or revise any unclear reasons or consequences. Then write a topic sentence that specifies the focus of your paragraph. Turn your list of causes or effects into smoothly connected supporting sentences using transitions such as *because* or *as a result*.

Exercise 11.7   **Considering Purpose in Cause and Effect Paragraphs**

This chapter features several sample cause and effect paragraphs. The names of the authors of these paragraphs, with the appropriate page numbers, are listed below. Working with a partner, take another look at the paragraphs and then on the lines next to the names list the primary purpose and any secondary purposes for each paragraph.

1. Alice Walker, page 148 _Most students will agree that Walker's primary purpose_

is to entertain, and her secondary purpose is to inform.

2. Cynthia Hahn, page 149 _Most students will agree that Hahn's purpose is to inform._

3. Steven Pinker, page 151 _Most students will agree that Pinker's primary purpose_

is to inform, and his secondary purpose is to entertain.

Challenge 11.2   **Composing a Cause and Effect Paragraph**

For Challenge 11.1 on page 151, you completed a prewriting on how a type of clothing, music, or dance became popular or on what resulted from the fad. Now compose a cause and effect paragraph of about 100 words on this subject.

Discovering Connections 11.2

Activity
11.3

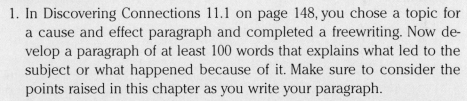

1. In Discovering Connections 11.1 on page 148, you chose a topic for a cause and effect paragraph and completed a freewriting. Now develop a paragraph of at least 100 words that explains what led to the subject or what happened because of it. Make sure to consider the points raised in this chapter as you write your paragraph.

2. Exchange your paragraph with a partner. If you completed a paragraph for Challenge 11.2 above and you feel that paragraph is better, use it for this exercise instead. Evaluate the paragraph you receive, using the cause and effect paragraph checklist below. Write your answers on a separate sheet of paper, and then return the paragraph and your assessment to the writer.

3. Using your reader's comments to guide you, revise your own paragraph.

Cause and Effect Paragraph Checklist

☐ Does the topic sentence focus on either cause or effect?

☐ Does the paragraph distinguish between direct and related causes and effects? Underline any details that seem like coincidences rather than true causes or effects.

☐ Does the writer provide a sufficient number of causes or effects to support the main idea? If you feel more specific details are required, write "I'd like to know more about _____" in the margin next to the appropriate sentence or passage.

☐ In your judgment, what is the best part of the paragraph? Explain.

☐ Which detail or example would be even better if it were expanded? Why?

 CAUSE AND EFFECT

Activity 11.4

New terms in this chapter	Definitions
● **cause and effect**	● the writing technique that explains why things happen (**cause**) and what occurs when they do (**effect**)
● **direct causes**	● primary or main reasons
● **direct effects**	● primary or principal results
● **related causes or effects**	● contributing reasons or results
● **coincidence**	● events, ideas, or experiences that occur by accident at the same time
● **oversimplification**	● error in reasoning that causes one to overlook the complexity in a cause and effect relationship ***Example*** "She doesn't want a career because her mother was never home when she was a child."

Writing a Cause and Effect Paragraph

Identify a **subject** that focuses on the **reasons for** or the **results of** an event or phenomenon.

↓ ↑

Establish the **focus—cause** or **effect**—in a clear topic sentence.

↓ ↑

Be sure the reader will understand the differences between **direct** and **related** causes and effects in your paragraph.

↓ ↑

Provide details to convey the **complexity** of the cause and effect relationship you are describing.

Chapter 12

Division and Classification

Getting Started... **Q:** The topic I've chosen is really complicated, so I doubt most people will understand it unless I simplify it. I know I have to find a way to present it in more manageable parts. How do I do that?

Audio
12.1

A: Whenever you have to simplify a complicated topic, the secret is to analyze it. With some subjects, you'll need to break them into their basic components: division. With other subjects, you'll need to arrange the component parts, elements, or sections into smaller groups, making it easier for somebody unfamiliar with the subject to see your point: classification. Regardless of the approach, division and classification will help your reader gain a better understanding of the complicated issues you write about.

Overview: Analyzing the Whole in Terms of the Parts

Audio
12.2

Writing often involves simplifying complex subjects in order to communicate them clearly to a reader. Two important techniques for this purpose are **division** and **classification**. Although division and classification are separate processes, they are usually discussed together and often appear together in writing. Both processes involve **analysis**, looking at something large or complex by breaking it down into parts. *Division* refers to the separation of a subject into component parts. *Classification* refers to the arrangement of component parts into groups on the basis of some principle or characteristic.

Division and classification would dominate in a paragraph about weekend activities available in our city, including cultural events, wellness presentations, and dance clubs. A paragraph discussing an effective sales presentation would also employ division and classification, focusing on the *pitch, product demonstration, summary of benefits,* and *close.*

Weblink
12.1

Weblink
12.2

This chapter will explore the basic requirements for writing an effective division or classification paragraph:

- providing a topic sentence that defines the scope of the discussion and indicates an emphasis on either division or classification

- establishing a logical method of analysis

- maintaining a consistent presentation

- using distinct and complete groupings

Once you have mastered these basics, you'll be prepared to use division and classification to write longer papers.

Discovering Connections 12.1

Discovering Connections 12.2 at the end of the chapter will allow students to apply what they learn in this chapter by composing and revising a division or classification paragraph.

Choose one of the following topics. Then, employing one of the strategies that you practiced in Chapter 2, complete a prewriting on this subject. Think of categories, or types, within the topic as you write.

1. college students
2. popular music
3. television commercials

Save your work for later use.

Specifying Scope and Emphasis through a Topic Sentence

In a division or classification paragraph, the topic sentence specifies the scope of the subject that the writer will examine. It also often indicates whether the emphasis in the paragraph will be on division or classification.

A typical topic sentence for a classification paragraph will name the large group to be divided and then specify the *basis of classification*. This is the principle or characteristic used for making subdivisions or *classes*. The topic sentence may also name the classes, as in the following example:

EXAMPLE

                large group   *basis for classes*

We can classify *any rock* into one of three groups *according to the way in which it was formed: igneous, sedimentary, or metamorphic.*
                               classes

Consider this paragraph from "Risk," an article by Paul Roberts about so-called "extreme" activities:

Ask students to identify the transitions that are used in this paragraph and in other sample paragraphs in this chapter. How do these transitions help readers understand the division and classification analysis?

> Risky business has never been more popular. Mountain climbing is among America's fastest growing sports. Extreme skiing—in which skiers descend cliff-like runs by dropping from ledge to snow-covered ledge—is drawing wider interest. Sports like paragliding and cliff-parachuting are marching into the recreational mainstream while the adventure-travel business, which often mixes activities like climbing or river rafting with wildlife safaris, has grown into a multimillion-dollar industry. "Forget the beach," declared *Newsweek* last year. "We're hot for mountain biking, river running, climbing, and bungee jumping."

As you can see, the topic sentence identifies the group to be discussed in the paragraph—risky activities. It also indicates how their popularity has grown beyond any previous level. The supporting sentences then divide that topic into the various risky sports: extreme skiing, paragliding, cliff-parachuting, river rafting, mountain biking, mountain climbing, and bungee jumping.

Establishing a Logical Method of Analysis

Whether your focus is division or classification, you need to establish a logical method of analyzing the group or subject you choose. Any subject can be presented in a variety of ways. You need to choose divisions or categories that will enable your reader to understand your subject.

Imagine that you are writing about e-commerce: doing business on the Internet. You could approach this broad topic from a number of directions. One promising way is to use division and classification to detail different types of e-commerce the average consumer might use. As one category, you could talk about completing applications online, such as license renewal, financial aid forms, and tax returns. Then you could discuss using the Internet to complete banking transactions, and finally, to purchase various goods, from books to vacations. You could also use division and classification to discuss types of companies that have attempted to sell their products over the Web. Such a paragraph could focus on grocery sales services, gasoline sales programs, personal counseling centers, and pet food delivery services.

Look at this paragraph from *Gifts Differing*, by Isabel Briggs Myers and Peter B. Myers. They divide the way people perceive the world around them into two categories:

> Of the two very different kinds of perception, sensing is the direct perception of realities through sight, hearing, touch, taste, and smell. Sensing is needed for pursuing or even casually observing hard facts; it is equally essential to enjoying the moment of a sunrise, the crash of surf on a beach, the exhilaration of speed, and the smooth workings of one's body. Intuition is the indirect perception of things beyond the reach of the senses, such as meanings, relationships, and possibilities. It translates words into meaning and meaning into words whenever people read, write, talk, or listen; people use intuition when they invite the unknown into their conscious minds or wait expectantly for a possibility, a solution, or an inspiration. Intuition works best for seeing how situations might be handled. A thought that starts "I wonder if" is probably intuition, and the thought "Aha!" indicates that intuition has brought to mind something enlightening and delightful.

In this paragraph, Myers and Myers use division to explain the two ways people interpret the world. The method of analysis is clear and logical. The writers separate perception into *sensing* and *intuition*, which they then explain in detail.

Certain words and phrases will help you to stress the divisions or classifications you establish in your paragraph. The list below gives you some possibilities.

Transitional Expressions That Show Division or Classification

can be categorized (classified)	the first type (kind), second type, etc.
can be divided	the last category

Exercise 12.1   **Understanding Division and Classification**

1. In your own words, explain how division and classification differ.

   Division and classification are processes of analysis. When you write a paragraph

   using division, you break up a broad subject into separate parts. When you write a

   paragraph using classification, you arrange component parts into groups on the

   basis of a principle or characteristic.

2. Briefly explain the meaning of *logical method of analysis.* _____

   A logical method of analysis means choosing reasonable divisions or groupings. You

   need to break up your broad subject into groups that make sense to your reader.

Exercise 12.2   **Identifying the Basis of Classification**

Each group of things, places, or people below has been classified according to a principle or characteristic. This principle or characteristic is the basis of classification. On the blank line, write a phrase that explains the basis of classification. Next, see if all the items fit this basis properly. Some groups have an item that does not belong. Cross it out. Use the example to guide you.

EXAMPLE   *plants*   a. full sunlight   b. partial sunlight   c. ~~blooming~~   d. shade

basis of classification: ___ *amount of light required to thrive* ___

1. *cereals*   a. oat-based   b. corn-based   c. wheat-based   d. ~~cooked~~

   basis of classification: _____ type of grain used to create cereal _____

2. *movies*   a. action   b. comedy   c. ~~R-rated~~   d. sci fi

   basis of classification: _____ genre or general type of movie _____

3. *sports icons*   a. "bad boys"   b. ~~basketball stars~~   c. record-holders
   d. grand old legends

   basis of classification: _____ reason for claim to fame _____

4. *travel accommodations*   a. bed and breakfast   b. resort lodge
   c. motel   d. hotel

   basis of classification: _____ services and structure of facility _____

5. *outdoor activities*   a. running   b. hiking   c. ~~reading~~   d. walking

   basis of classification: _____ means by which people move about by foot _____

Exercise 12.3   **Developing Classes for a Classification Paragraph**

Working with a partner, choose one of the classified groups in Exercise 12.2. Change or add to the list of classes if you wish. Add explanations, descriptive details, or examples, making sure they are parallel for each class.

Challenge 12.1   **Prewriting for a Division or Classification Paragraph**

Complete a prewriting on the tasks involved in performing your job or in completing assignments for one of your courses. Think in terms of the divisions or classes into which your topic may be organized. Save your work for later use.

Maintaining a Consistent Presentation

Activity 12.2

As you decide on the focus of your division or classification paragraph, you also need to maintain **consistency** in the component parts or classes you establish. A **consistent presentation** involves divisions or classes established on a set basis, with no unrelated categories.

Imagine you were writing a paragraph about your expenses. You would be likely to discuss such items as *rent, food, clothing, savings,* and *entertainment.* You wouldn't discuss an upcoming raise or an expected tax return because these are *sources of income,* not *expenses.*

Take a look at this well-constructed classification paragraph about reinforcement from a psychology textbook by Zick Rubin, Letitia Anne Peplau, and Peter Salovey:

> **Reinforcement** is the process of using rewards—or reinforcers—to strengthen particular responses. A *reinforcer* is any event that strengthens the response it follows—that is, that increases the likelihood of that response occurring again. One of the most important challenges for anyone trying to teach something to an animal or person is to figure out just what things are reinforcing to that individual. Some things, such as food, water, and affection, seem to be naturally reinforcing; these are called **primary reinforcers**. Other things or events become reinforcing as a result of their association with primary reinforcers; these are called

> **secondary reinforcers**. Secondary reinforcers play a big part in shaping our behavior. Think of all the behaviors we engage in to earn awards, pats on the back, and grades. We have learned that the awards, pats, and grades are rewarding because they tend to go along with other more basic rewards, such as affection and esteem.

As you can see, this paragraph divides reinforcers into two similar categories: primary reinforcers and secondary reinforcers. It defines and explains each type through closely related examples: Food and water are primary reinforcers; awards and pats on the back are secondary reinforcers. Therefore, both the types it establishes and the details about those types are consistent.

> *Fast Fact* Right now there are some thirty million registered Web addresses ending in *.com*, *.org*, or *.net*. To alleviate the continuing demand for Web addresses in these classifications, the following seven new top-level domains are on the way: *.biz*, *.info*, *.museum*, *.aero*, *.coop*, *.name*, and *.pro*.

Using Distinct and Complete Groupings

Activity 12.3

As you develop a division and classification paper, you also need to use **distinct and complete groupings**. When a grouping is *distinct*, it is clearly distinguished from others. When it is *complete*, it is expressed in full detail.

Imagine that you are writing a paragraph on community theater that focuses on the people who attend the plays. If you were to divide these people into only two groups—family members of the cast and other people from the community—the second category would be too general. Your groupings would be incomplete. In fact, *other members of the community* is actually composed of several groups: senior citizens, invited city officials, high school students, families with young children, and so forth. None of these groupings overlap; each one has a distinctive set of members. In order to make your analysis complete, you would want to be sure that these categories did not overlook anyone who attends the plays.

Consider the way this paragraph from "Cellular Divide," an article about stem cell research by Sharon Begley, discusses types of cells:

> The cells that make up days-old embryos embody a world of potential. Four days after fertilization, the embryo is a hollow ball of cells called a blastocyst. Cells in the outer layer are destined to become the placenta. Those in the inner layer have not yet decided what they will be when they grow up: they are "pluripotent," able to differentiate into any of the 220 cell types that make up a human body, from the kidney, heart and liver to the skin, neuronal and pancreatic. These are the famous embryonic stem cells. For a few short days they are blank slates waiting for destiny (or the complex interplay of genes and biochemistry) to write their future.

In this paragraph, Begley ensures that her groupings are distinct and complete. To do so, she divides the types of cells constituting a human embryo in the first days after conception into two groups. The first group includes those on the outer layer, which become the placenta. The other group is made up of the *stem cells:* the undifferentiated cells that will become one of the 220 human cell types.

Exercise 12.4	**Understanding Consistency, Distinctness, and Completeness in Groupings**

Have students refer to the Rhetorical Index to choose an essay that includes the division and classification mode and discuss these questions: What is the logical method of analysis? Are the groupings consistent, distinct, and complete?

1. What is a consistent presentation? _____

    A consistent presentation means that you stick to your logical groupings and that you

    don't introduce any points that aren't directly related to the group under discussion.

    _____

2. In your own words, briefly explain how to keep groupings in a division

    or classification paragraph distinct and complete. _____

    When groupings are distinct, each one is clearly different from all the others. When

    they are complete, they include all the details that are necessary.

    _____

    _____

Exercise 12.5	**Explaining Consistency, Distinctness, and Completeness in Groupings**

1. Take another look at the paragraph about types of cells on page 160. Are

    the divisions consistent? Why or why not? _____

    The divisions are consistent because they relate directly to the basis of classifica-

    tion: the types of cells present in a recently conceived embryo. Details about each

    division cover both these points.

    _____

2. Reread the paragraph about reinforcement on pages 159–160. Explain

    why the classes it presents are distinct and complete. _____

    The classes (primary and secondary reinforcers) are distinct because none of the members of any one class can belong to another class at the same time. They are

complete because details about the characteristics of each class are given.

Exercise 12.6 **Creating Consistent, Distinct, and Complete Groupings**

1. Working with a partner, choose one of the following subjects, and divide it into groups or types you might know or have observed: people at an airport, types of jobs within the criminal justice system, ways the Internet can be used to communicate with others and obtain information.

   Answers will vary.

2. Exchange your paper with another team. Evaluate whether the classes are consistent, distinct, and complete. Return the paper, with your suggestions, to its writers.

Exercise 12.7 **Considering Purpose in Division and Classification Paragraphs**

This chapter features several sample division and classification paragraphs. The names of the authors of these paragraphs, with the appropriate page numbers, are listed below. Working with a partner, take another look at the paragraphs and then on the lines next to the names list the primary purpose and any secondary purposes for each paragraph.

1. Paul Roberts, page 156 _Most students will agree that Roberts's purpose is to_ entertain, and his secondary purpose is to inform.

2. Isabel Briggs Myers and Peter B. Myers, page 157 _Most students will agree_ Myers and Myers's primary purpose is to inform, and their secondary purpose is to entertain.

3. Zick Rubin, Letitia Anne Peplau, and Peter Salovey, pages 159–160 _____

   Most students will agree that Rubin, Peplau, and Salovey's primary purpose is to in-

   form, and their secondary purpose is to persuade.

4. Sharon Begley, page 160   Most students will agree that Begley's primary purpose

   is to inform, and her secondary purpose is to entertain.

Challenge 12.2   **Writing a Division and Classification Paragraph**

Using the prewriting material you developed for Challenge 12.1 on page 159, draft a paragraph of at least 100 words on the tasks involved in your job or in completing assignments for one of your courses.

Discovering Connections 12.2

1. In Discovering Connections 12.1 on page 156, you chose a topic for a division or classification paragraph and completed your prewriting. Now develop a paragraph of at least 100 words that analyzes the subject by dividing or classifying it. As you develop your paragraph, consider the points raised in this chapter.
2. Exchange your paragraph with a classmate. If you completed the paragraph for Challenge 12.2 above and you feel that that paragraph is better, use it for this exercise instead. Evaluate the paragraph you receive, using the division and classification paragraph checklist below. Write your answers on a separate sheet of paper, and then return the paragraph and your assessment to the writer.
3. Using your reader's comments to guide you, revise your paragraph.

Division and Classification Paragraph Checklist

☐ Does the topic sentence define the scope of the discussion and indicate an emphasis on either division or classification?

☐ Is a logical, consistent method of analysis maintained throughout?

☐ Should any details or examples be further subdivided? If so, underline them.

☐ Are the elements used distinct and complete? If you think any of the material needs to be made clearer or more specific, write, "I'd like to know more about _____" in the margin next to it.

☐ In your judgment, what is the best part of this paragraph? Explain.

☐ Which detail or example would be even better if it were expanded? Why?

 DIVISION AND CLASSIFICATION

Activity
12.4

New terms in this chapter	Definitions
● division and classification	● writing techniques used to break down a subject (**division**) or group ideas (**classification**) for analysis so that the subject is easier to grasp
● consistent presentation	● using the same principle of division or classification for all the parts of a topic under discussion and providing parallel elements of description or analysis for each
● distinct and complete groupings	● categories for classification or division that are clearly distinguished from others and expressed in full detail

Writing a Division or Classification Paragraph

Indicate your subject and your focus—**division** or **classification**—in a clear **topic sentence**.

↓ ↑

Choose a **logical method of analysis**.

↓ ↑

Keep your **presentation consistent**.

↓ ↑

Make all **categories distinct** and **complete**.

Argument

Getting Started... **Q:** I really feel strongly about this subject. But I'm a little worried about whether I can convince somebody else about my point of view. How can I present my ideas so that they will be persuasive?

Audio 13.1 **A:** To convince your reader that you have something worthwhile to say, find the strongest support for your point of view. Also, carefully consider what someone holding an opposing view might say. Finally, always think of what persuades you to consider somebody else's point of view. Approach your subject in a similar way, and you'll be all set.

Overview: Understanding Persuasion

Audio 13.2 As Chapter 5 notes, **argument** differs from the modes presented in the last eight chapters. Argument is not a mode but an aim or **purpose**. With argument, you use a variety of modes to *persuade* your reader to accept a point of view.

A paragraph asserting that television advertisements for beer and other alcoholic beverages should be banned would be argument. So would one maintaining that ownership of pit bulls, hybrid wolf dogs, and other aggressive breeds should be restricted.

Weblink 13.1
> *This chapter will explore the basic requirements for writing an effective argument:*
>
> ● expressing a clear stance on the issue in a topic sentence
>
> ● providing sufficient support
>
> ● using a tone that is reasonable and convincing
>
> ● avoiding errors in logic
>
> ● arranging your support in emphatic order

Once you have mastered these basics, you'll be ready to write multi-paragraph arguments.

Weblink
13.2

Choose one of the following topics. Then, following one of the strategies that you practiced in Chapter 2, prewrite on the subject. Consider your position on the topic and your reasons for your conclusion.

Video
13.1

1. State governments should institute testing for all prospective teachers.
2. Bikers, in-line skaters, and skateboarders should be required by law to wear helmets.
3. People convicted of drunk driving should be forced to have special license plates indicating their offense.

Save your work for later use.

Discovering Connections 13.2 at the end of the chapter will allow students to apply what they learn in this chapter by composing and revising an argument paragraph.

Providing a Topic Sentence That Expresses a Clear Stance on the Issue

Audio
13.3

Activity
13.1

The topic sentence of an argument paragraph should clearly state the **stance** you are taking on the issue. In other words, it should indicate whether you are *in favor of* or *against* the point being raised. For example, imagine you were writing a paragraph about a National Health Care program to provide health insurance for all U.S. citizens. If you were writing to support this initiative, you might write a topic sentence like this:

EXAMPLE

The federal government owes it to its citizens to establish a National Health Care Program.

But if you were writing to oppose a National Health Care program, you might write a topic sentence like this one:

EXAMPLE

A National Health Care program, covering all citizens, is a luxury that the United States simply can't afford.

In both cases, your reader would be aware of the issue and your opinion of it.

Consider the stance set forth by the topic sentence in this paragraph about a controversial aspect of adoption:

Weblink
13.3

To introduce concepts discussed later in the chapter, ask students to identify the reasons that are provided to support the author's stance about adoption. Which reason is most important? Where is this reason placed in the paragraph?

Adopted children should be able to read through their sealed adoption files and make contact with their biological parents if they choose. Many adoptees feel that something is missing in their lives. They feel an emotional gap that can only be filled by learning more about their biological parents. Also, adoptees should have the same rights as everyone else to learn about their heritage, race, and ethnicity. Most people consider this kind of knowledge important. If their adoption records remain sealed, how can adoptees gain a full understanding of their own background? However, the most important reason for unsealing adoption records is medical. Researchers have proven that many diseases and medical conditions, such as diabetes and heart disease, tend to run in families. Therefore, without a full medical history of their biological relatives, some adoptees may actually be at medical risk.

In this paragraph, the topic sentence provides a clear direction for the reader. Both the issue and the writer's stance are explicitly stated: Adoptees should have full access to their adoption records. As a result, the reader is prepared for the supporting sentences that follow.

Developing Sufficient Support through Sound Reasons

Audio
13.4

Activity
13.2

Discuss the importance of limiting a topic sentence and focusing on a topic and stance that can be supported sufficiently in an effective paragraph. Ask students how they could sufficiently explain and illustrate a position on abortion, gun control, welfare reform, or another complex subject in a paragraph. Review Chapter 3 for practice focusing on one aspect of a broad subject and developing a specific topic sentence.

No absolute guideline exists about the amount of information needed to develop a sound argument. Think of a subject about which you are undecided: How much support would you need to see before *you* would accept that position? You would probably require several solid supporting details and examples before you would be convinced. Your reader demands the same of you when you write. As a general rule, include at least three reasons, or *points*, to support your stance.

As you develop your reasons with details and examples, keep in mind the relationship between *fact* and *opinion*. A **fact** is a verifiable truth. That driving on icy roads is dangerous is a fact. There is no room for discussion. An **opinion**, however, is a belief. It may be founded on impressions, experiences, or a person's base of knowledge. Saying that city officials who fail to treat icy roads don't care about the danger is an opinion. The validity of an opinion depends on how well it is supported by facts. Therefore, incorporate facts as often as possible to support your examples.

To help develop your argument, first list points that support your position. Next, list points that someone holding the opposite point of view might raise. The value of the first list is obvious. These are the points that will form the framework for your argument. The second list is also important, however. By addressing some of these points, you may be able to refute them completely or turn them to your advantage.

Imagine that you are against a proposal to establish English as the official national language of the United States, and you plan to write about that. Here are two lists of ideas you've generated about the subject, one against the proposal and one supporting it.

Video
13.2

Against the proposal

- The United States was founded so all could enjoy freedom, regardless of background.
- When we force people to reject their heritage, we all lose.
- The proposal discriminates against immigrants—it's prejudice.

In favor of the proposal

- It saves money on things like bilingual education and government forms that now have to be printed in several languages.
- If people want to live here, they should learn to speak English.

- Learning a new language is too difficult a burden for many old people.
- English language classes aren't readily available, especially for working people.
- If we become English-speaking only, some people won't be able to work—added to welfare lists.

- The majority rules.
- Some jobs are advertised only for people who can speak another language besides English. Native speakers shouldn't lose out on jobs because they can't speak another language.

The points you've developed to oppose the proposal are valid, so you could feel comfortable including any of them in your writing.

In addition, you could also adapt and use a couple of the points from the list in favor of the proposal. Your thought process might go something like this: Yes it's true that printing government forms in multiple languages and providing bilingual education cost taxpayers money. But as the most prosperous nation on earth, we should put people's needs ahead of dollar signs. And, yes, people who become permanent residents of the U.S. should learn English, but not because a law mandates it. Clearly, knowing the primary language of the U.S. opens up economic doors, making life easier overall. Rather than punishing people for not knowing English, our government should more aggressively educate newcomers concerning how speaking English will benefit them.

Now here's an argument paragraph that might result from the material on the lists:

A law making English the official national language of the United States would be a terrible mistake. For one thing, such a law would discriminate against immigrants. The United States was established on the principle of freedom for all, regardless of background, and it was settled and made great by immigrants. It's unfair to make the newest groups coming to the United States face a greater burden than earlier groups of immigrants faced. Certainly, people should learn English because knowing the main language of the country provides many economic and social benefits. But mastering English isn't that easy, especially if the people are older. Also, except in major cities, language classes aren't always readily available, particularly at convenient hours for people who work. In addition, if we become an English-only nation, some immigrants who don't speak English will be unable to get jobs. Rather than working to support themselves, they will be forced to turn to welfare. But most of all, when we force people to abandon their own language, we are also suggesting that they abandon their culture. Our society has evolved as it has because of *the positive contributions of so many groups. When we discourage a group from contributing, we all lose.*

As you can see, points from the list opposing the proposal to make English the official national language of the United States dominate here. In addition, some points from the list in favor of the proposal have been refuted and added to the other points. The result is an effective argument paragraph.

Video 13.3

As Chapter 4 (pages 83–85) indicates, if you use information from another document or individual to support your argument, you must include the source of that information. In most of the argument paragraphs you will write, you can acknowledge your sources in a simple, in-text explanation: "According to a recent report in *U.S. News and World Report,* the number of college students selecting computer science as their major has increased for the seventh straight year."

Video 13.4

In many cases, especially with longer, more formal assignments, you will need to provide more specific documentation for your sources. You'll need to include such details as the author's name, the title of the work, the publisher, the date of publication, the pages involved, and so on. Always ask which style of formal documentation your instructor prefers. The reference section of your college library will have guidelines for several methods of documentation.

Video 13.5

Remind students that if they use the exact words from another source, they must enclose the material in quotation marks and lit the source.

You will probably find that your instructors will want you to use one of two common systems. One is the Modern Language Association (MLA) method, generally called for with assignments in English or other humanities disciplines. The other is the American Psychological Association (APA) method, generally appropriate for assignments in education, the social sciences, and the natural and physical sciences. Chapter 4 (pages 83–85) provides brief examples of both systems.

Exercise 13.1   **Understanding Argument**

Video 13.6

1. What makes argument different from the writing techniques (*narration, description, definition,* etc.) that you have studied in the last several chapters?

   Argument is not a writing technique like narration or description. It is a *purpose,* an

   intent: to persuade the reader to accept the writer's point of view.

2. What gauge could you use to decide if you have provided enough support for your argument? _____

You could ask how much support you yourself would require to accept another position.

Video
13.7

3. Why should you think through the points of the opposing argument as you develop your plan for an argument paragraph? _____

If you can anticipate and answer points against your case, you stand a better chance

of swaying readers to see things as you do. Also, you may be able to use these

points to your advantage by including them and then refuting them in your paper.

Exercise 13.2   **Explaining the Stance and Reasons in an Argument Paragraph**

1. Find the topic sentence in the argument paragraph about English as the official national language of the United States on pages 168–169. Explain its role in the paragraph. _____

   The topic sentence of the paragraph clearly states the writer's position on English as

   the official national language of the United States. The writer is against such a

   movement.

2. How many reasons are given to prove the writer's case? Summarize them on the lines given. _____

   Four reasons are given: (1) The law would discriminate against immigrants. (2)

   Learning English can be difficult, especially for older people. (3) It might prevent

   people from getting and keeping jobs. (4) We would lose out on what different cul-

   tures have to offer.

Exercise 13.3   **Analyzing Fact and Opinion and Developing Persuasive Reasons**

1. On a separate sheet of paper, list three facts. Then underneath each fact, write an opinion about that fact.

2. Look again at the paragraph about adoption on pages 166–167. Working
with a partner, develop on a separate sheet of paper a list of reasons to
support the opposite point of view. Then list as many facts as you can to
support those reasons.

Challenge 13.1   **Prewriting for an Argument Paragraph**

Prewrite on a controversial subject. For example, take a stand on the issue
of banning certain books in U.S. public schools or on adding a surcharge at
gas stations for people who own gas-guzzling sports-utility vehicles.

Fast Fact It's not just those political types on Sunday morning political discussion shows who
enjoy arguing. The World Debating Championships, for instance, involve some 270 teams
from forty nations, making it the world's second largest student event.

Using a Reasonable, Convincing Tone

Audio
13.5

Another factor that will affect your reader's acceptance of your point of
view is your **tone**, the attitude you express about your subject. If your tone
is sarcastic, superior, or patronizing, you may alienate a reader who might
otherwise be swayed to agree with your point of view. On the other hand, if
your tone is sincere and respectful, you'll enhance the chance that your
point of view will be favorably received.

One way to make your writing reasonable and convincing is by avoiding **absolute** terms. For instance, it is better to say that people without sur-
vival suits *rarely* survive more than a few minutes in the frigid winter waters
of the North Atlantic rather than to say they *never* do. Here is a list of more
moderate terms that you can substitute for absolute language:

Absolute Word	*Moderate Substitute*
all	most
always	frequently
every	many
never	rarely

Avoid personally attacking or insulting opponents of your argument
(see Argument *ad hominem,* page 173). With an emotionally charged subject like gun control, for example, it's easy to understand how sentences
such as these might appear in an early draft:

Activity
13.3

Most people who buy handguns do so for personal protection.
However, a person would have to be stupid not to know that handguns
are statistically more likely to be stolen or to cause accidental injury
than to be used effectively for protection.

The message in these sentences is valid, but the name-calling is insulting to both the opponents of the writer's position and readers who are merely poorly informed about this issue.

Now, consider this version of the sentences:

> Most people who buy handguns do so for personal protection. *However, many people are unaware* that handguns are statistically more likely to be stolen or to cause accidental injury than to be used effectively for protection.

The message is the same in the second version, but the simple change in phrasing eliminates inflammatory name-calling. Instead, the writer is providing information in an objective tone that is much more likely to make poorly informed readers want to learn more about the issue.

Using Sound Logic

Weblink
13.4

To persuade a reader, an argument must feature logical reasoning leading to a valid conclusion. You can establish such a *line of reasoning* by engaging in one of two reasoning processes: induction or deduction. Although the goal of these two reasoning processes is the same, they come at the subject from opposite directions.

With **induction**, you move from a series of specific instances or pieces of evidence to a general conclusion. Physicians employ inductive reasoning in diagnosing an illness. For example, a dermatologist might conclude that a patient's skin rash is a form of eczema because every other rash like this one that she has examined has proven to be eczema.

An answer reached in this way involves an *inductive leap.* Although this diagnosis is a reasonable conclusion based on the evidence, it isn't the only possible valid explanation. The rash may closely resemble eczema, but it may actually be the result of another condition. The more specific instances backing it up, the more likely the conclusion is sound.

As an ongoing journal assignment, have students collect and explain examples of logical fallacies they hear or read.

Deduction, in contrast, involves reasoning from a general statement to a specific conclusion. Say, for example, you know that flat, low-lying inland areas are especially vulnerable to tornadoes. You also know that your cousin lives in a flat, low-lying inland area. You could therefore conclude that your cousin's neighborhood is a likely target for a tornado.

Video
13.8

Use of sound logic will strengthen your argument. Faulty logic or **logical fallacies**, like those described in the table on pages 173–174, will weaken it.

Avoid Logical Fallacies

Fallacy	Examples of Fallacious Logic	Instead Use Sound Logic
Argument *ad hominem* (Latin for "argument to the man")		
Attacking the person	That editorial writer criticizes the entertainment business for its portrayal of the American family, yet she is divorced herself.	Respond to the opposing positions.
Bandwagon approach		
Urging acceptance because "everybody does it"	Everyone wants the City Council to institute new zoning requirements.	Cite objective, qualified authorities of statistics.
Begging the question		
Assuming as fact what must be proven	NASA's call for increased funding in these hard times is more proof that these scientists care about nothing but their pet programs.	Provide relevant, documented evidence.
Circular reasoning		
Restating your opinion and calling it a reason	That car is the best choice because, compared to the competition, it is superior.	Give real reasons.
Creating a red herring		
Diverting attention to an unimportant point	Senator Hogg says that genetic engineering is too much like playing God, but she isn't even responsible enough to file her campaign finance reports on time.	Provide compelling evidence.
Either/or reasoning		
Suggesting only two alternatives when many possibilities exist	If we don't institute statewide testing in high schools, we will face another generation of poorly educated students.	Explore all relevant possibilities.
Hasty generalization		
Making an assumption based on insufficient evidence	I've used that medicine for two days and my cough is still not gone, so it's obvious that the pills aren't working.	Base conclusions on many objective facts.
Non sequitur (Latin for "it does not follow")		
Coming to an incorrect conclusion in relation to the evidence	Homeless people don't have permanent places to live, so it's obvious that they have no pride.	Think through relationships using logic.

(continued)

Avoid Logical Fallacies (*continued*)

Fallacy	Examples of Fallacious Logic	Instead Use Sound Logic
Oversimplification		
Wrongfully reducing a complex subject	Using solar energy will eliminate all our energy problems.	State all important aspects; admit inconsistencies.
Post hoc, ergo propter hoc (Latin for "after this, therefore because of this")		
Assuming a cause-effect relationship between two things that occurred by coincidence	The killer had just eaten at a fast-food restaurant, so something in the food must have triggered his aggression.	Check your thinking for irrational statements.

Find the logical fallacy in this paragraph on banning some material on the Internet:

> Censoring the discussion of certain topics on the Internet is wrong for several reasons. First, censorship of any sort is a violation of the First Amendment to the U.S. Constitution, which guarantees U.S. citizens freedom of speech. Banning particular words and subjects from websites violates this right. Second, many proponents of a ban are seeking censorship because the ideas being communicated are offensive to their religious beliefs. However, the United States was established on the principle of the separation of church and state. No religion must be allowed to dictate what is correct or moral for the majority. If we allow these extremists to decide what is acceptable and what isn't, before long we won't have any rights left. Third, and most important, restricting the flow of knowledge of any sort is counterproductive to society at large. Censoring an important means of worldwide communication creates the possibility that ignorance and hatred might prevail over peace and understanding.

You probably identified the seventh sentence, indicating that failing to stop this act of censorship will lead to an elimination of all our rights. This is a case of *either/or reasoning*. True, if a ban is established, we do face a limitation on *one* right, but it will not lead to a complete elimination of the First Amendment, nor will it affect the other freedoms we enjoy in the United States. Leave this sentence out and you improve the paragraph by eliminating this flaw in logic.

Arranging Your Support in Emphatic Order

Most often writers arrange ideas in an argument paragraph in emphatic order. Using *emphatic order* means arranging your details and examples in such a way that each point builds in greater importance. Presented this way, the reasons compel your reader to continue on. (Emphatic order is discussed at length on pages 72–73.) Your initial point should be lively enough to spark and hold your reader's interest and to begin cultivating acceptance of your point of view. Each point should grow increasingly stronger so that your argument builds to a forceful, convincing conclusion.

Consider the order of the reasons in the following paragraph about keeping animals in captivity and forcing them to perform for humans:

> We humans don't have the right to capture animals and force them to perform for our pleasure in circuses, zoos, or aquatic parks. First of all, even under the best of circumstances, the environments in which these animals are kept differ vastly from what they would enjoy in the wild. For example, in their natural environments, animals like killer whales, polar bears, and dolphins cover territories that measure hundreds of miles. In captivity, they are held in compounds that are a fraction of that size. Receiving regular meals doesn't seem like a fair trade for this loss of freedom to roam. In addition, creatures such as elephants, great apes, and other primates are highly social and accustomed to living in large groups. But most animals in captivity live in far smaller groups, depriving them of the wider interaction they would enjoy in the wild. Worst of all, when we force animals to perform for us, we fail to respect their native intelligence, grace, and dignity. Instead, we allow them to be subjected to long hours of training to make them behave in ways that are simply not normal for these highly intelligent animals. That's what people should think when they see an elephant standing on a tiny stool or a dolphin dancing on its tail across a pool.

Have students refer to the Rhetorical Index and choose an essay that presents an argument. Discuss the following: What is the author's stance? Try to describe the author's tone. Does the author present supporting information in emphatic order? Do you agree with the author's position? Why or why not?

As you can see, the supporting sentences follow emphatic order. The initial reason—that the environments in zoos, circuses, and aquatic parks are considerably different from and considerably smaller than the ones in the wild—is strong. It is a compelling reason to support the idea that keeping animals in captivity to perform for people's pleasure is wrong. The second point—that these animals are often kept in isolation—is even stronger. Depriving animals accustomed to living in groups the comfort of others seems especially cruel. But the final point—forcing animals to endure training so they will behave in ways that they don't in nature—is strongest of all. Forcing animals to perform in this fashion goes against their nature. Their behaviors are shaped simply for our pleasure. This final point is a suitable conclusion to the paragraph.

Transitional phrases can help guide your readers through your line of reasoning and highlight the emphatic order. The list below gives some of these transitions.

Transitional Expressions for Argument

To Establish Reasons	*To Answer the Opposition*	*To Conclude*
first (second, third, etc.)	some may say	therefore
most important	on the other hand	thus

Exercise 13.4 **Understanding Tone and Logical Reasoning**

1. Explain how you can establish a reasonable, convincing tone in an argument paragraph. _____

   Tone refers to the attitude you express in your writing. A reasonable tone is established through word choices that convey a serious, respectful attitude and straightforward presentation of facts, not overstatement.

2. Briefly explain the difference between induction and deduction. _____

   Induction and deduction are means of logical reasoning. Induction moves from specific evidence to a general conclusion. Deduction moves from a general truth to a specific conclusion.

Exercise 13.5 **Eliminating Logical Fallacies**

1. Turn again to the list of logical fallacies on pages 173–174. Working with a partner, choose three of the categories on the list. On a separate sheet of paper, write additional examples for them.

2. Exchange papers with another team. Evaluate the statements you receive. Mark statements that do not illustrate the specific fallacy as intended. Then for each fallacy, write a contrasting statement that is logical, factual, and reasonable. Return the papers to their writers.

Exercise 13.6 **Writing and Evaluating Arguments**

1. Reread the sample paragraphs on censoring material on the Internet (page 174), and on keeping animals captive and making them perform (page 175). First, decide which topic interests you more. Then imagine you hold a point of view that opposes the view expressed by the writer. On a separate sheet of paper, make a list of reasons to support your stance.

2. Exchange your list with a partner. Evaluate the list you receive. Put a + beside strong, convincing reasons. Label any logical fallacies with the appropriate phrase (*begging the question, non sequitur,* and so forth), using the list on pages 173–174 as a guide.

3. Return the paper to its writer. Adjust your own list as needed.

Exercise 13.7 **Considering Additional Purposes in Argument Paragraphs**

This chapter features several sample argument paragraphs. The specific points of these paragraphs, with the appropriate page numbers, are listed below. Because they are argument paragraphs, their primary purpose is obviously to persuade. Working with a partner, take another look at the paragraphs and then on the lines next to the specific points list the secondary purposes for each paragraph.

1. Allowing adopted children to view sealed adoption records, pages

   166–167 _____

   Most students will agree that the secondary purpose is to inform. Some students

   may also point out that the piece entertains in that it makes its case clearly and

   holds the reader's attention.

   _____

2. Objecting to making English the official language of the United States,

   pages 168–169 _____

   Most students will agree that the secondary purpose is to inform. Some students

   may also point out that the piece entertains in that it makes its case clearly and

   holds the reader's attention.

   _____

3. Censoring the discussion of certain topics on the Internet, page 174

   Most students will agree that the secondary purpose is to inform. Some students

   may also point out that with the problematic sentences removed, the paragraph also

   entertains in that it makes its case clearly and holds the reader's attention.

   _____

4. Prohibiting the captivity and forced performance of animals, page 175

   Most students will agree that the secondary purposes are to inform and to entertain.

   _____

   _____

   _____

Challenge 13.2 **Writing an Argument Paragraph**

Working from the prewriting material you generated for Challenge 13.1 on page 171, complete a paragraph of at least 100 words in which you either support or reject a ban on the topic you chose there.

Discovering Connections 13.2

1. In Discovering Connections 13.1 on page 166, you chose a topic for an argument paragraph and completed your prewriting. Now develop a paragraph of at least 100 words that expresses a stand for or against the subject. As you write your paragraph, keep in mind the points raised in this chapter.

2. Exchange your paragraph with a partner. If you completed the paragraph for Challenge 13.2 above and you feel that paragraph is better, use it for this exercise instead. Evaluate the paragraph you receive, using the argument paragraph checklist below. Write your evaluation on a separate sheet of paper, and then return the paragraph and your assessment to the writer.

3. Using your reader's comments to guide you, revise your own paragraph.

Argument Paragraph Checklist

☐ Does the topic sentence clarify the writer's stance on the issue?

☐ Are there sufficient examples and details to support the stance?

☐ Is the tone reasonable, sincere, and serious? Put a ✓ next to any places where you see a problem in tone.

☐ Is the presentation logical? Underline and label any logical fallacies.

☐ Is material effectively arranged in emphatic order or some other method of arrangement? Explain.

☐ In your judgment, what is the best part of this paragraph? Explain.

☐ Which detail or example would be even better if it were expanded? Why?

RECAP ARGUMENT

Activity
13.5

New terms in this chapter	Definitions
● argument	● writing that seeks to persuade a reader to accept the writer's point of view
● stance	● the position taken on a subject—the writer's opinion

New terms in this chapter	Definitions
● **fact**	● a verifiable truth ***Example*** The city is in the process of tearing down several historic buildings.
● **opinion**	● a belief based on impressions, experiences, or knowledge base In argument, opinions must be backed up by facts. ***Example*** The city should be trying to preserve historic buildings instead of tearing them down.
● **documentation**	● the process of acknowledging the source of supporting information taken from another document or individual
● **tone**	● the attitude you express about your subject
● **induction**	● a system of reasoning that moves from specific examples to a general conclusion
● **deduction**	● a system of reasoning that moves from general premises to a specific conclusion
● **logical fallacies**	● common errors in reasoning: argument *ad hominem;* bandwagon approach; begging the question; circular reasoning; creating a red herring; either/or reasoning; hasty generalization; *non sequitur;* over-simplification; *post hoc, ergo propter hoc*

Writing an Argument Paragraph

Use the topic sentence to **express a clear stance** on the issue.

↓ ↑

Include **sufficient support**.

↓ ↑

Maintain an **effective tone**.

↓ ↑

Keep your presentation **logical**.

↓ ↑

Consider **emphatic order** to arrange the supporting material.

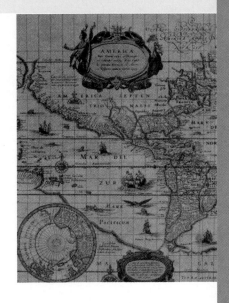

Moving On to the Essay

Chapter 14

Developing an Essay

Getting Started... **Q:** Instead of a simple paragraph, now I have to write an essay. I really feel intimidated because it seems like such an enormous task. What should I do to help me write an effective essay?

Audio 14.1 **A:** To help you write an essay, first relax. The process you follow is the same you've followed to write paragraphs—prewriting, composing, revising. The main difference is in scope. A paragraph discusses a subject in fairly limited detail. An essay covers a broader topic in much greater detail. You'll probably find this a good thing because it will liberate you to explore and express more of your thoughts.

Overview: Understanding the Essay

Audio 14.2 Up to this point, we have focused on writing paragraphs as a way to develop your skills. But as a college student and as a professional beyond the classroom, you will often be asked to prepare longer pieces of writing. Most college assignments call for multi-paragraph writings, called **essays**, that deal with a subject in greater detail than is possible in a single paragraph. The main difference between a paragraph and an essay is *scope*. A paragraph deals with a subject in a limited way. An essay covers a subject more thoroughly, exploring many facets and angles.

Paragraphs are the building blocks of essays, so what you have already learned about paragraphs will help you write essays. What you have learned about paragraphs is also important for another reason. You follow the same basic process to write an essay that you do when you write a paragraph.

Weblink 14.1 **In this chapter you will learn what you need to know about writing an essay, including:**

- the structure of an essay

- the stages of essay writing: prewriting, composing, and revising

- the importance of the thesis

- the importance of meeting your reader's needs

- the role of the introduction and conclusion

Discovering Connections 14.1

As students complete the Discovering Connections exercises in this chapter, they will compose and revise an essay, following the writing process explained in this chapter.

Later in this chapter, you will read an essay about a first day on the job. Before you read this essay, prewrite on a complaint—perhaps about work, school, local or national policy, and so on. Then highlight the most promising ideas and save your work for later use.

Understanding the Structure of an Essay

Video 14.1 An essay consists of three parts: an *introduction,* a *body,* and a *conclusion.*

The Introduction

The **introduction** of an effective essay is usually a single paragraph that indicates the subject and direction of the paper. This paragraph sparks the interest of the reader and compels that reader to continue reading. The most important part of the introduction is the **thesis**, the element that specifies the subject and focus of the entire essay.

The Body

The **body** of an essay is the series of paragraphs that support and illustrate the thesis. How many paragraphs should be provided in the body of an essay depends on the focus and direction of the writing. With an essay of 500 to 700 words, the body will likely consist of four to ten paragraphs, depending on the length of the paragraphs themselves. Regardless of the number of paragraphs, however, each paragraph must contain a clear topic sentence and supporting details, all relating to the thesis.

The minimum number of paragraphs constituting the body of an essay is three. One type of essay featuring a three-paragraph body is called the **five-paragraph essay**. As the name suggests, the five-paragraph essay has five paragraphs total, one introductory paragraph, three body paragraphs, and a concluding paragraph. Each of the three paragraphs of the body discusses one of the three points raised about the topic in the introduction. The five-paragraph essay may prove particularly useful with some timed writing assignments like essay examinations and writing assessments. (See Chapter 16, "Adjusting Your Process: Time Writing and Summaries," for a more complete discussion of the five-paragraph essay.)

The Conclusion

The **conclusion** of an essay, usually a paragraph, strengthens the overall message expressed by the thesis and the supporting examples and details. The conclusion brings the essay to a logical and appropriate end, summing up the *significance* of the essay. Although most conclusions don't introduce new ideas, sometimes they raise issues that readers may want to pursue.

The following figure shows the structure of an essay:

Some students may note that they have read effective essays that don't follow this structure exactly. Discuss with students how this model will help them successfully complete academic writing assignments and express their ideas clearly and efficiently as they develop their writing skills.

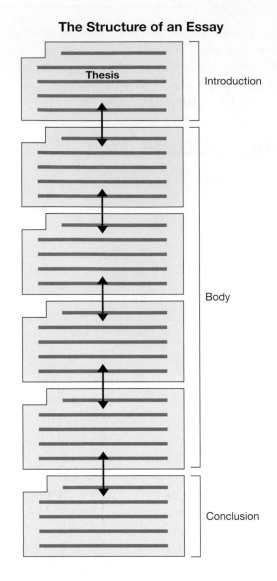

The Structure of an Essay

Thesis

Introduction

Body

Conclusion

Note that the arrows between paragraphs point in both directions. That's because each paragraph should relate both to the thesis and to the paragraphs before and after it.

Exercise 14.1   Understanding Essay Structure

1. Briefly explain the structure of the essay. _____

   An essay has three parts: an introduction, a body, and a conclusion.

2. What role does the introduction play in an essay?

   The introduction of an essay prepares the reader for the discussion to follow in the body.

3. What is the purpose of the conclusion? _____

The conclusion sums up the significance of the essay, bringing the paper to a logical

and appropriate end.

Challenge 14.1   **Developing Essay Awareness**

1. What do you think will be the biggest difference you will find in writing

an essay versus writing a paragraph? _____

Answers will vary, although most students will indicate that the task of writing an

essay is far more involved than the process of writing a paragraph.

2. Working with a classmate, choose one of the readings from Part Seven. After you both read the piece, on a separate piece of paper identify the introduction, the body, and the conclusion of the essay.

Examining an Effective Essay

Consider the following essay:

Making Their Marks: The Popularity of Tattooing and Body Piercing

Many people seem content enough to go through life looking like everybody else. But for others, nothing seems more important than distinguishing how they look from the rest of society. Some set themselves apart by how they dress. Others show their individuality by how they wear their hair. Today, people with an independent streak have found another way to make themselves stand out from the crowd. These people are choosing tattooing or body piercing as their marks or distinctions. These ancient forms of body art are among the most popular trends of the past decade.

The history of decorating the body in these ways goes back thousands of years. Originally, members of a tribe would undergo elaborate tattooing, piercing, or scarring to signify membership in the group. For example, natives of some islands in the South Pacific would tattoo their faces with intricate designs, while ancient tribes in other lands would cut parts of their bodies to leave scars in particular designs.

Tattoos and piercings have been around in more modern times, too. However, until the past 15 years or so, they have been largely associated with bikers and sailors. They held little appeal for the average person. Until recently, tattooing wasn't even legal in many states. The only way for many people to get a tattoo was to find an illegal tattoo parlor or travel to a country where tattooing was legal. Either way, people endured great pain and risked infection just to decorate their skin.

All that has changed today, however. For one thing, tattooing and piercing are legal in many areas throughout the country. Tattoo parlors are now licensed and inspected regularly to make sure they are sanitary. The instruments used are sterilized, in many cases using the same technology that is used to purify dental instruments.

But the biggest change is the clientele who seek tattoos and piercings. No longer is it just outlaws looking to get a skull on their biceps. Today bikers and rock stars share the waiting room at the tattoo parlor with teenaged football players, fraternity members, stockbrokers, and other ordinary people looking for something that will mark them as different from the next person.

Nobody knows how long this new interest in tattooing and piercing will last. Right now, though, the number of people with colorful skin decorations and nose, tongue, and belly button jewelry seems to be on the increase. It looks like none of the new tattoo parlors will be closing any time soon.

This writing illustrates all the required elements of an effective essay. Its introduction has a clear thesis: *These ancient forms of body art are among the most popular trends of the past decade.* The thesis is fully supported and explained in the body—four paragraphs that discuss aspects of tattooing and body piercing. The essay then closes with a conclusion that restates the topic and reemphasizes the significance of the points made in the essay.

But how did the essay come to be in this form? The rest of the chapter will show you, walking you step by step through the process of writing an essay.

Exercise 14.2   Explaining the Parts of the Model Essay

1. Briefly explain how the introduction in the essay about tattooing and body piercing prepares the reader for the body to follow. _____

   The introduction prepares the reader for the body to follow because it states that

   although these forms of body art are not new, they are current ways that people use

   to indicate their individuality. Therefore the reader is ready for a discussion of the dif-

   ferent aspects of this trend.

2. For each of the paragraphs in the body, summarize the details that support the thesis. (2) Tattooing has a long history, including South Pacific tribesmen who tattooed their faces.

(3) In modern times, tattooing used to be relegated to bikers and sailors. It was illegal in most states, painful, and potentially infectious.

(4) Tattooing is now legal in many areas. Tattoo parlors are licensed and regulated, and instruments are carefully sterilized.

(5) The clientele seeking tattooing now include everyday people—teenagers, housewives, stockbrokers.

3. How does the conclusion sum up the significance of the material presented? The conclusion points out that it's hard to tell how long the new wave of this old tradition will remain. It also restates that tattooing and body piercing continue to grow in popularity.

Examining the Process of Writing an Essay

ESL Note
See "Writing Essays" on pages 585–586.

Video
14.2

To write an essay, you follow a process that is similar to the one you follow to write a paragraph. When you write an essay, however, you use the stages of *prewriting, composing,* and *revising* to explore the subject in far greater detail.

The first stage of essay writing is prewriting, during which you generate the ideas you'll need to complete you essay. In Chapter 2, "Generating Ideas through Prewriting," you discovered which prewriting technique—or which combination of techniques—you prefer to develop examples and details about a subject. When you are developing an essay, you also prewrite to develop a manageable focus, just as you do when you write a paragraph.

You then develop this focus into your **thesis**, your main point for the essay, expressed in sentence form. Developing a draft thesis is your bridge from prewriting to composing. In this stage, you turn your prewriting ideas into sentences that support, illustrate, or explain the thesis. You then arrange the sentences in paragraphs, including an **introduction** and a **conclusion**, that address the needs of the reader.

With a first draft completed, you **revise**, or refine and polish your draft. When you revise, you first **reassess** its *unity, coherence,* and *use of language.* Then you **redraft** to address any problem spots. Finally, you **edit** to eliminate any remaining errors. Take a look at this figure, which illustrates the process of writing an essay:

The Process of Writing an Essay

Prewrite	Draft a Thesis	Compose
Develop ideas and narrow your subject		Develop paragraphs that explain the thesis

Repeat steps as needed

Revise

Assess, identify problem spots, and redraft

Edit

Eliminate errors

FINAL DRAFT

As the two-way arrows show, the process or writing an essay often requires you to repeat some steps. In other words, the process is *recursive*.

Imagine, for example, that during the revising stage you find that one or more of the paragraphs need additional detail. You simply return to the prewriting stage to generate new information. You then move to the composing stage to turn the new ideas into correct, reader-centered sentence form. Finally, you would edit this newly generated material to make sure that it is expressed correctly.

Think again of the essay on tattooing and piercing. It was created following the same process. Now let's examine that essay in its various stages.

Prewriting: Generating Ideas and Identifying a Manageable Focus

All writing starts with **prewriting**. Here is a freewriting on *fads and trends*, which contains initial facts and details about tattooing and body piercing:

Ok, what fads and trends are around? Music? Maybe. Different types like Alternative, Retro, Rap? They've all been around for a while, though, so are they really fads or trends? How about clothes? Fashions change so fast. If you spend a lot of money on clothes this year, you are out of style by next year-so annoying! And so expensive. I paid $70 for one pair of shoes last year. How about people getting tattoos? That seems more like it-tattooing and piercing are hot now. Even before it was legal in this state, people got cool tattoos at these illegal tattooing and piercing parties at somebody's house. Nick and Kara went to the next state where tattooing was legal. Three places here in town now. Really safe now-the city health inspector has to check out the places and they have to have special devices like at the dentist to keep the instruments germ free. Piercing-it must hurt a lot, especially depending where you get it. Alikia said it didn't hurt to have her belly button pierced, but she has to be lying. And somebody told me that getting a tattoo on the small of your back hurts the most. How about on your butt? Willy had one of a leprechaun there-now that had to hurt! And tongue rings-ouch! People get piercing and tattoos to make them different from everyone else-body art. My grandmother says that only trashy people get tattoos. She's almost 80, and when she was growing up, only criminals and sailors had tattoos-nobody had piercings. But tattooing goes way back in time-some tribes used to decorate their faces or purposely scar themselves to indicate their membership in a group. Now all kinds of people go-housewives, teenagers, you name it. I should talk to Urbano about how much it costs-his cousin is a tattoo artist. Today I'll look around at people at the Metro station to see how many of them have piercings, scarrings, or tattoos-I hope nobody sees me staring.

As you can see, this freewriting contains a number of interesting details about tattooing and piercing. The writer has highlighted the most promising ideas. From the highlighted material, it's easy to identify a likely focus: tattooing and body piercing as a current popular fad, but with a history.

Discovering Connections 14.2

For Discovering Connections 14.1 on page 183, you completed a prewriting on a complaint and highlighted the most promising ideas. Now, drawing from this material, develop a thesis. Save your work for later use.

Developing an Effective Thesis

Weblink
14.2

The bridge between prewriting and composing is developing a draft thesis. Think of the thesis as a signpost in sentence form that lets the reader know what is to come in the rest of the paper. A topic sentence states the main idea of a single paragraph, but a thesis states the main idea of the *entire* essay.

An effective thesis, like an effective topic sentence, is generally composed of two parts: a *subject* and the *writer's attitude about* or *reaction to* that subject. This structure clarifies the purpose of the essay and establishes the reader's expectation about the way the subject will be discussed. For example, if you were writing an essay about the greatest technological advance of the past 50 years, your thesis might look like this:

EFFECTIVE THESIS

|—————— subject ——————| |—————— attitude or opinion ——————|
The development of the Internet is **the most important technical innovation of the past 50 years.**

This thesis is effective because it features both a subject and an attitude or opinion about the subject. In addition, it indicates that the primary purpose of the piece is to persuade and that the rest of the paper will likely provide examples demonstrating that the Internet was indeed the most significant technological development of the past half century.

One way to remember what a good thesis *is* is to remember what a thesis *isn't*. An effective thesis is **not**

- an **announcement** of your intent, featuring words like *I plan, I intend,* or *This paper concerns,* since these expressions merely repeat what you should make obvious with your thesis.

INEFFECTIVE THESIS

I want to talk about how important the development of the Internet has been.

- a **statement of fact**, because a fact is a verifiable truth, leaving no room for discussion or debate:

INEFFECTIVE THESIS

People link to the Internet with a modem.

- a **title**, since a title is not usually a sentence and is generally intended to provide only a broad hint of the subject of your essay:

INEFFECTIVE THESIS

The Internet: The Innovation That Changed the Whole World

This may be an appropriate time to discuss the role of titles. Ask students why titles are important. What titles in the essays and readings in the text do they find effective? What should the title suggest to readers about the essay that follows?

Exercise 14.3 **Understanding the Thesis**

1. What is the role of the thesis in an essay? _____

   The thesis is a sentence that lets the reader know the primary point of the entire

   essay.

   _____

Weblink
14.3

2. What are the two parts of the thesis? _____

   The two parts of the thesis are the subject and the writer's attitude about or reaction

   to that subject.

   _____

3. How does the thesis act as a bridge between prewriting and composing?

   The thesis is developed on the basis of ideas generated during prewriting. Once a

   thesis exists, the focus of the writing process changes to identifying and then devel-

   oping ideas into supporting sentences.

Exercise 14.4 **Revising Ineffective Theses**

COLLABORATION

Working with a partner, turn each of the following sentences or titles into an effective thesis. Study the example first.

Answers will vary. Representative answers are shown.

EXAMPLE

Ask students to explain if asking a question is an effective way to present a thesis. Group answers to Exercise 14.4 can be shared and discussed with the class.

The Hovel Where I Grew Up

Although the house where I spent my childhood was a shack, I have many good memories of the days I spent playing there.

1. The metric system is a system of measurement based on units of ten.

   Although the metric system is an excellent system of measurement, U.S. citizens

   continue to resist adopting it.

2. I plan to show that having a good educational experience in kinder-

   garten can have an enormous impact on a child's self-image. _____

   Having a good educational experience in kindergarten can have an enormous im-

   pact on a child's self-image.

3. Tabloids like the *National Enquirer* sell millions of copies a week.

   People who buy the *National Enquirer* and other tabloids—which sell millions of

   copies a week—can be classified into four major groups.

   _____

4. The Ideal Occupation One person's idea of an ideal occupation can be another

   person's idea of daily torture.

   _____

5. I want to show that insurance companies shouldn't be allowed to termi-

   nate coverage for people who face extraordinary medical bills. _____

   Insurance companies shouldn't be allowed to terminate coverage for people who

   face extraordinary medical bills.

   _____

6. Manatees are large aquatic mammals that live within the intercostal wa-

   terways of Florida. Recreational boaters in Florida's intercostal waterways are

   rapidly moving manatees toward endangered status.

   _____

7. I plan to show that taking music lessons can help preschoolers develop

   a greater ability to learn. Taking music lessons can help preschoolers develop

   greater ability to learn.

   _____

8. More and more people are doing their holiday shopping through the

   Internet. Holiday shopping on the Internet will never replace traditional shopping

   experiences.

   _____

9. Electric Cars: Transportation of the Future _____

   Speed-obsessed American drivers will refuse to drive electric cars until they perform

   as well as gas-powered vehicles.

   _____

10. I want to show that directors of youth leagues should enact strict rules regarding acceptable behavior for parents at games. _____

Directors of youth sports leagues should enact strict rules regarding acceptable be-

havior of parents at games.

Activity 14.1

Challenge 14.2   **Developing Support for a Thesis**

The section on developing an effective thesis (pages 190–193) presents the following thesis for an essay:

EXAMPLE

> The development of the Internet is the most important technical innovation of the past 50 years.

Working with a partner, make a list on a separate sheet of paper of several details and examples that could be used to support this thesis.

Composing

Once you have developed a draft thesis, you move to the **composing** stage, during which you complete a draft of your essay. You've already highlighted the ideas that you initially felt held the most promise for development. Now you should *filter* this material, identifying the information that offers the best support for the thesis you have developed.

With these ideas identified, you need to list them, putting related ideas together. Restated more completely, in correct sentence form, the ideas in these groups will become the basis for the supporting paragraphs of your essay. Therefore, you should also consider the best way to arrange the groups to fulfill the purpose of the essay. This order will serve as a tentative blueprint for your essay.

Here are the most promising ideas about tattooing and piercing from the highlighted material in the freewriting on fads and trends. The thesis indicates that the primary purpose will be to inform—to explain the historical background of tattooing. Therefore, arranging this information in chronological order makes sense.

1. That seems more like it—tattooing and piercing are hot now.
   People get piercing and tattoos to make them different from everyone else—body art.
2. But tattooing goes way back in time—some tribes used to decorate their faces or purposely scar themselves to indicate their membership in a group.

3. My grandmother says that only trashy people get tattoos. She's almost 80, and when she was growing up, only criminals and sailors had tattoos.

   Even before it was legal in this state, people got cool tattoos at these illegal tattooing and piercing parties at somebody's house.
4. Three places here in town now.

   Really safe now—the city health inspector has to check out the places and they have to have special devices like at the dentist to keep the instruments germ free.
5. Now all kinds of people go—housewives, teenagers, you name it.

   Nick and Kara went to the next state where tattooing was legal.

Once you have grouped and arranged your best prewriting material, the next step is to express it more completely and clearly, using additional details, examples, and illustrations. As with paragraph writing, should you include any information that you have taken from a specific source, make sure to acknowledge that source. (See pages 83–85 for a more complete discussion of **documentation**.)

As you organize your ideas and write them down, keep your reader's needs in mind so that the essay will be *reader centered*. In other words, your goal is to create an essay that will make sense to somebody else. You know a great deal about most of the subjects you will write about. For this reason, you might incorrectly conclude that your reader has the same background and frame of reference as you do.

The secret to meeting your reader's needs is to think of yourself *before* you learned what you know about the subject. What specific examples and details did you need to understand the subject yourself?

Discovering Connections 14.3

Review the ideas and thesis you generated in Discovering Connections 14.1 (page 183) and 14.2 (page 189). Then organize the details you have chosen in a logical order, grouping related ideas. Compose a paragraph for each group of supporting details. Be sure each supports the thesis. Use the list on pages 193–194 as a guide. Save your work for later use.

Fast Fact Don't you just hate it when the word you want is "on the tip of your tongue," but you can't actually say it or get it down on paper? You aren't alone. In fact, it's a phenomenon that's so common that it has a name. And what is that name? Psychologists commonly refer to it as the tip-of-the-tongue phenomenon. Ah, those experts . . .

Creating an Effective Introduction and Conclusion

Weblink
14.4

An essay contains two important paragraphs that perform specialized functions: the introduction and the conclusion. The introduction contains the thesis, engages the reader, and previews the structure of the essay. The conclusion summarizes the point of the essay, restating the significance of the ideas while bringing the paper to a logical and appropriate end.

Introduction You have several techniques available to help you develop an effective introduction. One technique is to use an **anecdote**—a brief, entertaining story that emphasizes the thesis.

Video
14.3

Imagine a paper discussing the media's intrusion into the lives of people in the news. The introduction to this paper might include the following story about a victim of the media:

> When my friend Cerene opened the newspaper one morning last year, she saw a story that made her physically sick. There, on page two, was a story about her father's arrest for tax evasion. Included in the story were her name and age. What the story didn't mention was that Cerene's parents had been divorced four years earlier. Her father hadn't contacted her or provided any financial support in all that time. These facts didn't stop the newspaper from dragging her name into the story, even though she had nothing at all to do with her father or his legal troubles. Cerene was perfectly innocent, yet she still had to face the embarrassment of seeing her name published in an unflattering situation. The media shouldn't be able to drag anyone's name into a story that doesn't genuinely involve that person.

Bring copies of several magazine articles to class and have students discuss the effectiveness of various techniques that writers use to develop introductions. Ask students if they've noticed other methods besides those explained here. Continue this activity by also examining the conclusions of the articles.

Another technique is to use relevant facts or statistics:

EXAMPLE   A recent *USA Today* poll found that 75 percent of all Americans think the media focus too much on the private lives of news makers.

To show the reader what direction the essay will take, the next sentence could state that the discussion will focus on examples from politics, business, show business, and sports.

Still another technique is to begin the introduction with a relevant saying or quotation:

EXAMPLE   My grandmother's favorite expression was, "Keep your nose out of other people's business, and they'll keep their noses out of yours."

Another technique is to begin with a **rhetorical question**. This type of question is designed not to be answered, but to provoke thought or discussion:

EXAMPLE   How would you like to suffer a personal loss and then read all the personal details in the paper the next morning?

Activity
14.2

Placing your thesis as the first or second sentence of your introduction lets your reader know the point of your essay immediately. Placing it toward or at the end of the introduction, however, can arouse interest, drawing your reader into your subject. Regardless of where you place the thesis, keep in mind that your introduction should always suggest the direction the essay will take.

Weblink
14.5

Conclusion The conclusion is the writer's last word on the subject, a final thought or a question for the reader to consider. In general, conclusions don't present new information in detail. The place to develop new thoughts and ideas fully is the body, not the conclusion.

As with an introduction, concluding an essay with an anecdote that embodies the point of the paper is a good technique. Other times a relevant question or quotation will be the best alternative. The technique you ultimately choose should depend upon the particular situation. Whatever technique helps you bring the essay to an effective close is the correct choice for that essay.

Here is an effective conclusion for a paper discussing the media's intrusion into the lives of people in the news:

> No one is saying that news reporters shouldn't have the right to publish or broadcast the news. But they do have a responsibility to make sure that the material they broadcast or publish is actually news and not gossip. Everybody has the right to personal privacy, even public figures, and the media should respect this right.

Exercise 14.5   **Reviewing the Principles for Composing an Essay**

Activity
14.3

1. What advantage do you gain by grouping ideas that you develop for your essay during prewriting? _____

   Grouping your prewriting ideas on the basis of some common point will make it easier for you to establish a tentative order and to develop paragraphs.

2. Briefly explain reader-centered writing. _____

   Reader-centered writing is writing that makes sense not just to the writer but to another person as well.

Exercise 14.6   **Understanding Techniques for Introductions and Conclusions**

1. Of the list of techniques available to use in introductions or conclusions (pages 195–196), which do you find most interesting? Why? _____

   Answers will vary.

2. On a separate sheet of paper, briefly explain which you think you would find easier to write for an essay, an introduction or a conclusion, and why.

Challenge 14.3   **Examine Introductions and Conclusions**

For Challenge 14.1 (page 185), you and a classmate were asked to read one of the essays from Part Seven, "Connecting: Responding to Reading." Now, working with the same partner answer the following questions on a separate sheet of paper:

1. What is the thesis of this essay? Write it down.

2. Does the writer use any special techniques to introduce or conclude the essay? Explain.

Understanding the Relationship between Topic Sentences and the Thesis   As Chapter 3, "Composing: Creating a Draft," indicated, the main sentence in any paragraph is called the *topic sentence*. An essay is a multiparagraph writing, so it contains several topic sentences, each of which is directly connected to the thesis.

Here is the thesis from a paper about honesty in the United States:

EXAMPLE

> In the United States today, it seems as if people don't care about honesty and lawful behavior anymore.

As the thesis indicates, the rest of the essay deals with examples of dishonesty or illegal behavior. The first paragraph of the body, for example, discusses regular violations of drug laws. The next paragraph deals with employee theft, and the next one discusses incompetence and dishonesty in public works projects. The final paragraph in the body discusses the public reaction following the impeachment of the President of the United States. The conclusion then restates the significance of the thesis—that in all areas of life, society no longer values honesty as it once did.

The figure on page 198 illustrates the relationship between the thesis and the topic sentences of this essay. As the figure shows, each topic sentence deals with some form of dishonesty or unlawful behavior. In terms of the relationship between the thesis and these topic sentences, *dishonesty or unlawful behavior* represents the *common thread*, the element that all the paragraphs share. This thesis indicates that honesty is no longer valued. Each topic sentence directly supports, illustrates, or explains this thesis by presenting a different aspect of dishonesty.

The Relationship between Topic Sentences and the Thesis

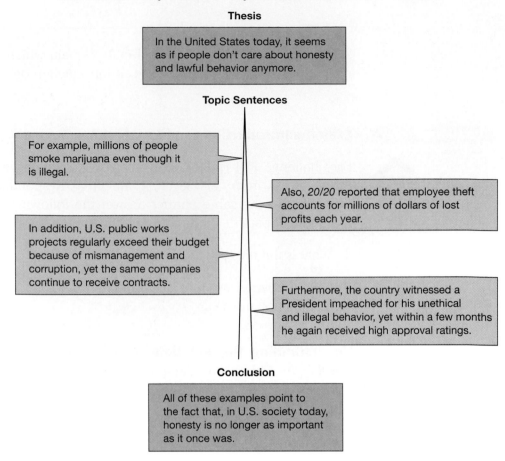

Thesis

In the United States today, it seems as if people don't care about honesty and lawful behavior anymore.

Topic Sentences

For example, millions of people smoke marijuana even though it is illegal.

Also, *20/20* reported that employee theft accounts for millions of dollars of lost profits each year.

In addition, U.S. public works projects regularly exceed their budget because of mismanagement and corruption, yet the same companies continue to receive contracts.

Furthermore, the country witnessed a President impeached for his unethical and illegal behavior, yet within a few months he again received high approval ratings.

Conclusion

All of these examples point to the fact that, in U.S. society today, honesty is no longer as important as it once was.

Challenge 14.4 **Relating Thesis and Topic Sentences**

Review the final draft of the essay about tattooing and piercing on pages 185–186. Find the topic sentence of each paragraph. Working with a partner, show the relationship between the thesis, the topic sentences in the body, and the topic sentence in the conclusion. Create a figure like the one above.

Developing a Solid First Draft Once you have organized selected details into a list like the one on pages 193–194, then it's time to develop a solid first draft of the essay. Using your list to guide you, you should be able to compose an introduction, body, and conclusion, all expressed in complete sentence form.

Here is the *first draft* of the paper on tattooing and piercing:

Making Their Marks: The Popularity of Tattooing and Body Piercing

(1) Today a number of people are choosing tattooing or body piercing to make them feel different. Right now these forms of body art are really popular.

(2) In modern times, tattoos have usually been associated with bikers and sailors. Until recently, it was illegal. People went to illegal tattoo parlors to get them. They had to put up with pain and possible infection.

(3) The history of decorating the body goes back thousands of years. Natives of some islands in the South Pacific would tattoo their faces with intricate designs. Some of these islands are still experiencing volcanic eruptions. One eruption a few years ago destroyed most of a small town. Some ancient tribes cut other parts of their bodies to leave scars in particular designs.

(4) All that has changed. Tattooing and piercing are legal in many areas throughout the country. Tattoo parlors are licensed and inspected. The instruments used are sterilized.

(5) A big change is who goes for tattoos today. Besides tough guys getting some designs done, everybody goes, too, so that they can all be different.

(6) Nobody knows how long fads like tattooing and piercing will stay in fashion. People still seem to be interested, so it will probably be around for a while.

This first draft contains the basics: a thesis, prewriting ideas expressed in sentence form, and paragraphs arranged into an introduction, body, and conclusion. At this point, however, it is in a limited and rough form. Before it fulfills the promise that it holds, it needs to be reexamined and reworked. In other words, it needs to be revised.

Discovering Connections 14.4

For Discovering Connections 14.3 on page 194, you developed supporting sentences for the thesis you had created earlier. Now compose a first draft of an essay on that topic. Don't forget to include an introduction and a conclusion. Save this first draft for later use.

Revising

Once you have completed a draft of your essay, it is a good idea to take a break of a day or so. This way you will bring a rested and refreshed eye to the final stage of the writing process: **revising**. When you revise, you *refine* and then *polish* your draft. You follow the same steps to revise an essay that you follow to revise a paragraph. First, you *reassess* your draft, then you *redraft*, and finally you *edit*.

Reassessing When you **reassess** a piece of writing, you reexamine the essay for several factors. For example, a successful essay must be

- *unified*—all examples and details must be directly connected

- *coherent*—all the material must have clear transitions and be expressed in standard English and be arranged in a logical order
- *effectively worded*—all ideas must be specific and concise.

Revising for Unity   In a successful essay, all the elements work together to support the thesis. When you reassess your draft, examine each component to make sure it is directly connected to your main idea. Sometimes, an entire paragraph is not connected to the thesis. In other cases, individual sentences within a paragraph lack unity. In both cases, the result is the same: the reader is distracted from your main point.

Look again, for example, at paragraph 3 of the draft essay on tattooing and piercing. As the topic sentence indicates, the main point of the paragraph concerns the history of tattooing. In order for the paragraph to be unified, all the sentences must be directly connected to that point. Which material breaks the unity?

> The history of decorating the body goes back thousands of years. Natives of some islands in the South Pacific would tattoo their faces with intricate designs. Some of these islands are still experiencing volcanic eruptions. One eruption a few years ago destroyed most of a small town. Some ancient tribes cut other parts of their bodies to leave scars in particular designs.

You probably identified the third and fourth sentences, which concern volcanic eruptions. Because these sentences aren't directly related to tattooing and piercing, they must be eliminated to maintain unity.

Discovering Connections 14.5

Check the draft you completed for Discovering Connections 14.4 (page 199) to make sure it is unified. First, be sure that all your paragraphs relate to the thesis. Then be sure that every sentence within each paragraph relates to the paragraph's topic sentence. Cross out any sentences or paragraphs that do not belong in your essay.

Revising for Coherence   An effective essay is one in which one idea flows smoothly on to the next. This quality, called *coherence*, is achieved (1) by providing adequate *transitions* between paragraphs and between sentences and (2) by *organizing* your ideas in a logical order.

Transitions   As Chapter 4, "Refining and Polishing Your Draft," showed, transitions help establish a smooth flow of ideas. Both *synonyms* and *common transitional expressions* help show relationships among your ideas. (See page 65 for lists of transitions.) When you reassess a draft, examine it closely for any gaps or points where the flow between sentences or paragraphs should be improved.

Consider again paragraph 4 from the first draft essay about tattooing and piercing:

> All that has changed. Tattooing and piercing are legal in many areas throughout the country. Tattoo parlors are licensed and inspected. The instruments used are sterilized.

This paragraph from the draft essay contains good information. Right now, however, the paragraph is choppy and doesn't flow smoothly. Part of the reason is that the information itself is not as complete and detailed as it should be. In addition, however, it needs some transitions. Without transitions the paragraph isn't as coherent as it should be.

Now look at the final draft of the same paragraph. Notice how much better this paragraph is, thanks to the additional details (italics) and transitions (boldface):

This may be an appropriate place to reinforce the concept of the *common thread* running throughout the essay.

> All that has changed **today, however**. **For one thing**, tattooing and piercing are legal in many areas throughout the country. Tattoo parlors are **now** licensed and inspected *regularly to make sure they are sanitary*. The instruments used are sterilized, **in many cases** *using the same technology that is used to purify dental instruments*.

Challenge 14.5 Assessing the Need for Transitions in a Rough Draft

Working with a partner, assess the need for transitions in the paragraphs (other than paragraph 3) of the first draft essay on pages 198–199. Put a ✓ next to places where transitions are needed.

Discovering Connections 14.6

Reassess the draft you completed for Discovering Connections 14.4 (page 199) to make sure you have used transitions effectively. Insert transitional expressions where they are needed to help the flow of ideas. Save your changes to use later, when you redraft.

Proper Organization   The second element of coherence is logical order. A successful essay is organized in such a way that the reader can easily follow it. Chapter 4 discussed several methods of establishing order:

1. *Emphatic order*   arranging points according to their importance
2. *Spatial order*   arranging descriptive details on the basis of their physical relationship with each other

3. *Chronological order*   arranging events on the basis of order of occurrence

When you reassess a draft, check the arrangement to make sure it is consistent
and logical. If the essay features spatial order, reevaluate the presentation to
make sure that the reader is able to visualize the scene. If the essay follows emphatic order, check the presentation to ensure that it sustains the reader's interest and effectively accentuates the thesis. If the writing is arranged in
chronological order, look closely at the sequence of events, making sure each
event is presented in the order in which it actually occurred. Because the essay
discusses tattooing through the years, following chronological order would
make great sense. But take a look at paragraphs 2, 3, and 4 of the first draft
essay on tattooing and piercing (with the sentences breaking the unity of paragraph 3 removed). Is there a problem with the order of these paragraphs?

> In modern times, tattoos have usually been associated with bikers and
> sailors. Until recently, it was illegal. People went to illegal tattoo parlors to
> get them. They had to put up with pain and possible infection.
>
> The history of decorating the body goes back thousands of years.
> Natives of some islands in the South Pacific would tattoo their faces with
> intricate designs. Some ancient tribes cut other parts of their bodies to
> leave scars in particular designs.
>
> All that has changed. Tattooing and piercing are legal in many areas
> throughout the country. Tattoo parlors are licensed and inspected. The
> instruments used are sterilized.

You probably noticed that paragraph 2 discusses the present, paragraph 3
discusses the past, and paragraph 4 discusses the present again. As Chapter
4, "Refining and Polishing Your Draft," explains (page 68), writers occasionally use flashbacks to provide necessary background information. But the
reader would likely find the information in these paragraphs easier to follow if they were presented from past to present, as this version shows:

> The history of decorating the body goes back thousands of years.
> Natives of some islands in the South Pacific would tattoo their faces
> with intricate designs. Some ancient tribes cut other parts of their bod-
> ies to leave scars in particular designs.
>
> In modern times, tattoos have usually been associated with bikers
> and sailors. Until recently, it was illegal. People went to illegal tattoo par-
> lors to get them. They had to put up with pain and possible infection.
>
> All that has changed. Tattooing and piercing are legal in many areas
> throughout the country. Tattoo parlors are licensed and inspected. The
> instruments used are sterilized.

Of course, these paragraphs still need some attention before they are suitable for a final draft. Now, at least, the order has been effectively adjusted to
make things easier for the reader.

Discovering Connections 14.7

Reassess the draft you completed for Discovering Connections 14.4 (page 199) to make sure it is organized logically. In the margin, draw an arrow from any sentence that is not in the proper order to the place it should be moved. Note any other errors in logic that may affect the structure of your essay. Save your notes to use later, when you redraft.

Revising for Effective Language   A successful essay is one in which the language captures the meaning the writer intends. When you reassess a draft, look for any spots in which the language is vague, general, or unclear. Then replace this weak language with specific and concise terms. If they will help to re-create the experience or clarify your point, you should include additional examples or details.

Here is a paragraph from "The Brown Wasps," an essay by writer Loren Eiseley. He discusses what happens when he makes a visit hoping to see a cottonwood tree. He and his father had planted it some sixty years earlier, and he has now discovered that the tree is gone. Which details help the reader visualize and understand the experience presented here?

> I came close to the white picket fence and reluctantly, with great effort, looked down the long vista of the yard. There was nothing there to see. For sixty years that cottonwood had been growing in my mind. Season by season its seeds had been floating farther on the hot prairie winds. We had planted it lovingly there, my father and I, because he had a great hunger for solid and live things growing, and because none of these things had long been ours to protect. We had planted the little sapling and watered it faithfully, and I remembered that I had run out with my small bucket to drench its roots on the day we moved away. And all the years since it had been growing in my mind, a huge tree that somehow stood for my father and the love I bore him.

Chances are that you identified details such as *the white picket fence, the long vista of the yard,* the *seeds floating,* and *the hot prairie winds.* In addition, you probably noticed *the little sapling* that the young Eiseley *watered faithfully* with a *small bucket* that he remembers using to *drench its roots on the day* his family *moved away* from the area. These specific details and examples bring the scene and situation into sharp focus.

Take another look at paragraph 5 from the first draft of the essay on tattooing and piercing:

> A big change is who goes for tattoos today. Besides tough guys getting some designs done, everybody goes, too, so that they can all be different.

As you can see, this paragraph fails to create a clear picture for the reader. In the first sentence, *who goes for tattoos* is awkward and unclear. In the second sentence, *tough guys getting some designs done* doesn't specify who was involved or what was done. Worst of all, *everybody* is an indefinite pronoun, so it is general and nonspecific. In addition, the statement isn't true. As popular as tattooing may seem, a large segment of the population is not tattooed.

Now consider this version:

> But the biggest change is the clientele who seek tattoos and piercings. No longer is it just outlaws looking to get a skull on their biceps. Today bikers and rock stars share the waiting room at the tattoo parlor with teenaged football players, fraternity members, stockbrokers, and other ordinary people looking for something that will mark them as different from the next person.

As you can see, the ineffective *who goes for tattoos* has been replaced by *the clientele who seek tattoos and piercings,* phrasing that is far more specific and effective. In addition, the general phrases *tough guys getting some designs done* has been changed to *outlaws looking to get a skull on their biceps,* and *bikers and rock stars,* phrasing that specifies who is under discussion and what was done. Finally, the indefinite *everybody* is replaced by a list specifying exactly what groups of people are now seeking tattoos. These groups include *teenaged football players, fraternity members, stockbrokers, and other ordinary people.* Changed in this way, the language in this paragraph is clearer and far more specific than the language in the first draft version.

Challenge 14.6   Assessing Use of Effective Language in a Rough Draft

Working with a partner, check the effectiveness of the language in the other paragraphs in the first draft of "Making Their Marks: The Popularity of Tattooing and Body Piercing" (pages 198–199). Circle or highlight any words that are too vague or too general to be effective. Discuss possible replacements.

Discovering Connections 14.8

> Reassess the draft you completed for Discovering Connections 14.4 (page 199) to make sure you have used language effectively. Replace any wordy or vague language with specific, concise phrases; add details as needed to allow readers to understand the experience fully. Save your changes to use later, when you redraft.

Seeking Help from an Objective Reader   In addition to reassessing your draft yourself, it's always a good idea to get feedback from an objective reader. Choose someone who will respond honestly and intelligently to your work. Your reader will find the following reader assessment checklist useful in responding to your first draft.

Reader Assessment Checklist

☐ Do you understand the point I am making? Does my thesis statement clearly state the topic along with my perspective on it? (thesis)

☐ Do I stick to that point all the way through? Does the topic sentence of each paragraph relate to the thesis? (unity)

☐ Are all my ideas and examples clearly connected and easy to follow? (coherence)

☐ Are the words I've used specific and concise? (effective language)

☐ Are my introduction and conclusion effective?

☐ What changes do you think I should make?

Here are a reader's comments in reaction to the first draft essay on tattooing and piercing:

I learned a lot from your paper—it's good. You have a good thesis, and the paragraphs in the body are all connected to it. The introduction and conclusion are also pretty good. The best feature is the topic. I know lots of people with tattoos, so I was really interested in the ideas you provided. I think a couple of things would make your paper even better. I was a little confused in the beginning with the order of the paragraphs. Maybe you could rearrange a couple so that the history would be easier to follow. And the stuff about the volcanoes doesn't really seem to have much to do with tattoos—maybe you should eliminate it. But my biggest suggestion is that you expand your paper. The stuff you have included is really interesting, and as I read I wanted to know even more. I think if you expand your discussion, including the introduction and conclusion, and add other examples in the body, your paper would be outstanding.

With these kinds of suggestions, you are prepared to move to the next step: redrafting.

Exercise 14.7   **Understanding Effective Revision**

1. Of the questions making up the reader assessment checklist above, which

   do you find easiest to answer? Why? _____ Answers will vary. _____

   _____

   _____

2. Why is it a good idea to give yourself a break between the composing and revising stages of writing? _____

<u>It gives you a little distance, or objectivity, so you can review the material with a</u>

<u>fresh eye. It also allows you to be rested before looking for errors.</u>

_____

_____

3. How can an objective reader help you improve your essay? _____

<u>An objective reader will be honest and will see errors that you may miss.</u>

_____

_____

Challenge 14.7   **Providing Feedback on a Student Essay**

Working with a partner, select a student essay from Part Seven. Pretend that a classmate has written this essay and has asked for your reaction. Use the reader assessment checklist on page 205 to review and evaluate it.

Redrafting   With the various weaknesses in your essay identified, you are ready to being **redrafting**. When you redraft, you need to rethink your essay, considering the best way to bring the scene or situation into even better focus. Redrafting involves addressing any problem spots in unity, coherence, logical order, and specific language identified by you or your objective reader.

You also need to **amplify**: to provide additional specific examples and details to support your ideas and fill any gaps. As Chapter 3, "Composing: Creating a Draft," (pages 52–53) indicates, the transitional expressions *for example* and *for instance* are helpful to you and your reader. They remind you to supply a specific supporting example and they cue your reader that a specific illustration will follow.

Discovering Connections 14.9

Revise the draft you completed for Discovering Connections 14.4 (page 199). Incorporate the lessons you have learned in this chapter and the changes you made as you completed the last several Discovering Connections exercises.

Editing: Eliminating Errors   The final step in revising an essay is **editing**. The purpose of this part of the revising process is to eliminate any remaining grammatical or spelling errors. Make it a point to be well rested whenever you edit. Fatigue can make it easy to overlook obvious errors.

When you edit, use the following proofreading checklist, which lists several of the most common writing problems, to identify specific weaknesses in your essay. Next to each listing is the abbreviation commonly used to identify this error when it appears in a paper. The inside back cover of this book includes a more complete list of errors and abbreviations.

Proofreading Checklist

☐ Have I eliminated all sentence fragments (*frag*)?
(See Chapter 18 for more on sentence fragments.)

☐ Have I eliminated all comma splices (*cs*)?
(See Chapter 20 for more on comma splices.)

☐ Have I eliminated all run-on sentences (*rs*)?
(See Chapter 20 for more on run-on sentences.)

☐ Is the spelling (*sp*) correct throughout?
(See Chapter 29 for more on spelling.)

☐ Is the verb tense (*t*) correct throughout?
(See Chapters 22, 23, and 24 for more on verb tense.)

☐ Do all subjects agree with their verbs (*subj/verb agr*)?
(See Chapters 21 and 25 for more on subject–verb agreement.)

☐ Do all pronouns agree with their antecedents (*pro/ant agr*)?
(See Chapter 27 for more on pronoun–antecedent agreement.)

When it comes to your own essay, you may find that you have no problems with some items on the list. At the same time, your paper may contain weaknesses not covered on the list. Therefore, the best thing to do is adapt the list so that it covers your own particular problem spots. Then use this personal proofreading checklist every time you write, regardless of whether it's an essay, a term paper, or a letter.

Working with a proofreading partner, someone who can look for errors with a fresh perspective, is also a great idea. Also, if you are using a computer, take full advantage of any spell checking or style checking features. Always proofread your paper one more time after using these functions, however, to make sure that all errors have been corrected. Despite all the advances in computer software, a computer still doesn't reason the way a human does. If you write *desert* when you actually mean *dessert*, the computer may not discover this oversight because *desert* is a correctly spelled word.

Fast Fact One problem with proofreading has to do with *selective perception*. Studies have shown that experienced readers don't actually read every word and so cover somewhere between 180 and 600 words a minute. This is when selective perception comes into play. Because we know how to spell simple or familiar words, we perceive them on the page as we know they *should be* rather than as they actually *are*. The secret to effective proofreading, then, is to *slow down*. Force yourself to read every word, meaning you will read about one word every 1.75 seconds—35 words per minute.

Exercise 14.8 **Understanding Redrafting and Editing**

1. What does it mean to *amplify?* _____

   Amplifying means providing additional specific examples and details to make it eas-

   ier for a reader to understand the point being made.

   _____

2. Briefly explain the purpose of editing. The purpose of editing is to eliminate

   any remaining errors in grammar, usage, spelling, and so on.

   _____

   _____

3. Working with a classmate, discuss your answers to the following question:

   EXAMPLE

   > Of the categories on the proofreading checklist (page 207), which do you
   > feel most confident dealing with? Why?

   Now, on a separate sheet of paper, briefly explain what the two of you
   have in common and how you differ.

Discovering Connections 14.10

1. Exchange the final draft you completed for Discovering Connections
   14.9 (page 206) with a partner. Using the proofreading checklist (page
   207), check the essay you receive. Identify any errors you see in the
   paper, using the abbreviations presented in the checklist and on the inside back cover of this book. Then return the paper to the writer.
2. Correct any errors your proofreading partner identified in your essay.

Looking Again at the Final Draft

Remember the final draft of "Making Their Marks: The Popularity of
Tattooing and Body Piercing" you saw earlier on pages 185–186? Here it is
again, this time in annotated form. The various notations point out how the
essay has changed from first to final draft.

Making Their Marks: The Popularity of Tattooing and Body Piercing

Many people seem content enough to go through life looking like everybody else. But for others, nothing seems more important than distinguishing how they look from the rest of society. Some set themselves apart by how they dress. Others show their individuality by how they wear their hair. Today, people with an independent streak have found another way to make themselves stand out from the crowd. These people are choosing tattooing or body piercing as their marks or distinctions. These ancient forms of body art are among the most popular trends of the past decade.

The history of decorating the body in these ways goes back thousands of years. Originally, members of a tribe would undergo elaborate tattooing, piercing, or scarring to signify membership in the group. For example, natives of some islands in the South Pacific would tattoo their faces with intricate designs, while ancient tribes in other lands would cut parts of their bodies to leave scars in particular designs.

Tattoos and piercings have been around in more modern times, too. However, until the past 15 years or so, they have been largely associated with bikers and sailors. They held little appeal for the average person. Until recently, tattooing wasn't even legal in many states.

Details and examples have been added. In this amplified form, the introduction provides a more complete direction for the reader. Instead of two sentences, the introduction is now seven.

The order of these paragraphs has been adjusted to maintain chronological order.

Additional details and examples appear throughout about the history of tattooing.

Additional details and examples appear throughout about the history of tattooing.

Unrelated sentences have been removed, so the paragraph is now unified.

Note the additional specific details about the state of tattooing until recently.

The only way for many people to get a tattoo was to find an illegal tattoo parlor or travel to a country where tattooing was legal. Either way, people endured great pain and risked infection just to decorate their skin.

Note the additional specifics about safety measures as well as the added transitions.

All that has changed today, however. For one thing, tattooing and piercing are legal in many areas throughout the country. Tattoo parlors are now licensed and inspected regularly to make sure they are sanitary. The instruments used are sterilized, in many cases using the same technology that is used to purify dental instruments.

The general language is now specific, and it is supported with several detailed examples of people who seek tattoos.

But the biggest change is the clientele who seek tattoos and piercings. No longer is it just outlaws looking to get a skull on their biceps. Today bikers and rock stars share the waiting room at the tattoo parlor with teenaged football players, fraternity members, stockbrokers, and other ordinary people looking for something that will mark them as different from the next person.

Nobody knows how long this new interest in tattooing and piercing will last. Right now, though, the number of people with colorful skin decorations and nose, tongue, and belly button jewelry seems to be on the increase. It looks like none of the new tattoo parlors will be closing any time soon.

The conclusion is now three sentences rather than two. The details are more specific. As a result, the conclusion brings the essay to a more complete, logical close.

As the notations show, developing this final draft involved making a significant number of changes. The point here is that writing isn't a one-shot process. Often you will find that you need to work through several drafts before your essay is as effective as it could be.

When you compare the first draft of this essay with the final draft, one thing is obvious. Revision works, as the following instructor's comments indicate:

> *Congratulations—this revision is excellent. You have improved the paper in so many ways. The new supporting examples make your point about these trends much clearer. Your introduction is much more detailed and effective—it really prepares the reader for the rest of the essay. You've also adjusted the presentation of some of the paragraphs so that they are in chronological order. In each paragraph, you've made sure to include solid examples and plenty of transitions. And your conclusion does a great job of encapsulating the significance of your essay. You should definitely include a clean copy of this essay in your portfolio. You should also submit it to be included in the class anthology that we will be putting together at the end of the course.*

Challenge 14.8 **Evaluating a First Draft Essay**

After all pairs of students have completed Challenge 14.8, ask them to discuss their answers with the class. Do all pairs agree about what is effective and what areas need further work? As an alternative, have individual students complete this exercise as an instrument to evaluate their understanding of the concepts in this chapter.

1. Read the following first draft essay on home shopping. Then, working with a partner, answer the questions that follow on a separate sheet of paper.

The Home Shopping Phenomenon

(1) Home shopping has become a popular alternative for busy shoppers.

(2) There are a couple of different home shopping networks. All the shows seem to work the same, a host introduces the product, describes it, and posts the price. Then a phone number is flashed. You can get a good deal on collectibles and sports memorabilia.

(3) The home shopping networks sells designer clothing, including outerwear and shoes. Occasionally, a fashion designer comes on to discuss the clothing while fashion models walked around displaying them.

(4) Celebrities come on to sell her own brands of fragrances or jewelry. Cheap rings, bracelets, or necklaces can cause allergic reactions. The celebrities chat with the hosts and encourage viewers to buy.

(5) What makes it all especially convenient is that you never have to leave your couch to shop. When you see what you want on the screen, you dial the 1-800 number, give a credit card number, and the item is on it's way to your door. No crowded mall parking lots, no long lines at the registers.

(6) In today's fast-paced world, it's often hard to find time to go out shopping, especially during the holiday season.

a. Evaluate the introduction and conclusion. In what way would you suggest they be changed?

b. Which paragraph in this draft supplies the best support for the thesis? Explain why.

c. Turn again to the reader assessment checklist (page 205) and the proofreading checklist (page 207), and use them to assess and edit this first draft. On a separate sheet of paper, make a list of problem spots and errors that need to be addressed.

2. Imagine that the writer has asked you to write a critique (a short paragraph of around ten sentences) in which you indicate (a) what is good in the essay and (b) what still needs work. On a separate sheet of paper, write that critique.

 DEVELOPING AN ESSAY

 Audio 14.4

New terms in this chapter	Definitions
● essay	● a multi-paragraph writing that deals more extensively with a subject than a paragraph does
● introduction	● a paragraph that opens an essay, providing a clear thesis and engaging the reader
● thesis	● the sentence in the introduction that specifies the main subject of the essay and the writer's attitude or position on it
● body	● the series of paragraphs that provide support and illustration for a thesis
● conclusion	● a paragraph that closes the essay, summarizing the essay's point and bringing it to a logical and appropriate end
● anecdote	● a brief, entertaining story, often used to make a point An anecdote may be used effectively in an introduction or a conclusion.
● rhetorical question	● a question designed not to be answered, but to provoke thought or discussion A rhetorical question may be used effectively in an introduction to engage readers.
● amplifying	● the process of providing additional, specific details and examples

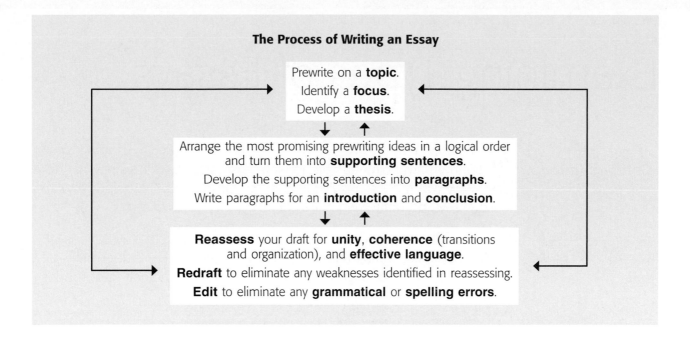

The Process of Writing an Essay

Prewrite on a **topic**.
Identify a **focus**.
Develop a **thesis**.

Arrange the most promising prewriting ideas in a logical order
and turn them into **supporting sentences**.
Develop the supporting sentences into **paragraphs**.
Write paragraphs for an **introduction** and **conclusion**.

Reassess your draft for **unity**, **coherence** (transitions
and organization), and **effective language**.
Redraft to eliminate any weaknesses identified in reassessing.
Edit to eliminate any **grammatical** or **spelling errors**.

Chapter 15

Examining Types of Essays

Getting Started... **Q:** I know I am going to have to write essays on a wide variety of subjects. How can the lessons I've learned so far in this book help me write these essays no matter what the subject?

 Audio 15.1 **A:** You will find that understanding the characteristics of the various modes will make writing an essay on any subject much easier. You'll soon find it simple enough to include the perfect combination of modes to fulfill your purpose and create an effective essay.

Overview: Understanding How to Use the Modes to Develop Essays

 Audio 15.2 As the previous chapters point out, effective writing fulfills a purpose while communicating the writer's ideas. Chapters 5 through 12 show how to use the various **modes** or techniques to develop paragraphs: *narration, description, example, process, definition, comparison and contrast, cause and effect,* and *division and classification.* Chapter 13 explains that *argument* differs from the modes because it is a **purpose** or aim, not a mode.

Chapter 14 introduces the essay, explaining how this type of writing differs from a paragraph. Probably the most significant difference is in scope. When you write an essay, you deal with a subject in far greater detail than you can with a single paragraph. To write an essay, you actually use a number of modes in combination. This chapter explores ways to use the modes to help you create effective essays.

> ***In this chapter, you will learn how to use the modes to write***
> - narration essays
> - description essays
> - example essays
> - process essays
> - definition essays

214

- comparison and contrast essays

- cause and effect essays

- division and classification essays

- argument essays

The Relationship between Your Purpose and the Modes

Audio
15.3

Video
15.1

Video
15.2

Video
15.3

Understanding the connection between your purpose and the modes is crucial. As Chapter 1, "Ensuring Success in Writing," explains, people write to fulfill one of three purposes: to *inform,* to *entertain,* or to *persuade.* The modes are your means to fulfill the purpose you choose. In most essays, one mode will dominate, with other modes providing additional support.

Open your favorite magazine, and read a few of the articles. Perhaps one article reports recent findings about fat consumption and heart disease. In this case, the writer's primary purpose is to *inform* readers about the data linking diet and heart disease. Another article takes a lighthearted look at the shopping habits of U.S. families. In this case, the writer's primary purpose is to *entertain.* Of course, not all writing that entertains is intended to make you laugh. For example, a story about a small town raising money to send a promising young musician to college might not be funny, but it would entertain you. Finally, the primary purpose of an article asserting that nuclear power plant construction should be halted until safety concerns are addressed would be to *persuade.*

Look closely at the articles, and you will also see the modes in action. For example, the article about the scientific research might feature *cause and effect* as its primary mode to link coronary disease to diet. It might also feature such modes as *example* to develop specific case studies and *definition* to explain the terms used in the article.

The essay about people's shopping habits might have *division and classification* as a primary mode to explain the various ways that people approach shopping. It might also include such modes as *description* to create images of the shoppers in action and *narration* to follow them as a video-camera might.

The essay about nuclear power plants might feature *example* as the primary mode to illustrate the dangers at specific nuclear power plants. It might also feature *process* to show how nuclear power plants generate electricity. In addition, it might include *cause and effect* to show how radiation leakage could affect nearby residents' health. Finally, it might include *description* to show in vivid terms the destruction that could result from a nuclear accident.

Most essay assignments will call for one particular mode to dominate. Remember, though, that you will actually use a combination of modes to fulfill your purpose. The rest of this chapter will examine ways to use the modes to develop essays.

Have students bring in newspaper or magazine articles, and, working in small groups, identify the writer's purpose and the modes used. As an alternative, ask students to identify the purpose and supporting modes of the model essays in this chapter or in the essays in Part Seven, "Connecting: Responding to Reading." Readings in Part Seven can also serve as examples of specific modes in action.

Using Narration to Develop an Essay

Students may find it useful to review the Recaps at the end of Chapters 5 through 13 as they examine the types of essays in this chapter.

As Chapter 5 explained, writing that relates a series of events is *narration*. For example, if you were writing a paper about your first day at a new job, narration would be a natural choice. Like narrative paragraphs, **narrative essays** are usually arranged in *chronological order*. In addition, narrative writing is often presented from the *first person point of view* (using *I, me, my*), although it may be written in the *third person* (using *he, she, her, him, they*). In order to be effective, a narrative essay must also be *unified* and include plenty of specific details for support.

Examining a Narrative Essay

 Audio 15.4

Take a look at this narrative essay about the first day at a new job:

Lost and Confused: My First Day in the Hospital Halls

(1) Any change is difficult to handle. Beginning a new job is no different, especially when the new job involves more responsibility than the last one. My first day as a dietary aide at City Hospital was such an ordeal, I don't think I'll ever forget it. <u>By the end of that first workday, I was so frustrated and embarrassed that I never wanted to return.</u>

(2) <u>Here's how it all began.</u> At 6:45 on that first morning, half an hour before my shift officially started, I entered the imposing building and headed to the first floor, where the kitchen and cafeteria are located. In spite of my nervousness, I found my time card and punched in. I then introduced myself to the woman sitting at the desk next to the time clock and asked her where I should go next. She told me to report to Mr. Javits in the kitchen.

(3) <u>Just as I was beginning to think I would make it through the day, I met Mr. Javits, and I became convinced that I wouldn't.</u> First, he looked at me and yelled, "Who the hell are you?" After I explained that I was a new dietary aide, he quickly assigned me to set up and deliver morning meals to the entire cardiac unit. Mr. Javits warned me that any mistake in preparation or delivery of the meals could have serious consequences for the patients. By the time he finished talking, my shirt was soaking wet.

(4) <u>My first round of deliveries was a disaster.</u> The cardiac unit was being renovated, and the painting crew had removed the room numbers. I figured that once I identified one room, I would be able to find the rest easily. The rooms weren't arranged sequentially, however, so I had to personally identify all the patients and go through their menu choices with them. As a result, I fell behind schedule at each room. I began to know what salmon must feel like as they try to swim upstream.

(5) <u>The worst was yet to come.</u> When I returned to the cafeteria with the trays, Mr. Javits was waiting for me. He began yelling and demanding to know where I had been. As I pointed to the notice on the wall an-

nouncing the renovation of the cardiac floor, I accidentally bumped Mr. Javits' hand and spilled his cup of coffee over the front of his uniform. At this point, I felt that the end of the day would never come.

(6) <u>The lunch shift was almost as bad as the breakfast shift.</u> This time, Mr. Javits assigned me to the orthopedic area. To distribute the meals, I had to travel the length of the hospital and take two different sets of elevators. By the time I collected the trays and returned them to the cafeteria, I was late again. My shift was scheduled to end at 2:30, and it was almost 3 P.M. Fortunately, Mr. Javits had already left.

(7) After this kind of start, it is hard to believe that I soon became an expert on the hospital. Within a couple of days, I knew my way around the building. After a month, Mr. Javits even put me in charge of training new workers. I also found out that most of my co-workers had had similar experiences on their first day working in the hospital cafeteria. Like me, they had been completely intimidated at the prospect of something new.

Activity
15.1

Challenge 15.1   **Analyzing the Sample Narrative Essay**

After students complete each Challenge in this chapter, ask them to diagram the relationship between the thesis and topic sentences (see page 198) and explain the method of arrangement. This can be a journal assignment, a small group exercise, or a class activity.

Refer to the sample narrative essay above to answer each question.

1. Reread the introduction of the essay. Underline the thesis.

2. Underline the topic sentences of paragraphs 2 through 6. In an essay, each topic sentence relates back to the thesis, but it also serves as a building block for its own main idea. Work with a partner to analyze the role of these sentences. On a separate sheet of paper, explain (a) how each topic sentence in the essay is related to the thesis and (b) how each one is developed by its supporting paragraph information.

3. On the same sheet, list transitional expressions that help establish the sequence of events.

Discovering Connections 15.1

1. Using the essay above to guide you, write a narrative essay on your first day at a new job or on one of the following topics:
   a. a time when you witnessed a crime
   b. the best phone call you ever received
   c. a family (or school, team, or club) reunion
   d. a time you were caught in a lie
   e. an accident you witnessed

2. Exchange your draft with a partner. Evaluate the essay using the narrative essay checklist on page 218. Write your answers on a separate sheet of paper, and then return the essay and your assessment to the writer.

3. Using your reader's comments to guide you, revise and redraft your narrative essay.

Narrative Essay Checklist

- ☐ Does the introduction set the scene for the sequence of events to follow?
- ☐ Is a *first person* or *third person* point of view used consistently?
- ☐ Does the paper follow chronological order? If a flashback has been used, has the switch in time been made clear for the reader?
- ☐ Is the essay unified, with all supporting ideas and examples related to the main idea? Circle any material that isn't unified.
- ☐ Are there enough specific details and examples to guide the reader? Put a ✓ next to any spot that you'd like to know more about.
- ☐ In your judgment, what is the best part of this essay? Explain.

Using Description to Develop an Essay

Audio 15.5

As Chapter 6 showed, writing that uses words to paint a picture of a scene, individual, or experience is *description*. Effective description emphasizes specific sensory details, as it would in an essay about an unusual experience. **Descriptive essays** often combine both *objective* description (observable details and sensations) and *subjective* description (the impressions that the details and sensations create within the writer). In addition, descriptive writing often uses *spatial order* to organize details for the reader.

Fast Fact Not all people find it easy to provide sensory details when they use description. People who suffer from *anosmia,* for example, would have difficulty, as would those who suffer from *ageusia.* A person who has *anosmia* is unable to detect smells, and a person who has *ageusia* is unable to taste.

Examining a Descriptive Essay

Take a look at this descriptive essay about an unusual experience:

Bright Lights, Loud Music:
Not Your Average Planetarium Show

Discuss the techniques the author uses to develop this introduction. Ask students if they think the introduction is effective and why.

(1) If someone invited you to a planetarium show, what would you expect? You are probably thinking of seeing pictures of stars and constellations. You may even be thinking, "Boring!" At first, that's what I thought when two friends invited me to a show at the Hayden Planetarium in New York City, but I was mistaken. <u>On that night my eyes and ears were exposed to more sensation and stimulation than they had ever been exposed to at one time.</u>

(2) I was on vacation visiting friends who go to school in New York City, and they told me that we were going to the planetarium that evening. I had been to other planetarium shows before, and I had always enjoyed seeing images of the various constellations projected on the inside of a dome. I was a bit surprised, though, that my friends, two of the wildest people I have ever met, had picked such a tame adventure. After all, it was Friday night, and we were in one of the most exciting cities in the world.

(3) When we arrived at the planetarium at 8:30, I began to wonder exactly what was going on. About 300 people, most of them under twenty-five, were just starting to stream through the doors under the sign that said "Genesis Laser Show." Like the other planetariums I had been in before, this one had rows of soft seats that reclined so that people could comfortably look up at the ceiling. I settled into my seat just as the lights began to dim, and a display of the various constellations appeared on the ceiling. **O O O**

(4) That's when I got my second surprise of the night. The constellations on the ceiling suddenly disappeared, plunging the planetarium into darkness. Then a series of speakers practically exploded with a tune by the rock group Genesis. Suddenly, rows of red, blue, and yellow lasers projected a series of brilliantly colored designs that moved to the beat of the music all across the inside of the domed ceiling. **O O O**

(5) The music was so loud that I felt as if I were on stage with the group. I could feel each beat of the drum reverberate right through my body. I felt as if I was completely surrounded by the music through all fifteen of the songs. **S S S**

(6) But what I was hearing was nothing compared to what I was seeing. The designs pulsed and glowed and blinked all across the dome. Even if I tried to close my eyes, the light seemed to break through my eyelids. It was as if those lasers had some magical power to force me to keep looking. It was like being able to look at the sun without having to worry about burning your eyes. The light was brilliantly bright, yet cool and comfortable at the same time. **O S S S S**

(7) Finally, after forty-five minutes, the music stopped, the lights came on, and the crowd filed out the double doors into the hot July night. I felt exhausted but exhilarated at the same time. Outside, the bright street lights and the blaring New York City traffic seemed mild compared to what I had just experienced. **O S S**

(8) An evening that I expected to be merely calm and pleasant turned out to be a true adventure for my ears and eyes. Now every time I hear a song by Genesis on the radio, I immediately think back to one of my favorite vacation memories, a night filled with sound and light.

Challenge 15.2 **Analyzing the Sample Descriptive Essay**

Refer to the sample descriptive essay (pages 218–219) to answer each question.

1. Reread the introduction of the essay. Underline the thesis.

2. Working with a partner, analyze paragraphs 2 through 7 of the essay. On a separate piece of paper, explain how each one develops this thesis. Rate these six paragraphs according to how effectively they use description: 1 = very effective; 2 = somewhat effective; 3 = not effective.

3. Working with the same partner, bracket each sentence of description in paragraphs 3 through 7. In the margin, write *S* next to each sentence of subjective description; write *O* next to each sentence of objective description.

4. Does the essay use spatial order? On your paper, explain where and how it is used.

Discovering Connections 15.2

1. Using the sample descriptive essay to guide you, write an essay on an unusual experience of your own or on one of the following topics:
   a. a normally busy place, now deserted
   b. a physical injury or bout with illness
   c. the feeling of being alone
   d. a unique restaurant, deli, bakery, or bar
   e. what you see in a painting or photograph

2. Exchange your draft with a partner. Evaluate the essay using the descriptive essay checklist below. Write your answers on a separate sheet of paper, and then return the essay and your assessment to the writer.

3. Using your reader's comments to guide you, complete the final draft of your descriptive essay.

Descriptive Essay Checklist

- ☐ Does the introduction engage the reader? Does the thesis prepare you for the event to be described?
- ☐ Does the essay include effective use of both objective and subjective description?
- ☐ Are the paragraphs arranged so that the reader can picture the scene being painted? Explain.
- ☐ Does each paragraph feature a number of specific, concrete sensory details to support the thesis?
- ☐ In your judgment, what is the best part of this essay? Explain.
- ☐ Which detail or example would be even better if it were expanded? Why?

Using Example to Develop an Essay

Audio
15.6

As Chapter 7 discussed, *example* uses specific instances to illustrate, clarify, or back up some point you've made. An **example essay** would be a natural choice to discuss various superstitions. When you write an essay that relies heavily on this technique, make sure that the examples you include are *relevant* and *specific*. In addition, *amplify*—provide enough examples to develop your main idea fully. Don't forget to take advantage of the transitional expressions *for instance* and *for example* to alert your reader that a specific example is to follow.

Examining an Example Essay

Consider this example essay about superstitions:

As students read this essay, ask them to underline or highlight the transitions that the author uses. Ask what order the author uses to arrange the examples and whether this order is effective.

Superstitions: The Irrational Beliefs That Influence Our Behavior

(1) All cultures seem to have some beliefs that can be thought of as superstitions. All over the world, people believe that doing or possessing certain things can bring them good luck or cause them bad luck. The most common groups of superstitions involve objects that can bring good luck, behaviors that can influence luck, and actions that can cause bad luck.

(2) The belief in good luck charms is one of the best-known superstitions. Many people keep special objects that they believe will somehow keep them safe or provide an extra edge. For some people, the good luck charm is a particular shirt or key chain. For others, the good luck charm is the more traditional rabbit's foot or four-leaf clover.

(3) In addition to lucky objects, many people believe that performing certain rituals can provide good luck. If you've ever watched a professional sporting event, you've probably seen players performing a series of movements. Sometimes a basketball player will take a certain number of bounces—no more, no less—before shooting a foul shot. Some baseball players, while waiting for a pitch, will adjust their equipment, from batting helmet to wristbands to gloves, always in the same order. Regardless of the particular actions, the players perform them because they believe they will bring them good luck.

(4) Other well-known superstitions are those bits of advice to ward off bad luck passed down from generation to generation. For instance, from childhood, people are often told that breaking a mirror will bring seven years' bad luck. Others warn us not to walk under a ladder, not to open an umbrella inside a house, and not to let a black cat cross our paths. Of course, no evidence exists that any of these things cause bad luck, but people often follow these directions, just to be sure.

(5) Exactly why people believe in superstitions is difficult to understand. Maybe it is because life in general is so uncertain. In any case, when you notice people holding a special object, performing some little ritual, or following some old directive, wish them luck. They need it, or at least they think they do.

Challenge 15.3 **Analyzing the Sample Example Essay**

Refer to the sample example essay above to answer each question.

1. Working with a partner, analyze paragraphs 2 through 5 of the essay. On a separate piece of paper, summarize the example each presents to support the thesis that there are several common groups of superstitions.

2. Working with the same partner, analyze each example. On your paper, list the number of the paragraph that you find most effective. Explain why its example is effective.

Discovering Connections 15.3

Activity
15.2

1. Using the example essay to guide you, write an essay on superstitions or rituals you follow or have witnessed or on one of the following topics:
   a. college challenges
   b. dating complications
   c. proper manners
   d. ways to save money
   e. duties as a pet owner

2. Exchange your draft with a partner. Evaluate the essay using the example essay checklist below. Write your answers on a separate sheet of paper, and then return the essay and your assessment to the writer.

3. Using your reader's comments to guide you, complete the final draft of your example essay.

Example Essay Checklist

☐ Does the introduction spell out the concept or principle to be illustrated?

☐ Are all the examples directly connected to the thesis? Put a ✓ next to any example that you feel is not relevant.

☐ Are all the examples specific? Put an * next to any example that you feel needs to be made more specific.

   ☐ Are there enough examples to support the thesis? Write *for example* or *for instance* next to any passage that you think could use another example.

   ☐ In your judgment, what is the best part of this essay? Explain.

   ☐ Which example would be even better if it were expanded? Why?

Using Process to Develop an Essay

Audio
15.7

Chapter 8 introduced *process*, the writing technique used to explain how to do something, how something occurs or is done, or how you did something. For instance, an essay explaining how to burn a CD would clearly be a **process essay**. When you are explaining how to do something, you should use the *imperative mood* to address the reader directly. The imperative mood is usually not appropriate for other types of process writing. If you were writing an essay explaining how acid rain affects the environment or an essay detailing how you investigated your family history to create a family tree, you would not address the reader directly. Many process essays are organized in linear order, using transitional words such as *first, next, then, afterward,* and so on. Be sure that each step describes a small and manageable part of the task, and that you warn your reader about any particularly difficult or potentially confusing steps.

Examining a Process Essay

Weblink
15.1

Consider this essay, which explains the process of creating a CD:

The Burn That Saves You Money: Creating Your Own CD

At one time, if you wanted to play recorded music, you listened to a vinyl record. Then came eight track tapes and then cassette tapes. These innovations improved sound quality and made listening more convenient. But the development of the compact disc has taken sound quality and convenience to an even higher level. At the cost of about $18, however, CDs can be expensive, especially if you aren't interested in all the songs. Now there's a solution to this problem. <u>The answer is to create or burn your own CD, a simple process that requires a computer, a CD burner, a blank CD, and a little bit of your time.</u>

<u>To begin the process,</u> decide on the song or songs you want to copy and then put the CD into the CD drive on your computer. <u>Now</u> put a blank CD in the CD burner. Some CD burning programs auto-start, but if yours doesn't, just open the program from the start menu.

The menu that appears when the program begins will ask which type of CD you want to make. Select audio. <u>At this point,</u> you'll be asked about burn speed. Higher speeds generally increase the chances for a faulty CD burn, so you might want to select a low or moderate speed for this first time.

Once you have selected a burn speed you'll be asked to select from three commands: *test, copy,* or *test and copy.* Choosing *test and copy* is the best alternative because it will identify any corrupted material and keep the new disc free from problem audio tracks. At this point, you can also choose to copy the source material to your hard drive. Having the track on your computer is a good idea, just in case you encounter difficulty and need the backup copy.

When you've completed these steps, a screen, split horizontally into two windows, will appear. In the top window, a list of the tracks of the source CD will appear. The bottom window will be blank. Click and drag the audio tracks you want to copy from the top window to the bottom. Repeat this step for each audio track you want to add to the blank CD.

With all the tracks you want to copy in the lower window, look at the toolbar at the top of the screen. Click on the button with a red circle that says "Create CD." Now just let the computer do the work. Depending on how many audio tracks you are copying, the actual burning will take somewhere between 20 and 60 minutes. When the new CD is complete, the computer will eject it, and you'll have your own personalized CD, with just the songs you want.

The process of burning a CD may seem a little confusing at first, but after one time you'll be turning out CDs like a pro. Your reward for your efforts will be a collection of CDs containing all the songs you want, at a fraction of the cost. How can you lose?

Challenge 15.4 Analyzing the Sample Process Essay

Refer to the sample process essay above to answer each question.

1. Working with a partner, find and underline the thesis in the introduction.

2. What are the steps of burning a CD? List them in order on a separate sheet of paper.

3. Find and underline transitional expressions that help establish linear order in the essay.

4. With your partner, evaluate each step in the process. Do you need more information about any steps? What questions would you ask the writer to get the information you need?

Discovering Connections 15.4

1. Using the sample process essay to guide you, write your own essay that tells how to carry out a process such as changing a flat tire. If you prefer, write on one of the following:

    a. how to build a campfire

    b. how a natural phenomenon—a thunderstorm, a tornado, a tsunami (tidal wave)—occurs

    c. how to make a bed

    d. how to balance a checkbook

    e. how you conducted a study or experiment

2. Exchange your draft with a partner. Evaluate the essay using the process essay checklist below. Write your answers on a separate sheet of paper, and then return the essay and your assessment to the writer.

3. Using your reader's comments to guide you, complete the final draft of your essay.

Process Essay Checklist

- ☐ Does the introduction identify the procedure or technique to be presented?

- ☐ Is the reader addressed directly through the imperative mood (*you*)? Is it appropriate for this essay? Why?

- ☐ Are the steps presented in linear order? Underline any step that is out of order, and then draw an arrow to the spot in the essay where it actually belongs.

- ☐ Is each step simple and clear? Put a ✓ next to any step that you think should be divided or explained further.

- ☐ In your judgment, what is the best part of this essay? Explain.

- ☐ Which detail or example would be even better if it were expanded? Why?

Using Definition to Develop an Essay

Audio
15.8

Chapter 9 introduced *definition,* the writing technique used to identify the essential characteristics or qualities of an object, location, or individual. An essay setting forth the characteristics of road rage, for example, would use definition. To write a **definition essay,** you need to recognize the *elements of an effective definition:* The term is placed in its appropriate class and then differentiated from the other elements in its class. In general, you should provide a *working definition* in the introduction and then build an *extended definition* throughout the body of the paper. This is done by supplying *clear, specific,* and *detailed* examples and illustrations. At the same time, take into consideration both the *denotation,* the literal meaning of the term, and its *connotations,* additional subjective or emotional impact it will have on readers. In addition, you should present the material you include in an order that enhances understanding.

Examining a Definition Essay

Look at this essay, which defines road rage:

As they read, ask students to identify sections of this essay that include other modes: narration, example, description.

Road Rage: The Anger That Can Kill

(1) You've probably witnessed the behavior yourself. You are in a car someplace and you are stalled in traffic. After a minute or two, someone behind you begins honking the horn, revving the engine, and yelling and swearing out the window. In some cases, the driver gets out of the car and walks up to where the traffic is stalled and begins yelling and gesturing. Sometimes, the behavior escalates until the driver is pounding or kicking the other car and perhaps physically fighting with other drivers. This kind of behavior occurs often enough that it has a name. It's called road rage.

(2) Occasionally becoming annoyed while driving is normal. People aren't always as careful as they should be when they drive. Also, construction, accidents, and rush hour traffic can often slow progress on the roads to a crawl. But when simple annoyance turns into burning anger, that is road rage.

(3) One thing that makes road rage different from normal annoyance is the degree of emotion involved. When road rage hits, it's not as if there has been a gradual build-up. Instead, road rage is more like the sudden eruption of a volcano. At one moment, a person seems calm, and at the next, that person is completely transformed, screaming, gesturing wildly, and sometimes threatening whoever has caused the problem.

(4) When people suffer from road rage, they seem unable to differentiate between minor and major problems. It makes no difference if the delay is caused by a simple breakdown or a serious multi-car crash. The reaction is the same intense, unreasonable anger.

(5) Unfortunately, road rage isn't limited to honking a horn repeatedly or yelling at others. Often, road rage leads to serious violence and sometimes death. News reports frequently include stories of road rage that escalates until someone has been killed. A few years ago, for example, a driver became convinced that another driver had cut him off. He chased the other car at high speed, forced it off the road, and then used a hunting bow to shoot the other driver to death.

(6) Life is full of annoyances, and people need to learn how to deal with them, especially when it comes to driving. But for some people, irritation quickly grows to enormous proportion. When it does, it becomes road rage, and the results are bound to be unpleasant and, sometimes, deadly.

Challenge 15.5 **Analyzing the Sample Definition Essay**

Refer to the sample definition essay above to answer each question.

1. Find and underline the thesis in the first paragraph. On a separate sheet of paper, write the term that is defined and the writer's working definition of it.

2. Working with a partner, analyze paragraphs 2 through 5. First, underline the topic sentence in each. Then study the way each topic sentence is developed. On your paper, summarize the way each paragraph develops or extends the definition.

3. Why are the supporting paragraphs presented in this order? On your paper, explain why you think the writer organized the paper in this way. Would you change the order? Tell how and explain why.

Discovering Connections 15.5

1. Using the essay on page 226 to guide you, write an essay on your definition of good manners or on one of the following topics:
   a. a sports (or music, surfing, dance, computer, religious) fanatic
   b. a perfect date
   c. true charity
   d. success
   e. a masterpiece of literature, music, or art

2. Exchange your draft with a partner. Evaluate the essay using the definition essay checklist below. Write your answers on a separate sheet of paper, and then return the essay and your assessment to the writer.

3. Using your reader's comments to guide you, complete the final draft of your definition essay.

Definition Essay Checklist

- [ ] Does the introduction introduce the term or principle to be defined?
- [ ] Does the essay begin with a working definition and then develop an extended definition?
- [ ] Does the extended definition reflect both the denotations and connotations of the term defined?
- [ ] Are the supporting details and examples clear and specific? If you find any that are too general or too abstract, suggest a way to clarify or sharpen them.
- [ ] Are the supporting paragraphs effectively arranged in an appropriate order? Explain.
- [ ] In your judgment, what is the best part of this essay? Explain.
- [ ] Which detail or example would be even better if it were expanded? Why?

Using Comparison and Contrast to Develop an Essay

Audio
15.9

As Chapter 10 discussed, the writing technique that focuses on examining alternatives is called *comparison and contrast. Comparison* means examining similarities, and *contrast* means examining differences. For example, an essay evaluating electronic books versus printed texts would call for comparison and contrast. In your college courses, you will often be called on to explain how two people, objects, or phenomena are alike or how they are different. With most comparison and contrast essays, restrict your focus to *two subjects* that have some common ground. In addition, be sure you have an adequately developed *basis of comparison* using at least three points.

To arrange a **comparison and contrast essay**, use either a *block format* or an *alternating format*. For the block format, include a thesis in your introduction, and then present the first point, the second point, the third point, and so on for Subject A. Afterward, examine the first point, the second point, and the third point for Subject B.

For the alternating format, examine the two subjects at the same time. In other words, after the introduction, address the first point for Subject A and Subject B, then the second point for Subject A and Subject B, then the third point for Subject A and Subject B, and so on. This method is helpful for longer papers. It may be hard for a reader to keep all the points for Subject A in mind while reading the second half of such a paper. See pages 141–143 for illustrations of both the block and alternating formats.

Fast Fact Where can you see comparison and contrast at work on a regular basis? Pick up any copy of *Consumer Reports,* a magazine that has earned its solid reputation by closely examining competing brands of everything from food products to appliances.

Examining a Comparison and Contrast Essay

Weblink
15.2

Here's a comparison and contrast essay that contrasts electronic books and printed books:

E-Books? Will They Replace the Printed Text?

(1) For hundreds of years, when people picked up a book, they could count on one thing. The book would look pretty much like books have looked since the development of the printing press. But consumers now have a new choice: electronic books. The development of E-books makes it possible for people to read on a special computerized reader, about the size of a hardcover book. The text to be read can be downloaded from the Internet or accessed from a CD. The manufacturers promise that this innovation will change the reading habits of readers in the 21st century, but I don't agree. When it comes to cost, availability of texts, and convenience, you can't beat an old-fashioned printed book.

(2) One thing that manufacturers of E-book technology don't talk much about is the cost. It's true that E-books themselves, whether online or from a CD, are fairly inexpensive, often costing under $10. The computerized device needed to be able to read the E-books, however, costs between $250 and $500. The price is expected to decline as the technology improves, but right now, that's a hefty investment to read a book. In contrast, when it comes to traditional books, even a hardcover best seller costs under $30. Paperbacks and discounted hardcover books

cost far less. Of course, with an actual book no additional device is needed, either. All you have to do is open the cover and turn the pages.

(3) Another concern for consumers is the availability of titles. At this point, some publishers have just begun creating electronic versions of their books. Experts believe it will be a number of years before the number of available E-book titles comes anywhere close to matching the number of print books. Therefore, even if you were to make the investment in an E-book reader, you might still not have access to electronic versions of all the books you want to read. You would never face such a situation with traditional books. Major traditional booksellers like Barnes and Noble have thousands of titles on hand. If you can't find it on their shelves, you can order it from Internet giant Amazon.com. If a printed book exists, someone can get it for you, and often within a few days.

(4) When it comes to reading, maybe the biggest concern for the average person is convenience. In this category, E-books don't yet measure up well. For example, the screens of many of the systems can be hard to read, and battery life can be a problem. In addition, the devices require careful handling to avoid damaging their sensitive electronics. You don't have any of these concerns with a traditional book, however. What could be easier and more convenient? You don't have to worry about screen brightness or batteries. If you drop it, you just pick it up, dust it off, and resume reading. If you want to read at the beach or in the bathtub, go right ahead. If you spill something on it, just wipe off the page. It's just that simple.

(5) In today's world, computers continue to play an increasingly large role. In most cases, they make our lives better or easier in some way. But when it comes to reading, I don't think the computer has yet been able to improve on what already exists. For now, a traditional printed book is far superior to any electronic version.

Challenge 15.6 **Analyzing the Sample Comparison and Contrast Essay**

Refer to the sample comparison and contrast essay above to answer each question.

1. In the introduction, what point is made about E-books versus printed books? What does the introduction tell you about the purpose of this essay? Write your answers on a separate sheet of paper.

2. Working with a partner, analyze paragraphs 2 through 4. What bases of comparison are used to examine the two types of books? List the bases of comparison on your paper.

3. Still working with a partner, identify the format used to arrange this essay. On your paper, prepare a diagram like the one on page 140 in Chapter 10 to illustrate the organizational plan.

Discovering Connections 15.6

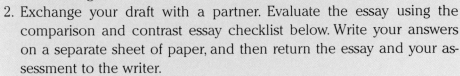

1. Using the essay just presented to guide you, write a comparison or contrast essay on selecting a laptop computer versus a traditional model or on one of the following topics:
   a. the typical family today versus the typical family twenty-five years ago
   b. two jobs you've held
   c. two dates you've gone on
   d. two politicians, musical groups, or professional athletes
   e. two religions
2. Exchange your draft with a partner. Evaluate the essay using the comparison and contrast essay checklist below. Write your answers on a separate sheet of paper, and then return the essay and your assessment to the writer.
3. Using your reader's comments to guide you, complete the final draft of your comparison or contrast essay.

Comparison and Contrast Essay Checklist

Activity
15.3

☐ Does the introduction specify the essay's focus and the subjects to be compared or contrasted?

☐ Does the essay concentrate on two subjects?

☐ Is a basis for comparison established and followed? Make sure that each characteristic or element is discussed in detail for each subject. Put a ✓ at any point where an element or characteristic is missing, and write *amplify* above any point that should be discussed in greater detail.

☐ Has the block format or the alternating format been used to arrange the paragraphs? Would the essay be more effective if it were arranged differently, for example, using block format instead of alternating format or vice versa?

☐ In your judgment, what is the best part of this essay? Explain.

☐ Which detail or example would be even better if it were expanded? Why?

Using Cause and Effect to Develop an Essay

Audio
15.10

Cause and effect, the writing technique you use to focus on what led to something or what happened as a result, is discussed in Chapter 11. Cause is *why* something occurred, and effect is the *outcome* or *consequence* of an occurrence. An essay in which you discuss how a new job has changed your life would be a cause and effect essay.

For a **cause and effect essay**, remember that most events or experiences have *more than one* cause and *more than one* effect. Therefore, don't oversimplify. Furthermore, be sure that any cause and effect relationships you suggest aren't actually *coincidence*—events that occur close to the same time by accident. Finally, arrange the various causes or effects you present in a logical order.

Examining a Cause and Effect Essay

Look at this essay about the various consequences of advancing to a more responsible job:

More Than a Promotion

(1) When I was about ten years old, I spent two weeks at my cousin's house just outside of Chicago. One day we went into the city with my aunt to see the department store that she managed. She showed us around the store and then took us up to her office. I sat quietly watching her make phone calls and instruct her staff on what she wanted done that day. After half an hour, I knew I wanted to do just what she did for a living when I grew up. Six months ago, I got my chance to fulfill my dream when I was made the night and weekend manager at a large drug store. Almost overnight, I went from simply doing my job as a part-time clerk to keeping the ten people I supervise happy and productive. The many changes my promotion has brought about have definitely made me a different person.

(2) One way the promotion has changed my life is financial. When I was a clerk, I worked twenty hours a week at $7 an hour with no benefits. After taxes, my weekly pay was about $115. As a manager, I work at least forty hours a week for a weekly salary of $500, and I have full insurance coverage. Since I've become a manager, I have been able to buy a car and save money on a regular basis. With a little luck, I should be able to afford to move out of my mother's house and into my own apartment in six months or so.

(3) My new responsibilities have also helped build up my self-confidence. At first, I almost didn't take the job because I wasn't sure I could handle the responsibility. My supervisor convinced me to take it by telling me that she wouldn't have recommended me if she didn't feel I was capable. After the first few weeks on the job, I found out something about myself that I had never realized. Not only was I able to handle responsibilities such as motivating other workers, setting work schedules, and doing the payroll, but I was actually good at all these things. Because of these successes, I'm more confident whenever I face a new task.

(4) Taking the promotion has also meant I had to grow up a lot. For one thing, I had to learn to budget my personal time. As a manager, I work almost twice as many hours as I did when I was a clerk. Furthermore, managers often have to attend meetings at night or on weekends and do paperwork at home. No longer do I have time to ride around with my friends. I also can no longer do things like call in sick when I just don't feel like working. A clerk might be able to get away with that, but a manager can't. Managers are paid to be responsible.

(5) I've also had to adjust to a new relationship with the people I supervise. Before, I was one of them, but now I'm their boss. I have to make decisions about such things as who has to work Friday and Saturday nights and who gets extra hours when business is good. I now also have to evaluate them every four months to see who gets merit raises and who doesn't. Some of the people I was friendliest with when I was a clerk barely talk to me now because I won't play favorites when it comes to schedules and raises. I sometimes feel guilty when I have to give someone a bad evaluation for job performance or lack of punctuality. I know that when I was a clerk, I sometimes was lazy and showed up late or left a few minutes early. But I'm a manager now, and I have a responsibility to make sure that my company is getting its money's worth.

(6) I've been a manager for four months now, and I can honestly say that I enjoy the job far more than I ever expected to. I like earning more money, and the idea that people are willing to put their trust in me has made me more confident overall. I also like the fact that I've learned to take responsibility. I know that, overall, this job has helped to make me a better person.

Challenge 15.7 **Analyzing the Sample Cause and Effect Essay**

Refer to the sample cause and effect essay above to answer each question.

1. What event is the focus of this cause and effect essay? Does the essay explore the causes for this event or the consequences of it? Write your answers on a separate sheet of paper.

2. Working with a partner, analyze paragraphs 2 through 5 of the essay. First, underline the topic sentence of each paragraph. Then, on your paper, write the specific changes that occurred in the writer's life.

3. Imagine that the focus of this essay was on causes, not effects. Consider the causes of the promotion—diligence at work, a positive attitude, natural leadership ability, and a supervisor's confidence. Working with your partner, write a cause and effect paragraph that focuses on these causes. (Remember—your thesis should state the effect and reveal that you will explore the causes.)

Discovering Connections 15.7

1. Using the essay "More Than a Promotion" to guide you, write an essay on the cause(s) or effect(s) of a change in employment, schools, or personal relationships. If you prefer, choose one of the following topics:

   a. your interest in music, art, or sports

b. an automobile, motorcycle, or bicycling accident you were involved in or witnessed

c. a major environmental disaster like an oil spill from an ocean-going tanker, a volcanic eruption, a forest fire, or an earthquake

d. lack of consumer confidence in a product or company

e. cheating in high school or college

2. Exchange your draft with a partner. Evaluate the essay using the cause and effect essay checklist below. Write your answers on a separate sheet of paper, and then return the essay and your assessment to the writer.

3. Using your reader's comments to guide you, complete the final draft of your cause and effect essay.

Cause and Effect Essay Checklist

- ☐ Does the introduction indicate a focus on either cause or effect?

- ☐ Are the cause and effect relationships supported with enough examples and details to avoid oversimplification? If you feel more specific details are required, write "I'd like to know more about _____" in the margin next to the poorly explored passage.

- ☐ Does the essay distinguish between direct and related causes and effects? Underline any details that seem like coincidences rather than true causes or effects.

- ☐ Are the supporting paragraphs effectively arranged in a logical order?

- ☐ In your judgment, what is the best part of this essay? Explain.

- ☐ Which detail or example would be better if it were expanded? Why?

Using Division and Classification to Develop an Essay

Audio
15.11

Chapter 12 discussed the writing techniques you use to analyze a complex subject. *Division* is separation of a subject into its component parts. *Classification* is arrangement of the subcategories into *groups* on the basis of some principle or characteristic. An essay in which you discuss types of televised sports would use both division and classification. When you write a **division and classification essay**, choose a logical *method of classification*, and keep the groupings as *distinct* and *complete* as possible.

Fast Fact If you were asked to classify the greatest writers of all time, what choices would you make? When the editors and staff of *The World Almanac and Book of Facts 2001* were asked, these are the choices making up their top ten list: 1. John Steinbeck; 2. William Shakespeare; 3. Pat Conroy; 4. Jane Austen; 5. Charles Dickens; 6. Barbara Kingsolver; 7. Emily Dickinson; 8. Henry James; 9. Emily Bronte; 10. Thomas Hardy.

Examining a Division and Classification Essay

Weblink
15.4

Look at this essay about the various types of televised sports:

Television: The Sports Fan's Paradise

(1) One of the most popular activities in the country is watching sports. Most sports fans would prefer to attend games in person, but cost and other life responsibilities keep most people from attending more than a few games a year. Fortunately, for sports fans, network television and cable outlets make it possible to watch some kind of sporting activity on a daily basis. Most of the sports available on television for fans to enjoy can be grouped in four basis categories.

(2) The first group is probably the type that has been featured on television the longest: major league professional sports. This group includes Major League baseball, NFL football, NBA basketball, and NHL hockey. More recently, WNBA basketball and Major League soccer have also enjoyed wide exposure. Fans love these games because of long-standing rivalries between teams and the opportunity to see a sport's elite players.

(3) Another category that draws fans includes individual sports like golf and tennis. These sports, unlike the major league group, have no organized leagues or seasons. Instead, fans have the chance to see the stars of these sports compete all year long in both national and international competitions.

(4) College sports represent another group of televised sporting events. This category of sports remains among the most watched, especially football and basketball games. The various Bowl Games at the end of the football season and the NCAA March Madness basketball tournament games are among the ratings leaders each year.

(5) The fourth group is one that has grown in popularity over the past 10 years. This category might be termed alternative sports. These sports, which once appeared only on such sports cable stations such as ESPN and ESPN2, have gradually become more mainstream. Events such as the World's Strongest Man contests, bodybuilding events, and Ultimate Frisbee games now often appear for wider audiences to enjoy. The events that have attracted the most attention in this group are various extreme sports featured in competitions like the X-Games. These competitions feature stunt BMX biking and skateboarding events as well as such innovations as street luge.

(6) Certainly, there are other popular sporting events besides those in these categories. NASCAR racing, bowling, Summer and Winter Olympics, and skating competitions all draw big television audiences. But these four categories do include the sports that American fans find most captivating, at least for now. Stay tuned.

Discuss the techniques the author uses to develop a conclusion. Ask students if they think the conclusion is effective and why.

Challenge 15.8 **Analyzing the Sample Division and Classification Essay**

Refer to the sample division and classification essay above to answer each question.

1. Find and underline the thesis statement in the first paragraph. Then, on a separate sheet of paper, list the essay's subject and the classes into which it is divided.

2. Find and underline the topic sentences of paragraphs 2 through 5. Working with a partner, analyze these paragraphs. On your paper, name each class of televised sports and describe the characteristics of each type that is discussed.

3. Working with a partner, identify another category of televised sports or subdivide one of the existing categories. Then write a paragraph that illustrates or explains this new classification.

Discovering Connections 15.8

1. Using the essay on televised sports to guide you, write a division and classification essay on types of movies or sitcoms, or on one of the following topics:
   a. types of rock 'n' roll music
   b. kinds of shoppers at the mall
   c. types of responsibilities a first-year college student faces
   d. types of indoor sports
   e. kinds of clothing in your closet

2. Exchange your draft with a partner. Evaluate the essay using the division and classification essay checklist below. Write your answers on a separate sheet of paper, and then return the essay and your assessment to the writer.

3. Using your reader's comments to guide you, complete the final draft of your essay.

Division and Classification Essay Checklist

☐ Does the introduction specify the focus of the discussion and indicate an emphasis on either division or classification?

☐ Are the elements distinct and complete? If you think any divisions or classes need to be subdivided further to make them clearer or more specific, write, "I'd like to know more about _____" in the margin next to them.

☐ Does the essay feature a logical, consistent method of analysis throughout?

☐ Are the supporting paragraphs presented in an effective order?

☐ In your judgment, what is the best part of this essay? Explain.

☐ Which detail or example would be even better if it were expanded? Why?

Writing an Argument Essay

Audio
15.12

As Chapter 13 explained, *argument* isn't a writing technique or a mode. It is writing that uses a combination of modes to persuade. An **argument essay** takes a firm stand on an issue and then attempts to convince readers to agree with that stand. For example, an essay suggesting that child beauty pageants are harmful to participants would be an argument because its purpose would be to convince readers to accept the writer's viewpoint.

Video
15.4

When you write an argument essay, it's important to make your stance on the issue clear in the introduction. In the body, supply at least three convincing reasons why readers should agree with you. Back up each reason with sound support. Should you draw any of your supporting information from a document or individual, always acknowledge your source. Also, adopt a reasonable tone; avoid an emotional or condescending view. It's often better to use qualifying terms such as *most, rarely,* and *frequently* rather than absolute ones such as *all, never,* and *always.* In addition, make sure that your argument essay has a logical line of reasoning and that you have avoided the errors in logic known as *logical fallacies.* See the list of logical fallacies on pages 173–174. Finally, be sure to arrange your points in a logical order, such as order of importance.

Examining an Argument Essay

Look at this argument essay about child beauty pageants:

The Beast Is the Beauty Contest

(1) On Christmas Day, 1996, six-year-old JonBenet Ramsey was murdered in Boulder, Colorado. Shortly after her tiny body was discovered, the story of her brief life became public, especially details about her involvement in child beauty pageants. Within a few weeks, the spotlight was turned on the pageants themselves. The public quickly learned that at these events, held in nearly every state across the United States, children as young as ten months old don makeup and fancy clothing to compete for crowns and titles. Despite the large number of people who claim that these events are a form of innocent fun and recreation, these reports clearly indicate that children's beauty pageants can have a negative and lasting effect on their young participants.

(2) Proponents of child beauty pageants, including promoters and parents of contestants, compare these events to other childhood pastimes such as Little League or playing "dress-up." They argue that the competitions can help youngsters develop poise and self-confidence. A lucky few, they point out, even earn scholarships or launch careers in acting or modeling. However, these people are ignoring the fact that the lessons these competitions teach are damaging to a child's future.

(3) The first lesson children learn is that personal appearance is everything. The "dressing-up" that they do in these pageants is far from

innocent play. Right from the start, they see that the right hairstyle, the most stylish outfit, the perfect makeup win the prizes. How you look, not who you are, is what is truly important in this world. Unfortunately, this harmful attitude may stay with a child well into adulthood, coloring the way she interacts, forms relationships with others, and values herself.

(4) Those who compare beauty pageants with Little League are also forgetting that beauty, unlike a sport, cannot be developed and improved through practice. If a child's appearance does not conform to society's standards for beauty, then winning the competition is out of the question. Children who fail at these events may learn to feel unattractive, rejected, and worthless before they even have a chance to develop an adult body. Moreover, even those who enjoy success as children may run into trouble when they reach adolescence. When they grow taller or heavier, or when they develop acne, they may no longer meet society's standards for beauty. If they have based their sense of self-worth on their appearance, then these children are in danger of developing disorders such as depression, anorexia, or bulimia.

(5) The most damaging aspect of child beauty pageants, however, is that children learn to display themselves as sex objects before they can possibly understand what sexuality is all about. As the news reports have shown, many of the contestants have to appear before adult judges in elaborate makeup, scaled-down versions of provocative dresses, and bathing suits. They also learn to flirt and use their bodies to attract attention. In a world in which sex crimes against children make daily headlines, such practices are deeply disturbing and potentially harmful.

(6) Although it is tempting to argue that child beauty pageants should be banned, that is not a good long-term solution. Instead, parents should think carefully about the lessons and values that children are likely to learn from these events. If parents really considered the consequences of those lessons, then the competitions might die a natural death. Vermont, for example, failed to produce a Miss America candidate a few years ago because the women in that state refused to enter a contest that judges people on looks and other superficial qualities.

(7) If parents do not want their children to grow up thinking that appearance is all that matters, then they should keep their children away from activities that twist and exploit a child's natural desire for attention. Beauty contests are far more likely to make children, like poor JonBenet, the victims of adult desires than to deliver the fame and fortune they seem to promise.

Challenge 15.9   Analyzing the Sample Argument Essay

Refer to the sample argument essay above to answer each question.

1. Find the thesis statement in the first paragraph. Write it on a separate sheet of paper.

2. Working with a partner, analyze the paragraphs in the body of the essay. How many reasons does the writer give to support this thesis? On your paper, list each reason.

3. Analyze the support given for each reason. Which is most convincing to you? Which reason is least convincing? Working together, brainstorm further support for this reason (or develop an alternative reason) and revise or replace this paragraph.

Discovering Connections 15.9

1. Using the essay on child beauty pageants to guide you, write an argument essay taking a stance on whether beauty contests—for adults or children—are harmful. If you prefer, choose one of the following topics instead, and write an argument essay in which you support or refute it:

   a. Presidential elections should be decided on the basis of the popular vote only.
   b. Dress codes should be imposed in public schools.
   c. Attendance should be mandatory in college classrooms.
   d. People receiving government assistance should be required to perform community service in return.
   e. A C average should be a minimum requirement for high school and college students who wish to participate in sports.

2. Exchange your draft with a partner. Evaluate the essay using the argument essay checklist below. Write your answers on a separate sheet of paper, and then return the essay and your assessment to the writer.

3. Using your reader's comments to guide you, complete the final draft of your argument essay.

Argument Essay Checklist

Weblink
15.5

- [ ] Does the introduction clarify the stance on the issue?
- [ ] Are there at least three reasons, properly documented if necessary, to support the stance?
- [ ] Is the tone throughout the essay respectful and concerned? Put a ✓ next to any sentence in which the tone seems inappropriate.
- [ ] Is the presentation logical? Underline any errors in logic.
- [ ] Does the essay feature qualifying terms rather than absolute ones when appropriate?
- [ ] Are the supporting paragraphs effectively presented in emphatic order or some other method of arrangement? Explain.

☐ In your judgment, what is the best part of this essay? Explain.

☐ Which detail or example would be even better if it were expanded? Why?

 EXAMINING TYPES OF ESSAYS

Activity
15.4

New terms in this chapter	Definitions
● **narrative essay**	● a multi-paragraph writing that relates a sequence of events in story fashion
● **descriptive essay**	● a multi-paragraph writing that uses concrete, sensory language to recreate a scene, situation, or individual
● **example essay**	● a multi-paragraph writing that uses specific instances to illustrate, clarify, or back up a thesis
● **process essay**	● a multi-paragraph writing that spells out how to do something, how something is done, or how you did something
● **definition essay**	● a multi-paragraph writing that specifies the characteristics or elements of some object, location, or individual
● **comparison and contrast essay**	● a multi-paragraph writing that examines similarities and differences between two or more subjects
● **cause and effect essay**	● a multi-paragraph writing that considers reasons leading to some situation or condition or the outcomes or consequences of an event or phenomenon
● **division and classification essay**	● a multi-paragraph writing that analyzes a complex subject either by separating it into its component parts or by grouping its parts into categories Some division and classification essays use both approaches.
● **argument essay**	● a multi-paragraph writing that takes a firm stand on an issue and then attempts to convince readers to agree with that stand

The Relationship between the Purpose of an Essay and the Modes

Determine the *purpose* of the writing task	Choose your *main* mode	Employ *supporting* modes
Example topic: What is sexual harassment? purpose: to **inform** →	Identify the characteristics of sexual harassment using **definition**. +	Support your definition using **example**, **cause and effect**, and **comparison and contrast**.

Chapter 16

Adjusting Your Process: Timed Writing and Summaries

Getting Started... **Q:** I'm beginning to feel comfortable and confident when I can tackle a
Audio 16.1 writing assignment at home, on my own schedule and based on my own
ideas. But what do I do when I have to complete some kind of timed
writing or condense what someone else has written?

Activity 16.1 **A:** To feel comfortable and confident with timed writings and summaries, you first need to understand the nature of the specific writing
task. Once you do, it's a simple matter of choosing and applying the
strategy—the particular *approach*—that matches the task.

Overview: Understanding How to Deal with the Pressure of Timed Writing

Audio 16.2

Video 16.1

It doesn't make a difference what field you are talking about—sports, business, music, medicine, law, or engineering. With few exceptions, people do
their best work best when they have time to think through a task, to plan,
concentrate, and reexamine it. As the previous chapters illustrate, taking
your time to plan, concentrate, and reexamine helps you produce your
best writing.

No matter what field, however, people will face situations in which they
have no time to spare. In these situations, they must *adapt* the process they
normally follow so that they can perform effectively in less-than-ideal conditions. A journalist, for example, must be prepared to deviate from a
planned series of questions if the interview takes an interesting turn but
the deadline is looming. An athlete on the field or court must make imme-
diate adjustments if someone misses a shot or commits a foul. An actor
must be ready to ad-lib if another actor "drops a page," leaving out crucial
dialogue. An EMT must be prepared to treat the victim of an auto accident
in the vehicle if the person is trapped. In each of these cases, the situations

Weblink
16.1

give these people little choice. If they don't adapt, they won't succeed. It's as simple as that.

With writing, you will also occasionally face circumstances calling for you to adjust the process you follow. For instance, answering an **essay question** and completing a **writing assessment** generally involve tight time constraints. Preparing a **summary** may not always involve a strict time limit, but it does require you to work in a different direction. Instead of developing your own ideas in full detail, you reduce someone else's ideas to their essence.

Weblink
16.2

This chapter discusses strategies that will lead you to success whenever you must

- answer essay questions

- complete a writing assessment

- prepare a summary

Fast Fact Don't panic at the panic you might feel when you see an essay question. Your goal should be to reduce your apprehension, not eliminate it completely. That's because research suggests that a little test anxiety can actually enhance performance.

Answering an Essay Question Effectively

As a group discussion topic or journal assignment, ask students to describe essay test situations they have faced or know they will face. Have essay tests been difficult? Why? What specific challenges do these tests present? What questions do students have about how to answer essay questions successfully? Encourage students to share strategies or return to their questions after reading this chapter.

An **essay question** is a specific writing assignment given as part of an examination. It calls for a clear, concise, multi-paragraph response within a limited period of time. Answering an essay question isn't all that different from completing other writing tasks. Your goal is the same: to work through the writing process and to communicate to your reader what you know about the question.

Keep this point in mind: An essay question can be easier to answer than multiple-choice or short-answer questions. Because these nonessay kinds of questions focus on single bits of information, they can focus you on what you *don't know.* But essay questions test you on what you *do know.* In other words, an essay question provides you with the opportunity to demonstrate in detail what you understand about the subject.

Developing an effective strategy for writing a successful essay answer involves following three simple steps: **preparation**, **anticipation**, and **rehearsal**. Consider this figure:

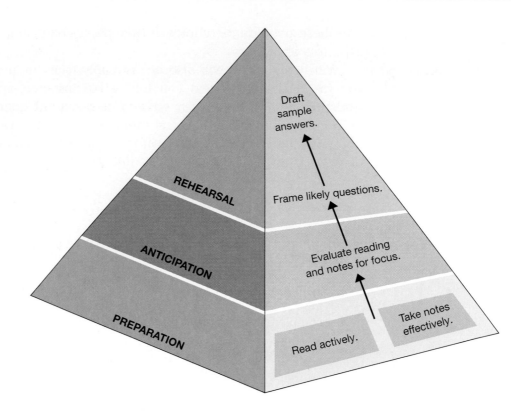

As the figure shows, the three steps are closely connected. Preparation gives you the foundation for the rest of the process, and anticipation gears you up for rehearsal.

Preparation

The best way to *prepare* yourself to answer essay questions is to apply yourself in your coursework. Learn the information you will need during an exam by (1) reading actively and (2) taking effective classroom notes.

Active Reading   To get the most out of your assigned reading, read *actively.*

Suggest students try these reading strategies with this chapter. Then ask students to compare and discuss the summaries they have prepared. Are all the summaries similar in content?

- Read the introduction and conclusion to each chapter for an overview of the material.
- Preview all headings and subheadings in the selection. They highlight main ideas in the chapter.
- Read any *charts, boxed areas,* or *lists.* They summarize important information.
- If the book or article you are reading belongs to you, highlight or underline information you judge to be important—*specific* names, dates, distances, conditions, and so on.
- Look for any *definitions* and information presented *in order* (*first, second, third,* and so on). Be alert for *transitional expressions* and words like *important, crucial,* and *vital* that signal important material will follow.
- Write any points that you feel are especially important in the *margin* or in your *notebook.*

- Use the material you have highlighted or underlined to prepare a *summary*, a greatly reduced version of the original, expressed in your own words. A discussion of summary writing appears later in this chapter.

Effective Note-Taking   To take effective notes, follow these guidelines:

- Filter what you hear in class. Concentrate on recording information that is new to you or that you are unsure of.
- Assume that any material your instructor puts on the board is important.
- Listen when your instructor uses words like *important, vital, crucial,* and so on. These words are clues to what the instructor feels you need to know.
- Focus on definitions and material the instructor repeats or presents in sequence (*first, second, third*).
- Keep your notes as neat and orderly as possible, writing on every other line so that you always have room to add information.
- Use abbreviations or your own personal shorthand system.
- Reread your notes an hour or so after the class is over and flesh out, clarify, and tie together the information.
- Write a summary, interpretation, or analysis of the material.

Anticipation

Activity 16.2

In addition to learning your course material, it is wise to think strategically about an upcoming essay exam. Begin by evaluating your notes and readings to identify the topics your instructor might use for essay questions. To *anticipate* these essay questions, consider the following guidelines:

- Focus on the ideas you've identified as important in your reading.
- Note the focus of any questions or checklists your instructor has provided or discussed.
- Reconsider your classroom notes, paying particular attention to material that your instructor described as *important, crucial, vital,* and so on or that he or she repeated several times.
- Discuss important ideas with your classmates. This will help you clarify your own thinking, and it may provide additional perspectives on those ideas.

Rehearsal

Once you have identified the information you feel is likely to be included on the examination, you should *rehearse*. In this context, rehearsal means creating several **practice questions**, or the type of query that might appear on an exam, and then drafting answers.

Drawing Up a Practice Question   Imagine, for instance, that you are studying for an essay exam in your introductory psychology class. Over the past two weeks, you've discussed a great many topics in relation to the sensation of pain. From your notes and reading, you have identified the psychological factors involved in the perception and management of pain as the likely focus of essay questions.

With this focus identified, you create the following practice question, intended to be answered within 20 minutes or so:

> Research in the area of pain management suggests that psychological factors are involved in the perception of pain. What are three psychological factors that influence pain perception? Be sure to provide a concrete example for each factor. Also, what are three treatments that are commonly used to manage pain? Again, be sure to provide a concrete example for each treatment and an explanation as to why the treatment works.

On a real exam, you must first identify exactly what the essay question is asking you to do. Even though you have developed the sample question yourself, you should follow the same strategy. That way, each practice session will mirror the process you will follow during an exam.

In this case, the question asks you to supply a total of *six* points, with a specific example of each. *Three* of the points must be psychological factors, and *three* must be common treatments. With this information identified, you are ready to move to the next step: answering a practice question.

Developing a Sample Essay Answer   As indicated above, you have set a time limit of 20 minutes to develop an effective answer, so you need to get to work. Incidentally, with such a tight time constraint, don't expect that your writing will be perfect. Perfection takes hours, not minutes. Instead, plan to do the best writing you can under those circumstances. Concentrate on making your answer *complete* in terms of **content** and *correct* in terms of **form**.

Here are the steps you should follow when answering an essay question. The time estimate is based on the 20 minutes set aside to develop an effective answer:

Students sometimes are not sure of what the question asks them to do. Before they begin to compose, suggest that they identify *key words* in the question, such as *describe, define, argue, compare;* explain the *process;* and note if the question asks them to provide *examples*.

Prewriting (5 minutes or so)

- Read the question thoroughly, making sure you understand what is expected.
- On a piece of scrap paper, the back of the exam, or the inside cover of the exam book, use the technique you like best for developing preliminary information that will address the question.
- Identify the most promising ideas and the direction you want to follow with your answer.

Composing (10 minutes or so)

- Write a sentence—your *thesis*—that expresses the direction you want to take by restating or responding to the question.
- Express your most promising preliminary ideas in sentence form. In certain cases, list your most important ideas first, in case you run out of time.
- Write on every other line so that you'll have room to add information or make changes or corrections later.

Revising (5 minutes or so)

- Reevaluate what you've written, making sure you have addressed the question.
- Proofread, concentrating on the particular errors you are prone to.
- Make any last-minute corrections or additions by drawing a line through the material to be deleted and placing a caret (^) below the line and inserting the new material immediately above it.

EXAMPLE

> A second factor that influences pain is ~~different cultures~~.
> a person's culture
> ^

Here again is the essay question:

> Research in the area of pain management suggests that psychological factors are involved in the perception of pain. What three psychological factors influence pain perception? Be sure to provide a concrete example for each factor. Also, what are three treatments commonly used to manage pain? Again, be sure to provide a concrete example for each treatment and an explanation as to why the treatment works.

Now, here are the prewriting ideas you've generated in response to the question:

> OK, 3 psy. factors? 1. anxiety, like worrying about a date making a headache worse 2. culture, your culture tells you how to react, like men not complaining 3. experience with pain, the pain you have from an injury or from having a baby makes you expect to have the same pain or more the second time. Now 3 effective treatments? 1. acupuncture is used to treat things like headaches—works by releasing endorphins 2. medication-pain killers like percodan following surgery work by keeping Substance P from being released—the result is euphoria 3. cognitive therapy, learning new ways to deal with

pain. Instead of saying "I can't stand this pain," tell yourself "the pain is only temporary"—works because people feel more in control

As you can see, the prewriting material includes the six points the question calls for. Now you need to express your focus—the *thesis*. In this case, you can simply restate the main idea of the question, that psychological factors play a role in both the perception and treatment of pain:

Research shows that psychological factors are involved in pain perception and treatment.

At this point, convert your promising prewriting ideas into correct sentences that support or illustrate your thesis. Always take a moment to identify the best order to present the material. The question itself indicates how you should arrange your supporting ideas. For example, the essay question about pain asks first about perception and second about treatment. Therefore, it makes sense to present your points in that order. Once you have completed your answer, take a few moments to reevaluate what you have written. Does it actually answer the question? Finally, proofread and neatly make any last-minute corrections.

Here is the resulting answer, with annotations pointing out the key features.

Clear thesis expressing the main idea —— Research shows that psychological factors are involved in pain perception and treatment. (One factor) that will make

First psychological factor with an example —— pain worse is anxiety. For example, if you have a headache and feel anxiety that the headache will prevent you from going on a date, the headache is likely to hurt even more than it originally did. A (second factor) that influences pain is a person's culture

Second psychological factor with an example —— ~~different cultures~~. Different cultures have different rules ——**Note correction**
about how people should react to pain. For example, some cultures believe that men should not complain about pain. A man from this type of culture might feel severe pain but still not see a doctor because he doesn't want to seem

Third psychological factor with an example —— unmanly. A (third factor) that is involved in pain perception is past experience. For instance, if a woman has a lot of pain when her first baby is born, she is likely to expect a lot of pain when her second baby is born. This expectation,

based on past experience, is likely to make the pain ~~worst~~ worse ⌐ Note
because you experience what you expect to experience.   └ correction

Three types of pain treatments are acupuncture,

First pain treatment with an example —
medication, and cognitive therapy. (Acupuncture) involves inserting small needles into the body to lessen pain. For example, if you get migraines, you might go for acupuncture in order to lessen the pain. It is thought that acupuncture works by closing gates and releasing endorphins.

Second pain treatment with an example —
(Medication) involves taking drugs to stop the pain. For example, if you have surgery, you might take percodan. It is thought that medications work by blocking the release

Third pain treatment with an example —
of Substance P and creating euphoria. (Cognitive therapy) involves learning new ways to interpret pain. For example, the person with back pain might be taught to think, "This pain is only temporary" instead of "I can't stand this pain." It is thought that cognitive therapy lessens pain by increasing the person's sense of control.

As you can see, this process led to an effective answer that directly addresses the question. It identifies and illustrates three psychological factors related to pain perception and three methods to treat pain. The points are presented in sentence form and arranged in a logical order. In short, the answer is simple, clear, complete, and correct, exactly what you need to get the best grade possible on your essay examination.

Exercise 16.1   Focus on Answering Essay Questions

1. What advantage do you gain when you face an essay question rather

   than a multiple-choice or short-answer question? _____

   With an essay question, you have the opportunity to demonstrate what you know

   about a subject. With multiple-choice or short-answer questions, you might not know

   the one fact being asked, even though you know many other related facts.

   _____

2. How do reading actively and taking effective class notes prepare you to deal with essay questions? _____

   Reading actively and taking effective notes prepare you to answer essay questions

   because these two techniques help you identify the most significant material from

   your reading and from classroom discussion and presentation.

3. What are two ways you could identify likely essay question topics for a class you are currently taking? _____

   Answers will vary.

Challenge 16.1 **Developing and Answering Essay Questions**

As an alternative, have students develop essay questions based on the material in one of the chapters in Part One, "Starting Out."

1. Imagine that you are preparing for an essay examination in one of your courses. Go through the reading you have done and your relevant classroom notes. On a separate sheet of paper, list the key information that appears in both your reading and your notes.

2. From this list of material, develop three essay questions. Write each question on a separate sheet of paper.

3. Prepare answers of 200 to 300 words for each question. Write each answer immediately under the appropriate question.

4. Exchange your questions and answers with a partner. Evaluate the material you receive, using the essay answer checklist below. Return the answer and your assessment to the writer.

5. Correct the problem spots your reader has identified in your answers.

Essay Answer Checklist

☐ Does the essay answer directly address the question being asked? Make a note in the margin next to any point that does not relate to the question.

☐ Should any section of the answer be amplified? Put a ✓ next to the section that needs more explanation.

☐ Are there any mistakes in spelling or usage? Circle any errors.

Fast Fact A few years ago, Educational Testing Services of Princeton, New Jersey, quietly changed the name of the college admissions test familiar to thousands upon thousands of high school students, teachers, and parents. What was once known as the Scholastic *Aptitude* Test is now the Scholastic **Assessment** Test. What a difference a word makes—or does it? To most people, it's still just the SAT.

Completing a Writing Assessment Effectively

U.S. college students today face a number of challenges that their counterparts a decade ago generally did not. Among these new challenges in an increasing number of institutions are mandated entrance and exit assessments. Students must complete these tests to be admitted to a particular course or to receive credit for it. In many cases, these evaluations require that a student prepare an effective writing in accordance with specific guidelines on a particular topic, often within a given time period.

To succeed with this kind of **writing assessment**, you do many of the same things you do when you answer an essay question. Consider these guidelines:

If your institution has a writing assignment of some kind, consider discussing its particulars in class.

- Be realistic when facing a timed writing assessment. Don't expect to write a perfect paper. Your job is to write an essay that proves your overall competence. In most cases, the resulting writing won't be the best paper you are capable of. That takes much more time than the assessment conditions are likely to allow.
- Make sure you understand exactly what the assessment is asking you to do. That means carefully examining the topic and any information accompanying it before you begin developing ideas. Underline or write down key words and phrases from the assignment that suggest the direction or focus you are expected to take. These words and phrases will guide you as you begin to work through the writing process.
- Pay close attention to time management. Once you know how much time you will have, divide the writing process up accordingly. For instance, if you have 50 minutes total, devote approximately 10 minutes to prewriting and approximately 25 minutes for composing. You will then have at least 10 minutes for the revising stage.
- Make sure that the paper you write is as complete and correct as possible under the circumstances. Doing so means including an introduction with a clear thesis, several body paragraphs supporting that thesis, and a conclusion closing the paper effectively. Make any last-minute corrections or additions neatly the same way you do with answers to essay questions.

Understanding the Five-Paragraph Essay

Activity 16.3

Because you are working such a tight time line, you may want to consider using a format called the **five-paragraph essay**. With this format, you use the thesis to specify three main points relative to the topic. Then, in the next three paragraphs—the body of the essay—you discuss each subtopic, one per paragraph. Finally, you add a conclusion that restates the thesis and three supporting points.

In the previous chapter, you may have noticed that some of the sample essays followed this format. For example, here again is the essay from pages 221–222 on superstitions, with annotations highlighting the format:

Superstitions: The Irrational Beliefs That Influence Our Behavior

As an alternative, refer students to "E-Books? Will They Replace the Printed Text?" on pages 228–229.

Thesis

(1) All cultures seem to have some common beliefs that can be thought of as superstitions. All over the world, people believe that doing or possessing certain things can bring them good luck or cause them bad luck. The most common groups of superstitions involve objects that can bring good luck, behaviors that can influence luck, and actions that can cause bad luck.

Three points relative to superstitions

Discussion of point ①, with examples

(2) The belief in good luck charms is one of the best-known superstitions. Many people keep special objects that they believe will somehow keep them safe or provide an extra edge. For some people, the good luck charm is a particular shirt or key chain. For others, the good luck charm is the more traditional rabbit's foot or four-leaf clover.

Discussion of point ②, with examples

(3) In addition to lucky objects, many people believe that performing certain rituals can provide good luck. If you've ever watched a professional sporting event, you've probably seen players performing a series of movements. Sometimes a basketball player will take a certain number of bounces—no more, no less—before shooting a foul shot. Some baseball players, while waiting for a pitch, will adjust their equipment, from batting helmet to wristbands to gloves, always in the same order. Regardless of the particular actions, the players perform them because they believe they will bring them good luck.

Discussion of point ③, with examples

(4) Other well-known superstitions are those (bits of ③ advice to ward off bad luck) passed down from generation to generation. For instance, from childhood, people are often told that breaking a mirror will bring seven years' bad luck. Others warn us not to walk under a ladder, not to open an umbrella inside a house, and not to let a black cat cross our paths. Of course, no evidence exists that any of these things cause bad luck, but people often follow these directions, just to be sure.

Conclusion with a sentence recapping the three points

(5) Exactly why people believe in superstitions is difficult to understand. Maybe it is because life in general is so uncertain. In any case, when you notice people (holding a special object,) ① (performing some little ritual,) ② or (following some old directive,) ③ wish them luck. They need it, or at least they think they do.

Examining a Sample Writing Assessment

Writing assessments appear in a variety of forms. One common type presents a brief excerpt. Students are instructed to read the excerpt and then respond to a specific writing assignment related to the passage. Here's an example of this type of assessment:

Exit Assessment

Name _____

Student ID Number _____

Date _____

Read the following passage and then write an essay of 300 to 500 words on one of the options that follow the excerpt. Use the pages attached to this sheet. You have 50 minutes to complete all work. Your essay will be judged on its overall effectiveness. Therefore, try to develop a writing that features

- a clear thesis

- solid supporting examples, effectively arranged

- appropriate, specific language

- correct usage, spelling, and punctuation

Assignment

Consider this excerpt from Isabel Briggs Myers' *Taking Type into Account in Education.*

Children in all the grades should be given maximum opportunity to learn the things that have meaning and interest for them in terms of their own kind of perception and their own kind of judgment. To the extent that they are given this opportunity, they gain not only in interest but in application and intelligence as well. People of any age, from six to sixty, apply themselves with greater vigor to the task in hand when they are interested. People of any age are more intelligent when they are interested than when they are bored.

Now choose *one* of the following options and develop a writing that responds to it:

Option A: Based on Briggs Myers's statement and your own experiences with school, what specific changes would you suggest to make sure that every school becomes the kind of place where more learning takes place?

Option B: In this passage, Briggs Myers uses the word "interest" several times to emphasize how important this element is to success in learning and in life. Consider the examples Briggs Myers provides along with what you've seen, read, and experienced. Then give your view of the types of interest or curiosity that can lead to success in school and the world beyond.

The guidelines provided indicate that the maximum amount of time available to complete the writing is 50 minutes, so it's important to get to work immediately. When an assessment assignment offers more than one possibility, the first step is to select the option that holds the most appeal. Then spend about 10 minutes doing some prewriting.

Here, for example, is some brainstorming in response to Option B:

Different kinds of curiosity lead people to success

- Curiosity about the world

kids want to learn about clouds and rain,

about plants and animals

about where they come from

helps them understand their relationship with the rest of the world

- Curious about their families

what about their history

any famous ancestors?

- Interest in letters and numbers

in school kids are curious about letters and numbers

understand them, words and math suddenly make sense—like magic

- Curiosity about what jobs involve

what their parents do for jobs

what other kinds of workers do, what equipment they use

leads them to careers

Thesis: The types of interest that most help to foster success include curiosity about nature, about letters and numbers, and about the work world.

With prewriting material generated, the next step is to use the most promising ideas to create a draft. Under these time constraints, about 20 minutes is available. As with any essay, an assessment essay should include an introduction, several body paragraphs, and a conclusion. The introduction should restate the significance of the assignment itself and include a clear thesis. The body paragraphs should explain and support that thesis, and the conclusion should reemphasize the point being made in the essay. Then, once the draft is complete, the remaining time can be used to revise, making any last-minute corrections or additions.

Here is the assessment essay that results from this process, with annotations to illustrate the key points:

In this excerpt from Taking Type into Account in Education, Isabel Briggs Myers discusses what children need in order to develop fully. She believes that keeping children interested in what they are doing is the secret to success.

Thesis indicating three key points about the topic

In my view, the types of interest that foster success

include (curiosity about nature,) (about letters and numbers,) ① ②
and (about the work world.) ③

Discussion of point ①, with examples

① From the time they are able to speak, children ask questions about the world around them. They are clearly interested in all aspects of their world. They want to know where clouds come from, why sometimes ~~its~~ it's cold and sometimes ~~its~~ it's not, and why dogs and cats don't get along. — **Note corrections**

As they learn the answers, they ask more questions. Life is confusing. If people are going to succeed, they need to be able to understand their environment. With each round of questions and answers, children begin to be able to make sense of the world around them. This curiosity drives them toward success. — **Note addition**

Discussion of point ②, with examples

② Curiosity about letters and numbers is also crucial if children are going to succeed in school and in the world outside school. Before ~~they~~ children can read, write, and calculate, — **Note correction**

letters and numbers must seem like some kind of magic. But once they learn how letters form words and how numbers are added and subtracted to solve problems, the mystery is solved. Suddenly they can understand what a book or sales receipt means. When this interest is stimulated, they are developing — **Note addition**

the foundation for a life of success.

Discussion of point ③, with examples

③ A third type of interest that will lead to success is a curiosity about the world of work. It starts when kids ask their parents about their jobs. As they are growing up, they also observe other people at work. For example, from day to day, they see police officers, pediatricians, teachers, construction workers, etc. doing their jobs. Then they are introduced — **Note addition**

to other occupations in school, learning about the tools and specialized equipment involved. These experiences draw children to consider different career possibilities. Once they become interested in a particular field, they have a reason to concentrate more in school. As a result, their prospects for future success are enhanced.

Conclusion with a sentence recapping the three points

> Many things influence whether children eventually succeed in life. One of those things is making sure that children remain ~~curiosity~~ *curious*. In particular, (maintaining their interest in their environment,) (in language and mathematics,) and (in different career possibilities) gives them the best chance for future success.

Note correction

This writing assessment essay is effective for several reasons. For one thing, the introduction directly addresses the assignment and contains a clear thesis. For another thing, the body contains several supporting ideas expressed in detail. Finally, it has a conclusion that reemphasizes the points made in the essay.

As the annotations indicate, this assessment essay follows the format of the five-paragraph essay presented earlier. If the time available permits, however, always feel free to include more than three points about your subject. Think of three as the minimum number of points you need to present, and you'll be all set.

Exercise 16.2   **Understanding the Characteristics of a Writing Assessment**

1. Why is it important to be realistic when facing a timed writing assessment?

   If you hope to do your best possible work on a timed writing assessment, you are

   bound to be disappointed. Good writing demands time. Therefore, you need to be

   realistic—expect to do the best work you can under such circumstances rather than

   the best work you are capable of.

2. How does good time management lead to success with a writing assessment? Good time management skills lead to success with a writing assessment be-

   cause they enable you to budget time, allowing you to plan, develop, and revise a

   complete writing.

3. In your own words, explain the structure of the five-paragraph essay.

   With the five-paragraph essay, the introduction contains a thesis that notes three factors relative to the subject of the paper. Each of these factors is discussed, one at

a time, in the three paragraphs of the body. The conclusion then restates the main

and supporting ideas.

Challenge 16.2   **Completing a Writing Assessment**

You might want to conduct the assessment in class and then have a class discussion about it during the next class. Doing so will help normalize the experience for your students.

1. Here again is **Option A** of the sample exit assessment provided earlier:

> Based on Briggs Myers's statement and your own experiences with school, what specific changes would you suggest to make sure that every school becomes the kind of place where more learning takes place?

Now take 50 minutes and complete an assessment essay that responds to this option.

2. Exchange your completed assessment essay with a writing partner. Evaluate the essay you receive, using the writing assessment checklist below. Return the essay and your evaluation to the writer.

3. Correct any problem spots your reader has identified.

Writing Assessment Checklist

☐ Does the introduction have a clear thesis that directly addresses the topic or scenario assigned in the assessment? Write a brief note in the margin if you think the introduction is off target.

☐ Do all the paragraphs provide specific support for the thesis? Put a ✓ next to any paragraph that doesn't offer support.

☐ Does the conclusion restate the significance of what has been presented? Write a brief note in the margin next to the introduction if you think the conclusion doesn't bring the assessment to an effective close.

☐ Are there mistakes in spelling or usage? Circle any errors.

Fast Fact One magazine that operates on the principle that less is more is *Reader's Digest*, which has turned the process of summarizing writings into an art form. And people certainly seem to like it. *The New York Times 2001 Almanac* reported that in 1999 *Reader's Digest* was the third-best-selling American magazine, with a circulation of 12,962,369.

Writing an Effective Summary

As part of your studies, you will often have to take some document, identify the key points in it, and then express them in a greatly reduced form. The resulting writing is called a **summary**. In some fields, a summary is called an

Consider bringing in and distributing examples of summaries from a couple of fields: informative abstract at the beginning of an annual report and an excerpt from *Dissertation Abstracts.*

abstract or *précis.* Depending on the length of the document itself, a summary may be as little as five to ten percent of the original. You therefore need to focus on only the most important or significant points in the original. That way, you will produce a document that expresses the essence of the original.

As with an essay answer and a writing assessment, an effective summary is the product of a series of steps, which are listed below. Follow this process, and you'll find writing a summary much easier:

1. Read the original document *actively.*
   a. Read the title, introduction, headings and subheadings, conclusion, and other features designed to indicate the key points in the writing.
   b. Reread the writing, highlighting key ideas.
      ✓ Note any **signal words** emphasizing importance, for example, *crucial, vital, significant, prominent, extraordinary.* These words generally indicate the value the author has placed on the material.
      ✓ Note any charts, boxed information, or lists as well as specific names, dates, distances, amounts, conditions, and statistics. These elements often represent a brief version of what the writer considers important.

2. Make a list of the key ideas you've identified.
   a. Express these ideas in your own words. Consult a dictionary for any word in the original that is unfamiliar to you so that you express its meaning correctly.
   b. Write these ideas out in complete sentence form.

3. Eliminate the *least* essential ideas from your preliminary list.
   a. Avoid more than one reference to the same point.
   b. Trim or discard lengthy examples and explanations.
   c. Cut any material taken from footnotes.

4. Use the sentences you have written to create a draft summary.
   a. Include enough information so that the summary makes sense for someone who has not read the original.
   b. Present the material in your summary in the same order as the original document.
   c. Unless instructed otherwise, don't include your own opinion of the original.
   d. Provide transition wherever it is needed so that your draft seems like a coherent paragraph and not just a list of sentences.

5. Revise your draft summary.
   a. Make sure that the summary makes sense independent of the original.
   b. Make sure you have supplied sufficient transitions.
   c. Make sure you have eliminated any of your own commentary of the original.
   d. Make sure you have eliminated any errors.

Examining the Summarizing Process
of Preparing a Summary

Here is a passage from E. D. Hirsch's *Cultural Literacy: What Every American Needs to Know*. Creating an effective summary begins with the identification of the most essential information in the original, as the highlighted sections indicate:

As a journal entry, have students discuss their reaction to what Hirsch has to say.

My son assures me that his pupils are not ignorant. They know a great deal. Like every other human group, they share a tremendous amount of knowledge among themselves, much of it learned in school. The trouble is that, from the standpoint of their literacy and their ability to communicate with others in our culture, what they know is ephemeral and narrowly confined to their own generation. Many young people strikingly lack the information that writers of American books and newspapers have traditionally taken for granted among their readers from all generations. For reasons explained in this book, our children's lack of intergenerational information is a serious problem for the nation. The decline of literacy and the decline of shared knowledge are closely related, interdependent facts.

The evidence for the decline of shared knowledge is not just anecdotal. In 1978 NAEP [The National Assessment of Educational Progress] issued a report which analyzed a large quantity of data showing that our children's knowledge of American civics had dropped significantly between 1969 and 1976. The performance of thirteen-year-olds had dropped an alarming 11 percentage points. That the drop has continued since 1976 was confirmed by preliminary results from a NAEP study conducted in late 1985. It was undertaken both because of concern about declining knowledge and because of the growing evidence of a causal connection between the drop in shared information and in literacy. The Foundations of Literacy project is measuring some of the specific information about history and literature that American seventeen-year-olds possess.

Although the full report will not be published until 1987, the preliminary field tests are disturbing. If these samplings hold up, and there is no reason to think they will not, then the results we will be reading in 1987 will show that two thirds of our seventeen-year-olds do not know that the Civil War occurred between 1850 and 1900. Three quarters do not know what *reconstruction* means. Half do not know the meaning of *Brown decision* and cannot identify either Stalin or Churchill. Three quarters are unfamiliar with the names of standard American and British authors. Moreover, our seventeen-year-olds have little sense of geography or the relative chronology of major events. Reports of youthful ignorance can no longer be considered merely impressionistic.

This passage doesn't have any title, headings, or subheadings, but as the highlighting shows, it does contain a number of specific names, situations, conditions, and classifications. In addition, a number of points are introduced by or related to signal words such as *serious, significantly, alarming,* and *disturbing.* All together, roughly half of the original has been identified as essential to some degree.

Once the list has been trimmed so that it contains only the most essential ideas, they are expressed in correct sentence form and combined to create the summary:

> E. D. Hirsch states that today's American high school students generally lack information that American writers believe everyone knows. For example, reports from the National Assessment of Educational Progress show significant declines in students' knowledge of American civics, which supports this view. Also disturbing are the preliminary results of the Foundations of Literacy study. They indicate that two-thirds of those tested didn't know when the Civil War occurred. In addition, large proportions couldn't define *reconstruction,* explain the *Brown decision,* or identify prominent historical figures such as Churchill and Stalin.

This summary is 88 words long, one-quarter the length of the original passage, so it more than fulfills the requirement that it be one-third or less than the original. Even more important, the summary effectively captures and communicates the meaning of the original.

Exercise 16.3 **Understanding and Practicing Summarizing**

1. In your own words, define *summary*. _____

   A summary is a greatly reduced version of a writing, sometimes as little as 5 to 10

   percent of the original, that captures and expresses the essence of the original.

   _____

   _____

2. What are the five steps in writing a summary? _____

   The five steps include (1) actively reading the original; (2) making a list of the key

   ideas; (3) eliminating the least essential ideas; (4) creating a draft summary; and (5)

   revising the draft.

   _____

3. On a separate sheet of paper, answer the following questions: Which do you find more difficult, identifying the essential information of a document or expressing that information in your own words? Why?

Challenge 16.3 **Developing an Effective Summary**

1. Make a copy of a passage of approximately 500 words from a newspaper, magazine, or book. Following the guidelines presented, create a summary on a separate sheet of paper that is one-third the length of the original.

2. Exchange the passage you used as well as your draft summary with a writing partner. Read the passage you receive, and then on a separate sheet of paper evaluate your partner's summary, using the summary checklist below. Return the passage and draft summary, along with your notes, to your reader.

3. Using your partner's comments to guide you, revise your summary.

Summary Checklist

Weblink
16.3

☐ Is the main point of the summary clear? Write a brief note in the margin near the beginning of the summary if you think the main point should be stated more directly.

☐ Is there any portion that you think could be reduced or eliminated without making the summary less effective? Put a ✓ next to any section that could be trimmed or cut.

☐ Is there sufficient transition throughout? Put a ✓ next to any spot that could use some transition.

RECAP

ADJUSTING YOUR PROCESS: TIMED WRITING AND SUMMARIES

Activity
16.4

New terms in this chapter	Definitions
● **essay question**	● a specific writing assignment given as part of an examination that calls for a clear, concise, multi-paragraph response within a limited period of time
● **practice question**	● an essay question that a student creates to rehearse for an exam Formulate practice questions by identifying key topics in readings and notes.
● **writing assessment**	● a writing assignment, often administered with strict time limits, required to qualify for or complete a course or level of education
● **five-paragraph essay**	● a format that involves an introductory paragraph introducing three aspects of a subject, a three-paragraph body discussing each of these aspects, and a conclusion recapping these points
● **summary**	● a greatly reduced version of a document that effectively captures and communicates the essence of the original. ● sometimes called an *abstract* or *précis*
● **signal words**	● language that emphasizes importance: *crucial, vital, significant, prominent, extraordinary*

The Process of Preparing for an Essay Exam

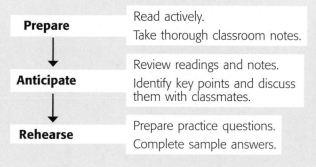

Prepare — Read actively.
Take thorough classroom notes.

↓

Anticipate — Review readings and notes.
Identify key points and discuss them with classmates.

↓

Rehearse — Prepare practice questions.
Complete sample answers.

Points to Consider When Completing a Writing Assessment

- Recognize the difficulties of writing under time.

- Identify exactly what is being asked.

- Divide the stages of the writing process up on the basis of the time available.

- Consider using the five-paragraph essay format.

- Make your writing as clear and complete as possible.

The Process of Creating a Summary

1. **Actively read the original document.**
   Note title, the introduction, any headings, and conclusion.
   Reread, highlighting key ideas.
   - Note signal words.
   - Note charts, boxed information, and lists.
   - Note statistics and specific names, dates, amounts, and distances.

2. **List the key ideas.**
   Express them in your own words.
   Write them in sentences.

3. **Edit the list to reflect only the most essential information.**
   Eliminate multiple references.
   Cut lengthy examples and supplemental information.

4. **Use the sentences you have written to create a draft summary.**
   Make the summary coherent and complete.
   Don't include your own opinion.
   Add necessary transition.

5. **Revise the draft.**
   Does it make sense independent of the original?
   Is there enough transition?
   Is it free from any commentary?
   Are there any remaining errors?

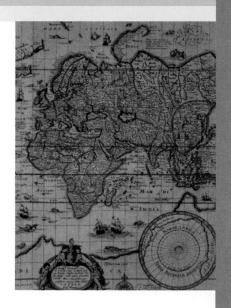

Developing Sentence Sense

Chapter 17

The Sentence

Getting Started... **Q:** I've completed some prewriting on my subject and developed a focus for my paper. Now I have to turn my prewriting ideas into complete sentences. How do I make sure that I communicate my focus and supporting ideas in proper sentence form?

Audio 17.1 **A:** To make sure that you express your focus and your good supporting ideas in complete sentence form, you need to check for the basic components of a sentence in each unit you write. That means you need to make sure that each verb has a subject and that the resulting unit expresses a complete thought.

Overview: Understanding Sentence Basics

ESL Note
See "Sentence Basics" on pages 572–574 and "Word Order" on pages 574–575.

Audio 17.2

Learning to recognize and construct complete sentences is crucial to your success as a writer. For a group of words to be a **sentence**, it must contain a *subject* and *verb* and express a complete thought. The verb represents the action or condition presented. The subject is the doer of the action or the person, place, thing, or idea that is being described. Keep in mind that many of the sentences you write will have more than one subject–verb unit. But to qualify as a sentence, a group of words must have at least one subject–verb unit that makes independent sense.

> *In this chapter, you will discover how to identify and use*
>
> - action verbs, linking verbs, helping verbs, verb phrases, and compound verbs
> - simple subjects, complete subjects, and compound subjects

Discovering Connections 17.1

Discovering Connections 17.2 provides an opportunity for students to apply the skills they learned about recognizing and constructing complete sentences. They will be asked to compose and revise an essay based on one of the topics suggested here.

Using one of the techniques you practiced in Chapter 2, "Generating Ideas through Prewriting," prewrite on one of the following topics:

1. the use of cameras in the courtroom
2. the behavior of tourists

Or, focus on this picture.

Save your work for later use.

Understanding Verbs

Audio 17.3

Audio 17.4

By definition, a **verb** is a word that shows action or a link between the subject and another word that renames or describes it. In most English sentences, the subject precedes the verb. However, when you're identifying the components in the sentence, look for the verb before you look for the subject. Without a verb, there would be no subject.

A verb that describes what the subject did, does, or might do is called an **action verb**:

EXAMPLE   Sally *sang* six songs at the party last night.

EXAMPLE   We *enjoyed* her performance.

Not all verbs are action verbs. A **linking verb** links the subject and a word that identifies or describes it, indicating a state of being. Take a look at these common linking verbs and the examples that follow:

Common Linking Verbs

Audio 17.5

| forms of *to be* (am, is, was, were, will be, might have been, etc.) | feel become appear | look seem taste, smell |

EXAMPLE   In high school, Sun Yee *was* a member of the Student Council.

EXAMPLE   Gregory *seems* happy with his choice.

Was is a linking verb because it connects *Sun Yee* with a word that identifies her: *member.* The linking verb *seems* links *Gregory* with the descriptive word *happy.*

To identify the verb in a sentence, try asking yourself *what word describes action or shows a connection between two things?*

Sometimes the verb in a sentence is composed of more than one word. These verbs may be either verb phrases or compound verbs. A **verb phrase** is a *main verb* plus a *helping verb,* as the italicized words in the following examples show:

> helping verb ⎤ main verb ⎤
>
> **EXAMPLE** Rosa *is managing* the office.

> helping verb ⎤ main verb ⎤
>
> **EXAMPLE** They *had bought* several sweaters last month.

Study the list of common helping verbs shown here:

Common Helping Verbs

am	being	do	have	must	were
are	can	does	is	shall	will
be	could	had	may	should	would
been	did	has	might	was	

Audio 17.6

A **compound verb** consists of two or more verbs connected by *and* or *or,* which share the same subject. Study the italicized verbs in the following examples:

EXAMPLE During the rainstorm, the house lights *blinked* and *flickered.*

EXAMPLE Uncle Tony *was, is,* and always *will be* a Red Sox fan.

Fast Fact It isn't a verb but a form of a verb called a *verbal*—in this case, an *infinitive*—that makes one of the single most famous and recognizable sentences in all of literature so memorable. This infinitive, repeated twice in a row, in both positive and negative form, is spoken by Hamlet in Act III, Scene I, line 56, of William Shakespeare's magnificent tragedy of the same name: "To be, or not to be—that is the question . . . ."

Exercise 17.1 **Identifying Verbs**

Activity 17.1

Underline the verbs in the following sentences. In the space above each, label the verb *A* (action) or *L* (linking). Remember—some verbs may be phrases or compound; check to be sure you have underlined the whole verb. Study the example first.

$$A$$

EXAMPLE Attitudes toward technology in education <u>have changed</u> in recent years.

Have students save these sentences and identify the subjects in each as they read the next section, "Recognizing Subjects."

(1) Since the beginning of the 20th century, many women have fought
(A)
(L)
for equal rights. (2) Because of their efforts, life for today's women is clearly better than in any other time in American history. (3) In the early 1900s, for example, Margaret Sanger took a stand on an issue of great significance: (A) birth control. (4) During this time, Sanger bravely challenged vice laws con- (A) cerning birth control. (5) She took the extraordinary step of distributing in- (A) formation about contraception. (6) In addition, she researched and wrote (A) (A) *Family Limitation,* a book dealing with this controversial subject. (7) An edu- (L) cational tool for family planning like this one was not available to the gen- (A) eral public before this. (8) Sanger actually served time in jail because of her (L) activism. (9) The availability of safe, legal birth control today is the result of (A) her crusade for reform. (10) Women today enjoy greater freedoms and a better quality of life because of Sanger's efforts.

Exercise 17.2 **Using Verbs in Your Writing**

Activity 17.2

Choose ten of the following verbs, verb phrases, and compound verbs. Use them to write ten sentences on a separate sheet of paper.

pass and dribble	has found	records	opens
scurries	decays	celebrated	protested
had called	are discussing	jogs	have thought
have moved	study or fail	mix	triumphed

Challenge 17.1 **Identifying and Evaluating Verbs in an Essay**

COLLABORATION

1. Working with a partner, choose a selection from Part Seven that you would both like to read. Then, reading the essay together, identify verbs that the author has used in ten sentences.

2. On a separate piece of paper, copy these sentences, and label the verb(s) in each: *action* or *linking*. Also label any *verb phrases* or *compound verbs.*

3. Share the sentences with your classmates. Which of the action verbs that you have identified are the most effective? Why?

Recognizing Subjects

Activity 17.3

In addition to a verb, the second component required for a group of words to be a sentence is a **subject**. In a sentence, the subject is the word that performs the verb's action or condition. It is either a **noun**, a word that names a person, place, thing, or idea, or a **pronoun**, a word that substitutes for a noun. Finding a subject is easy. First, find the verb, and then ask yourself *who or what is doing the action being discussed?* The word that answers the question is the subject.

What are the verbs and the subjects in the sentences below?

> **EXAMPLE** The sales representative asked several preliminary questions.

> **EXAMPLE** The bus will be late because of the accident downtown.

In the first example, the verb is *asked.* Now ask *who or what asked several preliminary questions?* The subject is *sales representative.* In the second example, the verb is *will be.* Ask *who or what will be late because of the accident downtown?* The subject is *bus.*

For more discussion of modifiers, refer to Chapter 27.

Most sentences have both a simple subject and a complete subject. The **simple subject** is an individual word that identifies who or what is doing the action or being discussed. The **complete subject** is that simple subject plus any words or phrases that describe or modify it. A **modifier** is a word or a group of words that describe a noun or pronoun, telling *which one* or *what kind.*

In the sentences below, both the verbs and complete subjects are identified. Find the simple subject of each sentence.

> **EXAMPLE**
>
> ┌──── complete subject ────┐   ┌ verb ┐
> *Inexpensive wireless phones with Internet capability have* recently *been introduced.*

> **EXAMPLE**
>
> ┌── complete subject ──┐ ┌ verb ┐
> *An apartment in those complexes offers* an affordable option for working families.

In the first sentence, the simple subject is *phones.* In the second sentence, it is *apartment.*

For more information and practice on subject–verb agreement, see Chapter 21, "Subject–Verb Agreement."

Being able to identify the simple subject is important because the verb must *agree with* or match the simple subject. Modifiers in the complete subject can mislead you into selecting the wrong verb form, especially if the words are in a **prepositional phrase.** For more about subject–verb agreement see Chapter 21. A prepositional phrase begins with a *preposition* and ends with a noun or pronoun called the *object of the preposition.* The preposition *relates* that noun or pronoun to another word in the sentence, often by indicating location, direction, or time. Here is a list of common prepositions:

Common Prepositions

about	behind	during	on	to
above	below	except	onto	toward
across	beneath	for	out	under
after	beside	from	outside	underneath
against	besides	in	over	unlike
along	between	inside	past	until
among	beyond	into	since	up
around	but (except)	like	than	upon
as	by	near	through	with
at	despite	of	throughout	within
before	down	off	till	without

Consider again the examples above, this time with the prepositional phrases italicized:

EXAMPLE   Inexpensive wireless phones *with Internet capability* have recently been introduced.

EXAMPLE   An apartment *in those complexes* offers an affordable option for working families.

In the first sentence, the preposition is *with,* and the object of the preposition is the singular word *capability.* In the second, the preposition is *in,* and the object of the preposition is the plural word *complexes.* Writers sometimes make the mistake of making the verb agree with the object of the preposition rather than with the simple subject. Remember—*an object cannot be a subject.* Therefore, be careful to identify the simple subject.

Sometimes a **compound subject** answers the question *who or what is doing the action or being discussed?* Compound subjects consist of two or more nouns or pronouns, usually connected by *and* or *or.* These subjects may cause confusion for writers, who must decide whether the subject is singular or plural.

EXAMPLE   *Dana or Rebekka* answers the phone in the office after 5 P.M.

EXAMPLE   *Squirrels, birds, and opossums* live in the trees behind the cafeteria.

In the first sentence, the verb is *answers,* and the answer to the question *who or what answers?* is the compound subject, *Dana or Rebekka. Or* implies a choice. Only one person answers the phone, so the verb is singular. In the second sentence, the verb is *live*, and the answer to the question *who or what live?* is the compound subject, *squirrels, birds, and opossums. And* implies addition, making the subject plural. All these animals live in the trees, so the verb is plural.

> *Fast Fact* The shortest complete sentence in English is two letters long: the command, "Go!" The shortest declarative sentence is three letters long: "I am."

As Chapter 8, "Process," explains, with the **imperative mood** or **command**, the subject is *understood* rather than explicitly stated. When you write, "Place your shoes in plastic bags before packing them in your suitcase," the subject isn't actually expressed. Yet, it is obvious that you are saying, "**You** place your shoes in plastic bags before packing them in your suitcase." In other words, the subject is *understood* to be **you**.

Exercise 17.3   **Distinguishing between the Simple and the Complete Subject**

Activity
17.4

Underline the complete subject, and circle the simple subject in the sentences below. Remember—the simple subject is the specific noun or pronoun that is doing the action or being discussed. Study the example first.

EXAMPLE

The (crowd) in the streets waited impatiently for the beginning of the fireworks display.

(1) Sports (championships) on television attract huge viewing audiences. (2) The NCAA Final Four Basketball (tournament) in March is one such ratings-boosting program. (3) Tennis (fans) can cheer for their favorite players in the popular Wimbledon tournament during July. (4) The glitzy (Super Bowl) with its hours of pregame shows attracts the most armchair quarterbacks all year. (5) However, the traditional (favorite) of many couch potato fans is still October's World Series.

Exercise 17.4   **Identifying the Principal Parts of Compound Subjects**

Each sentence in the following paragraph has a compound subject. Underline these compound subjects and then circle the principal parts—the simple subjects—making up the compound sentence, as the example shows.

EXAMPLE   (Ceiling fans) and (window fans) can help cool a room and avoid the high

cost of air conditioning.

(1) My (brothers) and (sisters,) our (friends,) and (I) used to treat the Greene

Schoolyard in our old neighborhood as our personal playground. (2) My

best friend (Benni) and (I) would have a jump rope contest near the front door

of the school every afternoon. (3) My sister (Linna) or (another) of the older

girls would be the contest judge. (4) Around back, my older brothers

(Ronnie) and (Ramon) had drawn a big chalked square on the brick wall for

speed ball games. (5) During speed ball, a form of baseball, the older (boys)

and a (few) of the girls would pitch a rubber ball against the square. (6) A

chalk (mark) on the ball or a (smudge) in the square was evidence of a strike.

(7) Late (summer) and early (spring) marked football and soccer season. (8)

The narrow (lawn) at the side of the building and the dirt (yard) behind it were

perfect fields for these sports. (9) Every afternoon after school, my brother

(James) and (one) of the other big kids would divide up the rest of us into two

teams. (10) The (lawn,) the dirt (yard,) and the (rest) of the schoolyard are all

gone now, with two big additions to the school filling space.

Challenge 17.2   **Using Compound Subjects in Your Writing**

1. Below is a list of compound subjects. Choose ten of these subjects, and
   on a separate piece of paper, write a sentence using each one. Add modifiers if you wish.

heat and humidity	a shovel and rake
swimming or sailing	soccer and football
red meat, eggs, and cheese	travel and tourism
hardcovers and paperbacks	Macintosh and Gateway
wind and rain	my father and mother
winning or losing	breakfast and lunch

2. Exchange sentences with a partner. Underline the verbs in each sentence;
   then return the draft to its writer. Do all of your sentences have a verb that

agrees with the subject? If not, revise your sentences to be sure they are correct and complete.

Chapter Quick Check: Sentence Basics

In each sentence in the following passage, identify all subjects and verbs. Underline each complete subject, and then circle each simple subject. With any compound subjects, circle each of the simple subjects within it. Double underline all verbs, verb phrases, and compound verbs. Put an X in front of any sentence in the imperative mood.

EXAMPLE   The (lawyer) with her briefcase and her client with a small notebook had been stopped and searched by the police officer at the door.

(1) Because of a recent technological development, a complete (book) can be produced in less than an hour. (2) (Experts) in this field refer to this innovation as Print on Demand and believe strongly in its future. (3) With this technology (books) and other (documents) are digitized and stored in electronic form. (4) Individual (customers) and small (businesses) can then select books and print them up right in the bookstore. (5) As a result of this development, the (problem) of out-of-print books should be greatly reduced or completely eliminated. (6) In electronic form, a (book) will never go out of print or be out of stock. (7) Major (publishers) of commercial and academic books can now publish smaller batches of books and save money as a result. X (8) Think of the possibilities. (9) For instance, without a contract, (novelists,) short story (writers,) and (poets) have few publishing opportunities. (10) With Print on Demand, these (people) can fulfill their publishing dreams and distribute their work themselves.

Discovering Connections 17.2

1. In Discovering Connections 17.1 on page 265, you prewrote on one of three suggested topics. Now, using this prewriting material as

your basis, work your way through the rest of the writing process, and complete a draft essay of about 500 words on this subject.

2. Exchange your draft with a partner. Using the material in this chapter to guide you, check the draft you receive. Make a note in the margin to indicate errors in subject–verb usage, and mark any word groups in which a subject or a verb is missing. Return the draft to its writer.

3. Revise your essay, correcting any errors your partner noted.

Summary Exercise: Sentence Basics

Weblink
17.1

In each sentence in the following passage, identify all subjects and verbs. Underline each complete subject, and then circle each simple subject. With any compound subjects, circle each of the simple subjects within it. Double underline all verbs, verb phrases, and compound verbs. Put an X in front of any sentence in the imperative mood.

(1) Honor students are not always the smartest students in class. (2) They probably organize, plan, and prepare the most effectively, however.

(3) Organized students purchase necessary tools for their classes. (4) The items and equipment at the top of their shopping list might include an assignment notebook and calendar, highlight markers, and folders. (5) A pocket dictionary and computer disks are other useful tools.

(6) Successful students with job or family commitments have scheduled manageable study time in advance. (7) They have analyzed their time needs for study and balanced their schedules. (8) Study schedules must be flexible and realistic. (9) Emergencies can happen and may interrupt work on assignments. (10) A list of assignments and due dates is an excellent planning tool. (11) Less serious students do the fun, easy assignments first. (12) Successful students, however, complete the assignments in a logical order. (13) They tackle challenges a step at a time.

(14) Preparation also leads to good grades. (15) One good study technique is called prereading. (16) Smart students preview the textbook materi-

als before the lecture. (17) Introductions, chapter highlights, and review sections often emphasize key points. (18) Successful students read assignments on time, take good class notes, and anticipate test questions. (19) This preparation before the day of a test repays them with good scores as well as better learning.

(20) Good grades are within your reach. (21) Make effective study habits your number one priority.

 THE SENTENCE

 Weblink
17.2

New terms in this chapter	Definitions
● **sentence**	● a series of words containing a subject and verb and expressing a complete thought
● **verb**	● a word or words that describe the action or the condition of the subject
● **action verb**	● a word or words expressing action completed by the subject **Example** Marcel *held* the door for his sister.
● **linking verb**	● a word or words connecting the subject with other words that identify or describe it The most common linking verbs are the forms of *to be.* **Example** Katherine *is* an excellent athlete.
● **verb phrase**	● a main verb plus one or more helping verbs **Example** Karen *has been taking* dancing lessons for five years.
● **compound verb**	● two or more verbs connected by a conjunction and relating to the same subject **Example** Shannon *cooked* and *served* the meal.
● **subject**	● the noun or pronoun that is the doer of the action or the focus of the verb Find the subject by answering the question *who or what is doing the action or being discussed?* **Example** *Paul* enjoyed the party.

New terms in this chapter	Definitions
● **noun**	● a word that names a person, place, or thing ***Example*** The *river* overflowed its banks.
● **pronoun**	● a word that substitutes for a noun ***Example*** *He* loves to tell ghost stories.
● **simple subject**	● the noun or pronoun that answers the question *who or what is doing the action or being discussed?*
● **complete subject**	● the simple subject plus any words or phrases that describe or modify it ***Example*** The *books on that shelf* are best-sellers.
● **modifier**	● a word or group of words that tell you *which* or *what kind* when used with a noun or pronoun ***Example*** *My older, wiser* sister gave me *some good* advice.
● **prepositional phrase**	● a group of words beginning with a preposition and ending with a noun or pronoun that is the object of the preposition The subject of a sentence can *never* be in a prepositional phrase. ***Example*** The clothes *on the floor* are dirty.
● **subject–verb agreement**	● a state in which the subject and verb agree in number
● **compound subject**	● two or more nouns or pronouns connected by a conjunction and acting as the subject for the same verb ***Example*** Our wonderful *friends* and our dear *neighbors* collected money to help us after the fire.

The Basic Elements of a Sentence

Subject ———————— Verb

Expression of a Complete Thought

Chapter 18

Fragments

Getting Started... **Q:** I know that sentence fragments are serious sentence errors, but I'm not sure what they are. How can I avoid fragments in my writing if I'm not sure how to identify them?

Audio 18.1 **A:** Avoiding sentence fragments is easier than you think, as long as you take the time to focus on what makes a sentence a sentence. In other words, make sure each unit you write contains a subject and verb and expresses a complete thought.

Overview: Recognizing and Writing Complete Sentences

Audio 18.2 To communicate your full meaning to your reader, you must make sure you express your good ideas in correct sentence form. That means you must avoid **sentence fragments**, units in which one of the elements required for a complete sentence is missing. In other words, sentence fragments lack a verb or a subject or fail to communicate a complete thought to the reader. Sentence fragments are serious errors. The reason is simple. Because they do not convey complete ideas, fragments can leave readers unclear about your intended meaning.

Video 18.1

> *In this chapter, you will learn how to avoid and correct fragments created by*
>
> ● omitting a subject or a verb
>
> ● mistaking a phrase for a sentence
>
> ● mistaking a subordinate clause for a sentence
>
> ● mistaking an appositive for a sentence

Discovering Connections 18.1

Discovering Connections 18.2 provides an opportunity for students to apply the skills they learned about avoiding and correcting fragments. They will be asked to compose and revise an essay based on one of the topics suggested here.

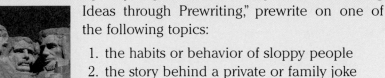

Using one of the techniques you practiced in Chapter 2, "Generating Ideas through Prewriting," prewrite on one of the following topics:

1. the habits or behavior of sloppy people
2. the story behind a private or family joke

Or, focus on this picture.

Save your work for later use.

Correcting Fragments with Missing Subjects or Verbs

ESL Note
See "Sentence Basics" on pages 572–574.

Fragments occur for several reasons. One common cause is the lack of a verb or subject. As the previous chapter shows, to be a sentence, a group of words must contain a verb and subject. When you are checking your own sentences, first identify the verb. If you cannot find an action or linking verb, the group of words is a fragment. Look at the following group of words:

FRAGMENT   The use of acupuncture to treat rheumatoid arthritis.

There is no verb here, only a noun and its modifiers, so this group of words is a fragment. To change it to a sentence, add a verb and complete the thought.

REVISED   The use of acupuncture to treat rheumatoid arthritis *shows* the growing influence of alternative medicine.

Weblink
18.1

Sometimes a group of words has a subject and a word or group of words that seems to be a verb but in fact cannot function as a verb. These words, called **verbals**, are verb forms that can't communicate a complete action or meaning.

Consider the italicized verbals in the following groups of words:

FRAGMENT   The front-end manager *looking* for volunteers for an overtime shift.

FRAGMENT   Daisy *spoken* to Clarise an hour before the accident.

FRAGMENT   Eddie *to run* the Chicago Marathon again.

All three groups of words are fragments because they contain verbals, not verbs. To make them into sentences, substitute true verbs for the verbals, as these versions show:

SENTENCES   The front-end manager *looked* for volunteers for an overtime shift.

or

The front-end manager *is looking* for volunteers for an overtime shift.

SENTENCES   Daisy *spoke* to Clarise an hour before the accident.

or

Daisy *had spoken* to Clarise an hour before the accident.

SENTENCES   Eddie *ran* the Chicago Marathon again.

or

Eddie *will run* the Chicago Marathon again.

See Part Five, "Understanding Subjects and Verbs," for more on using verbs correctly.

Even if a group of words has a verb, it's not a sentence unless it also has a subject. As the previous chapter showed, the subject is the word or group of words that answers the question *who or what is doing the action or being discussed?* If no word answers the question, then there is no subject, and the group of words is a fragment.

Weblink
18.2

Consider the following group of words:

FRAGMENT   Told Sally's boss about Sally's excellent computer skills.

This group of words is not a sentence. There is a verb—*told*—but if you ask *who or what told*, there is no answer.

To correct this fragment, simply add a subject:

                     ┌──── subject ────┐
SENTENCES   *Professor Tessier* told Sally's boss about Sally's excellent computer skills.

Fast Fact On occasion, experienced writers use what can be called an *intentional fragment*, a group of words that is deliberately expressed as an incomplete sentence, to create some effect. Perhaps the longest and best-known intentional fragment appears in James Joyce's extraordinary novel *Ulysses*. The final section of the book, which records Molly Bloom's thoughts as she lies in bed, is a 46-page fragment, beginning and ending with the same word, "Yes."

Exercise 18.1   **Correcting Fragments with Missing or Incomplete Verbs**

Audio
18.3

The following groups of words are fragments because they contain verbals, not verbs. Correct each fragment by (1) crossing out the misused word and writing an appropriate verb above it or (2) adding a verb. There is more than one way to correct each fragment. Study the example first.

Answers may vary. Likely answers are given.

EXAMPLE   The dry cleaner ~~pressing~~ *pressed* my good white shirt.

(1) My aunt Julia ~~baking~~ *baked* the most delicious sweets. (2) The whole family ~~to gather~~ *gathered* at her home every Sunday evening for dessert. (3) She ~~serving~~ *served* hot apple pie, rich chocolate cake, or creamy pudding. (4) We ~~eating~~ *ate* and ~~visiting~~ *visited* for a couple of hours. (5) This tradition ~~being~~ *was* our family's favorite weekend activity.

Exercise 18.2   **Correcting Fragments with Missing Subjects or Verbs**

 Audio 18.4

The following groups of words are fragments because they lack a subject, a verb, or a helping verb. On the lines provided, write an appropriate subject or verb, and complete the thought. Label your added portions *S* or *V*. Study the example first.   Answers will vary. Labels and representative answers are shown.

EXAMPLE   Wildflowers ___*bloomed*(V)___ by the roadside.

1. ___*The victim*(S)___ picked the robber from a police lineup.

2. Shirley ___*began*(V)___ running after the bus.

3. ___*Wine*(S)___ is a good gift to give if you don't know the recipient very well.

4. The cookbook ___*includes*(V)___ the complete recipe in Spanish.

5. The chocolate roses ___*were*(V)___ melting in the hot midday sun.

Exercise 18.3   **Identifying and Correcting Fragments with Missing Subjects and Verbs**

The following passage contains several fragments that lack either a subject or a verb. Underline each fragment, and then correct each by adding a subject or a verb above the appropriate spot and a ^ below it. Use the example to guide you.

EXAMPLE   *The food in the cooler had*
^ ~~Had~~ to be thrown out because of contamination.

(1) A few weeks ago, I visited a wonderful place, a newly opened butterfly sanctuary. (2) <u>The sanctuary itself *is* a large closed area within a larger building.</u> (3) In this area, flowering plants are arranged in a number of small

Several paths crisscross

garden settings. (4) ~~Crisscross~~ the sanctuary, allowing people easy access to
∧
                              live
the entire area. (5) The butterflies in a completely safe environment, with no
                                          ∧
predators of any kind. (6) As a result, they are able to fly around and feed

           Visitors can
freely. (7) ~~Can~~ walk right up to brightly colored butterflies for a close look
            ∧
at their delicate features and distinct wing patterns. (8) Sometimes, butter-

flies land on people's clothing. (9) Above the exit, a sign asks people to

check themselves to avoid accidentally taking butterflies out the door upon

            The beautiful scene within that sanctuary
leaving. (10) ~~Will~~ remain with me for a long time.
              ∧

Challenge 18.1   **Writing Supporting Sentences for a Paragraph**

Working with a partner, compose a paragraph of at least five sentences to
support one of the topic sentences listed below.

1. Knowledge of a second language is important in today's global economy.

2. Reading a book is more satisfying than watching a movie based on that
   book.

Exchange your sentences with another writing team. Check the paper you receive for fragments. Write *frag* in the margin beside each fragment you find.
Return the paper to its writers. Make any corrections needed to your paper.

Correcting Phrase Fragments

Audio
18.5

A *phrase* is a group of two or more related words that lacks a subject–verb
unit. As the previous chapter indicated, two common types of phrases are
verb phrases (page 266) and *prepositional phrases* (pages 268–269). When a
phrase is left to stand alone, it is a **phrase fragment**.
    Look at the following groups of words:

FRAGMENT   Will soon be sleeping.

FRAGMENT   Inside the house.

The first example is a verb phrase, and the second is a prepositional phrase.
They both lack a subject–verb combination, so both are fragments.
    To correct phrases that are incorrectly used as sentences, you need to
supply the missing elements, as these versions show:

SENTENCE
$\overline{\text{subject}}$
My grandfather will soon be sleeping.

SENTENCE
$\overline{\text{subject}}\overline{\text{verb}}$
Daryl left his jacket inside the house.

Exercise 18.4 | **Identifying and Correcting Phrase Fragments**

The following passage contains several fragments resulting from phrases used incorrectly as sentences. Underline these fragments. Then, on a separate piece of paper, rewrite the paragraph, turning the fragments into sentences. Use the example to guide you.   Answers will vary.

EXAMPLE   Under the porch.
The frightened kitten hid under the porch.

(1) Being a musician demands a lot of dedication. (2) Have to practice hours daily. (3) Some musicians keep an unusual schedule. (4) Until the early morning hours. (5) Then they sleep until the afternoon. (6) Family life becomes difficult. (7) With this work schedule. (8) Sometimes musicians face weeks without employment. (9) Through all this, musicians keep playing. (10) Have a need to bring the joy of music to their audiences.

Exercise 18.5 | **Rewriting Phrases as Sentences**

On a separate sheet of paper, turn the following verb phrases and prepositional phrases into sentences by adding subjects or verbs or both and completing the thoughts. Study the example first.   Answers will vary.

EXAMPLE   over the lake
The sun dawning over the lake was beautiful.

1. throughout the neighborhood

2. inside my room

3. were laughing

4. on the subway

5. have been warned

6. behind the warehouse

7. will leave soon

8. through the back door

9. are playing

10. was canceled

Challenge 18.2   **Identifying Subjects and Verbs**

Exchange the sentences that you and a partner wrote for Challenge 18.1 on page 280 with another pair of students. Underline the subjects and verbs in each sentence, and return the paragraph. Make revisions that are necessary to eliminate any fragments in your own work.

Correcting Subordinate Clause Fragments

For more information about identifying and using subordinate clauses, see Chapter 19, "Subordination and Coordination."

Even if a group of words contains a subject and a verb, it is still a fragment if it does not express a complete thought. For example, a **subordinate clause fragment** contains a subject and a verb, but it cannot stand on its own. Its function is to explain or describe another portion of the sentence. It is called *subordinate* because it depends on a **main clause**, the primary subject–verb unit of the sentence, to make complete sense.

Look at these subordinate clause fragments:

FRAGMENT   After the *EMT's arrived.*
(subject) (verb)

FRAGMENT   That *Michaela saw* outside the bus station.
(subject) (verb)

Both examples have subjects and verbs, but neither one expresses a complete thought. Each leaves the reader waiting for more information.

To correct this type of fragment, you have a couple of choices. You could add or delete words so that the clause makes sense on its own:

SENTENCE   The EMTs arrived within minutes of receiving the emergency call.

SENTENCE   Michaela saw Theo outside the bus station.

In the first sentence, *after* has been deleted, and *within minutes of receiving the emergency call* has been added. In the second sentence, *That* has been deleted, and *Theo* has been added. Both groups of words are now sentences. Furthermore, the meaning of both groups of words has changed considerably.

You can also choose to correct this type of fragment by adding a main clause to the subordinate clause. Together, they should express a complete thought:

SENTENCE   After the EMTs arrived, *they began treating the injured people immediately.*

SENTENCE   *The car* that Michaela saw outside the bus station *was broken down.*

These changes make the meaning of the original clauses clearer and more specific. They do not alter the meaning as the preceding corrections do.

Fast Fact   The nature of conversation helps to explain why some fragments occur in writing. In spoken discussion, when one person asks, "Why didn't you call?" the other person generally doesn't repeat the words just expressed in the question. Instead, the second person gives just the answer, something like, "Because I lost your number." It works in conversation because both people are present. But writing isn't talking. You need both parts of the discourse to make a complete sentence, and when people forget to do so, a fragment results.

Exercise 18.6   Identifying Subordinate Clause Fragments

The following passage contains several subordinate clause fragments. Underline these fragments, as the example shows.

EXAMPLE   <u>Even though the new movie had received poor reviews.</u> The crowd waiting to see it was huge.

(1) In the near future, your pockets or purse may no longer jingle the same way. (2) <u>Because the penny may soon disappear from use.</u> (3) <u>Although not everyone agrees with their stance.</u> (4) Some merchants and retail groups are asking the government to eliminate this coin. (5) In their view, the penny no longer serves a useful purpose. (6) <u>That it had served over its long history.</u> (7) These critics complain about the nuisance factor of dealing with all those pennies. (8) <u>Unless the purchase is for an even amount of money.</u> (9) Every cash transaction involves the use of several pennies. (10) According to people pushing to eliminate the penny, a better plan is to round off all final prices to denominations ending in 5 or 10.

Exercise 18.7   Rewriting Subordinate Clauses as Sentences

On a separate sheet of paper, turn the following subordinate clauses into sentences by adding a main clause. Check your work for correct use of capitals and punctuation. Study the example first.   Answers will vary.

EXAMPLE   even though the class had ended

The students continued their discussion, even though the class had ended.

1. who plans to ride to the game on the team bus

2. whenever a false alarm is sounded

3. which hung on a chain around her neck

4. until I get a haircut

5. so that I can improve my keyboarding skills

6. unless management agrees to give them a raise

7. although it won two Academy Awards

8. in order that my wife and I could both attend the concert

9. because the neighborhood parents petitioned the school department

10. since it wasn't my fault

Exercise 18.8   **Identifying and Correcting Subordinate Clause Fragments**

The following passage contains several subordinate clause fragments. Underline these fragments. Then, on a separate piece of paper, rewrite the paragraph, turning the fragments into sentences. Study the example first.

EXAMPLE   Who has a quick temper.

My boss, who has a quick temper, should learn how to relax.

(1) Sweetgrass basket making is a historic craft. (2) Which dates back to the late 1600s in this country. (3) When slaves from West Africa were brought to South Carolina. (4) They brought their skills in cultivating rice. (5) Their knowledge was essential to plantation owners. (6) Because these Europeans had little experience with growing rice. (7) To winnow the rice, slave women made durable, pliable household baskets. (8) The women chose the plentiful sweetgrass to work with. (9) Although more and more coastal farmers started to cultivate rice. (10) The craft of sweetgrass basket making stayed locally in and around Charleston, South Carolina, among the descendants of these slaves.

Challenge 18.3   **Analyzing and Completing Sentences**

To make sure each sentence you revised in Exercise 18.8 expresses a complete thought, ask a partner to read your completed revision aloud, pausing for a few seconds after the period at the end of each sentence. Note any groups of words you hear that can't stand on their own. Turn these groups of words into complete sentences. Repeat this process for your partner.

Correcting Appositive Fragments

An **appositive** is a word or group of words that rename or explain another noun or pronoun. Some appositives contain subjects and verbs, but like subordinate clauses, appositives don't express complete thoughts on their own.

Look at the following appositives:

FRAGMENT   The spot where my *car had broken* down.

FRAGMENT   A talent *she* usually *kept* hidden.

Both groups of words have subjects and verbs, but both are fragments because they don't express complete thoughts.

To eliminate this kind of fragment, you can change and adjust the order of the words to express a complete thought:

SENTENCE   My *car had broken* down at that spot.

SENTENCE   *She* usually *kept* that talent hidden.

Alternatively, you can join the fragment with a main clause so that it expresses a complete thought:

SENTENCE   *Fortunately, a car dealership was on the corner,* the spot where my car had broken down.   (*The appositive now focuses on* corner.)

SENTENCE   *Tami entertained the crowd by singing,* a talent she usually kept hidden. (*The appositive now modifies* singing.)

Exercise 18.9   **Identifying and Correcting Appositive Fragments**

The following passage contains several appositive fragments. Underline these fragments. Then, on a separate piece of paper, turn those fragments into complete sentences. Use the example to guide you.

EXAMPLE   A task that frustrates him.

Tim had to balance his checkbook, a task that frustrates him.

(1) Last year, I worked during the summer as a nanny. (2) The best temporary job I ever had. (3) My duties included dressing, feeding, and entertaining two children. (4) The nicest, most well-behaved kids I have ever known. (5) They enjoyed the zoo, the beach, and the park. (6) Only a few of the places I took them. (7) They were always excited, no matter what we did. (8) They especially liked the school playground. (9) A place that was always nearly deserted in the summer. (10) I was sorry to see that summer end.

Exercise 18.10   **Rewriting Appositives Correctly as Sentences**

On a separate sheet of paper, turn each of the following appositives into a sentence by adding a main clause containing a word for the appositive to rename or explain. Use the example to guide you.   Answers will vary.

EXAMPLE   a park on the outskirts of the city

Evergreen Acres, a park on the outskirts of the city, is the best place to view the comet.

1. the quietest person in the office

2. the minister who led the protest

3. an inexpensive, plastic toy

4. the most influential musician of the decade

5. a dangerous intersection for pedestrians

6. the welcoming smell of fresh-brewed coffee

7. the person who always cheers me up

8. a color that I love

9. the best seat in the auditorium

10. a required course in my major

Challenge 18.4   **Working with Subordinate Clauses and Appositives**

Working with a partner or writing group, read one or more of the essays in Part Seven. Find at least three subordinate clauses and at least two appositives. On a separate piece of paper, write the sentences that contain these elements, and discuss with your partner or group how they contribute to the ideas in the sentences that contain them.

Chapter Quick Check: Fragments

Underline the fragments in the following passage. Then, on a separate sheet of paper, revise the essay by correcting the fragments, using the techniques you practiced in this chapter. Remember that fragments can be corrected in a variety of ways.

(1) One of the best-known U.S. monuments, the Vietnam Veterans' Memorial, has had a controversial history. (2) <u>After the government announced their plans for a memorial to honor Vietnam combat casualties.</u> (3) A number of architects submitted designs for consideration. (4) <u>By a blue ribbon selection committee.</u> (5) <u>Chose a design by a young Asian-American woman, Maya Lin.</u> (6) Lin's plans called for a wedge-shaped black, polished-granite wall. (7) <u>With the names of the war dead inscribed in rows across its surface.</u> (8) <u>Although some people immediately praised Lin's design.</u> (9) One critic described it as a "black scar in the earth." (10) <u>Despite this rocky beginning, the Memorial among the most visited of all the historical sites in Washington, D.C.</u>

Discovering Connections 18.2

Activity 18.1

1. In Discovering Connections 18.1 on page 277, you completed a prewriting on one of three suggested topics. Now work your way through the rest of the writing process, using this prewriting material as your foundation, and complete a draft essay of about 500 words on this subject.
2. Exchange your draft with a partner. Using the material in this chapter to guide you, check the draft you receive for fragments. Underline any fragments, and then return the draft to your partner.
3. Revise your essay, correcting any fragments discovered by your reader.

Summary Exercise: Fragments

Underline the fragments in the following essay. Then, on a separate piece of paper, revise the essay by correcting the fragments, using the techniques

Activity 18.2

Activity 18.3

Activity 18.4

you practiced in this chapter. Remember that fragments can be corrected in a variety of ways.

(1) One of the major stars of the world of cooking is Chef Emeril Lagasse. (2) Referred to by his many fans simply by his first name. (3) Emeril has enjoyed an enormously successful career in the arenas of world-class restaurants and television.

(4) Emeril's success had simple beginnings. (5) Born in Fall River, Massachussetts, an old New England mill town. (6) As a youngster, he worked in a Portuguese bakery (7) An ideal place to learn to make bread and pastries. (8) Also worked in the kitchen of the St. John's Club, a small ethnic restaurant in Fall River, mastering many aspects of food preparation.

(9) He studied culinary arts at Diman Regional Vocational Technical High School in Fall River. (10) Although he was offered a college music scholarship. (11) Emeril chose to study culinary arts at Johnson and Wales University in Providence, Rhode Island.

(12) After graduating and traveling to France to learn the secrets of French cuisine. (13) Emeril returned to the United States to work in major restaurants in Philadelphia, Boston, New York, and then New Orleans. (14) He made his mark in New Orleans, over the years opening three restaurants there. (15) Several other restaurants in Las Vegas and Orlando. (16) With his trademark exclamation, "Bam!" Emeril has also captivated television audiences with his two Food Network shows, *The Essence of Emeril* and *Emeril Live*. (17) Which are broadcast into approximately 70 million households each day.

(18) From his first work in a small Fall River bakery. (19) Emeril has seen his career grow to almost unbelievable levels. (20) Along the way, he has inspired much interest in cooking throughout the United States.

Have students share their revised sentences within small groups and discuss the ways they corrected the fragments.

RECAP FRAGMENTS

Weblink
18.3

New terms in this chapter	Definitions
• **sentence fragment**	• a group of words that fails to express a complete thought because it lacks a subject, a verb, or other needed words ***Example*** Although they tried not to laugh [not a complete thought]
• **verbal**	• a verb form that is used as another part of speech and therefore doesn't communicate a complete action or meaning A verbal cannot substitute for a verb in a sentence. ***Example*** *Running* down the stairs
• **phrase fragment**	• a group of two or more related words that lacks a subject–verb combination, used incorrectly as a sentence ***Verb phrase*** Are looking ***Prepositional phrase*** About time
• **subordinate clause fragment**	• a group of words that contains a subject and a verb but does not express a complete thought A subordinate clause must be joined to a main clause to express a complete thought. ***Example*** That had struck the coast
• **main clause**	• the primary subject–verb unit of a sentence ***Example*** *The hurricane* that had struck the coast *was not expected.*
• **appositive**	• a word or group of words that renames or explains a noun or pronoun next to it An appositive must be connected to a main clause to express a complete thought. ***Example*** A retired police officer

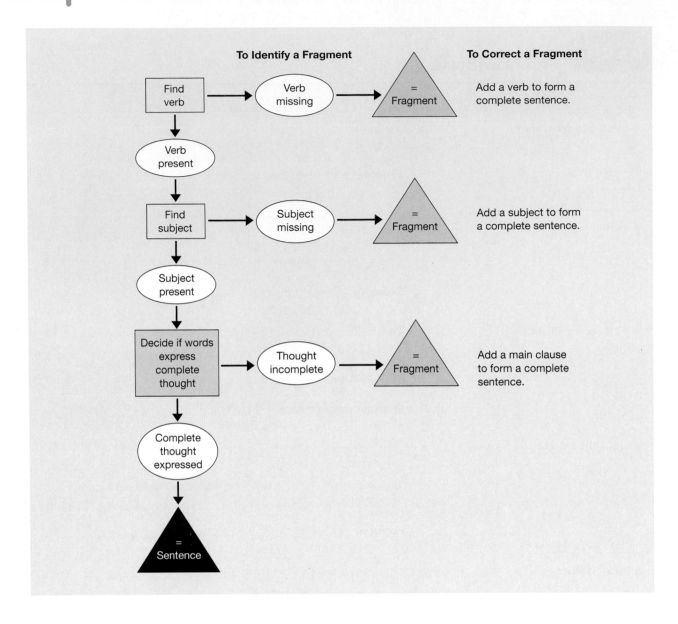

Chapter 19

Subordination and Coordination

Getting Started... **Q:** I'm concerned that my writing might be a little boring because I've written all short sentences. What can I do to make my sentences more interesting?

Audio 19.1 **A:** One way to improve the flow of your writing is to combine short sentences so that they hold a reader's interest. In some cases, you will want to use a coordinating conjunction or a semicolon to connect them so that they are equally balanced—that's coordination. And sometimes you will want to connect them with a subordinating conjunction so that one section depends on the other to make sense—that's subordination. Both methods will help you keep your writing lively and highly readable.

Overview: Combining Clauses for Sentence Complexity

Audio 19.2 When you write, you must express your ideas in complete sentence form. As the previous two chapters emphasize, this means that you must make sure each unit contains a subject and verb expressing a complete thought. When a group of words contains a single subject–verb unit expressing a complete thought, the structure is called a *simple sentence*. If you used only simple sentences, however, your writing style would be pretty boring. You can emphasize some ideas by using **subordination**, which means combining an idea in a main clause with an idea in a **subordinate clause**. The subordinate clause depends on the main clause to make sense. Alternatively, you can join ideas through **coordination**, in which two main clauses (or simple sentences) are linked by a semicolon or by a coordinating conjunction and comma.

Video
19.1

In this chapter, you will learn to

● identify and use simple and complex sentences to express your ideas with variety

● use subordinating conjunctions to connect and show relationships between clauses

● use relative pronouns to introduce subordinate clauses that describe a noun or pronoun

● use a coordinating conjunction and a comma, a semicolon, or a semicolon and a conjunctive adverb to create a compound sentence

Using one of the techniques you practiced in Chapter 2, "Generating Ideas through Prewriting," prewrite on one of the following topics:

1. the advantages or disadvantages of cable television
2. the most effective print, television, or radio advertising you've been exposed to

Or, focus on this picture.
    Save your work for later use.

Using Subordination

Activity
19.1

To use **subordination** effectively, you need to understand the difference between a simple sentence and a complex sentence. A **simple sentence** consists of only one subject–verb unit or *clause*, as this example shows:

subject   verb

SIMPLE SENTENCE   The *reporter* on the scene *detailed* the degree of damage.

As a writer, you will also rely on **complex sentences**, which combine a main, or independent, clause, and a **subordinate**, or dependent, **clause**. Subordinate clauses are introduced by either **subordinating conjunctions** or **relative pronouns**:

Common Subordinating Conjunctions

after	before	since	when
although	even though	so that	whenever
as	if	than	where
as if	in order that	though	wherever
as soon as	once	unless	whether
because	rather than	until	while

To be sure that students understand the concept of subordination, ask them to define the word *subordinate.*

Relative Pronouns

that	who
what	whom
which	whose

If you join a simple sentence and a subordinate clause in a complex sentence, the simple sentence becomes the **main clause**, as this example shows:

COMPLEX SENTENCE

main clause ─── subordinate clause

The reporter on the scene detailed the degree of damage where the explosion had occurred.

In a complex sentence, you may also place the subordinate clause before the main clause. In this case, a comma is needed before the conjunction. No matter where it is placed, the main clause of a complex sentence contains the most important idea.

Subordinating conjunctions do more than connect clauses. They also indicate the *relationship* between the two clauses in terms of time, purpose, result, condition, or cause. Study the following complex sentences:

EXAMPLE

main clause ─── subordinate clause

My car insurance increased $500 this year *because* I received a speeding ticket.

EXAMPLE

subordinate clause ─── main clause

If Linda concentrates on her studies, she could earn a scholarship.

In the first sentence, *because* indicates that the first occurrence—the increase in insurance rates—is the result of the second occurrence. In the second, *if* suggests under what condition Linda will earn a scholarship.

Relative pronouns are used to introduce subordinate clauses that either *describe* a noun or *specify* a noun or pronoun in the sentence. Look at the following sentences, with the subordinate clauses italicized:

EXAMPLE

Any person *who provides encouragement and emotional support* is a true friend.

EXAMPLE

Food *that is low in fat* is better for a healthy heart.

In the first sentence, the relative pronoun *who* introduces the subordinate clause specifying what kind of person qualifies as a true friend. In the second, the relative pronoun *that* indicates which type of food is heart healthy.

Exercise 19.1   Identifying Subordinate Clauses

The following sentences are complex, containing both a main and a subordinate clause. Underline the subordinate clause in each sentence, and circle the subordinating conjunction or relative pronoun that introduces it, as the example shows.

EXAMPLE

Caring for a young child (who) is sick can be a stressful job for any parent.

(1) Today, people have easy access to newspapers from around the world (because) electronic versions of these papers are available on the Web. (2) Even small hometown newspapers (that) are delivered to doors every morning can be read on a computer. (3) (Once) an Internet browser is opened, it is easy to find a particular newspaper. (4) (If) the Web address is already known, users simply have to enter the address and hit Return. (5) The newspaper Web site (that) has been requested will quickly appear. (6) A search engine like Google or Yahoo can find a newspaper (when) the specific Web address isn't known. (7) (After) a line for the home page of the paper appears, users simply have to click on that line. (8) Within seconds, the electronic version of the newspaper fills the screen, (which) contains some top stories as well as links to other parts of the paper. (9) (Because) a link to the newspaper's archives is often provided, readers can also review stories from previous editions of the paper. (10) The pages (that) are prepared by the nation's large newspapers are also regularly updated, giving readers the most current news possible.

Exercise 19.2 **Combining Simple Sentences to Create Complex Sentences**

Before students revise the paragraph, read the original version out loud. Do students like the way it sounds? Why or why not? Compare the original paragraph with the final versions students create in Challenge 19.1.

The following paragraph is composed of simple sentences. On a separate piece of paper, rewrite it, joining ideas to create complex sentences. Use subordinating conjunctions and relative pronouns to introduce subordinate clauses. (Refer to the lists on pages 292–293.) Be sure that the ideas you want to emphasize are in the main clauses of your new sentences. You may decide to leave some simple sentences just as they are for variety. Be sure you use punctuation and capitals correctly.

(1) I have made taking a walk a top priority in my daily routine. (2) I walk two miles in the park. (3) The park is near my apartment. (4) My walk is important to me for many reasons. (5) First, the exercise helps me deal with

stressful situations. (6) These may come up at work. (7) I have many responsibilities, including preparing the work schedule for all workers. (8) Some mornings it is cold or raining. (9) I refuse to give up the most important hour of my day. (10) All in all, my morning walk is an invigorating way to start my day.

Challenge 19.1   **Evaluating Your Use of Subordination**

Exchange the paragraph you revised in Exercise 19.2 with a partner. Compare your versions, and discuss why you made the changes that you did. Did you leave any sentences as simple sentences? Did you emphasize the important ideas by making them the main clauses of the complex sentences? Choose the sentences in each version that you both agree are most effective. Then write a final version of the paragraph, and read it to your class.

Using Coordination

Another way to join related ideas is to use **coordination**. This is a technique for connecting two or more sentences to give each one equal emphasis. The resulting sentence is called a **compound sentence**.

Achieving Coordination by Using Coordinating Conjunctions

The most common way to create a compound sentence is to connect simple sentences with a **coordinating conjunction** and a comma. Writers may also use coordination to join complex sentences to simple ones or to join complex sentences to one another. The parts of a compound sentence are called **independent clauses** because each part is essentially a simple sentence and can stand on its own. Coordination cannot be used to join clauses that could not function on their own as complete sentences.

The coordinating conjunction in a complex sentence shows the relationship between the equally important ideas that it joins. Here is a list of the coordinating conjunctions.

Coordinating Conjunctions

and	for	or
but	nor	so

Using coordination can help you eliminate choppiness from your writing. Consider these two pairs of sentences:

CHOPPY	The heavy rain flooded the streets. Lightning started two small fires.

CHOPPY	The toddler started to fall from the top step. A woman coming up the stairs managed to steady him.

Suggest students keep a copy of subordinating conjunctions, coordinating conjunctions, and conjunctive adverbs in a journal or notebook for reference. They can also refer to the Recap on pages 301–303 at the end of this chapter.

As they are now, these two sets of sentences sound choppy. Now consider the same pairs of sentences when a conjunction and comma are used to join each pair of sentences:

| COMBINED | The heavy rain flooded the streets, *and* lightning started two small fires. |

| COMBINED | The toddler started to fall from the top step, *but* a woman coming up the stairs managed to steady him. |

These compound sentences are more fluid than the sets of simple sentences. The coordinating conjunctions clearly show how the two ideas within each subject–verb pair are related.

> *Fast Fact* U.S. President Abraham Lincoln made good use of subordination and coordination in his famous Gettysburg Address. The final sentence of the speech is a whopping 82 words long, which is nearly a third of the length of the entire address.

Exercise 19.3 **Developing Skills with Coordination**

Join each pair of simple sentences in the paragraph below with a comma and a coordinating conjunction to create one compound sentence. Insert the new material in the space above, using the example to guide you.
Answers will vary. Sample answers are given.

| EXAMPLE | The doors opened. The lines inched slowly ahead. |

, and the (inserted above, with "The" struck through)

Coordinating conjunctions suggest a relationship between the clauses that they join. Have students identify which conjunction they used to join the simple sentences and explain why.

(1) Last Monday, Marisol walked to the Transit Office. She bought a pass for a full week's transportation. *, and she* (2) She paid for the pass with a check. Then she forgot to put her checkbook back in her backpack. *, but then* (3) With her new pass in hand, she took the bus to school for a full morning of classes. She didn't think about her checkbook until lunch. *, and she* (4) At that point, Marisol had to act fast. She faced the loss of all the money in her account. *, or she* (5) She immediately called the Transit Office. Luckily, the head clerk had put her checkbook aside for her. *, and luckily,*

Exercise 19.4 **Using Coordination**

Fill in the blanks, adding a clause that is related to the existing clause before or after the coordinating conjunction. Answers will vary. Sample answers are given.

EXAMPLE   The basketball game was tied, **so** _the coach left the starting five on the court._

1. The restaurant that I wanted to go to was closed, **so** _____
   we tried the new Thai restaurant next door.

2. _The Thai restaurant was not open_ _____, **nor** was the coffee shop open down the street.

3. Our stomachs were growling, **so** _we decided to take the bus to another restaurant across town._

4. The wait at the bus stop was long, **but** _we bought hot pretzels to snack on._

5. _It's a good thing the pretzel vendor came by_ _____, **or** I would have fainted from hunger.

Challenge 19.2   **Analyzing the Clauses in Compound Sentences**

Each of the clauses in a compound sentence must be *independent*, or able to stand on its own as a complete sentence. Underline the subjects and verbs in the clauses you wrote for Exercise 19.4. Could each clause stand on its own as a sentence? If not, make any changes necessary to make each one an independent clause.

Achieving Coordination by Using Semicolons

Another way to achieve coordination is to use a *semicolon* (;) to connect independent clauses. A semicolon, which has the same power to connect as a coordinating conjunction with a comma, makes the connection more direct. You will learn more about the use of semicolons in Chapter 31, "Other Punctuation and Capitalization."

Consider the two versions of the following sentence:

EXAMPLE   The day had been long and hot, *and* all I wanted to do was take a shower.

EXAMPLE   The day had been long and hot; all I wanted to do was take a shower.

In the first version, the coordinating conjunction *and* joins the two clauses, *adding* the second thought. In the second version, the semicolon joins the two ideas directly, emphasizing the close relationship between them. Semicolons are used to join sentences that have such a clear, obvious connection.

In addition to using a semicolon alone, you can add a twist to this technique by including a **conjunctive adverb** after the semicolon. Study the following list of conjunctive adverbs:

Common Conjunctive Adverbs

also	however	similarly
besides	instead	still
consequently	meanwhile	then
finally	moreover	therefore
furthermore	nevertheless	thus

Conjunctive adverbs *suggest a relationship* between two thoughts, as the following compound sentences show:

EXAMPLE   In-line skating is great exercise; *furthermore*, it's great fun.

EXAMPLE   I had planned to get to work early; *however*, two accidents on the highway delayed me for 45 minutes.

Neither *furthermore* nor *however* is used to connect the sentences. The semicolon does that. Note that this technique requires two punctuation marks: a semicolon *before* the conjunctive adverb and a comma *after* it.

Fast Fact And you thought the semicolon was just a strange-looking mark of punctuation. The 1870–1873 Texas Supreme Court was given the derogatory name of Semicolon Court by contemporary lawyers in the Lone Star State. The Court earned this title because the justices ruled that a semicolon in one article of state election law made the general election of 1873 unconstitutional and invalid. The ruling was never enforced, however, and the government that came into power removed the three judges that made up the Semicolon Court.

Exercise 19.5   **Achieving Coordination by Using Semicolons**

As you read the sentences in the paragraph below, decide which ones are closely related in meaning. On a separate sheet of paper, create a new version of the passage, using a semicolon to join these closely related sentences. Use the example to guide you.

EXAMPLE   Janet had always considered Michelle a courageous, ethical person. ;
Michelle's actions that morning only reinforced her belief. ∧

(1) Getting contact lenses was one of the best decisions I ever made. (2) My vision is so much better now. (3) I am also much happier with my appearance. (4) I have had to wear glasses since the tenth grade. (5) No high school student wants to look at the world through thick lenses. (6) At the end of the year, I asked my parents to get me contact lenses. (7) Unfortunately, they simply couldn't afford to buy them for me. (8) I decided at that point to save up myself. (9) All together, it took my two months of

overtime to pay for the examination, fitting, and lenses. (10) It was time and money well spent.

| **Exercise 19.6** | **Combining Sentences Using Conjunctive Adverbs and Semicolons** |

Complete each sentence by adding a conjunctive adverb and an independent clause after the semicolon. Use the list of conjunctive adverbs on page 298. Don't forget a comma after the conjunctive adverb. Study the example first.   Answers will vary. Representative answers are given.

EXAMPLE   The waiting room at the clinic was crowded; *however, I decided to stay until the doctor was available.*

1. Washington, D.C.'s Metro system is clean and efficient; therefore, visitors to the nation's capital enjoy using it.

2. The wheels on the subway cars are made of special material that reduces noise; consequently, you can hear announcements made in the stations.

3. Last year a record number of visitors used the system; nevertheless, the cars never looked dirty or littered.

4. The New York subway system is quite different; instead, it is noisy and dirty.

5. New Yorkers often choose the bus over the subway; however, it remains one of the country's busiest systems.

Before students revise the paragraph in Exercise 19.7, read the original version out loud. Do students like the way it sounds? Why or why not? Compare the original paragraph with the revised paragraphs students create in this exercise.

| **Exercise 19.7** | **Using Coordination and Subordination** |

Activity 19.3

The paragraph below contains simple sentences. Decide where it can be improved through coordination and subordination. Then rewrite the new version on a separate piece of paper. Use all the methods you have practiced in this chapter to create compound and complex sentences. You may decide to leave some sentences as they are.

EXAMPLE   Many people try to avoid taking Statistics I. It is a difficult course.
Many people try to avoid taking Statistics I because it is a difficult course.

(1) Asthma is a chronic, dangerous lung condition. (2) It can be treated. (3) The causes of asthma are increasing. (4) More and more people suffer

from asthma every year. (5) Asthma attacks can be triggered by air pollution, dust, a cold, and even exercise. (6) During an asthma attack, bronchial tubes in the lungs get irritated and constrict. (7) Patients cough, wheeze, and struggle to breathe as a result. (8) Asthma sufferers can lead normal lives. (9) They need proper medication and medical supervision. (10) They also need to understand and avoid the conditions that trigger their asthma attacks.

Challenge 19.3 **Evaluating Your Sentence Combining Techniques**

Share the paragraph you revised in Exercise 19.7 with a partner, and compare the choices you each made to combine ideas. In your discussion, answer the following questions: What options did you use for achieving coordination? Where did you use subordination? Why did you make the changes that you did? Where is your revision different from your partner's? Which ideas did you leave expressed as simple sentences? Why?

Chapter Quick Check: Subordination and Coordination

The writing below is composed of simple sentences. On a separate sheet of paper, revise it by combining sentences to emphasize ideas, to show connections among ideas, and to make the writing smooth. Use the methods you have practiced in this chapter to create complex or compound sentences. In some cases, you may decide to leave a particular sentence as it is.
Answers will vary.

(1) Memory is a fascinating subject. (2) Scientists continue to study different aspects of this mental capability. (3) One area of continued focus is the connection between aging and a weakening of memory processes. (4) The ability to remember seems to diminish with age. (5) This point may be true to some extent. (6) People of all ages sometimes forget where they have parked their cars or left their keys. (7) Current research points to lack of attention rather than some problem in the brain as the cause of some memory lapses. (8) The desire to suppress traumatic recollections accounts for others. (9) In their recollections, trauma victims often innocently include untrue or inaccurate details or events. (10) Courts are now having to rethink their attitudes about the accuracy of eyewitness reports of crimes.

Discovering Connections 19.2

1. In Discovering Connections 19.1 on page 292, you prewrote on one of three suggested subjects. Now use this prewriting material as the basis, and work your way through the rest of the writing process to complete a draft essay of about 500 words on this topic.
2. Exchange your draft with a partner. Using the material in this chapter to guide you, check the sentences in the draft to see whether subor-

dination and coordination have been used effectively. Put a ✓ next to any pairs or groups of sentences that could benefit from either of these techniques; then return the draft to the writer.

3. Revise your essay, using subordination or coordination where it is appropriate.

Summary Exercise: Subordination and Coordination

Activity
19.4

The writing below is composed of simple sentences. On a separate piece of paper, revise it by combining sentences to emphasize ideas, to show connections among ideas, and to make the writing smooth. Use the methods you have practiced in this chapter to create complex or compound sentences. In some cases, you may decide to leave a particular sentence as it is.
Answers will vary.

Ask small groups of students to discuss the changes they made and explain how subordination and coordination improved the sentences.

(1) Important documents in our nation's history are housed in the National Archives in Washington, D.C. (2) Many of the documents are old and fragile. (3) They are carefully protected from further deterioration. (4) Many people see these documents. (5) They are impressed both by their importance and by the care taken to preserve them for the future.

(6) The Constitution, signed by representatives of twelve of the original states in 1787, is housed in the Archives. (7) It is only four pages long. (8) The Constitution contains the foundation of our democratic system. (9) Visitors can see two pages of this famous document. (10) They are housed in bronze and glass cases. (11) The cases are filled with helium gas to preserve the old parchment.

(12) The Archives also displays the Declaration of Independence and the Bill of Rights. (13) The Declaration of Independence, written primarily by Thomas Jefferson, was adopted on July 4, 1776. (14) The Bill of Rights was ratified more than two hundred years ago. (15) Citizens, judges, and scholars still discuss it today. (16) This document speaks about freedom of the press, freedom of religion, freedom of speech, and the right to bear arms. (17) These are still controversial issues today.

(18) All of these documents are stored every night in a special vault. (19) The bronze and glass cases are lowered electronically to the bottom of a vault. (20) It is twenty-two feet below the ground.

Weblink
19.1

Weblink
19.2

 RECAP SUBORDINATION AND COORDINATION

New terms in this chapter	Definitions
● **subordination**	● a way to combine unequal ideas, giving emphasis to one and making the other dependent upon the former
● **simple sentence**	● a sentence consisting of a subject and a verb and their modifiers ***Example*** A mouse had eaten a hole in the bag of popcorn.
● **complex sentence**	● a sentence consisting of a main clause and a subordinate clause
● **subordinate clause**	● a subject–verb unit that doesn't express a complete thought; also called a *dependent clause* Subordinate clauses are introduced by *subordinating conjunctions* or *relative pronouns*.
● **subordinating conjunction**	● one of a group of connecting words used at the beginning of a subordinate clause to join it to an independent clause: *after, although, as, as if, as soon as, because, before, even though, if, in order that, once, rather than, since, so that, than, though, unless, until, when, whenever, wherever, whether, while* The subordinating conjunction expresses the relationship between the two clauses. ***Example*** The downtown flooded *because* we had torrential rains.
● **relative pronoun**	● one of a group of words used to introduce subordinate clauses that describe or specify a noun or pronoun in a main clause: *that, what, which, who, whom, whose* ***Example*** An author *whose* work I admire is Jamaica Kincaid.
● **main clause**	● a subject–verb unit that can stand on its own but is combined with another subject–verb unit A main clause is an *independent clause*.
● **coordination**	● the combining of independent clauses of equal importance into *compound sentences* to eliminate choppiness and repetition
● **compound sentence**	● a sentence containing two or more independent clauses joined by a connector: (1) a *coordinating conjunction* and a comma, (2) a *semicolon*, or (3) a semicolon plus a *conjunctive adverb*
● **coordinating conjunction**	● one of a set of joining words used to connect words or ideas of equal rank: *and, but, for, nor, or, so,* and *yet*

New terms in this chapter	Definitions
● **independent clause**	● a clause with a subject and a verb that can stand alone as a sentence A compound sentence consists of two or more independent clauses joined by a connector. ***Example*** *Spring is on the way,* and *the temperature is rising.*
● **conjunctive adverb**	● one of a group of words used with a connector to link ideas by showing how they are related: *also, besides, consequently, finally, furthermore, however, instead, meanwhile, moreover, nevertheless, similarly, still, then, therefore,* and *thus* A conjunctive adverb cannot connect simple sentences itself but does emphasize the connection provided by semicolons. A conjunctive adverb requires a comma after it when used with a semicolon connecting simple sentences. ***Example*** Cheetahs are an endangered species**;** *however,* many cheetahs were born at zoos last year.

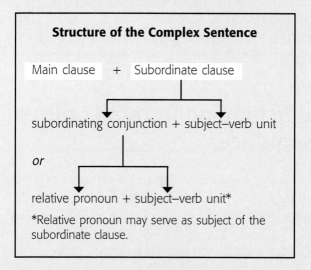

Structure of the Complex Sentence

Main clause   +   Subordinate clause

subordinating conjunction + subject–verb unit

or

relative pronoun + subject–verb unit*

*Relative pronoun may serve as subject of the subordinate clause.

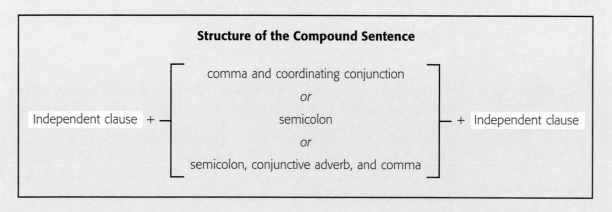

Structure of the Compound Sentence

Independent clause +

comma and coordinating conjunction

or

semicolon

or

semicolon, conjunctive adverb, and comma

+ Independent clause

Chapter 20

Comma Splices and Run-On Sentences

Getting Started... **Q:** I'm happy with the ideas I've developed, and I know I have to express them in correct sentence form. Right now, though, I'm concerned that my thoughts run together. What can I do to make sure that I end each sentence where it's supposed to end?

Audio 20.1 **A:** You have developed good ideas, so you already have what you need to create an effective writing. To avoid comma splices and run-on sentences, answer this simple question: Do I want to keep these units separate or connect them? To separate them, use a period, question mark, or exclamation point. To connect them, use a coordinating conjunction with a comma, a subordinating conjunction, or a semicolon. That's all there is to it.

Overview: Understanding Comma Splices and Run-On Sentences

Audio 20.2 Two of the most common and most serious sentence errors are the **comma splice** and the **run-on sentence**. A comma splice is an error in which sentences are incorrectly connected by a comma, a mark of punctuation that *can't* connect. A run-on sentence is an error in which two sentences are run together without proper punctuation or an appropriate connector. Both errors are serious because they distract readers from the point you are making. To avoid these two sentence errors, you must first recognize and then correct them in your writing.

Weblink 20.1 *In this chapter, you will learn how to recognize and avoid comma splices and run-on sentences. You will practice correcting these errors by using*

- a coordinating conjunction and a comma

- a subordinating conjunction

- a semicolon (or a semicolon and a conjunctive adverb)

- a period

Discovering Connections 20.1

Discovering Connections 20.2 provides an opportunity for students to apply the skills they learned about recognizing and avoiding comma splices and run-on sentences. They will be asked to compose and revise an essay based on one of the topics suggested here.

Using one of the techniques you practiced in Chapter 2, "Generating Ideas through Prewriting," prewrite on one of the following topics:

1. the responsibilities and dangers of credit cards
2. maintaining a healthy diet

Or, focus on this picture.
Save your work for later use.

Identifying Comma Splices and Run-On Sentences

ESL Note
See "Sentence Basics" on pages 572–574 and "Punctuation and Capitalization" on pages 583–584.

Audio
20.3

The first step in correcting comma splices and run-on sentences is to identify them. Start by locating the subjects and verbs in your sentences. Then check if you have joined two subject–verb units with only a comma. If so, you have a comma splice. *Commas cannot connect independent clauses.* Commas indicate a pause, or they separate elements within a sentence, but they can't connect.

Take a look at this example:

COMMA SPLICE

The *flashlight flickered* out, the *batteries were* obviously dead.

Video
20.1

Each unit contains a subject and verb, and each could stand alone as a simple sentence. But a comma can't connect, so the result is a comma splice.

To check for run-on sentences, follow the same method. First, locate the subjects and verbs in your sentences. Then check to see whether you have joined two subject–verb units without any *connector* or *separator.* If so, you have created a run-on sentence.

Read out loud the following example, which has a / where one unit ends and the next begins:

RUN-ON SENTENCE

My car *horn is* broken again / *I have replaced* it twice already.

Audio
20.4

As you can see, this example consists of two subject–verb units, each of which could stand on its own. Nothing either connects or separates these units. Instead, the first unit just *runs into* the second, which is why this type of error is called a run-on sentence, or simply a run-on.

Incidentally, one reason comma splices occur is that the ways that commas function are often misunderstood. Therefore, one way to avoid making comma splices is to understand what commas do. When you write, you use commas in the following ways:

● To indicate the pause between clauses connected by conjunctions

EXAMPLE   The door was closed, but it wasn't locked.

- To separate items in a series

EXAMPLE We looked for the missing ring around the apartment, in the backyard, and in the car.

- To set off introductory material

EXAMPLE With the additional memory, the computer performed much faster.

- To set off elements that interrupt sentence flow

EXAMPLE Showing up early on your first day, for instance, is a great way to impress a new boss.

- To set off direct quotations

EXAMPLE "I'm just not interested in that class," Vincente explained.

- To fulfill several other purposes, including

> setting off the salutation of a personal letter (Dear Zelda,)
> setting off the parts of dates from the rest of the sentence (March 31, 1982, was the day Jacqueline was born.)
> setting off parts of addresses (His last permanent address was 44 Bogle Street, East Ridge, NM 34268.)
> indicating thousands within numbers (3,211 or 3,211,000)
> setting off a name when you address someone directly (I want you to know, Marilyn, that you have made a tremendous impact on this office.)

If you use commas for these purposes only, you decrease your chances of making a comma splice. For a more complete discussion and additional examples of proper comma use, see Chapter 30, "Commas."

Exercise 20.1   **Identifying Comma Splices and Run-On Sentences**

By reading aloud, students can sometimes hear sentences that run together. They can then determine where a strong pause is needed to separate the units.

The paragraph below contains several comma splices and run-on sentences. To identify them, first underline every subject and verb. Then note where one idea ends and the next begins and put a / between these units. If the subject–verb units are joined by only a comma, put *CS* for comma splice in front of it. If there is no connector or separator, put *RS* for run-on sentence in front of it. Use the example to guide you.

EXAMPLE   *RS* The city should lower the speed limit on Plymouth Avenue / the area is

very congested.

CS (1) Over the past few years, youth sports leagues in the United States

have been the focus of much attention, / the behavior of adult fans and parents <u>is</u> the primary reason for this concern. RS (2) News <u>reports</u> across the country <u>have recorded</u> numerous incidents involving parents yelling and interrupting games and practices/these <u>confrontations</u> sometimes <u>have</u> even <u>led</u> to physical violence. CS (3) In one infamous incident, a <u>parent</u> physically <u>attacked</u> a coach,/the <u>coach died</u> as a result. RS (4) Clearly, some <u>reform</u> is necessary/some <u>people have suggested</u> banning any adult spectators as a solution to the problem. CS (5) The <u>purpose</u> of these leagues <u>is</u> to give children the chance to have fun,/<u>adults need</u> to let the kids play without any interference.

Exercise 20.2   **Recognizing Comma Splices and Run-Ons**

The following paragraph contains several comma splices and run-on sentences. Put an ∗ in front of any comma splice or run-on, and insert a / where one sentence should end and the next should begin. Use the example to guide you.

EXAMPLE   ∗Jennifer didn't show up for class again today,/this is the fifth time she has been absent this month.

(1) ∗In national politics, money talks/a candidate can't expect to win today without enormous financial backing. (2) It isn't unusual for a congressional campaign to cost each candidate several million dollars or more. (3) ∗People simply can't afford to run a campaign alone,/they must count on donations. (4) Incumbents have a great advantage over challengers in terms of fund-raising. (5) ∗Incumbents already have contacts,/businesses are therefore more willing to donate to them. (6) ∗With a little luck, the donations will pay off/the incumbents will act on behalf of those businesses once they are re-elected. (7) ∗Challengers have no power and no influence,/they have difficulty getting corporate support. (8) ∗Of course, there are exceptions/misconduct or criminal charges against an incumbent will often shift popular and financial support to a challenger. (9) ∗Our campaign finance system is

not productive or fair/we need to reform the laws that govern it. (10) We should have a system that enables us to elect the best candidate, not the one with the biggest campaign chest.

Challenge 20.1 | **Checking for Comma Splices and Run-Ons in Your Writing**

Take a recent assignment that you are working on, and exchange it with a partner. Underline the subjects and verbs in each sentence of the paper you receive. Then put a / between any clauses you see that can stand alone. If you discover any comma splices or run-ons, mark these errors. Return the draft to your partner. Save your own draft for later use.

Correcting Comma Splices and Run-Ons by Using Coordinating Conjunctions

Stress that all of these techniques are correct; each one represents a choice that writers make to communicate their ideas clearly. Discuss how each technique creates a slightly different meaning.

One way to correct comma splices and run-on sentences is to use a coordinating conjunction such as *and, but,* and *or* between independent clauses. (See page 295 for a complete listing of coordinating conjunctions.) Besides providing connection, these conjunctions help you eliminate choppiness and repetition.

Consider these examples, with corrections added:

COMMA SPLICE

$$yet$$
The clock is over 100 years old, it keeps perfect time.
$$\wedge$$

RUN-ON

$$, and$$
Karen does volunteer work at an extended-care facility she also has a
$$\wedge$$
weekend job.

In the first sentence, *yet* provides the connection and shows opposition between ideas. In the second, a comma plus *and* now link the two clauses; *and* suggests addition of ideas. The sentences now flow better, and, more important, they are now correct. By the way, as the examples above show, always include a comma *before* a conjunction used to connect simple sentences.

Fast Fact Among English words, *and* ranks as the third most commonly used word. This little word is versatile, too, serving as a means of correcting comma splices and run-on sentences, and it links individual words, phrases, and clauses. Depending on the items being connected, *and* can also provide a comic connection, as it does in these actual street locations identified by State Farm Insurance: the intersection of Grinn *and* Barret in West Chester, Ohio; the intersection of Ho *and* Hum in Carefree, Arizona; the intersection of Antonio *and* Banderas in Santa Margarita, California; and the intersection of Hickory *and* Dickory *and* Dock in Harahan, Louisiana.

Exercise 20.3   **Using Coordinating Conjunctions to Connect Clauses**

Each numbered item in the following paragraph is either a run-on sentence or a comma splice. If the item is a run-on, put a / between the independent clauses. Then above the /, add a comma and the coordinating conjunction (*and, or, but, for, nor, so,* or *yet*) that best connects the thoughts in the independent clauses. If the item is a comma splice, simply insert a / and the correct coordinating conjunction between the clauses. Use the examples to guide you.   Answers may vary.

EXAMPLE   I had completed my art project on time/I forgot to bring it.   ⟨, but⟩

EXAMPLE   Annie has black hair,/it curls naturally.   ⟨and⟩

(1) Finally, Martin Luther King Day is celebrated in all 50 states,/it certainly took a while. ⟨but⟩ (2) For a time, it was a federal holiday/most states celebrated it. ⟨, and⟩ (3) A few states, however, did not observe it,/schools, businesses, and government offices in those states remained open. ⟨and⟩ (4) Many individuals in these states were outraged about this/they stayed home from work and kept their children out of school in protest. ⟨, so⟩ (5) A special day in Dr. King's honor is well deserved,/he gave his life to improve civil rights for all of us. ⟨for⟩

Exercise 20.4   **Using Coordinating Conjunctions to Correct Comma Splices and Run-On Sentences**

Audio 20.5   The following paragraph contains several comma splices and run-on sentences. Put an * in front of any comma splice or run-on sentence. Then put a / between independent clauses. Choose an appropriate coordinating conjunction from the list below and insert it above where one sentence should end and the next should begin. Don't forget to add a comma if it isn't already there. Use the example to guide you.

and	nor
but	so
for	yet
or	

EXAMPLE   *The officer was clearly lying/the judge allowed his testimony.   ⟨, yet⟩

Representative answers are given. Actual answers may vary somewhat.

*(1) A new bakery and coffee shop in my neighborhood has been open for only three weeks/already business seems excellent. ⟨, but⟩ *(2) The shop

is called The Stafford Road Stop/ , and it sells a wide variety of bagels, muffins, doughnuts, and other pastries.*(3) The shop is located right across the street from a Metro stop,/ so many of the patrons stop by on their way into the downtown area. (4) The shop itself is bright and clean, with a large display case and ten small tables, each with two chairs in front of it.*(5) A counter with stools is against the front wall/ , so patrons can enjoy their food while looking at the busy street scene outside.*(6) The staff doesn't hesitate to ask customers about their favorite selections,/ and they don't hesitate to inquire about the need for new products.*(7) According to the owner, Ms. Liliana Godek, they will have your favorite baked goods on hand/ , or they will add them to the menu. *(8) She also prides herself on her coffee,/ and patrons can choose from several types, including at least two types of decaffeinated coffee.*(9) The quality of all her products is excellent,/ yet yet the prices are reasonable. (10) All in all, the Stafford Road Stop gives every sign of becoming a success story.

Challenge 20.2   **Working with Coordinating Conjunctions**

Consider again the list of coordinating conjunctions in Exercise 20.4. Then, working with a partner, write two sentences for each conjunction and use the conjunction to connect the simple sentences. When you are done, explain in a few sentences which conjunction you found most useful and why.

Correcting Comma Splices and Run-Ons by Using Subordinating Conjunctions

Audio
20.6

Another way to eliminate comma splices and run-on sentences is to add a subordinating conjunction such as *after, because, if,* and *unless* to connect clauses. (See page 292 for a complete listing of subordinating conjunctions.) As Chapter 19, "Subordination and Coordination," showed, subordinating conjunctions indicate a relationship between the ideas they connect. Consider the following examples:

COMMA SPLICE   *Because oil*
~~Oil~~ from the leaking barge fouled the water for over 20 square miles, more than 1,000 birds were killed.

RUN-ON   On Wednesday afternoon, the needed items were still not here, *even though* they promised to deliver them by Tuesday.

In the first example, *because* joins two ideas related by cause and effect: The death of the birds *resulted from* an oil spill. In the second example, *even though* links the ideas and also indicates the relationship between them: Items were not delivered *despite the fact that* they had been promised.

Exercise 20.5   **Using Subordinating Conjunctions to Correct Comma Splices and Run-On Sentences**

Each numbered item in the following paragraph is either a run-on sentence or a comma splice. First, put a / between the independent clauses. Then add one of the subordinating conjunctions listed below to show a relationship between the clauses. In some cases, more than one correct answer is possible. With a comma splice, you'll need to add only the subordinating conjunction, but with a run-on sentence, you'll need to add a comma as well as the conjunctive adverb. Study the example first.

after	before
although	since
because	when

EXAMPLE   *Before the*
~~The~~ police arrived,/traffic was backed up for three miles.

(1) *Before* I started work/I never saw the importance of knowing a second language. (2) Having bilingual workers is important,/*because* the needs of all customers can be met. (3) *When* I thought about it/learning a second language seemed like a great idea for me. (4) *Although* I am training to be a paralegal,/I will have to deal with people from a wide variety of backgrounds. (5) *Since* I know more than one language/a law office will be more interested in hiring me.

Exercise 20.6   **Correcting Comma Splices and Run-On Sentences by Using Subordinating Conjunctions**

In the following paragraph, find the comma splices and run-ons, and put an * in front of each one. Then choose an appropriate subordinating conjunction (*because, since, even though, when, although,* or *so that*), and insert it in the proper place above the line to make the sentence correct. Make sure to add a comma if it is needed. Study the example first.

EXAMPLE

> *because*
> *They were late leaving the campground ∧ they had to wait for Gil and Sheila.

(1)*Some people are counted as unemployed or underemployed by the

although
government ∧ they actually have an income. (2) They are part of the "under-

so that
ground economy." (3)*Most people in this situation work for cash only, ∧ they

can hide their income from government agencies. (4)*In most cases, they

because
charge substantially less ∧ their salary is tax free. (5) Sometimes these workers

are amateurs just picking up a little extra cash on the weekends or nights.

since
(6)*They don't want to declare their earnings, ∧ the extra income might raise

their overall tax burden. (7)*Sometimes trained specialists and union arti-

when
sans join the underground economy ∧ they are between jobs or laid off. (8)

Many members of the underground economy have no other means of sup-

because
port. (9)*They work below the minimum wage ∧ they would have no employ-

even though
ment otherwise. (10)*The underground economy continues to thrive, ∧ the

government has tried to control it.

Challenge 20.3 **Working with Subordinating Conjunctions**

For Exercise 20.5, you corrected comma splices and run-on sentences by using subordinating conjunctions to connect the subject–verb units. Working with a partner, choose three of these sentences, and, on a separate sheet of paper, substitute different subordinating conjunctions. Then discuss how these new conjunctions change the meaning of the sentences.

Correcting Comma Splices and Run-Ons by Using Semicolons

A semicolon (;) has the same power to connect simple sentences that conjunctions have. Using a semicolon to provide the link between sentences enables you also to emphasize the connection between the units, adding another dimension to your meaning, as these examples, with corrections, show:

COMMA SPLICE   The new store features specialty paper products;their greeting cards are

all printed on recycled paper.

RUN-ON   The guest speaker waited for questions from the class;nobody said a word.

In the first example, the clause about the nature of the store is now properly joined to the clause explaining one of the products. In the second example, the clause explaining the speaker's expectation is connected by a semicolon to the clause describing the class's lack of response.

To clarify the relationship between the clauses, you can use a conjunctive adverb (*also, furthermore, instead, however, moreover, then, therefore*, etc.) with a semicolon. (See page 298 for a complete list of conjunctive adverbs.) Consider these examples:

EXAMPLE   The suit was expensive; *however,* it was very well made.

EXAMPLE   After playing for five minutes, the band suddenly left the stage; *meanwhile,* two technicians began to check the sound system.

In each example, the semicolon joins the ideas, and the conjunctive adverb clarifies why the ideas are linked. Notice that a comma is needed after each of these conjunctive adverbs.

Fast Fact   A case of mistaken identity can explain some comma splices and run-on sentences. Because it indicates something contrary, people often assume that *however* is a conjunction, like *but*. It isn't, though—it's a *conjunctive adverb*. You can tell because *however* can be moved to several spots in a clause without changing the meaning. For example:

• The front parking lot is full. *However,* the three lots behind the building are empty.
• The front parking lot is full. The three lots behind the building, *however,* are empty.
• The front parking lot is full. The three lots behind the building are empty, *however.*

Exercise 20.7   **Working with Semicolons to Correct Comma Splices and Run-On Sentences**

Each numbered item in the following paragraph is either a comma splice or a run-on sentence. First, put a / between the independent clauses. Then insert a semicolon, alone or with an appropriate conjunctive adverb, to connect the clauses. If you add a conjunctive adverb, write it followed by a comma above the point where the first clause ends and the second begins. (A complete list of conjunctive adverbs appears on page 298.) Use the examples to guide you.

EXAMPLE   At first, the puppy wouldn't come out from behind the chair/Caitlyn eventually coaxed it out with a doggie biscuit.

or

> ; *however,*
EXAMPLE   At first, the puppy wouldn't come out from behind the chair/Caitlyn even-
> ^
tually coaxed it out with a doggie biscuit.

Representative conjunctive adverbs are given. Actual answers may vary somewhat.

    ; moreover,
(1) The city is sponsoring its first Summer Arts Festival/the goal is to
    ^
have such a festival to mark the beginning of each season. (2) The Summer
    ; however,
Arts Festival will take place under a large tent in Wachusetts Park/the other
    ^
three festivals will be held in the Historical Center Annex downtown.
(3) Visual and performance artists in the surrounding area have been invited
    ; furthermore,
to take part/vendors selling everything from ethnic food to specialty clothing
    ^
to craft items will set up booths. (4) The city's tourist board has hired a com-
    ; nevertheless,
pany specializing in such events to coordinate the festival/various city offi-
    ^
cials have remained closely involved in the planning. (5) Everyone involved
    ; however,
is hoping for a big success at this first festival/the city has stated its determi-
    ^
nation to provide support for a one-year cycle regardless of attendance at
the initial event.

Exercise 20.8   **Using Semicolons to Correct Comma Splices and Run-On Sentences**

The following paragraph contains several comma splices and run-on sentences. Put an ***** in front of any comma splice or run-on sentence. Then insert a semicolon, with or without a conjunctive adverb. If you use a
conjunctive adverb, insert it above where one sentence should end and the
next should begin, and put a comma after it. Study the examples first.
Answers may vary.

    ;
EXAMPLE   The injury to her ankle was severe/she was in great pain.

or

    ; *consequently,*
EXAMPLE   The injury to her ankle was severe/she was in great pain.

(1) Jasmine earns money for college by delivering the morning newspa-
    ;
per. (2)*An adult can make a pretty good paycheck this way/the person just
    ^
has to be willing to get out of bed at 5 A.M. every day. (3)*Her route covers

ten miles outside the city ; she delivers a total of 200 papers on weekdays and 100 on Sundays. (4)*Jasmine never complains ; however, her job is far from easy. (5)*She spends the first hour folding papers and putting them in plastic bags ; these steps are vital in order to keep the papers dry. (6) She then piles the papers into the passenger's seat in her car and begins driving. (7)*The process of delivering the papers is a little dangerous ; therefore, she puts her emergency blinkers on and drives slowly along her route. (8)*Her delivery method is interesting ; she grabs a paper from the seat and throws it completely over the car and into the subscriber's yard. (9) By 6:30, she has finished her entire route. (10)*She then stops at the bakery at the end of her route for coffee ; she is too tired to read the paper, though.

<table>
<tr><td>**Exercise 20.9**</td><td>**Using Semicolons with Conjunctive Adverbs to Correct Comma Splices and Run-On Sentences**</td></tr>
</table>

The following passage contains a number of comma splices and run-on sentences. Correct them by using a semicolon and one of the conjunctive adverbs listed below, as the example illustrates.

also	meanwhile	then
consequently	moreover	therefore
furthermore	nevertheless	thus

EXAMPLE The heavy rains destroyed the old earthen dam ; therefore, the mayor was forced to declare a state of emergency.

Answers in terms of conjunctive adverbs are representative. In some cases, more than one answer is acceptable.

(1) Advances in photography have made it possible for the average person to record the world in a professional way. (2) Digital cameras, many costing less than $300, capture sharp, precise images and record them on a photo storage card ; then the images can be transferred to a computer and turned into prints. (3) Through various easy-to-use computer programs, the pictures can be manipulated to eliminate minor blemishes or to enhance the

; furthermore,
images in some way, in their electronic form, digital pictures can be e-mailed.

(4) With a few easy steps, a person can use these images to illustrate Web

; moreover,
pages, they can be combined with music and text to create an inviting and

informative website. (5) With digital photography, no film is wasted on out-

; also,
of-focus pictures nobody has to spend additional money to develop a roll

of film. (6) The advances have been just as dramatic in the area of video

; nevertheless,
recording. (7) Today's video cameras are light, compact, and powerful, they

capture events with far greater clarity than the huge video cameras of the

past. (8) The color display available on most models makes it easy to see

; therefore,
exactly what the lens is recording the operator is able to make any adjust-

ments with ease. (9) The cost of these compact video cameras has contin-

; consequently,
ued to drop, many vacationers and even people on the street carry them.

(10) As a result, accidents, natural catastrophes, and other incidents that

might have gone unrecorded are captured on video by someone who just

happened to be on the scene.

Challenge 20.4 **Working with Semicolons and Conjunctive Adverbs**

For Exercise 20.7, you made some choices about how to connect clauses in
a paragraph by using either a semicolon or a semicolon and a conjunctive
adverb. Now, working with a partner, compare your two versions of the passage. Discuss why you made your choices. If, after your discussion, you prefer another way of joining some of your sentences, make those changes.

Correcting Comma Splices and Run-Ons by Using Periods

Another way to correct comma splices and run-on sentences is to use a period between the subject–verb units to create separate sentences. This option isn't a good idea if the simple sentences are short because it may make
your writing seem choppy. If the sentences are longer, however, separating
them may be a good choice, as these examples show:

COMMA SPLICE   Larry's plan is to earn his two-year degree in Business Administration and

Marketing, ~~he~~ then will enroll at the university to earn his undergraduate

. He

degree.

RUN-ON   Serena and Venus Williams have brought genuine excitement back to

women's tennis ~~their~~ matches, especially the ones against each other, have

. Their

been ratings blockbusters.

You could certainly eliminate these errors by using a conjunction and a comma or a semicolon. The sentences that would result would be a bit long, however, and long sentences can be difficult to follow. Therefore, using a period to create separate simple sentences is a better choice. When you use this option to correct run-on sentences and comma splices, remember to capitalize the first word of the second sentence.

Exercise 20.10   **Using a Period to Separate the Units**

In this paragraph, using a period to separate the independent clauses is probably the best option because the clauses are long. Put a / between the clauses, and then insert a period to eliminate the run-on sentence or comma splice. Start the first word of a new sentence with a capital letter. Use the example to guide you.

EXAMPLE   By noontime on opening day, the line leading into the stadium was al-

ready a quarter of a mile long / ~~inside~~ 10,000 people had already taken

. Inside,

their seats, waiting for the first ball to be thrown out.

(1) The recent hurricane changed the entire landscape at Horseneck

Beach / ~~fortunately,~~ only a few of the houses along the edge of the beach suf-

. Fortunately,

fered from the effects of severe erosion. (2) The most severely damaged house

was owned by Mr. Lionel Partridge, one of the oldest residents of the commu-

nity / ~~the~~ storm ripped off the front of the house, sending all his belongings

. The

into the churning ocean. (3) The contour of the beach itself showed the most

dramatic change of all / ~~the~~ dunes separating the beach from the road were

. The

completely flattened. (4) Foundations of several homes destroyed by earlier

> . They
hurricanes were visible again /~~they~~ had been buried for over 25 years.
> . The
(5) Even with the changes, Horseneck Beach is still beautiful /~~the~~ whole expe-

rience should remind everyone of the tremendous power of nature.

Exercise 20.11   **Working with a Period to Separate the Units**

The following paragraph contains several comma splices and run-on sentences. Put an **∗** in front of any comma splice or run-on sentence. Then put
a / between the independent clauses. Insert a period where the first sentence should end, and then start the word that begins the second sentence
with a capital letter. Study the example first.

EXAMPLE

> . The
∗The landscapers spent the afternoon digging up the dead sod/~~the~~ grass

had been completely destroyed by grubs.

> . Even
(1)∗Max's first experience with a credit card was not a good one/~~even~~

at age twenty-one, he wasn't ready for the responsibility. (2) Five years ago,

he filled out an application for a credit card at his favorite clothing store.
> . His
(3)∗A week later, the card came in the mail/~~his~~ troubles began at that point.
> . He
(4)∗His original plan was to buy one item a week/~~he~~ would then pay off

the entire bill at the end of the month. (5)∗For the first two months, he had
> . As
no trouble keeping up with the payments/~~as~~ a result, Max decided to buy

more things. (6) However, his bill for the third month was over $800, and he
> . For
had put aside only $200. (7)∗Max panicked and didn't pay the bill/~~for~~ the

next two months he received the same bill, plus a finance charge. (8)∗A few
> . It
weeks later, Max received a letter from the credit department of the store/~~it~~

instructed him to call the department. (9) He was scared and ashamed, so

he also ignored that letter. (10)∗Shortly after that, Max received a letter
> . After
threatening him with legal action/~~after~~ that warning, he began to make pay-

ments again, and he cut up his credit card.

Challenge 20.5   **Correcting Comma Splices and Run-Ons in Your Writing**

Return to the work you completed for Challenge 20.1 (page 308). Using the methods you have learned in this chapter, correct any comma splices and run-ons that your partner marked. Then reassess your writing. Do your ideas flow more smoothly? Are the relationships among the ideas clear?

Chapter Quick Check: Comma Splices and Run-On Sentences

The following passage contains a number of comma splices and run-on sentences. First, identify these errors by putting an * in front of each one. Then, using the various techniques discussed in this chapter, correct the errors. In some cases, more than one solution is possible.

Answers may vary. Sample answers are shown.

(1) Among the most persistent urban myths circulating on the Internet are those involving scientific or medical matters. *(2) One group of myths involves great suffering and sometimes painful death for people, [after] they have been exposed to exotic poisons or flesh-eating bacteria. *(3) The twists in the stories involve the method of transmission of the afflictions, [;] these people allegedly were infected from contact with everyday items like vending machines and pay phones. *(4) Everybody is exposed to such common objects [, so] the stories seem vaguely possible. *(5) Some of the myths involve rare, deadly insects or spiders, [and] the bite of these creatures, which apparently lurk in public restrooms, fast-food restaurants, and convenience stores, causes paralysis or death. *(6) Of course, these insects or creatures either don't actually exist or don't pose a threat to humans, [; nevertheless,] people still believe in them. *(7) In one persistent myth, a pet owner flushes a baby alligator down a toilet in a big city like New York or Chicago [, and] the alligator eventually grows to gargantuan size in the sewer system below, waiting to attack some unfortunate worker. *(8) In some myths, the U.S. government or some sinister force adds a

dangerous drug or compound to prepared foods ˌ, and in some cases a particular

brand is actually named. (9) This kind of hoax can cause widespread damage to an innocent manufacturer by weakening consumer confidence in

their product.*(10) The nature of the Internet guarantees the fast spread of any new rumors ˌ; consequently, millions of people hear and pass on the latest hoax in a

matter of minutes.

Discovering Connections 20.2

COLLABORATION

1. In Discovering Connections 20.1 on page 305, you prewrote on one of four suggested subjects. Now, using this prewriting material as the foundation, work your way through the rest of the writing process, and complete a draft essay of about 500 words on this topic.
2. Exchange your draft with a partner. Using the material in this chapter to guide you, check the draft you receive for any comma splices and run-ons. Mark these errors with a *CS* or an *RO,* and then return the draft to the writer.
3. Revise your essay, correcting any comma splices or run-ons identified by your reader.

Summary Exercise: Comma Splices and Run-On Sentences

Students can share their revised sentences and discuss the techniques they used to correct the comma splices and run-on sentences.

Activity 20.1

The following passage contains a number of comma splices and run-on sentences. First, identify these errors by putting an ✱ in front of each one. Then, using the various techniques discussed in this chapter, correct the errors. In some cases, more than one solution is possible.

Answers may vary. Sample answers are shown.

(1) In the neighborhood where I grew up, there was an old, abandoned house. (2)*According to all the kids in the neighborhood, it was haunted ˌ; however, I didn't believe them. (3)*At age eleven, I finally explored that house with my two best friends, ˌ and I always regretted it.

(4)*The house was located across the street from our school ˌ; therefore, it seemed to call to us every time we passed it. (5)*Jack and Nickie wanted to break in, but

I kept talking them out of it. (6)*Finally, I could resist no longer˄ we made our   **;**

plans to enter the haunted house on the following Saturday night.

      Activity
      20.2

    (7)*At eight o'clock that evening, we met in my backyard˄ I had told my   **. I**

mother we were going to play basketball under the lights at nearby Pulaski

Park. (8) We often played at night, so she wasn't suspicious. (9)*We left my

yard quickly and headed off to the house ~~we~~ were all set for the big break-in.   **. We**

    (10) We had spent a few days planning our caper, so we had come well

prepared. (11)*Nickie brought a hammer and a crowbar˄ Jack took his fa-   **;**

ther's big flashlight. (12)*I brought a screwdriver and a pair of pliers˄ we   **;**

wanted to be prepared for every possibility.

      Activity
      20.3

    (13)*Twenty minutes later, we reached the house˄ it was pitch dark and   **;**

very quiet. (14)*We went around back and snuck in through the cellar

door ~~the~~ lock was badly rusted, so we only had to pry a little with the crow-   **. The**

bar. (15)*Once inside, we crept down the stairs to the dirt˄ cellar it was dark   **;**

and clammy. (16)*Jack shined his light around the cellar˄ ~~everything~~ was   **. Everything**

covered with dust and cobwebs. (17)*We never made it upstairs˄ ~~the~~ floor-   **. The**

boards squeaked, and we ran out at lightning speed.

      Activity
      20.4

    (18)*We ran two blocks before stopping ~~none~~ of us had ever been so   **. None**

scared in our whole lives. (19) We all headed home and agreed not to tell

anyone else. (20)*I've kept the secret˄ I don't know if Nickie or Jack ever told.   **; however,**

RECAP COMMA SPLICES AND RUN-ON SENTENCES

Weblink 20.3

New terms in this chapter	Definitions
● **comma splice**	● an error in which sentences are incorrectly connected by a comma ***Example*** The storm dumped four inches of rain across the region, / several cities and towns suffered heavy flooding.
● **run-on sentence**	● an error in which two sentences are run together with no punctuation or connectors ***Example*** James forgot his wallet at home / he didn't realize it until he arrived at the register.

To Identify Comma Splices and Run-On Sentences

1. Identify all subject–verb units.

2. Establish whether the clauses can stand alone.

Four Ways to Correct Comma Splices and Run-On Sentences

1. subject–verb unit + *comma and coordinating conjunction* + subject–verb unit

2. subject–verb unit + *subordinating conjunction* + subject–verb unit

   or

   subordinating conjunction + subject–verb unit and *comma* + subject–verb unit

3. subject–verb unit + *semicolon* + subject–verb unit

   or

   subject–verb unit + *semicolon, conjunctive adverb, and comma* + subject–verb unit

4. subject–verb unit + *period* + subject–verb unit (begin with capital)

Understanding Subjects and Verbs

Chapter 21

Subject–Verb Agreement

Audio
21.1

Getting Started... **Q:** Sometimes, when I read back what I've written, I can tell that my subjects and verbs don't match up. What can I do to make sure that the verb form I choose is the correct one?

A: The good news is that, for the most part, problems with subject–verb agreement occur in only the present tense. That narrows things down a bit. Avoiding problems with subject–verb agreement comes down to isolating the subject so you can verify whether it is singular or plural. Once you do this, check that the verb form matches the number of the subject, and you'll be all set.

Overview: Understanding Subject–Verb Agreement

Audio
21.2

When two parties, either companies or individuals, plan a joint enterprise, they draw up an **agreement**, a document outlining the details of their relationship. That way, both parties know the roles they will play to ensure that everything runs smoothly. In writing, agreement means essentially the same thing. Each subject must agree in **number** with its verb in order for your sentences to run smoothly. As the term suggests, number refers to the **quantity** or **amount** the word indicates, either *singular,* meaning one, or *plural,* meaning more than one. Singular subjects call for singular verb forms, and plural subjects call for plural verb forms. Maintaining subject–verb agreement is essential because subjects and verbs communicate the basic meaning of your sentences.

> *In this chapter, you will learn how to recognize and avoid the following difficulties with subject–verb agreement:*
>
> - problems when the subject follows the verb
>
> - problems when words come between subjects and verbs
>
> - problems with indefinite pronouns
>
> - problems from other causes, including compound subjects; collective nouns; singular nouns ending in -s; and words referring to measurements, money, time, and weight

Discovering Connections 21.2 at the end of this chapter provides an opportunity for students to apply the skills they have learned about subject–verb agreement. They will be asked to compose and revise an essay based on one of the topics in Discovering Connections 21.1.

Using one technique you practiced in Chapter 2, "Generating Ideas through Prewriting," prewrite on one of the following topics:

1. the appeal of computer games
2. the reason people gossip or the consequences that can result when they do

Or, focus on this picture.

Save your work for later use.

Avoiding Agreement Errors When the Subject Follows the Verb

ESL Note
See "Sentence Basics" on pages 572–574 and "Agreement" on pages 576–578.

**Audio
21.3**

The secret to avoiding errors in **subject–verb agreement** is to identify the subject. To do this, as Chapter 17, "The Sentence," shows, ask yourself *who or what is doing the action or being discussed?* The answer to that question is the subject.

In the majority of the sentences you write, the subject comes before the verb, as these examples show:

EXAMPLE

subject — verb

Volunteer relief workers provide a valuable service at the scenes of fires, accidents, and natural disasters.

EXAMPLE

subject — verb

The *Internet puts* the world at a person's fingertips.

**Video
21.1**

But not all sentences follow this pattern. In some sentences, the subject appears after the verb. One type of sentence in which the subject follows the verb is a question:

EXAMPLE

verb — subject — verb

Do division supervisors attend weekly planning meetings?

EXAMPLE

verb subject — verb

Is ESPN planning to broadcast the X-Games again?

**Weblink
21.1**

In the first sentence, *supervisors* is the subject; in the second, *ESPN* is the subject. Note, however, that in each case, part of the verb precedes the subject: *do* in the first sentence and *is* in the second.

Sentences beginning with *there* or *here* also feature subjects that follow the verb. *There* and *here* are adverbs, and only a noun or pronoun can be the subject of a sentence. So in sentences beginning with *there* or *here*, the actual subject follows the verb, as these examples show:

EXAMPLE

verb — subject

There *are* several new *signs* near the new highway exit.

EXAMPLE

verb

subject

Here *comes* the guest *speaker* on the subject of health care reform.

In the first sentence, *signs* is the subject, even though it follows the verb *are*. In the second sentence, the subject is *speaker*, even though it follows the verb *comes*.

Fast Fact In typical sentences that begin with *there* or *here*, what do these words mean? Nothing. Used to open sentences in this way, *there* and *here* are called **expletives**. They simply serve to start a sentence. To strengthen your writing, use words that MEAN something. In other words, avoid using *there* and *here* to begin your sentences.

Exercise 21.1 **Identifying Subjects That Follow the Verb**

For each sentence in the following passage, identify the verbs and subjects, circling the verbs and underlining the subjects. Use the following example as a guide.

EXAMPLE Here (is) the missing notebook.

(1) Decades after their introduction, there (are) still many game shows on television. (2) There (is) nothing challenging about some of them, for instance *Wheel of Fortune*. (3) Then there (is) *Jeopardy!* (4) (Is) there a harder game show anywhere? (5) (Don't) the producers of *Jeopardy!* (have) any mercy for the poor contestants?

Exercise 21.2 **Maintaining Agreement When Subjects Follow the Verb**

Each of the sentences in the following paragraph contains a pair of verbs in parentheses. First, find and underline the subject with which the verb must agree. Then circle the verb that agrees with that subject, using the example to guide you.

EXAMPLE (Has/(Have)) Mary Beth and Joe rented their apartment yet?

(1) (Doesn't/(Don't)) people know how easy it is to register as a bone marrow donor? (2) According to recent news articles, there ((is)/are) a shortage of bone marrow donors. (3) It's too bad, because here ((is)/are) a wonderful opportunity to help save someone's life, and people are missing out on it because of misconceptions about the procedure itself. (4) First, there ((is)/are) a blood test. (5) ((Is)/Are) there a simpler form of testing available?

(6) Once a blood sample is taken, there (is/are) some sophisticated <u>tests</u> done at a special lab, and the results are entered into a special bone-marrow-donor registry. (7) Here (is/are) the <u>point</u> at which everyone waits for a match between someone in need of a transplant and a potential donor. (8) Once a match is identified and the donor is notified, there (is/are) a few simple <u>steps</u> during which marrow is extracted from the donor's hip. (9) For the donor, the good news is that there (is/are) very little <u>discomfort</u>. (10) (Does/Do) <u>people</u> have to know any more than this to get involved?

Challenge 21.1   **Examining Subjects and Verbs in Your Writing**

1. Exercise 21.1 discusses two television game shows, *Wheel of Fortune* and *Jeopardy!* What is your favorite game show? Why do you like it? Write a paragraph of 100 to 150 words on this subject, using present tense verbs only.

2. Exchange your paragraph with a partner. On the paper you receive, identify the subjects and verbs by underlining the subjects and circling the verbs. Put a ✓ next to any sentence that contains an error in subject–verb agreement. When you are finished, return the paragraph to your partner, and check the work your partner did on your paragraph.

Avoiding Agreement Errors When Words Come between the Subject and Verb

Often, problems with subject–verb agreement occur because of the words you use *between* subjects and verbs. Don't be fooled by the noun closest to the verb, which may not actually be the subject. Instead, be sure that you identify the person or thing that is performing the action or that is being discussed.

In some cases, what comes between a subject and verb is a *prepositional phrase.* As Chapter 17, "The Sentence," explains, a prepositional phrase begins with a preposition and ends with a noun or pronoun. Common prepositions include *about, against, around, behind, beneath, by, down, during, inside, out, through, to, up, within,* and *without.* Here is an example of a sentence with a prepositional phrase coming between the subject and the verb:

EXAMPLE   The spare tire *under the tools* was flat.

In this sentence, the verb *was* agrees with the singular subject *tire,* not with the noun closest to it, the plural object of the preposition, *tools.*

Other times, a subject and a verb are separated by a *subordinate clause*. As Chapter 19, "Subordination and Coordination," explains, a subordinate clause is a subject and verb unit introduced by a subordinating conjunction or relative pronoun. Common subordinating conjunctions include *after, although, because, if, since, unless, until, when, whether,* and *while.* Common relative pronouns include *that, which, who,* and *whose.* Here is a sentence in which the subject and verb are separated by a subordinate clause:

EXAMPLE

[subject]————————[subordinate clause]————————[verb]
Students *who have computer network experience* enjoy great job prospects.

In this sentence, the verb agrees in number with the actual subject, *students,* not with the word closest to the verb, *experience.*

Exercise 21.3   **Identifying Subjects Separated from Verbs by Other Words**

For each sentence in the following passage, identify the verbs and subjects, circling the verbs and underlining the subjects. This task will be easier if you cross out any words that come between subject and verb, as the example shows.

EXAMPLE   On some days, the <u>crowd</u> ~~in the cafeteria lining up for lunch~~ (reaches) the back of the building.

(1) <u>Advertisements</u> ~~on the Internet, especially on Web pages and search engines,~~ (continue) to generate controversy. (2) For one thing, some <u>people</u> ~~using the Web, especially those using it for work,~~ (find) the advertisements annoying. (3) The most distracting <u>ones,</u> ~~according to these users,~~ (feature) words or characters "crawling" across the top of the screen. (4) Other <u>critics</u> ~~of the practice~~ (dislike) the lack of government regulation over the advertisements. (5) Yet many other <u>people</u> ~~using the 'Net for pleasure or work simply~~ (pay) little attention to the ads.

Exercise 21.4   **Maintaining Agreement with Subjects Separated from Verbs by Other Words**

Each of the sentences in the following passage contains a pair of verbs in parentheses. First, find and underline the subject with which the verb must agree. Then circle the verb that agrees with the subject you have underlined, as the example shows.

EXAMPLE   The burners on the stove, which are now covered with drips of paint from the ceiling, (needs/(need)) to be replaced soon.

(1) A good general contractor who can perform a wide variety of tasks ((remains)/remain) a rare individual. (2) Too often, people needing work done on an apartment or home (enters/(enter)) the process with uncertainty and trepidation. (3) The stories they've heard about unscrupulous contractors doing inferior work (does/(do)) nothing to reassure them. (4) But my friend Lou Ledoux, the owner of South-End-Boys Contracting, the company he started after doing carpentry work part time for years, ((qualifies)/qualify) as that rare individual. (5) Lou, who can do any kind of work, from new construction to general repairs, ((does)/do) no advertising. (6) Nevertheless, his schedule, particularly during the good-weather months, ((remains)/remain) full. (7) That's because people, especially those operating on a strict budget, (needs/(need)) a contractor who is skilled, dependable, and honest. (8) Nobody who has seen the quality of one of his finished projects ((has)/have) any doubts about Lou's ability. (9) In terms of dependability, the needs of his clients to see the work completed according to schedule (represents/(represent)) a top priority for Lou. (10) But Lou's honest dealings in terms of sticking to his original price regardless of any complication (impresses/(impress)) people most of all.

Challenge 21.2   **Identifying Subjects and Verbs to Achieve Subject–Verb Agreement**

Working with a partner, choose one of the readings from Part Seven, "Connecting: Responding to Reading," and select three paragraphs from it. Working together, identify the subjects and verbs, crossing out all prepositional phrases, subordinate clauses, and other words between the subjects and verbs. Then, on a separate sheet of paper, identify which subjects and verbs you found most difficult to identify, and explain why.

Avoiding Agreement Errors with Indefinite Pronouns

See Chapter 26, "Pronouns," for further information about using indefinite pronouns.

Another potential difficulty with subject–verb agreement involves indefinite pronouns. *Indefinite pronouns* are used to refer to general rather than specific people and things, for instance, the indefinite *somebody* rather than the specific *Bill*, the indefinite *anything* rather than the specific *a burrito*. See pages 399 and 406–408 in Chapter 26, "Pronouns: Understanding Case, Clear Pronoun–Antecedent Agreement, and Nonsexist Pronoun Usage," for a further discussion and a complete list of indefinite pronouns.

Some indefinite pronouns are singular, some are plural, and some are singular or plural depending on how you use them. Of these words, *another, anybody, anyone, anything, each, either, everybody, everyone, everything, much, neither, nobody, no one, nothing, one, somebody, someone,* and *something* are singular and call for singular verb forms:

EXAMPLE *Nobody wants* to deal with stress on a daily basis.

EXAMPLE *Someone has* to find the owner of that puppy.

Both, few, many, and *several* are always plural and call for plural verb forms:

EXAMPLE *Both* of the apartments *look* well maintained.

EXAMPLE *Many* of the over one hundred people attending the presentation now *want* to participate in the training program.

All, any, more, most, none, and *some* are either singular or plural depending on the word they refer to in the sentence. With one of these pronouns, check the word it refers to. If that word is singular, choose a singular form of the verb; if it is plural, choose a plural form of the verb, as these examples show:

EXAMPLE *All* her *enthusiasm* suddenly *disappears* at the thought of rehearsing.

EXAMPLE *All* their *books are* missing.

Exercise 21.5 **Maintaining Agreement with Indefinite Pronouns**

Underline the verbs in the following sentences. Then fill in the blank in each sentence with an appropriate indefinite pronoun from the list below. In some cases, you may need to use the same pronoun more than once.

anyone   everyone   no one   none   some

EXAMPLE   Of the new medications available to combat asthma, ____*some*____ have proven to be especially effective.

(1) ____Everyone____ likes to save money. (2) Now, ____no one____ has to pay high long-distance fees, thanks to the Internet. (3) With the right Internet service provider and computer hardware, ____anyone____ can route long-distance calling through the Internet. (4) Because of occasional problems in sound quality, ____some____ view this innovation as a waste of time. (5) But according to a recent article on the subject, ____none____ of the small business owners currently paying $500 or more a month in standard long-distance fees seem to agree.

Exercise 21.6   **Identifying Correct Agreement with Indefinite Pronouns**

For each sentence in the following passage, identify the subject by underlining it. Then circle the verb that agrees with that subject from the pair of verbs in parentheses. Study the example first.

EXAMPLE   Nobody in the office (has/have) a personal parking space.

(1) Springfield, like most medium-sized cities, (has/have) several major neighborhoods. (2) The east end of the city is called "the Flint," and nobody (seems/seem) to know where the name came from. (3) Many of the people living in the Flint (traces/trace) their heritage to Canada. (4) Everyone who lives in the south end of the city (refer/refers) to this neighborhood as "Maplewood." (5) Some of the larger homes in this part of the city (displays/display) the elegance of the Victorian Age. (6) The neighborhood in the center of the city is called "Below the Hill," and many of the young professionals working in the city (lives/live) here. (7) This part of the city is undergoing a rejuvenation, and everyone (has/have) been rushing to buy and restore the brownstone buildings that line the streets. (8) "The Highlands"

and "the Lowlands" in the hilly north end of the city are the other two neigh-

borhoods, and everybody in the city ((enjoys)/enjoy) the beauty of these two

areas. (9) Both (has/(have)) tree-lined streets and large homes with big yards.

(10) Each also ((features)/feature) a clear view of the Springfield River.

Challenge 21.3 **Writing Sentences Using Indefinite Pronouns That Can Be Either Singular or Plural**

Here again is the list of indefinite pronouns that are either singular or plural depending on what they refer to:

all	any	more
most	none	some

Working with a partner, write two sentences for each, one in which the word refers to a singular word and one in which the word refers to a plural word.

Avoiding Agreement Errors from Other Causes

The following situations can also create confusion as you make decisions about subject–verb agreement.

When the Subject Is Compound

As Chapter 17, "The Sentence," indicates, not all subjects are individual words. Many are *compound subjects:* more than one noun or pronoun connected in most cases by *and* or *or.* Compound subjects connected by *and* are almost always plural. The exceptions are subjects that are commonly thought of as one, such as *pork and beans, peanut butter and jelly, peace and quiet, ham and eggs,* and *rock and roll.*

EXAMPLE
A *headache* and a *bruise* on her arm *were* the only indications that Margarita had been in an accident.

If the two subjects are singular and connected by *or,* use a singular form of the verb:

EXAMPLE
A *doughnut* or a *muffin is* not going to help anyone on a diet.

But if the subjects are both plural, use a plural form of the verb:

EXAMPLE
Doughnuts or *muffins are* not going to help anyone on a diet.

When the compound subject consists of one singular word and one plural word connected by *or*, make the verb agree with the subject closest to it:

EXAMPLE

The *supervisor* or the *workers are* responsible for the decreased level of production.

Workers is closer to the verb, so the correct choice is the form that agrees with *workers*.

When the Subject Is a Collective Noun or Is Introduced by a Cue Word

Refer students to Chapter 25, "Nouns," for more information about collective nouns.

Collective nouns are words that name *groups* of items or people. Common collective nouns include *audience, class, committee, faculty, flock, herd, jury, swarm,* and *team*. (See Chapter 25, "Nouns: Working Effectively with Words That Name," for more on collective nouns.) Collective nouns are singular, so they call for singular verb forms:

EXAMPLE

This year's *team has won* twenty-five games so far.

In some cases, certain words, called *cue words*, help you to identify whether a subject is singular or plural. Common singular cue words include *a, an, another, each, either, every, neither,* and *one*. A subject introduced by one of these words will be singular and call for a singular verb form:

EXAMPLE

Neither sales representative *recalls* the meeting.

Common plural cue words include *all, both, few, many, several,* and *some*. Subjects introduced by these words call for a plural verb form:

EXAMPLE

Few great novels ever *make* good movies.

When the Subject Is a Singular Word Ending in -s, a Word Referring to an Amount, or a Word That Has the Same Singular and Plural Form

Certain words that end in *-s* may look plural, but they are actually singular and call for singular verb forms. Common words in this category include *economics, ethics, mathematics, measles, mumps, news, physics,* and *politics*.

EXAMPLE

Physics appears to be growing in popularity in schools across the nation.

Nouns used to refer to measurements, money, time, and weight can also cause some confusion in terms of subject–verb agreement. These words may seem plural, but because they are used to refer to the entire amount as one unit, they are actually singular and call for singular verb forms:

EXAMPLE　*Fifty dollars is* much more than any ticket is worth.

Finally, with certain words such as *antelope, deer, fish,* and *species,* use either a singular or plural form of the verb depending on whether you mean one or more than one:

EXAMPLE　That *moose has broken* out of its holding area.

EXAMPLE　Those *moose look* so peaceful as they stand together.

Fast Fact　The word "news" is actually an *acronym,* a word that draws its name from the initials of the words it refers to. For example, *scuba* is an acronym for *self-contained underwater breathing apparatus.* And what is news an acronym for? It gets its name from the four directions from which information appears and is gathered: *north, east, west,* and *south.*

Exercise 21.7　**Maintaining Agreement with Compound Subjects**

Each of the sentences in the following passage includes a pair of verbs in parentheses. First underline the compound subject, and then circle the verb that agrees with that subject. Study the example first.

EXAMPLE　Even after working all afternoon, David and Bobbie still (has/**have**) not

been able to start the car.

(1) In today's modern world, eye specialists and patients looking to improve their eyesight (has/**have**) a number of alternatives available. (2) For those still interested in glasses, ultra-thin lenses and smaller shapes (has/**have**) replaced coke-bottle lenses and clunky frames. (3) Today, style and comfort (**do**/does) not have to be sacrificed, thanks to the advent of low-cost designer frames. (4) In addition, bifocals or trifocals (has/**have**) been replaced in many cases with an innovative type of lens that allows the wearer to see clearly regardless of the distance. (5) For those wanting to do without glasses altogether, daily-wear contact lenses or extended-care contact lenses (remains/**remain**)

the most common options. (6) <u>Colored lenses and patterned lenses</u> (is/(are))
among the variations of contacts available to the daring and style-conscious
wearer. (7) <u>Bifocal contacts and contacts</u> that reshape the lens (is/(are)) recent
innovations in this field. (8) Also, <u>conventional surgery or laser surgery</u> ((enables)/enable) people with vision problems to go without glasses or contacts.
(9) Of course, any surgery has risks, so with this type of procedure, either the
<u>eye specialist or a specially trained technician</u> thoroughly ((explains)/explain)
to the patient what will occur. (10) The <u>improved vision and freedom from vision aids</u> of any type (makes/(make)) these surgical alternatives an increasingly
popular choice among the young and physically active.

Exercise 21.8   **Maintaining Agreement with Collective Nouns, with Singular Words Ending in -s, and with Words Referring to Amounts**

Each of the following sentences contains the infinitive of a verb (*to* + a simple form of the verb—*to speak*) in parentheses. Identify the subject of the
verb by underlining it, and then write the proper *present tense* form of the
verb on the line provided. Remember—the story is told in the present, so
use present tense forms only. Study the example first.

EXAMPLE   The <u>audience</u> (to be) _____*is*_____ clearly enjoying the concert.

(1) The <u>committee</u> in charge of selecting the Youth Center's Volunteer of
the Year (to have) _____has_____ an important job. (2) A nominating <u>team</u> of
five committee members first (to select) _____selects_____ five semifinalists
from the many nominations. (3) In most years, 50 to 100 <u>nominations</u>
(to be) _____are_____ not unusual. (4) The <u>ethics</u> of the situation (to require)
_____requires_____ careful, objective scrutiny of the nominations. (5) That's because <u>politics</u> often (to play) _____plays_____ a part in the nominating
process, with companies and organizations lobbying for the opportunity to
highlight the activities of one of their employees to thousands of people
across the state. (6) <u>Economics</u> (to do) _____does_____ not come into play,

however, because no monetary reward is attached to the award. (7) After the initial selections are made, two <u>hours</u> (to pass) _____passes_____ while the team ranks the candidates in ten categories on a 1–5 scale. (8) Ultimately, simple <u>mathematics</u> (to determine) _____determines_____ the winner, with the nominee holding the highest composite score being unanimously named Volunteer of the Year. (9) Despite efforts to keep the results secret until the annual recognition banquet, <u>news</u> often (to spread) _____spreads_____ among the rest of the committee. (10) On the night of the recognition banquet, as the <u>audience</u> (to applaud) _____applauds_____ for the winner, the committee sits back and enjoys what their hard work has brought about.

Challenge 21.4   Revising to Achieve Subject–Verb Agreement

Working with a partner, help the writer of the following Letter to the Editor revise to eliminate the errors in subject–verb agreement. Cross out the wrong verb form and write the correct one above it. Some sentences are correct as they are.

Dear Editor:

(1) Right now, few members of the City Council ~~appears~~ appear to be taking the city's traffic problems seriously. (2) Thirty minutes ~~are~~ is clearly an unreasonable amount of time to spend stuck in downtown traffic. (3) Under the worst cir-cumstances, drivers should be able to complete this two-mile drive in half OK that time. (4) The streets blocked off to make the pedestrian mall five years ago ~~represents~~ represent the main impediment to improving the flow of traffic. (5) As a result, anyone who travels on the downtown streets ~~have~~ has to take a series of narrow one-way streets in order to get around the mall. (6) When buses or a tractor trailer ~~enter~~ enters the area, traffic slows down even more than usual. (7) Even the blue-ribbon committee that originally lobbied in favor of the pedestrian mall to bring more consumers downtown ~~want~~ wants it removed. (8) Of course, eliminating the pedestrian mall will cost money, and so most mem-

bers of the council ~~seems~~ ^{seem} hesitant to vote in favor of the change. (9) But each of our elected officials ~~have~~ ^{has} a responsibility to act in the best interest of the citizens. (10) There ~~is~~ ^{are} many voters who are watching carefully and will make sure that the councilors who won't act will be out of a job.

Chapter Quick Check: Mastering Subject–Verb Agreement

The following passage contains the various kinds of errors in subject–verb agreement discussed in this chapter. Consider again the ways to correct these errors illustrated in this chapter. Then identify errors in agreement, crossing them out and writing the correct verb form above the incorrect one, as the example shows:

EXAMPLE   Several of my friends from my old neighborhood still ~~plays~~ ^{play} basketball together two nights a week in the City League.

(1) Speed and convenience ~~seems~~ ^{seem} to be what most customers are looking for when they go grocery shopping. (2) Because everyone, especially those who have demanding work schedules, ~~want~~ ^{wants} to spend less time in line, some retailers are experimenting with an innovation. (3) Under this new system, a customer with fewer than 20 items ~~go~~ ^{goes} to a self-service area. (4) In this area, there ~~is~~ ^{are} 15 stations, each with a computer screen and a small platform containing an electronic scanner. (5) The steps involved in the process ~~requires~~ ^{require} no special training. (6) All the instructions ~~appears~~ ^{appear} on the computer screen. (7) The UPC code, printed on all items, ~~are~~ ^{is} the key to the process. (8) This series of vertical bars and numbers ~~indicate~~ ^{indicates} the name and price of the item. (9) The customer runs the UPC code of each item in front of the scanner, and an electronic tone and visual image on the screen ~~tells~~ ^{tell} the customer that the sale has been recorded. (10) A team of three workers ~~monitor~~ ^{monitors} the fifteen checkout stations, ready to address any problems customers encounter.

Discovering Connections 21.2

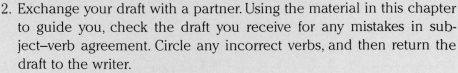

COLLABORATION

Weblink
21.2

1. In Discovering Connections 21.1 on page 325, you did prewriting on one of three suggested subjects. Now, using that material as your foundation, work your way through the rest of the writing process, and complete a draft essay of about 500 words.
2. Exchange your draft with a partner. Using the material in this chapter to guide you, check the draft you receive for any mistakes in subject–verb agreement. Circle any incorrect verbs, and then return the draft to the writer.
3. Revise your essay, correcting any errors in subject–verb agreement identified by your reader.

Summary Exercise: Mastering Subject–Verb Agreement

Activity
21.1

The following passage contains the various kinds of errors in subject–verb agreement discussed in this chapter. Consider again the ways to correct these errors illustrated in this chapter. Then identify errors in agreement, crossing them out and writing the correct verb form above the incorrect one.

Activity
21.2

(1) There ~~is~~ ^are^ many choices available for the person looking for a laptop computer. (2) Thanks to price cuts by most major manufacturers, anybody wanting the option of a portable computer now ~~have~~ ^has^ that possibility. (3) This new class of laptops ~~appear~~ ^appears^ to consist of the first portables with broad consumer appeal.

(4) Attractive laptop computers with huge amounts of memory now ~~costs~~ ^cost^ far less than ever before. (5) Only a few years ago, $3,000 ~~were~~ ^was^ considered a bargain-basement price for a basic portable computer. (6) Right now, a laptop with 10 times as much memory and many more built-in features ~~run~~ ^runs^ under $2,000.

Activity
21.3

(7) In the past two years alone, there ~~has~~ ^have^ been improvements almost beyond belief. (8) Today, for example, five pounds ~~are~~ ^is^ considered heavy for these powerhouse portables. (9) A tiny keyboard or awkward pointer was a negative feature of many of the older portable computers. (10) Today, how-

ever, everybody trying the new generation of laptops ~~give~~ ^{gives} positive marks to

these features.

(11) Either a brighter active-matrix color screen or the many built-in fea-

tures ~~is~~ ^{are} also cited by consumers as factors that cause them to consider pur-

chasing a laptop. (12) In addition, there ~~have~~ ^{has} been great interest in the

compact CD-ROM drives, extended-life batteries, and fast modems available as

accessories. (13) All these features ~~has~~ ^{have} been applauded by prospective buyers.

**Activity
21.4**

(14) According to consumer responses, here ~~are~~ ^{is} the most popular im-

provement: speed. (15) Everyone trying these new laptops ~~remark~~ ^{remarks} on this

improvement, especially with complex tasks. (16) Many of these laptops

~~features~~ ^{feature} the newest generation of Pentium chips. (17) Now some of the

most complex functions ~~takes~~ ^{take} only a few seconds.

(18) ~~Does~~ ^{Do} manufacturers expect these innovations in laptops to lead

most people to abandon their desktop computers? (19) Nobody ~~seem~~ ^{seems} to

know for sure. (20) But with prices for portable computers so low, a real

choice between desktop computers and this new generation of laptops

~~exist~~ ^{exists} for the first time.

RECAP   SUBJECT–VERB AGREEMENT

New terms in this chapter	Definitions
● **subject–verb agreement**	● a state in which the subject and verb agree in number Use a singular form of a verb with a singular subject. Use a plural form of a verb with a plural subject.

Ways to Maintain Agreement

● When the **subject follows the verb**

in a question ⟶ *Does* she *know* the directions to the party?

in a sentence beginning with *there* or *here* ⟶ There *are* six days left in the term.

Identify the verb and ask "who or what?" to find the subject.

- When the **subject and verb are separated** by other words

  prepositional phrases ⟶ The *baby* across the hall *cries* all night.

  subordinate clauses ⟶ The substitute *teacher,* because she is strict, *controls* the class.

Identify the verb and ask "who or what?" to find the subject.

- When the **subject is compound**

  with *and* the subject is usually plural ⟶ *Marcus and Simon are* friends.

  unless the compound is considered one ⟶ *Rock and roll is* here to stay.

  with *or* the subject can be singular ⟶ *Red or blue is* my favorite color.

  with *or* the subject can be plural ⟶ *Pancakes or waffles are* good for breakfast.

Find the conjunction and determine what is being connected.

- When the **subject is an indefinite pronoun**

  singular ⟶ *Everyone is* late today.

  plural ⟶ *Both* of my grandparents *are* immigrants.

Use singular verbs with singular pronouns and plural verbs with plural pronouns.

- When the **subject is a collective noun or singular noun ending in *-s***

  collective noun ⟶ The *jury returns* today.

  singular noun ending in *-s* ⟶ The *news follows* my favorite comedy.

If the subject is a unit, use a singular verb.

Singular Indefinite Pronouns

another	each	everything	nobody	somebody
anybody	either	neither	nothing	someone
anyone	everybody	no one	one	something
anything	everyone			

Plural Indefinite Pronouns

both	few	many	several

Indefinite Pronouns Affected by the Words That Follow Them

all	more	none
any	most	some

Chapter 22

Basic Tenses for Regular Verbs

Getting Started... **Q:** From time to time, I have trouble with my verb endings. For example, I mix them up, adding a *-d* or an *-ed* to the end of a verb or putting *will* in front of one, for no good reason. It's so frustrating. Why do verbs in English have to have different forms?

Audio
22.1 **A:** Actually, having various verb tenses to work with is a plus for you as a writer. You will often write about things that have already occurred or that are yet to occur, so it's to your advantage to have specialized forms of a verb to signify these periods of time. If you stop periodically as you are composing a draft and check for any incorrect switches in verb tense, you'll avoid a lot of frustration with this aspect of writing.

Overview: Understanding Tense

ESL Note
See "Agreement" on pages 576–578.

Audio
22.2

To a writer, no words hold more importance than verbs. As Chapter 17, "The Sentence," demonstrates, verbs convey action or link elements in a statement. Through verbs, you communicate about people, events, concepts, or possibilities. Verbs also indicate the period of time involved, whether it is *past, present,* or *future.* This time element is called **verb tense**. You indicate a change in verb tense by changing the form. Most verbs in English are **regular**, meaning that you convert their present form to past and future tenses in consistent ways.

> ***In this chapter, you will discover how to use the following for regular verbs:***
>
> ● the present tense to describe a fact, an action, or a situation that is happening now or that happens habitually
>
> ● the future tense to describe an action or situation that hasn't occurred yet
>
> ● the past tense to describe an action or situation that has already occurred
>
> ● the past participle and perfect tenses to describe an action or situation that was either completed in the past or will be completed in the future

Discovering Connections 22.1

Discovering Connections 22.2 at the end of this chapter provides an opportunity for students to apply the skills they have learned about using simple tenses. They will be asked to compose and revise an essay based on one of the topics in Discovering Connections 22.1.

Using one of the techniques you practiced in Chapter 2, "Generating Ideas through Prewriting," prewrite on one of the following topics:

1. the impact of the entertainment industry on the lives of average people
2. the reluctance of many people to take personal responsibility for their actions

Or, focus on this picture.

Save your work for later use.

Using the Simple Present, Simple Future, and Simple Past Tenses

Weblink 22.1

Weblink 22.2

The **present tense** signifies a fact, action, or situation that is happening *at the moment* or that happens habitually. For regular verbs, the simple present tense is the basic form of the verb, the one you would use in the simplest "I" statement: I laugh, I jump.

What makes the present tense a little confusing is that its form changes depending on the subject. If the subject is *singular,* meaning *one* person or thing, then the verb ends in *-s* or *-es.* If the subject is plural (or the singular *I*), the verb has no *-s.*

EXAMPLE   All day long, that dog *digs* holes in the yard.

EXAMPLE   Most children *enjoy* a magic show.

Audio 22.3

The subject in the first example is singular (*dog*), so the verb ends in *-s: digs.* In the second example, the plural subject *children* calls for a verb without an *-s* ending: *enjoy.* The exceptions to this guideline are the pronouns *I* and *you.* Even though *I* is singular, you don't add an *-s* to the present tense verb when *I* is the subject:

EXAMPLE   I *play* basketball every weekend.

You also don't add an *-s* to a present tense verb when *you* is the subject, even when it is singular:

EXAMPLE   You always *clean* your apartment on Saturday.

Audio 22.4

The simple **future tense** conveys an action or relationship *that hasn't occurred yet.* For regular verbs, the future tense for both singular and plural subjects is formed by adding *will* to the basic form of the verb. No *-s* or *-es* is necessary.

EXAMPLE   The actors *will prepare* for the play. The director *will coach* them.

Audio
22.5

The simple **past tense** indicates an action or situation *that has already oc-curred*. For regular verbs, the simple past tense is formed by adding *-ed* to the basic verb form. If the verb ends in *-e*, only a *-d* is added. For some regular verbs that end in *-y*, or with a single consonant preceded by a single vowel, forming the past tense requires a little more work. You must either change the last letter or add a letter before you add the *-d* or *-ed* ending. Chapter 29, "Spelling: Focusing on Correctness," discusses ways to treat these verbs. Again, the simple past tense is the same for both singular and plural subjects.

| EXAMPLE | Osvaldo *answered* many questions in botany class. |

| EXAMPLE | Several dozen applicants *responded* to our ad for an assistant manager. |

How to Form Simple Tenses for Regular Verbs (Example verb—*call*)

	Simple Present Tense (Use the basic form of the verb, adding *-s* or *-es* for singular subjects except *I* and *you*.)	**Simple Past Tense** (Use the basic form of the verb plus *-d* or *-ed*.)	**Simple Future Tense** (Use the basic form of the verb plus *will*.)
Basic or "I" form	I *call* friends in the evening.	I *called* friends last night.	I *will call* friends tomorrow evening.
Singular	Ami *calls* friends in the evening.	Ami *called* friends last . night	Ami *will call* friends tomorrow evening.
Plural	Joe and Estella *call* friends in the evening.	Joe and Estella *called* friends last night.	Joe and Estella *will call* friends tomorrow evening.

For more on the use of present tense verbs, see Chapter 21, "Subject–Verb Agreement."

Fast Fact Khmer, the native language of Cambodia, has no past or future tense. Writers and speakers use other words to mark changes in the time under discussion.

Exercise 22.1   Working with Future Tense Verbs

Complete the following sentences by adding a completing thought containing a future tense verb. Use the example to guide you.

Answers will vary. Representative answers are given.

| EXAMPLE | When the warm weather arrives, ___the campus will look beautiful.___ |

1. At the end of this century, _____

   we will look back at an era of enormous technological growth.

Write a list of regular verbs on the blackboard. Then ask each student to write three sentences, using one of the verbs in three different tenses, as the table on page 343 shows. Have students exchange sentences with a partner and identify the tenses that their partner used.

2. When the election results are finally tabulated, _____

   we will measure the success of our campaign strategy.

3. After Albert shaves his moustache and cuts his hair, _____

   his family will not recognize him.

4. As soon as the semester is over, _____

   Professor Hall will return to Paris.

5. The proposed increase in property taxes _____

   will fund the city hall addition.

6. Once the jury reaches a verdict, _____

   the newspapers will have a field day.

7. A new manufacturing plant is opening up in town, so _____

   new shops and restaurants will open up, too.

8. If you learn to speak a second language, _____

   you will expand both your horizons and your job skills.

Activity 22.1

9. Soon, high-speed trains _____

   will connect the two capital cities.

10. When the parade is over, the city's public works department _____

    will clean the streets along the parade route.

Exercise 22.2   **Working with Past Tense Verbs**

The italicized verbs in the sentences below are in the present tense. Change them to the past tense by adding -d or -ed. Cross out the present tense verb, and write the revised verb in the space above as the example shows.

EXAMPLE

During the first few classes, the instructor ~~tries~~ *tried* to make the class comfortable with the subject matter.

(1) My friend Andrea ~~works~~ *worked* with stained glass. (2) She ~~constructs~~ *constructed* small items such as holiday ornaments. (3) She also ~~creates~~ *created* larger items. (4) For example, she ~~designs~~ *designed* wall displays. (5) My favorite ~~shows~~ *showed* an open door leading into a cozy room, as a way to say "Welcome."

Exercise 22.3   **Using Past Tense Verbs to Complete Sentences**

Use the following list of basic verbs to complete the paragraph below. Make all verbs past tense by adding *-d* or *-ed*.

purchase	line	wash	measure	redecorate
brush	fold	pick	start	place

(1) Last weekend, my friend Kathy _____redecorated_____ the living room in her apartment by wallpapering. (2) First, she _____measured_____ the walls to find out how much wallpaper to buy. (3) Then she _____purchased_____ the paper, along with a kit containing several wallpapering tools. (4) She also _____picked_____ up two containers of premixed wallpaper paste. (5) She then _____washed_____ the walls down to make sure the surface was clean. (6) Once the walls dried, she _____started_____ to hang the wallpaper. (7) After cutting a strip of paper to the correct length, she _____brushed_____ paste onto the back of the paper. (8) Next, she _____folded_____ the strip of paper in half and carried it from the table to the wall. (9) She unfolded the paper and _____placed_____ its top edge against the ceiling. (10) She then _____lined_____ up the right side of the paper against the guideline she had drawn to ensure that the paper was straight.

Challenge 22.1   **Analyzing the Formation of Past Tense Verbs**

Activity 22.2

Select a reading in Part Seven, "Connecting: Responding to Reading," and re-view it to find ten sentences that include past tense verbs. Write these sentences on a separate piece of paper, and exchange sentences with a writing partner. Underline the past tense verb in each sentence, and write the basic form of the verb above it. Are all the past tense verbs formed the same way? Discuss your conclusions with the rest of the class.

Using the Perfect Tenses

Audio 22.6

Writers use another verb form called the **past participle** to form additional tenses: past perfect, present perfect, and future perfect. All of the **perfect tenses** are formed by adding a helping verb to the past participle of a verb. For regular verbs, the past participle is the same as the simple past tense: the basic verb form plus *-d* or *-ed*.

This chapter discusses perfect tense verbs that use *has, have,* or *had* as helping verbs. Chapter 24, "Passive Voice, Additional Tenses, and Maintaining Consistency in Tense," will discuss progressive tense verbs that use *am, is, was,* and *were* as helping verbs.

To form the perfect tenses for regular verbs, use the helping verbs shown below:

Perfect Tense	=	*Helping Verb*	+	*Past Participle*	*Example*
Past perfect		had		walked	I *had walked.*
Present perfect		has, have		walked	I *have walked.*
Future perfect		will have		walked	I *will have walked.*

Perfect tense verbs cover time in a slightly different way than simple past, present, and future tenses do.

- The *past perfect tense* expresses action completed in the past before some other past action or event. (Jim *had bought* Nikki's birthday gift before they broke up.)
- The *present perfect tense* expresses action completed at some indefinite period in the past, or action that began in the past and is still going on. (Jim *has bought* me a birthday gift every year since 1988.)
- The *future perfect tense* refers to actions that will be completed in the future before some other future event or action. Note that this tense requires the word *will* before the helping verb. (By August, Jim *will have bought* all his Christmas gifts.)

Study the time line below, which shows the relationship of all the tenses discussed in this chapter.

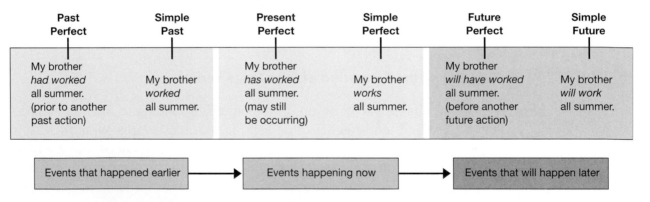

Fast Fact When you change the form of a word to indicate time or condition, as you do with verbs in English, the words are said to be *inflected.* If you feel bad about having to deal with inflection with verbs, just be thankful we don't speak Old English, one of the ancestor languages of modern English, anymore. According to scholars, Old English, which was spoken from around 450 to 1100 A.D., was heavily inflected, meaning that nearly all types of words were changed depending on the time, person, case, mood, or number being discussed.

Exercise 22.4   **Practice Working with the Perfect Tenses**

On another sheet of paper, rewrite the following sentences, changing the present tense verb to either the present perfect, past perfect, or future perfect form. In some cases, more than one tense can be used. Use the example to guide you.

EXAMPLE   Josh earns all of his tuition money.

Josh will have earned all of his tuition money. [Future perfect]

1. The blue jay eats the blueberries on the ground below the bush.

2. The pie chills in the refrigerator at least two hours before dinner.

3. Bryan asks his friend for help with algebra.

4. The meteorologist forecasts a stormy weekend.

5. Dan states his preferences for vacation before anyone else.

6. The class turns in a teacher evaluation.

7. The secretary sorts the papers on the manager's desk.

8. I revise my essay one more time before submitting it.

9. The artist sketches the scene for an oil painting.

10. The baseball team practices every day for six weeks.

Exercise 22.5   **More Practice Working with the Perfect Tenses**

Each of the sentences in the following paragraph contains a past participle that is missing a helping verb. Write the correct helping verb in the space provided to form a complete verb in the perfect tense. Then, label these verbs in the space above the line. Use *PaP* for past perfect tense, *PP* for present perfect tense, and *FP* for future perfect tense. Remember that the future perfect tense requires the word *will* along with the helping verb. Use the example to guide you.

EXAMPLE   My daughter was delighted that the groundhog ⎯⎯*had*⎯⎯ failed to see his [PaP] shadow this year.

Activity 22.3   (1) When mid-September comes to the northeastern United States, the hot days of summer ⎯⎯*have*⎯⎯ passed for good. [PP] (2) The heat that several weeks earlier __had__ (PaP) felt so oppressive is now just a memory. (3) The lawns that __had__ (PaP) suffered from the combination of intense sun and low rainfall __have__ (PP) become lush again, at least for another few weeks. (4) In the most northern areas, the first frost __has__ (PP) even occurred, which for some plants indicates the end of one cycle of their lives. (5) By this point, the woods __have__ (PP) also entered another phase. (6) They __have__ (PP) begun the beautiful show that year after year amazes locals and draws thousands of tourists. (7) Throughout the region, the various shades of dark green seen in the spring and summer __have__ (PP) largely disappeared. (8) In their place, brilliant shades of red, orange, and yellow __have__ (PP) appeared. (9) Unfortunately, by the time winter arrives, the explosion of color __will have__ (FP) disappeared, with the once-colorful leaves lying in dull heaps under the trees.

Challenge 22.2 **Writing with the Perfect Tenses**

1. Using the paragraph in Exercise 22.5 as a model, write a five-sentence paragraph about the signs of spring in your part of the country. Use at least one perfect tense verb in each sentence.

2. Exchange your writing with a partner. On the paper you receive, underline the perfect tense verbs and label them, using the abbreviations you used in Exercise 22.5. Then return the paragraph to the writer. Check to see whether all the labels are accurate. Which perfect tense did you choose most often? Which perfect tense did your partner choose most often? With the class, discuss how the topic affected your choices.

Chapter Quick Check: Working with Basic Verb Tenses

For each italicized verb in the following passage, identify the tense, using the labels listed below.

Pr = present tense   *F* = future tense   *PP* = present perfect tense
Pa = past tense   *PaP* = past perfect tense   *FP* = future perfect tense

(1) Quincy Jones *ranks* (Pr) as one of the true giants in American popular music. (2) Born in 1933 on Chicago's South Side and raised in Seattle, Jones

Pa   *Pa*

knew from age 11 that he *loved* music. (3) During his more than 50 year ca-

Pr   *PP*

reer in music, "Q," as he *is* known to his friends, *has affected* popular music

PaP

to a profound degree. (4) Early in his career Jones *had worked* with such

musical giants as Dizzy Gillespie, Count Basie, Duke Ellington, Frank Sinatra,

PP

and Sarah Vaughan. (5) As a producer, arranger, and conductor, Jones *has put*

his mark on the work of a number of rock and roll artists, including Ray

Pa

Charles, Diana Ross, and Stevie Wonder. (6) In the 1970s, he *suffered* two

Pa   *Pa*

brain aneurysms that *left* him with a metal plate in his head, but he *refused*

Pa

to let them slow him down. (7) In fact, in 1982, Jones *stepped* back into the

spotlight as the producer of pop star Michael Jackson's *Thriller,* one of the

PP

best-selling recordings of all time, and more recently, he *has worked* with a

number of Rap artists, including Ice-T. (8) In addition to his work in the

PP

music studio, Jones *has enjoyed* great success in a number of other areas.

Pa

(9) For instance, in 1961, Jones *became* the vice-president of Mercury

Pr

Records, the first African-American to serve in such a capacity, and he *is* co-

founder of *Vibe* magazine. (10) His induction into the American Academy

Pr   *F*

of Arts & Sciences *is* a fitting acknowledgment for someone who *will certainly*

continue to influence popular music.

Discovering Connections 22.2

1. In Discovering Connections 22.1 on page 342, you completed a prewriting on one of the subjects suggested. Now work your way through the rest of the writing process, and create a draft essay of about 500 words on this topic.
2. Exchange your draft with a partner. Using the material in this chapter to guide you, check the essay you receive for any problems with simple tenses. Underline any errors, and then return the essay to the writer.
3. Revise your draft, correcting any errors in tense identified by your reader.

Summary Exercise: Working with Basic Verb Tenses

The chapter Recap on pages 351–352 will help students complete this Summary Exercise.

For each italicized verb in the following passage, identify the tense, using the labels listed below.

Pr = present tense *F* = future tense *PP* = present perfect tense
Pa = past tense *PaP* = past perfect tense *FP* = future perfect tense

(1) Recent research on the human brain *offers* us a number of interesting findings about the "wiring" of this fascinating organ. (2) Scientists are now theorizing that, before your birth, your brain *programmed* itself. (3) It *dedicated* large numbers of nerve cells to performing basic functions. (4) However, it *reserved* even more nerve cells for specialized functions that help you learn about the world. (5) These findings *add* great significance to the way that we *treat* children. (6) We now believe that a child's neurons *will thrive* with appropriate stimulation. (7) Without direct stimulation and use, however, these nerve cells *will wither* away.

(8) This research *will encourage* parents and teachers to change some of our old views about learning. (9) For one thing, the findings *suggest* that there are certain peak periods of opportunity for learning. (10) They *indicate* that children will make the greatest strides in learning mathematics between birth and four years. (11) The same thing *appears* to be true for learning music. (12) Parents who *had played* simple number games and *had introduced* their children to music during this period *saw* impressive results.

(13) The findings also *urge* us to examine how we *have treated* language. (14) Children *learn* language most easily from birth to age ten. (15) The first few years of life *matter* most. (16) It now *appears* likely that those infants and toddlers who master language quickly *have heard* more words than other children. (17) In addition, children who *have listened* to many words before they reach age two *will have developed* large vocabularies by the time they reach adulthood.

Weblink
22.3

Pr
(18) If these preliminary findings *prove* to be true, parents and schools *will want* to make some serious adjustments. (19) For one thing, teachers *will expect* parents to be much more involved at home, since a great deal of valuable learning time occurs before children attend public school. (20) In addition, schools *will arrange* to offer instruction in a second language much earlier, perhaps as early as the first few grades.

 **RECAP** ## BASIC TENSES FOR REGULAR VERBS

Activity 22.4

New terms in this chapter	Definitions
• **verb tense**	• the form of a verb which tells when the action or situation occurs, either in the present, future, or past
• **present tense**	• the basic form of the verb signifying a fact, action, or situation that is occurring now or habitually Many singular present tense verbs end in *-s* or *-es*. ***Example*** My son *cleans* our apartment on the weekend. ***Example*** We *ignore* the dust during the week.
• **future tense**	• the form of the verb signifying a future action or state of being; the basic verb plus *will* ***Example*** This weekend he *will wash* the kitchen floor.
• **past tense**	• the form of the verb signifying an action or state of being that has already occurred; the basic form of the verb plus *-d* or *-ed* ***Example*** He *shopped* for groceries on Saturday.
• **past participle**	• for regular verbs, a form created by adding *-d* or *-ed* to the basic form Use the past participle with a helping verb to form the perfect tenses. ***Example*** Martha *had ended* the relationship months ago.
• **perfect tenses**	• verb tenses formed by adding some form of *to have* to the past participle of another verb Perfect tenses express actions that are complete with reference to another indicated time. ***Example*** We *have shared* the work this way for a few months. ***Example*** I *had finished* the rest of the chores earlier. ***Example*** We *will have succeeded* in sharing responsibilities.

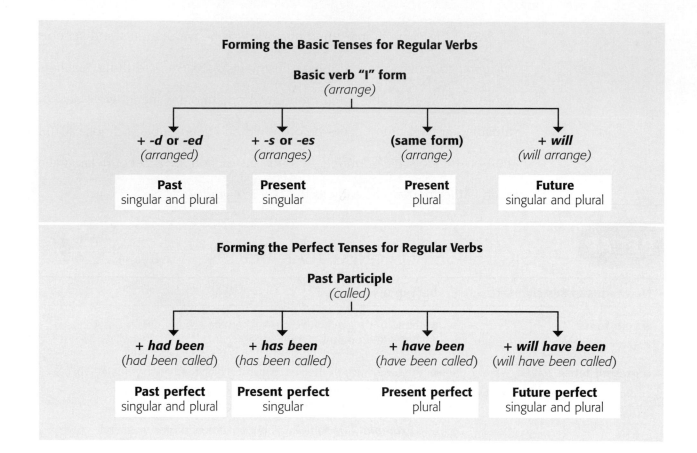

Forming the Basic Tenses for Regular Verbs

Basic verb "I" form
(arrange)

+ -d or -ed *(arranged)*	+ -s or -es *(arranges)*	(same form) *(arrange)*	+ will *(will arrange)*
Past singular and plural	**Present** singular	**Present** plural	**Future** singular and plural

Forming the Perfect Tenses for Regular Verbs

Past Participle
(called)

+ had been *(had been called)*	+ has been *(has been called)*	+ have been *(have been called)*	+ will have been *(will have been called)*
Past perfect singular and plural	**Present perfect** singular	**Present perfect** plural	**Future perfect** singular and plural

Chapter 23

Irregular Verbs and Frequently Confused Verbs

Getting Started... **Q:** The verbs that give me the most trouble aren't the ones that follow the rules—the regular verbs. It's the ones that don't follow the rules—plus a few others like *can* and *could* and *will* and *would*—that I keep mixing up. If I can't rely on rules to show me how to form the verb tenses, how am I going to keep them straight?

Audio
23.1

A: It's not surprising that the irregular verbs and verb pairs like *can* and *could* and *will* and *would* cause you the most difficulty. Sadly, there is no easy solution. Probably the best way to keep the irregular verb forms straight is to go through the list of irregular verbs provided in this chapter. Highlight the ones you didn't realize were irregular and the ones that you often have difficulty with. From this material, make a list of your own personal problem verbs and memorize them. Look at the guidelines about *can* and *could* and *will* and *would* and memorize them, too. It's not a foolproof method, but it will definitely improve your chances of selecting the proper verb form.

Overview: Understanding Irregular Verbs and Other Verb Problems

Audio
23.2

Chapter 22, "Basic Tenses for Regular Verbs," illustrated how to form the basic tenses of regular verbs. As that chapter pointed out, forming the past and past participle forms for regular verbs is easy and predictable. You simply add either *-d* or *-ed* to the end of the basic verb form: *create—created, talk—talked*. The problem, of course, is that all verbs don't form their past or past participle forms in predictable ways. These **irregular verbs** hold the most potential to confuse writers. The verb *to be* is perhaps the most troublesome of these irregular verbs because it has so many forms. Other verbs that give writers trouble are the confusing pairs *can* and *could* and *will* and *would*.

In this chapter, you will learn how to

● form the present, past, and past participle forms of common irregular verbs

● work effectively with forms of *to be*

● choose correctly between *can* and *could* and between *will* and *would*

Discovering Connections 23.1

Discovering Connections 23.2 at the end of this chapter provides an opportunity for students to apply the skills they have learned about using irregular verbs and confusing pairs of verbs. They will be asked to compose and revise an essay based on one of the topics in Discovering Connections 23.1.

Using one of the techniques you practiced in Chapter 2, "Generating Ideas through Prewriting," prewrite on one of the following topics:

1. the elements that constitute heroism
2. how a religion or some other system of belief can help—or hurt—people

Or, focus on this picture.
Save your work for later use.

Identifying Irregular Verbs

See the Recap at the end of this chapter for strategies for forming and remembering irregular verbs. Have students create lists of irregular verbs that fit each of the four categories presented there.

The verbs in the following list are all irregular. As you learned in Chapter 22, "Basic Tenses for Regular Verbs," the past participle form (column three below) is used with a helping verb to form a perfect or progressive tense verb.

Weblink
23.1

Irregular Verb Forms

Present Tense	Past Tense	Past Participle (+ a helping verb)
am/is/are	was/were	been
arise	arose	arisen
awaken	awoke, awaked	awoke, awaked
become	became	become
begin	began	begun
bend	bent	bent
bind	bound	bound
bite	bit	bitten, bit
bleed	bled	bled
blow	blew	blown
break	broke	broken
bring	brought	brought
build	built	built
burn	burned, burnt	burned, burnt
burst	burst	burst

(continued)

Refer students to pages 345–346 in Chapter 22, "Basic Tenses for Regular Verbs," for more information about past participles and forming the perfect tense.

Irregular Verb Forms *(continued)*

Present Tense	Past Tense	Past Participle (+ a helping verb)
buy	bought	bought
catch	caught	caught
choose	chose	chosen
cling	clung	clung
come	came	come
cost	cost	cost
creep	crept	crept
cut	cut	cut
deal	dealt	dealt
dig	dug	dug
dive	dived, dove	dived
do/does	did	done
draw	drew	drawn
dream	dreamed, dreamt	dreamed, dreamt
drink	drank	drunk
drive	drove	driven
eat	ate	eaten
fall	fell	fallen
feed	fed	fed
feel	felt	felt
fight	fought	fought
find	found	found
flee	fled	fled
fling	flung	flung
fly	flew	flown
forbid	forbade, forbad	forbidden
forget	forgot	forgotten, forgot
freeze	froze	frozen
get	got	got, gotten
give	gave	given
go/goes	went	gone
grind	ground	ground
grow	grew	grown
hang	hung	hung
hang (execute)	hanged	hanged
have/has	had	had
hear	heard	heard
hide	hid	hidden, hid
hold	held	held
hurt	hurt	hurt
keep	kept	kept
kneel	knelt, kneeled	knelt, kneeled
knit	knit, knitted	knit, knitted
know	knew	known
lay	laid	laid
lead	led	led
leap	leaped, leapt	leaped, leapt
leave	left	left

**Weblink
22.3**

(continued)

Irregular Verb Forms (continued)

Present Tense	Past Tense	Past Participle (+ a helping verb)
lend	lent	lent
let	let	let
lie	lay	lain
light	lighted, lit	lighted, lit
lose	lost	lost
make	made	made
mean	meant	meant
meet	met	met
mistake	mistook	mistaken
pay	paid	paid
plead	pleaded, pled	pleaded, pled
prove	proved	proved, proven
put	put	put
quit	quit	quit
raise	raised	raised
read	read	read
ride	rode	ridden
ring	rang	rung
rise	rose	risen
run	ran	run
say	said	said
see	saw	seen
seek	sought	sought
sell	sold	sold
send	sent	sent
set	set	set
sew	sewed	sewn, sewed
shake	shook	shaken
shine	shone, shined	shone, shined
shine (polish)	shined	shined
shoot	shot	shot
show	showed	shown, showed
shrink	shrank, shrunk	shrunk, shrunken
shut	shut	shut
sing	sang, sung	sung
sit	sat	sat
sleep	slept	slept
slide	slid	slid
sling	slung	slung
slink	slunk, slinked	slunk, slinked
sow	sowed	sown, sowed
speak	spoke	spoken
speed	sped, speeded	sped, speeded
spend	spent	spent
spit	spit, spat	spit, spat
spring	sprang, sprung	sprung
stand	stood	stood
steal	stole	stolen
stick	stuck	stuck
sting	stung	stung

(continued)

Irregular Verb Forms (continued)

Present Tense	Past Tense	Past Participle (+ a helping verb)
stink	stank, stunk	stunk
stride	strode	stridden
strike	struck	struck, stricken
string	strung	strung
strive	strived, strove	striven, strived
swear	swore	sworn
sweat	sweat, sweated	sweat, sweated
swell	swelled	swelled, swollen
swim	swam	swum
swing	swung	swung
take	took	taken
teach	taught	taught
tear	tore	torn
tell	told	told
think	thought	thought
throw	threw	thrown
understand	understood	understood
wake	woke, waked	woken, waked, woke
wear	wore	worn
weave	wove, weaved	woven, weaved
weep	wept	wept
win	won	won
wind	wound	wound
wring	wrung	wrung
write	wrote	written

Video 23.1   As the table shows, the past and past participle forms of irregular verbs are often different. Consider these examples:

EXAMPLE   The windows in the building *shook* each time the furnace started up.

EXAMPLE   The front picture window *had shaken* so much that it actually cracked.

Because of their unpredictability, irregular verbs in all their forms must be memorized. As you learn the irregular verb forms, keep two things in mind: (1) You *don't* use a helping verb with the past tense, and (2) You *must* use a helping verb with the past participle.

Fast Fact One way we learn things is to group them on the basis of some similarity and then memorize the pattern. This method generally works well, but don't count on having just one group when you need to form the past and past participle forms of irregular verbs ending in -ng. With *sing,* for example, the past is *sang* and the past participle is *sung.* The pattern is the same for *ring* (*rang* and *rung*) and *cling* (*clang* and *clung*). But with *fling,* the *a* disappears, and the past and past participle is *flung.* The same is true for *sting* (*stung* and *stung*), *swing* (*swung* and *swung*), and *wring* (*wrung* and *wrung*). For *spring,* the past participle is *sprung,* but the past can be either *sprang* or *sprung.* That brings us to *bring.* It stands alone, with its past and past participle both *brought.*

Exercise 23.1   Forming Perfect Tenses for Irregular Verbs

Activity
23.1

In the following paragraph, fill in the blanks with the past participle form of the verb in parentheses to form a perfect tense verb. Remember to provide the appropriate helping verb (*have, has,* or *had*) for each past participle. Then label these verbs in the space above the line. Use *PaP* for past perfect tense, *PP* for present perfect tense, and *FP* for future perfect tense. Use the example to guide you.

EXAMPLE

PP

It looks as though Caryl's eye (swell) _____*has swollen*_____ shut.

PaP

(1) When I asked my friend Jarod how he (cut) ____*had cut*____ his fore-

head, he began to laugh. (2) Then Jarod told me that he (fall)

PaP

____*had fallen*____ while roller blading, but he hadn't hurt himself. (3) Feeling

very proud of himself for having avoided any injury, he stood up, but he

PaP

(forget) ____*had forgotten*____ to tighten the binding on his left skate boot. (4) He

fell again, and when he wiped his forehead and saw red on his fingers, he

PaP

realized he (hurt) ____*had hurt*____ himself. (5) He said that his friends

PP

(make) ____*have made*____ him captain of the Olympic klutz team, but he vows

FP

he (prove) ____*will have proven*____ them wrong by the end of the roller blading

season.

Exercise 23.2   Using Irregular Verbs in Your Writing

Activity
23.2

On a separate sheet of paper, write three related sentences for each of the irregular verbs listed below: one each for the present tense, the past tense, and the past participle forms. Remember—the past participle requires a helping verb to form a perfect tense verb. Use the example to guide you.

EXAMPLE

Kathy and John always <u>hear</u> the noise from the Fourth of July fireworks.

Last night, they also <u>heard</u> the oohs and ahhs of the crowd.

In previous years, Kathy and John <u>have heard</u> the band as well as the fireworks.

1. keep	3. sleep	5. freeze	7. write	9. raise
2. bite	4. shake	6. speak	8. become	10. stand

Exercise 23.3   **Using Irregular Verbs Correctly**

The following narrative takes place in the past. Each sentence contains a present tense verb in parentheses. Write the correct past form of this verb on the line that follows. Use the form that the context calls for; include a helping verb if necessary. In some cases, more than one correct answer is possible. Use the example to guide you.   Answers may vary.

EXAMPLE   When I was growing up, I always (do) ___*did*___ my assigned chores as quickly as I could.

(1) Recently I (spend) ___spent___ a most memorable evening when several friends and I attended a production by Blue Man Group. (2) Our seats were in the front row, and what I (see) ___saw___ and (hear) ___heard___ that night still amazes me. (3) We saw everything the Blue Men (do) ___did___ up close, from drumming on huge PVC pipes to splashing fluorescent paint across the stage to burying part of the audience in tissue paper. (4) The theater program explained that Blue Man Group (begin) ___began___ as a kind of musical and theatrical "happening" in New York City in 1987. (5) Eventually, the concept of the Blue Men emerged: three performers who (wear) ___wore___ deep blue makeup and interacted on stage with everyday items like breakfast cereal, tissue paper, and, of course, television, to great comic effect. (6) From that point on, the original Blue Men, Matt Goldman, Phil Stanton, and Chris Wink, (know) ___knew___ they had a hit on their hands, both in terms of the stage show and the hard driving music backing the action on stage. (7) They (bring) ___brought___ such energy and fun to their performance that word rapidly spread about the production. (8) In fact, the original shows (become) ___became___ so popular that Blue Man troupes were established in several other cities, including Boston and Las Vegas. (9) They received some national attention when they (make) ___made___ a series of television advertisements for Pentium Processors. (10) The Grammy

nomination Blue Man Group received in 2001 for their original music (prove) _____proved_____ that they are more than just three pretty, blue faces.

Challenge 23.1 **Revising the Tense of a Paragraph**

Have students read their paragraphs aloud. Did any students use more than five verbs? Which paragraph did the class enjoy most? Why?

Ten verbs are listed below. On a separate sheet of paper, use at least five of these verbs in the present tense to write a paragraph. Exchange your work with a partner, and rewrite the paragraph you receive, changing the tense of each verb to either the past or past perfect form. Consult the list of irregular verbs (pages 354–357) as necessary.

feed	eat
give	sit
make	grind
see	bring
break	forget

Working with Forms of *To Be*

The most irregular of the irregular verbs is the verb **to be**. For example, it is the only verb that uses different forms for different persons in the past tense. However, memorizing the various forms of *to be* is not that difficult because many do *not* change when the subject changes.

Look at the table below, which shows the most common forms of the verb *to be:*

Tell students that another form of *to be*—the present participle *being*—is also the same for first, second, and third person subjects. Present participles are discussed in Chapter 24.

Common Forms of the Verb *To Be*

When the subject is ...	the present tense is ...	the past tense is ...	the future tense is ...	the past participle is ...
I	am	was	will be	been
he, she, *or* it	is	was	will be	been
we, you, *or* they	are	were	will be	been

As you can see, *will be* and *been* are used with *all* subjects, although different helping verbs are needed for *been*.

To simplify your understanding of *to be*, concentrate on those forms that *do* change, as this version of the same table shows:

When the subject is . . .	the present tense is . . .	the past tense is . . .	Examples
I	am	was	I *am* tired tonight. I *was* more energetic yesterday.
he, she, or it	is	was	He *is* late for his dental appointment. She *was* early for her guitar lesson.
we, you, or they	are	were	You *are* the best friend I've ever had. They *were* childhood sweethearts before they were married.

If you keep these forms straight, you'll have far fewer problems using *to be*. In addition, keep in mind two rules when you are using forms of *to be*.

1. Never use *been* without *has, have,* or *had*:

EXAMPLE   For some time, we ~~been~~ have been looking for a house.

EXAMPLE   Just a year earlier, that superstar comedian ~~been~~ had been a complete unknown.

2. Never use *be* by itself as the verb in a sentence:

EXAMPLE   We ~~be~~ are proud of your achievement.

EXAMPLE   You ~~be~~ are the reason for this celebration.

Although you may hear violations of these rules in informal speech, such usages are not acceptable for the writing you will do in college and the workplace.

Exercise 23.4   **Working with Forms of *To Be***

In the following paragraph, complete each sentence by writing the correct form of the verb *to be* in the space provided. Use the tables on page 360 and above for help with the most irregular forms of *to be*. Use the example as a guide.

EXAMPLE   Annette ____will be____ thirty on her next birthday.

(1) Today, one way to get a brighter smile ____is____ to use a chemical whitener. (2) Some observers of trends in business believe that these whiteners ____are____ among the fastest growing personal care products

in this decade. (3) These analysts note that many people _____are_____ embarrassed by stains on their teeth but don't want to pay $300 to have a dentist bleach them. (4) Unfortunately, until now, there _____was_____ no alternative. (5) Now, however, an over-the-counter product _____is_____ finally available for the general public.

Exercise 23.5   **Correcting Errors in the Forms of *To Be***

In the following paragraph, correct the errors in the use of *be* and *been*. Cross out the error, and write the verb correctly above it as the example shows.

EXAMPLE

is
Mary ~~be~~ the most experienced worker in the office.

is
(1) With all the injuries suffered in professional boxing each year, it ~~be~~ hard to understand why we allow the sport to continue. (2) Nevertheless,

is
boxing is still legal, and it ~~been~~ causing permanent damage to hundreds of

is
people every year. (3) The brutality of boxing ~~been~~ no longer reserved for

Activity 23.5

men only, either. (4) A few years ago, the first professional bouts between fe-

were
male boxers ~~been~~ broadcast. (5) Regardless of the sex of the combatants, the

is   are
impact of a punch ~~be~~ unbelievably damaging. (6) Fighters ~~be~~ often lifted off

are
their feet when they ~~been~~ hit. (7) The physical state of former heavyweight

is
champion Muhammad Ali ~~was~~ the greatest argument that boxing should be

was
banned. (8) At the beginning of his career, Ali ~~been~~ among the most articu-

is
late people in the world of sports. (9) Now he ~~be~~ barely able to speak.

is
(10) Ours ~~are~~ a civilized society, so why do we allow this brutality to continue?

Exercise 23.6   **Working with Forms of *To Be***

Change the verbs in the following paragraph to the past tense. Cross out the present tense verb, and write the past tense form above it. Use the example to guide you.

EXAMPLE

was
Marcy ~~is~~ the right person to run the business.

(1) In the city, a group of volunteers ~~is~~ was organized to clean up the water-front area. (2) These workers ~~are~~ were organized by the local chapter of the Sierra Club. (3) The hope of the organizing committee ~~is~~ was to attract fifty vol-unteers. (4) Many spots ~~are~~ were in terrible shape. (5) After years of neglect, the three-mile stretch of beach near Reflecting Lake ~~is~~ was full of litter like old tires and beer cans. (6) The worst area ~~is~~ was the spot near the abandoned Kerr Mill. (7) This section ~~is~~ was the hardest to reach because of a city barrier to keep peo-ple out. (8) Nevertheless, the area ~~is~~ was a frequent party spot for teenagers in the city. (9) Glass slivers from hundreds of windows broken by vandals ~~are~~ were everywhere on the pavement around the old mill building. (10) However, the volunteers ~~are~~ were so dedicated that the area ~~is~~ was soon clean and attractive enough for family picnics.

Challenge 23.2   **Explaining Problem Verbs**

Activity 23.4

Identify the form of *to be* that you think is most difficult to use, and write a paragraph in which you explain why you find this form confusing. Include brief sentences illustrating how you use the form incorrectly, and then show what you must do to use it correctly. Share your paragraph and example sentences with a partner. Did you both choose the same form of *to be* to write about?

Choosing between *Can* and *Could* and between *Will* and *Would*

Beginning writers often have trouble choosing between *can* and *could* as helping verbs. These two verbs both mean *to be able to. Can* is used to indi-cate the present tense, and *could* is used to indicate the past tense:

> **EXAMPLE**   At this moment, no one in the conference *can beat* our relay team.

> **EXAMPLE**   Last season, no one in the conference *could beat* our relay team.

Sometimes *could* is also used to indicate a *possibility* or *hope* of doing something:

EXAMPLE Our competitors wish they *could beat* our relay team.

Beginning writers also have trouble deciding between the helping verbs *will* and *would*. Although both verbs are used to indicate the future, each links the future with a different period of time.

Look at the following versions of the same sentence, with the verbs italicized:

present tense

EXAMPLE Carlos *thinks* that he *will major* in computer programming.

past tense

EXAMPLE Carlos *thought* that he *would major* in computer programming.

The first sentence says that *right now* Carlos intends to focus on computer programming in the future. The second sentence indicates that *at an earlier time*, he had intended to study computer programming.

In some instances, *would* is also used to indicate a *hope* or *possibility* rather than a certainty, as this sentence shows:

EXAMPLE Many people *would* be able to save if they budgeted carefully.

Fast Fact *Can* means to be physically or mentally able. *May* means to be allowed or permitted to do something. A common error is to make a request using *can* when *may* is the logical choice. For example, as long as mobility isn't a problem for you, asking "*Can* I go out the open front door?" would be incorrect because you are certainly able to move through the doorway. The correct phrasing, because you are asking if doing so is all right, is "*May* I go out the open front door?"

Exercise 23.7 **Choosing between *Can* and *Could* and between *Will* and *Would***

In each sentence in the following paragraph, circle the correct verb in parentheses as the example shows.

EXAMPLE If he didn't work, Arnie (will, (would)) take an evening class.

(1) From personal experience, I know that being able to speak a second language ((can,) could) make a real difference in your chances to get a job. (2) If you are able to converse with people who don't speak English, you ((will,) would) be a great candidate for a number of jobs that involve customer contact. (3) Before I learned to speak Spanish, I saw advertisements for several good jobs that I knew I (can, (could)) never get because I didn't speak Spanish. (4) Instead of feeling sorry for myself, I decided I (will, (would))

work harder in my conversational Spanish class. (5) Thanks to that class, I
(can) could) now apply for those good jobs with confidence.

Exercise 23.8   **Correcting Errors in the Use of *Can* and *Could* and *Will* and *Would***

The following passage contains a number of errors in the use of *can* and
could and *will* and *would*. Correct the errors by crossing out the incorrect
word and writing the correct word above it. If a sentence is correct as written, write *OK* above it. Use the example as a guide.

EXAMPLE   *will*
I don't know if I ~~would~~ be available to begin work on Monday.

will
(1) Soon, physicians ~~would~~ have a new weapon in their battle to help
OK
burn victims. (2) The Food and Drug Administration (FDA) recently approved an artificial skin that can be used in grafting procedures. (3) Up until
could
now, patients ~~can~~ expect attempts at skin grafting to fail more often than not.

(4) When a person is severely burned, in many cases only the outer layer of
will
skin ~~would~~ grow back. (5) If the skin graft cannot attach itself to healthy tis-
will
sue, the procedure ~~would~~ fail. (6) So, before the artificial skin became avail-
could
able, the best that burn patients ~~can~~ hope for was to minimize the number of
would
failures. (7) Each time a graft failed, the surgeon ~~will~~ harvest a new graft and

begin the procedure again. (8) Now, however, it appears that the new artifi-
will   *OK*
cial skin ~~would~~ dramatically improve the success rate for grafting. (9) The

new material, which eventually breaks down to be absorbed by the body,

will provide an anchor for the skin graft. (10) Now that the FDA has ap-
will
proved the use of this artificial skin, doctors ~~would~~ soon begin using it in

their surgical procedures.

Challenge 23.3   **Analyzing Correct *Can/Could* and *Will/Would* Choices**

Working with a partner, write a brief paragraph that explains the differences
between *can* and *could* and between *will* and *would*. Provide examples of
correct and incorrect usage for each word.

Chapter Quick Check: Eliminating Problems with Irregular Verbs and *Can* and *Could* and *Will* and *Would*

Proofread the following sentences, and revise any errors you find in the use of irregular verbs, *can* and *could*, or *will* and *would*. Cross out the incorrect word or words, and write a correct version above it, as the example shows. If a sentence is correct as written, write *OK* above it. In some cases, more than one answer is possible.

EXAMPLE

    had drunk
The fifteen-year-old driver ~~had drank~~ an entire six-pack of beer before he stole my car and crashed it.

(1) Thanks to the wonders of modern technology, the old-fashioned trea-
    is
sure hunt ~~be~~ now a brand new game. (2) This modern variation of an old activity is called Geocaching, Geo for geography and cache for something
    has grown   *OK*
hidden, and it ~~has grew~~ in popularity in the past couple of years. (3) Right now, across the world, thousands of "stashes," generally plastic containers filled with inexpensive trinkets, have been hidden and are waiting to be dis-
                                 thought
covered. (4) The sport was created by a man in Oregon who ~~think~~ of a way to use the formerly classified radio signals from a network of government
                               OK
navigational satellites to explore for "buried treasure." (5) To participate in Geocaching, participants need a computer, a compass, and a hand-held
                               go
Global Positioning System, or GPS. (6) Participants first ~~went~~ to geo-caching.com, a website listing the longitude and latitude of caches in a par-
             take
ticular area. (7) Players then ~~took~~ these coordinates and enter them into
                               sends
the GPS unit. (8) The GPS device taps into the satellite system, which ~~sent~~ players to within 35 feet of the stash. (9) Once participants have this infor-
        can
mation, they ~~could~~ use hints provided on the website to do some old-fash-ioned detective work and find where in that 35-foot radius the stash is
           find
hidden. (10) Once participants ~~found~~ a particular stash, they often remove one object, replace it with another, record their success on the website, and start some research for their next adventure.

Discovering Connections 23.2

1. In Discovering Connections 23.1 on page 354, you completed a prewriting on one of three suggested subjects. Now work your way through the rest of the writing process, drawing from this prewriting material, and complete a draft essay of about 500 words on this topic.
2. Exchange your draft with a partner. Using the material in this chapter to guide you, check the draft you receive for any errors in the use of irregular verbs, *can* and *could*, or *will* and *would*. Circle any errors, and then return the draft to the writer.
3. Revise your essay, correcting any errors that your reader identified.

Summary Exercise: Eliminating Problems with Irregular Verbs and *Can* and *Could* and *Will* and *Would*

Proofread the following sentences, and revise any errors you find in the use of irregular verbs, *can* and *could,* or *will* and *would.* Cross out the incorrect word or words, and write a correct version above it. If a sentence is correct as written, write *OK* above it. In some cases, more than one answer is possible.
Some answers may vary.

(1) Today, you ~~could~~ [can] buy a greeting card for just about any occasion or person. (2) As might be expected, there ~~be~~ [are] plenty of cards for standard events such as birthdays, weddings, and so on. [OK] (3) What is surprising is the range of holidays, occasions, and special needs and concerns addressed through greeting cards.

[OK]

(4) If you have had no luck in buying the perfect birthday present for someone, you can find a card that apologizes for your failure. (5) You can also ~~bought~~ [buy] birthday cards for every variety of relative you can imagine.

(6) For example, if you want to get a card created specifically for great-grandmothers or stepsons, you ~~could~~ [can] find one.

(7) In addition to the cards commemorating traditional events, such as Thanksgiving, Christmas, Hanukkah, and Valentine's Day, you ~~would~~ [will] find cards for special occasions, such as St. Patrick's Day and Halloween. [OK] (8) The

list continues to grow, too. (9) For example, cards celebrating Kwanzaa re-

cently ∧ been added to stores across the nation.
(have)

(10) If your boss just gave birth, you don't need to worry. *(OK)* (11) There ~~be~~ *are*

cards to mark the occasion. (12) You can ~~chosen~~ *choose* between pink ones for

girls and blue ones for boys. *(OK)* (13) Do you need a card to apologize to your

old friend for not writing sooner? (14) Just check the racks, and you ~~could~~ *can*

find one.

(15) These cards ~~isn't~~ *aren't* just for family and close friends, either. (16) They

~~came~~ *come* in different levels of familiarity. (17) For example, if you need a sym-

pathy card for someone you barely ~~known,~~ *know* one is available. (18) There even

~~been~~ *are* greeting cards for ex-spouses and ex-in-laws.

(19) Finally, whether you like humor, sentimentality, or inspirational mes-

sages, you ~~would~~ *will* discover a greeting card that suits you. *(OK)* (20) Just head to

the nearest card store, and plan to spend some enjoyable time reading over

the possibilities.

IRREGULAR VERBS AND FREQUENTLY CONFUSED VERBS

New terms in this chapter	Definitions
● irregular verbs	● verbs that do not form their past tense and past participle in typical ways

Strategies for Learning Irregular Verb Forms: Grouping by Pattern

	Present	Past	Past Participle
All tenses use the same form	let	let	let
	burst	burst	burst
Past tense and past participle use the same form	feel	felt	felt
	mean	meant	meant
In each tense, one letter changes	ring	rang	rung
	drink	drank	drunk
In past tense, one letter changes; in past participle, one letter is added	throw	threw	thrown
	blow	blew	blown

New terms in this chapter	Definitions
● *to be*	● the most challenging irregular verb for writers Always use *has, have,* or *had* with *been*. Never use *be* alone as a verb. Follow the chart below for tenses of *to be*.

Common Forms of the Verb *To Be*

When the subject is . . .	the present tense is . . .	the past tense is . . .	the future tense is . . .	the past participle is . . .
I	am	was	will be	been
he, she, *or* it	is	was	will be	been
we, you, *or* they	are	were	will be	been

Verb pairs often confused	

● *can/could*	● helping verbs that mean *to be able to*
	Use *can* to show present tense.
	
	   Example Jose *can* win the contest.
	
	Use *could* to show past tense, or the possibility or hope of being able to do something.
	
	   Example If I *could* sing, I'd join the chorus immediately.

● *will/would*	● helping verbs that indicate the future
	Use *will* to point to the future from the *present*.
	
	   Example Howard promises he *will* return before midnight.
	
	Use *would* to point to the future from the *past* and to indicate a hope or possibility.
	
	   Example Howard promised he *would* return before midnight.

Chapter 24

Passive Voice, Additional Tenses, and Maintaining Consistency in Tense

Getting Started... **Q:** Just when I thought I had verbs figured out, I discovered I've still got more to learn about them. Why do I need to be concerned about *voice* when I write? What other tenses are there? And how can I keep my verb tense consistent throughout a document?

Audio 24.1 **A:** When it comes to verb use, there is probably more to keep straight than with any other aspect of writing. But this complexity works to your advantage. For instance, you can present a subject of a sentence so that it either does the action or is acted upon. In writing, that's *voice.* You can also discuss something developing or happening over time. The *progressive* and *perfect progressive* tenses make this possible. Both voice and these additional tenses enable you to record and present information more accurately. As long as you are consistent in your use of verb tense, your writing will express the right time relationship. That way, your reader will get your point.

Overview: Understanding Additional Elements of Verb Use

Audio 24.2 To work effectively with verbs, you need to do more than master such essentials as basic and perfect tenses for regular and irregular verbs. As a writer, you also need to consider the differences between active and passive voice. In addition, you need to learn to deal with the progressive and perfect progressive tenses. And finally, you need to understand the importance of being consistent with verb tense in a piece of writing.

> ***In this chapter, you will learn how to***
>
> ● form the passive and active voices and when each is appropriate
>
> ● form and use the progressive and perfect progressive tenses correctly
>
> ● maintain consistency in verb tense

Discovering Connections 24.1

Discovering Connections 24.2 at the end of this chapter provides an opportunity for students to apply the skills they have learned about using passive and active voice, the progressive tenses, and maintaining consistency. They will

Using one of the techniques you practiced in Chapter 2, "Generating Ideas through Prewriting," prewrite on one of the following topics:

1. the influence of fate
2. a situation made worse by hypocrisy

Or, focus on this picture.

Save your work for later use.

be asked to compose and revise an essay based on one of these topics.

Forming the Passive and Active Voice

Weblink 24.1

When you combine the past participle form of a verb with a form of *to be*, such as *am, is, was,* or *were,* you are using the **passive voice**. In a sentence with a passive voice verb, the subject *receives* the action:

PASSIVE

[subject] [verb]
Madeleine was told the good news about her promotion by the manager of the production team.

PASSIVE

[subject] [verb]
Several *improvements were made* in the customer service area by David.

Weblink 24.2

Video 24.1

In general, the passive voice is considered less forceful than the active voice; it can sound awkward (The game *was won* by us). With a verb in the **active voice**, the subject *performs* the action and is the *focus* of the sentence.

ACTIVE

[subject] [verb]
The *manager* of the production team *told* Madeleine the good news about her promotion.

ACTIVE

[subject] [verb]
David made several improvements in the customer service area.

Audio 24.3

Audio 24.4

Using a string of passive verbs in your writing tends to weaken it. The active voice generally makes your language sound more direct, powerful, and concise. In addition, because it indicates the doer of the action, the active voice also establishes responsibility for that action. Therefore, the passive voice should be used sparingly. However, it is useful for expressing actions in which the actor is unknown or for emphasizing the receiver of an action.

EFFECTIVE PASSIVE VOICE

[subject] [verb]
The stolen *necklace was returned*; no questions were asked.

> **Fast Fact** Here are a couple of points to consider about passive voice: (a) Writers sometimes hide behind passive voice, using it to avoid identifying who did, initiated, or should be held accountable for what is under discussion. For example: A serious error in accounting was made last month, resulting in a $50,000 budget deficit. (b) Legal and governmental documents often feature passive voice. Interesting, isn't it?

Exercise 24.1 Identifying Passive and Active Voice

Weblink
24.3

Underline the simple subjects and verbs in the following sentences. Watch for compound subjects and verbs and compound sentences. Label active voice verbs with an *A* and passive voice verbs with a *P* Remember—if the subject receives the action, the sentence is in the passive voice. Use the example to guide you.

EXAMPLE

During the police chase, several <u>shots</u> <u>were fired</u>. *(P)*

Activity
24.1

(1) Last month, my <u>roommate Trey and I</u> <u>held</u> *(A)* a yard sale to get rid of our unwanted things. (2) During the week before the sale, the <u>items</u> for sale <u>were</u> *(P)* all <u>identified</u>. (3) <u>We</u> <u>spent</u> *(A)* several nights deciding on prices and putting little tags on each item. (4) <u>We</u> also <u>placed</u> *(A)* a small ad in the community newsletter, and <u>we</u> <u>posted</u> *(A)* signs throughout the neighborhood. (5) By 9 A.M. on the Saturday of our sale, our <u>treasures</u> <u>were piled</u> *(P)* on tables in front of the apartment house. (6) <u>People</u> <u>started</u> *(A)* arriving by 10. (7) For the next two hours, every <u>item</u> <u>was handled</u> *(P)*, but not one <u>thing</u> <u>was bought</u> *(P)*. (8) At 2 P.M., <u>Trey and I</u> <u>called</u> *(A)* off our sale. (9) Then <u>everything</u> <u>was carried</u> *(P)* upstairs where <u>it</u> <u>was</u> *(P)* originally <u>found</u>. (10) Finally, by 7 P.M. the <u>apartment</u> <u>was straightened</u> *(P)* out, and <u>we</u> <u>began</u> *(A)* to laugh about our short careers as entrepreneurs.

Ask students to think of more situations in which the doer of the action is unknown (*The store was robbed*) or the receiver of the action should be emphasized (*The concert was canceled*).

Exercise 24.2 Using Passive Voice

In the paragraph below, fill in the blanks with the passive forms of the verbs in parentheses. Use the example to guide you.

EXAMPLE

The championship game (to televise) <u>was televised</u>.

(1) Recently, a bicycle path (to complete) <u>was completed</u> along the edge of the Allen River, right near downtown. (2) The path (to intend) <u>was intended</u> to beautify the old abandoned railroad route. (3) The tracks (to tear) <u>were torn</u> up and smooth asphalt (to lay) <u>was laid</u> over the track bed. (4) The path (to design) <u>was designed</u> to be wide enough for four bicyclists. (5) In addition, all the lighting along the path (to repair)

___was repaired___ so that the path could be used late at night. (6) On the first weekend, a local television camera crew (to send) ___was sent___ to film the opening day crowd. (7) The officials who attended were delighted when they noted that helmets (to wear) ___were worn___ by most of the cyclists. (8) The first weekly amateur bike race (to conduct) ___was conducted___ at 5 P.M. (9) Prizes (to supply) ___were supplied___ by several local businesses. (10) When the day ended, police estimated that the new path (to enjoy) ___was enjoyed___ by more than 150 bicyclists.

Challenge 24.1   **Analyzing the Effect of Active and Passive Voice**

With a partner, rewrite the paragraph in Exercise 24.1 on page 372 two ways. In one version, use every verb in the active voice; in the other, make every verb passive. Use a separate sheet of paper for your paragraphs. Evaluate both versions of the paragraph, and then answer the following questions. Discuss your answers with the rest of the class.

1. Who or what is the subject in each sentence?

2. Who or what should be emphasized in each sentence?

3. Which version of each sentence do you think is most effective? Why?

Using the Progressive and Perfect Progressive Tenses

In addition to using the basic tenses, you also need to master the progressive and perfect progressive tenses.

The Progressive Tenses

The simple and perfect tenses that you learned about in Chapter 22, "Basic Tenses for Regular Verbs," and Chapter 23, "Irregular Verbs and Frequently Confused Verbs," also have **progressive** forms to indicate ongoing action. For the simple past, present, and future, progressive tenses are formed by adding a form of *to be* to the **present participle** (the *-ing* form) of a verb.

Progressive Tense	=	*Form of* To Be	+ *Present Participle*	*Example*
Present progressive		am, are, is	going	I *am going.*
Past progressive		was, were	going	I *was going.*
Future progressive		will be	going	I *will be going.*

Show students that *being,* the present participle of the irregular verb *to be,* is the same for first, second, and third person subjects.

- The *present progressive tense* indicates something that is currently ongoing. (I *am taking* piano lessons.)
- The *past progressive tense* indicates something that was ongoing in the past. (She *was serving* an internship while she attended the university.)
- The *future progressive tense* indicates something that will be ongoing in the future. (They *will be showing* slides continuously throughout the open house.)

The Perfect Progressive Tenses

You form the **perfect progressive tenses** by using the *-ing* form of a verb with *have been, has been, had been,* or *will have been.*

Perfect Progressive Tense	Helping Verb +	Present Participle	Example
Present perfect progressive	has been, have been	studying	She *has been studying.*
Past perfect progressive	had been	studying	She *had been studying.*
Future perfect progressive	will have been	studying	She *will have been studying.*

- The *present perfect progressive tense* indicates an action that began in the past but that is still ongoing. (Our membership *has been growing* steadily for five years.)
- The *past perfect progressive tense* indicates an action that had been happening in the past but that stopped before the present. (Until 1996, our membership *had been growing.*)
- The *future perfect progressive tense* indicates an action that will be ongoing in the future but that will end before something else begins. (By 2005, our membership *will have been growing* for six straight years.)

Remember—all of these tenses allow you to express actions in time with great precision. It is much more important to learn how to use them than it is to be able to name them or even identify them. When you do the exercises below, refer back to this section if you get confused about the correct tense.

Students will also find the Recap at the end of this chapter a helpful reference. For classroom practice, ask students to write a simple sentence, such as *She dances,* in simple, perfect, progressive, and perfect progressive tenses. Then place the sentences along a timeline written on the blackboard.

Exercise 24.3 **Recognizing the Progressive and Perfect Progressive Tenses**

In the sentences below, underline the progressive and perfect progressive tense verbs. Then, in the space above the line, label those verbs, as the example shows. Use the following abbreviations to label the verbs.

PPr = present progressive *PPPr* = present perfect progressive
PaPr = past progressive *PaPPr* = past perfect progressive
FPr = future progressive *FPPr* = future perfect progressive

PPPr

EXAMPLE   Lately, I have been spending all my spare time surfing the Internet.

PPr

(1) As a result of my government class, I am becoming a news junkie.

PaPPr

(2) In the first week of this class, we had been discussing current affairs.

PaPr

(3) One morning, the instructor was lecturing on the role played by the

PaPPr

media in all news events. (4) I had already been considering a subscription

to *Newsweek*, so I decided to follow through. (5) Within a couple weeks, I

PaPr

was also scanning two or three newspapers online every day. (6) The more

PPPr

I do, the more I have been noticing the different ways print reporters pre-

PPPr

sent the news (7) My television viewing habits have been changing, too.

(8) Now instead of watching sitcoms or some prime-time dramas, I find that

PPr   PPPr

I am turning on CNN every night. (9) In addition, I have been watching

FPPr

other all-news stations like MSNBC, Fox News, and CNBC. (10) I will soon be

declaring a major, and my new interest in the news is leading me to con-

sider history, government, and pre-law.

Exercise 24.4   **Using the Present Progressive Tense**

Activity 24.2   For each sentence below, change the present tense verb in parentheses to a progressive tense verb. Write the correct verb form in the blank space as the example shows.

EXAMPLE   My sister (watches) *is watching* _____ *Nightline* now.

(1) Right now at work, I (take) ____am taking____ a safety course. (2) The in-

structor (try) ____is trying____ hard to make the class interesting, and I think she

(succeed) __is succeeding__. (3) At this point, we (evaluate) ____are evaluating____ our

work environment to make sure our building is as safe as possible.

(4) In fact, two of my co-workers (create) ____are creating____ a crisis management

plan. (5) In particular, they (concentrate) ____are concentrating____ on ensuring that everyone in the building knows exactly where to go in the case of fire. (6) Also,

the course (cover) ___is covering___ basic first aid techniques. (7) For example,

we (learn) ___are learning___ how to recognize things like shock, complications

from diabetes, and allergic reactions. (8) In addition, we (review) ___are reviewing___

how to help someone who (choke) ___is choking___ by using the Heimlich ma-

neuver. (9) Most important of all, everybody (learning) ___is learning___ how to

perform CPR. (10) So far, all the people on my crew feel that we (gain)

___are gaining___ a truly valuable education.

Exercise 24.5   **Using the Perfect Progressive Tense**

Choose at least five verbs from the following list. Then, on a separate sheet
of paper, write a paragraph in which you use perfect progressive tense forms
(a form of *to have* plus the present participle) of the verbs you have selected. Use the example as a guide.

to ask	to answer
to complain	to reassure
to think	to observe
to speak	to laugh
to look	to find

EXAMPLE   to think

I had been thinking about dropping out before I spoke to Dennis.

Challenge 24.2   **Working with Verb Tenses in Your Writing**

1. Choose two verbs from the list of irregular verbs on pages 354–357 and
   two regular verbs. Write three sentences for each, using verbs in the progressive and perfect progressive tenses.

2. Exchange your writing with a partner. On the paper you receive, underline the verbs and label them either progressive (*P*) or perfect progressive (*PP*). Then return the sentences to the writer.

Maintaining Consistency in Tense

Activity
24.3

In addition to choosing the correct tense for your sentence context, you
must use that tense *consistently.* To maintain **consistency in tense**, use a

ESL Note
See "Agreement" on pages 576–578.

Discuss the need to change tense when using a flashback as a narrative strategy (see pages 97–98 in Chapter 5, "Narration").

logical pattern for your verb choices, and avoid switching carelessly from one tense to another. Actions or situations occurring now call for the present tense. If they happened earlier, the past tense is needed, and if they have not yet happened, then the future tense is called for.

It's important to use a consistent time frame within a paragraph and especially within a sentence. To write about past events, use the past tense; don't switch, without good reason, to the present or the future. Use present tense verbs to write about events occurring now.

PAST TENSE
The pitcher ~~stands~~ *stood* on the mound and *stared* at the batter.

PRESENT TENSE
The pitcher *stands* on the mound and ~~stared~~ *stares* at the batter.

The tense you choose will depend upon the context of your writing. You must make the choice that is most logical to help readers understand the thoughts or events you are writing about.

Fast Fact   The way we speak helps to explain a number of errors in writing because we sometimes transfer a habit from one method of communication to another. Incorrect switches in verb tense may fall into this category. Look at this familiar way of telling a story: "I walked over to the counter and sat down. All of a sudden, this man gets up and starts screaming at the cashier." In speech, the switch from past tense in the first sentence to present tense in the second can be explained as an attempt to make the scene seem more alive or real. On paper, however, these kinds of switches aren't acceptable.

Exercise 24.6   **Maintaining Consistency in Tense**

Fill in the blanks in the following sentences with the correct form of the verb in parentheses to maintain consistency in verb tense. Use the example as a guide.

EXAMPLE   Once the police arrived, a crowd (to start) ___*started*___ to gather.

(1) When I first started doing my work in college, the main thing that (to hold) ___*held*___ me back was my lack of self-esteem. (2) When it came to studying, I was so sure I couldn't do the work that I (to do) ___*did*___ not even bother. (3) For the first few weeks, I (to fail) ___*failed*___ every quiz and examination I took. (4) As a result, I (to become) ___*became*___ more convinced that I had no ability. (5) My lack of confidence (to begin) ___*began*___ to influence other aspects of my life. (6) I (to think) ___*thought*___ that nobody liked me. (7) Of course, because

I didn't bother with anybody, nobody (to bother) ___bothered___ with me either, so I became more convinced that I had no worth. (8) I was just about ready to drop out when my business instructor (to talk) ___talked___ to me and said that I could do the work. (9) Her words (to shock) ___shocked___ me. (10) I (to decide) ___decided___ that if she thought I could do it, I would give college one more try.

Exercise 24.7   **Keeping Verb Tense Consistent**

Several sentences in the following passage suffer from inconsistency in verb tense. Cross out each error, and write the correct verb form above it. Use the example as a guide.

> **EXAMPLE**
>
>   *saw*
>
> As I walked along Main Street, suddenly I ~~see~~ my friend Kelly with somebody I didn't recognize.

    (1) One of the most unusual places I've seen is Clarkin Caverns. (2) Even though we ~~go~~ [went] there almost nine years ago, I still remember what a strange and wonderful place it is. (3) The last time I ~~am~~ [was] there, I first ~~have~~ [had] to go into a small ticket center. (4) Once there were enough people to make up a group, a guide ~~walks~~ [walked] us to an extra large elevator, which quickly ~~lowers~~ [lowered] us about sixty feet beneath the surface of the earth. (5) When I stepped out of the elevator, I ~~am~~ [was] amazed at what I saw. (6) All around me were beautiful rock formations, and as the group ~~walks~~ [walked] around, the guide talked about the cavern. (7) She ~~explains~~ [explained] the differences between *stalactites*, which "grow" down from the roof of the cavern, and *stalagmites*, which "grow" up from the ground. (8) As we walked, I ~~keep~~ [kept] looking all around, because I was afraid a bat was going to fly down and get caught in my hair. (9) At the end of the tour, our guide ~~puts~~ [put] out the lights for a minute so we ~~can~~ [could] experience total darkness. (10) It ~~is~~ [was] so dark that I ~~can't~~ [couldn't] even see my hands in front of me; never had a place felt peaceful and spooky at the same time.

Exercise 24.8 **Evaluating Tenses for Effectiveness**

In each sentence below, fill in the blanks with a form of the verb in parentheses, using a consistent tense. Then, on a separate sheet of paper, copy the paragraph over, using verbs in a different tense to fill in the blanks. Reread both versions, and write a brief paragraph in which you explain which tense you feel is most effective and why. Use the example as a guide.

EXAMPLE   The young boy (to kick) _____*kicked*_____ an empty can into the vacant lot.

or

EXAMPLE   The young boy (to kick) _____*kicks*_____ an empty can into the vacant lot.

(1) My old computer (to be) __is (was)__ such a piece of junk. (2) Every day I (to switch) __switch (switched)__ it on and (to hope) __hope (hoped)__ for the best. (3) On some days, the screen (to light) __lights (lit)__ right up. (4) On other days, however, it (to remain) __remains (remained)__ blank, with no sign of life. (5) Every time this (to happen) __happens (happened)__, I (to unplug) __unplug (unplugged)__ the unit for a couple of minutes. (6) I (to check) __check (checked)__ all the connections before plugging it in again. (7) This process (to be) __is (was)__ usually enough to get the computer to start up. (8) Once started, however, the computer (to crash) __crashes (crashed)__ frequently. (9) As a result, I sometimes (to lose) __lose (lost)__ some documents. (10) That computer often (to cost) __costs (cost)__ me as much time as it (to save) __saves (saved)__ me.

Challenge 24.3 **Analyzing the Effect of Inconsistent Tense**

Reread the paragraph in Exercise 24.7 in its original (uncorrected) form. Then, working with a partner, write a brief paragraph in which you explain what effect inconsistent verb tense has on the reader's ability to understand the point of the writing.

Chapter Quick Check: Mastering Voice, Progressive and Perfect Progressive Tenses, and Consistency in Verb Tense

The following passage contains a number of the errors and weaknesses in verb used outlined in this chapter. Using the various examples throughout the chapter to guide you, identify problems with voice, tense, and consistency. Cross out the incorrect form, and write the correct form above it, as the example shows. In some cases, more than one correct answer is possible.

EXAMPLE

entered
After Karen and Eddie ~~enter~~ the plane, they quickly stored their carry-on

luggage and took their seats.

(1) Car-sharing programs, an idea popular for some time in Europe and
beginning
Canada, is ~~begun~~ to catch on in such U.S. cities as San Francisco, Boston,
will be establishing
Seattle, and Portland, Oregon. (2) Soon, organizers ~~had been establishing~~ car-

sharing groups in several other major U.S. cities, including Boulder, Colorado,

and Honolulu, Hawaii. (3) These kinds of programs benefit both the individ-
operate
uals involved and the cities in which they ~~operated~~. (4) After all, when sev-
are sharing
eral people ~~will be sharing~~ rather than owning cars exclusively, fewer cars
participants pay a yearly fee
clog busy city streets. (5) To join a group, ~~a yearly fee is paid by participants~~
are
in the range of $200 to $500. (6) In return, members ~~were~~ able to use cars

owned by the organization for a nominal fee, perhaps $1.50 to $2.00 an hour.
covers
(7) The yearly fee ~~covered~~ registration, insurance, and maintenance costs, so

members are generally responsible only for a small mileage charge, if any-
are going
thing. (8) When they ~~had been going~~ to need a car, members call or log into
Users then pick
the organization's Web site and make a reservation. (9) ~~Then a car is picked~~
up a car
~~up by the users~~ at one of several lots around the city. (10) When users are
return
done with the car, they simply ~~returned~~ it to the same site, turn in the keys,

and head for home, free from the headaches that car owners face.

Discovering Connections 24.2

1. In Discovering Connections 24.1 on page 371, you prewrote on one of three suggested subjects. Now, using this prewriting material as the foundation, work your way through the rest of the writing process, and complete a draft essay of about 500 words on this topic.

2. Exchange your draft with a partner. Using the material in this chapter to guide you, check the draft you receive for any errors in voice, progressive tenses, or consistency in tense. Underline any errors, and then return the draft to the writer.
3. Revise your essay, correcting any errors identified by your reader.

Summary Exercise: Mastering Voice, Progressive and Perfect Progressive Tenses, and Consistency in Verb Tense

As a small group exercise, have students compare the changes they made and discuss why they made them.

The following passage contains a number of the errors in verb use outlined in this chapter. Using the various examples throughout the chapter to guide you, identify errors in voice, tense, and consistency. Cross out the incorrect form, and write the correct form above it. In some cases, more than one correct answer is possible. Some answers may vary. Representative answers are given.

                                had spent

(1) I often wish I ~~spend~~ more time reading as a child. (2) If ~~more read-~~

I had done more reading

~~ing has been done by me~~, I wouldn't feel so embarrassed and frustrated

                       sit

now every time I ~~sat~~ down to read.

              started

(3) When I ~~start~~ elementary school, I missed almost half of first grade

                                         were

because of illness. (4) While all my classmates ~~are~~ learning the basics of

reading, I was at home in bed. (5) In spite of this, at the end of the year, I

was

~~am~~ promoted anyway, and my difficulties began.

                               my teachers always gave me breaks

(6) I never misbehaved in class, so ~~breaks were always given to me by~~

                          hesitated

~~my teachers~~. (7) When I read aloud, if I ~~hesitate~~ over a word, my teacher

                       became

would say it for me. (8) As a result, I ~~become~~ very good at pretending to be

able to read.

                fell   *kept*

(9) Although I ~~was fall~~ further behind each year, I ~~keep~~ getting pro-

                     I failed courses

moted. (10) When ~~courses were failed by me~~, I went to summer school.

                                    was

(11) Even though I attended summer classes, I ~~am~~ still not learning anything.

                                  earned

(12) In my senior year of high school, I ~~have earned~~ straight D's for the

                                failed   *was*

first term, except for English, which I ~~will be failing~~. (13) Because she ~~is~~ con-

cerned about me, my English teacher arranged for me to take a reading test. (14) When ~~the test was finished by me,~~ I discovered that I ~~am~~ not even

I finished the test

was

reading on the sixth grade level. (15) My teacher ~~gets~~ me a special reading

got

∧

tutor, and after working hard the rest of the year, I ~~am~~ able to read well

was

enough to graduate with my class.

(16) However, when I ~~am~~ ~~thinking~~ about college, all my shame and frus-

thought

tration returned. (17) I failed the college's reading placement test, and ~~a reme-~~

~~dial reading course had to be taken by me.~~ (18) I ~~will be~~ determined not to

I had to take a remedial reading course.

was

lose this chance to make something of myself, so I ~~work~~ as hard as I could.

worked

(19) I'm proud to say that by the end of that course, I ~~am~~ reading better

was

than any of the other students in the class. (20) However, I still ~~felt~~ insecure

feel

about my ability, and I ~~was~~ planning to keep working to change my attitude.

am

 PASSIVE VOICE, ADDITIONAL TENSES, AND MAINTAINING CONSISTENCY IN TENSE

Activity 24.4

New terms in this chapter	Definitions
● **passive voice**	● a characteristic of sentences in which the subject receives the action of the verb ***Example*** Her bicycle was stolen.
● **active voice**	● a characteristic of sentences in which the subject does or is responsible for the action ***Example*** A photographer took a picture of the scene.
● **progressive tenses**	● forms of a verb created by combining some form of *to be* with the present participle of another verb Progressive forms express ongoing actions or situations. ***Example*** Monique and Bill *are talking* about buying a house. ***Example*** Louis *was reading* in the library. ***Example*** Laura *will be wallpapering* her room soon.
● **present participle**	● formed by adding *-ing* to the basic form of regular and irregular verbs ***Examples*** play*ing*; ris*ing*

New terms in this chapter	Definitions
● **perfect progressive tenses**	● forms of a verb created by combining some form of *to have* with the present participle of another verb Perfect progressive forms express actions or situations that occur over a period of time.
	Example Monique and Bill *have been talking* about buying a house.
	Example Louis *had been reading* in the library.
	Example By 8 P.M., Laura *will have been wallpapering* her room for five hours.
● **consistency in tense**	● refers to a logical pattern for the verbs within a sentence, paragraph, or essay Consistency requires avoiding careless mixing of verb tenses and maintaining a unified time frame within a piece of writing.
	Inconsistent I *answer* all the questions that were asked.
	Consistent I *answered* all the questions that were asked.

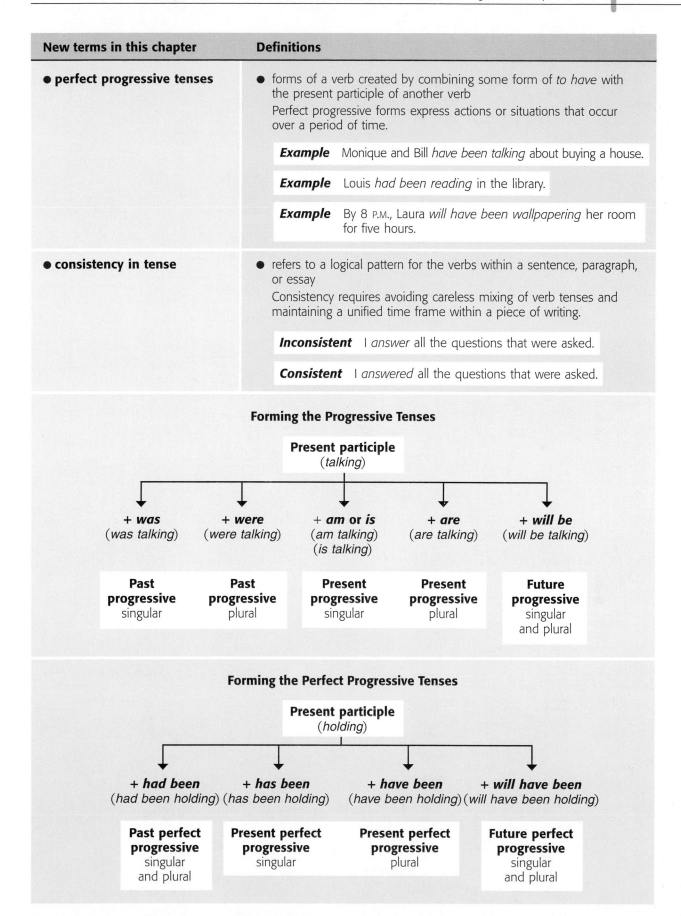

Forming the Progressive Tenses

Present participle
(*talking*)

+ ***was***
(*was talking*)

+ ***were***
(*were talking*)

+ ***am* or *is***
(*am talking*)
(*is talking*)

+ ***are***
(*are talking*)

+ ***will be***
(*will be talking*)

Past progressive singular

Past progressive plural

Present progressive singular

Present progressive plural

Future progressive singular and plural

Forming the Perfect Progressive Tenses

Present participle
(*holding*)

+ ***had been***
(*had been holding*)

+ ***has been***
(*has been holding*)

+ ***have been***
(*have been holding*)

+ ***will have been***
(*will have been holding*)

Past perfect progressive singular and plural

Present perfect progressive singular

Present perfect progressive plural

Future perfect progressive singular and plural

Keeping Your Writing Correct

Chapter 25

Nouns: Working Effectively with Words That Name

Getting Started... **Q:** When I write, the words that often seem to dominate are the ones that name people and things. What can I do to make sure I use these words effectively and correctly?

Audio 25.1 **A:** Because nouns appear so frequently in writing, it makes sense to concentrate on using them properly. The good news is that, for the most part, working with nouns is fairly straightforward. The most frequent problems involve determining the *number* of the word—whether the word is singular or plural. As long as you make sure to use the correct plural form and to recognize any cue words that signal number, you will be fine.

Overview: Understanding Nouns

Audio 25.2 To understand and keep straight all the elements and aspects of the world around us, we name them. The words we use to do so are **nouns**. Nouns are classified into two groups. Those that name a nonspecific person or thing—*a police officer, a continent, a short story*—are called **common nouns**. Those that name a particular person or thing—*Officer Donna Boyd, Asia, "Everyday Use"*—are called **proper nouns**, and are always introduced by a capital letter. More important, nouns have two forms. Those that name individual people or things are *singular,* and those that name several are *plural.* Mastering this aspect of noun use is crucial to your success as a writer, since it holds potential for error.

> **In this chapter, you will learn how to**
>
> - turn a singular noun into a plural one
> - recognize singular nouns that end in *-s*
> - use collective nouns effectively
> - use cue words to identify the number of a noun

Discovering Connections 25.1

Discovering Connections 25.2 at the end of this chapter provides an opportunity for students to apply the skills they have learned about using nouns correctly. They will be asked to compose and revise an essay based on one of the topics in Discovering Connections 25.1.

Using one of the techniques you practiced in Chapter 2, "Generating Ideas through Prewriting," prewrite on one of the following topics:

1. a family or cultural tradition you are familiar with
2. reasons for the wide variety of greeting cards

Or, focus on this picture.

Save your work for later use.

Reviewing the Function and Form of Nouns

 Audio 25.3

Nouns are the most versatile part of speech in English. Although writers don't generally think about all of them when they write, nouns can perform six different functions in a sentence:

- Nouns can serve as a **subject** of a sentence, as this example shows:

EXAMPLE

Many small *farms* [subject] have gone out of business in the past decade.

- Nouns can also serve as a **predicate nominative**, the word that answers "Who or What?" *after* a linking verb (such as *is* or *was*), as this example shows:

EXAMPLE

Kevin was the *goalie* [predicate nominative] for the varsity soccer team.

- In addition, nouns can serve as a **direct object**, the word that answers "Whom or What?" *after* an action verb, as this example shows:

EXAMPLE

Karen mailed the *letter* [direct object] at the campus mail center.

- Nouns can serve as an **indirect object** as well, the word that answers "To Whom or For Whom?" or "To What or For What?" *after* an action verb, as this example shows:

EXAMPLE

The pharmacist gave the *customer* [indirect object] a brochure explaining the drug's side effects.

- Nouns can also serve as the **object of a preposition**, the word that follows a preposition and completes a **prepositional phrase**, as this example shows:

EXAMPLE

The coat in the *closet* [object of the preposition] originally cost $200.

● Finally, nouns can serve as an **appositive**, a word that helps explain or illustrate another noun, as this example shows:

appositive

EXAMPLE
The child clutched her favorite *toy*, a small stuffed *kitten*.

Regardless of a noun's function, you must select the proper form—singular or plural—for each situation. Fortunately, changing nouns from singular to plural is generally easy. To make most nouns plural, simply add -*s* to the singular form:

Singular	*Plural*
cup	cup**s**
decision	decision**s**
flower	flower**s**

Some nouns form their plurals in other ways. For example, most words that end in -*ch, -sh, -x,* and -*s* form their plurals by adding -*es*:

Singular	*Plural*
brush	brush**es**
mix	mix**es**
pass	pass**es**
watch	watch**es**

For words that end in a -*y* preceded by a consonant, form the plural by changing the -*y* to -*i* and adding -*es*:

Singular	*Plural*
candy	cand**ies**
enemy	enem**ies**
eulogy	eulog**ies**
mystery	myster**ies**

Certain words that end in -*f* or -*fe* form their plurals by changing the ending to -*ves*:

Singular	*Plural*
half	hal**ves**
leaf	lea**ves**
shelf	shel**ves**
wife	wi**ves**

Combined or *hyphenated* words form their plurals by adding -*s* to the main word:

Singular	*Plural*
attorney-at-law	attorney**s**-at-law
brother-in-law	brother**s**-in-law
maid of honor	maid**s** of honor
runner-up	runner**s**-up

Some common words form their plurals by changing letters within the word :

Singular	Plural
foot	fe**e**t
man	m**e**n
mouse	m**ice**
tooth	te**e**th

Some words have the same singular and plural forms:

Singular	Plural
deer	**deer**
rice	**rice**
sheep	**sheep**
species	**species**

Activity
25.1

This section may provide an opportunity for a discussion about using the dictionary and reviewing the types of information in each entry.

In addition, some words that end in *-o* form their plural by adding *-s*: *sopranos* and *pros*. Other words that end in *-o* form their plural by adding *-es*: *tomatoes* and *heroes*. Some words from foreign languages form their plurals in keeping with their original language: *analysis/analyses* and *crisis/crises*.

If you have a question about the plural form of a noun, a dictionary should be your first stop. It gives the plural ending after the singular form if the noun forms its plural in an irregular way.

Fast Fact Besides being names for garments that cover the lower part of the body and that have separate coverings for both legs, what do the nouns *pants* and *trousers* and *slacks* have in common? They are all plural words for a singular item of clothing.

Exercise 25.1 **Identifying the Function of Nouns**

In each of the following sentences, a noun is underlined. Using the discussion of the function of nouns on pages 387–388 to guide you, write the function of each underlined noun above it, as the example shows:

EXAMPLE
predicate nominative
The manager of the club was once a professional <u>musician</u> herself.

direct object
(1) Rock guitarist Carlos Santana has enjoyed a remarkable <u>career</u> in music that has now spanned five decades. (2) Santana first came into na-
object of the preposition
tional <u>prominence</u> at the original Woodstock music festival with his captivating performance before the half million fans in attendance. (3) From that
subject
point, his <u>infusion</u> of Latin and Afro-Cuban flavors into a rock rhythm caught
appositive
the ears of America. (4) *Santana,* his 1969 debut <u>album,</u> and *Abraxas,* his 1970 multiple platinum follow-up album, produced several hit songs.

(5) Some of these songs, including "Evil Ways," "Black Magic Woman," and

predicate nominative
"*Oye Como Va*," are still favorite <u>selections</u> on radio stations across the coun-

object of the preposition
try. (6) Throughout the <u>years</u> that followed, Santana continued recording and

performing, using the opportunity to remind the world of the need for peace,

subject
tolerance, and compassion. (7) In 1998, Santana's <u>accomplishments</u> were rec-

ognized by his peers when he was inducted into the Rock and Roll Hall of

Fame. (8) In 1999, Santana's star rose once again with *Supernatural*, his 36th

appositive   indirect object
<u>album</u>. (9) *Supernatural* earned the <u>guitarist</u> nine Grammys and to date has

sold well in excess of 10 million copies. (10) With this album, on which he

collaborated with contemporary artists like Wyclef Jean, Rob Thomas, and

predicate nominative
Lauryn Hill, Santana is a household <u>name</u> once more.

Exercise 25.2   **Making Nouns Plural**

In the paragraph below, change the italicized singular nouns to their plural
forms. Cross out each singular noun, and write the plural noun above it.
Review the rules above. Use the example to guide you.

> *churches*   *museums*
> **EXAMPLE**   As we drove through the city, we saw the ~~church~~ and the ~~museum~~.

skyscrapers   cathedrals   universities   barns   years
(1) The bus tour I took last spring introduced me to Midwestern archi-
tecture, from ~~skyscraper~~ and ~~cathedral~~ to ~~university~~ and ~~barn~~. (2) After ~~year~~

magazines   books
of reading ~~magazine~~ and ~~book~~ about architecture, I finally decided to take

treasures
a firsthand look at some ~~treasure~~ of Americana. (3) Our group, which filled

buses   individuals   countries
two ~~bus~~, was a chatty, friendly group of ~~individual~~ from a variety of ~~country~~.

buildings
(4) Our first stop was Chicago, where we toured famous ~~building~~: the Sears

Tower, the Hancock Observatory, and Water Tower Place. (5) The view from

roofs   pools
the Observatory was breathtaking: sparkling ~~roof~~, swimming ~~pool~~ like gems

skyscrapers   streets
atop ~~skyscraper~~, bustling ~~street~~, and a vast expanse of Lake Michigan spread

tours
out before us. (6) After several brief walking ~~tour~~ in the city, we were off for

sandwiches   ^ stories
the country, munching ~~sandwich~~ and swapping ~~story~~ about the history we

had learned. (7) Our ~~guide~~ ^guides^ pointed out interesting ~~style~~ ^styles^ of ~~barn~~ ^barns^ and ~~silo~~ ^silos^ and explained the ~~influence~~ ^influences^ that produced them as we glided past big, prosperous ~~farm~~ ^farms^. (8) In ~~community~~ ^communities^ along the Mississippi River, quaint little ~~church~~ ^churches^ and ~~house~~ ^houses^ on ~~stilt~~ ^stilts^ enchanted us. (9) We even toured several Victorian ~~mansion~~ ^mansions^ and the ~~home~~ ^homes^ of two former U.S. ~~president~~ ^presidents^. (10) Inspired by my adventure, I am preparing slide ~~show~~ ^shows^ and ~~article~~ ^articles^ about the ~~structure~~ ^structures^ I saw and the ~~theory~~ ^theories^ and ~~history~~ ^histories^ behind them.

Challenge 25.1   **Recognizing the Function of Nouns**

Choose two consecutive paragraphs from one of the reading selections in Part Seven, "Connecting: Responding to Reading." Then, working with a partner, make a list on a separate sheet of paper of each noun in the passage and the function it is serving.

Considering Singular Nouns Ending in -s, Collective Nouns, and Cue Words

Audio
25.4

Although most nouns are made plural by adding -s, not all nouns that end in -s are plural. Words that fall in this category include the following:

Singular Words That End in -s

economics	mathematics	mumps	physics	statistics
ethics	measles	news	politics	

Because these words end in -s, it's easy to choose the incorrect verb form when one of these nouns is the subject. Remember—these words are singular and therefore call for singular verb forms. See Chapter 21, "Subject–Verb Agreement," for more information.

Collective nouns are words that stand for *groups* of items or individuals. Here is a list of common collective nouns:

Common Collective Nouns

audience	faculty	group	populace
class	family	herd	school
committee	flock	jury	team
congregation	government	office	tribe

For more on subject–verb agreement, see Chapter 21.

Even though they represent a number of people or things, collective nouns are singular in form. In most cases, a collective noun used as a subject requires a singular form of the verb, as the following sentences illustrate:

EXAMPLE The *jury wants* to see a copy of the trial transcript.

EXAMPLE The *faculty looks* forward to meeting the incoming students.

You should also become familiar with the following **cue words**. When they precede the subject, they alert you that it is singular and therefore calls for a singular verb.

ESL Note
See "Articles" on pages 580–581.

Common Singular Cue Words

a, an	every
another	neither
each	one
either	

EXAMPLE *Every* student *needs* a notebook to use as a journal.

EXAMPLE *Either* book *is* a good choice as a gift.

Also be aware of the following words. When they precede the subject, they cue you that it is plural and therefore calls for a plural verb.

Common Plural Cue Words

all	many
both	several
few	some

EXAMPLE *Many* children *are* actually afraid of clowns.

EXAMPLE *Several* stray cats *live* in my neighborhood.

Exercise 25.3 **Working with Collective Nouns and Cue Words**

Underline the collective noun or cue word in each sentence below. Decide whether the subject is singular or plural. Then circle the correct verb. Study the example first.

EXAMPLE Each class (<u>(has)</u>, have) its unique demands on my time and energy.

(1) A <u>group</u> that (<u>(seems)</u>, seem) to be diminishing day by day is people who read newspapers. (2) From all appearances, the average <u>family</u> today (<u>(is)</u>, are) far less interested in print journalism than the family of thirty years ago. (3) As a result, the <u>audience</u> that a reporter reaches with a story today (<u>(has)</u>, have) lessened—in some cases by more than 25 percent. (4) The <u>jury</u> (<u>(is)</u>, are) still out as to why readership has dropped off so drastically.

(5) Several recent studies (has, (have)) indicated that people prefer to get their news from television. (6) Some critics (maintains, (maintain)) that newspapers' continuing emphasis on sensationalism has turned many people away. (7) The government ((has) have) recently funded a major study, but the results won't be available for several months. (8) Meanwhile, a blue ribbon committee of editors and publishers ((has) have) decided to conduct a separate study. (9) At this point, each member of the committee ((feels), feel) that if action isn't taken, the number of newspapers published will continue to plummet. (10) One concern shared by both the industry and the government ((is), are) the indication that the populace overall ((is), are) reading less than it did a decade ago.

Fast Fact If you've ever wondered where new words come from, read the news. Every time something is invented, discovered, or developed, we have to name it. Consider the situation in which a woman agrees to carry the fertilized embryo resulting from the egg and sperm of another couple. What should this activity be called? For the time being, physicians and other professionals have offered these names: *gestational carriers, gestational surrogacy,* and *gestational care.*

Exercise 25.4   **Using Collective Nouns and Verbs Correctly**

Activity 25.2   Complete the following sentences by adding a present tense verb with modifiers. Underline the collective noun or cue word in the first part of the sentence to help you choose the correct present tense verb. Study the example first.   Answers will vary. Representative answers are shown.

EXAMPLE   The herd of cows ___heads for the barn like clockwork at 5 P.M.___

Students may find it helpful to review the difference between simple subjects and complete subjects in Chapter 17, "The Sentence," before completing Exercise 25.4.

1. Every time we try to eat outdoors, a swarm of wasps _____
   descends on our feast.

2. Each month, the congregation at that church _____
   collects food and clothing for a shelter for homeless people.

3. Few chairs in the waiting room _____
   are comfortable enough to sit on.

4. <u>Neither</u> winner of the tri-state lottery _____

   seems to mind sharing the fortune. _____

5. <u>Many</u> students enrolled in this college _____

   hold part-time jobs and take care of families as well. _____

6. The <u>audience</u> at the opening night performance of most plays usually

   notices a few glitches in the production. _____

7. By next year, the <u>team</u> of twenty scientists _____

   hopes to identify a reason for the change in water quality. _____

8. <u>Many</u> art museums throughout the country _____

   offer reduced-price admission for college students. _____

9. Every year, the activities <u>committee</u> at the neighborhood center _____

   arranges for tax advice for senior citizens. _____

10. Another <u>sign</u> encouraging government officials _____

    is the slow but steady reduction in the unemployment rate. _____

Challenge 25.2   **Writing Sentences Using Singular Words Ending in –s and Cue Words**

1. On a separate sheet of paper, write a sentence for each of the following words in which the word is the subject of a present tense verb. Review the examples in Chapter 21, "Subject–Verb Agreement," if you need further guidance:

economics	audience	government	statistics	jury
mathematics	committee	news	politics	audience

2. Exchange your list of sentences with a partner. Check the sentences you receive to make sure the words have been used correctly and then return the sentences to the writer.

Chapter Quick Check: Working with Nouns

Each sentence in the following passage contains an error in noun or cue word use. First review the discussion of the number of nouns, collective nouns, and cue words. Then correct each error by crossing out the incorrect word and writing the correct form above it, as the example shows.

EXAMPLE   It took me over an hour to install the new ~~shelfs~~. *shelves*

(1) ~~Storys~~ *Stories* of computer hackers appear frequently in the news because of the ingenious ways that these computer whizzes manipulate computer programs and networks. (2) Often, the articles discuss such actions as illegal ~~entrys~~ *entries* into classified government networks, the release of computer viruses, or the theft of credit card numbers. (3) But ~~each~~ *many or some* hackers argue that they are being unfairly accused of such crimes. (4) They say that the problem isn't with hackers but with a group of computer vandals and ~~thiefs~~ *thieves* called *crackers*. (5) True hackers aren't interested in using computers to create serious ~~worrys~~ *worries* or problems for others. (6) Even when a few ~~hacker~~ *hackers* break into some network, they do so for the thrill of doing it, not to cause trouble. (7) With crackers, however, the ~~motivationes~~ *motivations* are quite different. (8) Some crackers use their considerable computer ~~abilitys~~ *abilities* to break into a network and corrupt or destroy files, often costing the affected organizations thousands and thousands of dollars. (9) Others intentionally commit illegal acts such as pirating software, making free long-distance calls, or obtaining supposedly "secure" information on individuals and ~~companys~~ *companies*. (10) Hackers, who take pride in their knowledge and ~~skilles~~ *skills*, object to being lumped together with a group that misuses their expertise.

Discovering Connections 25.2

1. In Discovering Connections 25.1 on page 387, you prewrote on one of three suggested topics. Working from this prewriting material, work through the rest of the steps in the writing process, and complete a draft essay of about 500 words on your topic.

2. Exchange your draft with a partner. Using the material in this chapter to guide you, check the draft you receive for any errors in the use of nouns. After checking the paper, return it to the writer.

3. Revise your essay, correcting any errors your reader has identified in the use of nouns or pronouns.

Summary Exercise: Working with Nouns

Each sentence in the following passage contains an error in noun or cue word use. First review the discussion of the number of nouns, collective nouns, and cue words. Then correct each error by crossing out the incorrect word and writing the correct form above it. In some cases, other correct versions are possible. Answers may vary.

(1) Because of advances in technology, ~~every~~ many/some educators feel that cursive writing is fast becoming a thing of the past. (2) At one time, good penmanship was considered one of the most important ~~signes~~ signs of professionalism. (3) Even today, many people still view handwriting styles as ~~indicationes~~ indications of individuality and maturity. (4) Now, however, with ~~many~~ an emphasis on using computers for writing, the art of handwriting is losing its status.

(5) At one time, ~~all~~ every student was taught handwriting as a separate subject in school. (6) In ~~each~~ many/some cases, handwriting teachers were chosen because their own writing was considered excellent. (7) Students learned cursive by first practicing different strokes and ~~ovales~~ ovals that they copied from handwriting books. (8) Once these ~~beginneres~~ beginners had mastered the various shapes, they would begin work on actual letters and numbers. (9) The ~~childs~~ children were then graded on the precision and accuracy of their handwriting.

(10) In ~~every~~ many schools today, however, nobody seems concerned about handwriting instruction. (11) According to a recent article, a typical elementary ~~classes~~ class spends very little time on handwriting. (12) Apparently, the various other educational ~~crisies~~ crises that must be handled in the classroom take priority over handwriting.

(13) Not everyone is concerned that those ~~dayes~~ days are a thing of the past in some regions. (14) In fact, many people see this change as one of the

                     journeys
many ~~journeyes~~ students must follow to become part of the electronic age.

(15) In some elementary schools today, as soon as children learn the alpha-

                              shows
bet, a team of teachers ~~show~~ them how to use a word processor. (16) They

                                  stories
quickly learn to write all their ~~storys~~ electronically, using a keyboard.

                                                              scenarios
(17) Some proponents of the change say that in the future the only ~~scenarioes~~

that will call for handwriting will be taking notes in class, completing writ-

ten tests, or writing signatures.

                                                        centuries
     (18) Cursive writing of one sort or another has been around for ~~centurys,~~

so no one should seriously expect it to disappear. (19) In fact, good ~~argu-~~

arguments
~~mentes~~ can be made to ensure that it doesn't. (20) Probably the best solu-

tion is to teach students handwriting and word processing so that they can

                            ways
take advantage of both ~~wayes~~ of recording their ideas.

NOUNS: WORKING EFFECTIVELY WITH WORDS THAT NAME

New terms in this chapter	Definitions
● **noun**	● a word that names a person, place, thing, or idea Form plural nouns by adding *-s* or following spelling guidelines.
● **proper noun**	● a noun introduced by a capital letter that names a specific person or thing
● **predicate nominative**	● a word that answers "Who or What?" *after* a linking verb
● **direct object**	● a word that answers "Whom or What?" *after* an action verb
● **indirect object**	● a word that answers "To Whom or For Whom?" or "To What or For What?" *after* an action verb
● **appositive**	● a word that helps to explain or illustrate another noun
● **collective noun**	● a noun that stands for a group of items or individuals Collective nouns are singular in form, and generally call for the singular form of the verb. ***Example*** The *team is* about to win the tournament.
● **cue word**	● a word such as *another* or *both* that indicates the number of a noun

Pronouns: Understanding Case, Clear Pronoun–Antecedent Agreement, and Nonsexist Pronoun Usage

Getting Started... **Q:** In my writing, I often use pronouns, but I'm not always sure I'm using the right ones. I have the most trouble choosing the correct pronoun when it is the subject or an object. Figuring out whether a singular or plural pronoun is called for is also hard for me. How can I make sure that I always use the proper pronoun?

Audio
26.1

A: Choosing the right pronoun for each situation is a matter of understanding the features of the types of pronouns. For instance, when it comes to subjects and objects, you really need to worry only about *personal pronouns*. That's because personal pronouns are the ones that have separate forms for subject and object. And *number* isn't an issue with most pronouns, since deciding which ones are singular and which ones are plural is usually obvious. *Indefinite pronouns* can be a problem in this regard, however, because some of them are singular, some are plural, and some can be either. Once you understand these characteristics, you'll find working with them much easier.

Overview: Choosing the Correct Pronoun

ESL Note
See "Agreement" on pages 576–578.

Audio
26.2

Pronouns are the words that substitute for nouns. Think of pronouns as a kind of verbal shorthand. They enable you to use a brief, easily recognizable alternative for a noun rather than repeating that noun several times. Thus, they add variety to your language. There are several types, including **personal pronouns**, **indefinite pronouns**, **demonstrative pronouns**, **reflexive/intensive pronouns**, **relative pronouns**, and **interrogative pronouns**. To work effectively with pronouns, you need to attend to several concerns. You must consider the form, or *case*, of personal pronouns and the *number* and *gender* with indefinite pronouns. You also need to make sure that the pronouns and the words they refer to, called **antecedents**, match or *agree*. Otherwise, the people, places, things, and ideas being referred to won't be clear for your reader.

> **In this chapter, you will learn how to**
>
> ● recognize the types of pronouns
>
> ● understand the cases of personal pronouns
>
> ● identify number and gender with indefinite pronouns
>
> ● ensure that pronouns and antecedents agree in number and gender

Discovering Connections 26.1

Discovering Connections 26.2 at the end of this chapter provides an opportunity for students to apply the skills they have learned about using pronouns and their antecedents correctly. They will be asked to compose and revise an essay based on one of the topics in Discovering Connections 26.1.

Using one of the techniques you practiced in Chapter 2, "Generating Ideas through Prewriting," prewrite on one of the following topics:

1. the need for universal health care
2. the advantages—or disadvantages—of fame

Or, focus on this picture.

Save your work for later use.

Examining Pronoun Types

Weblink
26.1

Because we use pronouns as alternatives to nouns, pronouns appear frequently in writing. They can be grouped in several classes:

- **personal pronouns**, which refer to *specific* people, places, things, and ideas

I, me, my, mine	we, us, our, ours
you, your, yours	she, he, her, him, hers, his
it, its, their, theirs	

Video
26.1

- **indefinite pronouns**, which refer to *general* persons and things

all	each	little	nobody	others
another	either	many	none	several
any	everybody	more	no one	some
anybody	everyone	most	nothing	somebody
anyone	everything	much	one	someone
anything	few	neither	other	something
both				

- **demonstrative pronouns**, which point out *particular* people or things referred to

this	that
these	those

Weblink
26.2

- **reflexive/intensive pronouns**, which add emphasis to antecedents

myself	ourselves
yourself	yourselves
himself, herself, itself	themselves
oneself	

- **relative pronouns**, which introduce dependent clauses, called *relative clauses*, within a sentence

who	which
whom	that
whose	

- **interrogative pronouns**, which begin questions

Who . . . ?	Whom . . . ?	Whose . . . ?
Whoever . . . ?	Whomever . . . ?	Which . . . ?
Whichever . . . ?	What . . . ?	Whatever . . . ?

For the most part, working with pronouns is fairly straightforward. But two issues can make working with some pronouns potentially confusing. The first is *case*, the particular one of three *forms* of a personal pronoun called for in a specific situation. The second is the *number* of the *antecedent*, that is, whether the word the pronoun refers to is singular or plural.

Understanding and Applying Pronoun Case

Weblink
26.3

Among the pronouns that you use most often as a writer are the **personal pronouns**, which point out *particular* people, places, things, and ideas. As the table shows, personal pronouns have three separate forms, or *cases*: *subjective*, *objective*, and *possessive*.

Students can identify direct objects by asking *what?* or *whom?* after the verb. Indirect objects answer the questions *to whom, to what, for whom,* or *for what is the action of the verb being done?* Objects can also follow a preposition. A list of common prepositions appears in Chapter 17 on page 269.

Personal Pronouns

	Subjective	Objective	Possessive
First person	I, we	me, us	my, mine, our, ours
Second person	you	you	your, yours
Third person	she, he, it, they	her, him, it, them	her, hers, his, its, their, theirs

Use the *subjective* case pronouns as *subjects* of sentences.

EXAMPLE *We* were stuck in traffic for over an hour.

EXAMPLE *They* sat in front of the fireplace.

Use the objective case pronouns as *objects;* objects receive the action of the verb (as *direct objects*) or are governed by a preposition (as *objects of prepositions*). See pages 268–269 for a discussion of prepositional phrases.

EXAMPLE In the final inning, the pitcher threw four straight *balls.*
                                         direct object

EXAMPLE All the trees *around them* looked the same to the lost children.
             preposition | *object of the preposition*

Use possessive pronouns to show ownership.

EXAMPLE *Your* class has been canceled for today.

EXAMPLE *Her* friends were planning a surprise birthday party.

Fast Fact The pronoun *you* always takes a plural verb, even when it is being used as a singular word.

You need to keep a few points in mind when using personal pronouns.

● *An objective pronoun can never serve as a subject.*

The exceptions are *you* and *it*, which can serve as either subjects or objects. *Her, him, me, us,* and *them* are never subjects. Be careful when you are writing sentences with compound subjects linked by *and* or *or.* Make sure that each word in the compound subject could be used alone with the verb in the sentence.

                   she
EXAMPLE *Muriel, Billy, and ~~her~~* are taking a drawing course together.

                  I
EXAMPLE *Either the hostess or ~~me~~* will seat the guests at the reception.

● *A subjective pronoun can never serve as an object.*

Errors in the use of objective case also tend to occur in compound objects. Again, try using each element in the compound object alone to see if it can serve as an object.

                                     him
EXAMPLE The boss had to make a choice between *Joe and ~~he.~~*

                                                her
EXAMPLE My mother could not remember whether Grandpa taught *my uncle or ~~she~~* to drive first.

These homonyms and other commonly confused word pairs appear in a list in Chapter 29, "Spelling."

Finally, do not confuse the possessive pronoun *its* with the contraction for *it is (it's)*. *Its* needs no apostrophe because the word is already possessive. To avoid this error, try inserting *it is* whenever you want to use *its*. If *it is* fits, use *it is* or the contraction *it's*. If *it is* doesn't fit, use the possessive form, *its*.

EXAMPLE

It's
~~Its~~ too late to go to the movies now.

EXAMPLE

its
The owl flew to ~~it's~~ nest.

Exercise 26.1   Identifying Pronoun Case

In the following passage, underline all personal objective pronouns. Write an *S* above subjective pronouns, an *O* above objective pronouns, and a *P* above possessive pronouns, as the example shows. Use the table of personal pronouns on page 400 for guidance.

EXAMPLE

    S   O   S   P
I wanted to show him how important he was in my life.

                                S   P   S
(1) Every Monday when we were in elementary school, my sister and I used to go to the municipal library downtown. (2) It was almost three miles from our apartment, and our parents didn't want us to walk all that way. (3) So after school, Laura and I would go to the bus stop a block away and wait for the downtown bus to pick us up. (4) Because we were so young, riding the bus was an adventure for us. (5) We were always a little nervous until the driver gave us back our bus passes with new holes punched in them. (6) When we finally reached the library, she and I would go right to the shelves to look for books to take home. (7) It was a challenge to see which one of us could find books that would impress the head librarian more. (8) Adventure stories were my favorite, so I always ended up with a pile of them. (9) My sister wasn't as lucky because the library didn't have as many of her favorites—science fiction—in its collection. (10) As we were leaving, the head librarian would always say, in his formal, bass tone, "Be careful going home, girls, and take care of the books because they belong to all of us."

Exercise 26.2 **Using Personal Pronouns and Identifying Pronoun Case**

Fill in each blank in the following paragraph with an appropriate personal pronoun. Then label the pronoun you have supplied with an *S* for subjective, an *O* for objective, or a *P* for possessive case. Use the example as a guide.

EXAMPLE

Children need to learn a great deal more about ____*our*____ world than
children did twenty-five years ago.

(1) After a decline in ____*their*____ numbers stemming back thirty years or

more, bald eagles are making a major comeback throughout North America.

(2) During the 1960s, ____*they*____ were affected by both industrial pollution

and toxic pesticides like DDT. (3) At that time, ____*we*____ didn't have a full

understanding of the effect of these compounds on the environment.

(4) However, as we later learned, these poisons worked ____*their*____ way

through the food chain, becoming more concentrated in each species.

(5) Eagles were especially hard hit; the concentrated chemicals made it impos-

sible for ____*them*____ to produce the calcium needed for eggshells. (6) In

essence, ____*our*____ industrial society was making reproduction impossible for

eagles. (7) In the 1970s, ____*our*____ government acted to preserve the bald

eagle by declaring ____*it*____ an endangered species and banning DDT.

(8) ____*Its*____ decisions proved to be the correct ones. (9) Across the United

States today, the number of nesting pairs of bald eagles is somewhere between

4,000 and 5,000, and ____*their*____ species designation has been changed from

endangered to threatened. (10) Now it appears that ____*we*____ won't bear

responsibility for the extinction of one of nature's most majestic creatures.

Exercise 26.3 **Avoiding Usage Errors with Personal Pronouns**

Each sentence in the following paragraph contains an error in personal pronoun use. Cross out the incorrect pronoun, and write the correct form
above it. Use the example as a guide.

EXAMPLE

she
Traci and ~~her~~ were able to settle their differences.

me
(1) Between you and ~~I~~, computer dating services are not the best way to meet other single people. (2) My friend Brendan said that his cousins Greg and Mike and ~~him~~ *he* all tried different services and were all disappointed. (3) For one thing, ~~them~~ *they* had to pay $50 just to register for the services. (4) In addition, Greg explained that the questionnaire he filled out was too general to give an accurate picture of ~~he~~ *him*. (5) Also, the dating services didn't provide ~~he~~ *him* and Mike enough information about prospective dating partners. (6) For ~~they~~ *them*, the dates felt more like blind dates than arranged meetings between compatible people. (7) Mike agreed, because the woman that the dating consultant and ~~him~~ *he* chose on the basis of her profile just didn't appeal to him. (8) On the night of their date, it was obvious right away that ~~him~~ *he* and his date had nothing in common. (9) After about an hour, the woman asked Mike to take ~~she~~ *her* home. (10) Before he dropped her off, however, ~~her~~ *she* and ~~him~~ *he* agreed that computer dating services are not for them.

Activity 26.1

Challenge 26.1 **Evaluating Your Use of Personal Pronouns**

1. Take a look at some of the writings you have already created. Copy several sentences in which you have used personal pronouns. Make sure your sentences include at least one subjective pronoun, one objective pronoun, and one possessive pronoun. If necessary, write new sentences.

2. Exchange the sentences with a partner, and check for any pronoun errors. When you get your sentences back, revise any in which your reader found an error.

Maintaining Agreement in Number

Weblink 26.4

A pronoun must agree with its antecedent in *number:* Both must be singular, or both must be plural. Use singular pronouns to refer to singular antecedents and plural pronouns to refer to plural antecedents.

| singular antecedent | | singular pronoun |

EXAMPLE

Rachael dropped *her* book bag to the floor with a crash.

> plural antecedent ┐   plural pronoun
>
> The *students* in health class volunteered *their* time to run the blood drive.

Video
26.2

The use of *collective nouns* such as *class, herd, jury,* and *team* can cause confusion in pronoun–antecedent agreement. Remember that collective nouns represent groups of people or things but are generally considered singular, so they call for singular pronouns (see pages 391–392).

> singular antecedent ┐   singular pronoun

EXAMPLE   Last night, the Ordinance *Committee* closed *its* meeting, in violation of the Open Meetings Act.

Exercise 26.4   **Maintaining Pronoun–Antecedent Agreement**

Weblink
26.5

Each of the following sentences contains a pair of pronouns in parentheses. For each sentence, underline the antecedent, and circle the correct pronoun. Study the example first.

EXAMPLE   Five <u>children</u> had misplaced (his or her, (their)) books.

(1) Last week, several <u>employees</u> of P. A. Cummings International Airport were hospitalized after experiencing nausea and tingling in (his or her, (their)) arms. (2) When an airport <u>official</u> was first contacted by the media, ((she), they) refused to comment. (3) Instead, the <u>official</u> scheduled a news conference for the next morning, saying ((she), they) would respond to questions at that time. (4) In the meantime, state environmental <u>officials</u> studied the airline terminal to see if (he, (they)) could discover the cause of the illness. (5) The officials first tested the <u>air</u> to see if ((it), they) contained carbon monoxide. (6) After that test proved negative, the <u>chemicals</u> used to clean the carpet were checked to see if (it, (they)) could have caused the illness. (7) The officials discovered that maintenance <u>workers</u> had used too much cleaning solution when (he, (they)) cleaned one portion of carpeting on the previous evening. (8) The excess solvent dried to a powder behind the ticket counter, and when the <u>employees</u> walked across that area, (his, (their)) shoes released the chemical. (9) The employees then breathed in the <u>powder</u>, and ((it), they) made them ill. (10) At the news conference, the <u>director</u>

of the airport announced that (she, they) would have the carpet in that terminal replaced immediately.

Exercise 26.5   Maintaining Agreement with Collective Nouns

Below is a list of collective nouns. Working with a partner, write a sentence using each collective noun as an antecedent with an appropriate pronoun. Write your sentences on a separate sheet of paper. Underline both the collective noun and its replacement pronoun.

| association | committee | crowd | gang | mob |
| club | company | family | group | union |

EXAMPLE   *The __union__ has ordered a strike if __it__ can't get management to authorize a wage increase.*

Challenge 26.2   Revising a Paragraph and Maintaining Pronoun–Antecedent Agreement

1. In each of the sentences in Exercise 26.4 above, you chose the pronoun that agrees with the antecedent. Now, working with a partner, rewrite the paragraph, using the *other* pronoun in parentheses and then changing its antecedent. Keep in mind that you may also have to change some of the verbs to maintain subject–verb agreement.

2. Still working together, write a brief paragraph in which you explain which version is better and why.

Maintaining Agreement with Indefinite Pronouns

Indefinite pronouns refer to someone or something general. For instance, the pronoun *somebody* could refer to one of any number of people, and the indefinite pronoun *anything* could refer to one of any number of items or events. The following indefinite pronouns are always singular:

Singular Indefinite Pronouns

another	each	everything	nobody	other
anybody	either	little	no one	somebody
anyone	everybody	much	nothing	someone
anything	everyone	neither	one	something

Singular indefinite pronouns call for singular verbs. In addition, they must be referred to by singular pronouns (*he, him, his, she, her, hers, it, its*).

EXAMPLE   *Everyone* standing in line to pay a fine *looks* unhappy.

EXAMPLE *Anyone* who wants to compete in the drama festival must memorize *his or her* lines by Friday.

The following indefinite pronouns are always plural:

Plural Indefinite Pronouns

both	others
few	several
many	

EXAMPLE *Several* of the students *have* started a rowing club.

EXAMPLE The officials gave high scores to *both* dancers for *their* originality.

Some indefinite pronouns are either singular or plural, depending on the word to which they refer:

Indefinite Pronouns Affected by the Words That Follow Them

all	more	none
any	most	some

When you encounter one of these pronouns, check the word to which it refers. If that word is singular, choose a singular form of the verb, and if it is plural, choose a plural form of the verb.

Encourage students to keep a list of singular and plural indefinite pronouns, as well as those that can be either, as a quick reference list in their journals.

> plural antecedent   plural verb

EXAMPLE *Some* of the *shirts* on sale *were* seconds.

> singular antecedent   singular verb

EXAMPLE *All* of the *soil* at that construction site *is* contaminated with chemicals.

When an indefinite pronoun is the antecedent for another pronoun, maintaining agreement can be tricky. To avoid making an error in pronoun–antecedent agreement in this situation, first isolate the two pronouns and then check to see if they are both singular or both plural. If they don't match up, you can either change one of the pronouns or replace the indefinite pronoun with a definite noun so that the pronoun and its antecedent agree, as these examples show:

Problems concerning gender and sexist language are discussed on pages 419–421 in this chapter. As an introduction to these issues, ask students which of the corrected versions they prefer and why.

SINGULAR ANTECEDENT
his or her
Anyone needing more information about financial aid should bring ~~*their*~~ questions to the Financial Aid Office.

or

PLURAL ANTECEDENT
students
~~*Anyone*~~ needing more information about financial aid should bring *their* questions to the Financial Aid Office.

PLURAL ANTECEDENT
their
Few of the parents understood the relief that ~~*his or her*~~ children felt when the test was postponed.

> *or*
> *Each*
> SINGULAR ANTECEDENT — ~~Few~~ of the parents understood the relief that *his or her* children felt when the test was postponed.

Exercise 26.6 **Selecting Indefinite Pronouns for Correct Agreement**

In each of the following sentences, underline the verb that must match the missing word. Then fill in the blank in each sentence with an appropriate indefinite pronoun from the list below. You may use the same pronoun more than once. Study the example first. *Answers may vary.*

few	everyone	some
somebody	all	many
nobody	no one	none

EXAMPLE — _____*Many*_____ of the delegates <u>have</u> never before <u>attended</u> a political convention.

(1) _____*Everyone*_____ hopes that he or she will do the right thing when faced with a crisis. (2) For example, _____*all*_____ of us <u>like</u> to believe we would rush into a burning building to save the people inside. (3) _____*No one/Nobody*_____ <u>wants</u> to think she or he would stand there, paralyzed with fear. (4) But the truth is that _____*no one/nobody*_____ <u>knows</u> for certain how he or she would react. (5) It is true that, faced with such a situation, _____*some*_____ <u>are</u> able to run right through the flames. (6) Not _____*everyone*_____ <u>is</u> able to play the role of a hero, however. (7) _____*Many*_____ of us <u>experience</u> a kind of paralysis in crisis situations. (8) A _____*few*_____ even <u>become</u> sick or <u>pass out</u>. (9) Faced with the same crisis, _____*none*_____ of us <u>is</u> likely to react in exactly the same way. (10) Even _____*somebody*_____ who <u>is</u> a leader in everyday situations may not be able to take charge in a crisis.

Exercise 26.7 **Maintaining Agreement with Indefinite Pronouns**

Circle the indefinite pronouns in each of the following sentences, and then fill in the blanks with a pronoun that agrees with this antecedent. Use the example to guide you.

EXAMPLE   (Few) of the people sitting in the waiting room had already filled out

_____*their*_____ applications.

For additional practice, ask students to rewrite the sentences in Exercise 26.7. If the antecedents and pronouns are singular, have students change them to plural. If they are plural, students should change them to singular.

(1) Sometimes it's easy to get the impression that (nobody) wants to get involved in helping _____his or her_____ neighbors. (2) News accounts regularly appear, for example, relating how (someone) took advantage of _____his or her_____ power or money to make life difficult for other people. (3) As a result, (many) begin to change _____their_____ attitudes, becoming increasingly cynical. (4) After a while, people in general begin to doubt whether (anyone) is actually willing to reach out and help in _____his or her_____ city. (5) However, a restaurant owner in my town has proved that not (everyone) is apathetic about what happens in _____his or her_____ neighborhood. (6) This restaurant owner serves holiday dinners for free to (all) in the surrounding area who otherwise couldn't afford to pay for _____their_____ meals. (7) (Several) of the city's most prominent citizens sacrifice time with _____their_____ families to serve people who are experiencing hard times. (8) (Most) of the employees of the restaurant also volunteer _____their_____ time to serve the meals. (9) (Many) even contribute _____their_____ tips from the prior week to pay for gift packages of clothing and blankets for those seeking a meal. (10) What's especially noteworthy is that (none) of the people serving the meals earns a dime for _____their_____ work, yet they volunteer year after year.

Exercise 26.8   **Correcting Errors in Agreement with Indefinite Pronouns**

Each sentence in the following passage contains an error in agreement with an indefinite pronoun. Cross out each error, and then write the correct pronoun above it. Change the verb if necessary. More than one answer may be possible, as the example shows:

his or her
EXAMPLE   Anybody could improve ~~their~~ grades by working harder.

_or_

Most students
~~Anybody~~ could improve their grades by working harder.

(1) An interview is uncomfortable enough for a job seeker without the
interviewer trying to give ~~them~~ **him or her** a hard time. (2) On my last two interviews,
everybody in the office seemed to do ~~their~~ **his or her** best to put me on edge.
(3) Obviously, no one in these places remembered what ~~their~~ **his or her** first interview
was like. (4) For example, at a firm looking for a receptionist, several supervisors asked me for an evaluation of ~~her~~ **their** desktop publishing software. (5) Some
of my friends work as receptionists, and ~~he does~~ **they do** not even do any writing, let
alone desktop publishing. (6) I later learned that many managers at that company ask such questions to test the poise of the people ~~he is~~ **they are** interviewing.
(7) At the other firm, somebody asked me if I would mind doing ~~their~~ **her/his** personal errands on my lunch hour. (8) Even worse, someone else asked if I
would be willing to give ~~them~~ **him/her** a back rub. (9) That subject was clearly a matter of sexual harassment, but no one in the room even raised ~~their~~ **his or her** eyebrows
at the question. (10) I wish that someone at a decent company would just
offer me a job in ~~their~~ **his or her** office so I wouldn't have to do any more interviewing.

Challenge 26.3 **Maintaining Agreement with Indefinite Pronouns in Your Writing**

Students can
share their
sentences
within small groups and
discuss how they have
maintained agreement.

As you now know, the indefinite pronouns *all, any, more, most,* and *none* are
either singular or plural depending on the word following them. Working with
a partner, write two sentences for each of these indefinite pronouns, using
each one first as a singular antecedent and then as a plural antecedent.

Maintaining Agreement with Demonstrative and Reflexive or Intensive Pronouns

Audio
26.4

You may occasionally experience difficulties in maintaining pronoun–antecedent agreement with **demonstrative pronouns**, which point out a particular person or thing.

Demonstrative Pronouns

Singular	Plural
this	these
that	those

As the list indicates, two demonstrative pronouns are singular (*this* and *that*), and two are plural (*these* and *those*). *This* and *these* point out things that are near or point to things in the future. *That* and *those* point out things that are farther away or point to things in the past.

When you use a demonstrative pronoun to begin a sentence in a paragraph or essay, you may be referring to the antecedent in the previous sentence. In these cases, check for any errors in pronoun–antecedent agreement by identifying that antecedent. If the antecedent is singular, use *this* or *that;* if it is plural, use *these* or *those*.

EXAMPLE

┌──── antecedent ────┐

There have been *four major accidents* near the park entrance.

Those have

~~*That has*~~ caused the city to install warning signs.

EXAMPLE

The Civic Improvement League is donating $15,000 to establish an

┌──────── antecedent ────────┐   *This*

urban entrepreneur's scholarship at the college. ~~*These*~~ will be given

to students majoring in marketing or accounting.

Often writers add a clarifying word to the demonstrative pronoun to make the reference more precise. In this case, the demonstrative pronoun then becomes a *demonstrative adjective,* as in the following versions of the sentences that appear above:

EXAMPLE

┌ antecedent ┐ | demonstrative adjective |

There have been four major *accidents* near the park entrance. *Those*

| clarifying word |

crashes have caused the city to install warning signs.

EXAMPLE

The Civic Improvement League is donating $15,000 to establish an urban

┌ antecedent ┐ | demonstrative adjective | clarifying word |

entrepreneur's *scholarship* at the college. *This award* will be given to students majoring in marketing or accounting.

Another potential problem in maintaining pronoun–antecedent agreement involves the use of **reflexive** or **intensive pronouns**, which are used to emphasize the words to which they refer.

Reflexive or Intensive Pronoun Forms

myself	oneself
yourself	ourselves
himself, herself	yourselves
itself	themselves

You should never use reflexive or intensive pronouns in a sentence unless you have included the word to which the pronoun refers. These pronouns may not be used as subjects.

| REFLEXIVE | The capsized sailboat righted *itself.* [*To direct verb's action back to subject*] |

| INTENSIVE | The president *himself* will testify. [*To emphasize*] |

If these pronouns are used incorrectly as subjects, replace the reflexive or intensive form with a personal pronoun that suits the situation.

| EXAMPLE | Connie and ~~myself~~ *I* did most of the work on that presentation. |

Exercise 26.9   Maintaining Agreement with Demonstrative Pronouns

Each sentence in the following passage contains an error in pronoun–antecedent agreement involving demonstrative pronouns. In each sentence, cross out the incorrect demonstrative pronoun, and above it write one that matches the antecedent. If necessary, turn the demonstrative pronoun into a demonstrative adjective and add a clarifying word. Use the example to guide you.

| EXAMPLE | During a storm, a huge tree fell across the power lines, and ~~these~~ *this OR this incident* caused a major power outage. |

(1) Yesterday, the Red Cross held a blood drive on campus, and ~~these~~ [that OR that event] proved to be a big success. (2) At most drives the Red Cross runs, around thirty to forty people donate, and ~~those~~ [that OR that response] is considered good. (3) At this drive, however, more than a hundred donors showed up, and ~~these~~ [that OR that number] was beyond anyone's hope. (4) Many participants were donating for the first time, and in the beginning ~~these~~ [those OR those people] complicated work a little for the officials. (5) Some newcomers were visibly nervous, and ~~these~~ [those OR those participants] seemed to affect the mood of others waiting in line. (6) To help settle everyone down, the Red Cross workers spoke directly with ~~that~~ [those OR those people] appearing especially anxious. (7) They explained the steps involved, while stressing the simplicity and safety of ~~that~~ [those steps OR those]. (8) After the first few newcomers donated blood without a problem, ~~that~~ [those] people behind them in line began to relax. (9) ~~Those~~ [That development OR That] made all the difference, and the time passed more quickly and pleasantly for everyone in-

Activity 26.3

That day OR That

volved. (10) ~~Those~~ was such a success that the Red Cross plans to schedule

another drive for the end of the semester.

Exercise 26.10   **Using Reflexive and Intensive Pronoun Forms Correctly**

Audio
26.5

Fill in the blanks in the following sentences with an appropriate reflexive or intensive pronoun form from the list on page 411. Study the example first.

EXAMPLE   After waiting at the register for five minutes, the woman finally decided to

check the price _____*herself*_____.

1. I will be picking you up at the airport _____myself_____.

2. The participants _____themselves_____ criticized the organizers of the natural healing seminar most harshly.

3. At the end of this semester, perhaps you will decide to major in business _____yourself_____.

4. After several hours, the storm finally blew _____itself_____ out.

5. Rather than wait for the city crew to arrive, we cleaned up the field _____ourselves_____.

6. The exhausted horse still managed to force _____itself_____ up the steep slope.

7. Instead of consulting a map, Lenna decided to try to figure out a route _____herself_____.

8. When Susie and Brian didn't arrive, we enjoyed the dessert all by _____ourselves_____.

9. Jeremy's ankle _____itself_____ wasn't broken, but all the ligaments were sprained.

10. When you face a stressful situation, you must force _____yourself_____ to remain focused on the task.

Maintaining Agreement with
That, Who, and *Which* Clauses

Clauses introduced by a **relative pronoun**, *that, who,* or *which,* may also create problems with pronoun–antecedent agreement. If the antecedent that the clause describes is singular, then the verb in the clause must be singular. If the antecedent of the clause is plural, then the verb must also be plural.

EXAMPLE

| singular antecedent |

sells

The *store that sell* baked goods at half price is always crowded.

| plural antecedent |

allow

The *special parking stickers, which allows* a student to park in the campus garage, may be purchased in the bookstore.

Exercise 26.11   **Maintaining Agreement with *That, Who,* and *Which* Clauses**

The italicized clauses in the following paragraph contain errors in agreement. Circle the antecedent, and then correct the error by crossing out the incorrect verb and writing the correct one above it. Study the example first.

EXAMPLE

was

The (firefighter) *who were involved in the rescue* received a citation for bravery.

(1) Most (people) *who was questioned in a recent survey* felt that their

were

memories weren't as sharp as they'd like. (2) These (respondents,) *who was*

were

between the ages of forty-five and sixty-five, felt that their memories had

weakened. (3) For example, their (ability) to match a name with a face, *which*

was

a few years earlier were strong, seemed now far less reliable. (4) Also, the

were

(details) of meetings or public gatherings *that in the past was easy to keep*

straight, now seemed fuzzier. (5) To these people, these (memory lapses,)

were

which was really upsetting, seemed to be signs of old age. (6) Like many of

are

the beliefs about aging, however, (some of the issues) *that is associated with*

growing older are more stereotype than fact. (7) According to many experts

were

consulted, the (kinds) of memory problems *that was reported* aren't necessar-

involve

ily related to age. (8) Genuine memory (deficits,) *which involves serious and*

sometimes permanent loss of recognition of otherwise familiar people and

places, affect many segments of society. (9) In fact, (anyone) who ~~experience~~ ^experiences^
a sudden memory loss, regardless of age, should see a doctor immediately.
(10) True memory (problems,) *which fortunately* ^are^ ~~is~~ *not common,* could be a
symptom of serious neurological problems or drug interactions.

Exercise 26.12   **Identifying and Correcting Agreement Problems with *That, Who,* and *Which* Clauses**

The following passage contains several errors in agreement with *that, who,* and *which* clauses. Cross out any incorrect verb, and write the correct verb above it. If a sentence does not contain an error, write *OK* above it. Study the example first.

EXAMPLE   Because of the crowd, many people who usually ^ride^ ~~rides~~ the 8 A.M. crosstown bus had to wait for the 8:30 bus.

(1) I attended a great workshop that ^was^ ~~were~~ held at school the other day.
(2) A counselor who ^works^ ~~work~~ in the counseling center on campus presented
the workshop. (3) ^OK^ The program, which was called "How to Build an Effective
Personal Relationship," attracted about twenty participants, both male and
female. (4) She first discussed several common misconceptions that people
^have^ ~~has~~ about love. (5) For example, "love conquers all," a concept which ^is^ ~~are~~ be-
lieved by many people, isn't always true. (6) ^OK^ In some cases, a person can
have so many problems that love alone isn't enough to maintain a relationship. (7) ^OK^ She also disproved the naive idea that there is only one right person in the world for each of us. (8) Then she showed how people who
^think^ ~~thinks~~ the right partner will be the salvation for all their problems in life are
setting themselves up for disappointment. (9) All of us who ^were^ ~~was~~ participating in the session were impressed, because we had all had fantasies like
those she described. (10) I'm looking forward to the follow-up session,
which ^is^ ~~are~~ scheduled for next Friday.

Keeping the Relationship between Pronoun and Antecedent Clear

To help your reader understand your meaning, you must also make the relationship between the pronoun and the antecedent clear. Look at this sentence:

AMBIGUOUS   *Ed* and *Bill* had a fight, and *he* broke *his* nose.

The problem with this sentence is obvious. It does not make clear who did what to whom. The simplest way to correct this type of error is to restate the sentence completely to eliminate the ambiguity, as this version shows:

REVISED   During their fight, *Ed* broke *Bill's* nose.

Exercise 26.13   **Identifying the Pronoun–Antecedent Relationship**

In each of the following sentences, a pronoun is italicized. Circle the antecedent for each of these pronouns, and draw an arrow from the pronoun to the antecedent, as the example shows. Remember—the antecedent to the pronoun may be in a different sentence.

EXAMPLE   The (lock) on the suitcase was broken, so I asked my uncle to fix *it*.

(1) Although (voice mail) has become very popular over the past few years, many (people) don't like *it*. (2) *They* prefer the human touch that voice mail can't supply. (3) When (people) have a question, all *they* want to do is talk to an actual person. (4) But many voice-mail (systems) force callers to follow a complicated series of commands, and *they* also often include a dizzying array of options. (5) With some voice-mail systems, if (callers) hit the wrong buttons, *they* can be disconnected and have to call back. (6) Even if (people) manage to reach the proper extension, *they* may not be out of the voice-mail loop yet. (7) If the (individual) at that extension is away or using the system to screen calls, *he or she* will not answer the call personally. (8) A (recording) will instruct the caller to leave a message, and then *it* will indicate which buttons to press to approve the message. (9) If the caller

pushes the wrong buttons, some (systems) delete the message, and then *they* ask the caller to go through the entire process again. (10) For the average person, such a (system) often increases the frustration *it* is meant to eliminate.

Exercise 26.14   **Correcting Unclear or Ambiguous Pronoun References**

Each sentence below contains an unclear or ambiguous relationship between a pronoun and an antecedent. Circle the unclear or ambiguous pronoun. On another sheet of paper, revise the sentence to clarify the relationship. There may be more than one way to correct each sentence. Study the example first.   Sentence revisions will vary.

EXAMPLE   When the vase she threw hit the window, (it) shattered.

The window shattered when the vase she threw hit it.

or

When the vase she threw hit the window, the window shattered.

(1) Last week's accident downtown involving a bus and a tanker truck caused major structural damage to a highway overpass, and (it) is still being investigated. (2) Heavy rain was falling and the truck was reportedly exceeding the speed limit, and (that) may have contributed to the accident. (3) Also that stretch of Whipple Avenue bends sharply and there are no stop signs along the way, and (that) didn't help the situation either. (4) When the tanker collided with the bus, (it) burst into flames. (5) The bus then hit a curb, and the driver couldn't handle (it.) (6) The bus wasn't carrying passengers at the time, and it was an older model, so (that) may have made the bus less stable. (7) The bus also hit a light pole, and (it) was badly damaged. (8) The cab and the tanker broke apart, and then (it) slammed into the side of the overpass. (9) Traffic was snarled and a crowd gathered on the sidewalk, and (that) created problems at rush hour. (10) The pavement under the overpass is badly gouged and the concrete over the entrance of the overpass is crumbling, and (that) is expected to be repaired within a month.

Challenge 26.4 | **Writing with Clear Pronoun–Antecedent Agreement**

Working with a partner, write a sentence to precede each of the sentences provided below. Make sure to include an antecedent that matches the pronoun that begins the second sentence. If necessary, add a clarifying word to those pronouns. Study the example first. Answers will vary. Sample answers are given.

Yesterday, Diane reminded me of the time the two of us locked our-
selves out of the office. That still makes me laugh.
                                             story
                                             ^

1. Margaret regrets what she did after witnessing a car crash yesterday.

   She left the scene of the accident before the police arrived.

2. A fire broke out in Mario's Kitchen last month.

   It caused the restaurant to be closed for an entire week.

3. The doors and hallways in this building are very narrow.

   These should be modified to make access easier for disabled people.
        entries
        ^

4. Tim and Ellen couldn't agree on what to do last Saturday night.

   They finally decided to rent a movie.

5. My family just gave me a large amount of money for my twenty-first birthday.

   That means I won't have to take out a loan to attend classes next semester.
        gift
        ^

6. Representatives from several government agencies set up temporary headquarters

   in town hall this afternoon.

   They will be available to answer questions for the next two days.

7. A small supermarket recently opened in the abandoned store in the strip mall downtown.

   It should make life easier for the people living in that area.

8. The company finally agreed to install new air filters throughout the building.

   That agreement was the solution everyone was hoping for.

9. Television networks are now offering fewer dramatic mini-series.

   It indicates that people are no longer interested in them.

10. The furniture was delivered by noon.

   That development left us with the rest of the afternoon to straighten everything out.

Avoiding Problems with Gender in Pronoun–Antecedent Agreement

If any students speak or study a language besides English, ask them to explain rules concerning gender in the other language.

Gender refers to whether a word is masculine or feminine. Making sure that pronouns agree in gender is usually much easier than making them agree in number. In English, inanimate objects and ideas don't have masculine or feminine forms as they do in languages such as Spanish and French.

With personal pronouns, identifying gender is easy. *I, me, we, you,* and *your* can be either feminine or masculine. Likewise, the plural pronouns *they, them, their,* and *themselves* apply to both genders. The personal pronoun *it* refers to objects only. In fact, you need to worry about gender only with third-person pronouns: *she, her, hers, he, him,* and *his.* To correct errors in agreement with any of these words, change the pronoun so that it matches the gender of the word to which it refers:

EXAMPLE

                    her
Mother Teresa devoted ~~his~~ life to helping the poor in India.

EXAMPLE

                                            his
As the man turned to leave, a ticket fell out of ~~her~~ coat.

Video 26.3

When you use pronouns, you should also eliminate any accidental *sexism* in your writing. **Sexist language**, as the National Organization for Women (NOW) and the National Council of Teachers of English (NCTE) have been pointing out since the 1970s, is language that inappropriately designates gender. The word *foreman*, for instance, suggests that only a man can direct a group of workers.

This section provides an opportunity to discuss the connotations of language before completing Challenge 26.5 (page 421), which calls for a discussion about the importance of avoiding sexist language.

Words have tremendous power. When you use words like *chairman, salesman,* or *mailman,* you send out the message that only males should conduct meetings, sell things, or deliver mail. The proper way to deal with these words is to make them gender-neutral, that is, with references to neither sex: *supervisor, chairperson, salesperson,* and *mail carrier.*

You must also be concerned with sexism when you use singular indefinite pronouns such as *anybody, someone,* or *everybody.* These words can be either masculine or feminine. It was once acceptable to use *he, him, himself,* and *his* to represent both sexes when referring to a singular indefinite pronoun. Today, however, this usage is considered sexist, so you should either use pronouns of both genders or rewrite the sentence to make both your pronoun and your antecedent plural.

Weblink 26.6

If you choose the first option, you can connect a feminine and a masculine pronoun with *or* to refer to the indefinite pronoun: *he or she, him or her,* and *his or her,* rather than *he, him,* and *his.* Reverse the pairs if you prefer: *she or he, her or him, her or his.*

EXAMPLE

Everybody should be prepared to do *her or his* best.

The other option is to make both pronoun and antecedent plural. This method is generally a better choice. It eliminates sexism and eliminates the possibility of making an error in gender agreement, as this version shows:

EXAMPLE *People* should be prepared to do *their* best.

Fast Fact One of the strangest stories concerning sexist language originated in a small town in New England. At a meeting of the town council, one official proposed renaming those familiar black discs in the middle of any town and city street across the nation from *manhole* cover to *personhole* cover.

Exercise 26.15 **Avoiding Problems with Gender in Pronoun–Antecedent Agreement**

In the following passage, identify errors in pronoun gender and uses of sexist language. Cross out each error you find, and write the correction above it in the space provided between the lines. More than one correct answer may be possible. Study the example first. Answers may vary.

EXAMPLE

People who ride motorcycles
~~Anyone who rides a motorcycle~~ should wear ~~his helmet~~ *their helmets*, even on short trips.

or

her or his
Anyone who rides a motorcycle should wear ~~his~~ helmet, even on short trips.

(1) My ambition is to finish school and begin a career in the business world. (2) My first step will be sales because ~~a good salesman~~ *good sales representatives* can earn a great salary and help ~~her~~ *their* company at the same time. (3) Of course, to be effective, ~~a salesman has~~ *sales representatives have* to develop contacts in the firms with which ~~he deals~~ *they deal*. (4) To do this, ~~a salesman~~ *sales representatives have* has to make regular rounds and get to know as many people as possible in the companies ~~she visits~~ *they visit*. (5) For example, when ~~a salesman visits~~ *sales representatives visit* a company, ~~he~~ *they* should first visit the ~~foreman~~ *supervisor* to find out what ~~her~~ *his or her* needs are. (6) Succeeding as part of the sales force is just the first step in my career plans. (7) Eventually, I hope to work my way up to chief executive officer, or even ~~chairman~~ *chairperson* of the board of directors. (8) ~~An effective~~ *Effective* ~~chairman~~ *chairpeople* can make money for ~~herself~~ *themselves* and ~~his~~ *their* corporation by ensuring that the managers are doing a good job. (9) Everybody has ~~her~~ *his or her* own management strategies, but I feel the best strategy is to make sure that people are treated fairly and paid according to their efforts. (10) With these kinds of simple ideas, anybody should be able to make ~~his~~ *his or her* mark in the business world.

Exercise 26.16   Avoiding Sexist Language

Below is a list of sexist words. In the spaces provided, write a neutral, non-sexist alternative for each one. Make sure you don't substitute another equally sexist word in its place. For instance, don't replace *stewardess* with *steward*. Instead, use *flight attendant*. Then, on a separate sheet of paper, compose a sentence using each of your substitutions.

fireman	firefighter	actor	performer
congressman	congressperson	anchor woman	anchorperson
mankind	humankind	businessman	businessperson
weatherman	weather forecaster [or meteorologist]	policewoman	police officer

Challenge 26.5   Evaluating Sexist Language and Nonsexist Alternatives

Make a list of the sexist words you have read or used in your own writing. Working with a partner, discuss your lists. Develop a nonsexist version for each word on your list. Then, still working with a partner, compose a brief paragraph in which you discuss the ways that sexist language may affect people.

Activity 26.5

Chapter Quick Check: Working with Pronouns

Proofread the following essay for problems with pronoun–antecedent agreement; agreement with *who, that,* and *which* clauses; and sexist language. Eliminate the problems by crossing out the incorrect word and writing a more effective choice above it. If a sentence is correct as written, write *OK* above it. In some cases, more than one solution is possible. Use the example to guide you.

EXAMPLE

The DVD player was out of stock, so I asked for a rain check in order to

                                                 it

purchase it at the same price when ~~they~~ came in.

                                                     is

(1) A recent development, which ~~are~~ called face-recognition technology, is being hailed as a way to track and identify criminals. (2) With face-recognition systems, computers record images of faces and then converts ~~it~~ into an-

                  them

other form. (3) ~~That~~ can come from a variety of sources, including pictures

      These images

taken of large groups of people at sports stadiums or busy city streets. (4) The face-recognition programs then isolate ~~each person~~ [each person OR the people] in the picture and carefully create an individual blueprint or map of ~~their faces.~~ [his or her face OR their faces] (5) To do so, the software focuses on ~~somebody's~~ [somebody's OR people's] unique features, such as ~~their~~ [his or her OR their] cheekbones, jaw shape and line, and eye shape, size, and location to each other. (6) The system converts this information into a computer code and stores ~~them~~ [it] in a database. (7) [OK] In the case of a crime, law enforcement officials can use the system to match these images to others taken by surveillance cameras in stores, banks, government buildings, and airports. (8) ~~Spokesmen~~ [Spokespeople] for face-recognition companies claim that these systems are nearly foolproof. (9) Some civil liberties organizations disagree, however, citing independent testing that ~~show~~ [shows] these systems to be only 60 to 70 percent accurate. (10) In addition, these groups warn of potential legal fallout, since ~~no one~~ [no one OR no individuals] in the pictures taken in public areas ~~has~~ [has given OR have given] permission for ~~their~~ [his or her OR their] images to be used and stored.

Activity 26.4

Discovering Connections 26.2

1. In Discovering Connections 26.1 on page 399, you completed a prewriting on one of three suggested subjects. With this prewriting material as a basis, work through the rest of the writing process to complete a draft essay of about 500 words on this topic.

2. Exchange your draft with a partner. Using the material in this chapter to guide you, check the draft you receive for errors in pronoun use. Then return the draft to the writer.

3. Revise your essay, correcting the errors identified by your reader.

COLLABORATION

Summary Exercise: Working with Pronouns

Proofread the following essay for problems with pronoun–antecedent agreement; agreement in *who, that,* and *which* clauses; and sexist language. Eliminate the problems by crossing out the incorrect word and writing a more effective choice above it. If a sentence is correct as written, write *OK* above it. In some cases, more than one solution is possible. Some answers may vary.

(1) I am godmother to my brother's five-year-old twins, a boy and a girl, and I recently went to the toy store to buy ~~him or her~~ ^{them} birthday presents.
(2) Unfortunately, the expedition turned out to be a depressing experience. ^{OK}
(3) I discovered that a person can find plenty of toys, but ~~they~~ ^{he or she} will find that most of them are unbelievably expensive or inappropriate for young children.
(4) First, I went to the game aisle. ^{OK} (5) With the exception of Candyland, ^{OK} Cootie, and a few other simple games, which the twins already owned, all the board games were too complicated or too expensive. (6) There were plenty of video game cartridges, but I couldn't afford to buy the game unit ~~them-~~ ^{itself} ~~selves~~. ^{OK} (7) Also, the one game cartridge that seemed as if it would be suitable for children their age was almost $80. (8) One of the ~~salesmen~~ ^{sales representatives} said that she had just reordered that cartridge because ~~they were~~ ^{it was} so popular.
(9) My niece and nephew also wanted some action figures. ^{OK} (10) Anybody who has ~~their~~ ^{his or her} own children or has ever babysat knows how much kids enjoy pretending. ^{OK} (11) James and Jenna are no different. (12) Both of them enjoy playing ~~his or her~~ ^{their} own special roles and pretending to have super powers.
(13) However, their favorite characters, which ~~changes~~ ^{change} colors when dunked in water, cost over $25 each. (14) That ^{overpricing} amazed me. ^{OK} ^
(15) Even more amazing and sickening was the number of realistic-looking guns and war toys in the store. (16) Why would ~~anyone~~ ^{people} want to spend a lot of money so their children could pretend to kill each other? (17) The huge arsenal I observed, however, made it seem as if ~~almost everybody~~ ^{most people} ~~wants~~ ^{want} to buy their children a toy machine gun. ^{OK}
(18) By the time I finished shopping, I was much sadder and poorer than I had been on the way in. (19) My godchildren loved ~~his or her~~ ^{their} cards and toys; that helped me feel better. (20) However, after spending an after-

noon seeing what kinds of toys are out there, I'm glad I don't have to make
~~those~~
~~that~~ choices for my own children yet.

PRONOUNS: UNDERSTANDING CASE, CLEAR PRONOUN–ANTECEDENT AGREEMENT, AND NONSEXIST PRONOUN USAGE

Activity
26.6

New terms in this chapter	Definitions
• **pronoun**	• a word used in place of a noun ***Example*** Georgie picked up a *rock* and threw *it* at the abandoned house.
• **antecedent**	• the word or words to which a pronoun refers Singular antecedents call for singular pronouns; plural antecedents call for plural pronouns. ***Example*** The little *girl* dropped *her* hat. Indefinite pronoun antecedents must agree with their pronouns. ***Example*** *Everyone* who has a coupon will receive 25 percent off *her or his* purchase.
• **personal pronoun**	• a pronoun that specifies a particular person, place, thing, or idea Personal pronouns have three separate forms, or cases, to show person.

Personal Pronouns

	Case		
	Subjective	**Objective**	**Possessive**
First person	I, we	me, us	my, mine, our, ours
Second person	you	you	your, yours
Third person	she, he, it, they	her, him, it, them	her, hers, his, its, their, theirs

• **indefinite pronoun**	• a pronoun used to refer to someone or something in general

Singular Indefinite Pronouns

another	each	everything	nobody	other
anybody	either	little	no one	somebody
anyone	everybody	much	nothing	someone
anything	everyone	neither	one	something

Plural Indefinite Pronouns

both	others
few	several
many	

Indefinite Pronouns Affected by the Words That Follow Them

all	more	none
any	most	some

● **demonstrative pronoun**

- singular: *this, that*
- plural: *these, those*

  If a demonstrative pronoun begins a sentence, find the antecedent in the preceding sentence.

  A demonstrative pronoun placed next to a noun is then called a *demonstrative adjective*.

  Example   Some clothes in *that* box are damaged. *Those* should be mended.

● **reflexive/intensive pronoun**

- a combination of a personal pronoun with *-self* or *-selves: myself, yourself, himself, herself, itself, ourselves, yourselves, themselves.*

  Reflexive or intensive pronouns are used for emphasis (Ginny *herself* paid for the repair) or to direct the action of the verb back to the subject (Peter threw *himself* across the saddle).

● **relative pronoun**

- *that, who, which, whom, whose*

  A relative pronoun introduces a clause that describes an antecedent; the verb in the clause must agree with the antecedent.

  Example   The *attorney* who *is* addressing my class this morning graduated from this college.

● **interrogative pronoun**

- What . . . ? Whatever . . . ? Which . . . ? Whichever . . . ? Who . . . ? Whoever . . . ? Whom . . . ? Whomever . . . ? Whose . . . ?

  An interrogative pronoun introduces a question.

  Example   *What* is the problem?

● **gender**

- refers to whether a word is masculine or feminine

  Pronouns must match the gender of their antecedents.

● **sexist language**

- language that inappropriately excludes one gender

  Try using plural antecedents and pronouns instead.

  Example   *All bicyclists* using the municipal bike path must wear *their* helmets.

Chapter 27

Adjectives, Adverbs, and Other Modifiers: Using Describing and Modifying Words Effectively

Getting Started… **Q:** I want to make my ideas as clear and specific as possible for readers, so I try to use plenty of words that describe. But I am not always confident that I've used these modifying words correctly. What can I do to make sure that I don't make any mistakes with their use?

Audio 27.1

A: Adjectives and adverbs are the words you can use to make your ideas clear and specific. To avoid errors in their use, you need to be aware of the most likely problems: using the wrong word form when making comparisons, placing a modifier in the wrong position in a sentence, and using two negatives (such as *no* and *not*) in the same clause.

Overview: Understanding the Roles of Adjectives and Adverbs

Audio 27.2

Nouns and pronouns name people and things, and verbs show the action or situations in which those people and things are involved. But writing that relies on nouns and verbs alone would be ineffective. It wouldn't be clear, precise, or colorful enough to communicate your ideas to your reader. To make your writing effective, you need to include **modifiers**, words that **describe** or **limit** other words in a sentence. **Adjectives** are words that modify nouns or pronouns, and **adverbs** are words that modify verbs, adjectives, and other adverbs. Both adjectives and adverbs are useful for making comparisons and expressing negation. If you look back at the paragraphs and essays you have written so far, you'll discover that you've used many adjectives and adverbs. You'll also see that they inject life into your writing, so it's important to master their use.

In this chapter, you will learn to

● use the positive, comparative, and superlative forms for adjectives and adverbs

● distinguish between commonly confused adjectives and adverbs

● avoid dangling and misplaced modifiers

● avoid double negatives

Discovering Connections 27.1

Discovering Connections 27.2 at the end of this chapter provides an opportunity for students to apply the skills they have learned about using adjectives and adverbs. They will be asked to compose and revise an essay based on one of the topics in Discovering Connections 27.1.

Using one of the techniques you practiced in Chapter 2, "Generating Ideas through Prewriting," prewrite on one of the following topics:

1. the most interesting things to do with the Internet
2. the effects of welfare reform

Or, focus on this picture.
    Save your work for later use.

Understanding Adjectives and Adverbs

Video
27.1

Adjectives and adverbs have three forms: positive, comparative, and superlative. The **positive form** of an adjective describes a noun or pronoun without making a comparison. It tells the reader *how many, what kind,* or *which one.*

> **EXAMPLE**   The *small* dog is *fierce.*

Weblink
27.1

In this sentence, the adjective *small* tells *which dog* and the adjective *fierce* describes *what kind* of dog.

The positive form of an adverb describes a verb, an adjective, or another adverb without making a comparison. It tells the reader *how, when,* or *to what extent.*

> **EXAMPLE**   *Finally,* the child spoke *quietly* to the nurse.

In this sentence, the adverb *finally* tells *when,* and the adverb *quietly* describes *how* the child spoke.

> **Fast Fact** *A, an,* and *the* are a subgroup of adjectives called *articles. A* and *an* are the *indefinite* articles, referring to a nonspecific person or thing (a professor, an apple) and *the* is the *definite* article, referring to a particular person or thing (the professor, the apple). And they are busy little words. For example, *an* is the forty-third most commonly used English word, and *a* is the fourth most frequently used. And *the*? It's number one—the word that appears most frequently in English.

Exercise 27.1 **Identifying Adjectives and Adverbs**

In the passage below, circle the positive form of the adjectives and underline the positive form of the adverbs. Use the example to guide you.

EXAMPLE Chika <u>often</u> organizes (athletic) activities for the children in her neighborhood.

Audio 27.3

Audio 27.4

Weblink 27.2

Weblink 27.3

Weblink 27.4

Weblink 27.5

(1) Last Saturday, my friends and I went for a (quick) lunch at the Granite Café, a (new) deli near the college. (2) The restaurant is located in a building that was <u>once</u> the office of the Mill City Granite Works. (3) The building itself is constructed of (massive) slabs of granite that were <u>actually</u> quarried at the Mill City Granite Works. (4) The (deep) cavity left when the quarry closed 50 years ago <u>gradually</u> filled with water, so the building is all that is left of this once <u>highly</u> (successful) business. (5) The city was planning to knock down the (run-down) building before the café owners bought and rehabilitated it. (6) The owners, Lynette and her brother Kevin, think that the (historical) significance of the building would <u>probably</u> help attract customers. (7) At noontime on Saturday, Genia, Shannon, Kathryn, and I <u>first</u> picked a (large) table near the window. (8) <u>Then</u> we examined the (extensive) menu to decide on our meals. (9) We <u>quickly</u> chose from the (full) array of sandwiches and (homemade) soups. (10) The (final) bill for the four of us was $14, which was a (real) bargain.

Discuss with students how adjectives and adverbs can create images and add clarity. Remind them that concrete, specific nouns and verbs also help to communicate ideas precisely.

Creating Comparative and Superlative Forms of Adjectives and Adverbs

Audio 27.5

The **comparative form** of an adjective or an adverb is used to compare *two* things.

ADJECTIVE   This new word processing program is *more complex* than the one I used last year.

ADVERB   The nursery school students play *longer* than the first graders.

In the first sentence, the adjective *more complex* compares one computer program with another. In the second sentence, the adverb *longer* compares the extent to which two groups of children play.

The **superlative form** of an adjective or an adverb is used to compare *more than two* things.

ADJECTIVE   This store has the *lowest* prices for name brand clothes as well as household appliances.

ADVERB   Of all the young women in the chorus, Eleanor was the one who danced *most gracefully.*

Audio 27.6   In the first sentence, the adjective *lowest* compares the prices of many stores. In the second sentence, the adverb *most gracefully* compares the style of many dancers.

For adjectives and adverbs of one syllable, create the comparative by adding *-er,* and create the superlative by adding *-est* to the end of the positive form of the word.

Positive	*Comparative*	*Superlative*
dark	dark**er**	dark**est**
high	high**er**	high**est**
far	farth**er**	farth**est**
hard	hard**er**	hard**est**

For adjectives and adverbs of more than two syllables, place *more* in front of the word for the comparative or *most* in front of the word for the superlative.

Positive	*Comparative*	*Superlative*
ridiculous	**more** ridiculous	**most** ridiculous
intelligent	**more** intelligent	**most** intelligent
remarkably	**more** remarkably	**most** remarkably
unfortunately	**more** unfortunately	**most** unfortunately

If the adjective or adverb is *two* syllables, which of these two methods should you use? The answer depends on the word. Some two-syllable words take an *-er* or *-est* ending:

Positive	*Comparative*	*Superlative*
early	earli**er**	earli**est**
angry	angri**er**	angri**est**
lazy	lazi**er**	lazi**est**
funny	funni**er**	funni**est**

Other two-syllable words require that you use *more* or *most* before them:

Positive	*Comparative*	*Superlative*
private	**more** private	**most** private
slowly	**more** slowly	**most** slowly
careful	**more** careful	**most** careful
safely	**more** safely	**most** safely

As an in-class exercise, have some students create a list of two-syllable modifiers, and have others look up those words in the dictionary. Ask the dictionary users to identify the correct comparative and superlative forms.

To avoid errors, look up two-syllable adjectives and adverbs in the dictionary. In addition to definitions, a dictionary gives the correct spelling for adjectives and adverbs that form their comparative and superlative forms by adding *-er* or *-est*. If no *-er* or *-est* forms are listed, then use *more* and *most*.

Regardless of the number of syllables, never use both *more* and *-er* or *most* and *-est* with the same adjective or adverb. Expressions like *more faster* and *most completest* are always wrong.

Some adjectives and adverbs form their comparative and superlative forms in irregular ways:

Positive	*Comparative*	*Superlative*
bad (adjective)	worse	worst
badly (adverb)	worse	worst
good (adjective)	better	best
well (adverb)	better	best
little	less	least
much	more	most

As you can see, two pairs of words on this list share the same comparative and superlative forms. However, these similar words have different functions. *Bad* and *good* are adjectives used to identify *what kind* of people, places, ideas, or things a writer is discussing. *Well* and *badly* are adverbs used to explain *how* something was done.

Exercise 27.2 **Using Comparative and Superlative Forms Correctly**

Each sentence in the following paragraph contains an incorrect positive, comparative, or superlative adjective or adverb. Cross out the incorrect form, and write the correct form above it, as the example shows.

EXAMPLE

fastest

Secretariat was the ~~most fast~~ racehorse I had ever seen.

(1) My friend Laura wants to be a singer, and she already sings *better* ~~more well~~

than most professionals. (2) She has the *sweetest* ~~most sweet~~ voice I've ever heard.

(3) She even does a great job with the National Anthem, which most singers

claim is the *most* ~~more~~ difficult song around. (4) Her sound is like Whitney

Houston's, except Laura's voice is ~~more deep~~. (5) Laura is so talented that she

~~deeper~~

tried out for a local talent show when she had the flu, had the ~~worse~~ audition

~~worst~~

of her life, and still won a place in the show. (6) A local agent who manages

Laura says that her abilities are improving ~~quicklier~~ than those of his other

~~more quickly~~

singers. (7) Even though it's ~~most~~ difficult now than it was ten years ago for

~~more~~

an unknown singer to get a record contract, Laura has been sending "demo"

CDs all over the country. (8) She figures that at ~~worse~~, all the record companies

~~worst~~

will turn her down, and she will have wasted a few dollars. (9) Meanwhile,

she is attending college, which has made her parents more ~~happy than~~ they

~~happier~~

were when she announced that she wanted to be a professional singer.

(10) Right now the ~~more~~ frustrating thing of all for Laura is finding time both

~~most~~

to study and to rehearse.

Working with Confusing Pairs of Adjectives and Adverbs

Some words have both adjective and adverb forms. Choosing the right form
can be confusing for writers. The list below contains the most commonly
confused pairs of adjectives and adverbs:

If students are creating
a reference section in
their journals, encour-
age them to enter this
list of commonly con-
fused modifiers, along
with notes about their
use.

Adjective	*Adverb*
awful	awfully
bad	badly
good	well
poor	poorly
quick	quickly
quiet	quietly
real	really

Deciding between *good* and *well* and between *bad* and *badly* probably
causes the most headaches for writers. *Good* and *bad* describe a person or
thing, whereas *well* and *badly* describe how something is done. In other
words, you can say that a person is a *good* singer or a *bad* singer, but you
must say that this individual sings *well* or sings *badly*.

Consider the following examples:

| EXAMPLE | Shannon is a *good* chef. |
| EXAMPLE | Elie cooks *well*. |

In the first sentence, the adjective *good* tells *what kind* of chef Shannon is. In the second, *well* acts as an adverb, describing *how* Elie cooks.

Exercise 27.3 **Working with Confusing Adjective and Adverb Pairs**

In the sentences below, underline the correct adjective or adverb from the choices given in parentheses. Use the example to guide you.

EXAMPLE Once again, the Orlando Magic played (poor, <u>poorly</u>) last night.

(1) To do my best schoolwork, no matter what the subject, I need a (<u>quiet</u>, quietly) place. (2) When I am in the back of the library or in my room, I can concentrate (good, <u>well</u>). (3) It's (awful, <u>awfully</u>) hard to arrange to be alone sometimes, but it is worth the effort. (4) When I'm around other people, I find it (real, <u>really</u>) difficult to stay focused. (5) Somebody will start talking about a movie or game, and I am (quick, <u>quickly</u>) part of the conversation. (6) Instead of concentrating on my statistics or sociology, I end up wasting time in a pointless discussion, and as a result I do (bad, <u>badly</u>) on my next quiz or exam. (7) I especially do (poor, <u>poorly</u>) when I try to write a paper with others around. (8) Again, I find what my friends are doing (awful, <u>awfully</u>) distracting, and the resulting paper shows it. (9) To make sure I become as (<u>good</u>, well) a writer as possible, I make it a point to write all my drafts when and where I am sure to be alone. (10) Since I changed my work habits, I have noticed a (<u>real</u>, really) improvement in the quality of my performance in all my classes.

Exercise 27.4 **Correcting Errors in the Use of Confusing Adjectives and Adverbs**

The following sentences contain some errors in the use of adjectives and adverbs. Cross out the incorrect form, and then write the correct one above it. If a sentence is correct as written, write *OK* above it. Use the example to guide you.

EXAMPLE The dog ran out from between the two cars so ~~quick~~ *quickly* that the driver couldn't avoid hitting it.

(1) For years, I needed eyeglasses ~~bad,~~ but I didn't know it. (2) In grade [*badly*]

school, I performed ~~poor~~ on any test that required me to read the black- [*poorly*]

board. (3) At first, my teachers thought I was being lazy and that I could do

~~good~~ if I paid more attention in class. (4) Then my third grade teacher sent [*better [OR well]*]

me for a vision test, and the doctor said I was ~~awful~~ nearsighted. (5) I was [*awfully*]

~~real~~ afraid I'd have to wear glasses like my grandfather's, with ugly frames. [*really*]

(6) As it turned out, my glasses didn't look so ~~badly,~~ and the difference they [*bad*]

made in my life was unbelievable. (7) Until I got glasses, I was used to sitting

~~quiet~~ in the back of the room, participating only when forced to. (8) After I [*quietly*]

got my glasses, all that changed ~~quick.~~ (9) When I could see every word on [*quickly*] [*OK*]

the board well, all I wanted to do was make up for lost time. (10) Although I

still received a few ~~poorly~~ test scores, school became a ~~more happy~~ experi- [*poor*] [*happier*]

ence for me.

Challenge 27.1   **Using Confusing Pairs of Adjectives and Adverbs in Your Writing**

COLLABORATION

Activity
27.1

Write topic sentences for three paragraphs. Include in each sentence an adjective or adverb from the list of confusing pairs on page 431. Then, working with a partner, develop one of the sentences into a paragraph. Include adjectives and adverbs to make your writing colorful and precise.

Avoiding Dangling and Misplaced Modifiers

ESL Note
See "Word Order" on pages 574–575.

Audio
27.8

As you saw in Chapter 24, "Passive Voice, Additional Tenses, and Maintaining Consistency in Tense," the present participle, or *-ing* form of a verb, can be combined with a helping verb to form a verb in the progressive tense. Without a helping verb, this form can't act as the verb in a sentence. When it describes another word or phrase, it is called a **participle**, as these examples show:

EXAMPLE   *Yelling* angrily, Dion left the room.

EXAMPLE   The teacher tried to quiet the *laughing* children.

In the first sentence, the participle *Yelling* is describing the proper noun *Dion*. In the second sentence, the participle *laughing* is describing the noun *children*.

Using participles can help you combine ideas and eliminate choppiness in your writing. Consider these sentences, none of which use participles.

EXAMPLE The telephone service workers had coffee in the small restaurant. They took a break from work.

EXAMPLE The teenaged girl behind the counter polished the glass pastry cabinets. She whistled softly.

Weblink 27.6 Although the sentences in each example are correct, they are choppy. By changing one of the sentences to a dependent clause beginning with a participle and making a few other changes in wording, you can combine these sentences:

EXAMPLE *Taking a break from work*, the telephone service *workers* had coffee in the small restaurant.

EXAMPLE *Whistling softly*, the teenaged *girl* behind the counter polished the glass pastry cabinets.

In the first example, the participle and the words that follow it, *Taking a break from work*, now describe *workers*. In the second example, the participle and the words that follow it, *Whistling softly*, now describe *girl*.

When you use a participle, be sure to place it near the word it describes in a sentence. Otherwise, your readers may not understand what word it is describing. Consider these examples:

FAULTY *Hanging from the ceiling*, Jacob saw the new lamp.

FAULTY *Looking for her dress*, the cat suddenly jumped onto Janet's back.

The participle in the first sentence is *Hanging*. Right now, however, the sentence suggests that it is *Jacob* and not the new lamp that is *hanging* from the ceiling. This type of error, which occurs when a modifier is placed near a word that it does not modify rather than near the word it does, is called a **misplaced modifier**. The participle in the second sentence is *Looking*. At this point, the sentence indicates that *Janet's cat* was *looking* for a dress. This type of error, which occurs when a modifier has no word that it can logically modify, is called a **dangling modifier**.

Avoiding these types of errors is simple. Always check any sentence in which you have included a participle to make sure the modifier is describing the correct word. If there is an error, you can correct it by putting the participle next to the word it modifies or by changing the wording of the sentence:

CORRECTED *Hanging* from the ceiling, the new lamp caught Jacob's eye.

or

CORRECTED Jacob stared at the new lamp *hanging* from the ceiling.

| CORRECTED | *Looking for her dress*, Janet suddenly felt her cat jump onto her back. |

or

| CORRECTED | *As Janet was looking for her dress*, her cat suddenly jumped onto her back. |

Weblink
27.7

Not all misplaced modifiers involve participles. Any modifier, whether it is an individual word or a group of words, is a misplaced modifier if it suggests a relationship between words when no such relationship does or could exist. Consider these examples:

| MISPLACED | *As a young child,* my great-grandfather often took my sister to the park. |

| MISPLACED | The new sales representative sold the portable stereo to the woman *with the built-in compact disc player.* |

The modifiers in these two sentences are obviously misplaced because the resulting sentences just don't make sense. A person can't be a young child and a great-grandfather at the same time. And people don't have stereo components in their bodies.

Avoid these kinds of misplaced modifiers by restating parts of the sentence or rearranging the order of the sentence so that the modifiers are next to the words they modify, as these corrected versions show:

| CORRECTED | As a young child, my sister often went to the park with my great-grandfather. |

| CORRECTED | The new sales representative sold the portable stereo with the built-in compact disc player to the woman. |

Exercise 27.5   **Identifying Participles**

Each sentence in the following paragraph contains a participle. Underline the participle and the word it describes. Draw a line connecting the two elements, as the example shows.

| EXAMPLE | <u>Staring</u> at the map, <u>Gracie</u> tried to determine where she was. |

(1) <u>Entering</u> a convenience store downtown last week, my brother <u>Joe</u> knew something was wrong. (2) <u>Trying</u> to figure out what the problem was, <u>he</u> looked around the store. (3) <u>Picking</u> up a few items and <u>talking</u>, two older <u>women</u> walked from the back of the store. (4) <u>Waiting</u> for them to finish their shopping, <u>Joe</u> looked around the rest of the store. (5) <u>Standing</u> behind the counter, the <u>clerk</u> seemed particularly nervous. (6) <u>Turning</u> around, <u>Joe</u> saw a figure all in black, with sunglasses and a baseball hat pulled low. (7) Quickly

striding toward the register, this <u>man</u> appeared to reach for something under his jacket. (8) <u>Pretending</u> he couldn't find what he wanted, <u>Joe</u> quickly inched toward the door. (9) <u>Driving</u> by the store at that moment, a <u>police car</u> caught his attention. (10) <u>Responding</u> to Joe's yells for help, the <u>officers</u> headed into the store in time to stop the robbery.

Exercise 27.6   **Working with Participles**

Each sentence below contains an underlined participle that acts either as a verb or a modifier. Label the word with a *V* or an *M* to indicate its function. For words labeled *V,* find and underline the helping verb. For words labeled *M,* find and underline the word being described. Study the examples first.

EXAMPLE   By the time Henry reached the finish line, he <u>was</u> <u>gasping</u>.
                                                            V

EXAMPLE   <u>Swirling</u> around the room, the <u>dancer</u> was dressed in red.
     M

1. <u>Laughing</u> uncontrollably, <u>Janine</u> finally had to sit down. *M*
2. A <u>group</u> <u>protesting</u> capital punishment demonstrated outside the prison. *M*
3. The bus <u>is</u> <u>leaving</u> right now. *V*
4. The pipe <u>had been</u> <u>leaking</u> for several weeks before anyone noticed. *V*
5. <u>Staring</u> straight into the camera, the <u>reporter</u> smiled and began her report. *M*
6. <u>Smiling</u>, the <u>President</u> accepted the gift and sat down. *M*
7. The <u>man</u> <u>walking</u> on the treadmill was at least seventy-five years old. *M*
8. Renee <u>was</u> <u>cooking</u> a gourmet dinner. *V*
9. The <u>woman</u> <u>changing</u> the tire was covered with grease. *M*
10. <u>Waving</u> happily, the <u>child</u> stepped out of the bus. *M*

Exercise 27.7   **Identifying and Correcting Dangling and Misplaced Modifiers**

Video 27.2

Each of the following sentences contains a dangling or misplaced modifier. First, underline the dangling or misplaced modifier. Then, on a separate piece of paper, restate or rearrange each sentence so that the modifiers are describing the correct words. More than one correct answer is possible. Use the example as a guide.

EXAMPLE   Flying around the lamp, the child was fascinated by the moth.

CORRECTED   Flying around the lamp, the moth fascinated the child.

or

The child was fascinated by the moth flying around the lamp.

(1) Expecting nothing but a normal day, the discovery Jennifer made one late spring afternoon changed her outlook for the summer. (2) She had been applying for a job for a month requiring computer skills. (3) Having taken a course in computer applications, spreadsheets and *PowerPoint* presentations were among her areas of expertise. (4) Sending out applications to several companies downtown, her hopes were that one of these places would come through for her (5) But the hopes seemed distant after three weeks for a good job. (6) But everything changed when lying under her refrigerator, Jennifer found a letter that she had dropped the previous day. (7) When she read the letter, she broke into a smile, informing her that she had been offered a job for the summer. (8) Shaking, the phone seemed to move as she called to accept the job. (9) As a prospective employee, her supervisor, Ms. Tally, told Jennifer about the various duties involved. (10) Hanging up the phone, her smile of happiness grew even broader.

Challenge 27.2   Using Participles to Combine Sentences

Working with a partner, combine the following simple sentences to eliminate choppiness by changing one of the sentences into a participle. All of these modifiers should be phrases rather than single words. Study the example first.

EXAMPLE   The puppy was waiting for its supper. It was wagging its tail.

Wagging its tail, the puppy was waiting for its supper.

1. Caroline was walking around the park. She was trying to get some exercise.

   Trying to get some exercise, Caroline was walking around the park. OR Walking

   around the park, Caroline was trying to get some exercise.

2. Reggie was reading a novel. He was sitting on the couch.

Sitting on the couch, Reggie was reading a novel. OR Reading a novel, Reggie was

sitting on the couch.

3. The strikers were marching in front of the factory. They were carrying signs.

Carrying signs, the strikers were marching in front of the factory. OR Marching in

front of the factory, the strikers were carrying signs.

4. The truck was fleeing from two police cars. It was traveling the wrong way on the highway.

Traveling the wrong way on the highway, the truck was fleeing from two police cars. OR

Fleeing from two police cars, the truck was traveling the wrong way on the highway.

5. The little boy was playing hide and seek. He was hiding from his friends.

Hiding from his friends, the little boy was playing hide and seek. OR Playing hide

and seek, the little boy was hiding from his friends.

6. Jeremy and Jackie enjoyed the reflection of the stars on the water. They sat on a bench overlooking the harbor.

Enjoying the reflection of the stars on the water, Jeremy and Jackie sat on a bench

overlooking the harbor. OR Sitting on a bench overlooking the harbor, Jeremy and
Jackie enjoyed the reflection of the stars on the water.

7. The skateboarders took advantage of the empty streets on the holiday afternoon. They practiced in front of City Hall Plaza.

Taking advantage of the empty streets on the holiday afternoon, the skateboarders

practiced in front of City Hall Plaza. OR Practicing in front of City Hall Plaza, the
skateboarders took advantage of the empty streets on the holiday afternoon.

8. The crowd at the comedy club laughed uncontrollably at the comedian. They were formerly reserved but came alive when she began her routine.

Laughing uncontrollably at the comedian, the formerly reserved crowd at the comedy

club came alive when she began her routine. OR Leaving their reserve behind and

coming alive when the comedian began her routine, the crowd at the comedy club
laughed uncontrollably.

9. Leslie opened the trunk and pulled out the tire. He got to work changing the flat.

Opening the trunk and pulling out the tire, Leslie got to work changing the flat. OR

Getting to work changing the flat, Leslie opened the trunk and pulled out the tire.

10. The scholarship winner waved in acknowledgment. She smiled at her grandmother.

Waving in acknowledgment, the scholarship winner smiled at her grandmother. OR

Smiling at her grandmother, the scholarship winner waved in acknowledgment.

Avoiding Double Negatives

Double negatives and other nonstandard usages are common in casual conversation. Discuss with students the various levels at which we use language — from informal to formal— depending on the situation and the audience. Identify a few rules and conventions for academic and professional

Expressing negation can also cause problems for writers. *No, never, nowhere, nobody, nothing, no one,* and *none* are all used to express the idea of *no.* Adverbs like *scarcely, hardly,* and *barely,* as well as *not,* the adverb used to create *contractions* (such as *did + not = didn't*), also express negation.

When two of these negative words are used in the same sentence, they form what is called a **double negative**. Double negatives are never acceptable in college or professional writing. To avoid double negatives in your writing, check your sentences to make sure you have only one negative in each.

Correcting a double negative is easy: Simply eliminate one of the negative words or change it to a positive form. Note the negatives in the examples below as well as the methods used to correct the errors.

EXAMPLE

Although my feet are very narrow, I have ~~not~~ had no trouble finding reasonable work shoes.

writing that people often break when speaking informally with friends. Why are these rules needed?

or

Although my feet are very narrow, I have not had ~~no~~ *any* trouble finding reasonable work shoes.

EXAMPLE

The firefighters could~~n't~~ do nothing to stop the forest fire.

or

The firefighters couldn't do ~~nothing~~ *anything* to stop the forest fire.

As corrected, each of these sentences expresses the point originally intended, but now each does so with a single negative.

Fast Fact   It wasn't always wrong to use a double negative. In fact double negatives can be seen in writings from the earlier days of modern English, including in the plays of Shakespeare. But some eighteenth-century English grammarians, intent on making English express the same kind of logic as mathematics, applied the mathematical rule that two negatives make a positive to language. Eventually, this application came to be the acceptable form, and the double negative came to be considered the nonstandard or illiterate form.

Exercise 27.8   **Avoiding Double Negatives**

In the following paragraph, circle the correct words in parentheses, avoiding double negatives. Use the material above and the following example as a guide.

EXAMPLE   Madeleine and David don't plan to travel ((anywhere,) nowhere) special this summer.

Activity 27.2

(1) Even though I don't know ((anything,) nothing) about professional sports, I enjoy going to see a professional baseball game once in a while. (2) In fact, I never turn down ((any,) no) invitation to see the Mud Hens. (3) This minor league team has not had ((any,) no) problem attracting crowds since they opened their new stadium five years ago. (4) The design of the stadium is a major factor, since the place has (any, (no)) obstructed-view seats. (5) I have never heard ((anybody,) nobody) who has attended a game there say a negative thing about the place. (6) In addition, the food services provider doesn't have ((any,) no) items for sale that cost more than $3, and they often publish discount food tickets in the paper. (7) As a result, even big families don't have ((any,) no) problem enjoying a few snacks during the game. (8) On game nights, when my cousin can't get ((anybody,) nobody) from work to drive him to the park, I drive and he buys me a ticket. (9) At most games, the crowd is large, and you can't find ((any,) no) empty seats behind home plate. (10) Unfortunately, it seems as if every time I go to a game, the team has (any, (no)) luck and ends up losing.

Exercise 27.9   **Identifying and Correcting Double Negatives**

Some of the sentences in the paragraph below contain double negatives. Put an * in front of any sentence containing a double negative, and then rewrite the sentence on a separate sheet of paper. More than one correct version is possible. Study the example first.

*

EXAMPLE   She wouldn't never leave town without contacting me first.

She would never leave town without contacting me first.

or

She wouldn't leave town without contacting me first.

(1) Bad habits are a plague not only for the offenders but also for the victims of the offending behavior. (2) For instance, many people who swear in public probably don't intend to offend nobody. (3) However, even if these people don't mean nothing by it, their bad habit can frighten, anger, or depress listeners. (4) Another bad habit many people share is not listening fully to those who are talking to them. (5) These offenders engage you in conversation, ask you a question, and then do not pay no attention as you try to answer. (6) There is not hardly anything more frustrating than trying to communicate with someone whose mind has moved on to other things. (7) The worst habit of all is gossiping about others. (8) Gossiping is particularly unfair because the people being discussed are not around to say nothing to defend themselves. (9) They never have no chance to confront the people talking about them. (10) Unfortunately, I am guilty of all these bad habits myself, so I don't have the right to lecture nobody else.

Challenge 27.3   **Building an Argument for Using Standard English**

Although some people use double negatives in casual speech, these errors aren't acceptable in college or professional writing. Imagine you have been asked to address a class of sixth graders on the subject of using proper language in writing and speaking. Working with a partner, list on a separate sheet of paper at least four reasons you would give to explain why double negatives and other nonstandard forms (*ain't, we be,* and so on) are unacceptable. Still working together, turn your list into a paragraph that could be handed out to the sixth grade students as a guide.

Chapter Quick Check: Working with Adjectives and Adverbs

The following passage contains errors involving double negatives, incorrect forms of adjectives and adverbs, and misplaced modifiers. Cross out each error and write the correct form above it. For misplaced modifiers, you may need to insert new words or cross out an entire clause and rewrite it. Also, there may be more than one way to correct the double negatives. Use the example to guide you.

EXAMPLE   Greg's new digital phone is ~~more~~ smaller than Krystall's.

(1) One of the ~~compellingist~~ *most compelling* literary voices of the current age is Jamaica Kincaid. (2) Best known for her beautiful coming-of-age novel *Annie John,* published in 1983, ~~the Caribbean island of Antigua is where Kincaid was born.~~ *Kincaid was born on the Caribbean island of Antigua* (3) Not experiencing ~~no~~ happiness or fulfillment while growing up, she decided to abandon Antigua and head to the United States. (4) She left her home at age 17 ~~in the Caribbean~~, *in the Caribbean* ∧ and she traveled to New York City where she became an *au pair,* a live-in babysitter. (5) After attending colleges in New York and New Hampshire but not earning ~~no~~ *a* degree, she began her professional writing career. (6) ~~She~~ *By this time, she* had also changed her name from Elaine Potter Richardson ~~by this time~~ to Jamaica Kincaid. (7) During the mid 1970s, Kincaid was writing so ~~good~~ *well* that she began to attract attention for her work in several periodicals, particularly the *New Yorker.* (8) After viewing her writing, the publisher ~~quick~~ *quickly* invited her to join the staff of this influential publication, and she remained associated with the periodical for twenty years. (9) Kincaid is considered to be one of the most ~~superbest~~ *superb* post-colonial writers, artists whose writing concerns countries formerly under the control of the British Empire. (10) In works like *Annie John, Lucy,* and *The Autobiography of My Mother,* Kincaid explores a number of ~~real~~ *really* intense and sensitive themes, including alienation, isolation, and mother-daughter relationships.

Activity 27.4

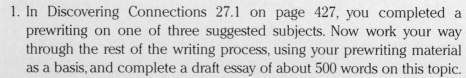

Discovering Connections 27.2

Activity 27.3

COLLABORATION

1. In Discovering Connections 27.1 on page 427, you completed a prewriting on one of three suggested subjects. Now work your way through the rest of the writing process, using your prewriting material as a basis, and complete a draft essay of about 500 words on this topic.

2. Exchange your draft with a partner. Using the material in this chapter to guide you, check the draft you receive for any errors in the use of adjectives or adverbs. Then return the draft to the writer.

3. Revise your essay, correcting any errors that your reader identified.

Summary Exercise: Working with Adjectives and Adverbs

The following passage contains errors involving double negatives, incorrect forms of adjectives and adverbs, and misplaced modifiers. Cross out each error, and write the correct form above it. For misplaced modifiers, you may need to insert new words or cross out an entire clause and rewrite it. Also, there may be more than one way to correct the double negatives.

(1) I didn't ~~never~~ think my life would improve when a 24-hour supermarket opened in my neighborhood, but I was in for a pleasant surprise. (2) I
a
have never been ~~no~~ believer that bigger always means ~~more~~ better. (3) Also,
awfully
the idea of grocery shopping at midnight seemed ~~awful~~ strange to me, but I decided to give it a try.

really
(4) I was ~~real~~ surprised to see how few people had the same idea.
small
(5) When I drove into the parking lot at midnight, I saw a ~~smallest~~ number of
a small crowd inspected   .
cars. (6) Cluttering the aisles, the produce section ~~had a small crowd.~~ (7) They
    ^   ^
were thumping melons, inspecting heads of lettuce, and picking apples just as
brightest
they would if the sun were shining its ~~most bright~~.

quickly
(8) I ~~quick~~ discovered the appeal of shopping at night. (9) First of all,
were   simpler
there ~~weren't~~ hardly any customers at midnight, so it was ~~more simple~~ to
any
maneuver in the aisles. (10) Also, I didn't have to fight ~~no~~ crowds, so I felt
~~more~~ freer to examine the selection of items at my leisure.
calmer   quietly
(11) The store seemed ~~calmest~~, too. (12) Speaking more ~~quiet~~ than they
were
do during the day, ~~I found~~ the workers ^ more pleasant~~er~~. (13) Even the
awfully   loudest
checkout area was ~~awful~~ still. (14) The ~~most loud~~ sound was the beep of
the computer scanners.
was [OR wasn't a]
(15) Best of all, there ~~wasn't~~ no long wait in line to check out and pay for
my groceries. (16) Normally, I am squeezed in between people who apparently
~~don't~~ have no limits on their grocery budgets. (17) Imagine my delight when I
quickly
found I could check out ~~quick~~, without the normal ten-minute wait in line.

I felt that

(18) Leaving the parking lot, ^this shopping trip was a positive experience. (19) I liked going about my shopping ~~quiet~~ quietly and ~~calm~~ calmly, without being bothered by other shoppers. (20) The only problem was that the next day I was ~~more~~ sleepier than usual.

RECAP   ADJECTIVES, ADVERBS, AND OTHER MODIFIERS: USING DESCRIBING AND MODIFYING WORDS EFFECTIVELY

New terms in this chapter	Definitions
● **modifier**	● a word that describes or limits other words in a sentence
● **adjective**	● a word that describes a noun or pronoun An adjective answers the question *which one, how many,* or *what kind?*
● **adverb**	● a word that describes a verb, adjective, or another adverb An adverb tells *how, when, where, to what extent,* or *how much.*
● **positive form**	● the form of an adjective or adverb that describes a noun or pronoun without making a comparison ***Example*** tall, poorly
● **comparative form**	● the form of an adjective or adverb used to compare two things ***Example*** **more** handsome, lovel**ier**
● **superlative form**	● the form of an adjective or adverb used to compare more than two things ***Example*** **most** remarkable, slow**est**
● **participle**	● a verb form that functions as an adjective in a sentence ***Example*** *Singing* sweetly, the nightingale darted from tree to tree. Use participles when combining sentences and eliminate choppiness.
● **misplaced modifier**	● a modifier placed near a word that it does not modify Place a participle near the word or words it describes in a sentence.
● **dangling modifier**	● a modifier with no word that it can logically modify
● **double negative**	● an incorrect construction using two negative words in the same unit of ideas ***Example*** *Nobody* should bring *nothing* flammable. Negative words include *no, not, never, nowhere, nobody, nothing, no one, none, scarcely, hardly, barely.*

Guidelines for Adjective and Adverb Forms

Type of word	Positive	Comparative	Superlative
One-syllable word	brave	positive form + -er brav**er**	positive form + -est brav**est**
Words of three or more syllables	enjoyable	*more* + positive form **more** enjoyable	*most* + positive form **most** enjoyable
Some two-syllable words	funny	change -y to -i + -er funn**ier**	change -y to -i + -est funn**iest**
Other two-syllable words	famous	*more* + positive form **more** famous	*most* + positive form **most** famous

Commonly Confused Adjectives and Adverbs

Positive	Comparative	Superlative
bad (adjective)	worse	worst
badly (adverb)	worse	worst
good (adjective)	better	best
well (adverb)	better	best
little	less	least
much	more	most

Chapter 28

Parallelism: Presenting Related Items in a Similar Form

Getting Started... **Q:** How can I present related ideas in a form that will sound right, *be* right, and flow in the best way for my readers?

Audio **28.1** **A:** Parallelism is the technique you use to make related ideas flow together, and it is actually simpler than it may seem at first glance. The key to maintaining parallelism is to focus on conjunctions because they are the words that form connections. Check any items connected by conjunctions, especially *and, or,* and *but,* and then use the first item in the series as a pattern for the others.

Overview: Balancing Ideas in Your Writing

Audio 28.2 Multiple births are often newsworthy events. You have probably seen a video clip or a picture in the newspaper of triplets or quadruplets, all dressed in identical clothes. When it comes to compiling a series of items in your writing, this is the image you should keep in mind. That's because you must also "dress" or present any related ideas so that they look the same—in other words, so they are parallel. Maintaining **parallelism** means presenting any series of ideas, whether the items are individual words or groups of words, in the same form. Faulty parallelism is a serious problem because the reader focuses on the items that don't match rather than on the good ideas being presented. Therefore it's important to spend some time mastering this aspect of writing.

> *In this chapter, you will discover how to maintain parallelism*
>
> ● with words in a series
>
> ● with phrases
>
> ● with words linked by correlative conjunctions such as *either/or*

Discovering Connections 28.1

Discovering Connections 28.2 at the end of this chapter provides an opportunity for students to apply the skills they have learned about maintaining parallelism. They will be asked to compose and revise an essay based on one of the topics in Discovering Connections 28.1.

Using one of the techniques you practiced in Chapter 2, "Generating Ideas through Prewriting," prewrite on one of the following topics:

1. the causes of or ways to reduce water or air pollution
2. an adventure or experience from a physical education class

Or, focus on this picture.
Save your work for later use.

Maintaining Parallelism with Words in a Series

Weblink 28.1

Video 28.1

When you use words in a series, all the words should have the same grammatical structure. Generally, coordinating conjunctions (*and, but, for, nor, or, so,* and *yet*) are used to join the words. To maintain parallelism, keep two things in mind:

1. *Connect only similar parts of speech.* Join nouns with nouns, verbs with verbs, adjectives with adjectives, and so forth. Do not connect a verb with an adjective, a noun with an adverb, and so forth.
2. *Do not connect individual words in a series to phrases or clauses.* Keep the structure of the series, as well as the number of words in it, parallel.

EXAMPLE   Steve Martin is an actor, a comedian, and ~~he writes plays.~~ *a playwright*

EXAMPLE   The weather this summer has been hot, rainy, and ~~a steam bath~~. *steamy*

> **Fast Fact** Rhyme is a form of parallel structure. But don't count on being able to employ this particular variation of parallelism with *month, orange, purple,* or *silver,* because no English words rhyme with them.

Exercise 28.1   Using Parallel Words in a Series

Audio 28.3

Complete each statement with a word that maintains the parallel structure of the sentence. Study the example first.

Answers will vary. Sample responses are given.

EXAMPLE   The antique painting was dusty, scratched, and _____*faded*_____.

Representative answers are shown. In some cases, more than one answer is possible.

To help students review the parts of speech, refer them to Chapters 17, 25, 26, and 27. Also, for guidelines about using commas to separate items in a series, refer them to Chapter 30.

(1) How can you tell whether someone is telling the truth or a ___lie___? (2) This question has stymied everyone, including parents, spouses, and ___criminal investigators___, as long as there has been a civilized society. (3) Existing polygraph tests measure truthfulness on the basis of such signs of anxiety as increased perspiration and ___heart rate___. (4) But polygraph results are not considered reliable because not everyone reacts to tragedy, adversity, or ___stress___ in the same way. (5) Some people react by shaking, sweating, and ___crying___, while others simply become seemingly emotionless. (6) Also, complicating the issue is that outright lies, denial, and ___exaggeration___ are all types of dishonesty, but people don't judge them all the same way. (7) Now new brain research may make it possible to tell if a person's statement is trustworthy or ___dishonest___. (8) To find out whether brain activity will signal when someone is being truthful or ___devious___, neuroscience researchers used an MRI to measure brain activity of eighteen volunteers. (9) The volunteers were given a specific playing card—for example, the jack of hearts or the ___ace of clubs___—and told to lie when a computer correctly identified the card. (10) The MRI results showed different levels of brain activity depending on whether the person was telling the truth or ___lying___.

Exercise 28.2   Maintaining Parallel Structure with Words in a Series

Each sentence in the following passage contains an error in parallelism. Cross out the errors, and, when necessary, write the correct version above the faulty one. In some cases, you can correct the sentence by simply eliminating words. In some cases, more than one correct answer is possible. Use the example as a guide.

EXAMPLE   Every time I try to stop smoking, I gain weight, get headaches, or ~~irritability takes over.~~ *become irritable*

(1) You need a good education and ~~to be ambitious~~ *ambition* to get a decent job today. (2) A few decades ago, people could find employment as long as they

were willing to work hard and ~~learning~~ _{learn} on the job. (3) Plenty of jobs existed
that didn't involve working with complex equipment or ~~to have~~ _{having} a specialized
math or science background. (4) Even if people had weak writing skills or
~~lacking~~ _{lacked} strong reading skills, they could still find regular work. (5) Now, however, even a high school diploma or ~~having~~ a G.E.D. doesn't automatically
land you a job. (6) I know from experience that employers in the twenty-first
century want employees who are intelligent, enthusiastic, and ~~they want them
to be~~ well educated. (7) After my military service, I missed out on a number
of good jobs because the employers said I lacked technical experience or
post-secondary education ~~was needed by me~~. (8) After a year of looking for a
desirable job, I became discouraged, angry, and ~~I was~~ depressed. (9) Now I
am in college, working in the computer lab and ~~computer science is being~~ _{studying computer science}
~~studied by me~~. (10) As a result, I will have some specific knowledge, confi-
dence, and ~~I will also have~~ experience to offer an employer.

Maintaining Parallelism with Phrases

Video
28.4

Phrases connected by *and* and *or* must also follow parallel structure. A
phrase is a group of words that acts as a single word. Common types of
phrases include prepositional phrases, *-ing* phrases, and *to + verb* phrases.
It's correct to connect prepositional phrases with other prepositional
phrases or *to + verb* phrases with other *to + verb* phrases. To correct errors
that join nonparallel phrases, all you have to do is change the incorrect
phrase to match the others, as these examples show:

EXAMPLE   The explosion affected people living *near the house, around the neighborhood, and the* ~~*entire city was involved*~~ *throughout the entire city*.

EXAMPLE   When she's not in art class, she is busy *sketching animals, painting nature
scenes, or* ~~*to draw portraits*~~ *drawing portraits*.

EXAMPLE   My grandmother always loved *to knit sweaters and* ~~*decorating*~~ *to decorate* *handkerchiefs.*

Exercise 28.3　　**Using Parallel Structure with Phrases**

Circle the coordinating conjunctions in each of the sentences below. Then underline the phrases that the conjunctions connect. If the connected phrases are not expressed in parallel form, change one so that it matches those to which it is connected. More than one correct answer may be possible. Study the example first.

EXAMPLE　　The car crashed <u>through the fence</u>, <u>across the yard</u>, (and) it went into the pool.

(1) Until I was ten years old, I was frequently in trouble <u>for breaking windows</u>, <u>beating up other kids</u>, (and) <u>~~to bother~~ old people</u> in my neighborhood.
   bothering

(2) I had a terrible attitude, whether I was <u>at school</u>, <u>on the street</u> (or) <u>~~I was home~~</u>, until I joined the Agnes Kidd Memorial Boys (and) Girls Club.
   at home
(3) The staff at the Club taught me <u>to respect others</u>, <u>to help those less able</u>, (and) <u>~~respecting~~ other people's property</u>.
   to respect
(4) Within a month, I became a different person <u>at home</u>, <u>around the neighborhood</u>, (and) <u>~~to spend time with~~ in school</u>.

(5) I had been having trouble <u>with math</u> (and) <u>~~reading was troublesome for me~~</u>, (so) I spent time with a tutor from the after school program at the Club.
   reading
(6) Because of the staff's influence, I began <u>to become more attentive to my younger sisters</u> (and) <u>~~doing my chores~~ without being reminded</u>.
   to do my chores
(7) Before long I was <u>bringing home good report cards</u>, <u>making new friends</u>, (and) <u>~~I was~~ feeling more confident</u>.

(8) I am determined to repay the staff for their help <u>with my attitude</u> (and) <u>~~they helped me~~ with school</u>.
(9) To do so, I intend <u>to study hard in college</u> (and) <u>~~earn~~ my degree in elementary education</u> with a minor in physical education.
   to earn
(10) Then I can begin working with children <u>in a community center</u> (or) <u>~~maybe to get a job~~ in an elementary school</u>.

Exercise 28.4　　**Keeping Phrases Parallel**

The sentences in the following passage contain errors in parallelism of phrases. Cross out these errors, and then provide correct versions above the faulty ones if necessary. In some cases, you can correct the sentence simply by eliminating words. In some cases, more than one correct answer may be possible. Use the example to guide you.

EXAMPLE   Elaine looked for her lost credit card under the bed, behind the bureau, and ~~she~~ even ~~looked~~ in her old pocketbook.

(1) Yesterday, a guest speaker in my American history class gave an outstanding lecture on racist attitudes, unfair stereotypes, and ~~on~~ race relations. (2) When my professor first announced that Dr. George Henry from City University would be showing a film, giving a speech, and ~~he would then answer~~ [answering] questions, I was annoyed. (3) In high school and ~~when I had presentations~~ in other college classes, I had never gained much from such performances. (4) In particular, I usually found the video presentations hard to follow because of the small monitor size and ~~the sound conditions was poor~~ [poor sound conditions]. (5) However, when the class began, I quickly discovered that whether he was discussing the video, asking questions, or ~~he related~~ [relating] a personal experience, Dr. Henry had my complete attention. (6) For example, he handed out a questionnaire delving into our racial fears and ~~to expose~~ [exposing] our hidden racist outlooks. (7) He urged us to read the questions carefully, to answer honestly, and ~~he told us~~ to consider the implications of our answers. (8) As I read over my answers, I began to realize that many educators, ~~people in the business world~~ [businesspeople], and politicians hold racist feelings without even being aware of them. (9) After his lecture, Dr. Henry led a discussion on ways to improve race relations, eliminate stereotypes, and ~~overcoming~~ [overcome] our unconscious racist feelings. (10) I left that classroom with a different perspective on racism and ~~my attitude about guest speakers was new~~ [on guest speakers].

Challenge 28.1   **Analyzing Effective Use of Parallel Structure**

Here is a brief passage from *Night*, Elie Weisel's powerful memoir of his experiences in Nazi death camps. Working with a partner, underline any parallel

Weblink
28.2

words or phrases. Circle the conjunctions. Find the most effective use of parallel structure, and explain to the class why it is effective.

Discuss with students the relationships among the ideas that are linked. How does parallel structure emphasize the balance or similarity among ideas?

All around me death was moving in, silently, without violence. It would seize upon some sleeping being, enter into him, ⟨and⟩ consume him bit by bit. Next to me, there was someone trying to wake up his neighbor, his brother, perhaps, ⟨or⟩ a friend. In vain. Discouraged in the attempt, the man lay down in his turn, next to the corpse, ⟨and⟩ slept too. Who was there to wake him up?

Fast Fact If you want an example of what correct parallelism can add to a piece of writing, look no further than the Declaration of Independence. As this passage shows, the strong repetition of *that* clauses hammers home the essence of the philosophy upon which our country was founded: "We hold these truths to be self-evident, that all men are created equal, that they are endowed by their Creator with certain unalienable Rights, that among these are Life, Liberty, and the pursuit of Happiness. That to secure these rights, Governments are instituted among Men, deriving their just powers from the consent of the governed. That whenever any Form of Government becomes destructive to these ends, it is the Right of the People to alter or abolish it. . . ."

Maintaining Parallelism when Using Correlative Conjunctions

Audio
28.5

You must also be careful to maintain parallelism when you use the following word pairs, called **correlative conjunctions**, to connect items:

both/and   not only/but also
either/or   whether/or
neither/nor

These pairs indicate two possibilities, alternatives, conditions, and so on. The words or phrases that these pairs connect must be parallel. To eliminate faulty parallelism in this kind of construction, make the second item match the first, as these examples show:

EXAMPLE I tried to sneak into the club *by both trying the back door* and ~~I showed~~ *by showing the guard a fake ID.*

EXAMPLE The salesclerk was *neither polite nor* ~~did she work efficiently.~~ *efficient*

Exercise 28.5 | **Maintaining Parallelism with Units Connected by Correlative Conjunctions**

Complete the following sentences by filling in the blanks with words or phrases that complete the thought and maintain sentence parallelism. Use the example as a guide. Answers will vary. Representative answers are shown.

EXAMPLE   By the time I get to the shower in the morning, either all the hot water is used up or ___*all the towels are missing*___ .

1. The fire at my neighbor's apartment last Christmas was terrifying not only for my friend but also ___for all the people on the block___ .

2. The fire started when one of her house guests either dropped a cigarette on a chair or couch or ___fell asleep while smoking___ .

3. Regardless of the cause, the damage was heavy, not only to the apartment itself but also ___to her belongings___ .

4. When I looked out the window on the night of the fire, the roof was not only smoking but also ___emitting bright orange flames___ .

5. At first I couldn't tell whether the smoke was coming from her apartment or ___from the apartment next to hers___ .

6. By the time the fire department arrived, both the front door and ___the side entrance___ were engulfed in flames.

7. Whether she was suffering from smoke inhalation or ___shock___ , my neighbor was hospitalized for three days.

8. Neither my family nor ___I___ could sleep until we knew that she and her guests were all right.

9. Fortunately, my neighbor was able to collect insurance money and ___replace her belongings destroyed in the fire___ .

10. Since then, she doesn't allow smoking in her apartment, so anyone wanting to smoke either steps out on the balcony or ___goes down the stairs and out to the street___ .

Exercise 28.6 | **Using Parallelism Correctly in Your Writing**

Weblink
28.3

One element in each of the following groups is not parallel. Cross out the nonparallel element, and revise it to make it parallel. Then, on a separate sheet of paper, write a sentence using each item.

Weblink
28.4

1. both a midterm and ~~we must write~~ three papers

2. either a situation comedy or ~~to watch~~ a talk show

3. near the cafeteria, _{past the gym} ~~the gym,~~ and beside the administration building

4. _{dribble} ~~dribbling,~~ pass, and shoot

5. not only interesting but ~~it was~~ funny, too

6. whether it is during the summer or the winter ~~is when it occurs~~

7. playing video games, _{using the Internet} ~~the Internet is used,~~ and watching DVDs

8. across the street and ~~she went~~ up the stairs

9. _{knowing} ~~to know~~ the answer but being afraid to volunteer in class

10. both the person _{who made} ~~making~~ the complaint and the person who was accused

Challenge 28.2 | **Analyzing Parallelism in Literature**

Speeches can also help students understand the power of parallel structure. Both "I Have a Dream" by Martin Luther King, Jr. and "The Gettysburg Address" by Abraham Lincoln contain effective examples. In addition, ask students to record and analyze in their journals any examples of parallelism they hear or read.

1. Read the following excerpt, which makes great use of parallelism, from John Steinbeck's *The Grapes of Wrath*. This powerful epic novel details the struggle of the Joads, a family who traveled west during the Great Depression in a vain search for work, security, and dignity. In this passage, Steinbeck describes one source of anguish for starving families like the Joads. They were forced to stand idly by while agribusinesses bent on controlling prices destroyed surplus food.

> The people come with nets to fish for potatoes in the river, and the guards hold them back; they come in rattling cars to get the dumped oranges, but the kerosene is sprayed. And they stand still and watch the potatoes float by, listen to the screaming pigs being killed in a ditch and covered with quick-lime, watch the mountains of oranges slop down to a putrefying ooze; and in the eyes of the people there is failure; and in the eyes of the hungry there is a growing wrath. In the souls of the peo-

Activity
28.1

ple the grapes of wrath are <u>filling</u> and <u>growing heavy</u>, <u>growing heavy</u> for the vintage.

2. Working with a partner, identify and underline the parallel elements you find in this passage.

3. Discuss ways in which the parallel structure helps you understand the point Steinbeck is making.

Chapter Quick Check: Maintaining Parallelism

Check the sentences in the following passage for the types of errors in parallelism described in this chapter. Cross out each incorrect form, and write any correction in the space above it. In some cases, more than one correct answer is possible. If a sentence is correct as written, write *OK* above it. Use the example as a guide.

EXAMPLE   The homeless woman who won the $20 million Big Game Lottery has been interviewed by newspaper reporters, radio personalities, and ~~she has been seen talking to~~ all the major national television news anchors.

(1) Some engineers are beginning to experiment with a surprising mate-
rial for building new structures and ~~to renovate~~ ^{renovating} old ones: cardboard. (2) Of course, cardboard has been around for a long time, but until recently almost everyone thought it wouldn't be any good as a primary structural component in houses and ~~to be used in~~ other buildings. (3) They think of how easy it is to tear up a cardboard gift box ~~or poking~~ ^{(to) poke} a hole in a cardboard shipping container, and they rule out other uses for this product. (4) As they see it, cardboard is too weak, flimsy, and ~~it is~~ insubstantial to be used for serious building projects. (5) But structural engineers have discovered that when it is properly prepared and treated, cardboard can be both durable and ~~it is also~~ ^{OK} surprisingly strong. (6) Cardboard is, after all, made from recycled paper, which means that it is actually composed of processed wood. (7) When it has been tightly compressed, coated with water-resistant

chemicals, and ~~it has been~~ manufactured for different lengths and widths. Cardboard has proven to be both strong and resilient. (8) In fact, some structural engineers in England demonstrated the strength of cardboard by designing and ~~they built~~ _{building} a cardboard bridge that they then drove a car across. (9) In addition, engineers recently constructed a school building that, except for the concrete foundation, ~~they used~~ glass windows, and roof framing, is largely made of treated cardboard. (10) The school building stands as proof that whether the cardboard is a small gift box or a large shipping container ~~is made from cardboard,~~ it may have another life that most of us have never considered.

Discovering Connections 28.2

1. In Discovering Connections 28.1 on page 447, you completed a prewriting on one of three suggested topics. Now take this prewriting material and work through the rest of the steps in the writing process to create an essay of about 500 words on this subject.
2. Exchange your draft with a partner. Using the material in this chapter to guide you, check the essay you receive for any problems with parallelism. Mark any errors in parallel structure, and return the draft to the writer.
3. Revise your draft, correcting the errors in parallelism identified by your reader.

Summary Exercise: Maintaining Parallelism

Activity 28.2

Check the sentences in the following passage for the types of errors in parallelism described in this chapter. Cross out each incorrect form, and write your correction in the space above. In some cases, more than one correct answer is possible. If a sentence is correct as written, write *OK* above it.

Answers may vary.

Ask small groups of students to compare and discuss the revisions they make. If more than one answer is correct, which version is the most effective? Why?

OK

(1) Alcohol abuse is one of the most misunderstood problems in the world. (2) Even though researchers have shown that alcoholism is a disease, many people still think that it's a sign of a defect, weakness, or ~~the per-~~

laziness
~~son is lazy.~~ (3) As a result, many individuals suffering from this disease are
to seek
more likely to hide the problem than ~~seeking~~ treatment.

(4) In the United States, drinking is treated as sexy, glamorous, and ~~you~~
~~can look~~ macho. (5) For example, television commercials for alcohol show
beautiful bars filled with attractive models, sports stars, or ~~some are~~ celebri-
OK
ties, all having fun. (6) People are encouraged to think that they can be like
those glamorous, famous people if they drink.

(7) However, for many, drinking is neither glamorous nor ~~it is not~~ special; instead, their genetic makeup means that drinking is as dangerous for
playing
them as ~~to play~~ Russian roulette. (8) Without even being aware of it, they
they change
become dependent on alcohol, and their patterns of living ~~can change, too.~~
OK   ^   ^
(9) As time passes, they need to drink more and more alcohol to function.
minds
(10) Without alcohol, both their bodies and their ~~mental state of being~~ go
through excruciating symptoms of withdrawal.
OK
(11) Alcoholism is a disease of denial, and many individuals suffering
from it are unable to admit they have a problem. (12) In some cases, they
lose their families, their jobs, their friends, and their self-respect ~~is gone~~ before they finally admit that they are addicted. (13) Unfortunately, some alco-
to acknowledge
holics choose to die rather than ~~acknowledging~~ that they have a problem.
OK
(14) Those who do accept that they are addicted can begin recovery
with a treatment program. (15) They can go into a detoxification center, ~~they~~
~~might go to~~ a public treatment center, or a private substance abuse clinic.
(16) With professional care, they undergo withdrawal from alcohol and also
receive
~~receiving~~ counseling to understand why they feel the need to drink. (17) For
recovering alcoholics, Alcoholics Anonymous provides a support group; they
can draw strength from others who have admitted they are alcoholics, are
are putting
taking steps to overcome their addiction, and ~~put~~ their lives back together.

Activity
28.3

(18) Most of us think of addiction as a problem with drugs such as co-caine, heroin, or amphetamines ~~are making a comeback.~~ (19) However, the

^

most common addicts do not stick needles in their arms or ~~are swallowing~~

in their mouths
pills; they abuse alcohol. (20) If more of us were aware that alcohol abuse

^

sex
affects people without regard for age, race, ~~people of both sexes,~~ or religion,

then perhaps fewer would start down that road to alcohol addiction.

 RECAP

PARALLELISM: PRESENTING RELATED ITEMS IN A SIMILAR FORM

Activity
28.4

New terms in this chapter	Definition
● **parallelism**	● a way of creating structural balance in writing by expressing similar or related ideas in similar form Individual words that are connected by a conjunction should be parallel. ***Example*** That car is *old* and *rusty.* Phrases that are connected by a conjunction should be parallel. ***Example*** She looked *in the closet* and *under the bed.* Words that follow pairs of correlative conjunctions should be parallel. ***Example*** *Neither* the police *nor* the insurance adjuster could identify the cause of the accident.
● **correlative conjunction**	● conjunctions used in pairs (like *both/and* and *either/or*) to connect items
● **Parallelism means balancing words.**	pens ... pencils **and, or**
● **Parallelism means balancing phrases.**	a package of pens was purchasing pens to use a pen ... a box of pencils was selling pencils to break a pencil **and, or**

● **Parallelism means balancing items with connecting pairs.**

neither sleet	**nor** hail
either signal agreement	**or** indicate disagreement
both newer	**and** shinier
not only attractive	**but also** intelligent
whether in the house	**or** at the park

Chapter 29

Spelling: Focusing on Correctness

Getting Started... **Q:** No matter how much time I have spent trying to learn the rules, I still seem to have trouble with spelling. Why is the spelling of English words so complicated, and what can I do to become a better speller?

Audio 29.1

Audio 29.2

A: American English is difficult to spell for a number of reasons that have to do with the history of the language and the influence of the various languages from which different words have come. As far as improving your spelling, you start by making yourself familiar with spelling rules. But as you've already discovered, it isn't the words that follow the rules that give you trouble. It's the many exceptions to the rules. Therefore, a second way to improve your spelling is to keep a list of those words that give *you* trouble. Every time you write, use this list to check your draft. Before long, you will find that your spelling is improving and that you notice errors more easily.

Overview: Understanding the Importance of Correct Spelling

ESL Note
See "Spelling" on page 581.

Students may be reassured to hear that most people face spelling challenges and that there are techniques to help them become better spellers. Ask students to discuss their spelling difficulties and to share how they have overcome some of them.

Any experienced writer will tell you the same thing: spelling *always* counts. One reason is that errors in spelling are often the most obvious flaws in writing, especially if the reader is someone who finds spelling easy. Make no mistake about it—some people simply don't have much difficulty with spelling, so for them spelling errors almost jump off the page. For others, however, the story is quite different. These people find spelling words correctly or noticing misspellings to be an enormous and frustrating task.

There are valid reasons why they do. For example, not all English words are spelled as they sound. Other words with different meanings sound the same. Some words conform to spelling rules, while others deviate from them. But as complicated as it is, those who find spelling difficult shouldn't expect much sympathy. Readers *always* expect correct spelling, and any misspelled words can spoil the effect of an otherwise excellent paper.

The good news is that a number of techniques can help you become a better speller. Besides learning basic spelling rules, you can review commonly confused words and maintain a personal dictionary of words that you have trouble spelling.

> **In this chapter, you will learn how to**
>
> ● spell plural forms correctly
>
> ● add prefixes and suffixes
>
> ● decide whether to double the final consonant of a word before adding *-ing* or *-ed*
>
> ● spell words with *-ei* or *-ie* combinations
>
> ● choose correctly among *-sede, -ceed,* and *-cede,* and other endings that sound alike
>
> ● deal with commonly confused words
>
> ● master the most commonly misspelled words

Discovering Connections 29.1

Discovering Connections 29.2 at the end of this chapter provides an opportunity for students to apply the skills they have learned about spelling correctly. They will be asked to compose and revise an essay based on one of the topics in Discovering Connections 29.1.

Using one of the techniques you practiced in Chapter 2, "Generating Ideas through Prewriting," prewrite on one of the following topics:

1. the appropriateness of vigilante justice
2. an issue or concern associated with organ donation

Or, focus on this picture.

    Save your work for later use.

Basic Rules for Forming Plurals

Video
29.1

As Chapter 25, "Nouns: Working Effectively with Words That Name," illustrated, the most basic rule for forming plurals is to add *-s* to the singular forms:

    book   book**s**   computer computer**s**   banana banana**s**

However, there are numerous exceptions to this basic rule, as the following guidelines show.

Nouns that end in *-ch, -sh, -x,* and *-s* For nouns that end in *-ch, -sh, -x, -s,* form the plural by adding an *-es:*

    porch porch**es**   fox fox**es**   lash lash**es**

Weblink
29.1

Nouns that end in -y   The plural for most nouns ending in -y depends on the letter preceding the -y. If that letter is a vowel (*a, e, i, o, u*), simply add -s:

> delay   delay**s**   key   key**s**   tray   tray**s**

If the letter before the -y is a consonant, change the -y to -i and add -es:

> worry   worr**ies**   duty   dut**ies**   sky   sk**ies**

Nouns that end in -o   For nouns that end in -o, look at the preceding letter to decide whether to add -s or -es. If the letter preceding the final -o is a *vowel*, simply add -s:

> radio   radio**s**   stereo   stereo**s**   trio   trio**s**

Weblink
29.2

If the letter before the -o is a *consonant*, you usually add an -es:

> potato   potato**es**   echo   echo**es**   veto   veto**es**

Exceptions   Nouns referring to music, such as *altos, falsettos, solos,* and *sopranos,* do not obey this rule. In addition, with a few nouns ending in -o preceded by a consonant, you may add either -s or -es:

> cargo   cargo**s** *or* cargo**es**   motto   motto**s** *or* motto**es**
> zero   zero**s** *or* zero**es**

Words that end in -f or -fe   Learn which plurals end in -fs or -fes and which ones must change to -ves. Some nouns that end in -f or -fe form plurals with a simple -s:

> safe   safe**s**   belief   belief**s**   chief   chief**s**

For others, however, you must change the -f to -ves:

> thief   thie**ves**   knife   kni**ves**   wife   wi**ves**

For some nouns, two forms are acceptable:

> scarf   scarf**s** *or* scar**ves**   hoof   hoof**s** *or* hoo**ves**
> dwarf   dwarf**s** *or* dwar**ves**

If you are in doubt about how to form the plural for one of these words, use the dictionary to find the proper spelling.

Video
29.2

Nouns with Latin endings   Make nouns with Latin endings plural in keeping with the original language:

> alumnus   alumn**i**   crisis   cris**es**

For some of these nouns, however, it is also acceptable to add -s or -es to form the plural:

> appendix   appendi**xes** *or* append**ices**
> memorandum   memorand**a** *or* memorand**ums**
> index   inde**xes** *or* indi**ces**

Hyphenated or combined nouns   For hyphenated and combined nouns, form the plural by adding -*s* to the main word:

sister**s**-in-law   leftover**s**   attorney**s** general

Irregular plurals   With some common words, form the plural by *changing letters within the word* or *adding letters to the end:*

man   m**e**n   foot   f**ee**t   louse   l**ice**   child   child**ren**

Nouns with the same singular and plural forms   A few common words have the same form whether they are singular or plural:

one deer   several deer   one sheep   many sheep
one species   five species

Nonword plurals and words discussed as words   For abbreviations, figures, numbers, letters, words discussed as words, and acronyms, form the plural by adding either an -*s* or -*'s* (apostrophe + -*s*). Use the -*'s* with all lowercase letters, with the capital letters *A, I, U,* or any other time when adding the -*s* alone might confuse the reader:

one A   four A**'s**   one i   several i**'s**   one the   many the**'s**

Exercise 29.1   **Identifying the Correct Plural Form of Words**

In each blank, write the plural form of the word in parentheses, as the example shows. Use the guidelines above for help.

EXAMPLE   Oak (leaf) ___*leaves*___ remain on the trees through the fall and into the winter.

(1) We love to ride our bikes along the bike (path) ___paths___ that run alongside the (highway) ___highways___ in surrounding (county) ___counties___. (2) We all wake up very early, pack our (lunch) ___lunches___ and (bottle) ___bottles___ of water, and hit the trail. (3) After a few miles, we are in the countryside where (farm) ___farms___ line the (roadside) ___roadsides___. (4) All the (quality) ___qualities___ of these calm places begin to work their magic, draining away (stress) ___stresses___ that have built up all week. (5) We love the leisurely way that (field) ___fields___, rustic barns and shiny (silo) ___silos___, house-

hold gardens with their rows of staked-up (tomato) _____tomatoes_____, and little

rural (church) _____churches_____ rise up to meet us and then slip past. (6) We

often spot (deer) _____deer_____, (fox) _____foxes_____, (rabbit) _____rabbits_____,

and assorted other wildlife. (7) Occasionally, wild (turkey) _____turkeys_____

break from the long grass beside the path and fly helter-skelter into the daz-

zling sunlight. (8) In the distance, the (roof) _____roofs_____ of townhouses

and office buildings glint. (9) This kind of peace, far from office (memoran-

dum) ___memoranda/memorandums___, and all the (stimulus) _____stimuli_____ that add

stress to our lives, is good for the soul. (10) We return home in the evening

tired but happy and ready to face our (responsibility) _____responsibilities_____.

Exercise 29.2   **Providing the Correct Plural Form of Words**

Following the guidelines on pages 461–463, provide the plural of each italicized word in the following passage. Cross out the singular form, and write
the plural above it, as the example shows.

EXAMPLE
    heroes   *men*
    The ~~hero~~ were two ~~man~~ who tackled the purse snatcher.

                                    illnesses
(1) Winter seems to bring with it a variety of ~~illness~~, and this past winter

               seasons   *families*   *children*
was one of the worst ~~season~~ in a long time for ~~family~~ with young ~~child~~. (2) I

               sons   *years*   *allergies*
am a single parent of two ~~son~~, both under five ~~year~~ old and both with ~~allergy~~.

          boys   *bouts*   *colds*   *infections*
(3) Last month, both ~~boy~~ had ~~bout~~ with ~~cold~~ or ~~infection~~. (4) It was hard for

          babies   *nights*
me to see my two ~~baby~~ suffer. (5) There were many ~~night~~ when I was still

     sheep
counting ~~sheep~~ at 2 or 3 A.M. (6) One morning, after staying up with them

                  pains   *knives*
most of the night, I awoke with ~~pain~~ in my chest. (7) It felt as though ten ~~knife~~

      lungs   *crises*
were cutting into my ~~lung~~. (8) "Why us?" I thought. "How many ~~crisis~~ do we

                         sisters-in-law
have to endure?" (9) Finally, I called one of my ~~sister-in-law~~ and asked her to

take me to the clinic. (10) The doctor diagnosed double pneumonia, which

         classes   *weeks*
kept me out of ~~class~~ for two ~~week~~. (11) I've never been one to fantasize

about ~~superhero,~~ but there were certainly ~~time~~ last winter when I dreamed
^{superheroes}   ^{times}

of being rescued.

Challenge 29.1   **Working with Plural Nouns**

   1. On a separate sheet of paper, choose five of the following singular nouns
      and make them plural. Then write a present tense sentence for each, as
      this example shows:

EXAMPLE
> leaf
> The **leaves** begin to fall during late September.

attorney-at-law	deer
play	birch
echo	wife
analysis	duty
glass	handkerchief

   2. Now exchange your sentences with a writing partner. In the sentences
      you receive, check that the plural forms are correct. Also check to make
      sure that the proper verb form is used. Note any problems and then re-
      turn the paper to the writer. Correct any problems your writing partner
      has identified.

Basic Rules for Prefixes and Suffixes

You can change the form and meaning of many words by adding *prefixes*
and *suffixes* to them. A **prefix** is a unit such as *un-, dis-, mis-,* or *semi-* added
to the beginning of a word. A **suffix** is a unit such as *-ness, -ing,* or *-ous*
added to the end of a word.

Prefixes   When you add a prefix to a word, do not change the spelling of
the word:

    believable **un**believable   obey **dis**obey
    understand **mis**understand

Suffixes -*ly* and -*ness*   In most cases, simply add *-ly* and *-ness* without
changing the spelling of the original word:

    real real**ly**   faithful faithful**ness**   usual usual**ly**

For words with more than one syllable that end in *-y,* you change the *-y* to *-i*
before you add *-ly* or *-ness:*

lonely lonel**iness**   easy eas**ily**   silly sill**iness**

Exception When you add -*ly* to *true*, you drop the final -*e*: *truly.*

Suffixes for words ending in -*e* For words ending in -*e*, drop the final -*e* when adding a suffix beginning with a vowel:

cope cop**ing**   disapprove disapprov**al**   fame fam**ous**

Keep the final -*e* if the suffix begins with a consonant:

care care**ful**   arrange arrange**ment**   safe safe**ty**

Exceptions With words such as *mile, peace,* and *notice,* you keep the final -*e* when you add suffixes beginning with a vowel: mile*age,* peace*able,* notice*able.*

Drop the final -*e* on such words as *whole, argue,* and *judge* when you add a suffix beginning with a consonant: whol*ly,* argu*ment,* judg*ment.*

Suffixes for words ending in -*y* For words ending in -*y* preceded by a consonant, change the -*y* to -*i* before you add the suffix, unless the suffix itself begins with -*i*, as with -*ing:*

bury bur**ied**   simplify simplif**ied**   *but*   hurry hurry**ing**

Doubling the final consonant when adding a suffix For one-syllable words that end in a *single* consonant preceded by a *single* vowel, *double the final consonant* before adding a suffix beginning with a vowel:

plan plan**ned**   slip slip**ping**   flat flat**ten**

However, if the final consonant is preceded by *another consonant* or by *more than one vowel,* do not double the final consonant. Just add the suffix beginning with a vowel:

brash brash**ness**   room room**ing**   fail fail**ure**

Multi-syllable words ending with a vowel–consonant pattern must be pronounced to identify which syllable is emphasized or *accented.* If the accent is on the *final syllable,* double the final consonant before adding the suffix:

begín begin**ning**   commít commit**ted**   contról control**lable**

If the accent is *not* on the last syllable, just add the suffix:

bénefit benefit**ed**   prófit profit**able**   súffer suffer**ing**

Fast Fact A 1990s study suggested that the ability to spell is much like hand–eye coordination and that spelling is therefore naturally more challenging for some than for others. In other words, some good spellers may be born, not made.

Exercise 29.3   **Adding Suffixes to Words**

Complete each sentence in the following passage by combining the word and suffix in parentheses. Refer to the guidelines on pages 465–466 for help. Use the example as a guide.

EXAMPLE   When it comes to (happy + ness) _____*happiness*_____, Jerome has more than his share.

(1) When I was growing up, I wanted to take piano lessons, but my parents could never afford to make the (arrange + ments) _____arrangements_____. (2) Year after year, I would listen wistfully to my favorite songs, (hope + ing) _____hoping_____ my parents could work out a way to pay for lessons. (3) I knew we didn't have much money to spare, so I never questioned their (judge + ment) _____judgment_____. (4) If they (true + ly) _____truly_____ felt we couldn't afford it, I understood. (5) I didn't want to cause any (argue + ments) _____arguments_____ between them. (6) At the same time, I was (whole + ly) _____wholly_____ convinced that I could be a good pianist if I got the chance. (7) When it came to my schoolwork, I learned (easy + ly) _____easily_____, and I was sure that music would be no different. (8) It wasn't that I wanted to become (fame + ous) _____famous_____ or anything; I just wanted a chance to learn to play the piano. (9) (Final + ly) _____Finally_____, last year, I was able to put aside enough money from my own job to start piano lessons. (10) Now, one afternoon a week, I travel to a small office downtown, and I (happy + ly) _____happily_____ indulge in my long-awaited lessons.

Exercise 29.4   **Deciding Whether to Double the Final Letter**

Each sentence in the following passage contains a word and a suffix in parentheses. Decide whether to double the final letter of the word before adding the suffix. Write the correct spelling of each word on the line provided. Use the example as a guide.

EXAMPLE   On my Caribbean vacation, I went (snorkel + ing) _____*snorkeling*_____ among brilliantly colored reefs and tropical fish.

(1) I'll never forget the day when I finally (stop + ed) _____stopped_____ smoking. (2) For years, my mother had been (beg + ing) _____begging_____ me to quit. (3) Even though I was only thirty, I found activities like (run + ing) _____running_____ almost impossible. (4) Nonetheless, it wasn't until I visited my grandfather in the hospital that I finally (realize + ed) _____realized_____ the damage I was doing to myself. (5) My grandfather had been a heavy smoker for forty years, and now he was (suffer + ing) _____suffering_____ from emphysema and lung cancer. (6) He and my grandmother had looked forward to his retirement so they could spend their time (travel + ing) _____traveling_____. (7) His sickness meant that they had done all that hoping and (plan + ing) _____planning_____ for nothing. (8) As I walked out of the hospital, I threw my pack of cigarettes in the trash, and I haven't (pick + ed) _____picked_____ up a cigarette since. (9) (Occasional + ly) _____Occasionally_____, I think of Grandfather. (10) I remember my (mortal + ity) _____mortality_____ and am no longer tempted.

The Basic Rule for *ie* or *ei*

Audio 29.3   The basic rule for words with *-ie* or *-ei* combinations is this:

> *I* before *e*
> Except after *c*
> And when sounded like *a*
> As in *neighbor* or *weigh*

These common words feature *-ie* combinations:

    gr**ie**f   bel**ie**ve   f**ie**ld   ach**ie**ve   hyg**ie**ne

And these common words need an *-ei* combination:

receive   perceive   ceiling   beige   freight

Receive, perceive, and *ceiling* call for *-ei* because these letters follow *c. Beige* and *freight* call for *-ei* because the combination sounds like *a.*

Exceptions   There are a number of exceptions to this rule. For instance, even though the combination doesn't follow *c, e* comes before *i* in the words *either, neither, leisure, seize, their,* and *weird.* And in *species, science,* and *ancient, i* comes before *e* even though the letters follow *c.* Whenever you come across these exceptions in your reading, make a note of them. Later in this chapter, you will learn how to make your own spelling dictionary.

Basic Rules for *-sede, -ceed,* and *-cede,* and Other Endings That Sound Alike

Words that end in *-sede, -ceed,* and *-cede*   Only one word in English ends in *-sede:*

super**sede**

Only three words in English end in *-ceed:*

pro**ceed**   ex**ceed**   suc**ceed**

All other words with this sound end in *-cede:*

pre**cede**   se**cede**   inter**cede**

Have* versus *of   The correct forms *could've, should've,* and *would've* sound like the incorrect forms *could of, should of,* and *would of.* When it comes to these three verbs, don't trust your ear; always write *could have, should have,* and *would have.* Then, if you still want to use the contraction, change the words in your final draft.

Used to* and *supposed to   In speaking, we often fail to sound the final *-d* in the expressions *used to* and *supposed to.* As a result, these two expressions are frequently misspelled as *use to* and *suppose to.* Always add the final *-d* in *used* or *supposed.*

A lot* and *all right   Two expressions that commonly appear in writing are *a lot* and *all right.* A common error is to use the nonstandard forms *alot* and *alright.* These forms are not correct, so always use the standard versions, *a lot* and *all right.*

Exercise 29.5   **Choosing the Correctly Spelled Word**

Circle the correctly spelled word in the sets of parentheses in each of the following sentences. Use the example as a guide.

EXAMPLE   If she doesn't (recieve, (receive)) the money she was awarded by the jury, Mrs. Andreas will have to take her former landlord to court again.

(1) Through recent experience, I have come to (beleive, (believe)) that the only way a supervisor can earn the respect of workers is to be fair and consistent. (2) When workers see that someone else is allowed (alot, (a lot)) of leeway as far as work schedules or punctuality, they naturally resent it. (3) I'll ((concede,) conceed) that a boss should be as flexible and accommodating as possible. (4) But what I experienced last week when I was (suppose to, (supposed to)) have Friday night off caused me to lose respect for my supervisor. (5) On Thursday, one of my co-workers said that she had to attend a party for her (neice, (niece)) and needed the night off. (6) My boss didn't even ((weigh,) wiegh) the consequences, and he agreed and told me I would have to fill her spot on Friday. (7) I angrily responded that I already had plans and that Diane (could of, (could've)) made the request before the schedule was posted. (8) When my boss finally said it would be ((all right,) alright) if I worked for only two hours instead of the full four, I agreed, but I wasn't happy about it. (9) I know it's unfair to expect that anyone can (acheive, (achieve)) a perfect record in terms of pleasing all employees. (10) Still, it's not always easy to be a worker and see problems that never (should of, (should've)) occurred.

Exercise 25.6   **Identifying and Correcting Misspelled and Misused Words**

Each of the sentences in the following passage contains at least one misspelled or misused word. Cross out each incorrect form, and write the correct version above it. Use the example as a guide.

                 proceeded   *leisurely*

EXAMPLE   The caravan ~~proceded~~ at a ~~liesurely~~ pace.

                                         believing

(1) Although many people have trouble ~~beleiving~~ it, thousands and thousands of adults in the United States cannot read. (2) It's ~~wierd~~ to think of
                                                               weird

adults being unable to do what schoolchildren can, but many are well behind second-graders in reading ability. (3) In my sociology class, a guest speaker from the Adult Literacy Program explained that these people ~~should of~~ been *(should have)* given special help in school but somehow "fell through the cracks." (4) As a result, they never ~~recieved~~ *(received)* the attention they needed. (5) The speaker explained that some of our friends and ~~nieghbors~~ *(neighbors)* might fall into this category. (6) In many cases, ~~niether~~ *(neither)* parents nor teachers noticed that these people were having difficulty during the course of growing up, so they did nothing to help. (7) It's amazing that many individuals manage to ~~succeede~~ *(succeed)* at various jobs despite their lack of literacy. (8) Somehow, they get ~~use to~~ *(used to)* bluffing their way through life. (9) The guest speaker explained that the greatest fear these people have is that someone will ~~percieve~~ *(perceive)* that they cannot read. (10) Fortunately, the Adult Literacy Program has a 90 percent success rate, so these people can hope to ~~acheive~~ *(achieve)* literacy if they are willing to try.

Students can highlight or copy the commonly confused words on this list that give them difficulty, or they can add the words to a personal spelling dictionary. If students use a spell-check program to edit their work, remind them that it will not notice words that are correctly spelled but incorrectly used.

Dealing with Commonly Confused Words

Sometimes, rather than misspelling a word, you wind up using a word that sounds like or reminds you of the one you intended to use. Such mistakes are common for *homonyms,* words that sound the same but have different spellings and meanings. They also occur with words that, for a number of reasons, people tend to confuse. On the following pages is a list of the most commonly confused words.

Commonly Confused Words

Words	Definitions	Examples
accept	to take or receive	The family refused to *accept* any financial support.
except	other than, excluding, but	They refused all donations *except* food.
advice	opinions, suggestions	The counselor tried to provide sound *advice*.
advise	to give suggestions, guide	To *advise* the man any further, she would need to know more about his finances.

(continued)

Words	Definitions	Examples
affect	(*verb*) to influence, stir the emotions	Exercising definitely *affects* me.
effect	(*noun*) a result, something brought about by a cause	One welcome *effect* is an increased energy level.
among	used to refer to a group or to distribution	Kerry stood *among* the crowd of students protesting the newly imposed dress code.
between	used to refer to individual relationships	The principal, standing *between* the superintendent and the mayor, glared at her.
all ready	everyone or everything prepared	When she returned from jury duty, her work was *all ready* for her to complete.
already	before, previously	She had *already* missed work the week before because of illness.
brake	(*noun*) a device to stop; (*verb*) to come to a halt	The driver's foot slipped off the *brake*. He could not *brake* in time to stop for the light.
break	to shatter, pause	He was lucky he didn't *break* his nose when he hit the windshield.
can	to be physically able to	I *can* usually get the new clothes priced and hung up on the display racks in about three hours.
may	to have permission to	*May* I leave once I've completed my work?
choose	to decide or select [present tense]	This semester, Terence will *choose* his own classes for the first time.
chose	decided or selected [past tense]	Last semester, he wasn't sure what classes to take, so his adviser *chose* all his courses.
conscience	inner sense of right and wrong	To live with a guilty *conscience* is a terrible ordeal.
conscious	aware, awake	All day long, you are *conscious* that you've done something wrong.
council	a group formally working together	The city *council* reacted angrily to the charge that the real estate agent had bribed them.
counsel	(*verb*) to give advice; (*noun*) a legal representative	The mayor tried to *counsel* the members to be quiet, but she was unsuccessful.

(continued)

Words	Definitions	Examples
desert	(*noun*) a dry, arid, sandy place; (*verb*) to abandon	The park was as hot and dry as a *desert*. One by one, the picnickers began to *desert* us and headed straight for the beach.
dessert	the final part of a meal	None of them even bothered with the *dessert* Kathy had made, a delicious blueberry pie.
fewer	refers to items that can be counted	During the last month, I've had *fewer* quizzes in accounting.
less	refers to amounts or quantities that can't be counted	Unfortunately, I've had *less* time to study.
good	used to describe persons, places, things, and ideas	My brother has had *good* results with his used computer.
well	used to specify how something is, was, or would be done	He told me that it has run *well* from the moment he plugged it in.
hear	to listen	I could barely *hear* the music.
here	refers to direction or location	Sit *here*, where the sound is better.
hole	an empty spot	One of the magazines in the collection has a *hole* in the cover.
whole	complete	But I don't think you should throw out the *whole* set.
its	possessive form of *it*	The kitten kept dunking *its* nose in the milk.
it's	contraction for *it is* and *it has*	*It's* funny to see the kitten with a milk mask.
knew	understood [past tense]	The senator *knew* her constituents well.
new	recent, unused, fresh	She felt that it was time for someone *new* to take a turn.
know	to understand [present tense]	You *know* what the problem is.
no	negative, the opposite of *yes*	The problem is that we get *no* direction from Jerry.
now	at this point	The question *now* is what are we going to do about it?
lay	to put down, spread out	Once you *lay* the chair on its side, disconnect the arms.
lie	to rest or recline	Then *lie* down on the floor and find the seam running up the back of the chair.

(continued)

Words	Definitions	Examples
lead	to go first, direct [present tense]	Parents should always *lead* their children by example.
led	went first, directed [past tense]	When they are grown, you'll be glad you *led* them well.
lead	soft metal; graphite [rhymes with *bed*]	The responsibilities of parenthood sometimes feel like a *lead* weight.
loose	not tight, unfastened	*Loose* clothing is better for exercise.
lose	to misplace, fail, not win	If you *lose* the game, don't *lose* your sense of humor.
of	stemming from, connected with or to	Peter is fond *of* late night TV.
off	away from, no longer on	On his day *off*, he sleeps late.
passed	went by [past tense of *pass*]	An ambulance suddenly appeared and *passed* us.
past	time gone by, former time	From *past* experience, I knew that it was heading to Parklane Hospital.
personal	individual, private	The shoplifter had a history of *personal* problems.
personnel	employees, staff	When the security *personnel* took her to the manager's office, she began cursing and kicking.
precede	to come before	One goal of this intervention program is to identify what *precedes* an incident of child abuse.
proceed	to go on	After they study the causes, they *proceed* through the formal process of filing an official complaint.
principal	(*noun*) the head of a school;	In high school, Giselle wanted to get back at the *principal* by ordering ten pizzas in his name.
	(*adjective*) primary, chief	My *principal* objection to this plan was that it was dishonest.
principle	a rule of conduct; a basic truth	One of my *principles* is to be honest.
quiet	still; silent	After Joanie finished yelling, the room was completely *quiet*.
quite	very; completely	Her friends were *quite* surprised that their party had disturbed her.
than	conjunction, used in comparisons	From a distance, people think John is older *than* his older brother Billy.
then	next, at that time	*Then* they take a closer look and see that Billy has wrinkles and gray hair.

(continued)

Words	Definitions	Examples
their	the possessive form of *they*	The reporters were ordered to reveal the names of *their* sources to the judge.
there	refers to direction or location	Immediately, the lawyers who were *there* objected.
they're	contraction for *they are*	The reporters will be going to jail because *they're* not going to follow the judge's orders.
threw	tossed, hurled [past tense]	The supervisor accidentally *threw* out the envelope containing the day's receipts for the store.
through	in one side and out the other, from beginning to end	We had to go *through* twenty bags of trash before we found the envelope.
to	in the direction of, toward	Joe and Marlene stopped at a gas station for directions *to* the hotel.
	also used to form an infinitive	They needed *to* fill the tank anyway.
too	also, excessively	They bought some snacks for the evening, *too*.
two	more than one, less than three	They had stopped just *two* blocks away from the hotel.
waist	middle part of the body	He constantly worries that his *waist* is getting bigger.
waste	use up needlessly; leftover material	If he'd eat less junk food, he wouldn't *waste* so much time worrying.
weak	not strong, feeble	No matter how much I study, my memory still seems *weak*.
week	seven days	Even after a *week* of study, I still don't know those math theorems
weather	atmospheric conditions	The *weather* has been unusually mild.
whether	indicating an alternative or question	Scientists are now trying to determine *whether* these warmer temperatures are due to global warming.
were	past tense plural of *are*	My mother and I *were* hoping to drive to Washington, D.C., in April.
we're	contraction for *we are* or *we were*	*We're* going to go in September instead.
where	indicates or raises a question about direction or location	The neighborhood *where* my uncle lives is near the National Zoo.
who	used as a subject	It took us several minutes to discover *who* had started the fight on the floor.
whom	used as an object	Once we cleared the room, we decided which shoes belonged to *whom*.

(continued)

Words	Definitions	Examples
who's	contraction for *who is* or *who has*	I'm not sure *who's* supposed to drive.
whose	possessive form of *who*	I don't know *whose* car we will use, either.
your	possessive form of *you*	Sometimes knowing all the rules governing *your* job is not enough.
you're	contraction for *you are*	Once *you're* on the job by yourself, rules don't help much.

Exercise 29.7 **Identifying the Correct Word from Pairs of Commonly Confused Words**

In each sentence in the following passage, circle the correct word from the pair in parentheses. Study the example first.

EXAMPLE A job can have a profound (affect, (effect)) on your whole life.

(1) If I had to ((choose,) chose) the strangest experience in my (passed, (past)), it would be the summer I worked third shift at the aluminum barrel factory. (2) When the interviewer asked me if I was willing to work from 11 P.M. ((to,) too) 7 A.M., I thought it was a great idea. (3) I figured I could ((lead,) led) a beachcomber's life by day and (than, (then)) go nightclubbing with my friends before my shift started. (4) My brother tried to tell me that the job would be (know, (no)) picnic, but I ignored him and took it. (5) After the first two days, I realized that I had planned on everything (accept, (except)) sleep. (6) Instead of going to the beach when I came home from work, I'd wash up and (than, (then)) crawl into bed. (7) I always had a tough time drifting (of, (off)) to sleep because there was no ((quiet), quite) around my house during the day. (8) I could ((hear,) here) every laugh and conversation and was aware of the beautiful summer ((weather,) whether) slipping by. (9) (Their, (There)) were few days when I could wake up in time to go to the beach. (10) My ((principal,) principle) goal became making it through each

week. (11) (Its, (It's)) no exaggeration to say that was the worst summer I ever

suffered (threw, (through)).

| Exercise 29.8 | **Identifying Errors with Commonly Confused Words** |

Each sentence in the following paragraph contains an error with one of the words from the list of commonly confused words. Cross out the incorrect words and write the correct ones above them, as the example shows.

| EXAMPLE |

principal
His ~~principle~~ objection to the job offer was that it involved a two-hour-a-day commute.

(1) I suffered my first serious injury a month ago when I stepped in a
hole
~~whole~~ in the sidewalk. (2) From the moment my right foot touched the edge
knew
of the broken sidewalk, I somehow ~~new~~ I was about to hurt myself. (3) I even
already
tried to shift the weight from that foot, but unfortunately I was ~~all ready~~ in the

middle of my stride. (4) As I came down on the side of my foot with all my
hear
weight, I could almost ~~here~~ the tissue tearing. (5) The pain was overpowering,
conscious   Then
and I had to sit down in order to remain ~~conscience~~. (6) ~~Than~~ I took a look

at my ankle and became sick to my stomach. (7) It was swollen to at least
its
three times ~~it's~~ normal size. (8) In addition, my entire right leg felt as heavy as
lead   there
a bar of ~~led~~. (9) Fortunately, ~~their~~ was a pay phone about five steps away, so I

called my brother for a ride to the hospital. (10) The doctor said it is gener-
break
ally better to ~~brake~~ an ankle than to tear several ligaments as I had.

| Challenge 29.2 | **Using Commonly Confused Words Correctly** |

1. The sentences in Exercise 29.8 contain ten incorrectly used words. Take each of these incorrectly used words and write a sentence in which you use the word correctly.

2. Exchange the sentences you have written with a writing partner. In the sentences you receive, make sure that the words are now used correctly. Note any problem spots and return the sentences to the writer.

Fast Fact Dyslexia is a condition that causes those affected to see some letters reversed, making reading and writing difficult. This disorder is less common among those speaking languages such as Italian, which look like they sound, than those speaking English, which so often doesn't sound like it looks.

Learning the Most Commonly Misspelled Words

Audio 29.4

Video 29.5

Encourage students to write a sentence for every word they include in their personal spelling dictionary.

In addition to remembering the various spelling rules and their exceptions, you should also keep your own personal spelling dictionary. Make a list, *in alphabetical order,* of words you misspell in your day-to-day writing. Keep this list with your dictionary for handy reference when you write.

A computer file is the best place to maintain your list. You can easily insert new words in alphabetical order and print out a new copy. If you handwrite your list, leave two or three lines between words. When you discover a misspelled word in one of your papers, add it on an extra line.

Look through the list of commonly misspelled words below and mark the ones that you misspell. Use these words to start your personal spelling dictionary.

Weblink 29.3

Commonly Misspelled Words

A

absence	acquired	all right	answer	assented
academic	acre	although	antarctic	association
acceptance	across	aluminum	anxious	athlete
accident	actual	always	apologize	attacked
accidentally	actually	amateur	apparatus	attempt
accommodate	address	among	apparent	attendance
accompany	administration	amount	appreciate	attorney
accomplish	advertise	analysis	approach	authority
accumulate	again	analyze	approval	auxiliary
accurate	agreeable	angel	argument	available
accustom	aisle	angle	arrival	awful
ache	alcohol	angry	article	awkward
achieve	a lot	anonymous	ascended	
acquaintance				

B

bachelor	bathe	believe	boundaries	bureau
balance	beautiful	benefit	breath	bury
bargain	because	biscuits	breathe	business
basically	beginning	bookkeeping	brilliant	
bath	belief	bottom	Britain	

C

cafeteria	careful	ceiling	change	children
calendar	careless	cemetery	characteristic	church
campaign	catastrophe	cereal	cheap	cigarette
cannot	category	certain	chief	circuit

(continued)

C (continued)

cocoa	comedy	comparative	continuous	courteous
collect	comfortable	competent	convenience	courtesy
colonel	commitment	competitive	cooperate	criticize
color	committed	conceivable	cooperation	curriculum
colossal	committee	condition	corporation	
column	company	consistent	correspondence	

D

daily	definitely	diameter	discuss	dominate
daughter	definition	diary	disease	doubt
dealt	dependent	different	disgust	dozen
debt	describe	direction	distance	drowned
deceased	description	disappointment	distinction	duplicate
decision	despair	disastrous	distinguish	
defense	despise	discipline	dominant	

E

earliest	emergency	environment	essential	exhausted
efficiency	emphasis	equip	exaggerated	existence
efficient	emphasize	equipment	excellent	experience
eligible	employee	equipped	excessive	extraordinary
embarrass	envelop	especially	excitable	extremely
embarrassment	envelope			

F

fallacy	February	fiery	fourth	fulfill
familiar	feminine	foreign	freight	further
fascinate	fictitious	forty	frequent	futile
fatigue				

G

garden	genuine	gracious	guarantee	guest
gauge	ghost	grammar	guardian	guidance
general	government	grateful	guess	gymnasium
generally				

H

handicapped	height	humor	hygiene	hypocrite
handkerchief	hoping	humorous	hypocrisy	

I

illiterate	incidentally	inevitable	intelligence	irresistible
imaginative	incredible	infinite	interest	irreverent
immediately	independent	inquiry	interfere	island
immigrant	indictment	instead	interpret	isle
important				

J

jealousy	jewelry	judgment		

K

kitchen	knowledge	knuckles		*(continued)*

L

language	leave	lengthen	library	literature
later	legitimate	lesson	license	livelihood
latter	leisure	letter	lieutenant	lounge
laugh	length	liable	lightning	luxury

M

machinery	mathematics	miniature	missile	mortgage
maintain	measure	minimum	misspell	mountain
maintenance	mechanical	minute	mistake	muscle
marriage	medicine	miscellaneous	moderate	mustache
marry	medieval	mischief	month	mutual
marvelous	merchandise	mischievous	morning	mysterious

N

naturally	necessity	nickel	noticeable	nuisance
necessary	negotiate	niece		

O

obedience	occurrence	omit	opportunity	organization
obstacle	official	opinion	oppose	original
occasion	often	opponent	optimism	ought
occurred				

P

pamphlet	perceive	phase	practically	probably
parallel	percentage	phenomenon	precisely	procedure
paralyze	perform	physical	preferred	professor
parentheses	performance	physician	prejudice	protein
participant	permanent	picnic	preparation	psychology
particularly	permitted	piece	presence	publicity
pastime	perseverance	pleasant	pressure	pursuing
patience	personality	politics	primitive	pursuit
peasant	perspiration	possess	priority	
peculiar	persuade	possibility	privilege	

Q

qualified	quantity	quarter	question	questionnaire
quality				

R

readily	recognize	relevant	renewal	resistance
realize	recommendation	relieve	repeat	responsibility
really	reference	remember	repetition	restaurant
reasonably	referring	remembrance	requirement	rhythm
receipt	regretting	reminisce	reservoir	ridiculous
receive	reign	removal	residence	
recipient				

S

salary	schedule	sensible	severely	sophisticated
sandwich	scissors	separate	similar	sophomore
scenery	secretary	sergeant	solemn	souvenir

(continued)

S *(continued)*

specimen	stomach	stretch	subtle	surprise
statistics	straight	subsidize	sufficient	surprising
statue	strategy	substantial	summarize	susceptible
stature	strength	substitute	superior	suspicion
statute				

T

technique	thorough	tournament	transferring	tremendous
temperament	thoroughly	tragedy	travel	truly
temperature	through	traitor	traveled	Tuesday
tendency	tomorrow	transfer	treasure	typical
theory	tongue			

U

unanimous	urgent	useful	utensil

V

vacancy	valuable	vein	villain	visibility
vacuum	vane	vicinity	violence	visitor
vain	vegetable			

W

warrant	Wednesday	weird	writing	written

Y

yesterday

Z

zealous

Exercise 29.9   **Identifying and Correcting Commonly Misspelled Words**

Each sentence in the following passage contains a misspelled version of a word from the list of commonly misspelled words. Cross out the misspelled word and write the correct version above the incorrect one as the example shows:

EXAMPLE   Their bank ~~balence~~ *balance* had already dropped below $100.

(1) Today, it seems as if there's more and more corruption in the ~~gover-ment~~ *government*. (2) The newspapers are filled with stories of public officials who have shown incredible lapses in ~~judgement~~ *judgment* leading to their arrests. (3) For example, a year ago our own mayor was accused of giving a big contract to one

of his ~~aquaintances.~~ ^{acquaintances} (4) On another ~~occassion,~~ ^{occasion} a state police officer was caught selling drugs he had confiscated. (5) Last ~~Wenesday,~~ ^{Wednesday} a high-ranking official in the Defense Department was accused of demanding kickbacks from the companies that supply military hardware. (6) With the ~~posibility~~ ^{possibility} of being caught so strong, you'd think that public officials would not be tempted. (7) Sometimes, you wonder how much ~~inteligence~~ ^{intelligence} these individuals possess. (8) Personally, I'm ~~discusted~~ ^{disgusted} with the whole situation. (9) I think that public officials convicted of a crime against the people they are representing should ~~definately~~ ^{definitely} be imprisoned. (10) It should be a maximum security prison, too, so they have to face the ~~embarasment~~ ^{embarrassment} of being known as common criminals.

Challenge 29.3 **Developing a Personal Dictionary and Using It to Correct Spelling in Your Writing**

Begin your own personal proofreading dictionary by scanning the list of commonly misspelled words on pages 478–481 and highlighting the ones you have trouble with. Make a separate list of just these words, in alphabetical order. Then review two or three assignments that you have recently written in this or other classes. Proofread for spelling errors, following the spelling guidelines in this chapter. Add any misspelled words you find in these writings to your own personal spelling dictionary.

Chapter Quick Check: Spelling Skills

The following passage contains numerous misspelled words. Using the various rules and examples in the chapter to guide you, find and cross out errors. Write the correct version above the incorrect one, as the example shows:

EXAMPLE The best ~~advise~~ *advice* I've ever heard is to treat everyone the way you want to be treated.

(1) The story of Rubin "Hurricane" Carter is an almost ~~unbeleivable~~ ^{unbelievable} tale of injustice. (2) Carter spent 20 years in a maximum security prison, half of it in solitary confinement, for a triple murder that he hadn't ~~commited.~~ ^{committed} (3) In 1966,

this contender for the ~~middlewieght~~ ^{middleweight} boxing crown was arrested and charged with a triple homicide in Paterson, New Jersey. (4) Despite his unwavering assertion of innocence, Carter was convicted and ~~than~~ ^{then} sentenced to three life terms, just narrowly escaping the electric chair. (5) But by the mid-1970s, the state's two key witnesses against Carter admitted that ~~there~~ ^{their} testimony was false. (6) This fact, along with the publication of Carter's autobiography and the hit song about the case by folk rocker Bob Dylan, enabled the world to ~~here~~ ^{hear} about Carter's situation. (7) Finally, after two retrials, a judge in 1988 declared that Carter's original conviction had been based on shoddy evidence and ~~predjudice~~, ^{prejudice} and Carter once again tasted freedom. (8) ~~Threw~~ ^{Through} the release a few years ago of *Hurricane*, a major motion picture starring Denzel Washington as Carter, another generation learned the story of this sad incident in the American justice system. (9) Now in his mid-sixties, Carter works on the behalf of the wrongfully accused and has ~~travelled~~ ^{traveled} the country lecturing on hope and tolerance. (10) Despite his years of false imprisonment, he refuses to give into anger and bitterness, just as he refused to allow the system to ~~brake~~ ^{break} his spirit.

Activity 29.3

Activity 29.4

Discovering Connections 29.2

1. In Discovering Connections 29.1 on page 461, you completed a prewriting on one of three suggested topics. Now, using this prewriting material as your basis, work your way through the rest of the writing process, and create a draft essay of about 500 words on this subject.
2. Exchange your draft with a partner. Using the material in this chapter to guide you, check the essay you receive for any problems with spelling. Circle any spelling errors, and return the draft to the writer.
3. Revise your essay, correcting the misspelled words your reader has identified.

Summary Exercise: Spelling Skills

Weblink 29.4

The following passage contains numerous misspelled words. Using the various rules and examples in the chapter to guide you, find and cross out errors. Write the correct version above the incorrect one.

(1) Peer pressure is one of the strongest forces people have to face in

their ~~lifes~~ *lives*. (2) Being ~~excepted~~ *accepted* is important to most people. (3) When people

go against peer pressure, though, they can find it a very lonely ~~expereince~~ *experience*.

Weblink
29.5

(4) Many times students ~~missbehave~~ *misbehave* in school because of peer pres-

sure. (5) The influence of this force is particularly ~~noticable~~ *noticeable* in middle and

high school classes. (6) If a group of kids in the hallway is making trouble,

for example, ~~quite~~ *quiet* kids will sometimes join in because they don't want the

other kids to think they are different. (7) By themselves, these quiet kids

would never make any fuss, but if ~~their~~ *there* is a group, peer pressure takes over.

(8) Kids ~~generaly~~ *generally* often have their first experiences with sex, alcohol, or

drugs because of peer pressure. (9) Even though they know they ~~should of~~ *should've OR should have*

refused, some young people have been pressured into doing things they

weren't ready for because, as they say, "everybody else is doing it." (10) If

kids are at a party and someone is drinking or ~~useing~~ *using* drugs, many kids find

it hard to resist trying. (11) They feel that if they don't, the other kids will

think they are ~~wierd~~ *weird* or childish.

Activity
29.1

(12) Peer pressure ~~effects~~ *affects* people after high school, too. (13) For exam-

ple, if people are in class in a college ~~wear~~ *where* hardly anyone asks or answers

questions, they may find themselves acting like their classmates. (14) Most

people don't want to look like a show-off or teacher's pet in front of their

~~freinds~~ *friends*. (15) If most people in a department don't like the boss, the others

may hesitate to ~~volunter~~ *volunteer* for any extra work. (16) With this kind of ~~oc-~~

~~curence~~ *occurrence*, most people will simply go along with the group because they

want to fit in so badly.

Activity
29.2

(17) Although peer pressure is a strong force, it is one that must be ~~resist-~~ *resisted*

~~ted~~. (18) People have to learn to do what is correct for them, even if it means

they won't win everyone's ~~approvel~~ *approval*. (19) When they ~~procede~~ *proceed* in this way, they will find that others respect them for who they are. (20) Once people begin

behaving in a way that is most authentic for them, they won't ~~waist~~ ^{waste} so much

time worrying what others think.

 SPELLING: FOCUSING ON CORRECTNESS

New terms in this chapter	Definitions
● **prefix**	● letter or letters added to the beginning of a word that change its meaning: *un-, dis-, semi-, re-, il-* ***Examples*** **un**able, **il**legible
● **suffix**	● letter or letters added to the end of a word that change its meaning: *-ness, -able, -ous, -ly, -er, -ed, -ing* ***Examples*** sad**ness**, slow**ly**

Spelling Guidelines for Adding Prefixes and Suffixes

(Check the dictionary for exceptions to these general guidelines.)

To add a prefix	prefix + word (no spelling change) dis + approve = **dis**approve

To add *-ly* or *-ness*	word + *-ly* or *-ness* (usually no spelling change)
	   clear + ly = clear**ly**
	
	Change *-y* to *-i* before adding *-ly* or *-ness*
	   silly + ness = sill**iness**

To add *-ed*	Change *-y* to *-i* before adding *-ed* carry + ed = carr**ied**

To add a suffix that begins with a vowel	Drop *-e* at the end of a word before adding suffix
	   cope + ing = co**ping**
	
	Double the final consonant if
	● the word has one syllable
	   stop + ed = stop**ped**
	● the final consonant is preceded by a single vowel
	   hot + est = hot**test**
	● the accent is on the last syllable of a word with two or more syllables
	   admit + ing = admit**ting**

To add a suffix that begins with a consonant	Keep *-e* at the end of a word hope + ful = hope**ful**

Chapter 30

Commas

Getting Started... **Q:** The mark of punctuation that I feel least confident using is the comma. I'm never really sure if I've used enough or too many. How can I make sure I'm using commas only when they are needed?

Audio 30.1 **A:** If you are concerned about comma use, join the crowd. Even experienced writers have difficulties with—and disagreements about—comma use. Commas primarily serve in seven ways in sentences. One way to strengthen your understanding of each of these functions is to write a brief sentence of your own in which commas fulfill that function. List your seven brief sentences on a separate sheet of paper and keep it in your writing notebook or next to your computer for fast reference.

Overview: Understanding Comma Use

ESL Note
See "Punctuation and Capitalization" on pages 583–584.

With speech, you frequently pause within thoughts to emphasize or clarify some point. With writing, you use the same technique. When you want to signal these pauses within a sentence, the mark of punctuation you will use most often is a **comma**. Your reader depends on these pauses to gain the full meaning of what you've written, so mastering the use of commas is important to your success as a writer.

Audio 30.2

In this chapter, you will learn how to use a comma to

- indicate a pause between two clauses connected by a conjunction

- separate items in a series

- indicate a brief break between introductory material and the main part of the sentence

- set off words, phrases, and clauses that interrupt the flow of a sentence

- set off a direct quotation from the rest of a sentence

- set off elements in certain letter parts, dates, addresses, and numerals

- set off nouns of direct address

Discovering Connections 30.1

Discovering Connections 30.2 at the end of this chapter provides an opportunity for students to apply the skills they have learned for using commas correctly. They will be asked to compose and revise an essay based on one of the topics in Discovering Connections 30.1.

Using one of the techniques you practiced in Chapter 2, "Generating Ideas through Prewriting," prewrite on one of the following topics:

1. what personal beauty truly is or should be
2. ways that creativity appears in day-to-day living

Or, focus on this picture.
Save your work for later use.

Using a Comma between Clauses Connected by Conjunctions

Video 30.1

A comma is used to indicate a pause between clauses connected by a conjunction or a pair of conjunctions.

COMPOUND SENTENCE

coordinating conjunction
The movie was good, *but* the book was better.

COMPOUND SENTENCE

correlative conjunction   *correlative conjunction*
Either the wind blew the campfire out, *or* the ranger put it out.

COMPLEX SENTENCE

subordinating conjunction
Even though the office was warm, everyone put in a full day's work.

Weblink 30.1

[*Use a comma when the subordinate clause comes first.*]

Exercise 30.1   **Working with Commas and Conjunctions**

Weblink 30.2

Commas alone cannot separate two simple sentences. Refer to Chapter 20 for more information about comma splices.   **EXAMPLE**

Add a comma, a conjunction, and another clause to complete the following sentences. Review Chapter 19, "Subordination and Coordination," to remember rules for creating complex and compound sentences and to find lists of subordinating and coordinating conjunctions. Use the example to guide you.   Answers will vary. Representative answers are given.

When Jerry misplaced his calculator, he had to buy a new one.

1. Many people do not want to serve as jurors, but

jury duty is part of every citizen's responsibility.

Audio
30.3

2. Serving on a jury can disrupt a person's life , and it may also cause financial hardship.

3. Although some people give pretty lame excuses, prospective jurors are often able to delay serving for a variety of reasons.

4. Being part of the judicial system is interesting , and some people find it an invaluable experience.

5. The juror's day at court starts at 8:30 A.M. , and it may sometimes last until 5:00 P.M.

6. Before the trial can begin, all the jurors are sworn in.

7. Then, the presentations by the lawyers begin , and the jurors usually listen carefully.

8. In my state, most jurors serve for only a day , but some trials take much longer.

9. Jurors may serve for up to a month for trials of capital crimes _____ , so they may be put up in a hotel.

10. Although it is not usually necessary, jurors are sometimes sequestered.

Using Commas to Separate Items in a Series

Commas are used to separate three or more items in a series. When only two items are connected by *and, or,* or *but,* no comma is needed.

| WORDS IN SERIES | Jacqueline spends her summer days *swimming, sailing, sunbathing,* or *sleeping.* |

| PHRASES IN SERIES | *In the fall, in the winter,* and *in the spring,* however, her schoolwork leaves her little time for these activities. |

Fast Fact During the 1980s, the style sheet of a major American corporation instructed its workers not to use the comma before *and* or *or* in a series such as "computers, printers and software," which amounted to one fewer keystroke. When asked for a reason, company officials argued that not including this comma would save time.

Exercise 30.2 **Using Commas in a Series**

Fill in the blanks in the following sentences, supplying the items to complete each series. Place commas where necessary. Use the example as guidance. Answers will vary. Comma placements are shown.

EXAMPLE The _____*city*_____ and _____*county*_____ cooperate on a recycling program that requires people to separate _____*plastic,*_____ _____*paper,*_____ and _____*glass*_____ from the rest of their trash.

(1) I work full-time on the third shift, so my workday begins at 11 P.M., when other people are _____ or _____. (2) The plant where I work makes plastic items such as _____, _____ and _____. (3) The machines I work with generate a great deal of _____ and _____, so I dress lightly and wear ear plugs. (4) In addition to running my machines, I supervise two other workers to make sure they _____ and _____. (5) The factory has a series of small windows near the ceiling, and if I look up from my machine, I can see _____, _____ and _____. (6) After three hours, I take my first break, during which I _____, _____ or _____. (7) When my break is over, I _____ and _____. (8) Before I know it, it's supper time, so I _____, _____ or _____. (9) During the rest of the shift, I have time to complete my paperwork, including _____ and _____. (10) At 7 A.M., I head home to bed

while everybody else is _____, _____, or

_____.

Using a Comma to Set Off Introductory Material

Audio
30.4

Often the main portion of a sentence is introduced by a word, phrase, or clause that indicates a time, place, or condition. If this introductory material consists of *four or more words* or contains a *verbal*, separate it from the rest of the sentence by a comma. (See page 277 for a discussion of verbals.)

EXAMPLE   *Within the pile of shredded paper,* the mouse nursed three babies.

EXAMPLE   *Yelling and splashing frantically,* Courtney drifted away from shore.

Ask students how the meaning of the sentence would be less clear if the comma after *Soon after* were omitted.

Occasionally, you will use a word or brief phrase to introduce a sentence. Use a comma to set off such an introductory element if it helps to emphasize or clarify the main point of the sentence.

EXAMPLE   *In fact,* the substitute teacher had never even been in the school before.

EXAMPLE   *Soon after,* the meeting was interrupted by strange noises.

Exercise 30.3   **Using Commas after Introductory Phrases and Clauses**

If the introductory phrase in each of the sentences in the following paragraph needs a comma, insert it. If a comma appears where it is not necessary, cross it out. Use the example to direct you.

EXAMPLE   At the major intersection near the entrance of the school, an accident was slowing/down traffic.

(1) After hatching on Florida beaches and crawling off into the surf, tiny loggerhead turtle hatchlings begin a journey that will take them across the Atlantic Ocean and back again. (2) Over, a period of several years, the baby loggerheads will travel thousands of miles as they swim and ride the warm currents of the Atlantic, feeding and growing. (3) For a number of years, no

one has been sure of exactly how they managed to navigate such an enormous trip while avoiding the colder waters that would kill them. (4) However, a recent study suggests that the answer lies in the innate ability of these creatures to react to natural magnetic fields marking a section of the ocean waters. (5) Called the Atlantic Gyre, this area is an oceanwide current of warm water that moves in a clockwise fashion, eastward across the Atlantic, along the coasts of Spain and Africa, and back westward to the east coast of the United States. (6) The turtles, apparently, follow a series of magnetic markers that keep them within the warmer waters that they need to survive. (7) For the study, that led to these findings, loggerhead hatchlings were placed in a specially designed saltwater tank. (8) To simulate particular magnetic fields, researchers equipped the tank with special copper coils. (9) Then, they outfitted the turtles with a device that would record the direction that the hatchlings were swimming. (10) As the scientists changed magnetic fields, the baby turtles responded by swimming in a direction that would keep them within the safe warm-water zone in the open ocean.

Using Commas to Set off Elements That Interrupt Sentence Flow

 Audio
30.5

Sometimes you use commas within a sentence to surround a word, phrase, or clause that interrupts the flow of the sentence. For instance, when a word adds emphasis, provides transition, or renames or illustrates another word in the sentence, use commas to set it off:

EXAMPLE   Our next car, *however,* ran like a top.

EXAMPLE   The crow, *for example,* is a highly intelligent bird.

EXAMPLE   We had skybox seats, *the best in the stadium,* for the game.

Also use commas to set off *nonrestrictive elements*, clauses or phrases that could be left out of the sentence without changing its basic meaning. Nonrestrictive clauses and phrases add extra but nonessential information:

EXAMPLE

nonrestrictive clause

This year's spring weather on Cape Cod, *which is usually calm and warm*, was cool and blustery.

If you were to leave *which is usually calm and warm* out of the sentence, the reader would still understand the main point. The clause is *nonrestrictive*.

Some clauses and phrases are *restrictive*, meaning that your reader needs them to identify or restrict the meaning of the word they modify. Therefore, you don't set them off with commas, as this example shows:

EXAMPLE

nonrestrictive clause

All students *driving vehicles with handicapped plates* may park in the first row of Parking Lot C.

Leave the italicized phrase out of this sentence, and you send the wrong message. Without these words, the sentence says that *all* students may park in a lot that is actually reserved for disabled students only. Therefore, *driving vehicles with handicapped plates* is restrictive, and no commas are used.

Exercise 30.4 **Using Commas around Elements That Interrupt Sentence Flow**

Read the sentences in the following paragraph. If a comma is needed in a sentence, write it in the blanks provided. If no comma is needed, put an **X** in the blank. Study the example first.

EXAMPLE

My asthma __,__ which usually doesn't cause me much trouble__,__ has been flaring up recently.

(1) Sometimes parents __X__ who are old enough to know better __X__ can go overboard in protecting their children. (2) A newspaper article about two children __,__ which I read in the dentist's office __,__ tells an incredible story about parental overprotection. (3) The mother of a three-year-old daughter __,__ according to the story __,__ obtained a restraining order to keep a three-year-old boy away from her child. (4) She said that her daughter __,__ who attends preschool with the boy __,__ is afraid to play in the park because of the boy's aggression. (5) Why didn't the judge __,__ who should temper justice with common sense __,__ tell the parents to straighten out the

difficulties between their children by themselves? (6) I wonder whether that

little girl _,_ with a mother like hers _,_ will ever learn to solve problems

on her own.

Exercise 30.5   **Considering Comma Use with Elements That Interrupt Sentence Flow**

In the following sentences, insert commas where you think they are needed
to set off words from the rest of the sentence. Put *OK* above any sentence
that doesn't require additional commas. Use the example as a guide.

EXAMPLE   Joie began singing lessons with her neighbor, a former professional, only to

discover that she really didn't enjoy studying voice.

(1) Although some people believe otherwise, I don't believe that *fate*, a

predetermined path that people are forced to follow, controls people's lives.
(2) I believe that all people, regardless of their stature in the world, have free

will and are not simply stepping in footsteps that some universal power has

placed there for them. (3) Consider, for example, the careers people pursue
                                        OK

or the individuals they associate with. (4) As I see it, people make specific

choices in terms of what they will do with their lives and who their friends

will be. (5) Although their personal skills, abilities, and interests will help to

shape their choices, the people themselves, not some universal force, will

make the final decision. (6) Rather than being born to become something,

people become successful in a field, which could be anything from teach-

ing to computers to medicine, by adapting their gifts and talents to suit it.
(7) With personal relationships, especially with the people we marry or live

with, destiny plays no role. (8) For example, the idea that everyone has a

predetermined soul mate, a person waiting to share another's every idea

and dream, just isn't realistic. (9) If fate determines our lives, then that

means that horrible tragedies, events that cause enormous pain, happen by

design. (10) I know that such terrible things do occur, but I refuse to believe that some all-powerful force, which can see and control everything that hap-

pens, would make people endure such sorrow on purpose.

Using Commas to Set Off Direct Quotations

Audio
30.6

Refer students to Chapter 31 for guidelines about using quotation marks.

Point out to students that periods and commas are placed inside closing quotation marks.

As a writer, you will sometimes want to *quote*, to write down word for word what other people say. When you do so, you let your reader know that the words are a *direct quote* by enclosing the passage in quotation marks (" "). (See Chapter 4, "Refining and Polishing Your Draft," for a discussion of the inclusion of direct quotations in a paper.) You then use a comma to set the direct quote off from the *attribution,* the part that identifies the speaker.

Note the placement of the comma in these three formats incorporating a direct quotation.

1. When the quote is at the beginning of a sentence, insert a comma within the closing quotation mark:

EXAMPLE

"My wallet—it's not in my pocketbook," Katlyn said, with an edge of panic in her voice.

2. When the quote is at the end of a sentence, place a comma before the opening quotation mark:

EXAMPLE

She said quietly, *"I can't find it anywhere."*

3. When the quote is interrupted in the middle by the attribution, insert a comma within the closing quotation mark of the first portion and a second before the opening quotation mark of the second portion:

EXAMPLE

"And I'm sure I had it," she cried, *"when we left the mall."*

Recognizing Other Situations in Which Commas Are Needed

Audio
30.7

In addition to these uses of commas, remember to use a comma

- to set off the salutation of a personal letter (not a business letter): *Dear Monique,*
- to set off the parts of dates from the rest of the sentence: *August 25, 2002,* was a crucial day for my family.
- to set off parts of addresses in a sentence: His last permanent address was *756 Craft Street, Tampa, FL 34268.*
- to indicate thousands within numbers: *9,870* or *9,000,000*
- to set off a name when you address someone directly: I'm telling you, *John,* that you need to save for retirement.

Fast Fact The comma may be the hardest working of the marks of punctuation, but at least the U.S. Postal Service has tried to give it a little rest. In order to make it easier for their Optical Character Recognition (OCR) system to sort mail, postal officials have suggested that all punctuation be omitted in addresses on envelopes. This step eliminates the comma that customarily appears between city and state. It's actually a good thing that the Postal Service made the request because computer databases create the labeling for much bulk mail, and in some computer language systems, commas have a meaning entirely different from the pause humans intend. These databases use commas as a *delimiter*—a sign that tells the computer to leave a space or start a new document or some other command—making it an addressing no-no.

Exercise 30.6   **Using Commas with Quotation Marks**

In the following paragraph, underline each attribution, and insert commas and quotation marks where needed to separate the attribution from the exact words of the speaker.

EXAMPLE   Then the <u>announcer</u> said, "I'm afraid I have some bad news to report."

(1) "Things aren't the way they used to be," my <u>Great-Aunt Mil</u> complained the other day. (2) <u>She</u> said, "I don't mean to complain, but you young people don't seem to have done much to make this world a better place." (3) "When I was young," <u>she</u> continued, "my generation worked to improve things around us." (4) <u>She</u> stopped for a minute, shook her head, and said, "Maybe I'm not being fair. (5) <u>Aunt Mil</u> then asked me outright, "What do you think of your generation?"

(6) When I could see that her concern was genuine, <u>I</u> smiled at her and answered, "Well, I think my generation is doing all right." (7) <u>I</u> paused for a minute to think and said, "People my age *do* care about the world around them." (8) <u>Aunt Mil</u> seemed unconvinced, so I asked, "What about the park clean-up program, the recycling drive, and the March for Justice, all sponsored by high-school and college students?" (9) As she nodded in agreement, <u>I</u> added, "Of course, I think your generation did much more, with your dedication to Civil Rights and work to eliminate poverty." (10) She smiled, and <u>I</u> added, "We will just have to try harder to emulate your generation."

Exercise 30.7   **Using Commas**

Ask students why using commas correctly is important in this letter.

Help this job applicant make a positive impression with this cover letter. Proofread and insert commas where they are needed. If a numbered item needs no commas, write *OK* above it.

325 Whipple Street
East Franklin, MA 02652
December 1, 2002

Ms. Mary Hayes
Director of Personnel
East Franklin Y.M.C.A.
49 Richmond Street
East Franklin, MA 02650

Dear Ms. Hayes:

(1) I am writing to apply for the part-time position as Assistant to the Director of Youth Services‸ which you have advertised in the *East Franklin Gazette*. (2) Having spent the past three summers as a youth counselor in the "Kids at Work" summer job program here in Taunton‸ I have the experience‸ enthusiasm‸ and qualifications your position requires.

Weblink
30.3

(3) I have just completed my first year at Bristol Community College‸ where I am majoring in criminal justice. (4) After I receive my degree‸ I plan to work full time with young people‸ either through a social agency or the State Police Outreach Center.

(5) As a counselor for "Kids at Work"‸ I was in charge of twenty teenagers between the ages of fourteen and eighteen. (6) In fact‸ this position called for both responsibility and leadership. (7) During my first two summers on the job‸ for example‸ I arranged work schedules‸ supervised work activities‸ and taught a job skills seminar. (8) The seminar was so successful that my director made it a permanent part of the summer program. (9) For the past two summers‸ I've also served as senior counselor‸ which means I was in charge of training all new counselors.

Weblink
30.4

(10) All in all, my experiences have prepared me well for the position of Assistant to the Director of Youth Services, and I look forward to meeting with you to discuss my qualifications in greater detail. (11) Please schedule me for an interview at your convenience. (12) Thank you.

OK

OK

(13) Sincerely,

Cosette J. Valjean

Cosette J. Valjean

Challenge 30.1 **Analyzing Comma Functions in Literature**

Read the following passage from Harper Lee's Pulitzer prize–winning novel *To Kill a Mockingbird.* In this passage, narrator Jean Louise Finch discusses the town's Halloween celebration.

Notice the various ways Lee has used commas in the passage. After you have finished reading the paragraph, discuss with a partner what function each of the commas serves. In the first sentence, for instance, the two commas set off a word that interrupts the flow of the sentence.

Activity
30.1

I soon learned, however, that my services would be required on stage that evening. Mrs. Grace Merriweather had composed an original pageant entitled *Maycomb County: Ad Astra Per Aspera,* and I was to be a ham. She thought it would be adorable if some of the children were costumed to represent the county's agricultural products: . . . Agnes Boone would make a lovely butterbean, another child would be a peanut, and on down the line, until Mrs. Merriweather's imagination and the supply of children were exhausted.

Our only duties, as far as I could gather from our two rehearsals, were to enter from stage left as Mrs. Merriweather (not only the author, but the narrator) identified us. When she called out, "Pork," that was my cue. Then the assembled company would sing, "Maycomb County, Maycomb County, we will aye be true to thee," as the grand finale, and Mrs. Merriweather would mount the stage with the state flag.

Chapter Quick Check: Comma Use

Add commas where they are needed in the sentences below. Review the functions of commas to help you as you proofread. Use the example to guide you.

EXAMPLE The open house at the hospital, sponsored by the new physical therapy center will begin at 9 A.M. on Saturday November 24.

(1) If it's true that we tend to overlook the value of things that are right in front of us then there is no better illustration than our lack of attention to estuaries. (2) An estuary is a partially enclosed wetland area where fresh water from rivers streams and other tributaries flows into the ocean, mixing fresh and salt water. (3) Here in the United States San Francisco Bay, Boston Harbor, Tampa Bay, and the Puget Sound are all examples of estuarine areas. (4) No one would argue that estuaries are beautiful areas noted for appealing to tourists as well as homeowners but they serve an even more vital role in terms of the environment. (5) As water flows through an estuary for example the marsh filters out pollutants and sediments, leaving the fresh and salt water cleaner. (6) In addition, the marsh land and various plants help to soak up and divert flood waters prevent erosion and protect property along the shore from damage. (7) Most important of all estuaries provide the perfect habitat for an enormous range of sea life, including migratory birds aquatic plants, crabs, lobsters shellfish, and reptiles. (8) Estuaries are generally protected from tides and ocean waves by sandbars, barrier islands, or reefs so they are ideal areas for reproduction. (9) In fact, some 75 percent of the commercial fish catch of the continental United States which is worth some $2 billion are dependent on estuaries. (10) When this fragile ecosystem is destroyed by filling or dredging the results can include such severe consequences as widespread fish kills and unsafe drinking water.

Discovering Connections 30.2

1. In Discovering Connections 30.1 on page 487, you completed a prewriting on one of three suggested topics. Now work your way through the rest of the writing process, using this material as a basis, and produce a draft of about 500 words on this topic.

2. Exchange your draft with a partner. Using the material in this chapter to guide you, check the draft you receive for any errors in the use of commas. After checking the paper, return it to the writer.
3. Revise your essay, correcting any errors in comma use identified by your reader.

Summary Exercise: Comma Use

Activity 30.2 Add commas where they are needed in the sentences below. Review the functions of commas to help you as you proofread.

(1) From what I have observed, most people spend too much time chasing after the wrong things in life. (2) The things that are truly valuable, such as good health, love, friendship, family, and spirituality, are right there in front of us. (3) Unfortunately, most of us don't see the obvious.

Activity 30.3 (4) Instead of noticing these marvelous gifts, we tend to concentrate on other aspects of life. (5) Some of us focus on such pursuits as making money, buying fancy cars or clothes, and gaining status. (6) In so many cases, people spend their whole lives driving themselves toward these goals.

(7) However, when they near the end of their lives, people sometimes begin to realize that material possessions are not fulfilling. (8) They've had the fancy cars, for instance, or the beautiful homes. (9) What they discover, though, is that they still feel empty. (10) When they realize how unfulfilled they are, they focus on the truly important things. (11) After years of ignoring their families, for example, they may desperately try to make up for lost time. (12) If they are lucky, they can still rebuild those bridges.

(13) In many cases, however, people don't have enough time left to attend to everything they've ignored. (14) If they haven't maintained their health, for instance, they may be saddled in old age with problems like ulcers, diabetes, heart disease, or cancer. (15) If they had acted earlier, perhaps they could

have avoided or at least controlled these conditions. (16) Now, after years of ignoring warning signs, they often must face permanent consequences.

Activity 30.4

(17) The answer, of course, is to reassess what we value most right now. (18) After all, at the end of life, nobody says, "I wish I had devoted more time to work." (19) The truly important things, the ones on which we should focus, are in front of us at all times. (20) Whenever I hear someone say, "The best things in life are free," I just nod my head and smile.

RECAP COMMAS

New term in this chapter	Definition
● comma	● a punctuation mark that indicates a pause within a sentence

Comma Functions

● To indicate a pause between two clauses connected by a conjunction

   Example   She picked up the pen, but then she put it down again.

● To separate items in a series

   Example   Accounting, marketing, and management are all areas that interest me.

● To separate an introductory phrase of four or more words from the rest of the sentence

   Example   Until the end of the race, I'll keep my fingers crossed.

● To set off words, phrases, or clauses that interrupt the flow of a sentence

   Example   The people in the front of the line, those who had camped out all night on the sidewalk, bought the first tickets.

● To set a direct quotation off from the rest of a sentence

   Example   "This course has been wonderful," said Lee-Ann.

● To set off the salutation in a personal letter

   Example   Dear Latisha,

● To set off parts of dates and addresses and names of direct address

   Example   Will you join us, Tim, on July 14, 2002, at Flying Y Ranch, Casper, Wyoming?

● To indicate thousands within numbers

   Example   6,950 or 1,000,000

Chapter 31

Other Punctuation and Capitalization

Getting Started... **Q:** Sometimes I feel so frustrated when I have to choose the proper mark of punctuation or decide which words to capitalize. It all seems overwhelming. What can I do to help keep all this information straight?

Audio
31.1

A: True, when it comes to punctuation and capitalization, there is a good deal to remember. The good news is that the various marks of punctuation are distinct from each other, so knowing which to choose is easier than you might think. The same is true for capitalization. Whether a word should be capitalized or not depends on where the word appears in a sentence and what class of word—proper or common—it is.

Overview: Maintaining Correctness and Clarifying Meaning through Punctuation and Capitalization

ESL Note
See "Punctuation and Capitalization" on pages 583–584.

Audio
31.2

When people use the expression "nuts and bolts," they generally mean the various bits and pieces that hold things together. In writing, think of *punctuation* and *capitalization* as the nuts and bolts, the elements that hold writing together. **Punctuation** involves the use of the various symbols that guide your reader through your writing. **Capitalization** involves the use of an uppercase letter at the beginning of a word to make it stand out or clarify its meaning. Like the nuts and bolts that hold the massive girders of a bridge together, these elements of writing play a vital role in communicating your ideas to your reader. Therefore, it's important that you master their usage.

> *In this chapter, you will learn how to use*
>
> - periods, question marks, and exclamation points to indicate the end of a sentence
>
> - quotation marks to indicate a person's exact words
>
> - apostrophes to indicate ownership or to take the place of letters left out when contractions are formed
>
> - colons to signal important information

- semicolons to emphasize a connection between independent clauses

- parentheses and dashes to signal additional information

- capitalization to emphasize words

Discovering Connections 31.1

Weblink
31.1

Discovering Connections 31.2 provides an opportunity for students to apply the skills they have learned about punctuating and capitalizing correctly. They will be asked to compose and revise an essay based on one of the topics discussed here.

Using one of the techniques you practiced in Chapter 2, "Generating Ideas through Prewriting," prewrite on one of the following topics:

1. what makes a movie, play, concert, computer game, or television show good
2. the conditions that might make someone engage in domestic or international terrorism

Or, focus on this picture.
Save your work for later use.

Fast Fact As he did about many things, Ernest Hemingway, a true giant in the world of writing, had some pretty strong feelings about the use of punctuation: "My attitude toward punctuation is that it ought to be as conventional as *possible.* The game of golf would lose a good deal if croquet mallets and billiard cues were allowed on the putting green. You ought to be able to show that you can do it a good deal better than anyone else with the regular tools before you have a license to bring in your own improvements."

Using Periods, Question Marks, and Exclamation Points

Audio
31.3

To indicate the end of a sentence, use one of three marks of end punctuation. Use a **period** to indicate a stop at the end of a sentence that makes a statement:

EXAMPLE   The old man sitting under the tree is my uncle**.**

Use a **question mark** when a sentence expresses a question directly:

EXAMPLE   Where did you park the car**?**

Use an **exclamation point** when a sentence expresses strong excitement or emotion:

EXAMPLE   Watch out for that hot pipe**!**

Video
31.1

Be careful not to overuse exclamation points. Use them only when you need to demonstrate profound excitement or emotion, not merely to spice up your writing.

Exercise 31.1   **Selecting the Correct End Punctuation**

Weblink
31.2

The sentences in the following passage all lack end punctuation. In the space provided, write the correct mark of end punctuation for each sentence, as the example shows.

EXAMPLE   The technician reported that the computer system wouldn't be repaired

for two weeks __.__

(1) Giant dinosaurs may have ruled the earth 100 million years ago, but a recent discovery indicates that even the giants among these giants may have had something to fear __.__ (2) According to paleontologists, that something was Sarcosuchus imperator, a cousin of the modern-day crocodile that was 40 feet long and weighted a whopping 10 tons __! OR .__ (3) The first evidence of this massive creature, a six foot skull, was found in a desert area of Niger, West Africa, in 1964 by a team of French scientists __.__ (4) Subsequent digs in 1997 and 2000 yielded additional skulls and enough other fossilized remains to create a skeleton that is nearly 50 percent complete __.__ (5) How fearsome was Sarcosuchus __?__ (6) For one thing, its jaws contained more than 100 teeth, including large numbers that could tear flesh and crush bone. (7) This mighty predator had other adaptations that made it especially suited for its life as a river dweller __.__ (8) For instance, it had a huge bulbous growth at the end of its snout, which experts believe enhanced its ability to breathe and smell, and its eyes tilted upwards __.__ (9) As this huge crocodile quietly lurked beneath the surface, almost completely hidden, even the largest dinosaurs of its time would easily be fast food __.__ (10) Imagine what a good Hollywood director could do with that lunchtime scene __! OR .__

Using Quotation Marks

Audio
31.4

When you record a person's words exactly as they were said, the resulting material is called a **direct quotation**. Direct quotations must be enclosed in **quotation marks**:

EXAMPLE   The smiling clerk said, "Thank you. Come again."

Notice that the first word of a direct quotation is capitalized and that the end punctuation is placed within the closing quotation mark. Notice also that a comma sets the direct quotation off from the *attribution,* the words that identify the speaker.

You can also place the direct quotation before the attribution:

EXAMPLE   "Thank you. Come again," the smiling clerk said.

Weblink
31.3
Notice that a comma is still needed to separate the direct quotation from the attribution. In this case, the comma is placed *within* the closing quotation mark. Punctuation of direct quotations is discussed further in Chapter 30, "Commas." In writing, an exchange of direct quotations between two speakers is called a **dialogue**. Start a new paragraph each time you switch speakers so that readers can keep track of who is talking.

EXAMPLE   "Marguerite, you know I can't stand the smell of tuna fish," said Brian. "But you know it's my favorite food. How could I give it up?" she replied.

Weblink
31.4
When you restate or explain what someone has said, the resulting expression is called an **indirect quotation**. No quotation marks are needed because indirect quotations do not represent a person's exact words.

EXAMPLE   Then the clerk behind the counter thanked us and said that she hoped we'd come again.

EXAMPLE   The company president said that profits for the third quarter were far lower than she had anticipated.

Quotation marks are also used to set off titles of short documents such as magazine or newspaper articles, book chapters, songs, short stories, and poems:

EXAMPLE   Leon read the fourth chapter, "Your Child's Brain," aloud to Joyce.

EXAMPLE   Listening to "Unchained Melody" always makes me cry.

Exercise 31.2   **Distinguishing between Direct and Indirect Quotations**

Some of the sentences below contain indirect quotations, and others contain direct quotations. Insert quotation marks in the space above the direct quotations, as the example shows.

EXAMPLE   "
Please check to make sure that you've locked the door, my grandmother "
^said as we left her apartment.   ^

(1) "The secret to success in life is self-confidence," said the speaker at the motivational seminar I attended recently. (2) As I sat in the audience, I asked myself if I had the kind of self-confidence she described. (3) I thought of how often my best friend had told me that I should believe in myself as much as others do. (4) The last time he said this, I finally said, "I think you're wrong. (5) I said, "Real confidence isn't necessarily what people see on the surface. (6) He told me he agreed, but he still felt that I didn't see myself in the positive way that others saw me. (7) The speaker at the seminar emphasized this same point when she said, "It's all a matter of recognizing your strengths and weaknesses. (8) She added, "Once you can do that, you can overcome your fears. (9) After the presentation I went up to the podium and told her she had helped me change my view of myself. (10) "My friend has told me the same thing," I said, "and hearing what you had to say made me realize how correct he was."

| Exercise 31.3 | **Converting and Punctuating Direct and Indirect Quotations** |

Weblink
31.5

Some of the sentences below contain indirect quotations, and others contain direct quotations. On a separate sheet of paper, rewrite each indirect quotation as a direct quotation, and rewrite each direct quotation as an indirect quotation. Use the examples to guide you.

EXAMPLE

Lauren explained that she found the hours too long and the work too confusing.

"I just find the hours too long and the work too confusing," Lauren explained. [Indirect to direct]

EXAMPLE

"I don't know why, but I love broccoli," said Peter.

Peter said that he doesn't know why, but he loves broccoli. [Direct to indirect]

Activity
31.1

(1) When I walked into the emergency room on the day I cut my head while running, the attendant behind the counter asked me to explain what had happened. (2) I felt myself blush as I said, "I ran into the side of a building." (3) He looked up from the desk and asked me to repeat what I had

said. (4) I told him again that I had run into a building. (5) "How could that happen?" he asked. (6) "A piece of the building was jutting out, and I didn't see it," I explained. (7) "Are you kidding me?" he asked, beginning to laugh. (8) I told him that I was serious and that I'd appreciate it if he would lower his voice. (9) "I'm sorry," he said, as he tried to stop laughing. (10) When he finally asked a doctor to examine me, he graciously refrained from laughing as he told her why I needed help.

Challenge 31.1   **Writing Dialogue**

After you have completed Exercise 31.3, use a separate sheet of paper to rewrite the exchange between the runner and the hospital attendant in dialogue form. Make all sentences direct quotations, and remember to begin a new paragraph every time the speaker changes. Exchange your work with a partner. On the paper you receive, circle any errors you find in the use of end punctuation or quotation marks. Return the paper to the writer. Correct any errors that your partner circled in your paper.

Using Apostrophes

Audio
31.5

Writers use **apostrophes** (') to show possession and form contractions. Make singular nouns possessive by adding an apostrophe and *-s*, even if the noun ends in *-s:*

EXAMPLES   artist**'s** easel; girl**'s** wallet; business**'s** assets

Video
31.2

If the possessive form sounds awkward to you, change it to a prepositional phrase. Rather than writing *Jonas's response,* write *the response of Jonas.*
    Make most plural nouns possessive by adding only an apostrophe:

EXAMPLES   artist**s'** easels; girl**s'** wallets; leopard**s'** spots

Direct students to Chapters 25 and 29 for information about making singular nouns plural.

For plural words that *don't* end in *-s,* form the plural by adding an apostrophe and *-s:*

EXAMPLES   men**'s** shirts; people**'s** attitudes; children**'s** toys

Pronouns such as *your* and *its* are already possessive, so they don't require an apostrophe. To make indefinite pronouns—such as *anybody, everybody, anyone, everyone,* and *nobody*—possessive, add an apostrophe and an *-s:*

EXAMPLES   everyone**'s** fault; anybody**'s** attention

Weblink
31.6

To make compound subjects possessive, determine whether you are discussing one item that is possessed jointly or separate items owned by each subject. If the subjects jointly possess something, put an apostrophe and an

-s after the last subject. If each subject possesses his or her own item, then add an apostrophe and an -s to each subject:

EXAMPLE | Lenny and Lila**'s** house   [*One item jointly owned*]

EXAMPLE | Lenny**'s** and Lila**'s** paychecks   [*Two items separately owned*]

For compound words like *maid of honor* and *father-in-law,* form the possessive by adding an apostrophe and an -s to the end of the word. Do the same for names of businesses and corporations that are compound:

EXAMPLES | brother-in-law**'s** car; Lord & Taylor**'s** sale

Apostrophes are also used to form contractions, words that you create by combining two words. The apostrophe takes the place of the letters left out when the words are combined.

Here is a list of common contractions:

Common Contractions

are**n't** are not	he**'s** he is, he has	should**'ve** should have
ca**n't** cannot	I**'d** I would	that**'s** that is
could**n't** could not	I**'ll** I will	they**'ll** they will
did**n't** did not	I**'m** I am	they**'re** they are
does**n't** does not	is**n't** is not	who**'s** who is, who has
do**n't** do not	it**'ll** it will	wo**n't** will not
had**n't** had not	it**'s** it is, it has	you**'d** you would
has**n't** has not	she**'d** she would	you**'ll** you will
have**n't** have not	she**'ll** she will	you**'re** you are
he**'d** he would	she**'s** she is, she has	
he**'ll** he will	should**n't** should not	

Notice that the letters in a contraction follow the same order as they do in the original two words. The exception is *won't,* the contraction for *will not.*

When you write, be sure to distinguish between *it's,* the contraction for *it is* and *it has,* and *its,* the possessive pronoun, which requires no apostrophe.

Exercise 31.4   **Using Apostrophes**

Each sentence below contains a number of italicized words. Some need an apostrophe to show possession; others can be combined into contractions. Write the appropriate contraction or possessive form above each italicized section, as the example illustrates.

EXAMPLE | *We'll*   *Franny's*
We will reach *Frannys* house in about twenty-five minutes.

               It's   hasn't

(1) *It is* hard to believe that the local commuter rail station *has not*

                       Didn't   mayor's

been replaced yet. (2) *Did not* the *mayors* task force recommend five years

                                           I'm

ago that the station be knocked down and rebuilt? (3) *I am* surprised that the

            commissioner's

public safety *commissioners* office has not condemned the structure. (4) After

                                            haven't

all, the building and the parking lot look as if they *have not* been maintained

                     that's   aren't

for ten years, and *that is* a shame. (5) The other stations along the line *are not*

           they're   hasn't

any older, and *they are* regularly cleaned and painted. (6) Why *has not* the

                     Troy's

same attention been given to *Troys* station? (7) Certainly the number of peo-

                    system's   hasn't

ple using the commuter rail *systems* Fast Trax trains from this station *has not*

                it's

lessened. (8) In fact, *it is* just the opposite, with 10 percent more city residents

           they'll   don't

deciding that *they will* ride these trains from this station. (9) I *do not* think I

                                     haven't

am overreacting when I say that city officials *have not* done everything they

     should've   Isn't   city's

should have. (10) *Is not* our well-being the *citys* first responsibility?

Exercise 31.5   **Correcting Errors in the Use of Apostrophes**

Activity 31.2

The following passage contains errors resulting from missing or misused apostrophes. Rewrite incorrect words, inserting an apostrophe wherever one is needed, and eliminating unnecessary apostrophes. Use the example as a guide.

                              brother's   its

EXAMPLE   After he smashed up his ~~brothers~~ car, Matt knew ~~it's~~ resale value would take a dive.

           can't

(1) You ~~cant~~ beat the companionship a dog gives, but you must be will-

                                you've

ing to invest a little time. (2) First of all, ~~youve~~ got to make sure that it gets

      its   dog's

all ~~it's~~ shots. (3) You must also make sure that the ~~dogs~~ other needs are met.

                  don't   You'll

(4) For example, ~~dont~~ buy just any dog food. (5) ~~Youll~~ find that your dog is

healthier and has more energy if you buy food that contains the right mix

                                       it's

of vitamins and minerals. (6) In addition, whether ~~its~~ you, a friend, or an-

other family member, somebody has to make sure that your pet gets exercise every day. (7) Also, unless the dog is a purebred that ~~youre~~ *you're* planning to

mate, you should have it spayed or neutered so that nobody ends up with a

bunch of unwanted ~~puppie's~~ *puppies*. (8) If ~~youre~~ *you're* patient, you can train your dog to

follow your commands very quickly. (9) That way, you ~~wont~~ *won't* have to worry

that your dog will misbehave. (10) If you follow these steps, ~~youll~~ *you'll* be able to

count on a number of ~~year's~~ *years* of companionship from a loving animal.

Exercise 31.6 **Using Apostrophes in Your Writing**

Use apostrophes to create contractions or phrases with possessive nouns from each of the following items. Then, on a separate sheet of paper, write a sentence that includes each word you create, as the example shows.

EXAMPLE the notebook of Bernard _____ *Bernard's notebook* _____

After a long search, I found Bernard's notebook under the couch.

1. do not _____ don't _____

2. the house of that family _____ that family's house _____

3. I would _____ I'd _____

4. the answer of the professor _____ the professor's answer _____

5. it is _____ it's _____

6. the sweater of Ray _____ Ray's sweater _____

7. should have _____ should've _____

8. the schedule of Nick _____ Nick's schedule _____

9. she will _____ she'll _____

10. the music of today _____ today's music _____

Challenge 31.2 **Using *Its* and *It's* in Your Writing**

As you can see from the list of common contractions on page 507, contractions of *it has* and *it is* are written as *it's*. For this Challenge, write ten sentences, five in which you use *its* and five in which you use *it's*. Then recopy the sentences, eliminating all apostrophes, and exchange your sentences with a partner. On the paper you receive, insert apostrophes where they are needed, and return the paper to the writer. Check to see whether you and your partner agree on the changes made to each of your papers.

Using Other Marks of Punctuation

Audio 31.6

Colons

A **colon** calls attention to what comes next. It is used to introduce a formal statement such as an explanation or announcement or a long or formal quotation. It is also used to introduce a list, often in combination with the words *as follows* or *the following*. Study the following examples:

Video 31.3

EXAMPLE

Now it was clear why Grandfather had been behaving so strangely: He had suffered a small stroke.

EXAMPLE

So far, I've test-driven four cars: a Geo Metro, a Dodge Neon, a Nissan Sentra, and a Ford Escort.

Weblink 31.7

In the first example, the colon introduces an explanation. If the explanation is a full sentence, it should begin with a capital letter. In the second example, the colon introduces a list.

Do not use a colon for a list that follows a verb or a preposition.

EXAMPLE

You must bring two pencils, a calculator, and a good eraser.

Colons have other functions, too:

- Use a colon after the salutation of a formal letter (*Dear Ms. Newman:*).
- Use a colon to separate hours and minutes (*10:45*), biblical chapter and verse (*John 4:11*), and the city of publication and the publishing company in bibliographic citations and footnotes (*New York: Longman*).

Exercise 31.7 **Using Colons**

Insert colons where they are needed in the space above the following sentences. If a sentence is correct, write *OK* above it. Use the example to guide you.

EXAMPLE

My goal was simple ; write a play, sell it to Broadway and Hollywood, and
∧

become filthy rich.

(1) Today, I had a 3 ; 30 P.M. appointment with Dr. Smits to ask her permis-
∧

sion to enroll in her advanced computer applications course. (2) I had not completed the course prerequisites :̬CPR 101, Introduction to Computers, and CPR 102, Networking. (3) However, I did have something that I thought might encourage her to add me to her class :̬three years experience working with computers at my job. (4) My plan was simple :̬explain what systems and software I had used and ask her to substitute my experience for the prerequisites. (5) I arrived early so that I could do the one thing that I hadn't done :̬organize my presentation. (6) By 3:̬25, I was well organized, but I was also feeling nervous. (7) If she refused, I would have to do something I considered ridiculous :̬take courses that duplicated all the experience I already had. (8) When she arrived, she quietly listened to my story and quickly gave her answer :̬yes. (9) Thanks to her willingness to credit my work experience, I can start out at the proper level and fill those two spots in my curriculum with other courses that will help me grow as a professional.

Semicolons

Audio 31.7

A **semicolon**, as you saw in Chapters 19, "Subordination and Coordination," and Chapter 20, "Comma Splices and Run-On Sentences," has the same power to connect as *and* preceded by a comma. But when you use the semicolon alone, you are saying that the connection between the clauses is so strong that no word is needed to signal it:

EXAMPLE

> By ten o'clock, Elaine's car had already been stuck in the snow three times**;** she just wanted to turn around and head for home.

The semicolon connects the two thoughts and emphasizes the connection between Elaine's experience and her wish to quit.

Weblink 31.8

The use of semicolons is also discussed in Chapters 19 and 20. Remind students that

As Chapter 19, "Subordination and Coordination," also showed, using a conjunctive adverb with a semicolon is another way to connect clauses. Conjunctive adverbs, which include words such as *however, finally,* and *therefore,* can suggest a relationship between sentences. A conjunctive adverb alone can't connect, though, so you must use a semicolon *before* the conjunctive adverb to connect the sentences:

EXAMPLE

> David has had plenty of experience as a pipe fitter**;** *however,* he hasn't done much welding.

semicolons are used to join independent clauses; colons serve a different function.

The semicolon connects the two sentences, and the conjunctive adverb *however* stresses that David's experience as a pipe fitter doesn't include welding.

Exercise 31.8 **Practice Using Semicolons**

Weblink
31.9

Many of the sentences in the following paragraph are missing semicolons. In the space above these sentences, insert semicolons where they are needed. Some sentences are correct. Just mark these sentences *OK*. Use the example first to direct you.

EXAMPLE

Cliff couldn't have been involved in the incident ; he was out of town on that day.

Activity
31.3

(1) Last year, my friend Lani's life was thrown into turmoil ; she discovered that she had been adopted. (2) This knowledge upset her greatly ; she felt more confused and insecure than she had ever felt before. (3) After twenty years, she suddenly discovered that she had other biological parents ; she couldn't understand why her Mom and Dad hadn't told her before now. (4) For the first time in her life, Lani felt anger and resentment toward her mother and father ; she felt that she could no longer trust them. (5) Lani's adoptive parents didn't help the situation much ; they just acted as if nothing had changed. *OK* (6) Furthermore, the discovery made her troubled relationship with her brother, her adoptive parents' biological child, much worse. (7) Lani had always felt that she and her brother were very different ; now she understood why she felt that way. (8) This feeling was replaced by insecurity ; Lani feared that her parents loved her brother more than her. (9) After a year of counseling, Lani has adjusted ; she has finally accepted that she was adopted. (10) She understands that her parents had good intentions ; they simply didn't consider the possible consequences.

Parentheses and Dashes

Audio
31.8

Parentheses enclose information added to a sentence but not vital to it. Added dates, asides, and explanations may be enclosed in parentheses.

EXAMPLE

The people in the car **(**all wearing seatbelts**)** escaped injury.

EXAMPLE

Hypothermia **(**dangerously low body temperature**)** threatens the elderly during these cold stretches.

**Audio
31.9**

In the first example, the parentheses enclose added information that the reader doesn't actually need to understand the sentence. In the second example, the parentheses enclose the definition of a specialized term.

Dashes are used to set off information that deserves special attention.

EXAMPLE

The murderer turns out to be—but I don't want to spoil the ending for you.

EXAMPLE

As the winners were announced—the crowd had been waiting more than an hour for this moment—a loud cheer filled the auditorium.

In the first example, the dash indicates an abrupt change in thought and sentence structure. In the second, the dashes set off information that emphasizes the importance of the main idea. Dashes and parentheses are sometimes interchangeable; however, dashes indicate a stronger interruption. Neither mark should be used frequently, or it will lose its effectiveness.

Exercise 31.9 **Using Parentheses and Dashes**

Some sentences in the following passage need either parentheses or dashes. Correct the sentences by inserting the proper marks of punctuation. In some cases, more than one correct answer is possible. Write *OK* above any sentence that is correctly punctuated. Study the example first.

Answers may vary.

EXAMPLE

In the back of the arcade $($ the one on Main Street, not the one on

Plymouth Avenue $)$ police found the missing boy.

(1) Working as an aide in two hospitals — St. Jude's and United — has proven
OK
to me that I want to become a nurse. (2) In the two years that I've worked at

these hospitals, I have gotten to know some of the most dedicated people

I've ever met. (3) These are people who put their patients before everything —
OK
even themselves. (4) I've seen some of them stay an hour beyond their shift

because a patient took a sudden turn for the worse. (5) In the cardiac inten-

**Weblink
31.10**

sive care units at St. Jude's — there is one for adults and another for infants — I've

seen nurses going out of their way to reassure patients and their families.
OK
(6) The nurses don't mind because they feel comforting people is an impor-

tant part of their job. (7) I've even seen them trying to calm the emergency

medical technicians $($ EMTs $)$ who have had to transport a badly injured per-

son. (8) When you consider the hours and the stress, the pay isn't great
(   )   OK
around $25,000 a year, but there are other things to be gained. (9) When you
       ^   ^
can see that you've made someone feel better, you can walk away with a
                                                          (   )
good feeling. (10) Sometimes not as often as you might think you can even
                                          ^   ^
help to save lives.

Understanding Capitalization

Video
31.4

Capitalization, the practice of using initial capital letters to distinguish words, is governed by basic guidelines for standard use.

- Always capitalize the first word of any sentence:

EXAMPLE

The bike was the first thing the thieves took.

- Always capitalize the personal pronoun *I:*

EXAMPLE

As far as **I** am concerned, Eileen is the only one of my childhood friends who ever understood me.

- Capitalize *proper names* of individuals or things, including holidays, countries, states, historical periods or events, buildings or monuments, months (but not seasons), days of the week, planets, races, religions, and nationalities:

Marge **H**ill	**A**rgentina	**L**incoln **M**emorial	**V**alentine's **D**ay
Renaissance	**M**ay (but **s**pring)	**C**ivil **W**ar	**M**onday
Venus	**I**slam	**C**hinese	**B**aptist
Maine (**ME**)			

- Capitalize words designating family relationships when these words are part of, or a substitute for, a specific name:

EXAMPLE

When I was in elementary school, **A**unt Mary always went with my parents to parent/teacher night.

- Capitalize the first letter of a formal title such as *Doctor, Senator,* or *Mayor* when the title is used with a name:

EXAMPLE

We expect **M**ayor Cummings to call a news conference soon.

Weblink
31.12

- Capitalize words like *Street, Avenue,* and *Boulevard* when these words are part of a specific address:

EXAMPLE

50 Earle **S**treet

● Capitalize geographical regions in the United States and other parts of the world, but not directions:

EXAMPLES After being stationed in the **F**ar **E**ast for three years, I settled in the **M**idwest on the **e**ast side of the **M**ississippi.

● Capitalize languages and the main words of *specifically* named courses:

EXAMPLES **I**ntroduction to **P**hysics; **E**cology of **N**orth **A**merica; **W**riting 101; **S**panish; **S**wahili

Weblink
31.13

● Capitalize the names of languages, whether or not they refer to specific academic subjects:

EXAMPLES **C**hinese; **K**hmer; **P**ortuguese

● Capitalize the main words in the titles of books, magazines, newspapers, television shows, songs, articles, poems, movies, and so on. Do not capitalize a preposition or conjunction of fewer than five letters or *a, an,* or *the* unless it is the first word in the title.

EXAMPLES *The Invisible Man; Rolling Stone; Of Mice and Men;* "**A R**ose for **E**mily"

● Capitalize the names of specific brands, companies, clubs, associations, and so on:

EXAMPLES **M**azda **P**rotege; **G**eneral **E**lectric; **N**ational **O**rganization for **W**omen

● Capitalize *acronyms,* words formed from the first letters of several words:

EXAMPLE **MADD** (**M**others **A**gainst **D**runk **D**riving)

EXAMPLE **AIDS** (**A**cquired **I**mmune **D**eficiency **S**yndrome)

● Capitalize the first words at the beginning of a letter, known as the *salutation,* and the first word of the ending, called the *complimentary close:*

Common Salutations	*Common Complimentary Closes*
Dear **D**r. **L**annon:	**S**incerely,
Dear **K**urtis,	**V**ery truly yours,
Dear **S**ir or **M**adam:	**R**espectfully,

Fast Fact The dot that you put over a lowercase *i* actually has a name. It is called a **tittle.**

Exercise 31.10   **Working with Capital and Lowercase Letters**

Circle the correct letter—capital or lowercase—from each set in parentheses. Refer to the guidelines above if you are in doubt. Use the example to direct you.

EXAMPLE (F/f)or any florist, the busiest days of the (Y/y)ear are (V/v)alentine's (D/d)ay and (M/m)other's (D/d)ay.

(1) (P/p)rofessor (G/g)odwin, my instructor for (I/i)ntroduction to (B/b)usiness, always stresses the importance of making a good appearance on the job. (2) (O/o)n the first day of (C/c)lass, (P/p)rofessor (G/g)odwin said, "(I/i)f you want (P/p)eople to take you seriously, you must dress as if you belong on the cover of (B/b)usinessweek."(3) (H/h)e urged us to go down to (S/s)outh (M/m)ain (S/s)treet and (W/w)est 53rd (S/s)treet, where (R/r)etail stores like (E/e)ddie (B/b)auer and (M/m)arshall (F/f)ield's and the (C/c)orporate offices for (T/t)imex and (J/j)ohn (H/h)ancock are located. (4) (T/t)here, he said, we would see (M/m)anagers and (E/e)xecutives dressed in (C/c)onservative (B/b)usiness suits. (5) (N/n)one of these (B/b)usinesspeople is dressed in (L/l)evi's (J/j)eans or (N/n)ike (S/s)neakers because all of them know the importance of dressing well on the job.

Exercise 31.11 **Correcting Errors in Capitalization**

Decide which words in the following business letter should be capitalized. Cross out the incorrect lowercase letter, and write the capital above it. Each line or sentence is numbered for you.

       B   V   W
(1) 49 buena vista way
     S C   IL
(2) st. charles, il 60174

      M
(3) march 31, 2002

     D   C   C   D
(4) director, consumer complaint division
     M   C   C
(5) megahertz computer company
     B   S
(6) 25 blythe street
     S   AK
(7) springfield, ak 67583

      D   D

(8) dear director:

     A   I   M

(9) a month ago, i purchased one of your megahertz 5000 personal computers,

                S   I   S C

model number 328. (10) since then, i have taken it to your authorized st. charles

            M   M   A

service center, microcomputers and more, five times for repairs. (11) although

                                     I

the costs were covered by my warranty, i feel that the number of repairs re-

                      I   I

quired has been excessive. (12) i have therefore decided that i want to return

the computer for a full refund.

     W   I   M E   I

(13) when i returned to mr. electronics, the store from which i had origi-

                      M   M T   L

nally purchased my megahertz 5000, ms. tamara lacey, who manages the

electronics department, told me that your company will not authorize a re-

                                          I

fund because the case of the computer had been opened. (14) i explained

    M L

to ms. lacey that the case had been opened by a service technician autho-

          M   S

rized by megahertz. (15) she insisted that since the computer was no longer

in its original condition, your company would not give me a full refund.

     I   M L

(16) i sincerely hope that ms. lacey is mistaken and that you will authorize

               I   M

my refund. (17) i originally decided to purchase a megahertz 5000 because

I   M   C   C

i had read that the megahertz computer company was particularly sensitive

                                      A

to the needs of its customers. (18) as the enclosed copy of my original sales

                                                   P

slip shows, my total purchase price, including tax, was \$1,453.55. (19) please

contact me if you need additional information.

          S

     (20) sincerely,

          S   H A

     (21) steven h. amster

Challenge 31.3   **Revising for Correct Capitalization**

1. As you revise your writing, check to be sure you have capitalized correctly. To practice focusing on this aspect of revising, select two paragraphs that you have drafted, and exchange them with a partner.

Activity
31.4

2. Using the guidelines on pages 514–515, check the paragraphs you receive to make sure the words are correctly capitalized. Circle any problems you notice, and return the paragraphs to the writer.

3. Correct any errors your reader has identified.

Chapter Quick Check: Punctuation and Capitalization

The following passage contains numerous errors in the use of end punctuation, quotation marks, apostrophes, colons, semicolons, dashes, parentheses, and lowercase and capital letters. Consult the examples throughout the chapter. Then correct all errors by inserting needed punctuation or by writing corrected words in the space above, as the example shows.

EXAMPLE

Until last year, my neighbor Pete, who served in ~~vietnam~~ *Vietnam*, didn't realize he had been exposed to ~~agent orange~~ *Agent Orange* during his tour of duty there.

(1) One of the most important steps for job-seekers is to make sure their resumes are widely circulated and reviewed. (2) Thanks to the Internet, people have another way to ensure that the maximum number of employers review work credentials: on-line resume-posting services. (3) When resumes are posted on the Web, an individual's qualifications can be quickly examined with a few clicks of a computer mouse. (4) The leading global careers site — several million hits monthly — is Monster.com, which traces its origins to a site called The Monster Board, created in 1994 by Jeff Taylor. (5) In 1999, the Monster Board merged with Online Career Center, and the resulting company became Monster.com, which is now based in ~~maynard, massachusetts~~ *Maynard, Massachusetts*. (6) Taylor, who is CEO (Chief Executive Officer) of the company, came up with the concept for the site while he was an undergraduate at the University of Massachusetts, in Amherst, Massachusetts. (7) In 1999, Taylor gambled on the power of conventional advertising when Monster.com spent $4 million to purchase three 30-second commercials during the ~~super bowl~~ *Super Bowl*. (8) As a result, Monster.com began to draw huge numbers of visitors to its

site, and Taylor didn*'*t make the mistake that other Internet companies had
made after an advertising blitz. (9) As Taylor later started a speech,*"*We're the
only Internet site that advertised on the Super Bowl that didn't crash because of added traffic.*"* (10) In 2001, not content to leave anything undone,
Taylor finished up something he had left behind eight years earlier*:* the requirements for his college degree.

Discovering Connections 31.2

1. In Discovering Connections 31.1 on page 502, you completed a
   prewriting on one of three suggested topics. Using this prewriting material as a basis, work your way through the rest of the writing
   process, and create a draft essay of about 500 words on the subject
   you've chosen.
2. Exchange your draft with a partner. Using the material in this chapter
   to guide you, check the draft you receive for any errors in punctuation
   and capitalization. After checking the paper, return it to the writer.
3. Revise your essay, correcting any errors your reader has identified in
   punctuation and capitalization.

Summary Exercise: Punctuation and Capitalization

Have students proof-
read and correct each
other's completed Sum-
mary Exercise.

The following passage contains numerous errors in the use of end punctuation, quotation marks, apostrophes, colons, semicolons, dashes, parentheses,
and lowercase and capital letters. Consult the examples throughout the
chapter. Then correct all errors by inserting needed punctuation or by writing corrected words in the space above.

There are acceptable alternative answers for some items.

(1) For almost forty years *(* 1905–1945 *)* Franklin ~~franklin~~ and Eleanor Roosevelt ~~eleanor roosevelt~~

forged one of the most remarkable partnerships in the history ~~History~~ of the United ~~united~~

States. ~~states.~~ (2) It began with marriage, moved on to public service, and ended

with contributions to political life and social reform that transformed our

nation's— ~~nations~~ indeed the world's— ~~worlds~~ history.

(3) The marriage of the wealthy, outgoing Roosevelt ~~roosevelt~~ to his shy fifth cousin, ~~Cousin,~~

Eleanor ~~eleanor~~ led first to the births of their children :Elliot, James, John, F.D.R, Jr., ~~elliot, james, john, fdr, jr.,~~ and

~~anna.~~ (4) ~~eleanor~~ put her ambition for ~~Public Service~~ on hold to raise the [Anna. Eleanor public service] children; meanwhile, the young ~~roosevelt~~ proved himself an able and progres- [; Roosevelt] sive leader to the ~~new york democrats.~~ [New York Democrats.]

(5) In 1921, the family suffered a staggering blow while they were vacation- [: While] ing at their summer home on ~~campobello island~~ in ~~new brunswick, canada,~~ [Campobello Island New Brunswick, Canada,] ~~roosevelt~~ was stricken with polio. (6) This was a terrible shock ~~roosevelt~~ had al- [Roosevelt —Roosevelt] ways been strong, active, and very able physically but the couple neither bent [—] nor broke. (7) Eleanor who later encouraged her husband to return to ~~Politics~~ [(politics)] now became both a physical and psychological support. (8) Although con- fined to a wheelchair for the rest of his life, F. D. R. went on to become a master politician and one of the ~~worlds~~ most revered leaders. [world's]

(9) Roosevelt was elected governor of ~~new york~~ in 1929 he became [New York ;] president of the ~~united states~~ in 1932. (10) For three consecutive terms [United States] 1932–1945, he led the ~~Country~~ through two of the most traumatic upheavals [( ) country] of the century the ~~great depression~~ and ~~world war ii.~~ (11) ~~the~~ Roosevelt [: Great Depression World War II. The] team proved equal to the challenge of these catastrophic events ~~they~~ con- [. They] ceived and implemented inventive programs and projects such as the ~~new~~ [New] ~~deal,~~ the ~~works progress administration,~~ the ~~tennessee valley authority,~~ and [Deal, Works Progress Administration, Tennessee Valley Authority,] the ~~civilian conservation corps.~~ [Civilian Conservation Corps.]

(12) When the ~~japanese~~ attacked ~~pearl harbor,~~ Roosevelt responded for [Japanese Pearl Harbor] an outraged nation, calling ~~december~~ 7, 1941, a day that will live in infamy, [December " "] a saying that is now a part of history. (13) Through the war years, he worked closely with ~~prime minister winston churchill~~ of ~~great britain.~~ (14) ~~these~~ two [Prime Minister Winston Churchill Great Britain. These] men personally determined military strategy for the ~~allies~~ in the ~~west.~~ [Allies West.]

(15) During all these years, Eleanor was a tireless worker for social causes, such as ~~Civil Rights~~ for ~~african-americans~~ and women. (16) She set a [civil rights African-Americans] standard for public involvement and accomplishment that is still unmatched.

(17) Her workday began at ~~600~~ [6:00] A.M. and ended after midnight. (18) She not only conducted press conferences and had her own ~~Radio Program,~~ [radio program,] but she also wrote the daily newspaper column, ~~my day.~~ ["My Day."] (19) Friends and enemies alike wondered, Was there an "end to this woman's energy." (20) ~~Eleanors~~ [Eleanor's] tireless work and travel, public speaking and leadership, and selfless advocacy of the underdog made her well known to the world and beloved to millions.

(21) F.D.R., exhausted and in terrible health, died in 1945, months before the ~~War~~ [war] ended. (22) Eleanor went on to serve as a ~~u.s.~~ [U.S.] delegate to the ~~united nations~~ [United Nations] and helped draft the ~~u.n. declaration~~ [U.N. Declaration] of ~~human rights.~~ [Human Rights.] (23) ~~in~~ [In] addition, she wrote two books ~~this I remember~~ [: This I Remember] and ~~the autobiography~~ [The Autobiography] of ~~eleanor roosevelt.~~ [Eleanor Roosevelt.] (24) When she died in 1962, ~~eleanor roosevelt~~ [Eleanor Roosevelt] was, as one ~~Biographer~~ [biographer] has said, ["] the most admired person in the world. ["] (25) The lives of these two remarkable people had ended, but this verse is an appropriate epitaph [: "] They are not dead who live in lives they leave behind. In those whom they have blessed, they live a life again. ["]

RECAP

OTHER PUNCTUATION AND CAPITALIZATION

New terms in this chapter	Definitions
● **punctuation**	● a system of symbols that signals starts, stops, and pauses in writing
● **capitalization**	● the practice of emphasizing words by beginning them with capital letters
● **period (.)**	● an end mark used to indicate the end of a statement **_Example_** I have a dream**.**
● **question mark (?)**	● an end mark used to indicate the end of a question **_Example_** Have we met before**?**
● **exclamation point (!)**	● an end mark used to indicate the end of an exclamation and to show great feeling **_Example_** Stop**!** That area is mined**!**

New terms in this chapter	Definitions
● **direct quotation**	● a record of someone's exact words *Example* Peter said, **"**If you'll wait, I'll go with you.**"**
● **quotation marks (" ")**	● marks used to set off someone's exact words

● **dialogue**	● an exchange of direct quotations between two or more people
	  Mark shifts in speakers with new paragraphs.
	
	Example **"**I said I wanted to go home at ten,**"** said Joe.
	                     "Yes, but you didn't specify A.M. or P.M.,**"** said Dianne.

● **indirect quotation**	● a restatement of someone else's words *Example* Peter asked me to wait and said he'd go with me.

● **apostrophe (')**	● a mark used in a noun to show ownership or possession or in a contraction to signify letters left out
	  To show possession:
	      add **'s** to singular nouns a child**'s** book
	      add **'** to plural nouns the students**'** answers
	      add **'s** to plural nouns that don't end in *-s* women**'s** concerns
	  To form contractions:
	      add **'s** to show letters omitted in the contraction haven**'t**

● **colon (:)**	● a mark that indicates a pause in a sentence and that introduces a quotation, formal statement, or list Begin full sentences following colons with a capital letter. *Example* The news was good**:** The test results were negative.
● **semicolon (;)**	● a connecting mark that separates related independent clauses but emphasizes the connection between them *Example* Shelley is dramatic**;** her twin sister is quite shy.
● **parentheses**	● marks that enclose non-vital information within a sentence *Example* The movie **(**which she saw with her sister**)** made Mavis cry.
● **dashes**	● marks that set off information to create emphasis *Example* Vincent Van Gogh**—**who mutilated his ear**—**was a genius.

Guidelines for Capitalization

● The first word in a sentence

    Example   **A** light bulb burned out in the kitchen.

● The personal pronoun *I* and the proper names of people, things, and places

    Example   **S**ean and **I** are going to **T**ulsa on **F**riday.

● Words that designate family relationships when they are part of, or a substitute for, a specific name

    Example   **U**ncle Rod always calls to check on **G**randma.

● Formal titles used with a person's name

    Example   **D**r. Warner has been selected for the award.

● Words that are part of a specific address or specific section of a country

    Example   Our plant in the **S**outhwest is located at 1411 **L**incoln **W**ay in **T**ucson.

● Main words in specific academic subjects, languages, and titles

    Example   In my **I**ntroduction to **E**nvironment class, we are reading Rachel Carson's ***Silent Spring***.

● Brand names, company and association names, and letters of acronyms

    Example   My sister works for **AT&T**.

● First letters of the salutation and complimentary close of a letter

    Example   **D**ear Paul,   **Y**ours truly,

Connecting: Responding to Reading

Overview: Responding to Reading

Video VII.1

Reading and responding to what other authors have written is another way to ensure your success as a writer. To read actively is to respond to the ideas other authors have developed and to discover the strategies they have used to express those ideas. This part of the text includes writings by both professional authors and students. After each selection, you will find questions to help you think about and respond to the ideas in the readings. Additional assignments will help you explore the connections between those ideas and your own experiences. The questions will also encourage you to use the various modes in your own writing.

> **In this section of the text, you can explore**
>
> ● a variety of modes that writers use to fulfill their purpose
>
> ● additional subjects for writing
>
> ● strategies writers use to express their ideas and experiences

Taking Notes

You have already learned that writing effectively has many benefits. In the same way, the more you practice reading actively, the more you will profit from what you read. As a way to improve your reading skills, your instructor may ask you to record in a journal your responses, questions, and comments about what you read. Some readers *annotate* or make notes in the margins of the pages they are reading or highlight sections for later reference. Still others collect responses in a computer file or on an audiocassette tape. Whatever method or methods you use, cultivate the habit of taking notes. Your notes will help you prepare for discussions with your classmates and explore ideas for your own writing assignments.

Active Reading Strategies

Sometimes it is difficult to know what questions to ask and what notes to take. The five guidelines below apply to any reading assignment. They will provide direction and help you focus your responses to the readings.

Review them before you begin to read each selection, and be sure to record your responses as you read.

1. **Establish the context**

   What's going on? Who is involved? When did it happen? Where? How? Why? These are the questions that news stories generally answer in their opening sentences to establish the *context* for readers. As you read, use these kinds of questions to identify details and examples that establish the context of the reading.

2. **Explore the modes**

   As you learned in Chapters 5 through 15, writers use techniques, or modes, to communicate their ideas to readers. These are narration, description, example, process, definition, comparison and contrast, cause and effect, and division and classification. To construct an argument, writers use a combination of these modes. As you read, first determine the author's purpose for writing. Is it to inform, to entertain, or to persuade? What is the dominant mode the author uses to fulfill this purpose? What other modes does the author use, and how are they combined?

3. **Explore the main ideas**

   As you read, highlight or record in your journal parts of the reading that state the author's thesis. Do the same for evidence that supports that idea. Finally, highlight or record the author's conclusions about the subject.

   Try to identify the main ideas or topic sentences of the paragraphs. Can you trace a common thread, the element that all the paragraphs have in common? Are there sentences or paragraphs that confuse you or sections that you don't understand? Make note of these to discuss with your classmates. Next, take note of supporting information that helps you understand the writer's points. What details catch your eye? Why are these effective?

4. **Respond to the ideas**

   What do you think of the essay? Why do you think the way you do? Do you agree with the ideas the author has expressed? Are you familiar with the context or the ideas in the reading? Does the author present an experience or view of the world that is new to you? Your answers to these questions will help you greatly in understanding the writing. As you talk or write about the piece, you will also be making sense of it. Remember as you read that a good piece of writing touches the reader. When you read, explore what the writer has done to make this happen.

5. **Read again**

   Active reading can be challenging and rewarding. Effective readers usually read a piece of writing more than once. You'll no doubt discover some elements or aspects in a second reading that you missed in the first. Regardless of what they are, these elements helped to make that writing successful. It is worth your effort to analyze them so that you will be able to use a similar approach in your own writing.

Active Reading Illustrated

Here is a brief excerpt from "The Future of TV Sports Is Glowing," by Ted Rose. This article explores and explains how technological innovations are changing the way televised sports are presented. The annotations illustrate the way active reading can help you uncover the writer's meaning and the various techniques that enabled the writer to communicate that meaning:

Modes: Main purpose—to inform

Main Ideas: Topic sentence

Context: Who

Context: What

The task presented many technical challenges, but [Stan] Honey was most concerned about how computers would locate the puck on the ice. Under normal conditions, baseballs and golf balls travel predictable—thus, mathematical—trajectories. Not so a hockey puck. Instead, surrounded by dozens of wooden sticks and metal skates wielded by aggressive hockey players, a puck can carom in any direction.

Modes: Process

Supporting ideas

Modes: Comparison and contrast

Modes: Cause and effect

Context: Why

Main Ideas: Topic sentence

Modes: Process and cause and effect

Context: Who

Working with a team of 12 engineers, Honey designed a special puck that emitted bursts of infrared energy, and a system of sensors to be placed around the arena to detect those emissions. With this sensor data, a computer could identify the puck's location. That, along with information from broadcast cameras themselves, produced the desired result: the TV-viewing fan could find the puck on the ice because a blue glow would illuminate it. When a player fired a puck at a high speed (usually more than 50 miles per hour), a red tail would follow in the wake. (*Brill's Content*, May 1999, 64–65)

Context: What

Context: How

Supporting ideas

Context: How

Modes: description

Response: Pretty cool! Just another way computers are changing the world. Lots of people wouldn't watch hockey on TV before because it was too hard to follow the puck. This innovation has changed that for sure.

As the annotations illustrate, active reading helps you isolate a number of elements of the writing. For instance, it helps you focus on the *context: what* was involved (the development of a hockey puck that would be easier to see on a television screen), *who* was involved (Stan Honey and a team of twelve engineers), and *how* they did it (they built a puck that emits signals and installed sensors throughout the ice rink).

Active reading also enables you to note the various *modes* (*comparison and contrast, process, cause and effect,* and *description*), as well as the *main ideas* (the *topic sentences* and the *supporting sentences*). And the *response* to the reading helps you focus on the significance or meaning of the passage to a more complete degree. When you understand how a writer communicates ideas to a reader, you are better able to communicate your own ideas to your reader. That's why active reading is so important.

5:00 A.M.: Writing as Ritual

Judith Ortiz Cofer

Franklin Professor of English and Creative Writing at the University of Georgia, Judith Ortiz Cofer has won awards and international recognition for her writing, which includes a novel, essays, short stories, and several volumes of poetry. In this selection from *The Latin Deli,* a book of prose and poetry, she writes about how she discovered the time she needed to create.

An act of will that changed my life from that of a frustrated artist, waiting to have a room of my own and an independent income before getting down to business, to that of a working writer: I decided to get up two hours before my usual time, to set my alarm for 5:00 A.M.

When people ask me how I started writing, I find myself describing the urgent need that I felt to work with language as a search; I did not know for a long time what I was looking for. Although I married at nineteen, had a child at twenty-one—all the while going through college and graduate school *and* working part-time—it was not enough. There was something missing in my life that I came close to only when I turned to my writing, when I took a break from my thesis research to write a poem or an idea for a story on the flip side of an index card. It wasn't until I traced this feeling to its source that I discovered both the cause and the answer to my frustration: I needed to write. I showed my first efforts to a woman, a "literary" colleague, who encouraged me to mail them out. One poem was accepted for publication, and I was hooked. This bit of success is really the point where my problem began.

Once I finished graduate school, I had no reason to stay at the library that extra hour to write poems. It was 1978. My daughter was five years old and in school during the day while I traveled the county, teaching freshman composition on three different campuses. Afternoons I spent taking her to her ballet, tap, and every other socializing lesson her little heart desired. I composed my lectures on Florida's I-95, and that was all the thinking time I had. Does this sound like the typical superwoman's lament? To me it meant being in a constant state of mild anxiety which I could not really discuss with others. What was I to say to them? I need an hour to start a poem. Will someone please stop the world from spinning so fast?

I did not have the privilege of attending a writers' workshop as a beginning writer. I came to writing instinctively, as a dowser finds an underground well. I did not know that I would eventually make a career out of writing books and giving readings of my work. The only models I knew were the unattainable ones: the first famous poet I met was Richard Eberhart, so exalted and venerable that he might as well have been the Pope. All I knew at that time was that at twenty-six years of age I felt spiritually deprived, although I had all the things my women friends found sufficiently fulfilling in a "woman's life" plus more; I was also teaching, which is the only vocation I always knew I had. But I had found poetry, or it had found me, and it was demanding its place in my life.

After trying to stay up late at night for a couple of weeks and discovering that there was not enough of me left after a full day of giving to others, I relented and did this odious thing: I set my alarm for five. The first day I shut it off because I could: I had placed it within arm's reach. The second day I set two clocks, one on my night table, as usual, and one out in the hallway. I had to jump out of bed and run to silence it before my family was awakened and the effort nullified. This is when my morning writing ritual that I follow to this day began. I get up at five and put on a pot of coffee. Then I sit in my rocking chair and read what I did the previous day until the coffee is ready. I take fifteen minutes to drink two cups of coffee while my computer warms up—not that it needs to—I just like to see it glowing in the room where I sit in semidarkness, its screen prompting "ready": ready whenever you are. When I'm ready, I write.

Since that first morning in 1978 when I rose in the dark to find myself in a room of my own—with two hours belonging only to me ahead of me, two prime hours when my mind was still filtering my dreams—I have not made or accepted too many excuses for not writing. This apparently ordinary choice, to get up early and to work every day, forced me to come to terms with the discipline of art. I wrote my poems in this manner for nearly ten years before my first book was published. When I decided to give my storytelling impulse full rein and write a novel, I divided my two hours: the first hour for poetry, the second for fiction; two pages minimum per day. Well or badly, I wrote two pages a day for three and one-half years. This is how my novel, *The Line of the Sun*, was finished. If I had waited to have the time, I would still be waiting to write my novel.

My life has changed considerably since those early days when I was trying to be everything to everyone. My daughter is eighteen and in college, not a ballerina, Rockette, or horsewoman but a disciplined student and a self-assured young person. Thus I do not regret the endless hours of sitting in tiny chairs at the Rock-Ette Academy of Dance or of breathing the saturated air at the stables as I waited for her. She got out of her activities something like what I got out of getting up in the dark to work: the feeling that you are in control, on the saddle, on your toes. Empowerment is what the emerging artist needs to win for herself. And the initial sense of urgency to create can easily be dissipated because it entails making the one choice many people, especially women, in our society with its emphasis on the "acceptable" priorities, feel selfish about making: taking the time to create, stealing it from yourself if it's the only way.

Exploring the Reading through Discussion

1. Why does Judith Ortiz Cofer begin to write poetry?

2. What is the problem to which Cofer refers at the end of the second paragraph? How does she solve her dilemma?

3. List the steps in Cofer's writing ritual.

4. What does Cofer create as a result of following her ritual? Did she gain anything else?

5. Cofer uses colons several times in her essay. Find those sentences that include colons. Why do you think she chose to use this punctuation mark when she did? Refer to Chapter 31, "Other Punctuation and Capitalization," as you explore this question.

Developing Vocabulary

List any words in this selection that are new to you. Write your understanding of each word from the context. Then look up each word in the dictionary, and write the definition that you think best fits the meaning in this writing.

Discovering Connections through Writing

1. Describe the steps you follow in your own writing ritual, if you have one. Include details to answer your readers' questions about when, where, and why you follow this process.

2. Do you take time to engage in an activity that makes you feel that you "are in control, on the saddle, on your toes"? Describe what you do and what the positive results are.

3. It took Cofer nearly ten years to write her first book of poetry and three and one-half years to finish her first novel. Do you have a long-term goal? Explain what your goal is and what steps you are taking to reach it.

Fish Cheeks

Amy Tan

Amy Tan is an acclaimed writer who has explored the relationships between immigrant Chinese mothers and their daughters. Her first novel, *The Joy Luck Club* (1989), is based on some of her own experiences. As you read this essay, first published in *Seventeen* magazine, try to understand the feelings of a little girl living in two cultures.

I fell in love with the minister's son the winter I turned fourteen. He was not Chinese, but as white as Mary in the manger. For Christmas I prayed for this blond-haired boy, Robert, and a slim new American nose.

When I found out that my parents had invited the minister's family over for Christmas Eve dinner, I cried. What would Robert think of our shabby Chinese Christmas? What would he think of our noisy Chinese relatives who lacked proper American manners? What terrible disappointment would he feel upon seeing not a roasted turkey and sweet potatoes but Chinese food?

On Christmas Eve I saw that my mother had outdone herself in creating a strange menu. She was pulling black veins out of the backs of fleshy prawns. The kitchen was littered with appalling mounds of raw food: A slimy rock cod with bulging eyes that pleaded not be thrown into a pan of hot oil. Tofu, which looked like stacked wedges of rubbery white sponges. A bowl soaking dried fungus back to life. A plate of squid, their backs criss-crossed with knife markings so they resembled bicycle tires.

And then they arrived—the minister's family and all my relatives in a clamor of doorbells and rumpled Christmas packages. Robert grunted hello, and I pretended he was not worthy of existence.

Dinner threw me deeper into despair. My relatives licked the ends of their chopsticks and reached across the table, dipping them into the dozen or so plates of food. Robert and his family waited patiently for platters to be passed to them. My relatives murmured with pleasure when my mother brought out the whole steamed fish. Robert grimaced. Then my father poked his chopsticks just below the fish eye and plucked out the soft meat. "Amy, your favorite," he said, offering me the tender fish cheek. I wanted to disappear.

At the end of the meal my father leaned back and belched loudly, thanking my mother for her fine cooking. "It's a polite Chinese custom to show you are satisfied," explained my father to our astonished guests. Robert was looking down at his plate with a reddened face. The minister managed to muster up a quiet burp. I was stunned into silence for the rest of the night.

After everyone had gone, my mother said to me, "You want to be the same as American girls on the outside." She handed me an early gift. It was a miniskirt in beige tweed. "But inside you must always be Chinese. You must be proud you are different. Your only shame is to have shame."

And even though I didn't agree with her then, I knew that she understood how much I had suffered during the evening's dinner. It wasn't until many years later—long after I had gotten over my crush on Robert—that I was able to fully appreciate her lesson and the true purpose behind our particular menu. For Christmas Eve that year, she had chosen all my favorite foods.

Exploring the Reading through Discussion

1. What is the lesson that the author appreciates after "many years"? Why doesn't she agree with her mother at the time?

2. Compare the responses of the two families to the dinner. How did the narrator feel? Why?

3. What sensory details does Tan use to describe the Christmas Eve menu? Can you find examples of both objective and subjective description in this essay?

4. What transitional expressions are included in the essay?

5. Do you think "Fish Cheeks" is a good title for this story? Explain why.

Developing Vocabulary

List at least three words in this selection that are new to you. Write your understanding of each word from the context. Then look up each word in the dictionary, and write the definition that you think best fits the meaning in this writing.

Discovering Connections through Writing

1. The narrator's mother tells her, "You must be proud you are different. Your only shame is to have shame." Do you agree? Write about a situation you know about or an experience you have had that supports her belief.

2. Have you participated in a traditional event or shared a special occasion with friends of another religion or culture as Robert and his family do? How did you feel? What did you learn? Provide plenty of concrete examples in your essay.

3. Write a narrative about a holiday celebration you remember well. In your essay, be sure to use effective description to put your readers at the scene.

Intimacy and Independence

Deborah Tannen

As you read this excerpt from Deborah Tannen's book You Just Don't Understand, *see if you can discover why Tannen thinks that spoken communication can be challenging.*

*I*ntimacy is key in a world of connection where individuals negotiate complex networks of friendship, minimize differences, try to reach consensus, and avoid the appearance of superiority, which would highlight differences. In a world of status, *independence* is key, because a primary means of establishing status is to tell others what to do, and taking orders is a marker of low status. Though all humans need both intimacy and independence, women tend to focus on the first and men on the second. It is as if their lifeblood ran in different directions.

These differences can give women and men differing views of the same situation, as they did in the case of a couple I will call Linda and Josh. When Josh's old high-school chum called him at work and announced he'd be in town on business the following month, Josh invited him to stay for the weekend. That evening he informed Linda that they were going to have a houseguest, and that he and his chum would go out together the first night to shoot the breeze like old times. Linda was upset. She was going to be away on business the week before, and the Friday night when Josh would be out with his chum would be her first night home. But what upset her the most was that Josh had made these plans on his own and informed her of them, rather than discussing them with her before extending the invitation.

Linda would never make plans, for a weekend or an evening, without first checking with Josh. She can't understand why he doesn't show her the same courtesy and consideration that she shows him. But when she protests, Josh says, "I can't say to my friend, 'I have to ask my wife for permission'!"

To Josh, checking with his wife means seeking permission, which implies that he is not independent, not free to act on his own. It would make him feel like a child or an underling. To Linda, checking with her husband has nothing to do with permission. She assumes that spouses discuss their plans with each other because their lives are intertwined, so the actions of one have consequences for the other. Not only does Linda not mind telling someone, "I have to check with Josh"; quite the contrary—she likes it. It makes her feel good to know and show that she is involved with someone, that her life is bound up with someone else's.

Linda and Josh both felt more upset by this incident, and others like it, than seemed warranted, because it cut to the core of their primary concerns. Linda was hurt because she sensed a failure of closeness in their relationship: He didn't care about her as much as she cared about him. And he was hurt because he felt she was trying to control him and limit his freedom.

A similar conflict exists between Louise and Howie, another couple, about spending money. Louise would never buy anything costing more than a hundred dollars without discussing it with Howie, but he goes out and buys whatever he wants and feels they can afford, like a table saw or a new power mower. Louise is disturbed, not because she disapproves of the purchases, but because she feels he is acting as if she were not in the picture.

Many women feel it is natural to consult with their partners at every turn, while many men automatically make more decisions without consulting their partners. This may reflect a broad difference in conceptions of decision making. Women expect decisions to be discussed first and made by consensus. They appreciate the discussion itself as evidence of involvement and communication. But many men feel oppressed by lengthy discussions about what they see as minor decisions, and they feel hemmed in if they can't just act without talking first. When women try to initiate a freewheeling discussion by asking, "What do you think?" men often think they are being asked to decide.

Communication is a continual balancing act, juggling the conflicting needs for intimacy and independence. To survive in the world, we have to act in concert with others, but to survive as ourselves, rather than simply as cogs in a wheel, we have to act alone. In some ways, all people are the same: We all eat and sleep and drink and laugh and cough, and often we eat, and laugh at, the same things. But in some ways, each person is different, and individuals' differing wants and preferences may conflict with each other. Offered the same menu, people make different choices. And if there is cake for dessert, there is a chance one person may get a larger piece than another—and an even greater chance that one will *think* the other's piece is larger, whether it is or not.

Exploring the Reading through Discussion

1. Tannen writes that "humans need both intimacy and independence." Do you agree? Why? Give examples.

2. How are the worlds of "connection" and "status" different? In which world would you rather live? Explain.

3. "Communication is a continual balancing act." Explain your understanding of this statement.

4. According to the author, how do men and women differ in the way they make decisions? Do you agree with Tannen?

5. What examples does the author provide to help readers understand the terms *intimacy* and *independence?*

Developing Vocabulary

List at least three words in this selection that are new to you. Write your understanding of each word from the context. Then look up each word in the dictionary, and write the definition that you think best fits the meaning in this writing.

Discovering Connections through Writing

1. Help Josh and Linda or Louise and Howie solve their communication problems. Write your advice, explaining how they can juggle their "conflicting needs for intimacy and independence."

2. Define the terms *masculine* and *feminine*. Provide examples, as Tannen does, to help readers understand what you mean by these terms.

3. Do men and women view the same situations in different ways, as Tannen suggests? Tell a story about a situation that supports this statement or about a situation that contradicts Tannen's opinion.

Nightwatch

Paul Fletcher

In this essay, originally published in 1990, Paul Fletcher writes about a minor car accident that led to more harm than a broken fender. As you read, see if you can discover the facts of what happened one night in a small town.

It is a quiet spring night. In the oak-paneled living room of one of the gussied-up old houses that line Main Street, my daughter, Rosemary, and her boyfriend, Dan, are watching TV. A fire burns in the nicely detailed fireplace.

Crash. Tinkle, tinkle, bang!

Dan leaps up.

"Damn! If that's my car. . . ."

He throws open the front door and runs out, with Rosemary at his heels.

The driver's side of Dan's station wagon is, as they might have said years ago in this old seacoast town, "stove in." Dan and Rosemary are just in time to see a Mustang take off.

Then, unaccountably, the car comes to a halt; it slowly backs into a driveway and stands there, idling. In the moonlight, one can just make out the head and shoulders of the driver, a young woman.

By now, several neighbors are out on the street, under the bare horse-chestnut trees. Against the old Colonial church, the shadows of the trees look like the ghosts of slaves. In the half-light, their bony arms seem to be warding off an overseer's whip.

From the back of the historic house on the corner, a young black man emerges. He is followed by another, and another, and yet another, until there are five young black men standing across the street from the driveway where the young woman sits in the Mustang.

The great tower of the old church, which has watched over the town since the days of the slave trade, chimes one.

A police car, its blue lights flashing, pulls up, and a young officer approaches the young woman in the car. She appears to be dazed. She is blonde, well dressed, in the preppie fashion—apparently a student at the local college.

"I didn't do any damage," she moans, more to herself or her absent parents than to anyone else.

Dan shakes his head as he looks at the large strip of chrome from his station wagon protruding from her front-wheel sprockets.

Under the great church tower, there in the moonlight, everyone seems to be frozen in time: the young woman; the police officer, joined now by a backup; the neighbors; the five young black men—all members, it turns out, of the college's basketball team. One of them seems to know the woman, and he steps toward her, to try to calm her.

"Take it easy," he seems to say, though his voice is muffled by those of the bystanders.

It appears that the young woman is intoxicated. One of the police officers tries to conduct a sobriety test, and she stands there flailing her slender arms as she tries to connect with the tip of her nose.

"Be cool," encourages the young man.

"Get away from her!" barks the officer. His even features turn distorted with rage.

"Get away from her!" he repeats.

"I'm only trying to help."

Now everything speeds up, and it seems that the policeman has struck the youth.

"That'll teach you," he says.

Did he jab the young man in the kidneys? Despite the bright, brittle moonlight, it's too dark to see.

Murmurs of protest emanate from the onlookers. The police officers hustle the young man into one of the patrol cars.

The church clock watches.

Gradually, the distorted mien of the angry policeman reverts to normal. He strides over to Dan.

"You wouldn't mind signing this report, would you, sir?" he says. "Just to witness that this young man was disorderly—don't want any stuff about police brutality."

Dan refuses. "I saw you manhandle that young man. He was only trying to quiet the girl."

The patrol car with the young woman and the young man drives off. Rosemary turns to go back into the house with Dan. She looks up at the church tower, which looms over the peaceful skyline of our old town, as it has always done, since the time when black people here were traded and transported.

Exploring the Reading through Discussion

1. Describe the neighborhood where this story takes place. Do you think the setting is important? Why?

2. Why is the police officer whose face is "distorted with rage" so angry?

3. Do you agree with Dan's decision to refuse to sign the report? Why?

4. Why do you think the author called his story "Nightwatch"? Who or what is watching?

5. What point of view does Fletcher use to write his narrative essay? Do you agree with his choice? Explain.

Developing Vocabulary

List at least three words in this selection that are new to you. Write your understanding of each word from the context. Then look up each word in the dictionary, and write the definition that you think best fits the meaning in this writing.

Discovering Connections through Writing

1. Have you ever seen an incident in which a person was treated unfairly because of his or her race, religion, ethnicity, or sexual orientation? Write about what happened, using effective description to create a vivid sense of the scene. Provide details that will clarify the causes and effects of the behavior.

2. Fletcher writes about the early history of the seacoast town in which his story takes place. Write about the history of your own community. How has it changed? How does the city or town commemorate its roots?

3. Describe an accident that you have witnessed or been involved in. Be sure to include descriptive details to help readers visualize the scene as you saw it.

Caesar

Therese C. MacKinnon

Therese MacKinnon's essay originally was published in 1995, in a book entitled *Circles of Compassion: A Collection of Humane Words and Work*. In this selection, you'll read about a unique cat whose life, unfortunately, comes to an all too familiar conclusion. As you read, see if you can discover why the author has such strong feelings for the animal.

Caesar, a "stray" cat, was euthanized today. I use the word *stray* in the loosest of terms, because, contrary to popular belief, cats very seldom stray from home. They're much too provincial for that sort of thing. More likely, that scraggly looking cat you see wandering through your yard has been abandoned, or it is the offspring of such a cat. Its family may have moved away, having decided that it was inconvenient to pack the cat along and that it would surely "find" another home. Or the cat may have been intentionally discarded when it reached maturity and began marking its territory and fighting, or when it became pregnant. Of course, these problems could easily have been solved with a simple spay or neuter operation.

Seldom does a cat choose to leave its home territory, so when a nameless, yellow, unaltered male cat was brought in to the animal shelter one morning in a wire trap it was no surprise to hear the bearer say that his neighbors had moved away, leaving kitty behind.

The man set the trap down by the counter. Huddled tensely in the steel mesh box, eyes wide with terror, the little animal didn't look like much, just another scared vagabond. I took down what sketchy information the neighbor could offer. The cat was about four years old—not so old—not, that is, until placed in a shelter, surrounded by cuddly, highly adoptable kittens. He had been on his own for several weeks and had been fighting with every cat in the neighborhood. He had the distinct musk odor of an unaltered male feline. Age, behavior and sex, I thought: three strikes, you're out. He was the classically unadoptable cat.

As I brought him into the holding room and set him up in a clean cage, I wondered what his personality would reveal once he settled in with us. Well, Caesar, as he was soon to be dubbed, was trouble from the very start, and it was not long before I was hopelessly in love.

He was a yellow tabby—yellow, not like buttercups or tangerines, but subtle, like cornmeal. He was compact and solid, all muscle, all tomcat, yet his fur was as soft as cotton balls and thicker than lamb's wool. His coat was short and silky along his flanks, and he had a long ruff around his neck that made him look like a handsome young lion. The fur on his belly was thick and downy and, oh, his tail! It was magnificent, dense and bushy so that pieces of litter and food were always getting caught up in it. I was constantly combing it out with my fingers. Diagonally across his nose and cheeks was painted a single white stripe, rather like the make-up of an Indian brave.

Caesar had clear, round eyes, yellow, the color of his fur. They weren't the kind of eyes that you might say, "could see right through you." Not at all. He wasn't a wise sort. But he was dashing and devil-may-care, and when I looked in his eyes and he gazed back at me, I knew that he trusted me and considered me his friend.

As I said, Caesar was trouble from the start. We all knew it the day he began picking the latch on his cage door and taking nightly excursions through the corridors of the shelter. We would come in mornings to find him staring down at us happily from some shelf or curled up on a pile of blankets in a storage cabinet. Murphy-Cat, our wimpy shelter mascot, never turned up with any wounds after these evenings of freedom, so I suppose they either never met or Caesar preferred exploring to ravaging. I like to think the latter. When we finally got wise and put a lock on his cage, Caesar began picking the latch on the door next to him. My little freedom fighter: If he couldn't be footloose, he was going to see to it that someone else was.

Although Caesar was a mature adult cat, he still had the heart of a kitten. That which remained still, was sniffed and passed by. But that which moved, or growled, or just looked inviting, was fair game for a pounce. It made perfect cat sense. One day, Carole, my co-worker, was moving a cat with an exceptionally fluffy and inviting tail. She passed too close to Caesar's cage, and he, always the opportunist, grabbed it—and tenaciously refused to let go. The more the poor gray Persian wailed, the more worth keeping hold of her tail. Caesar was finally persuaded, forcibly, to give it up. But the second time he grabbed someone, a sweet little black Angora, I knew his days were numbered. However, being not so wise, and not inclined to change for anyone, Caesar remained full of the mischief that was to be his undoing.

One day a young couple came in, hoping to adopt not one, but two adult cats! They had recently lost their cat to feline leukemia, a deadly disease. After looking at all of the available candidates, they chose Wiggins, a neutered, buff-colored Angora, and Caesar. This was the one chance for adoption that had come Caesar's way in the two months and a day that he had been with us. Knowing his impetuous nature, we feared there might be bloodshed, but wanting dearly for him to find a home, we decided to give it a try. We brought both cats and the couple into a visiting room to see how they would all get along. As we placed the cats on the floor in opposite corners, their eyes met. I held my breath and waited, tensed to intervene, should there be trouble. The cats ran straight at each other, sniffed a greeting and then, began to explore the room! I breathed a heavy sigh of relief—and then it happened. Caesar, with his flare for the unexpected, spied a mama cat nursing her three kittens in a nearby upper cage, and leaped. He leaped six feet in the air and landed vertically on the bars of the cage. The terrified mother cat, determined to defend her brood to the end, hissed and lashed with all her might, but Caesar held fast. As far as he was concerned, this was fun! The horrified couple looked on as we pried him from the bars and carried him back to his cage. They later adopted Wiggins and Whitey, both neutered males, highly adoptable and very lucky animals indeed.

I'd like to say that someone came in that very day, saw something in Caesar and realized that he was just the companion they were looking for. Or maybe I could say that the owner finally came in to claim him, their beloved long-lost pet. I'd love to say that I or one of the other shelter staff members was able to rescue him at the last moment and take him home to be our very own. But the reality is that there are just too many animals and not enough homes for them all. Pet breeding is out of control. It's not the fault of Caesar or any of the animals that come in to the hundreds of shelters across the country. It's something that only we, the pet owners, can do anything about. We must take the responsibility for curbing the thousands of unwanted domestic animal births that occur every day in our own little corners of the world. And we must make a lifelong commitment to the pets we choose to keep.

Caesar's fate was sealed that day, through no fault of his own. The next day he was placed on the list for euthanasia. *Euthanasia* is a Greek word in origin. Literally it means "good death" and is described as the act of killing painlessly for reasons of mercy. I wonder who the Greeks did it to, and how they did it, and was it really painless or did they just prefer to hope or wish it was, as we do at the animal shelter.

We killed several animals that day, two months and two days after Caesar had arrived. There were two dogs, seven cats, three kittens, and a rabbit. Two of the animals were old and sickly; the kittens were too young to survive in a shelter environment. The rest of the animals, one puppy, six cats, including Caesar, and the rabbit were killed simply and senselessly because no one wanted them. Too many animals, not enough homes.

That afternoon, I held Caesar in the corridor and waited for the veterinarian to finish with the rabbit. He lay in my arms, squinting up at me peacefully, purring as I scratched his neck and clucked at him. I thought, maybe it will be okay, maybe he won't struggle and it will be quick. But deep inside I knew that Caesar would not give up his life so easily, and I really expected nothing less of him.

It took four hands to restrain him on the table, to stop his thrashing, to silence his objections as the veterinarian pumped what seemed like a horse's dose of sodium pentobarbital into his veins. He did not die a good death, because death is never good outside of the natural order of things. Caesar was a victim of someone's thoughtlessness or perhaps just the simple ignorance of a society that thinks of other living creatures as objects, to be used for a while and then discarded. But if we would truly look into the eyes of another living being, our souls would be changed. We would realize their incredible worth. Like all living creatures, Caesar was unique, he was one-of-a-kind, I loved him, and he will never be again.

Exploring the Reading through Discussion

1. From what you know about Caesar, would you want to adopt him as a pet? Why?

2. What concrete details does the author include to help readers see what Caesar looked like?

3. Describe Caesar's personality. What specific examples help you understand him?

4. Why does the author tell Caesar's story? What is her purpose for writing?

5. MacKinnon begins her story by giving away the ending. Should she have waited until the conclusion before revealing Caesar's fate? Why?

Developing Vocabulary

List at least three words in this selection that are new to you. Write your understanding of each word from the context. Then look up each word in the dictionary, and write the definition that you think best fits the meaning in this writing.

Discovering Connections through Writing

1. Describe a pet that you have owned or have known so that readers can understand its personality.

2. What are some solutions to the problem of "too many animals, not enough homes"?

3. Do you feel strongly about a controversial issue involving animals, such as protecting endangered species, regulating the use of animals for research, or banning fur clothing? Write to argue your position on one of these issues.

Gullibles' Travels

John Yemma

Do you believe everything you read on the Internet? How do you distinguish between fact and rumor? As you read this column that first appeared in the Boston Globe Magazine, *see if you discover some ways to become a more knowing consumer of information.*

A relative e-mailed this story to me: A young man in Australia who was working as a trapeze artist was jumped by thugs one night and beaten to a pulp. Hideously disfigured, the man prayed and persevered and underwent a series of painful reconstructive surgeries. He is now, you will be amazed to learn, one of the most popular Hollywood stars around. His story will inspire you. His name will surprise you. He is a man with, let us say, a brave heart.

Another story, again by e-mail: the heartbreaking account of a Union officer in the Civil War who discovered a dying Rebel soldier on the battlefield at Harrison's Landing in Virginia. The soldier turned out to be the officer's son, who had secretly joined the Confederates. In the boy's pocket was a scrap of paper with the musical notes to the bugle call now known as "Taps." Think about the haunting music (and the words: "Safely rest, God is nigh") going through the father's mind as he cradled his son. How could you not get a lump in your throat?

Just one more: Leonardo da Vinci, painting his masterpiece, *The Last Supper,* chose a comely lad as his model for Jesus. Years went by, and the great artist needed a model for the 12th apostle, Judas. He looked far and wide. Finally, in a Rome prison, he found his Judas, a hardened criminal whose face bore the ravaged look of corrupt living. And who was this man? Why the same—the very same—as the model for Jesus so many years before. Whoa. How about that as a reminder of the wages of sin?

There are many more stories. They're urban legends, of course, also known as modern myths, folk tales, or by the relatively new Internet-age term "glurge." These are stories billed as true and usually sourced to a friend of a friend—a crucial aspect of urban myths that folklorist Jan Harold Brunvand identified in the 1960s.

Most of these tales have a chain-letter hook, urging you to pass them along. When an urban legend ends up in your inbox, you might think, "Hey, my Uncle Bob just sent me an e-mail!" But it turns out to be glurge. You read it, you wonder about it, you put a note at the top of the file saying: "A friend sent this to me. I don't know if it is true, but it's interesting." You hit the "forward" button. Congrats, you've just added to the Internet's supply of glurge.

Most glurges are tame, with morals like those of Greek myths and Grimm fairy tales: Have faith, don't sin, keep hope alive.

Often, there's a truth kernel submerged in a glurge. Mel Gibson, for instance, apparently did get in a bar fight the night before he auditioned for

Mad Max, and he once produced and starred in a movie called *The Man Without a Face.* And he's a handsome devil. But he is not known to have undergone reconstructive surgery or to list trapeze artist on his resume.

A general did compose "Taps" at Harrison's Landing during the Civil War. The general, Daniel Butterfield, was sitting in his tent, however, and based the tune on an earlier bugle call known as "Tattoo." There were a lot of dying men around, but his son was not among them.

Leonardo? Yes, he painted *The Last Supper.* Pretty much everything else about the story is bunk.

Angus Gillesspie, a professor of American studies at Rutgers University, points out that almost every new medium has been used by the mischievous to mislead the gullible. Orson Welles's *The War of the Worlds* broadcast upset people in the radio age. The Internet has had the same potential, Gillesspie says, but he notes, "Eventually skepticism comes in."

Happily, the Internet is as suited to skepticism as to glurging. All you have to do to verify a glurge is enter a few of the words in a search engine ("Gibson" and "disfigured" will do) or go to sites like www.snopes.com and www.urbanlegends.com to see the glurges debunked.

"Can anyone retain a charming level of naivete about these tales in the Internet age?" asks Robert Thompson, a professor of media and popular culture at Syracuse University. He doesn't think so. What may really be going on, he believes, is a kind of World Wrestling Federation [WWF] effect: "A small percentage of people may still naively believe, but most watch with tongue in cheek."

So forward the glurges if you want. Abide by the morals if you can. But believe the stories only if you also believe WWF smackdowns are real.

Exploring the Reading through Discussion

1. What does *gullible* mean? Explain your understanding of the title of this essay.

2. How does an urban legend spread on the Internet? Is there any harm in forwarding such stories by e-mail or other means?

3. In general, do you think that people believe the "glurge" found on the Internet? What evidence in the reading supports your answer?

4. How can the Internet be used to verify an urban legend?

5. John Yemma begins his essay with three examples. Why do you think he chooses to do so? Identify other examples that are used in this essay.

Developing Vocabulary

List any words in this selection that are new to you. Write your understanding of each word from the context. Then look up each word in the dictionary, and write the definition that you think best fits the meaning in this writing.

Discovering Connections through Writing

1. Have you heard or read about any urban legends? Do they have a moral or a kernel of truth in them as Yemma suggests? Following the guidelines for writing example paragraphs, write about one or more of these.

2. With the help of your college or public library staff, or by searching the Web, discover what happened on October 30, 1938, when Orson Welles presented a radio version of *War of the Worlds*. (The October 31, 1938, edition of the *New York Times* is a good source.) Write about the results of this broadcast or about why you think people reacted as they did.

3. Tell a story about a time when you were misled by a rumor. What made you believe the story was true? What happened as a result?

Remote Control—
How to Raise a Media Skeptic

Susan Douglas

Susan Douglas teaches in the Department of Communication Studies at the University of Michigan. She is a media critic, scholar, and author of many articles and several books, including the acclaimed *Where the Girls Are: Growing Up Female with the Mass Media*. As you read this selection, explore your own thoughts about the influence of television, especially on children.

"**M**ommy, Mommy, come here, now! Hurry, you're gonna miss it. It's Barbie's High-Steppin' Pony, and its legs really move! Hurreeeeey!"

"No!" I bark, as I'm wiping the dog barf up from the carpet, stirring the onions again so they don't burn, and slamming the phone down on a caller from Citibank who wants to know how I'm doin' today. It is 5:56 P.M., and I'm in no mood. "I don't come for commercials, and besides, the horse doesn't really move—they just make it look that way."

"Oh yeah?" demands my daughter, sounding like a federal prosecutor. "It can too. It's not like those old ones where you told me they faked it—this one really does move."

So now I have to go see and, indeed, the sucker takes batteries, and the stupid horse moves—sort of. "See, Mommy, the commercials don't always lie."

Moments like this prompt me to wonder whether I'm a weak-kneed, lazy slug, or, dare I say it, a hypocrite. See, I teach media studies, and, even worse, I go around the country lecturing about the importance of media literacy. One of my talking points is how network children's programming is, ideologically, a toxic waste dump. Yet here I am, just like millions of parents during that portion of the day rightly known as hell hour—dinnertime—shoving my kid in front of Nickelodeon so my husband and I can get dinner on the table while we whisper sweet nothings like "It's your turn to take her to

Brownies tomorrow" and "Oh, shit, I forgot to tell you that your mother called three days ago with an urgent message."

We let her watch Nickelodeon, but I still pop in to ridicule Kool-Aid commercials or to ask her why Clarissa's parents (on *Clarissa Explains It All*) are so dopey. I am trying to have it both ways: to let television distract her, which I desperately need, and to help her see through its lies and banalities. I am very good at rationalizing this approach, but I also think it isn't a bad compromise for overworked parents who believe Barbie is the anti-Christ yet still need to wash out grotty lunch boxes and zap leftovers at the end of the day.

It's best to be honest up front: My house is not media proofed. I am not one of those virtuous, haloed parents who has banished the box from the home. I actually believe that there are interesting, fun shows for my daughter to watch on TV. (And I'm not about to give up *ER*).

But I'm also convinced that knowing about television, and growing up with it, provides my daughter with a form of cultural literacy that she will need, that will tie her to her friends and her generation and help her understand her place in the world. So instead of killing my TV, I've tried to show my daughter basic bullshit-detecting techniques. Don't think your choices are either no TV or a zombified kid. Studies show that the simple act of intervening—of talking to your child about what's on television and why it's on there—is one of the most important factors in helping children understand and distance themselves from some of the box's more repugnant imagery.

I recommend the quick surgical strike, between throwing the laundry in and picking up the Legos. Watch a few commercials with them and point out that commercials lie about the toys they show, making them look much better than they are in real life. Count how many male and female characters there are in a particular show or commercial and talk about what we see boys doing and what we see girls doing. Why, you might ask, do we always see girls playing with makeup kits and boys playing with little Johnny Exocet missiles? Real life dads change diapers, push strollers, and feed kids, but you never see boys doing this with dolls on commercials. Ask where the Asian and African-American kids are. Point out how most of the parents in shows geared to kids are much more stupid than real-life parents. (By the way, children report that TV shows encourage them to talk back to their folks.) Tell them that all those cereals advertised with cartoon characters and rap music (like Cocoa Puffs and Trix) will put giant black holes in their teeth that only a dentist with a drill the size of the space shuttle can fix.

One of the best words to use when you're watching TV with your kids is *stupid,* as in "Aren't Barbie's feet—the way she's always forced to walk on her tiptoes—really stupid?" or "Isn't it stupid that Lassie is smarter than the mom on this show?" (My favorite Barbie exercise: Put your kitchen timer on for a minute and make your daughter walk around on her tiptoes just like Barbie; she'll get the point real fast.) *Cool*—a word that never seems to go out of style—is also helpful, as in isn't it cool that on *Legends of the Hidden Temple* (a game show on Nickelodeon) the girls are as strong and as fast as the boys?" Pointing out what's good on TV is important too.

See, I think complete media-proofing is impossible, because the shallow, consumerist, anti-intellectual values of the mass media permeate our culture. And we parents shouldn't beat ourselves up for failing to quarantine our kids. But we can inoculate them—which means exposing them to the virus and showing them how to build up a few antibodies. So don't feel so guilty about letting them watch TV. Instead, have fun teaching them how to talk back to it rather than to you.

Exploring the Reading through Discussion

1. What are Susan Douglas's objections to what is on television? Do you agree with her? Why does she allow her daughter to watch TV?

2. Douglas says she is "trying to have it both ways." Do you think her compromise solution works?

3. Douglas says that television provides her daughter with "a form of cultural literacy." Explain your understanding of that term.

4. Who do you think is the audience Douglas directs her writing to? What is her purpose for writing? What details in the writing lead you to this conclusion?

5. The author uses several voices and types of language in her writing. Find examples of language that let you hear Douglas the professor and media critic and examples of language that let you hear Douglas the busy wife and parent. Is the effect of this confusing? Interesting? Convincing?

Developing Vocabulary

List any words in this selection that are new to you. Write your understanding of each word from the context. Then look up each word in the dictionary, and write the definition that you think best fits the meaning in this writing.

Discovering Connections through Writing

1. "Pointing out what's good on TV is important too," states Douglas. Using specific examples, write about what you think is good on TV.

2. Watch several children's programs on network television, as well as the commercials aired before, during, and after, and take notes of what you see. What would you want to point out to a child to help him or her see through any "lies and banalities"?

3. Susan Douglas suggests that television programs don't portray us as we are in real life. Do you agree with her? Write an essay in which you take a stand and argue that television does or does not reflect people as you know them to be.

My Paradise

Naihsin Weng (student)

If you have ever left familiar surroundings for a new home, you might understand why everyday memories are so important to this student author. As you read, try to discover the details that help you imagine her home as she remembers it.

When I was twelve years old, living in Taiwan, my father bought a new apartment, which was close to our original apartment, only five minutes away. So my parents decided to move all our belongings by ourselves little by little. I was coming and going frequently, by riding my beloved pink bicycle with a basket in the front which was full of my treasures. At that time, I felt very excited because I was going to live in a brand-new apartment. Moving to a new apartment was so fresh to a twelve-year-old girl. I did not even feel sad about leaving my original house. Maybe that was because my parents still kept it, so I could go back any time. From then on, we started to call the original place "old house," and call our new apartment "new house."

After living in our new house for a month, I started to miss our old house. The simple reason was just that I could not find friends to play with me in our new building. So I needed to run back to my old house and play with my neighbors there. The neighbor kids were around my age. We were all innocent and friendly because of good education. Our parents were all teachers and colleagues in a high school. The school had several dormitories for teachers on the block. So we had all lived there and were like a big family.

Time did not make it easy to stay on course. After six months, I enrolled in the middle school. Homework occupied my playing time and made me say goodbye to my childhood. Later, I became a high school student, and then I was accepted as a student at the university. In those years, I hardly went back to the old house. There were several times I just passed in a rush. I noticed that something had changed, but I just let it go at that. The winter of 1999 I decided to study in the United States, so I went back to the old house and stayed there the whole afternoon to memorize my "home."

I opened the main door and heard some noises. The door was not easy to open and close because of its age. I touched some flakes of red paint that were peeling on the door, and the memories started to bring back my childhood.

It had been a Chinese New Year's Eve when my father decided to paint the door red, because red symbolized luck. I was a little girl and squatted beside my father. The red was bright, like a rose in full bloom. I told my father that it was beautiful, and my father was very proud of his painting because of my praise. From then on, I knew I was his little princess. My words could make him happy like walking in the clouds.

Being a princess, I had some privileges. I could play with other kids without finishing homework. I usually went to the high school with my neighbors. We played basketball, football, and volleyball until the sun was gone and the sky was black. There were always thousands of games we could play in such a large open space. One time we even roasted sweet potatoes on the playground and caught the fish in the school ponds for our BBQ. At that time, our parents were warned about our "bad" behaviors by the police at school. In our small world, we did not realize that we were doing something wrong. We just felt the whole school was like a paradise where we could play anything we wanted.

There was a shortcut from the old house to the high school. That was the way my father passed every day. At five-ten in the afternoon, I usually sat on a set of stone steps that were in the middle of the shortcut and waited for my father to come home. When he showed up at the head of the road, I would run as if I were flying, shouting "Pa-Pa," and jumping energetically into his arms.

One afternoon, I finished a homework assignment that involved making a swan by using thick paper. I was supposed to wipe oil on the bottom of the swan, so that it could float on the water. Unfortunately, I totally forgot this step. I put my white swan on the surface of water. But soon my swan could not float, and it sank like the *Titanic*. So my white swan became a gray one.

Then I cried and ran out to the stone steps. I sat there and waited for my father to save my poor swan. A second seemed to be a year. I stretched my neck many times looking for my father's shadow. I knew it was not five-ten yet, but I just hoped that a miracle would happen, which could bring my father here. I even counted the stone steps in three different languages, but my father still did not show up. Maybe because of my crying, I was so tired that I fell asleep on the stone steps. When I woke up, I was in the warm arms of my father. I forgot my sad story of the swan but just held my father tight, as he was my hero.

Standing on the playground and overlooking the dormitories, I tried to memorize every scene so that I could bring them to America. The laughter of my friends seemed to whisper in the wind. Most of them still lived there, but they were not at home. They might be studying in different cities now. I did not know if they missed me as now I missed them. Did they remember the taste of hot potatoes on the playground? Did all of them know that I was going to the other side of this earth? Now our worlds were not small any more, but had they found their own paradises yet?

I kept walking down and came to the shortcut. The stone steps looked so narrow. I could not imagine how I could sleep there. I looked at the head of the road, and tears came to my eyes. My father was still a teacher here. Will he feel sad when he walks on this road and I am on the other side of the earth? Will he expect a miracle to bring his little princess here?

Last September hundreds of powerful earthquakes happened in my country, Taiwan. I went back to my home this January and checked out both the old and new houses. I am glad that my beloved homes still look like the images that I have in my mind. All in all, home is my paradise that nothing can change.

Exploring the Reading through Discussion

1. What do you think the author means when she writes, "I touched some flakes of red paint that were peeling on the door, and the memories started to bring back my childhood"? Have you ever had a similar experience based on a sight or sound or smell?

2. What memories does Naihsin Weng describe? Which description do you think is the most effective? Why?

3. Find examples of objective description and subjective description in this essay.

4. The author's father is a central figure in her memories of her home and childhood. What details in the essay help you get to know him?

5. The author writes about several periods of time in her essay. Identify them. What clues does she include to help readers understand what time in her life she is describing?

Developing Vocabulary

List any words in this selection that are new to you. Write your understanding of each word from the context. Then look up each word in the dictionary, and write the definition that you think best fits the meaning in this writing.

Discovering Connections through Writing

1. Return to a favorite place that you remember from your childhood. Does what you see "still look like the images that [you] have in [your] mind"? What has changed? Compare your memory with the present reality.

2. Naihsin Weng concludes that "home is my paradise that nothing can change." Do you think she is referring only to the geographic location of her home or also to other aspects of her home? Write your definition of "home." Be sure to include both the denotation, or literal meaning of the word, and its connotations, all the associations that come with the word.

3. Have you moved from one home to another? Did you, as did Naihsin Weng, "[try] to memorize every scene" before moving on? Write to tell the story of your moving experience.

The Importance of Wearing a Safety Belt

Larissa R. Houk (student)

This student's essay challenges readers to explore the reasons for wearing a safety belt and to discover the effects on many lives when one person doesn't. Does this essay change your attitude about safety belts?

Many teenagers today seem to scoff at the idea of wearing a safety belt. Perhaps they do so because wearing a belt is not "cool." Maybe friends they drive with don't bother to wear a belt, and they fear being laughed at. Despite these and many other excuses that can be given for not wearing a safety belt, the concrete reasons for wearing a belt far outweigh these in significance.

Brian Machado's death is one example of a concrete reason.

"Mr. Machado died at Boston Medical Center from injuries received in a car accident. . . ." That's all the obituary had to say. The brief death notice failed to tell its readers the personal things that mattered most about Brian.

"Mr. Machado was a life-long resident of New Bedford," the notice read. The notice didn't mention the different houses in New Bedford where Brian had lived, how he used to tear little swatches of the wallpaper off from his bedroom wall in the house on Stapleton Street, how he and his brother wrestled each other in the living room countless times next to the brown couch their grandmother from Portugal had given them, or how very picky he was about everything that went into his room.

"He was a graduate of Roosevelt Jr. High School." Why didn't the article mention the secret crush he had on that cute girl in his math class when he was in seventh grade, how much he liked Tuesdays going home in the bus with his best friends, or how he was the real cause of that food fight that took place one November?

". . . and finished three years at Greater New Bedford Regional Vocational Technical High School." There was no mention of how much Brian hated going to Voke or how he and his friends rejoiced over the way the Packers had played their last game whenever they got together at Brian's locker on the second floor.

The obituary did say that Mr. Machado was eighteen.

It also said that Brian was employed by Stop & Shop and Burger King, but it failed to mention why he felt it necessary to work two part-time jobs when other kids his age struggled with just one. The article never mentioned Brian's plans.

The notice said that he died because of a car accident on Route 18, but it never said that Brian was on the highway because he was headed toward a Portuguese club with some of his new friends from Stop & Shop who had just ended their shift for the night.

"Mr. Machado was survived by . . ." and then a long list of names. If only those who had written the obituary had attended the funeral home, where Brian's mother sobbed loudly and bitterly, screamed and frantically clung to the still coffin surrounded with gaudy flowers, and cried out to her son in Portuguese. Maybe then they wouldn't have used the word "survived."

Perhaps the most important element of Brian's tragic death was the one thing that was most grueling to accept as fact. Bad enough that Brian was eighteen and just starting to feel more secure about himself. Bad enough that Brian's dreams for the future will never be realized. Bad enough that teenagers witnessed Brian's accident and were in the car with him when he drove. Bad enough that Brian's close friends and family lost a precious son, friend, brother, rival, and buddy that they will never see again. But worst of all, Brian's death could have been so easily prevented.

In the awful words of a state trooper at the scene of the accident, "the accident would not have been fatal if the victim had worn a belt."

If only Brian had taken a moment to click the safety belt into place over his waist, he would be alive today, working at Burger King, bagging at Stop & Shop, talking with friends, making plans for the future. Only one small click would have saved his life.

How many more of these horrible stories will we have to face? How many more times will we have to read the obituary of a teenage brother, student, sportsman, friend?

Brian's could be the last unnecessary death if only teenagers would take a moment from whatever it is they are doing in the car and simply click that safety belt over their waist. One small click. Please let's make Brian's death the last and learn from the tragedy of an eighteen-year-old boy who could have been and done so many things.

Exploring the Reading through Discussion

1. What are "the personal things that mattered most about Brian" according to Houk? Why aren't these details included in his obituary?

2. What do you think is the author's purpose in writing this essay? Does she succeed?

3. When you drive in a car, do you wear a seat belt or insist that your passengers do? Why?

4. Does Houk use a subject-by-subject or point-by-point organization of her comparison of the obituary and the personal details of her friend's life? Do you think the organization is effective? Why?

5. Several of the paragraphs in the essay are very short. Why do you think the author chose to write them this way?

Developing Vocabulary

List any words in this selection that are new to you. Write your understanding of each word from the context. Then look up each word in the dictionary, and write the definition that you think best fits the meaning in this writing.

Discovering Connections through Writing

1. Should using safety belts or wearing motorcycle helmets be mandated by law? Should the driving age be raised, or should increased restrictions be placed on drivers under age eighteen? Write an argument in which you clearly state and support your point of view on one of these

issues. Your instructor may ask you to research your topic and document the information you include.

2. Houk suggests in her introduction that peer pressure may be one reason that keeps teenagers from wearing safety belts. Write an essay in which you explore other examples of peer pressure. How do you define peer pressure? What are its causes? What effects does it have? Is peer pressure limited to people in their teens?

3. Write an essay about "the personal things that mattered most" about a friend or relative you have lost.

Exposed Toes

Diane Riva (student)

Are your old basketball shoes, the ones with the holes, your favorites? Maybe you couldn't spend a day without your floppy slippers? As you read student author Diane Riva's essay about shoes, try to discover the special connection she has to these everyday items.

The shoes scattered throughout the house belong to me. I will find a pair under the dining room table, a pair in the parlor, one or two pairs in the kitchen, and even a few in my bedroom. In my childhood memories, I can still hear my mother asking me to pick up my wayward shoes. Some habits are hard to break, and leaving my shoes wherever my feet release them is one I am still trying to overcome. When I look at my shoes, I see endless memories. They are part of my personality, and if they could talk, what colorful tales they would tell.

I own three pairs of black sneakers; they are my proud work shoes, and we spend the most time together. There are times when my feet melt when I enter them. My work as a bartender has enabled my sneakers to taste Guinness Irish stout, fine Russian vodkas, assorted hot coffee drinks, or whatever else I am rushing around the bar to make. They are the constant recipients of the overfilled glass of alcohol.

My black, tattered sneakers with tiny knots in the shoelaces have heard hours of endless stories from lonely travelers stopping in the hotel lounge, guests pouring out tales of love, heartache, job stress, divorce, battles won, battles lost, and hundreds of irritating jokes. At the end of my shift, if we are fortunate and it has rained, I give the bottoms of my hard-working sneakers a bath in a fresh puddle. It feels good to wash away work. When my feet arrive home, my sneakers are usually slipped off and left in the parlor to slumber. This is where they will quietly remain until I torture them for another eight hours of work.

Along with my sneakers, I own a pair of boat shoes. The tops are a reddish brown, the same color as an Irish Setter, and the soles are made of rubber. I have had these shoes for over six years, and still they do not age as I do. When I occasionally wear my boat shoes, I don't like the way they look on my wide feet, but they feel so good. They know me the least but struggle to be in my world. I will probably have these shoes for the rest of my life. They are like memories of past boyfriends: hard to get rid of.

When I open my closet door, my dress shoes lie dead in dusty boxes. About every four months, I will remove a pair and struggle into them. When I wear these high-heeled shoes, it is usually for a wedding, a Christmas party, or a night on the town. When I add one or two inches to my height, I end up having this pretty feeling, and my legs have a tendency to like the way they look. The sound of a high-heeled shoe on a polished marble floor at a posh restaurant, I will admit, has a certain appeal to me. I gather it is my whole look, from the top of my perfectly set hair to the ends of my smothered toes, that gives me this feeling of attractiveness.

But how I look forward to removing these falsely overstated dress shoes and returning them to their dusty coffins. Funny how these shoes never lounge around the house; they are always returned to their boxes. I would not want to insult the everyday, comfortable shoe with the high society heel.

Among my most treasured shoes is a pair of sandals. They can be worn throughout all the seasons, with or without socks. My huaraches are from Tiajuana, and on a hot day many years ago, I handpicked them myself from among many of their twins. The soles are made from black, recycled tires, and the upper portion consists of thick, tan leather strips that entwine to form an interesting open-toe design. They call my name constantly, but unfortunately, they are the most inappropriate shoe for all occasions. As I picked up my paycheck from work one cold November day, my boss commented on my unusual footwear for this time of year. He could not help but notice my well-worn extra-wide huaraches and my thick woolen socks, so he stated that it seemed an unsuitable time of year for sandals. I tried to explain the comfort zone of these broken-in shoes, but he just looked at me with confusion. I don't think that he could relate to the love–hate affair that women have with their shoes. I have had the pleasure of spoiling my feet with these huaraches for over eight years. Each spring they take a trip to the cobbler for their yearly checkup. I think the cobbler looks forward to this annual visit and admires the workmanship in these weary old sandals.

I must admit my shoes of choice were given to me by my parents, and I wear these constantly. Nothing has to be tied; they have no straps, no buckles, no leather between the toes, no heels. They are never too tight and always fit perfectly—my natural feet. Whenever possible, my feet are out of confinement, barefoot and happy. I love for my feet to touch and feel all the materials of life. They can be tickled, washed, counted, and colored. They hold all of my memories. They were on my honeymoon; they were at my daughter's birth; they feel spring and the ocean first; they have been bitten, cut, and bruised. I never have to look for them, they are always where I left them, and they never have to be put away.

As I search throughout my house and pick up my wayward shoes before my mother arrives for a visit, I look down at the bundle of leather and laces in my arms, and days of my past shout out to me. I know why these shoes are scattered about. They are my memories, and I do not want to put them away.

Exploring the Reading through Discussion

1. What is the main point the author wants to make about her shoes? On what basis does she categorize them?

2. What details help you picture the author's shoes and understand how she feels about them?

3. What are Riva's "shoes of choice"? Why are these her favorites?

4. How do the introduction and the conclusion contribute to the effectiveness of this essay?

5. In what order does the author arrange the types of shoes? Do you think this order is effective? Why?

Developing Vocabulary

List any words in this selection that are new to you. Write your understanding of each word from the context. Then look up each word in the dictionary, and write the definition that you think best fits the meaning in this writing.

Discovering Connections through Writing

1. Describe a favorite article of clothing that brings back fond memories or makes you feel good when you wear it. Help your reader understand your feelings by describing the clothing and explaining why it is special to you.

2. As Riva does with shoes, classify another type of clothing or accessory that you own, such as hats, T-shirts, or earrings. Be sure to follow a consistent method of classification.

3. The author writes about struggling into pairs of high-heeled dress shoes. Write an essay in which you support the thesis that being fashionable doesn't always mean being comfortable.

Childhood—Then and Now

Jane Patenaude (student)

Has anyone ever told you that "Life isn't the same as it used to be"? As you read this student's comparison/contrast essay, see if you agree with her about how life for children has changed.

As a child I had the freedom to roam most of North Fairhaven. Of course North Fairhaven to me was about four square blocks. Mom always knew where to find me, with friends or at the playground behind Oxford school. It seems to me that children today don't have the same type of childhood. I can't imagine a parent of today allowing a child to roam neighborhood streets as we did forty years ago. It appears to me that today's children of elementary school age have every minute of their lives filled with activities. They are kept busy with school work, soccer, or other activities. When do they have time to play?

For children growing up in the fifties our imaginations were the main source of our entertainment. Most families didn't have a television, so our entertainment came from other sources, such as dolls and balls. Barbie was just a doll then, not a collectible. We changed her outfits and created stories about her, Skipper, and Ken. We played board games, such as Clue and Parcheesi. I remember a Monopoly game that went on a whole summer. In the winter, it seemed to snow more then; we built forts of snow and had snowball fights. Our parents would have to beg us to come inside, even though our lips were turning blue from the cold.

Summer months were filled with riding bikes, running through the sprinkler in the back yard, riding on the swings and merry-go-round at the playground, and playing baseball. There were enough of us in the neighborhood to form teams and play Wiffle Ball in the street. Not many cars cruised down our side street to interrupt our game. Bike riding was a favorite pastime. One of my husband's childhood memories is of riding his bike out to Tinkham Pond in East Fairhaven. At a distance of about eight miles, it was an easy ride from the center of town, passing farms and wooded areas. Today this bike ride would entail crossing Route 6 as well as Route 240, a major highway, and two busy shopping centers, not a pleasant ride. To ride out that way today is still nice, but you would most likely transport the bikes to that part of town, then go for a bike ride, especially if you're riding with children. And it is unlikely any parents would let their children head that way on their own.

Today children have so much to keep them entertained. Electronic games, television, and videos occupy their time inside the house. Their parents spend a lot of time taxi-ing their children between activities such as soccer, T-ball, art classes, gymnastics, dance classes, and baseball. Kids today have so many diversions; it seems they have little freedom. Some adult is always there watching them or coaching them. I'm sure our parents were just as watchful, but they watched at a distance, checking on us by looking out the back window. They always knew where we were. It just wasn't obvious.

Just last summer I was at the beach with a friend. I asked where her eight-year-old son was. I couldn't believe it when she told me he was in the house watching a video. It was a beautiful day, and he was spending it inside watching a video he had seen at least five times. This kid actually has his own battery-operated car that he drives to the beach at the end of his street. As a kid the first thing I did after opening my eyes on a summer day was to look outside to see if the sun was out. I couldn't wait to go outside. And it was a huge treat if we could go to the beach for the day. The closest I came to having a car was one my mom fashioned out of sand with soda cans for headlights.

The family that lives across the street has three children, a son in elementary school, another son in middle school, and a daughter in high school. Each school has a different start time. Their mom takes three separate trips to deliver them to school. Two of these schools are within walking distance. Don't kids walk anymore?

I feel fortunate to have grown up in such an innocent time, a time when one income was enough to support a family. When I wasn't in school, I was playing in my back yard or at a neighbor's house. It bothers me to see the children at a nearby child care center playing outside in a penned-in area with adults watching over them, looking more like guards than teachers. While I'm sure there is good and bad in each generation, I'm just glad my childhood was when it was.

Exploring the Reading through Discussion

1. According to the author, what are the main differences between children of her generation and children today? Do you agree?

2. The author states that children are "kept [so] busy with school work, soccer, or other activities," that they don't have time to play. If asked, how do you think she would define "play"? Would you agree with her definition?

3. What are some of Jane Patenaude's reasons for suggesting that the type of childhood she had isn't possible today?

4. The author uses many proper and brand names in her essay. List as many of them as you can. Why do you think she includes these?

5. Is a block format or alternating format used in this comparison and contrast essay? Do you think this was a good choice? Explain.

Developing Vocabulary

List any words in this selection that are new to you. Write your understanding of each word from the context. Then look up each word in the dictionary, and write the definition that you think best fits the meaning in this writing.

Discovering Connections through Writing

1. The author writes about using her imagination as a source of entertainment. What do you think imagination is, and how do you use it? Write to explain your understanding of this term.

2. Do you agree that today's children "seem [to] have little freedom" and that our present time is a less innocent time in which to grow up? Write an essay in which you present the causes of this phenomenon. As you explore this topic, be sure to present enough details to help readers understand the complexity of this situation.

3. Ask a friend or relative who was a child in the 1950s to describe his or her childhood playtime experiences. Are they the same as Jane Patenaude's? Why? Using the mode of comparison and contrast, write about the differences or similarities.

A Bully Who Wore Bobby Pins

Amanda Beaulieu (student)

What image comes to your mind when you read the word *bully?* What is the difference between a child who is confident and a child who intimidates? As you read this story about a playground incident, explore your reactions to the narrator. Is she the proud ruler of her kingdom or a bully who should be reprimanded?

As a little girl, I was never too interested in dolls or patent leather shoes or other girls my age, for that matter. I suppose one might say I was a bit of a tomboy. I played sports, I liked bugs (except spiders, of course), and I wasn't afraid to get hurt or dirty. All my friends were boys because, in some small way, they could respect a girl who'd knock them out if they looked at her the wrong way. I guess they all figured that my "cooties" weren't as bad as the other girls'.

Being the bully with the pigtails was never an easy job, but it was a title I carried proudly. As a member of the boys' crowd, I valued my school playground as my kingdom. I could run the fastest, spit the farthest, and swing the highest. I was shameless and cruel, but I had a good time. If you were on my swing, you'd get a black eye. If you were in my way, you'd get pushed. If you had candy or a toy I liked, I took it, no questions asked. I was sitting on top of the world, and I was only in first grade!

Of course my reign was challenged over my four years on that playground. It was like going to war and having your home at stake. I can remember our playground having a jungle gym like no other I've seen. It was a massive bug with an arching tail, high eyeballs, and a gaping mouth. If the paint hadn't been so chipped and worn, it would have been green and red. Near the end of my second grade year, a myth started circulating. It was being said that only the toughest kids in school could climb to the top of the bug's eyes and jump down. Normally, myths and rumors never scared me, but this was a threat to my reputation. Of course no one had seen someone do it, so I did what anyone would have: I lied like a rug. I swore I'd done it last year. I'd done it dozens of times. Everything was perfect until another girl, with ripped corduroys and dirt-smudged cheeks, called my bluff.

She bet me a whole dollar that I couldn't do it. Then she bet me another dollar that she could. Now by this point, I was ready to move to another town, but I couldn't walk away from a challenge. I never had before. I accepted and shook her sticky hand, which was covered in McDonald's Band-Aids. It was agreed that we would meet at recess that day after lunch.

Eleven-thirty came too quickly, and I found myself standing in a ring of people waiting for my challenger. She came out late and with a clean face, as if she had washed it for the occasion. We glared at one another and began climbing. I moved up and up, one Barbie sneaker over the other, chewing my Chinese fortune gum and promising myself that even if I lost, I was going to beat the stuffing out of that girl. Finally I was at the very top. I looked down to see this sloppy girl, this threat, grinning back up at me. I was so angry, I jumped down without thinking. I landed on my feet, regained my balance, and punched her right in the stomach. I left her on her backside in the sand, holding her stomach and gasping for air. As I walked away and waited for the red to leave my cheeks, I realized what I'd done. I had climbed and jumped from the bug!

I had always liked being tough and boyish, but never so much as that day. And of all the boys and a few girls who ever dared challenge me, I was beaten only when the school closed down and they paved my little kingdom.

Exploring the Reading through Discussion

1. Do you like the little girl in this story? Why? Why is she proud to be called "the bully with the pigtails"?

2. What does the author mean when she says she was a tomboy? Do you agree with her description of what girls like to do?

3. Why does the author use the word *kingdom* to describe the playground? What other words does she use to develop this comparison? Do you think this metaphor is effective?

4. What is Beaulieu's tone in this essay? What details in the essay help you understand her attitude about this childhood experience?

5. Find examples of parallelism in this essay.

Developing Vocabulary

List any words in this selection that are new to you. Write your understanding of each word from the context. Then look up each word in the dictionary, and write the definition that you think best fits the meaning in this writing.

Discovering Connections through Writing

1. Describe a challenge that you met or a time you stood up for yourself when you were a child. Provide plenty of concrete details to help your reader understand why that experience was important.

2. What have you done that makes you particularly proud? Write an essay about that accomplishment, and be sure to describe how the achievement made you feel.

3. This story may raise some questions you would like to explore further. What should a child who is confronted by a bully do? What should children learn about resolving conflicts, and who should teach them?

Fear Not

Greg Andree (student)

Before this student author took a long walk across a dance floor, he considered what fear is and how it can affect us. As you read, ask yourself whether you have experienced each of the fears Greg Andree describes.

I looked across the dance floor; one of the most attractive women I had ever seen sat talking with some friends. She glanced toward me, but I turned away. Was she really looking at me? Why not? I'm a handsome guy. In fact, my mom tells me that all the time. I took a quick look back at her; she was still looking in my direction.

Why wouldn't she be looking at me? But she might just be looking at my friend who was sitting near me, or for that matter, she might just be trying to see what time it was (a clock hung just above my head). I could have misinterpreted a look at a clock for a glance in my direction.

What was keeping me from just getting up, walking over to her, and asking her to dance? Well, besides the fear of rejection from her and the dread of humiliation in front of her friends and mine, nothing at all.

I remember that as a kid I often sat alone in my basement doing my homework. It was the only place in the house I could go to be alone—well, besides the bathroom. If you spent too much time in there, though, people began to talk.

As daylight turned to dusk and then to darkness, the basement's shadows seemed to take on a life of their own; sounds that might have been ordinary before now sounded strange and menacing. I decided that this was no longer the ideal place for me to be alone with my thoughts. I got up and started walking slowly toward the steps that led to my family and the safety of their number. I wanted to run but refused to give the monster the satisfaction of knowing that it drove me from my own basement. I had to be brave and fight the panic that was welling up inside me. By the time I reached the stairs, I could feel its hot breath on my neck. I was sure that the creature was about to attack and drag me down into his hidden lair. Before it could, I ran, taking the stairs two at a time. If I could only reach the top, I would be safe.

Looking back now, it seems silly, but to a nine-year-old it was life or death. It's the same as when a thirteen-year-old, afraid of not fitting in, does everything within his power to belong. The worst thing in the world to a young teenager is the "problem" of being unique, having special talents or interests that are outside the margins of acceptability to the "popular" kids in school.

An example of this, from a boy's perspective, is that you're accepted if you excel in sports but are hopelessly doomed to exile if you are talented in music or art. As we get older, we realize these talents are gifts, not curses, and are grateful for our uniqueness, although knowing this now didn't make it easier then.

Now, as a college student, I have other fears. What if I fail in the career I've chosen, if I don't fulfill my dreams? How will I support myself, my family? Someday, if I do prosper in my career, will I look back at my college years and laugh at fears that now seem so enormous? What will my fears be then? Old age, senility, death? I don't really know.

What I do know is that no matter who we are or what our station in life is, we all have fears. Some are reasonable and keep us safe from the dangers that surround us constantly, and others are unreasonable and ridiculous, or seem so to those of us who don't share them. Some make us strive to do better; others keep us from attempting the things we would really like to do. If there's a fear holding you back from accomplishing your dreams, you have two choices: Either find a way to overcome it, or cower in its shadow and learn to live with what could have been.

But enough of all that. I was in the middle of one of my adventures. Now, where was I? Never mind, I remember. . . .

What should I do? Just sit there and not take the chance, or seize the day as Robin Williams would have in the movie *Dead Poets Society*? Which is best, to have loved and lost, or, in this case, tried and failed, or to have never tried at all? Finally, I thought of the advice Kevin Kline had given to a young pirate in Gilbert and Sullivan's *Pirates of Penzance:* "Always follow the dictates of your heart, my boy, and chance the consequences."

With this in mind, I got to my feet and made my way across the room to where she and her friends were sitting. I stood just a few feet from her. Doing my best Christian Slater imitation, I looked into her eyes and said, "Excuse me, Miss, would you care to dance?" She seemed to think it over for a moment, then took my hand and nodded her approval. "You do understand you'll be dancing with me, right?" I said. She laughed and said that she understood that I was included in the bargain.

As we danced, she leaned in close to me, her face inches from mine, and I felt her warm breath caress my cheek. She looked into my eyes and said, "Do you know what time it is? I really couldn't see the clock that well from where I was sitting."

Exploring the Reading through Discussion

1. What types of fear does the writer describe? In what order does he present these? Which fear do you think is the worst?

2. What did the author learn about what he feared as he grew older?

3. Some fears "are reasonable and keep us safe from the dangers that surround us constantly, and others are unreasonable and ridiculous." What examples can you think of to support this statement?

4. What is the thesis of this essay? Why do you think the author placed it where he did?

5. The author's story begins and ends at a dance. Where does the author shift from the chronological order of his narrative? How does he help readers understand that they are reading a flashback?

Developing Vocabulary

List any words in this selection that are new to you. Write your understanding of each word from the context. Then look up each word in the dictionary, and write the definition that you think best fits the meaning in this writing.

Discovering Connections through Writing

1. Write about a time you were afraid. Help readers understand not only what happened but also how the fear affected you. Did it hold you back or make you find a way to overcome it?

2. "If I only had known then what I know now." Have you ever had this thought? Write to explain why.

3. Andree quotes a line he heard in a film version of a Gilbert and Sullivan play: "Always follow the dictates of your heart, my boy, and chance the consequences." Do you agree with this advice? Provide specific examples to help your readers understand why you think the way you do.

R-E-S-P-E-C-T

Josh Trepanier (student)

Are people becoming increasingly more rude? Are parents shirking their duties to teach good manners? Or is etiquette less important in our fast-paced world? As you read this student's essay, explore your response to these and other questions that are raised.

Can you remember a time when men held doors for women and elders, and took off their hats when they were inside? Do you recall the days when youngsters wouldn't dare talk back to their parents or grandparents out of sheer respect? People who do remember those instances must be appalled at the lack of manners in today's society. It is becoming increasingly difficult to find people who still use the simple words *please* and *thank you* on a daily basis. Even "polite society" is no longer very polite. The general level of respect people have for other people has declined rapidly in the past few decades and it will continue to decrease until we teach ourselves and our children otherwise.

Who is to blame for the current decline in manners? The place where kids are most disrespectful is usually the place where they learn to be that way—at home. Children are refusing to obey parents more and more every day. Eight years ago, I could have never worn my hat at the dinner table; my mom would have thrown a fit. Nowadays, youngsters sit down to supper with their hats on, while playing hand-held video games, and parents don't blink an eye. Some kids are even allowed to use profane language in front of their parents. Such casual attitudes about disrespect are at the root of the growing problem America is having with unmannered youth. If impoliteness around the household continues to go unnoticed, the rude children will someday turn into rude adults, continuing the current trend of disrespectfulness. Of course, the media have also contributed to the growing problem by portraying the rudeness of our youth in a comical light in many modern family sitcoms.

Another way Americans show this loss of manners is in how they treat their elders. The number of senior citizens in nursing homes is on the rise, and I'm sure many of them could be just as well taken care of at home. However, some people don't have the patience and respect they once had for their parents, and a nursing home is becoming an easy alternative for rising numbers of elderly people across the country. Elders are also shown less and less respect on the roads. Older people who drive a little slower than the fast-paced younger drivers are harassed by the honking horns, flashing lights, and hand gestures of more youthful drivers. I'm sure the senior citizens of today are wondering why they don't get the same kind of respect they showed their elders. It is too bad that there isn't a single good reason to give them for the loss of manners Americans seem to suffer from.

Teachers across the United States experience the bad etiquette of students on a daily basis. For the most part, it is the high school teachers who see the biggest change in their pupils' attitudes. Teens are no longer afraid to talk back to teachers, which would have resulted in a few whacks from a ruler years ago. Maybe if we give the teachers their rulers back, kids might be a little more careful of what they say during school. The problem is that the instructors hear the disrespectful adolescents and let them get away with being totally ignorant. I suppose it's true that they aren't paid to babysit, but by allowing rude behavior to go unchastised for so long, teachers have only made their own jobs more irritating. The students will continue to use little or no manners in school until somebody puts an end to the everyday lack of respect they are allowed to show their teachers.

Basically, the problem America is now facing is one of neglect. We can no longer afford to ignore our children's bad manners. Had we put a stop to these lax attitudes about manners when they first showed up in kids, the problem most likely wouldn't have become as extreme as it is. We, as a nation, need to recognize and rectify the problems that exist due to the rudeness and disrespectfulness of our youth. Although chivalry may be a thing of the past, I think it's time for courtesy and respect to make a comeback in our society.

Exploring the Reading through Discussion

1. How many words with similar meanings to the tile, "R-E-S-P-E-C-T," can you identify in the essay? Do the words have different connotations?

2. Did you recognize anyone you know in any of the examples included in the essay? Do you also consider these behaviors to be bad manners?

3. What are some causes for the decline in manners that the author observes?

4. Do the examples of bad manners that the author includes in his writing differ in significance or importance? Are those differences reflected in the organization of the paragraphs?

5. Identify the topic sentences in each paragraph. Besides using topic sentences, what other methods does the author use to achieve coherence in his essay?

Developing Vocabulary

List any words in this selection that are new to you. Write your understanding of each word from the context. Then look up each word in the dictionary, and write the definition that you think best fits the meaning in this writing.

Discovering Connections through Writing

1. Do you agree with the author's thesis? Use plenty of specific examples to support your opinion.

2. Should teachers be stricter concerning student manners in the classroom? If you were a teacher, what specific behaviors do you think you would not allow?

3. The author writes that "*chivalry* may be a thing of the past." What is your understanding of that word? Should chivalry be forgotten? Would you like to see it come back? Be sure to provide reasons to support your argument.

Bilingual Education: The Need to Reform

Ana Gomes (student)

Is there a local or state education issue that is of concern to you? Have you expressed your views at election time? What facts and experiences influenced you? As you read student Ana Gomes's argument about bilingual education, try to discover what led her to develop her thesis.

Transitional Bilingual Education (TBE) is a program that was created to ease students who are non-English-speaking or have limited English-speaking skills into mainstream classes. I firmly believe that the TBE program can help bilingual students achieve self-esteem and academic achievement for success in years to come. Every year the children of immigrants start school without knowing how to speak English. It is not fair to just throw them into an all-English-speaking class and think that they will perform as well as the English-speaking students. Teaching bilingual students in their native language promotes self-esteem and academic achievement. However, I believe that two years of such teaching is sufficient for the elementary-level students and three to four years for the older students. After that, students need to move into mainstream classes so they will not become segregated from the general student population.

When I arrived in the United States I did not speak or understand the English language. I started attending school and immediately enrolled in a TBE program. We were taught all subjects in our native language, and English was rarely taught and never enforced. After I was in the TBE program for not even a year, I had to take art, physical education, and music classes with English-speaking students. I found this very difficult and traumatic because I was not prepared to function in an all-English-speaking class.

One particularly traumatic class that comes to mind is an art class that I had to take probably around the fourth grade. Only English was allowed in this class. This made me look like an outcast, especially when I could not do my work because I didn't understand the directions and had no one to interpret for me. This is an awful feeling to have as a child—not good for anyone's self-esteem. If I spoke in my native language, I was automatically staying after school. I never could understand how it was bad behavior to speak the only language I knew. I felt resentment from this particular teacher because she did not know how to handle us, much less communicate with us. When there are language barriers between teachers and students, it becomes very difficult to teach and to learn. These English-only classes became silent memories embedded in my mind, because I could not understand enough words to form a sentence.

Massachusetts is one of only nine states that requires a TBE program to be offered if there is a sufficient number of students within a school district (Rossell and Baker 1). Under the current system a student is allowed to spend three years in the TBE classroom. The program may be extended for up to seven years at the discretion of the school administration or the parents of a student (Duran 1). However, I found that spending more than four years in a TBE setting segregated me from the general student population.

The current bilingual education program needs reform. Observations of bilingual classes demonstrated that the quality of education varied from one school district to another (Rossell and Baker 1). In 1994, recommendations were made by the Bilingual Education Commission but were never put into effect (Duran 1). The recommendations included increasing the number of certified bilingual teachers, providing better training for those who work with bilingual students, supporting parent involvement, and ensuring that funds allocated for bilingual students were spent on bilingual programs only (Duran 2).

One great plan, a two-way bilingual program, is in effect at the Barbieri School in Framingham, Massachusetts. This program was started about twelve years ago because the TBE students had become segregated from the rest of the student population (Steiny 1). With this two-way bilingual program, students come together and have the opportunity to learn from one another. Bilingual students switch classes weekly—one week taking classes in English and the next week in their native language. These bilingual students have tested higher on the MCAS (the Massachusetts Comprehensive Assessment System) than bilingual students in the regular program, despite the fact that the two-way program does not have more gifted children and does not discriminate against special needs students (Steiny 2). This program has become so successful that it has a waiting list, and another school plans to try the same approach (Steiny 3). This is a great program that many school districts should learn from and that could improve bilingual education in Massachusetts.

Children who can use their native language in school have higher self-esteem and greater academic achievement. Still, bilingual students face a number of challenges: being segregated, being improperly placed, and being taught by unqualified staff. I found that the bilingual program had its ups and downs. For example, it helped me in the beginning, but after a while, I felt segregated from the general student population. This lowered my self-esteem when it came to education. I asked myself, Why am I being held in this TBE program? Am I not smart enough to be in an all-English-speaking classroom? Schools need to teach bilingual students how to speak English; it's not enough to teach all subjects in students' native language. The challenge is finding the right balance between teaching in the native language and in English. "Massachusetts has spent a great deal of time and money to improve public education. That all-out effort must include bilingual education, the weakest link in the school system" ("Bilingual Trap").

Works Cited

"Bilingual Trap." *Worcester Sunday Telegram & Gazette.* 15 Nov. 1998. <http://www.onenation.org/1198/11598.html>.

Duran, Rebecca. "Massachusetts Legislators Debate Fate of Bilingual Education System." *Boston University Free Press.* 12 Jan. 2000. <http://www.onenation.org/0001/011200.html>.

"Language Barrier." *Worcester Telegram & Gazette.* 24 Apr. 1996. <http://onenation.org/1996/042496.html>.

Rossell, Christine, and Keith Baker. *Bilingual Education in Massachusetts: The Emperor Has No Clothes.* 1996. <http://www.pioneerinstitute.org/research/pioppaper/summ10.cfm>.

Steiny, Julia. "These Kids Have It Both Ways." *Providence Journal-Bulletin.* 8 Oct. 2000. <http://www. Onenation.org/0010/100800c.html>.

Exploring the Reading through Discussion

1. What is the thesis of this essay?

2. Explain your understanding of the term *bilingual education*. Do you support the practice of bilingual education? Why or why not?

3. Ana Gomes uses her own experiences in the essay. Does this strengthen or weaken her argument? Why?

4. What evidence besides personal experience does the author provide to support her thesis? Is it sufficient?

5. What type of documentation does Ana Gomes use? Does she quote directly from other sources or does she summarize and paraphrase?

Developing Vocabulary

List any words in this selection that are new to you. Write your understanding of each word from the context. Then look up each word in the dictionary, and write the definition that you think best fits the meaning in this writing.

Discovering Connections through Writing

1. Have you studied another language besides your native language? What did you find challenging? What did you enjoy? What did you learn about yourself or others as a result? Describe your experience.

2. Ana Gomes writes about the "awful feeling" that resulted from being different from her classmates. Have you ever felt like an outcast? Tell your story.

3. Write an essay in which you inform your readers about bilingual education programs in your state or community. If you research your topic, be sure to document any material that you obtain from sources other than from your own experience.

Appendix A
Writing with a Computer

Most experienced college writers will tell you that they could not live without their computers. Before these powerful tools came on the scene, writers had to generate draft after draft by hand or on a typewriter. Now you can create one draft and then easily revise it many times without ever having to start again from scratch. If you know a few easy commands, you can change the order of your words, sentences, and paragraphs or add or delete either a single word or a whole chunk of text with little effort.

If you have not used a computer for word processing before, then this appendix will introduce you to some basic functions. If you will be using your school's computer lab, plan on spending some time with an instructional manual or tutorial. Your lab may also have advisers who can help you learn specific commands for the word-processing software you will be using. Especially important is the **Help** command, which provides answers to questions about the software right on the computer screen.

Because Microsoft® Word is one of the most widely used programs for both IBM and Macintosh computers, we will refer to its commands in our discussion below. However, every program is slightly different, so you may have to adapt some of the instructions you are about to read for the software you are using. Be sure to schedule enough lab time both for learning software and for writing.

If you are an experienced computer user, you will probably be familiar with all of the commands described below, and more. However, you may still discover some new ideas to help you become more efficient at writing and rewriting—so read on.

Creating Your First File

Most word-processing software will let you begin entering text as soon as you enter the program. Simply type as if you were using a typewriter, and the words will appear on the screen. The program will automatically put breaks in the lines, so do not use the **Enter** key unless you want to start a new paragraph.

Before you enter a great deal of text, however, you should use the **Save** command. This tells your program to store your work in an electronic file. These files are something like the folders you store in file cabinets, but they are on the computer's hard disk or on a floppy or zip disk that you can carry home with you. If you save your prewriting or draft in a file, then next time you want to work on it, you can retrieve it. If you do not save your words in a file, they will be lost when you switch off the computer.

When you use the **Save** command, the computer will display a prompt, or a request, for you to enter a file name. Some programs limit the number of letters you can use for a name, but try to choose one that describes the contents. For example, if you're doing a freewriting (see Chapter 2, "Generating Ideas through Prewriting," pages 17–18) to generate ideas for a psychology paper, then you might name the file "psycfree."

While you are writing, use the **Save** command *every fifteen minutes or so* to update the material stored in your file. When you are finished working, type the file name at the bottom of the page, and use the **Print** command to print out a hard copy that you can highlight or edit. Then, use either the **Close** command to leave the file or the **Exit** command to leave the word-processing program.

Writing Your First Draft

As you discovered in Chapter 2, "Generating Ideas through Prewriting," computers are excellent tools for prewriting activities, such as freewriting, clustering, and journal writing. Once you have worked out your ideas through one of these activities, you are ready to begin composing on your computer.

If you are writing a paragraph, you can start by working on a topic sentence. If you are writing an essay, then you can begin by developing your thesis statement. For either task, you can quickly draft sentences and leave them on the screen for reference as you expand and refine your statement.

Expanding and Revising Sentences

You can add words to a sentence by moving the cursor (the small flashing line on the screen) to the place where you want to insert them and then typing them in. Eliminate words by pressing the **Backspace** or **Delete** key. The series of thesis statements below shows how one writer expanded and revised her first sentence until she achieved the results she wanted.

First draft	This past year was the hottest one on record.
Second draft	After the hottest year on record, scientists wonder whether global warming is the cause.
Final draft	Although global warming may have played a role in this year's record-breaking heat, scientists say other factors were also at play.

Once you have a workable sentence, you may want to distinguish it with boldface type to help focus your attention on the topic as you compose. You can also distinguish the topic sentence of each paragraph in boldface as you write your draft. Most programs require that you select the words you want to boldface and then either press a boldface function key or choose boldface from a font style menu. Check with your lab instructor, use the **Help** function, or consult your manual for directions on selecting text and making it bold.

When you are satisfied with your sentence, you can delete your earlier versions. Or use the **Cut** and **Paste** functions in your program menu to place them at the end of your document. The **Cut** command will store a copy of the text you select on your program's *clipboard,* a temporary storage area. The **Paste** command will transfer the text from the clipboard to the screen. Again, your program may have different names or keys for these functions, so consult your lab instructor or manual or use the **Help** command.

When you begin composing your supporting sentences or paragraphs, check your manual or use the **Help** command to find out how to set your format for triple line spacing. As you write, you can continue using the **Cut** and **Paste** sequence to rearrange words, sentences, and paragraphs. You can also use the **Copy** command. This command will leave your words in the same place on the screen and will also store a copy of those words on the clipboard. Then you can **Paste** the copy anywhere else you need it in your paragraph or essay.

Remember, however, that it is best not to fuss too much over your first draft. Try to let your thoughts and words flow freely, and avoid criticizing what you have written. As you will recall from Chapter 4, "Refining and Polishing Your Draft," most writers like to put their first draft aside for a time and give it a fresh look later. Most writers also find it easier to review a hard copy than to reread an entire draft on a screen. So close your file: Type the name of the file at the bottom of your page so that you can easily locate the file later, and save your work. Then use the **Print** command to obtain a copy of your work from the closest printer. Finally, use the **Close** command to close the file.

Revising and Editing Your Draft

As you review the hard copy of your draft, write notes to yourself in the margin, and write any corrections or changes in the space between the lines. (Some software programs allow you to do this on the screen if you prefer.) If you have given your draft to a classmate, ask him or her to do the same. Then retrieve the file for your first draft using the **Open** command. When the file is open, use the **Save as** function to create an exact duplicate of it. Assign the duplicate file another name. For a paper on the thesis statement on page 568, for example, you might name your first revision file "Warmrev1." Then revise your paper, inserting and deleting words as you look at the notes on your hard copy, and rethink your thesis or topic sentence and supporting points. Again, use the **Cut** and **Paste** sequence to move text as needed.

Each time you revise your paper, save each new version to a new file so that you will have a complete record of your work. While you are working on a revision, you may decide that you could use a sentence or paragraph from an earlier draft in your paper. Simply open the file, place the text on your clipboard using the **Copy** command, and close the file. Then open your revision file, and use the **Paste** command to place the text in its new position. If you are working with a system that lets you open more than one file at a time, you can switch back and forth between drafts as you revise.

As you revise, you may want to check for logic and coherence by boldfacing all the transitional words in your paper to see whether you have given your reader enough help to understand the connections between your thoughts. Or you may want to boldface all the adjectives that appeal to the five senses to see whether you have described your thoughts in enough detail. When you are satisfied with your revision, eliminate the boldface by selecting the words and repeating your boldface command sequence. The words will then appear in regular type on the screen.

Next, use the spell checker, style checker, or any other tools your program offers to check your work. Do not assume, however, that these tools will do the whole job for you. See the section "Using Computer Tools to Your Advantage" in Chapter 4, "Refining and Polishing Your Draft," (page 87) for an explanation of their limitations. Change your format instructions for double line spacing, and then print out your paper. Finally, save your final version before closing the file and exiting the program.

Becoming a Power User

Once you have learned the basic functions we have described, do not stop there. Keep in mind that many of the commands just discussed offer an array of options and possibilities. Experiment with these and other commands that can help you prepare polished papers in your other courses. Your word-processing software may allow you to insert tables, draw boxes, vary your type size and font, and perform many other formatting operations. Moreover, some functions can save you time by storing and inserting text that you use frequently, such as your name and address.

If a short course is offered on your campus, consider signing up to learn even more applications. In addition, take advantage of the opportunities on your campus to join the global community of writers using networked computers to conduct research and work together on projects. Once you become comfortable working on a computer, you will discover countless ways to use and share your writing skills.

Basic Commands for Writers—A Quick Reference Guide Based on Microsoft® Word Software	
Command	**Basic Function**
Backspace	Moves the cursor back one space; deletes text one letter at a time.
Close	Closes the file in which you are working.

Command	Basic Function
Copy	Copies selected text from a document, leaving the original text in place. Stores the copy on the *clipboard,* a temporary storage area.
Cut	Removes selected text from a document and stores it on the *clipboard,* a temporary storage area.
Delete	Deletes either a single letter or a selected block of text.
Exit	Allows you to leave the word-processing program.
Help	Provides access to an online manual that displays procedures, defines terms, and explains commands on your computer screen.
Open	Retrieves an electronic file that you have saved and named.
Paste	Transfers text stored on the *clipboard* to a location that you select in your document.
Print	Sends your document to a printer that will produce a hard copy.
Save	Stores your document in an electronic file, using a file name that you assign.
Save as	Saves an exact copy of your document in a separate file, using a file name that you assign.

Appendix B
Tips for ESL Writers

As someone who can speak and write in a language—perhaps two or three—other than English, you should consider yourself truly fortunate. After all, the world is becoming a smaller place each year, and the knowledge of more than one language gives you a genuine advantage in a multicultural country and in a world where all major corporations are multinational.

But mastering writing in English must also feel frustrating at times. When you write in English, you must think about the many possible ways that English differs from your native language. For example, a sentence with an unusual word order will confuse your readers, so keep in mind the ways your language and English differ in sentence structure and word order. In addition, you must correct the common problems you have with English grammar so that you communicate clearly. The rules for capitalization, articles, spelling, and punctuation can also be very confusing. However, they help to make your writing correct, and correct standard English is more easily understood. Most important of all, you must think about the logic of paragraphs and essays written in English, which might be very different from the logical forms of composition in your language group and culture. If your goal is communication, you must learn to use the patterns that English speakers use to understand each other. The following guidelines will help you achieve this goal.

Sentence Basics

- Make sure each sentence has a subject and a verb. If a group of words does not have both, it does not express a complete idea. *See Chapter 17, "The Sentence," and Chapter 18, "Fragments."*

FAULTY   [verb] *Thought* of a good idea.   [*Subject missing*]

REVISED   [subject] [verb] *You thought* of a good idea.   [*A statement*]

In writing, the subject can be an implied *you* only if you are making a command. *See the section "Recognizing Subjects" on pages 277–278 in Chapter 17.*

EXAMPLE   [subject] [verb] [*You*] *Think* of a good idea!   [*A command*]

572

- Make sure that *is* and *are* verbs are linked to a subject. The words *it* and *there* and words describing a location can sometimes substitute in the normal location of a subject at the beginning of a sentence. In such cases, the actual subject is then found after the verb. (Usually, in English, the subject comes before the verb.) *See the section "Avoiding Agreement Errors When the Subject Follows the Verb" on pages 325–326 in Chapter 21, "Subject–Verb Agreement," and the section "Working with Forms of* To Be*" on pages 360–361 in Chapter 23, "Irregular Verbs and Frequently Confused Verbs."*

FAULTY

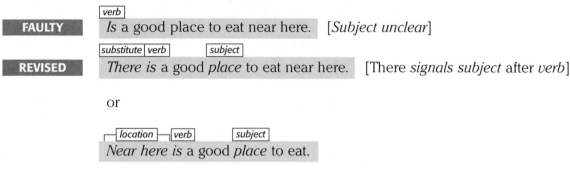

> verb
> *Is* a good place to eat near here.   [*Subject unclear*]

REVISED

> substitute | verb | subject
> *There is* a good *place* to eat near here.   [There *signals subject* after *verb*]

or

> location — verb | subject
> *Near here is* a good *place* to eat.

- In English sentences, the word *there* with some form of the verb *to be* is commonly followed by a noun or pronoun, which serves as the subject. The noun or pronoun may have modifiers, or it may be followed by a word or phrase that specifies a place.

EXAMPLES

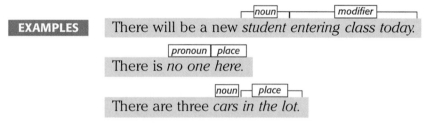

> noun | modifier
> There will be a new *student entering class today.*

> pronoun | place
> There is *no one here.*

> noun | place
> There are three *cars in the lot.*

- The word *it* with the verb *to be* is commonly followed by an adjective, an adjective with a modifier, an identification, or an expression of time, weather, or distance.

EXAMPLES

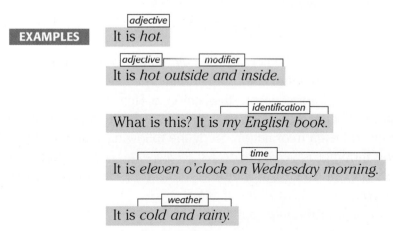

> adjective
> It is *hot.*

> adjective | modifier
> It is *hot outside and inside.*

> identification
> What is this? It is *my English book.*

> time
> It is *eleven o'clock on Wednesday morning.*

> weather
> It is *cold and rainy.*

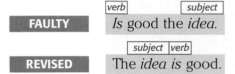

It is *twenty miles from school to home.*

The word *there* is not used in these expressions.

| FAULTY | *There* is long. *There* has been a long time. |

| REVISED | *It* is long. *It* has been a long time. |

Word Order

- In most English sentences, the subject comes first, followed by the verb.

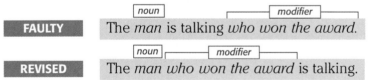

| FAULTY | *Is* good the *idea.* |

| REVISED | The *idea is* good. |

- Adjectives, even a string of adjectives, usually come *before* nouns. *See Chapter 27, "Adjectives, Adverbs, and Other Modifiers: Using Describing and Modifying Words Effectively," for more information about adjectives.*

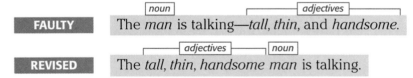

| FAULTY | The *man* is talking—*tall, thin,* and *handsome.* |

| REVISED | The *tall, thin, handsome man* is talking. |

- Groups of words that modify a noun, however, usually come immediately *after* the noun if they begin with a relative pronoun: *who, whom, whose, which, that,* and so forth.

| FAULTY | The *man* is talking *who won the award.* |

| REVISED | The *man who won the award* is talking. |

- In some cases, modifiers with an *-ed* or *-ing* verb form must go after a noun they identify. That is, they follow the noun if they add essential identifying information to the sentence. However, they can appear either immediately before or immediately after a noun about which they add extra information. Study the following examples, in which the *-ing* modifier is necessary to tell *which man. See the section "Avoiding Dangling and Misplaced Modifiers" on pages 433–435 in Chapter 27.*

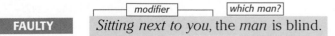

| FAULTY | *Sitting next to you,* the *man* is blind. |

REVISED

`noun`—`identifying modifier`

The *man sitting next to you* is blind.

Now compare the revised sentence above with the example below, in which the modifier adds extra information.

EXAMPLE

`modifier`   `noun`

Forgetting his promise, John is talking instead of listening.

- If the modifier is necessary to identify the noun, you don't use commas to separate it from the noun. If the modifier adds information about the noun, but the sentence makes sense without it, then set the modifier off with commas. *See the section "Using Commas to Set Off Elements That Interrupt Sentence Flow" on pages 491–492 in Chapter 30, "Commas."*

EXAMPLE

`noun` `modifier`

My *friend Frank* works hard.

The modifier is needed to identify which friend, *my friend Frank*, not *my friend Tom*, so no commas are needed.

EXAMPLE

`noun`   `modifier`

Frank, who lives next door, works hard.

The modifier provides extra information that isn't necessary for the sentence to make sense, so it needs commas.

- Adverbs usually are placed after *to be* verbs (*is/are/was/were*) but before other one-word verbs. *See the section "Understanding Adjectives and Adverbs" on page 427 in Chapter 27.*

EXAMPLE

`verb` `adverb`

They *are often* late.

EXAMPLE

`adverb`   `verb`

Birds *usually arrive* in the spring.

- Adverbs often go between verbs which have two parts (verb phrases).

EXAMPLE

`helping verb` `adverb`   `verb`

They *have often arrived* late.

- Pronouns that rename the subject in the same sentence are usually unnecessary and confusing—even when a long modifier separates the subject from the verb. The order of the words in a sentence makes the idea clear.

FAULTY

`subject`   `modifier`   `subject` `verb`

The *place* where they studied *it was* old.

REVISED

`subject`   `modifier`   `verb`

The *place* where they studied *was* old.

Agreement

- Make the subject and verb agree in number. Be especially careful about collective nouns, such as *family* and *class*, and words that specify uncountable things, such as *sugar* and *water. See the section "Considering Singular Nouns Ending in -s, Collective Nouns, and Cue Words" on pages 391–392 in Chapter 25, "Nouns: Working Effectively with Words That Name."*

- You can count *fingers, books,* or *students,* so they are called *count* words. You cannot count *freedom, advice,* or *machinery,* so they are called *noncount* words. Noncount words always take a singular verb and a singular pronoun reference.

	noncount noun | *plural verb*	*plural pronoun reference* | *plural verb*
FAULTY	*Sugar make* the recipe better. *They are* tasty.	

	noncount noun | *singular verb*	*singular pronoun reference* | *singular verb*
REVISED	*Sugar makes* the recipe better. *It is* tasty.	

- Some words are count with one meaning and noncount with another meaning.

EXAMPLES   Three *chickens are* in the yard.   [*Countable animals*]

Chicken is good with white wine.   [*Noncountable meat*]

Three pieces of *chicken is* enough.   [*Quantity of noncountable meat*]

- As the last example shows, some aspects of noncount words can be measured. You can count the number of *lumps* of sugar, *cups* of milk, *tablespoons* of flour, or *gallons* of water, but you cannot say *ten sugars, three milks, two flours,* and *four waters* as a complete grammatical form. Even though you can number *quantities* like *two pounds, six quarts, three minutes, five dollars,* and *ten gallons,* the "*of* phrase" with the noncount word makes a singular subject, which makes the verb singular (*two pounds of butter is*). You must use a *singular verb* with any quantity of noncount items. *See the sections "Using the Simple Present, Simple Future, and Simple Past Tenses" on pages 342–343 in Chapter 22, "Basic Tenses for Regular Verbs," and "Maintaining Agreement with Indefinite Pronouns" on pages 406–408 in Chapter 26, "Pronouns: Understanding Case, Clear Pronoun–Antecedent Agreement, and Nonsexist Pronoun Usage."*

	count noun
EXAMPLES	Twelve *cups are* necessary because we have twelve guests. [*12 items*]

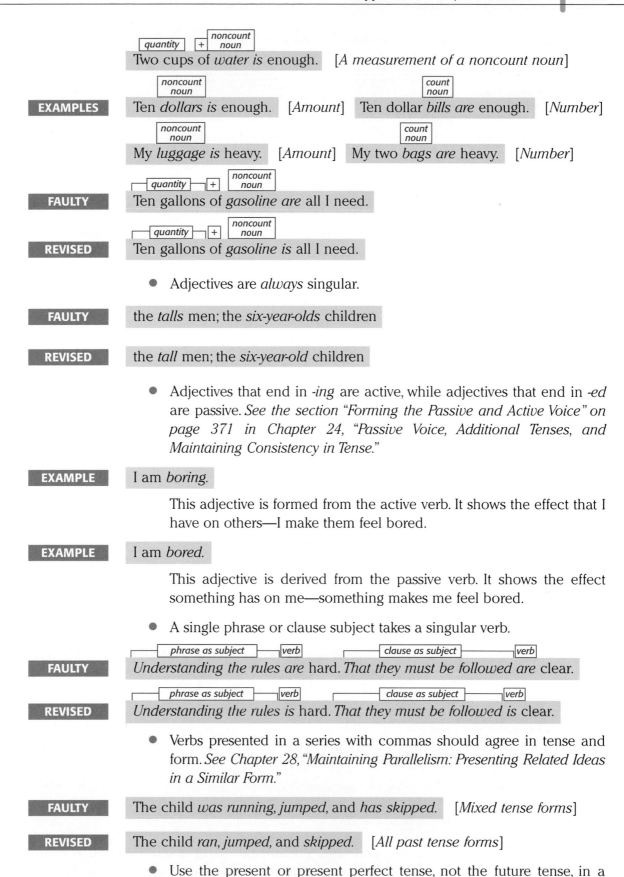

quantity + noncount noun

Two cups of *water is* enough.   [*A measurement of a noncount noun*]

EXAMPLES

noncount noun

Ten *dollars is* enough.   [*Amount*]

count noun

Ten dollar *bills are* enough.   [*Number*]

noncount noun

My *luggage is* heavy.   [*Amount*]

count noun

My two *bags are* heavy.   [*Number*]

FAULTY

quantity + noncount noun

Ten gallons of *gasoline are* all I need.

REVISED

quantity + noncount noun

Ten gallons of *gasoline is* all I need.

● Adjectives are *always* singular.

FAULTY   the *talls* men; the *six-year-olds* children

REVISED   the *tall* men; the *six-year-old* children

● Adjectives that end in *-ing* are active, while adjectives that end in *-ed* are passive. *See the section "Forming the Passive and Active Voice" on page 371 in Chapter 24, "Passive Voice, Additional Tenses, and Maintaining Consistency in Tense."*

EXAMPLE   I am *boring.*

This adjective is formed from the active verb. It shows the effect that I have on others—I make them feel bored.

EXAMPLE   I am *bored.*

This adjective is derived from the passive verb. It shows the effect something has on me—something makes me feel bored.

● A single phrase or clause subject takes a singular verb.

FAULTY

phrase as subject   verb

Understanding the rules are hard.

clause as subject   verb

That they must be followed are clear.

REVISED

phrase as subject   verb

Understanding the rules is hard.

clause as subject   verb

That they must be followed is clear.

● Verbs presented in a series with commas should agree in tense and form. *See Chapter 28, "Maintaining Parallelism: Presenting Related Ideas in a Similar Form."*

FAULTY   The child *was running, jumped,* and *has skipped.*   [*Mixed tense forms*]

REVISED   The child *ran, jumped,* and *skipped.*   [*All past tense forms*]

● Use the present or present perfect tense, not the future tense, in a subordinate time or *if* clause, whose main clause is future tense. *See the section "Maintaining Consistency in Tense" on pages 376–377 in Chapter 24 for more on keeping the voice of tense consistent.*

| | subordinate clause | main clause |

FAULTY   After I will do my homework, I will go out.

| | subordinate clause | main clause |

REVISED   After I have done my homework, I will go out.

Confusing Verb Forms

Don't omit the *-s* in the third person singular, present tense verb forms. *See the section "Using the Simple Present, Simple Future, and Simple Past Tenses" on pages 342–343 in Chapter 22.*

FAULTY   He *come* here every day.

REVISED   He *comes* here every day.

- Memorize the irregular verbs. *See the section "Identifying Irregular Verbs" on pages 354–357 in Chapter 23.* Some verb pairs such as the following can be confusing, but remembering which takes an object and which does not will help you tell the difference. The verbs *shine/shone, lie, sit,* and *rise* never have an object; the verbs *shine/shined, lay, set,* and *raise* always have an object:

No Object	*Object*
His shoes shone.	He shined *his shoes.*
She lay in the sun.	She laid *her books* on the floor.
She sat in the chair.	She set *the table* for four.
The sun rises every morning.	They raised *the flag.*

- Use complete passive verb forms; combine a form of *to be* with the past participle of another verb. *See the section "Forming the Passive and Active Voice" on page 371 in Chapter 24.*

FAULTY   His work finished.

REVISED   His work *was* finished.   [*Add form of* to be]

or

He finished his work.   [*Transform to active voice*]

- Use *-'s* to make contractions using *is* and *has,* but shorten *has* only when it is a helping verb. To sound more formal, avoid contractions like *she's.* Write *she is* instead.

| FAULTY | She's some money. |
| REVISED | She has some money. |

| INFORMAL | She's ready to help. |
| FORMAL | She is ready to help. |

- Verbs describing a completed mental process (*believe, consider, forget, know, remember, think, understand*), a consistent preference (*drink, swim, eat*), a state of being (*am, appear, have, seem, remember, forget, love*), or a perception (*feel, hear, see, taste*) can never be progressive. If the verb refers to an incomplete process, it can be progressive. *See the section "Using the Progressive and Perfect Progressive Tenses" on pages 373–374 in Chapter 24.*

EXAMPLES	I *consider* my choice good. [*An already completed decision*]
	I *am considering* going. [*A decision-making process not yet complete*]
	I *think* he should be president. [*A completed intellectual position*]
	I *am thinking* about what to do this summer. [*An incomplete thought process*]
	I *drink* coffee. [*A consistent preference*]
	I *am drinking* coffee. [*An incomplete action*]

| FAULTY | I *am seeing* you. I *am liking* you, but I *am loving* cheeseburgers. |

| REVISED | I *see* you. I *like* you, but I *love* cheeseburgers. |

- *Do* and *make* do not mean the same thing in English. *Do* often refers to action that is mechanical or specific. *Make* often refers to action that is creative or general: The teacher *makes* up the exercise (creative), but the student *does* the exercise (mechanical). However, there is no clear rule explaining the difference. You will just have to memorize their usage.

Mostly Mechanical or Specific	*Mostly Creative or General*
do the dishes	make the bed
do the homework	make an impression
do the laundry	make progress
do your hair	make up your mind
do (brush) your teeth	make (cook) a meal
do (write) a paper	make (build) a house
do the right thing	make mistakes

do someone a favor	make a speech
do good deeds	make a living
do away with	make arrangements

FAULTY   I have to *make the homework* before I can *do a speech*.

REVISED   I have to *do the homework* before I can *make a speech*.

- *Tell* and *say* do not mean the same thing in English:

tell time	say a prayer
tell a story or a joke	say hello
tell me	say that we should go
tell the difference	say, "Let's go!"

FAULTY   say me; tell hello; say a joke

REVISED   tell me; say hello; tell a joke

Articles

Articles (*a, an,* and *the*) can be very confusing in English, so you must pay special attention to them.

- Use *a* before words that begin with consonant sounds and *an* before words that begin with vowel sounds.

1. *A* and *an* mean the same as *one* or *each*: I want *an* ice cream cone. [*Just one*]
2. *A* and *an* go with an unidentified member of a class: *A* small dog came toward her, *a* bone in its mouth. [*Some unknown dog, some unknown bone*]
3. *A* and *an* go with a representative member of a class: You can tell by the way he talks that he is *a* politician.
4. *A* and *an* go with a noun that places an idea in a larger class: The car is *a* four-wheeled vehicle.

   See the section "Considering Singular Nouns Ending in -s, Collective Nouns, and Cue Words" on pages 391–392 in Chapter 25.

- *The* serves many functions:

1. *The* modifies known people, objects, or ideas: *the* mother of *the* bride, *the* head of *the* household in which he stayed, *the* Copernican theory
2. *The* goes with superlatives: *the* best, *the* least
3. *The* goes with rank: *the* first book, *the* third child with this problem
4. *The* goes with *of* phrases: the way of *the* world

5. *The* goes with adjective phrases or clauses which limit or identify the noun: *the* topic being discussed
6. *The* refers to a class as a whole: *The* giraffe is an African animal.
7. *The* goes with the names of familiar objects (*the* store) and the names of newspapers (*The Wall Street Journal*), but not the names of most magazines (*Time*).
8. *The* goes with the names of historical periods (*the* French Revolution), legislative acts (*the* Missouri Compromise), political parties (*the* Democratic Party), branches of government (*the* executive branch), official titles (*the* President), government bodies (*the* Navy), and organizations (*the* Girl Scouts).
9. *The* goes with rivers (but not lakes), canals, oceans, channels, gulfs, peninsulas, swamps, groups of islands, mountain ranges, hotels, libraries, museums, and geographic regions: *the* Panama Canal, *the* Mississippi River, Lake Superior, *the* Okefenokee Swamp, *the* Hilton, *the* Smithsonian, *the* South.

FAULTY   According to *New York Times,* the Lake Victoria is one of most beautiful lakes in world.

REVISED   According to *the New York Times,* Lake Victoria is one of *the* most beautiful lakes in *the* world.

Spelling

- Follow these steps to avoid common spelling errors:

1. Don't leave *h* out of *wh* words: *which,* not *wich*
2. Don't add an *e* to words that start with *s*: *stupid,* not *estupid*
3. Don't confuse words that sound alike in English but have different meanings and different spellings:

his/he's (he is)	which/witch	there/their
whether/weather	here/hear	through/threw
advice/advise (noun/verb)	too/to/two	though/thought

4. Don't confuse grammatical functions because of familiar sound combinations: *whose* or *who's* (*who is*), not *who his*
5. Don't confuse words that sound similar using your native language's pronunciation patterns but have different meanings and different sounds in English:

this (singular)/these (plural)	chair/share
read/lead	boat/vote
heat/hit	

See Chapter 29, "Spelling: Focusing on Correctness."

Other Common Grammar Problems

Double Negatives

- Never use a double negative; it is not acceptable in English. As in mathematics, two negatives equal a positive. *See the section "Avoiding Double Negatives" on page 439 in Chapter 27.*

$$(-) \;+\; (-) \;=\; (+)$$

FAULTY   I do*n't* have *no* money. [*Meaning becomes positive*]

$$(-) \;+\; (+) \;=\; (-)$$

REVISED   I do*n't* have *any* money. [*Meaning remains negative*]

Confusing Words

Some key words are confusing:

- *Too* does not mean *very. Very* is an intensifier that means *extremely* or *excessively.* It emphasizes quantity. *Too* is often negative and critical. It is sometimes attached to a word that goes with an infinitive (*to* + verb) to emphasize negative effects.

EXAMPLES   It is *very* cold, but we can walk to the restaurant. [Very = *intensely*]

It is *too* cold to walk, so we should take a taxi. [Too = *negative*]

FAULTY   He is *very* fat to play on the soccer team.

REVISED   He is *too* fat to play on the soccer team. [*He cannot play soccer because of excessive fat.*]

- *Hard* can be an adjective or an adverb, but *hardly* is always an adverb meaning *barely, almost none,* or *almost not at all.*

                    [adjective] [noun]

EXAMPLES   He learned a *hard* lesson. [*A difficult lesson*]

          [verb] [adverb]

He worked *hard.* [*With great effort*]

        [adverb] [verb]

He *hardly* worked. [*Barely, almost not at all*]

     [adverb] [noun]

Hardly anyone watches black-and-white television. [*Almost no one*]

- *A few* (count) and *a little* (noncount) mean *some,* while *few* and *little* mean *almost none.* The difference is between a positive attitude and a negative attitude.

EXAMPLES   I have *a little* money, so I can lend you some. [*Some, so positive*]

I have *little* money, so I can't lend you any.   [*Almost none, so negative*]

A few students came, so we were pleased.   [*Some, so positive*]

Few students came, so we were disappointed.   [*Almost none, so negative*]

- *Some* and *any* both mean an indefinite amount. However, *some* is used in positive statements, while *any* is used in negative statements.

EXAMPLES   I have *some* money.   [*Positive*]

I do*n't* have *any* money.   [*Negative*]

- Usually, *well* is an adverb, whereas *good* is an adjective. However, *well* can sometimes be an adjective referring to health. *See the section "Working with Confusing Pairs of Adjectives and Adverbs" on pages 431–432 in Chapter 27.*

EXAMPLES   The *boy* is *good*.   [*Well-behaved*]

He doesn't feel *well*.   [*Poor health*]

The *boy* is *well*.   [*Healthy, not sick*]

Prepositions

Prepositions can be very confusing. *See the section "Recognizing Subjects" on pages 268–270 in Chapter 17.*

- Use *on* when one thing touches the surface of another and *in* when one thing encloses another: *on* the desk (on top), *in* the desk (inside a drawer). Also, use *on* if you must step up to board (get *on* a motor-cycle/bus/train/large ship), but use *in* if you must step down (get *in* a small boat/car).
- *Since* goes with a specific initial time (*since* 3 P.M.; *since* July 3); *for* goes with duration, a length or period of time (*for* two hours; *for* ten days).

Punctuation and Capitalization

English rules for punctuation differ greatly from those in other languages.

- All sentences have an ending punctuation mark. Statements end with a period (**.**). Exclamations end with an exclamation mark (**!**). Questions end with a question mark (**?**). Statements, exclamations, and questions end with only one mark. Avoid multiple punctuation marks at the end of sentences. *See the section "Using Periods, Question Marks, and Exclamation Points" on page 502 in Chapter 31, "Other Punctuation and Capitalization."*

- Do not use commas to connect complete ideas or statements that can stand alone. Instead, use a period and a capital letter, a semicolon, or a comma and a coordinating conjunction. *See Chapter 20, "Comma Splices and Run-On Sentences."*

FAULTY   We finished class, then we got a pizza, later we went to a movie.
[*Comma splice*]

REVISED   We finished class. Then we got a pizza. Later we went to a movie.
[*Separate sentences*]

or

We finished class; then we got a pizza; later we went to a movie.
[*Clauses joined with semicolons*]

or

We finished class, then got a pizza, and later went to a movie.
[*Simple sentence with compound verb*]

- Commas go before and after a modifying word, phrase, or clause that adds extra information. This means that the sentence can stand alone without the added information. Modifying words, phrases, or clauses that are necessary for identification take no commas. In other words, if the material is crucial to the meaning of the sentence, then do not use commas. *See the section "Using Commas to Set Off Elements That Interrupt Sentence Flow" on pages 491–492 in Chapter 30.*

EXAMPLE

noun · modifier

Never eat chicken *that is undercooked.*

Without the modifier, the sentence meaning is changed and incorrect; use no commas.

EXAMPLE

noun · modifier

Supermarkets, *which we take for granted,* did not even exist a hundred years ago.

Without the modifier, the sentence retains its basic meaning; use commas.

- Semicolons are used to connect independent clauses. They may also be used to separate longer groups of words or lists that already contain commas.

EXAMPLES   Cats are lazy; dogs jump around.

Turn in your uniforms on Friday, May 24; Monday, May 27; or Wednesday, May 29.

- English rules for capitalization differ greatly from those in other languages. *See the section "Understanding Capitalization" on pages 514–515 in Chapter 31 for the English rules.*

Writing Paragraphs

Indentation Don't use a dash (—) to signal the beginning of a new paragraph. Instead, indent the first line of the paragraph to identify your change of subject or focus. *See the section "Recognizing the Structure of a Paragraph" on pages 36–37 in Chapter 3, "Composing: Creating a Draft."*

Unity Every sentence in a paragraph should be connected to the same topic, or main idea. In other words, the material should be unified. *See the section "Maintaining Unity" on pages 62–63 in Chapter 4, "Refining and Polishing Your Draft."* If you change direction in the middle of the paragraph to talk about another idea, even if it is related, your teachers may call it a *digression*. Digressions are allowed in some languages, but not in English. One way to avoid digression is to have a plan for organizing your examples. For example, move from most common to least common, or from the familiar to the unfamiliar, or from the least important to the most important.

EXAMPLES

most common traveler's problem in airports

next most common problem

not usual, but still a problem

EXAMPLES

an important study habit for final exams

a more important study habit for final exams

the most important study habit for final exams

Finally, avoid digression by keeping sentences short and tightly connected. Don't try to put too many unrelated ideas in one sentence or paragraph.

FAULTY

The writer warned us about the problem, he said it was very dangerous, he gave us convincing statistics. [*Three separate ideas; comma splice*]

REVISED

The writer used convincing statistics to warn about the dangerous problem. [*Ideas are combined and connected.*]

Writing Essays

Think about Audience Expectations Be businesslike: Go directly to your main idea. Don't try to tell your readers everything. Choose and limit your focus as much as possible. This narrowing of the topic may be much more extreme than you are used to in your language or culture.

Strive for Clarity   Most North American readers like everything important to be explained; they don't like to guess what something means. Thus, you must keep your writing clear and simple. At the same time, be as specific as possible with your ideas. Your readers will want facts, details, and examples, so provide as many as you can. In other words, **amplify**.

Don't try to be too formal, but don't rely too heavily on the pronoun *you*. Doing so will make your writing less specific and clear. Say *who* you mean: the student, the tourist, the opposition. Finally, when you revise your sentences, eliminate extra words and imprecise expressions.

FAULTY	the group of people who lead the university and decide on policy
REVISED	the board of governors

Reinforce Your Point with a "Close"   Never just stop writing. Always conclude with a few final words about your topic. This conclusion can repeat your main idea, but it should also show the significance of what you have said. Try to say how or why your topic idea is important and worth paying attention to.

Revise to Correct Errors   Proofread before you turn in your paper. When you proofread, watch for the common mistakes discussed above. If possible, have a native speaker in one of your classes or a writing lab look at it before you turn it in. *See Chapter 4, "Refining and Polishing Your Draft," Chapter 14, "Developing an Essay," and Chapter 15, "Examining Types of Essays," for guidelines on how to develop and write an essay.*

Appendix C
Exploring the Dictionary

Several chapters of this textbook have suggested that you refer to the dictionary to find information or to check the accuracy of your spelling. The dictionary is a tool writers use to verify the spelling of a word or to learn the meaning of an unfamiliar word. This reference tool can also provide other valuable information if you know what is available and where it is located. This appendix will help you learn how to explore the dictionary to gather all the information that is available to you.

Using the Dictionary

Good dictionaries are user friendly. They usually begin with a guide to using the dictionary, sometimes called a usage guide. The guide will probably include a pronunciation key, which uses symbols and phonetic spelling. Phonetic spelling shows the way the word sounds when pronounced correctly. It is necessary because the same letters can be pronounced different ways in English. For example, the double *o* is pronounced differently in *good* and *food*.

The usage guide also lists abbreviations that the dictionary's editors have used, along with the words they stand for. In addition, it may explain what each element of an entry means. Sometimes, you can find a pronunciation key and a list of abbreviations and symbols used in a dictionary on the inside cover. You can always refer to the usage guide to help you find the information you need when you are using the dictionary.

A Sample Dictionary Entry

Video
Appendix C.1

To help you discover what information is included in a dictionary, take a look at the entry for the word *knowledge* as it appears in *Webster's New World College Dictionary*.

> **knowl•edge** (näl´ ij) **n.** [ME *knoweleche*, acknowledgement, confession < Late OE *cnawlœc* < *cnawan* (see KNOW) + *-lœc* < *lācan*, to play, give, move about] **1** the act, fact or state of knowing; specif. *a*) acquaintance or familiarity (with a fact, place, etc.) *b*) awareness *c*) understanding **2** acquaintance with facts; range of information, awareness or understanding **3** all that has been perceived or grasped by the mind;

587

learning; enlightenment **4** the body of facts, principles, etc. accumulated by mankind **5** [ARCHAIC] carnal knowledge: see CARNAL **—*SYN.*** INFORMA-TION**—to (the best of) one's knowledge** as far as one knows; within the range of one's information

At first glance, this entry might seem confusing, but each dictionary entry follows a pattern. Once you understand what information is listed where, most entries will become clear. For example, here is an explanation of the information about *knowledge* that appears before the definitions of the word:

- The main entry, the word itself, is written in boldface: **knowl•edge**
- Each syllable of the word is separated by bold, centered periods: •
- The phonetic pronunciation follows, with a (´) over the accented, or stressed, syllable(s): (näl´ ij)
- The word's part of speech, in this case, is a noun: **n.**
- Finally, the etymology, or origin of the word, is also listed between brackets: [ ].

So before we read the definitions for this word, we know that the word has two syllables, that we should accent the first syllable when we pronounce the word, and that it is a noun. By referring to the usage guide for a list of abbreviations, we can also determine that the word has its roots in Old English (OE) and Middle English (ME). Knowing the etymology of a word helps writers understand its meaning more fully.

Following this information about the word are its definitions. Knowing how to define a word as it is used within a sentence or particular context is important. Some words have more than one meaning or sense, as *knowledge* does. Those multiple meanings are separated here by numbers in boldface. In some dictionaries, the different definitions are separated by a // or a double line. The five meanings of the noun *knowledge* provided in the definition above are as follows:

1. the act, fact or state of knowing; specif. *a*) acquaintance or familiarity (with a fact, place, etc.) *b*) awareness *c*) understanding
2. acquaintance with facts; range of information, awareness or understanding
3. all that has been perceived or grasped by the mind; learning; enlightenment
4. the body of facts, principles, etc. accumulated by mankind
5. [ARCHAIC] carnal knowledge: see CARNAL

In addition, this entry provides a **synonym**—the word *information*—and an example and explanation of an idiomatic expression or phrase that includes the word: **to (the best of) one's knowledge**.

Most dictionary entries will follow this basic pattern: the word, its pronunciation, its forms and part(s) of speech, the etymology, and the definition(s). The entry may contain other information, too. For example, you can use the dictionary to check the spelling of plurals (*pl.*), to find the comparative (*comp.*) and superlative (*superl.*) forms of modifiers, and to learn the various forms of a verb. If the verb will accept a direct or indirect object, that is also indicated by *vt.*, an abbreviation for *transitive verb.* The dictionary will also provide the correct spelling of the word with suffixes. Remember—if you are not sure what an abbreviation means within an entry, check the usage guide or list of abbreviations at the beginning of the dictionary.

Exercise C.1   Exploring the Usage Guide

1. Refer to the Usage Guide of your own dictionary and explain what *archaic* means in definition 5 of the word *knowledge.* _____

    _____

    _____

2. Using the Usage Guide, explain the following terms:

    obsolete: _____

    colloquial: _____

    rare: _____

Exercise C.2   Finding Additional Information

1. Look up the word *knowledge* in a dictionary that you use. How does the entry compare with the sample entry on pages 587–588? _____

    _____

    _____

2. Besides definitions, what additional information does your dictionary contain, such as maps, charts, or other reference information? _____

    _____

    _____

Challenge C.1   Searching the Library

Visit your college or municipal library, and explore the section of the reference collection that contains dictionaries. What did you discover about the number and variety of dictionaries that are available? Select one or two specialized dictionaries that you find interesting or unusual. Write a paragraph describing the content of the dictionary, and explain why you found it intriguing. Share the results of your exploration with your classmates.

If you have access to the World Wide Web, your instructor may ask you to complete this challenge by identifying and exploring on-line dictionaries.

Exercise C.3   **Exploring Etymologies**

1. Find and write the etymologies of the following words:

    a. education: _____

    _____

    b. college: _____

    _____

    c. student: _____

    _____

    d. write: _____

    _____

2. Does your dictionary include any of the following words? Be sure to use the most current edition of the dictionary.

cyberspace	diskette
World Wide Web	online
digital	hypertext
technology	laser

3. Working with a partner, see what you can discover about the etymologies of these words. Be sure to explore how adding a prefix changes the meaning, multiple definitions, and references to the root of the word in your search. Share your results with the class.

Challenge C.2   **Playing a Dictionary Game**

Play this game with four or five other students. Choose a word from the dictionary that you believe the students in the group do not know. Pronounce and spell the word for the group, distribute an index card or small piece of paper to everybody, and ask each person to write a definition for the word, including its part of speech. At the same time, you should write the correct definition from the dictionary on your own card. Collect the cards and read all the definitions. Ask each student in turn to guess which definition is correct. Students earn points by selecting the correct definition or by having their definition selected by another student. You earn a point for each incorrect answer. The game continues until every group member has a turn to choose a word.

Here is an example to get you started. Which of the following definitions is correct for the word *dibble?*

1. A dibble is a pointed gardening tool used to make holes for planting seeds and bulbs; it is a noun.
2. Dibble is an adjective that means small and without much worth.
3. Dibble is the technical name for the residue that remains after charcoal briquettes are burned. It is a noun.
4. Dibble is a verb that means to do something without much enthusiasm or seriousness.

After you've guessed, use the dictionary to find the right definition.

Rhetorical Index

Writers combine rhetorical modes to communicate their ideas in paragraphs and essays. Often, one mode is dominant, and one or more additional modes are used to provide illustration or support. To help you understand the characteristics of each mode, this index lists the paragraphs and essays in the text both by mode and by chapter. Paragraphs and essays that contain characteristics for more than one mode are listed more than once, under the headings for each of those modes.

Paragraphs and Essays by Mode

Paragraphs and Essays by Mode in Each Chapter

Credits

Text Credits

Greg Andree, "Fear Not." Used by permission of the author.

Amanda Beaulieu, "A Bully Who Wore Bobby Pins." Used by permission of the author.

Judith Ortiz Cofer, "5:00 A.M.: Writing as Ritual." As appears in *The Latin Deli*. The University of Georgia Press, © 1993.

Susan Douglas, "Remote Control: How to Raise a Media Skeptic." Copyright © 1997 by Susan Douglas. As first appeared in *Utne Reader* (January/February 1997).

Paul Fletcher, "Nightwatch," published in the *Providence Journal-Bulletin*, 20 April 1990. Used by permission of the author.

Ana Gomes, "Bilingual Education: The Need to Reform." Used by permission of the author.

Larissa Houk, "The Importance of Wearing a Safety Belt." Used by permission of the author.

Therese C. MacKinnon, "Caesar." First appeared in the book *Circles of Compassion: A Collection of Human Words and Work*, edited by Elaine Sichel. Used by permission of the author.

Jane Patenaude, "Childhood—Then and Now." Used by permission of the author.

Diane Riva, "Exposed Toes." Used by permission of the author.

Amy Tan, "Fish Cheeks." Copyright © 1987 by Amy Tan. First appeared in *Seventeen* magazine. Digitalized with permission of the author and the Sandra Dijkstra Literary Agency.

Deborah Tannen, "Intimacy and Independence," from *You Just Don't Understand* by Deborah Tannen. Copyright © 1990 by Deborah Tannen. Reprinted by permission of HarperCollins Publishers Inc. William Morrow.

Josh Trepanier, "R-E-S-P-E-C-T." Used by permission of the author.

Naihsin Weng, "My Paradise." Used by permission of the author.

John Yemma, "Gullibles' Travels." *The Boston Globe Magazine*, September 23, 2001.

Photo Credits

Chapters 1, 3, 5, 10, 11, 13, 14, 18: © FPG Int'l/Getty Images.

Chapters 2, 9, 12, 15, 17, 19: © Stone/Getty Images.

Chapters 4, 6, 16: © Image Bank/Getty Images.

Chapters 7, 8: © PhotoDisc/Getty Images.

Index